The Eisenhower Administration
1953–1961   A DOCUMENTARY HISTORY

ROBERT L. BRANYAN is Professor of History at the University of Missouri, Kansas City. He was awarded a Ph.D. from the University of Oklahoma in 1961. In addition to numerous scholarly articles, Professor Branyan has edited, with Lawrence Larsen, *Aspects of American History* (1970) and *Urban Crisis in Modern America* (1971).

LAWRENCE H. LARSEN is Professor of History at the University of Missouri, Kansas City. He was awarded a Ph.D. degree from the University of Wisconsin in 1962. In addition to his joint work with Professor Branyan, Larsen is the author of *The President Wore Spats: A Biography of Glenn Frank* (1965) and co-author, with Charles Glaab, of *Factories in the Valley: Neenah-Menasha, 1870-1915* (1969).

VOLUME II

The Eisenhower Administration
1953–1961   A DOCUMENTARY HISTORY

ROBERT L. BRANYAN
LAWRENCE H. LARSEN
UNIVERSITY OF MISSOURI, KANSAS CITY

Random House, Inc., New York

Reference Series Editors:

Fred L. Israel
William P. Hansen

FIRST EDITION

Copyright © 1971 by Random House, Inc.

All rights reserved under International and Pan-American
Copyright Conventions. Published in the United States by
Random House, Inc., New York, and simultaneously in Canada
by Random House of Canada Limited, Toronto.

Library of Congress Catalog Card Number: 71-164935
ISBN: 0-394-47241-1

MANUFACTURED IN THE UNITED STATES OF AMERICA by Trade
Composition, Inc. (composition) and Halliday Lithograph
Corp. (printing).

1 2 3 4 5 HL 9 8 7 6 5 4 3 2 1

Contents

Volume II

The Eisenhower Administration
1953–1961 A DOCUMENTARY HISTORY

3. THE AMERICAN ROLE IN THE SUEZ CRISIS

The Egyptian government nationalized the Suez Canal Co. on July 26, 1956. Great Britain and France, the two nations most immediately concerned, advocated immediate action, but the United States hoped for a negotiated settlement. The situation in the Middle East had deteriorated since communist arms shipments to Egypt. Western refusal to finance the Aswan Dam project also intensified the Cold War in that area. Throughout the late summer and early autumn of 1956, the United States sponsored conferences aimed at solving the situation without recourse to arms by creating an association of nations which used the canal.

Statement by Secretary John Foster Dulles
on the Suez Canal Crisis
September 17, 1956
[Department of State, *Bulletin,* XXXV (October 1,1956), 503.]

President Eisenhower and I have been talking over the Suez question in advance of my departure today for London. The United Kingdom has called together another meeting of the representatives of the 18 governments which supported the views put to the Government of Egypt by the five-nation mission headed by Prime Minister Menzies of Australia.

Let me make certain things quite clear:

1. The United States is dedicated to seeking by peaceful means assurance that the Suez Canal will carry out the international purpose to which it is dedicated by the convention of 1888.

2. We are not, however, willing to accept for ourselves, nor do we seek from other nations acceptance of, an operating regime for the canal which falls short of recognizing the rights granted to canal users by the 1888 convention.

3. We are not trying to organize any boycott of the canal, but we cannot be blind to the fact that conditions might become such that transit through the canal is impractical or greatly diminished. There must always be ways to assure the movement of vital supplies, particularly oil, to Western Europe.

Accordingly, we are carrying out planning as a prudent precaution. But our hope remains that satisfactory operating arrangements can be worked out with Egypt.

At London we will consider developments since the previous conference on the Suez adjourned August 23 and, I hope, find a common approach to the future.

Statement by Secretary John Foster Dulles on the Suez Canal Crisis Geneva, September 19, 1956

[Department of State, *Bulletin,* XXXV (October 1,1956), 503-04.]

Our meeting here last month gave rise to solid hope that the Suez Canal problem could be settled. Eighteen of us had come to an agreement. We represented nations of Europe, Asia, Africa, Australasia, and America. Our shipping constituted over 90 percent of all the Suez Canal shipping. Among us were those whose patterns of trade showed differing, yet important, dependence upon the canal. It was no small achievement that out of that diversity agreement was reached. That was possible only because there prevailed among us a spirit of conciliation, and of urgency, born out of the gravity of the situation with which the Government of Egypt has confronted us.

What we agreed upon was a program to assure permanently an efficient and dependable operation, maintenance, and development of the Suez Canal in accordance with the treaty of 1888. That program was scrupulously respectful of the sovereignty of Egypt.

However, as our Committee of Five has just reported to us, the Government of Egypt unqualifiedly refused to consider our proposal as a basis of negotiation. It made no counterproposal.

This attitude of Egypt has created a new and difficult situation.

Exercising the restraint enjoined by the charter of the United Nations, we continue to seek, by peaceful means, a solution of this difficult problem.

Certain things are, I think, clear.

1. The convention of 1888 gives our vessels the right at all times to pass through the Suez Maritime Canal as a free and open waterway.

2. Those rights are jeopardized by the action of the Egyptian Government in preventing the Universal Suez Canal Company from exercising its agreed functions and in Egypt itself usurping all of those functions.

It is true that, although the Egyptian Government has unilaterally terminated the concession to the Universal Suez Canal Company, which was part of the system referred to and established by the convention of 1888, that Government says that it will nevertheless live up to the convention itself and assure a fair and equal operation of the canal.

But the testing issue is whether the Government of Egypt accepts that the parties to, and beneficiaries of, the convention of 1888 may in fact have the facilities needed to assure them in the exercise of their rights. If the Government of Egypt insists that ships' masters be in the position of suppliants, who can never pass through the canal except under such conditions as the Government of Egypt may from time to time impose, then there is no guaranty of free and secure passage such as the convention of 1888 prescribes.

I know that the Government of Egypt has argued that it can always, by the use of force, interrupt traffic through the Suez Canal and that therefore transit must depend on Egypt's good faith and good will. But there are many sanctions against open and forcible interruption of free passage. The same is not true if any one government dominates and controls all phases of operation. The operation of the Suez Canal is a highly complicated, intricate affair. It offers infinite possibilities of covert violation and the practice, in obscurity, of preferences and discriminations. Lack of efficiency can be a grave hazard. It is against risks of this kind that the users can, and I believe should, protect themselves in the exercise of their rights under the 1888 treaty. The economic well-being of many nations and peoples is at stake, and there are no adequate sanctions against the dangers I describe.

3. The third point I would like to make is this: When vital rights are threatened, it is natural and elemental to join to meet the common danger.

The Government of Egypt has warned us not to join together in association. It is natural that it should prefer the canal users to be unorganized and divided. I recall that in its memorandum of September 10, 1956, to the Secretary-General of the United Nations and to many governments, the Egyptian Government seeks the creation of a negotiating body that will reflect what it calls "different views." But for those endangered to come together and to harmonize their views is an elemental right, not to be forgone. . . .

Declaration Providing for the Establishment of a Suez Canal Users Association September 21, 1956

[Department of State, *Bulletin,* XXXV (October 1, 1956), 508.]

I. The members of the Suez Canal Users Association (SCUA) shall be those nations which have participated in the second London Suez Conference and which subscribe to the present Declaration, and any other adhering nations which conform to criteria to be laid down hereafter by the Association.

II. SCUA shall have the following purposes:

(1) To facilitate any steps which may lead to a final or provisional solution of the Suez Canal problem and to assist the members in the exercise of their rights as users of the Suez Canal in consonance with the 1888 Convention, with due regard for the rights of Egypt;

(2) To promote safe, orderly, efficient and economical transit of the Canal by vessels of any member nation desiring to avail themselves of the facilities of SCUA and to seek the cooperation of the competent Egyptian authorities for this purpose;

(3) To extend its facilities to vessels of non-member nations which desire to use them;

(4) To receive, hold and disburse the revenues accruing from dues and other sums which any user of the Canal may pay to SCUA, without prejudice to existing rights, pending a final settlement;

(5) To consider and report to members regarding any significant developments affecting the use or non-use of the Canal;

(6) To assist in dealing with any practical problems arising from the failure of the Suez Canal adequately to serve its customary and intended purpose and to study forthwith means that may render it feasible to reduce dependence on the Canal;

(7) To facilitate the execution of any provisional solution of the Suez problem that may be adopted by the United Nations.

III. To carry out the above mentioned purposes:

(1) The members shall consult together in a Council on which each member will be represented;

(2) The Council shall establish an executive group to which it may delegate such powers as it deems appropriate;

(3) An Administrator, who shall, . . . make the necessary arrangements with shipping interests, will be appointed to serve under the direction of the Council through the executive group.

IV. Membership may at any time be terminated by giving 60 days' notice.

During the latter part of Dulles' "Face the Nation" appearance on October 21, the Secretary indicated that the United States and the Western European allies had a "common policy" on the Suez crisis. But, even as he spoke British-French-Israeli plans pushed ahead.

Interview with Secretary John Foster Dulles on "Face the Nation," October 21, 1956
[Official File 69, Eisenhower Papers.]

QUESTION. Mr. Peter Lisagor, *Chicago Daily News:* Mr. Secretary, since about September of 1955, when the Soviet Bloc sold Egypt arms, the Middle East seems to have been in one crisis after another, and I wonder whether you see any chance of retrieving the situation in the Middle East, unless the British and the French, who seem to be at odds with us about policy there, and the United States, develop some kind of a joint policy toward the Middle East.

SECRETARY DULLES: Well, now, just a minute. I want to go back to some of the premises in your question. You say since 1955, it's been in a crisis. I was out there in the spring of '53, and if there ever was a crisis, that was it. I couldn't even go to Iran because it was practically under Soviet control at that time. That is a Middle East country which the Soviets have long coveted and which they had within the grip of their hand at that time, so much so that I didn't dare go to the country, not that I was afraid of getting shot—

MR. LISAGOR: Well, let's take your starting date, Mr. Secretary.

SECRETARY DULLES: —but because I didn't want to give respectability to a Soviet dominated government.

When I was also out there in '53, the British were facing a desperate situation at the Suez Canal base. They were thinking then of having to take Cairo and Alexandria with their armed forces, and were moving their women and children out of the place.

When I went in my car from the airport at Cairo to the city, I was attacked by rotten tomatoes. Fortunately, the aiming was very bad and none of them hit me. So to say this dates from '55 is completely to lose track of history.

MR. LISAGOR: Well, I am willing to accept your '53 date, Mr. Secretary.

SECRETARY DULLES: All right. All right. You can say that for a long time, this has been a scene of great difficulty.

Now, what is the rest of your question?

QUESTION. Mr. Lisagor: Well, I wondered whether or not you see any chance of retrieving the situation in the Middle East without developing a joint common policy with the British and French?

SECRETARY DULLES: What do you mean, retrieving the situation?

MR. LISAGOR: Well, are you suggesting now that there are no crises in the Middle East today?

SECRETARY DULLES: I am sure there are crises and there have been crises. I want to know which one you want to retrieve.

Retrieve means going back to something, doesn't it? I don't want to go back to anything. There has been no time that I know of in the history of the last fifty years in that part of the world—you can go back further than that—that there has been a satisfactory situation in that part of the world. There has been turmoil. The Russians had been there. Why are the Russians parties to the Constantinople Convention of 1888? Everybody says this is the first time they have been there. Why, they were right in the middle of the Canal in 1888. I don't want to retrieve anything. There is nothing that has been lost that we would want to go back to. We want to go ahead to something that is better.

MR. LISAGOR: Well, perhaps my choice of words is wrong. It seems that the British and French are very unhappy about the situation in the Middle East, and there do seem to be crises there, if what we read is correct; and I wondered what you, how you feel we can develop a common policy toward easing the situation in the area.

SECRETARY DULLES: Well, we have developed a common policy, and I think it's just amazing the degree to which we have had a common policy. We have now had what you might call four Suez conferences, that I personally have attended, over the last three months, and while we have sometimes started out with somewhat different points of view, we have ended up together, and the fact that there are certain minor superficial differences as to details about just how you handle tolls or how much is going to get paid to Egypt and how much isn't, doesn't detract from the fact that basically we do have a common policy.

MR. MAX FREEDMAN, *Manchester Guardian*: Mr. Secretary, you reminded us last week that it's not always very easy to determine the guilt for aggression. As a practical matter, how would we fix the responsibility for aggression if serious fighting should develop on the Jordan-Israel frontier, and what would the United States do in that event?

SECRETARY DULLES: Well, that is primarily a job, in the first instance, for the United Nations Armistice Commissions that are there. They are out there to supervise the Armistice Commissions, and to get a report from them. Then the matter will go to the Security Council and there would be a vote presumably in the Security Council.

Now, that is assuming that the matter isn't clear-cut.

There sometimes is an aggression which is so open and obvious that you don't need to go through these exploratory appraising processes, but the normal way to do is when you have an Armistice Commission, you get its report, and it goes to the Security Council. . . .

On October 29—in the midst of the American presidential campaign—the Israelis attacked Egyptian positions in the Sinai. The next morning the United States called for a meeting of the United Nations Security Council, where it expressed shock, not only at the Israeli action, but also at a British-French ultimatum which threatened occupation of the Canal Zone unless the fighting ceased. Following Ambassador Lodge's remarks, a resolution was vetoed by the British and French governments. In marked contrast to the struggle over the Hungarian crisis and most other issues of the Cold War, the United States and the Soviet Union voted together.

Statement on the Middle East Crisis
by Ambassador Henry Cabot Lodge, Jr.
October 30, 1956
[Department of State, *Bulletin,* XXXV (November 12, 1956), 748–51.]

The United States has requested this urgent meeting of the Security Council to consider steps to be taken to bring about the immediate cessation of military action by Israel against Egypt.

The Security Council has been meeting on the Palestine question within the last few days and repeatedly in recent months to consider actions which the Council unanimously believed constituted a grave danger, and I am sure therefore that there can be no question about the adoption of the agenda.

I request, therefore, Mr. President, that you put to the vote the question of the adoption of the agenda, which I am certain each member of the Council will consider appropriate in these grave circumstances, and that the Council will act with the same unanimity now as it has on the Palestine question in numerous recent meetings.

After the adoption of the agenda, Mr. President, I would appreciate the opportunity to speak immediately on the substance of the question.

(The agenda was adopted unanimously, and Ambassador Lodge then made the following statement:)

We have asked for this urgent meeting of the Security Council to consider the critical developments which have occurred and are unfortunately still continuing in the Sinai Peninsula as a result of Israel's invasion of that area yesterday. It comes as a shock to the United States Government that this action should have occurred less than 24 hours after President Eisenhower had sent a second earnest, personal appeal to the Prime Minister of Israel urging Israel not to undertake any action against her Arab neighbors and pointing out that we had no reason to believe that these neighbors had taken steps justifying Israel's action of mobilization.

Certain things are clear.

The first is that, by their own admission, Israeli armed forces moved into Sinai in force "to eliminate Egyptian Fedayeen bases in the Sinai Peninsula." They have admitted the capture of Quseima and Ras el Naqb.

Secondly, reliable reports have placed Israeli armed forces near the Suez Canal.

Thirdly, Israel has announced that both the Egyptian and Israeli armed forces were in action in the desert battle.

An official announcement in Tel Aviv said that Egyptian fighter planes strafed Israeli troops. We have a report that President Nasser has called for full mobilization in Egypt today and that the Egyptian Army claims that it has halted the advance of major Israeli forces driving across the Sinai Peninsula.

The Secretary-General may receive more information from General Burns and the Truce Supervision Organization, and I am sure that we shall continue to be fully informed as we proceed with our deliberations here.

These events make the necessity for the urgent consideration of this item all too plain. Failure by the Council to react at this time would be a clear avoidance of its responsibility for the maintenance of international peace and security. The United Nations has a clear and unchallengeable responsibility for the maintenance of the armistice agreements.

The Government of the United States feels that it is imperative that the Council act in the promptest manner to determine that a breach of the peace has occurred, to order that the military actions undertaken by Israel cease immediately, and to make clear its view that the Israeli armed forces be immediately withdrawn behind the established armistice lines. Nothing less will suffice.

It is also to be noted that the Chief of Staff of the United Nations Truce Supervision Organization has already issued a cease-fire order on his own authority, which Israel has so far ignored. Information has reached us also that military observers of the United Nations Truce Supervision Organization have been prevented by Israeli authorities from performing their duties.

We as members of the Council accordingly should call upon all members of the United Nations to render prompt assistance in achieving a withdrawal of Israeli forces. All members specifically should refrain from giving any assistance which might continue or prolong the hostilities. No one nation certainly should take advantage of this situation for any selfish interest.

Each of us here, and all members of the United Nations, have a clear-cut responsibility to see that the peace and stability of the Palestine area is restored forthwith. Anything less is an invitation to disaster in this part of the world.

This is an immediate responsibility, Mr. President, which derives from the Council's obligations under its cease-fire orders and the armistice agreements between the Israelis and the Arab States and endorsed by this Security Council. It derives, of course, also from the larger responsibility under the United Nations Charter.

On behalf of the United States Government I give notice that I intend at the afternoon session to introduce a resolution whereby the Council will call upon Israel for a withdrawal and indicate such steps as will assure that she does. . . .

Now, Mr. President, in the interests of bringing the Council up to date so that the Council will be possessed of all the facts that we have, let me give this added information which has just been sent to me from Washington. As soon as President Eisenhower received his first knowledge obtained through press reports of the ultimatum delivered by the French and United Kingdom Governments to Egypt and Israel, planning temporary occupation within 12 hours of the Suez Canal Zone, he sent an urgent personal message to the Prime Minister of Great Britain and to the Prime Minister of France. President Eisenhower expressed his earnest hope that the United Nations organization would be given full opportunity to settle the issues in the controversy by peaceful means instead of by forceful ones.

Mr. President, the United States continues to believe that it is possible by such means to secure a solution which would restore the armistice conditions between Egypt and Israel as well as bring about a just settlement of the Suez Canal controversy.

United States Cease-Fire Proposal for the Near East
Security Council, October 30, 1956
[Department of State, *Bulletin*, XXXV (November 12, 1956), 750.]

The Security Council,

Noting that the armed forces of Israel have penetrated deeply into Egyptian territory in violation of the armistice agreement between Egypt and Israel;

Expressing its grave concern at this violation of the armistice agreement;

1. *Calls upon* Israel and Egypt immediately to cease fire;

2. *Calls upon* Israel immediately to withdraw its armed forces behind the established armistice lines;

3. *Calls upon* all Members

(a) to refrain from the use of force or threat of force in the area in any manner inconsistent with the Purposes of the United Nations;

(b) to assist the United Nations in ensuring the integrity of the armistice agreements;

(c) to refrain from giving any military, economic or financial assistance to Israel so long as it has not complied with this resolution;

4. *Requests* the Secretary-General to keep the Security Council informed on compliance with this resolution and to make whatever recommendations he deems appropriate for the maintenance of international peace and security in the area by the implementation of this and prior resolutions.

At a press conference on January 26, 1960, Eisenhower said that he had not been swayed by the "Jewish vote" in dealing with the 1956 Middle East crisis. At that time, six days before the presidential election, Eisenhower took a firm stand over national television and radio.

Address to the Nation by President Eisenhower on Developments in Eastern Europe and the Middle East October 31, 1956

[*Public Papers of the Presidents: 1956* (Washington, 1958), 1060–66.]

My Fellow Americans:

Tonight I report to you as your President.

We all realize that the full and free debate of a political campaign surrounds us. But the events and issues I wish to place before you this evening have no connection whatsoever with matters of partisanship. They are concerns of every American—his present and his future.

I wish, therefore, to give you a report of essential facts so that you—whether belonging to either one of our two great parties, or to neither—may give thoughtful and informed consideration to this swiftly changing world scene.

The changes of which I speak have come in two areas of the world—Eastern Europe and the Mid-East.

I

In Eastern Europe there is the dawning of a new day. It has not been short or easy in coming.

After World War II, the Soviet Union used military force to impose on the nations of Eastern Europe, governments of Soviet choice—servants of Moscow.

It has been consistent United States policy—without regard to political party—to seek to end this situation. We have sought to fulfill the wartime pledge of the United Nations that these countries, over-run by wartime armies, would once again know sovereignty and self-government.

We could not, of course, carry out this policy by resort to force. Such force would have been contrary both to the best interests of the Eastern European peoples and to the abiding principles of the United Nations. But we did help to keep alive the hope of these peoples for freedom.

Beyond this, they needed from us no education in the worth of national independence and personal liberty—for, at the time of the American Revolution, it was many of them who came to our land to aid our cause. Now, recently the pressure of the will of these peoples for national independence has become more and more insistent.

A few days ago, the people of Poland—with their proud and deathless devotion to freedom—moved to secure a peaceful transition to a new government. And this government, it seems, will strive genuinely to serve the Polish people.

And, more recently, all the world has been watching dramatic events in Hungary where this brave people, as so often in the past, have offered their very lives for independence from foreign masters. Today, it appears, a new Hungary is rising from this struggle, a Hungary which we hope from our hearts will know full and free nationhood.

We have rejoiced in all these historic events.

Only yesterday the Soviet Union issued an important statement on its relations with all the countries of Eastern Europe. This statement recognized the need for review of Soviet policies, and the amendment of these policies to meet the demands of the people for greater national independence and personal freedom. The Soviet Union declared its readiness to consider the withdrawal of Soviet "advisers"—who have been, as you know, the effective ruling force in Soviet occupied countries—and also to consider withdrawal of Soviet forces from Poland, Hungary and Rumania.

We cannot yet know if these avowed purposes will be truly carried out.

But two things are clear.

First, the fervor and the sacrifice of the peoples of these countries, in the name of freedom, have themselves brought real promise that the light of liberty soon will shine again in this darkness.

And second, if the Soviet Union indeed faithfully acts upon its announced intention, the world will witness the greatest forward stride toward justice, trust and understanding among nations in our generation.

These are the facts. How has your government responded to them?

The United States has made clear its readiness to assist economically the new and independent governments of these countries. We have already— some days since—been in contact with the new Government of Poland on this matter. We have also publicly declared that we do not demand of these governments their adoption of any particular form of society as a condition upon our economic assistance. Our one concern is that they be free—for their sake, and for freedom's sake.

We have also—with respect to the Soviet Union—sought clearly to remove any false fears that we would look upon new governments in these Eastern European countries as potential military allies. We have no such ulterior purpose. We see these peoples as friends, and we wish simply that they be friends who are free.

II

I now turn to that other part of the world where, at this moment, the situation is somber. It is not a situation that calls for extravagant fear or hysteria. But it invites our most serious concern.

I speak, of course, of the Middle East. This ancient crossroads of the world was, as we all know, an area long subject to colonial rule. This rule ended after World War II, when all countries there won full independence. Out of the Palestinian mandated territory was born the new State of Israel.

These historic changes could not, however, instantly banish animosities born of the ages. Israel and her Arab neighbors soon found themselves at war with one another. And the Arab nations showed continuing anger toward their former colonial rulers, notably France and Great Britain.

The United States—through all the years since the close of World War II—has labored tirelessly to bring peace and stability to this area.

We have considered it a basic matter of United States policy to support the new State of Israel and—at the same time—to strengthen our bonds both with Israel and with the Arab countries. But, unfortunately through all these years, passion in the area threatened to prevail over peaceful purposes, and in one form or another, there has been almost continuous fighting.

This situation recently was aggravated by Egyptian policy including rearmament with Communist weapons. We felt this to be a misguided policy on the part of the Government of Egypt. The State of Israel, at the same time, felt increasing anxiety for its safety. And Great Britain and France feared more and more that Egyptian policies threatened their "life line" of the Suez Canal.

These matters came to a crisis on July 26th of this year, when the Egyptian Government seized the Universal Suez Canal Company. For ninety years—ever since the inauguration of the Canal—that Company has operated the Canal, largely under British and French technical supervision.

Now there were some among our allies who urged an immediate reaction to this event by use of force. We insistently urged otherwise, and our wish prevailed—through a long succession of conferences and negotiations for weeks—even months—with participation by the United Nations. And there, in the United Nations, only a short while ago, on the basis of agreed principles, it seemed that an acceptable accord was within our reach.

But the direct relations of Egypt with both Israel and France kept worsening to a point at which first Israel—then France—and Great Britain also—determined that, in their judgment, there could be no protection of their vital interests without resort to force.

Upon this decision, events followed swiftly. On Sunday the Israeli Government ordered total mobilization. On Monday, their armed forces penetrated deeply into Egypt and to the vicinity of the Suez Canal, nearly one hundred miles away. And on Tuesday, the British and French Governments delivered a 12-hour ultimatum to Israel and Egypt—now followed up by armed attack against Egypt.

The United States was not consulted in any way about any phase of these actions. Nor were we informed of them in advance.

As it is the manifest right of any of these nations to take such decisions and actions, it is likewise our right—if our judgment so dictates—to dissent. We believe these actions to have been taken in error. For we do not accept the use of force as a wise or proper instrument for the settlement of international disputes.

To say this—in this particular instance—is in no way to minimize our friendship with these nations—nor our determination to maintain those friendships.

And we are fully aware of the grave anxieties of Israel, of Britain and of France. We know that they have been subjected to grave and repeated provocations.

The present fact, nonetheless, seems clear: the action taken can scarcely be reconciled with the principles and purposes of the United Nations to which we have all subscribed. And, beyond this, we are forced to doubt that resort to force and war will for long serve the permanent interest of the attacking nations.

Now—we must look to the future.

In the circumstances I have described, there will be no United States involvement in these present hostilities. I therefore have no plan to call the Congress in Special Session. Of course, we shall continue to keep in contact with Congressional leaders of both parties.

I assure you, your government will remain alert to every possibility of this situation, and keep in close contact and coordination with the Legislative Branch of this government.

At the same time it is—and it will remain—the dedicated purpose of your government to do all in its power to localize the fighting and to end the conflict.

We took our first measure in this action yesterday. We went to the United Nations with a request that the forces of Israel return to their own land and that hostilities in the area be brought to a close. This proposal was not adopted—because it was vetoed by Great Britain and by France.

The processes of the United Nations, however, are not exhausted. It is our hope and intent that this matter will be brought before the United Nations General Assembly. There—with no veto operating—the opinion of the world can be brought to bear in our quest for a just end to this tormenting problem. In the past the United Nations has proved able to find a way to end bloodshed. We believe it can and that it will do so again.

My fellow citizens, as I review the march of world events in recent years, I am ever more deeply convinced that the processes of the United Nations represent the soundest hope for peace in the world. For this very reason, I believe that the processes of the United Nations need further to be developed and strengthened. I speak particularly of increasing its ability to secure justice under international law.

In all the recent troubles in the Middle East, there have indeed been injustices suffered by all nations involved. But I do not believe that another instrument of injustice—war—is the remedy for these wrongs.

There can be no peace—without law. And there can be no law—if we were to invoke one code of international conduct for those who oppose us—and another for our friends.

The society of nations has been slow in developing means to apply this truth.

But the passionate longing for peace—on the part of all peoples of the earth—compels us to speed our search for new and more effective instruments of justice.

The peace we seek and need means much more than mere absence of war. It means the acceptance of law, and the fostering of justice, in all the world.

To our principles guiding us in this quest we must stand fast. In so doing we can honor the hopes of all men for a world in which peace will truly and justly reign.

I thank you, and goodnight.

Even as Eisenhower spoke, French and British aircraft bombarded Egyptian military installations, and on November 5 Anglo-French troops landed at Port Said. Although the military effort partially miscarried, a cease-fire was agreed to, primarily because of American and Russian pressure. The Americans offered no support to their allies; the Russians talked of sending volunteers to Egypt and of rockets landing on Paris and London. On November 7 all parties involved in the conflict accepted the UN cease-fire proposal. While the British and the French, their governments shaken by the crisis, appeared eager to withdraw, rumors reached Washington that Israel intended to continue its occupation of Sinai after the Anglo-French evacuation. Eisenhower's letter to Prime Minister Ben-Gurion on the very day of the UN action indicated a "deep concern" over Israel's intention. Nearly four months after the cease-fire the State Department again reiterated American desire for an Israeli withdrawal. The Administration's efforts succeeded a few days later (March 1, 1957) when Ben-Gurion agreed to withdraw Israeli troops to the 1948 boundaries. The President's letter to the Prime Minister indicated pleasure.

President Eisenhower to Prime Minister David Ben-Gurion
November 8, 1956
[*Public Papers of the Presidents: 1956* (Washington, 1958), 1091–92.]

Dear Mr. Prime Minister:

As you know, the General Assembly of the United Nations has arranged a cease-fire in Egypt to which Egypt, France, the United Kingdom and Israel have agreed. There is being dispatched to Egypt a United Nations force in accordance with pertinent resolutions of the General Assembly. That body has urged that all other foreign forces be withdrawn from Egyptian territory, and specifically, that Israeli forces be withdrawn to the General Armistice line. The resolution covering the cease-fire and withdrawal was introduced by the United States and received the overwhelming vote of the Assembly.

Statements attributed to your Government to the effect that Israel does not intend to withdraw from Egyptian territory, as requested by the United Nations, have been called to my attention. I must say frankly, Mr. Prime Minister, that the United States views these reports, if true, with deep concern. Any such decision by the Government of Israel would seriously undermine the urgent efforts being made by the United Nations to restore peace in the Middle East, and could not but bring about the condemnation of Israel as a violator of the principles as well as the directives of the United Nations.

It is our belief that as a matter of highest priority peace should be restored and foreign troops, except for United Nations forces, withdrawn from Egypt, after which new and energetic steps should be undertaken within the framework of the United Nations to solve the basic problems which have given rise to the present difficulty. The United States has tabled in the General Assembly two resolutions designed to accomplish the latter purposes, and hopes that they will be acted upon favorably as soon as the present emergency has been dealt with.

I need not assure you of the deep interest which the United States has in your country, nor recall the various elements of our policy of support to Israel in so many ways. It is in this context that I urge you to comply with the resolutions of the United Nations General Assembly dealing with the current crisis and to make your decision known immediately. It would be a matter of the greatest regret to all my countrymen if Israeli policy on a matter of such grave concern to the world should in any way impair the friendly cooperation between our two countries.

White House Statement on Withdrawal of Israeli Troops February 17, 1957

[*Public Papers of the Presidents: 1957* (Washington, 1958), 144–46.]

The Department of State is today making public a memorandum which the United States gave to the Government of Israel on February 11th. It relates to Israeli withdrawal to within the armistice lines as repeatedly called for by the United Nations. The memorandum outlines the policies which the United States would, thereafter, pursue in relation to the two matters—the Gulf of Aqaba and the Gaza Strip—which so far lead Israel not to withdraw.

Israel would prefer to have the future status of the Gulf of Aqaba and the Gaza Strip definitely settled to its satisfaction prior to its withdrawal, and as a condition thereto. But all members of the United Nations are solemnly bound by the Charter to settle their international disputes by peaceful means and in their international relations to refrain from the threat or use of force against the territorial integrity of any state. These undertakings seem to preclude using the forcible seizure and occupation of other lands as bargaining power in the settlement of international disputes.

The United Kingdom and France, which occupied portions of Egypt at about the time of Israel's attack upon Egypt of last October, withdrew promptly and unconditionally in response to the same United Nations Resolution that called for Israeli withdrawal. They deferred to the overwhelming judgment of the world community that a solution of their difficulties with Egypt should be sought after withdrawal and not be made a condition precedent to withdrawal. The United States believes that Israel should do likewise.

President Eisenhower's letter to Prime Minister Ben-Gurion of Israel of November 8, 1956, urged, as a matter of "highest priority" that "Israeli forces be withdrawn to the general armistice lines." "After which," the President said, "new and energetic steps should be undertaken within the framework of the United Nations to solve the basic problems which have given rise to the present difficulty."

Prime Minister Ben-Gurion in his reply said: "In view of the United Nations Resolutions regarding the withdrawal of foreign troops from Egypt and the creation of an international force, we will, upon conclusion of satisfactory arrangements with the United Nations in connection with this international force entering the Suez Canal area, willingly withdraw our forces."

The international force referred to by the Prime Minister has been created and, pursuant to arrangements which the United Nations has deemed satisfactory, has entered into and is now within the Suez Canal area. But while there has been a partial withdrawal of Israeli forces from Egypt, Israel persists in its occupation of Egyptian territory around the entrance of the Gulf of Aqaba and of the Gaza Strip.

The United States is aware of the fact that Israel has legitimate grievances and should, in all fairness, see a prospect of remedying them. The United Nations General Assembly by its second resolution of February 2d, endorsing the Secretary General's report, gave such a prospect. We believe that that prospect is further assured by the view which the United States has formulated and communicated to Israel in its memorandum of February 11th. There, the United States took note of Israeli views with reference to the Gaza Strip and the Straits of Aqaba and made clear what the United States would do, after Israel's withdrawal, to help solve the problems that preoccupy Israel. Our declaration related to our intentions, both as a Member of the United Nations and as a maritime power having rights of our own.

The United States believes that the action of the United Nations of February 2d and the statements of various governments, including the United States memorandum of February 11th, provide Israel with the maximum assurance that it can reasonably expect at this juncture, or that can be reconciled with fairness to others.

Accordingly, the United States has renewed its plea to Israel to withdraw in accordance with the repeated demands of the United Nations and to rely upon the resoluteness of all friends of justice to bring about a state of affairs which will conform to the principles of justice and of international law and serve impartially the proper interests of all in the area. This, the United States believes, should provide a greater source of security for Israel than an occupation continued contrary to the overwhelming judgment of the world community.

The United States, for its part, will strive to remain true to, and support, the United Nations in its efforts to sustain the purposes and principles of the Charter as the world's best hope of peace.

President Eisenhower to Prime Minister David Ben-Gurion
March 2, 1957
[*Public Papers of the Presidents: 1957* (Washington, 1958), 165–66.]

My dear Mr. Prime Minister:

I was indeed deeply gratified at the decision of your Government to withdraw promptly and fully behind the Armistice lines as set out by your Foreign Minister in her address of yesterday to the General Assembly. I venture to express the hope that the carrying out of these withdrawals will go forward with the utmost speed.

I know that this decision was not an easy one. I believe, however, that Israel will have no cause to regret having thus conformed to the strong sentiment of the world community as expressed in the various United Nations Resolutions relating to withdrawal.

It has always been the view of this Government that after the withdrawal there should be a united effort by all of the nations to bring about conditions in the area more stable, more tranquil, and more conducive to the general welfare than those which existed heretofore. Already the United Nations General Assembly has adopted Resolutions which presage such a better future. Hopes and expectations based thereon were voiced by your Foreign Minister and others. I believe that it is reasonable to entertain such hopes and expectations and I want you to know that the United States, as a friend of all of the countries of the area and as a loyal member of the United Nations, will seek that such hopes prove not to be vain.

4. THE EISENHOWER DOCTRINE AND ITS APPLICATION

In the weeks following the Middle East cease-fire, the Administration pondered ways to fill the power vacuum. The humiliation of the British and the French opened the door to extensive Russian influence and threatened long-term Western interests. On January 5, 1957, Eisenhower appeared before a joint session of Congress to urge a resolution granting him authority to use United States armed forces, if necessary, to protect the Middle East from communist aggression. The President promised that if military action did seem "called for," he "would, of course, maintain hour-by-hour contact with the Congress." In addition, the President asked for a massive military and economic aid program to help "our friends of the Middle East in ways consonant with the purposes and principles of the United Nations."

For the next two months Congress debated this proposal, generally called the Eisenhower Doctrine. Despite a consensus that something should be done, some members of Congress objected to either the scope or the cost of the President's proposals. J. William Fulbright of Arkansas, Chairman of the Senate Foreign Relations Committee, opposed the resolution, contending that it constituted an executive usurpation of legislative prerogatives. Another Democrat, Senator Richard Russell of Georgia, proposed an amendment to eliminate economic assistance aspects. The President's spirited defense of the whole plan came in a letter to Senate Minority Leader William Knowland of California. In the end the President got almost everything he wanted. The resolution passed the House by a vote of 355 to 61, and the Senate 72 to 19. Eisenhower was well pleased when he signed the resolution on March 9; again, he had worked well with a Democratic-controlled Congress.

Special Message to the Congress by President Eisenhower on the Middle East January 5, 1957

[*Public Papers of the Presidents: 1957* (Washington, 1958), 6–16.]

To the Congress of the United States:
    First may I express to you my deep appreciation of your courtesy in giving me, at some inconvenience to yourselves, this early opportunity of

705

addressing you on a matter I deem to be of grave importance to our country.

In my forthcoming State of the Union Message, I shall review the international situation generally. There are worldwide hopes which we can reasonably entertain, and there are worldwide responsibilities which we must carry to make certain that freedom—including our own—may be secure.

There is, however, a special situation in the Middle East which I feel I should, even now, lay before you.

Before doing so it is well to remind ourselves that our basic national objective in international affairs remains peace—a world peace based on justice. Such a peace must include all areas, all peoples of the world if it is to be enduring. There is no nation, great or small, with which we would refuse to negotiate, in mutual good faith, with patience and in the determination to secure a better understanding between us. Out of such understandings must, and eventually will, grow confidence and trust, indispensable ingredients to a program of peace and to plans for lifting from us all the burdens of expensive armaments. To promote these objectives, our government works tirelessly, day by day, month by month, year by year. But until a degree of success crowns our efforts that will assure to all nations peaceful existence, we must, in the interests of peace itself, remain vigilant, alert and strong.

I

The Middle East has abruptly reached a new and critical stage in its long and important history. In past decades many of the countries in that area were not fully self-governing. Other nations exercised considerable authority in the area and the security of the region was largely built around their power. But since the First World War there has been a steady evolution toward self-government and independence. This development the United States has welcomed and has encouraged. Our country supports without reservation the full sovereignty and independence of each and every nation of the Middle East.

The evolution to independence has in the main been a peaceful process. But the area has been often troubled. Persistent cross-currents of distrust and fear with raids back and forth across national boundaries have brought about a high degree of instability in much of the Mid East. Just recently there have been hostilities involving Western European nations that once exercised much influence in the area. Also the relatively large attack by Israel in October has intensified the basic differences between that nation and its Arab neighbors. All this instability has been heightened and, at times, manipulated by International Communism.

II

Russia's rulers have long sought to dominate the Middle East. That was true of the Czars and it is true of the Bolsheviks. The reasons are not hard to find. They do not affect Russia's security, for no one plans to use the Middle East as a base for aggression against Russia. Never for a moment has the United States entertained such a thought.

The Soviet Union has nothing whatsoever to fear from the United States in the Middle East, or anywhere else in the world, so long as its rulers do not themselves first resort to aggression.

That statement I make solemnly and emphatically.

Neither does Russia's desire to dominate the Middle East spring from its own economic interest in the area. Russia does not appreciably use or depend upon the Suez Canal. In 1955 Soviet traffic through the Canal represented only about three fourths of 1% of the total. The Soviets have no need for, and could provide no market for, the petroleum resources which constitute the principal natural wealth of the area. Indeed, the Soviet Union is a substantial exporter of petroleum products.

The reason for Russia's interest in the Middle East is solely that of power politics. Considering her announced purpose of Communizing the world, it is easy to understand her hope of dominating the Middle East.

This region has always been the crossroads of the continents of the Eastern Hemisphere. The Suez Canal enables the nations of Asia and Europe to carry on the commerce that is essential if these countries are to maintain well-rounded and prosperous economies. The Middle East provides a gateway between Eurasia and Africa.

It contains about two thirds of the presently known oil deposits of the world and it normally supplies the petroleum needs of many nations of Europe, Asia and Africa. The nations of Europe are peculiarly dependent upon this supply, and this dependency relates to transportation as well as to production! This has been vividly demonstrated since the closing of the Suez Canal and some of the pipelines. Alternate ways of transportation and, indeed, alternate sources of power can, if necessary, be developed. But these cannot be considered as early prospects.

These things stress the immense importance of the Middle East. If the nations of that area should lose their independence, if they were dominated by alien forces hostile to freedom, that would be both a tragedy for the area and for many other free nations whose economic life would be subject to near strangulation. Western Europe would be endangered just as though there had been no Marshall Plan, no North Atlantic Treaty Organization. The free nations of Asia and Africa, too, would be placed in serious jeopardy. And the countries of the Middle East would lose the markets upon which their economies depend. All this would have the most adverse, if not disastrous, effect upon our own nation's economic life and political prospects.

Then there are other factors which transcend the material. The Middle East is the birthplace of three great religions—Moslem, Christian and Hebrew. Mecca and Jerusalem are more than places on the map. They symbolize religions which teach that the spirit has supremacy over matter and that the individual has a dignity and rights of which no despotic government can rightfully deprive him. It would be intolerable if the holy places of the Middle East should be subjected to a rule that glorifies atheistic materialism.

International Communism, of course, seeks to mask its purposes of domination by expressions of good will and by superficially attractive offers of political, economic and military aid. But any free nation, which is the subject of Soviet enticement, ought, in elementary wisdom, to look behind the mask.

Remember Estonia, Latvia and Lithuania! In 1939 the Soviet Union entered into mutual assistance pacts with these then independent countries; and the Soviet Foreign Minister, addressing the Extraordinary Fifth Session of the Supreme Soviet in October 1939, solemnly and publicly declared that "we stand for the scrupulous and punctilious observance of the pacts on the basis of complete reciprocity, and we declare that all the nonsensical talk about the Sovietization of the Baltic countries is only to the interest of our common enemies and of all anti-Soviet provocateurs." Yet in 1940, Estonia, Latvia and Lithuania were forcibly incorporated into the Soviet Union.

Soviet control of the satellite nations of Eastern Europe has been forcibly maintained in spite of solemn promises of a contrary intent, made during World War II.

Stalin's death brought hope that this pattern would change. And we read the pledge of the Warsaw Treaty of 1955 that the Soviet Union would follow in satellite countries "the principles of mutual respect for their independence and sovereignty and noninterference in domestic affairs." But we have just seen the subjugation of Hungary by naked armed force. In the aftermath of this Hungarian tragedy, world respect for and belief in Soviet promises have sunk to a new low. International Communism needs and seeks a recognizable success.

Thus, we have these simple and indisputable facts:

1. The Middle East, which has always been coveted by Russia, would today be prized more than ever by International Communism.

2. The Soviet rulers continue to show that they do not scruple to use any means to gain their ends.

3. The free nations of the Mid East need, and for the most part want, added strength to assure their continued independence.

III

Our thoughts naturally turn to the United Nations as a protector of small nations. Its charter gives it primary responsibility for the maintenance of international peace and security. Our country has given the United Nations its full support in relation to the hostilities in Hungary and in Egypt. The United Nations was able to bring about a cease-fire and withdrawal of hostile forces from Egypt because it was dealing with governments and peoples who had a decent respect for the opinions of mankind as reflected in the United Nations General Assembly. But in the case of Hungary, the situation was different. The Soviet Union vetoed action by the Security Council to require the withdrawal of Soviet armed forces from Hungary. And it has shown callous indifference to the recommendations, even the censure, of the General Assembly. The United Nations can always be helpful, but it cannot be a wholly dependable protector of freedom when the ambitions of the Soviet Union are involved.

IV

Under all the circumstances I have laid before you, a greater responsibility now devolves upon the United States. We have shown, so that none can doubt, our dedication to the principle that force shall not be used internationally for any aggressive purpose and that the integrity and independence of the nations of the Middle East should be inviolate. Seldom in history has a nation's dedication to principle been tested as severely as ours during recent weeks.

There is general recognition in the Middle East, as elsewhere, that the United States does not seek either political or economic domination over any other people. Our desire is a world environment of freedom, not servitude. On the other hand many, if not all, of the nations of the Middle East are aware of the danger that stems from International Communism and welcome closer cooperation with the United States to realize for themselves the United Nations goals of independence, economic well-being and spiritual growth.

If the Middle East is to continue its geographic role of uniting rather than separating East and West; if its vast economic resources are to serve the well-being of the peoples there, as well as that of others; and if its cultures and religions and their shrines are to be preserved for the uplifting of the spirits of the peoples, then the United States must make more evident its willingness to support the independence of the freedom-loving nations of the area.

V

Under these circumstances I deem it necessary to seek the cooperation of the Congress. Only with that cooperation can we give the reassurance needed to deter aggression, to give courage and confidence to those who are dedicated to freedom and thus prevent a chain of events which would gravely endanger all of the free world.

There have been several Executive declarations made by the United States in relation to the Middle East. There is the Tripartite Declaration of May 25, 1950, followed by the Presidential assurance of October 31, 1950, to the King of Saudi Arabia. There is the Presidential declaration of April 9, 1956, that the United States will within constitutional means oppose any aggression in the area. There is our Declaration of November 29, 1956, that a threat to the territorial integrity or political independence of Iran, Iraq, Pakistan, or Turkey would be viewed by the United States with the utmost gravity.

Nevertheless, weaknesses in the present situation and the increased danger from International Communism, convince me that basic United States policy should now find expression in joint action by the Congress and the Executive. Furthermore, our joint resolve should be so couched as to make it apparent that if need be our words will be backed by action.

VI

It is nothing new for the President and the Congress to join to recognize that the national integrity of other free nations is directly related to our own security.

We have joined to create and support the security system of the United Nations. We have reinforced the collective security system of the United Nations by a series of collective defense arrangements. Today we have security treaties with 42 other nations which recognize that our peace and security are intertwined. We have joined to take decisive action in relation to Greece and Turkey and in relation to Taiwan.

Thus, the United States through the joint action of the President and the Congress, or, in the case of treaties, the Senate, has manifested in many endangered areas its purpose to support free and independent governments— and peace—against external menace, notably the menace of International Communism. Thereby we have helped to maintain peace and security during a period of great danger. It is now essential that the United States should manifest through joint action of the President and the Congress our determination to assist those nations of the Mid East area, which desire that assistance.

The action which I propose would have the following features.

It would, first of all, authorize the United States to cooperate with and assist any nation or group of nations in the general area of the Middle East in the development of economic strength dedicated to the maintenance of national independence.

It would, in the second place, authorize the Executive to undertake in the same region programs of military assistance and cooperation with any nation or group of nations which desires such aid.

It would, in the third place, authorize such assistance and cooperation to include the employment of the armed forces of the United States to secure and protect the territorial integrity and political independence of such nations, requesting such aid, against overt armed aggression from any nation controlled by International Communism.

These measures would have to be consonant with the treaty obligations of the United States, including the Charter of the United Nations and with any action or recommendations of the United Nations. They would also, if armed attack occurs, be subject to the overriding authority of the United Nations Security Council in accordance with the Charter.

The present proposal would, in the fourth place, authorize the President to employ, for economic and defensive military purposes, sums available under the Mutual Security Act of 1954, as amended, without regard to existing limitations.

The legislation now requested should not include the authorization or appropriation of funds because I believe that, under the conditions I suggest, presently appropriated funds will be adequate for the balance of the present fiscal year ending June 30. I shall, however, seek in subsequent legislation the authorization of $200,000,000 to be available during each of the fiscal years 1958 and 1959 for discretionary use in the area, in addition to the other mutual security programs for the area hereafter provided for by the Congress.

VII

This program will not solve all the problems of the Middle East. Neither does it represent the totality of our policies for the area. There are the problems of Palestine and relations between Israel and the Arab States, and the future of the Arab refugees. There is the problem of the future status of the Suez Canal. These difficulties are aggravated by International Communism, but they would exist quite apart from that threat. It is not the purpose of the legislation I propose to deal directly with these problems. The United Nations is actively concerning itself with all these matters, and we are supporting the United Nations. The United States has made clear, notably by Secretary Dulles' address of August 26, 1955, that we are willing to do much to assist the United Nations in solving the basic problems of Palestine.

The proposed legislation is primarily designed to deal with the possibility of Communist aggression, direct and indirect. There is imperative need that any lack of power in the area should be made good, not by external or alien force, but by the increased vigor and security of the independent nations of the area.

Experience shows that indirect aggression rarely if ever succeeds where there is reasonable security against direct aggression; where the government disposes of loyal security forces, and where economic conditions are such as not to make Communism seem an attractive alternative. The program I suggest deals with all three aspects of this matter and thus with the problem of indirect aggression.

It is my hope and belief that if our purpose be proclaimed, as proposed by the requested legislation, that very fact will serve to halt any contemplated aggression. We shall have heartened the patriots who are dedicated to the independence of their nations. They will not feel that they stand alone, under the menace of great power. And I should add that patriotism is, throughout this area, a powerful sentiment. It is true that fear sometimes perverts true patriotism into fanaticism and to the acceptance of dangerous enticements from without. But if that fear can be allayed, then the climate will be more favorable to the attainment of worthy national ambitions.

And as I have indicated, it will also be necessary for us to contribute economically to strengthen those countries, or groups of countries, which have governments manifestly dedicated to the preservation of independence and resistance to subversion. Such measures will provide the greatest insurance against Communist inroads. Words alone are not enough.

VIII

Let me refer again to the requested authority to employ the armed forces of the United States to assist to defend the territorial integrity and the political independence of any nation in the area against Communist armed aggression. Such authority would not be exercised except at the desire of the nation attacked. Beyond this it is my profound hope that this authority would never have to be exercised at all.

Nothing is more necessary to assure this than that our policy with respect to the defense of the area be promptly and clearly determined and declared. Thus the United Nations and all friendly governments, and indeed governments which are not friendly, will know where we stand.

If, contrary to my hope and expectation, a situation arose which called for the military application of the policy which I ask the Congress to join me in proclaiming, I would of course maintain hour-by-hour contact with the Congress if it were in session. And if the Congress were not in session, and if the situation had grave implications, I would, of course, at once call the Congress into special session.

In the situation now existing, the greatest risk, as is often the case, is that ambitious despots may miscalculate. If power-hungry Communists should either falsely or correctly estimate that the Middle East is inadequately defended, they might be tempted to use open measures of armed attack. If so, that would start a chain of circumstances which would almost surely involve the United States in military action. I am convinced that the best insurance against this dangerous contingency is to make clear now our readiness to cooperate fully and freely with our friends of the Middle East in ways consonant with the purposes and principles of the United Nations. I intend promptly to send a special mission to the Middle East to explain the cooperation we are prepared to give.

IX

The policy which I outline involves certain burdens and indeed risks for the United States. Those who covet the area will not like what is proposed. Already, they are grossly distorting our purpose. However, before this Americans have seen our nation's vital interests and human freedom in jeopardy, and their fortitude and resolution have been equal to the crisis, regardless of hostile distortion of our words, motives and actions.

Indeed, the sacrifices of the American people in the cause of freedom have, even since the close of World War II, been measured in many billions of dollars and in thousands of the precious lives of our youth. These sacrifices, by which great areas of the world have been preserved to freedom, must not be thrown away.

In those momentous periods of the past, the President and the Congress have united, without partisanship, to serve the vital interests of the United States and of the free world.

The occasion has come for us to manifest again our national unity in support of freedom and to show our deep respect for the rights and independence of every nation—however great, however small. We seek not violence, but peace. To this purpose we must now devote our energies, our determination, ourselves.

Senate Speech by J. William Fulbright on the "Eisenhower Doctrine" January 24, 1957

[U.S., *Congressional Record*, 85th Cong., 1st Sess., 1957, CIII, Part 2, 1855–57.]

MR. J. WILLIAM FULBRIGHT (Dem., Ark.) : Mr. President, the President of the United States and his Secretary of State have solemnly asked the Senate for an unprecedented delegation of authority to make wars and to spend money without restriction. The administration prepared Senate Joint Resolution 19, which was introduced by request.

The significant provisions of Senate Joint Resolution 19 are as follows:

> The President "is authorized to employ the Armed Forces of the United States as he deems necessary to secure and protect the territorial integrity and political independence of any such nation or group of nations (in the general

area of the Middle East) requesting such aid against overt armed aggression from any nation controlled by international communism," and to use "without regard to the provisions of any other law or regulation, not to exceed $200 million. The resolution shall expire as the President may determine.

Mr. President, the question Senate Joint Resolution 19 puts to this body is not whether America should help reinforce the independence of Middle East nations. It is not whether we should help check the expansion of international communism. It is not whether a President of the United States needs the backing of a united America when he acts as our agent in the search for world peace. It is not whether our constitutional system must make a due allowance for the use of discretionary Executive power in time of grave emergency.

On these broad points, there is wide agreement in this Chamber. We favor freedom for all peoples. We are opposed to international communism. We favor a vigorous American checkmate to international communism. We favor national unity in the search for world peace. Moreover, as Senators we know from experience that the opportunities and threats arising in the foreign field cannot always be foreseen and covered by law before they emerge. We know that some matters must be entrusted to the discretion of our chief officers of state. Above all, we know that they ought to be entrusted in greater or lesser measure, depending on whether these officers have shown themselves candid, wise, responsible, and respectful of constitutional tradition in the discharge of their powers and duties.

The real question Senate Joint Resolution 19 puts to us has two related parts:

First, shall we strike down the Senate's rights and duties in the conduct of foreign affairs, as defined by 168 years of constitutional practice?

Second, shall we say yes to a radical proposal whose adoption would mean that we are abandoning our constitutional system of checks and balances; that from now on, naked Executive power will rule the highest and most fateful interests of the Nation?

If I put the question this way, it is not from any personal taste for extravagant words. We have heard enough of them from a current Secretary of State, who greets the dawn with a boast about his triumphs, and meets the dusk with scare words of panic, saying that the Nation will be ruined unless it unites to ratify the mistakes he made during the day.

If I put the question as I have, it is because that is precisely the way Senate Joint Resolution 19 puts it. In form and substance, the resolution, as prepared by the administration, wants something from this Chamber, the mere asking of which would have led to a national outcry under any other administration back to Washington's. It asks for a blank grant of power over our funds and Armed Forces, to be used in a blank way, for a blank length of time, under blank conditions, with respect to blank nations, in a blank area. We are asked to sign this blank check in perpetuity or at the pleasure of the President—any President.

Who will fill in all these blanks?

The resolution says that the President, whoever he may be at the time, shall do it. And that is not all it says. It says that in filling in the blanks, the President need not consult, much less be accountable to any other constitutional organ of government. He shall be the counsel, the judge, and the jury of the national interest.

His judgment about world realities shall be the sole warrant for his deeds in committing our forces to battle, and our funds to who knows what purpose.

His office shall be the only archive holding the record of his transactions, except as he reports the results once a year to the Congress.

And finally, he shall decide autonomously when his autonomous powers shall expire.

To repeat, all things are placed within the exclusive province of the President. He is absolved in advance from consulting the Congress. If he alone deems it important to the security of the Nation, he can use $200 million in any way he wants. The only limitation on the use of these funds, or more importantly, on the use of American Armed Forces against overt armed aggression from any nation controlled by international communism, is not a limitation to be exercised by the Congress of the United States, or, indeed, by the United States itself. The limitation turns on whether or not a nation or a group of nations under Communist attack asks for American military help.

This is a dubious kind of limitation, because our own security may well depend on the use of American Armed Forces against overt armed aggression from international communism—regardless of whether the nation under attack asks for our help or not. Does it make sense, then, to serve advance notice that America's freedom of action in fighting for its own interest will be at the mercy of how some of the quite unstable Middle Eastern governments react to Communist aggression? Uncertainty and confusion as to who really governs some of these states is not uncommon. From whom must the request for aid come during a revolutionary period—the ousted prime minister or the usurper; or must we wait until the United Nations or the World Court determines the legitimacy of the applicant for assistance?

How are we as Senators to react to all this?

Is the form and substance of the resolution consistent with the kind of constitutional government all of us in this Chamber took an oath to uphold? In the name of defending liberty abroad, are we, as Senators, henceforth to be deaf, dumb, and blind in the way we discharge our constitutional rights and duties in the conduct of foreign affairs? Do my colleagues believe that the President, any President, and his Secretary of

State will be wiser and more effective, or more foresighted, in protecting the interests of our people if they are relieved of the necessity of consulting with and of justifying their actions to the Congress? Do you, my colleagues, representing 48 sovereign States, really desire to be rid of your power to influence the conduct of our foreign affairs?

You may ask: "In what way does the resolution abridge the constitutional principles of the separation of legislative and executive powers and the power of the Congress to declare war?"

The answer is that it does this in two ways:

First, there is the fact that this is not a Senate resolution or a concurrent resolution having only the force of advice on policy. It is a joint resolution. This means that it has the force of law.

The second way is related to the first. Since the joint resolution has the force of law, it represents, in its substantive content, a blanket transfer to the Executive of the constitutional right vested in the Congress to declare war. This, indeed, is a startling innovation. The Constitution, as we inherited it from the past, provided in effect that the Congress would declare war on a case-to-case basis. Under the joint resolution, however, the Congress stockpiles a batch of hypothetical declarations of war, covering a variety of possible contingencies. Then it says to the President: "Here they are. Now that you have them, you can take us into war—if that is your pleasure—in the confident knowledge that whatever you do, you have a legal basis for it."

I put this analogy to the Senate: Under the Constitution, the President has the power, by and with the advice and consent of the Senate, to appoint Cabinet officers, Ambassadors, members of the Supreme Court, and the like. But would any one of us say that as Senators we were carrying out our constitutional responsibilities if we authorized the President to appoint the next 10 Ambassadors, Cabinet officers, and members of the Supreme Court without the Senate passing on each one? The implications here are so preposterous that the question answers itself.

How much more preposterous is it, then, to say to the President, to any President, in the life and death matter of peace or war: "Here are blanket forms you may need if you want to wage war. Fill them in at your own discretion."

Read in this light, the claim put forward by the administration that the aim of the resolution is to have the President share his powers with the Congress in matters related to peace or war, is an affront to commonsense, for under this resolution, there is no sharing of power at all. Exclusive powers are given to the President. All that can be said is that the Congress is dragged in by the heels to share, not the power, but the responsibility for the consequences of the Executive's use or misuse of the power blindly put in his hands by the Congress.

Superficially, and as a matter of form, it might appear to the uninitiated that this resolution is a vehicle for consulting the Congress. However, there was no real prior consultation with Congress, nor will there be any sharing of power. The whole manner of presentation of this resolution—leaks to the press, speeches to specially summoned Saturday joint sessions, and dramatic secret meetings of the Committee on Foreign Relations after dark one evening before the Congress was even organized, in an atmosphere of suspense and urgency—does not constitute consultation in any true sense. All of this was designed to manage the Congress, to coerce it into signing this blank check. The main argument now is, that regardless of whether or not this is a proper method to express the Nation's will, it has now gone too far to draw back or to delay.

I am not unaware that cases can arise, as they have arisen in the past, where Presidents have employed the Armed Forces of the Nation in military operations without the express consent of the Congress. I am not unaware that the actions of the Executive in these emergency cases have well served the defense of the Republic. Experience tells us that when the highest interests of the country are at stake, an Executive who is timid represents a far greater danger to the preservation of our constitutional system than does one who exceeds the letter of the law in a vigorous use of Executive power to defend the Government, the Nation, and the Constitution. Yet experience also tells us something else. It tells us that we do a disservice to ourselves and the Executive if we try to define in exact terms what emergency power is. Why so?

An official who is required to justify the exercise of a power which he does not legally possess is in a very different situation from an official who is charged with abusing a power which is legally his, and who pleads necessity as a legal defense. The former will be very careful to see that the necessity which he pleads to excuse his act is clear and beyond question; he will also take care that the necessity he pleads did not arise from a fault of his own, lest his excuse be turned against him. The latter official can act with much less caution. An abuse of power, unlike the usurpation of power, is condoned by the nonaction of Congress. There is in this case no necessity for seeking the positive approval of the constitutional authority, that is, the Congress. And that is what this resolution would absolve the administration from doing.

Instead of coming to us after the fact, when all the circumstances are known, and asking for our approval, this administration, not being willing to trust the fairness and justice of this body, asks us for an acquittance in advance of the fact, when none of the circumstances justifying the acquittance can possibly be known. I, for one, am unwilling to accept such a drastic change in constitutional practice.

In the First Congress, in 1789, a distinguished Member from Virginia,

Alexander White, stated the applicable principle clearly and succinctly, as follows:

> It would be better for the President to extend his powers on some extraordinary occasions, even where he is not strictly justified by the Constitution, than the Legislature should grant an improper power to be exercised at all times . . . I say it would be better for the Executive to assume the exercise of such a power on extraordinary occasions, than for us to delegate to him authority to exercise an extraordinary power on all occasions.

A final question remains.

What would the effect be on world opinion if the Congress failed to pass the joint resolution? I am not sure that the effect would be very significant, for the resolution in no way offers a policy that gets at the root of the dangers in the Middle East.

Witness after witness before our joint committee has testified that peace between Israel and her neighbors is indispensable to stability and progress in this area. To promote this peace, the refugee problem must be solved, and this in turn appears to be dependent upon the provision of opportunities for the refugees to work through irrigation and other public works. The Suez Canal, of course, must be reopened to all nations or alternative means of transporting oil developed, and long-term basic improvements in the economic and social structures of the countries undertaken. This area has vast undeveloped resources, which could carry the major part of the cost of development, if efficiently organized. But none of these objectives are envisaged by this resolution. And yet, if adopted, our people will assume, and quite logically, that surely a significant step toward a solution to the problems of the area has been enacted. It will be difficult indeed to persuade our constituents that after all the fuss and fury involved in promoting and enacting this resolution, the real work remains to be done.

Nevertheless, in view of the presentation of this resolution, I believe it would be advisable to announce now that if the international Communist movement tries to expand its influence in the Middle East by force, the United States would regard such action as a threat to the security of the United States, and would take appropriate action to repel such force.

It is one thing to tell the Soviet Union that the United States is prepared to use force to counter aggression. It is a very different thing—an unwise and unnecessary thing—for the Congress to say that the President is unauthorized to use the Armed Forces as he deems necessary at some future time and under conditions which cannot now be foreseen.

I am willing to vote for an advisory resolution expressing the Senate's support of the President's policy of opposing the expansion of Communist influence in the Middle East.

Such a procedure is not without precedent. The resolutions preceding the formation of the United Nations and the Vandenberg resolution, preceding

NATO, were adopted with overwhelming support. They did not have the force of law. They did not pretend, or purport, or attempt to delegate additional powers to the President or to merge the legislative and Executive powers, but they evidenced the will of a united and determined people in support of a definite and constructive policy.

In both instances their final culmination depended upon future ratification by the Senate, when the conditions and the limitations were spelled out. This resolution does not so depend; and, by its character it cannot.

During the hearings on the resolution, the Secretary of State urged the committee and the Senate to act quickly, and suggested that constitutional questions should not be raised at such a time as this. I do not believe that even for a short time the Congress should abdicate its constitutional powers. History will demonstrate that the periods of greatest danger to the rights of the people, in a democracy, are those periods when adulation for a popular idol diverts their attention momentarily from the implications of their actions.

Consider for a moment the effect of this resolution as a precedent for future grants of power or for future appropriations.

Here we are asked for only $200 million without restrictions or safeguards. If we grant this, how can we deny a similar request for 2 billion next year? If we are willing to delegate our power to declare war, how can we conscientiously deny a request for a delegation of less important powers?

The effective participation of this Senate and this Congress in the Government of our country under our constitutional system is not a fortuitous circumstance of our history. Our Founding Fathers recognized the inherent tendency of the Executive to absorb all governmental power, and they provided safeguards against such instincts. I, for one, will not lend my vote to further the erosion of the power of this Senate.

President Eisenhower to Senator William Knowland
February 28, 1957
[Official File 116-MM, Eisenhower Papers.]

Dear Senator Knowland:

I appreciate your request for my views on the amendment which would strike economic and military assistance provisions from the Middle East Resolution.

Elimination of these features would gravely impair our ability to help these nations preserve their independence. The Resolution is directed against two dangers, direct armed aggression and indirect subversion. To counter one and not the other would destroy both efforts.

This I emphasize once again: We cannot wage peace with American arms alone. We must understand other national needs. We must respond to human wants. We must help nations and peoples satisfy those needs and wants in order to wage peace successfully.

The pending amendment ignores the danger of subversion. This we must not do. These nations need effective security forces. Their peoples need hope for improving economic conditions. The present Resolution serves these ends. Thus economic and military assistance provisions are more than desirable. They are essential to our efforts to bring peace to this area.

I trust it is clearly understood that these provisions do not make available one additional dollar. They simply authorize us to adapt these funds to the new conditions resulting from recent military action in the area and its economic consequences. It is hardly reasonable to insist that these funds, which are already appropriated, be spent only for programs approved before such drastic changes occurred.

And this I consider even more serious—the world-wide interpretation of such action. Approval of the amendment would suggest that our country wants only to wage peace in terms of war. This is neither the purpose nor the spirit of our nation's foreign policy. I should deplore any action by the Senate that could give the world a contrary impression.

Joint Congressional Resolution to "Promote Peace and Stability in the Middle East"
March 9, 1957
[Department of State, *Bulletin,* XXXVI (March 25, 1957), 481.]

Resolved by the Senate and House of Representatives of the United States of America in Congress assembled,

That the President be and hereby is authorized to cooperate with and assist any nation or group of nations in the general area of the Middle East desiring such assistance in the development of economic strength dedicated to the maintenance of national independence.

SEC. 2. The President is authorized to undertake, in the general area of the Middle East, military assistance programs with any nation or group of nations of that area desiring such assistance. Furthermore, the United States regards as vital to the national interest and world peace the preservation of the independence and integrity of the nations of the Middle East. To this end, if the President determines the necessity thereof, the United States is prepared to use armed forces to assist any such nation or group of such nations requesting assistance against armed aggression from any country controlled by international communism: *Provided,* That such employment shall be consonant with the treaty obligations of the United States and with the Constitution of the United States.

SEC. 3. The President is hereby authorized to use during the balance of fiscal year 1957 for economic and military assistance under this joint resolution not to exceed $200,000,000 from any appropriation now available for carrying out the provisions of the Mutual Security Act of 1954, as amended, in accord with the provisions of such Act: *Provided,* That, whenever the President determines it to be important to the security of the United States, such use may be under the authority of section 401 (a) of the Mutual Security Act of 1954, as amended (except that the provisions of section 105 (a) thereof shall not be waived), and without regard to the provisions of section 105 of the Mutual Security Appropriation Act, 1957: *Provided further,* That obligations incurred in carrying out the purposes of the first sentence of section 2 of this joint resolution shall be paid only out of appropriations for military assistance, and obligations incurred in carrying out the purposes of the first section of this joint resolution shall be paid only of appropriations other than those for military assistance. This authorization is in addition to other existing authorizations with respect to the use of such appropriations. None of the additional authorization contained in this section shall be used until fifteen days after the Committee on Foreign Relations of the Senate, the Committee on Foreign Affairs of the House of Representatives, the Committees on Appropriations of the Senate and the House of Representatives and, when military assistance is involved, the Committees on Armed Services of the Senate and the House of Representatives have been furnished a report showing the object of the proposed use, the country for the benefit of which such use is intended, and the particular appropriation or appropriations for carrying out the provisions of the Mutual Security Act of 1954, as amended, from which the funds are proposed to be derived: *Provided,* That funds available under this section during the balance of fiscal year 1957 shall, in the case of any such report submitted during the last fifteen days of the fiscal year, remain available for use under this section for the purposes stated in such report for a period of twenty days following the date of submission of such report. Nothing contained in this joint resolution shall be construed as itself authorizing the appropriation of additional funds for the purpose of carrying out the provisions of the first section or of the first sentence of section 2 of this joint resolution.

SEC. 4. The President should continue to furnish facilities and military assistance, within the provisions of applicable law and established policies, to the United Nations Emergency Force in the Middle East, with a view to maintaining the truce in that region.

SEC. 5. The President shall within the months of January and July of each year report to the Congress his action hereunder.

SEC. 6. This joint resolution shall expire when the President shall determine that the peace and security of the nations in the general area of the Middle East are reasonably assured by international conditions created by action of the United Nations or otherwise except that it may be terminated earlier by a concurrent resolution of the two Houses of Congress.

◀━◦━◀

For more than a year after the passage of the Eisenhower Doctrine, the Middle East simmered but did not boil over. During the spring of 1958 an internal constitutional crisis in Lebanon escalated into a minor civil war. Had nothing further happened, the United States would have remained aloof. However, on July 14, a revolt in Iraq overthrew a pro-Western government and raised the spectre of a series of communist-instigated upheavals throughout the Near East. At this point, both Jordan and Lebanon asked for Western aid, and Great Britain and the United States responded within hours. British paratroops landed in Jordan (July 17) and quickly stabilized the situation there. Eisenhower invoked his Doctrine and ordered United States forces into Lebanon. Shortly after American troops landed (July 15), the President issued a short statement justifying his decision. He then went on national radio and television to explain in greater detail why he had acted. The fear that the Iraqi revolt was part of an overall plot proved unwarranted. The United States went into Lebanon expecting opposition from leftist elements. Instead, little more than the normal political unrest was in evidence. The lack of any military contact puzzled American forces and even required a Presidential Message (July 19) to explain the need for their presence. The civil war ended quickly when the Lebanese made their own arrangements for a new President (September 23), but the world-wide implications of the American landing concerned the White House. A hastily taken Gallup poll indicated the reaction of several parts of the world to the problems involved.

Statement by President Eisenhower on Sending United States Forces to Lebanon
July 15, 1958
[*White House Press Release,* Official File 116-SS, Eisenhower Papers.]

Yesterday morning, I received from President Chamoun of Lebanon an urgent plea that some United States forces be stationed in Lebanon to help maintain security and to evidence the concern of the United States for the integrity and independence of Lebanon. President Chamoun's appeal was made with the concurrence of all of the members of the Lebanese Cabinet.

President Chamoun made clear that he considered an immediate United States response imperative if Lebanon's independence, already menaced from without, were to be preserved in the face of the grave developments which occurred yesterday in Baghdad whereby the lawful government was violently overthrown and many of its members martyred.

In response to this appeal from the government of Lebanon, the United States has dispatched a contingent of United States forces to Lebanon to protect American lives and by their presence there to encourage the Lebanese government in defense of Lebanese sovereignty and integrity. These forces have not been sent as any act of war. They will demonstrate the concern of the United States for the independence and integrity of Lebanon, which we deem vital to the national interest and world peace. Our concern will also be shown by economic assistance. We shall act in accordance with these legitimate concerns.

The United States, this morning, will report its action to an emergency meeting of the United Nations Security Council. As the United Nations charter recognizes, there is an inherent right of collective self-defense. In conformity with the spirit of the charter, the United States is reporting the measures taken by it to the Security Council of the United Nations, making clear that these measures will be terminated as soon as the Security Council has itself taken the measures necessary to maintain international peace and security.

The United States believes that the United Nations can and should take measures which are adequate to preserve the independence and integrity of Lebanon. It is apparent, however, that in the face of the tragic and shocking events that are occurring nearby, more will be required than the team of United Nations observers now in Lebanon. Therefore, the United States will support in the United Nations measures which seem to be adequate to meet the new situation and which will enable the United States forces promptly to be withdrawn.

Lebanon is a small peace-loving state with which the United States has traditionally had the most friendly relations. There are in Lebanon about 2500 Americans and we cannot, consistently with our historic relations and with the principles of the United Nations, stand idly by when Lebanon appeals itself for evidence of our concern and when Lebanon may not be able to preserve internal order and to defend itself against indirect aggression.

Statement by President Eisenhower Following the Landing of United States Marines at Beirut
July 15, 1958

[*Public Papers of the Presidents:1957* (Washington, 1958), 553–57.]

Yesterday was a day of grave developments in the Middle East. In Iraq a highly organized military blow struck down the duly constituted government and attempted to put in its place a committee of Army officers. The attack was conducted with great brutality. Many of the leading personalities were beaten to death or hanged and their bodies dragged through the streets.

At about the same time there was discovered a highly organized plot to overthrow the lawful government of Jordan.

Warned and alarmed by these developments, President Chamoun of Lebanon sent me an urgent plea that the United States station some military units in Lebanon to evidence our concern for the independence of Lebanon, that little country, which itself has for about two months been subjected to civil strife. This has been actively fomented by Soviet and Cairo broadcasts and abetted and aided by substantial amounts of arms, money and personnel infiltrated into Lebanon across the Syrian border.

President Chamoun stated that without an immediate show of United States support, the Government of Lebanon would be unable to survive against the forces which had been set loose in the area.

The plea of President Chamoun was supported by the unanimous action of the Lebanese Cabinet.

After giving this plea earnest thought and after taking advice from leaders of both the Executive and Congressional branches of the government, I decided to comply with the plea of the Government of Lebanon. A few hours ago a battalion of United States Marines landed and took up stations in and about the city of Beirut.

The mission of these forces is to protect American lives—there are about 2500 Americans in Lebanon—and by their presence to assist the Government of Lebanon to preserve its territorial integrity qnd political independence.

The United States does not, of course, intend to replace the United Nations which has a primary responsibility to maintain international peace and security. We reacted as we did within a matter of hours because the situation was such that only prompt action would suffice. We have, however, with equal promptness moved in the United Nations. This morning there was held at our request an emergency meeting of the United Nations Security Council. At this meeting we reported the action which we had taken. We stated the reasons therefor. We expressed the hope that the

United Nations would itself take measures which would be adequate to preserve the independence of Lebanon and permit of the early withdrawal of the United States forces.

I should like now to take a few minutes to explain the situation in Lebanon.

Lebanon is a small country, a little less than the size of Connecticut, with a population of about one and one half million. It has always had close and friendly relations with the United States. Many of you no doubt have heard of the American University at Beirut which has a distinguished record. Lebanon has been a prosperous, peaceful country, thriving on trade largely with the West. A little over a year ago there were general elections, held in an atmosphere of total calm, which resulted in the establishment, by an overwhelming popular vote, of the present Parliament for a period of four years. The term of the President, however, is of a different duration and would normally expire next September. The President, Mr. Chamoun, has made clear that he does not seek reelection.

When the attacks on the Government of Lebanon began to occur, it took the matter to the United Nations Security Council, pointing out that Lebanon was the victim of indirect aggression from without. As a result, the Security Council sent observers to Lebanon in the hope of thereby insuring that hostile intervention would cease. Secretary General Hammarskjold undertook a mission to the area to reinforce the work of the observers.

We believe that his efforts and those of the United Nations observers were helpful. They could not eliminate arms or ammunition or remove persons already sent into Lebanon. But we believe they did reduce such aid from across the border. It seemed, last week, that the situation was moving toward a peaceful solution which would preserve the integrity of Lebanon, and end indirect aggression from without.

Those hopes were, however, dashed by the events of yesterday in Iraq and Jordan. These events demonstrate a scope of aggressive purpose which tiny Lebanon could not combat without further evidence of support. That is why Lebanon's request for troops from the United States was made. That is why we have responded to that request.

Some will ask, does the stationing of some United States troops in Lebanon involve any interference in the internal affairs of Lebanon? The clear answer is "no."

First of all we have acted at the urgent plea of the Government of Lebanon, a government which has been freely elected by the people only a little over a year ago. It is entitled, as are we, to join in measures of collective security for self-defense. Such action, the United Nations Charter recognizes, is an "inherent right."

In the second place what we now see in the Middle East is the same pattern of conquest with which we became familiar during the period of

1945 to 1950. This involves taking over a nation by means of indirect aggression; that is, under the cover of a fomented civil strife the purpose is to put into domestic control those whose real loyalty is to the aggressor.

It was by such means that the Communists attempted to take over Greece in 1947. That effort was thwarted by the Truman Doctrine.

It was by such means that the Communists took over Czechoslovakia in 1948.

It was by such means that the Communists took over the mainland of China in 1949.

It was by such means that the Communists attempted to take over Korea and Indo China, beginning in 1950.

You will remember at the time of the Korean war that the Soviet Government claimed that this was merely a civil war, because the only attack was by North Koreans upon South Koreans. But all the world knew that the North Koreans were armed, equipped and directed from without for the purpose of aggression.

This means of conquest was denounced by the United Nations General Assembly when it adopted in November 1950 its Resolution entitled, "Peace through Deeds." It thereby called upon every nation to refrain from "fomenting civil strife in the interest of a foreign power" and denounced such action as "the gravest of all crimes against peace and security throughout the world."

We had hoped that these threats to the peace and to the independence and integrity of small nations had come to an end. Unhappily, now they reappear. Lebanon was selected to become a victim.

Last year, the Congress of the United States joined with the President to declare that "the United States regards as vital to the national interest and world·peace the preservation of the independence and integrity of the nations of the Middle East."

I believe that the presence of the United States forces now being sent to Lebanon will have a stabilizing effect which will preserve the independence and integrity of Lebanon. It will also afford an increased measure of security to the thousands of Americans who reside in Lebanon.

We know that stability and well-being cannot be achieved purely by military measures. The economy of Lebanon has been gravely strained by civil strife. Foreign trade and tourist traffic have almost come to a standstill. The United States stands ready, under its Mutual Security Program, to cooperate with the Government of Lebanon to find ways to restore its shattered economy. Thus we shall help to bring back to Lebanon a peace which is not merely the absence of fighting but the well-being of the people.

I am well aware of the fact that landing of United States troops in Lebanon could have some serious consequences. That is why this step was taken only after the most serious consideration and broad consultation. I have, however, come to the sober and clear conclusion that the action taken was essential to the welfare of the United States. It was required to support the principles of justice and international law upon which peace and a stable international order depend.

That, and that alone, is the purpose of the United States. We are not actuated by any hope of material gain or by any emotional hostility against any person or any government. Our dedication is to the principles of the United Nations Charter and to the preservation of the independence of every state. That is the basic pledge of the United Nations Charter.

Yet indirect aggression and violence are being promoted in the Near East in clear violation of the provisions of the United Nations Charter.

There can be no peace in the world unless there is fuller dedication to the basic principles of the United Nations Charter. If ever the United States fails to support these principles the result would be to open the flood gates to direct and indirect aggression throughout the world.

In the 1930's the members of the League of Nations became indifferent to direct and indirect aggression in Europe, Asia and Africa. The result was to strengthen and stimulate aggressive forces that made World War II inevitable.

The United States is determined that that history shall not now be repeated. We are hopeful that the action which we are taking will both preserve the independence of Lebanon and check international violations which, if they succeeded, would endanger world peace.

We hope that this result will quickly be attained and that our forces can be promptly withdrawn. We must, however, be prepared to meet the situation, whatever be the consequences. We can do so, confident that we strive for a world in which nations, be they great or be they small, can preserve their independence. We are striving for an ideal which is close to the heart of every American and for which in the past many Americans have laid down their lives.

To serve these ideals is also to serve the cause of peace, security and well-being, not only for us, but for all men everywhere.

Message from President Eisenhower to United States Forces in Lebanon
July 19, 1958
[*White House Press Release,* Official File 116-SS, Eisenhower Papers.]

This is the President.

I am talking to you from my office in the White House.

I want to speak personally to the officers and men of our forces—Marines, Sailors, Soldiers and Airmen—who are now in Lebanon, on the Mediterranean Sea, or in the skies over that area.

You are in Lebanon because the United States has responded to an urgent request from Lebanon, a friendly country, for help in preserving its cherished independence which has been gravely threatened. Lebanon is a free nation—properly proud of its history and its traditions. The Lebanese people—like us—want only to live in peace and in freedom. They do not want to impose their will on any other people; they do not want to conquer or enslave any other nation.

But unfortunately their hopes and aspirations to remain free are now threatened. A large part of that threat comes from outside forces which have sent men and munitions into Lebanon to help in destroying its democratic government, based upon free popular elections.

Lebanon had no recourse but to appeal for assistance. Their President, with the unanimous approval of the Cabinet, asked me to help them maintain their independence. After careful consideration and consultation with the leaders of our Congress, I decided that the appeal for help had to be honored—that unless Lebanon received help, pending necessary enlarged United Nations support which could not be immediately furnished, it would cease to exist as a free and independent country.

You are helping the Lebanese people to remain free.

You are there at their invitation—as friends—to preserve for them the same freedoms that we have here at home.

As your first elements were landing on the beaches of Lebanon, your government was taking action in the United Nations in an attempt to get increased United Nations effort to help the Lebanon Republic to protect its freedom. We have not yet succeeded in this attempt, but we will persevere.

As soon as the independence and integrity of Lebanon are secure, then you and your comrades will be withdrawn immediately from the country.

While you are in Lebanon, each of you is a personal representative of the United States—a symbol of the national aspirations for freedom for all people.

While on this duty you may be assailed by propaganda whipped up by skillful and ambitious men. There may be deliberate attempts to involve you as units—or individually—in incidents which will be greatly exaggerated by these propagandists to suit their own purposes.

Through it all, just remember you are representing the United States of America—that you are true to her ideals in helping a people to keep their freedom. We have no hostile intent toward any people anywhere in the world.

It will be a trying time for all of you. I know that.

But I also know that you are American servicemen, trained to do your duty to your country.

Right now, the performance of that duty is the greatest contribution you can make to the peace of the world—the saving of the freedom of a small and friendly country.

Through me our people here at home thank you.

God bless you all!

USIA Director George Allen
to Staff Secretary Andrew Goodpaster
July 21, 1958

[Official File 116-SS, Eisenhower Papers.]

Official Use Only

Attached are the results of a Gallup "Flash" survey of reactions in some major world opinion centers to the Middle East crisis. Findings are based upon small high-speed samples of about 200 personal interviews in each city surveyed, conducted between July 17th and 19th, 1958. This pre-publication summary has been provided by the Gallup organization as a courtesy to the U. S. Government.

The fact that emerges most clearly from this study is that the idea of sending a UN emergency force into Lebanon is predominantly approved in every city surveyed.

Secondly it appears rather clear that except in the two Middle Eastern cities surveyed, Athens and New Delhi, and to a lesser degree in Santiago, Chile, there is predominant disapproval of what Nasser is trying to do in the Near East.

As to the U. S. action in sending troops in Lebanon, or in general what the U. S. is trying to do in the Near East, opinion appears divided. A predominance of approval on one or the other query appears to be most evident in Melbourne, in Toronto, in the U. S. cities surveyed (New York, Chicago, San Francisco) and in Great Britain. Disapproval prevails most clearly in New Delhi, in Athens, and interestingly enough, in Paris.

"Do you approve or disapprove of United States action in sending troops into Lebanon?"

Western Europe	Net Approval[1]	Approve	Disapprove	No Opinion
W.E. AVERAGE	6	42%	36%	22%
Great Britain[2]	24	52	28	20
Copenhagen	18	45	27	28
Amsterdam	15	51	36	13
West Berlin	12	53	41	6
Milan	11	49	38	13
Helsinki	−10	31	41	28
Vienna	−13	23	36	41
Paris	−17	28	45	27
(Stockholm[3])				

Western Europe	Net Approval[1]	Approve	Disapprove	No Opinion
Near East				
Athens	−27	19	46	35
New Delhi[4]				
Far East				
Melbourne	50	69	19	12
Latin America				
Montevideo	15	37	22	41
Santiago	−17	26	43	31
(Mexico City[3])				
North America				
N.Y./Chicago/ San Francisco	32	59	27	14
Toronto[4]				

[1]"Net Approval" equals "Approve" minus "Disapprove."
[2]Great Britain figures are based on a nationwide sample of 1000 cases, including London. Only this first question was asked in Great Britain.
[3]Findings will be available by July 22.
[4]This question was not asked in New Delhi or Toronto because of errors in cable transmission.

*   *   *

"Do you favor or oppose the United Nations sending an Emergency Force into Lebanon?"

Western Europe	Net Favoring[1]	Favor	Oppose	No Opinion
W.E. AVERAGE	39	61%	22%	17%
Helsinki	58	71	13	16
Copenhagen	55	68	13	19
West Berlin	44	69	25	6
Milan	43	66	23	11
Vienna	33	53	20	27
Amsterdam	22	54	32	14
Paris	14	44	30	26
(Stockholm)				
Near East				
New Delhi	37	54	17	29
Athens	10	39	29	32
Far East				
Melbourne	44	65	21	14

Western Europe	Net Favoring[1]	Favor	Oppose	No Opinion
Latin America				
Montevideo	34	48	14	38
Santiago	15	47	32	21
(Mexico City)				
North America				
Toronto	74	82	8	10
N.Y./Chi./San Fran.	69	79	10	11

[1]"Net" equals "Favor" minus "Oppose".

*   *   *

"In general, do you have a favorable or unfavorable impression of what President Nasser of Egypt is trying to do in the Near East?"

Western Europe	Net Favorable[1] to Nasser	Favorable	Unfavorable	No Opinion
W.E. AVERAGE	−38	18%	56%	26%
West Berlin	−24	33	57	10
Milan	−28	25	53	22
Helsinki	−34	12	46	42
Vienna	−38	10	48	42
Copenhagen	−43	13	56	31
Paris	−46	14	60	26
Amsterdam	−53	15	68	17
(Stockholm)				
Near East				
New Delhi	47	52	5	43
Athens	39	48	9	43
Far East				
Melbourne	−72	6	78	16
Latin America				
Santiago	2	27	25	48
Montevideo	−16	11	27	62
(Mexico City)				
North America				
N.Y./Chi./San Fran.	−51	9	60	31
Toronto	−64	9	73	18

[1]"Net" equals "Favorable" minus "Unfavorable."

*   *   *

"In general, do you have a favorable or unfavorable impression of what the United States is trying to do in the Near East?"

Western Europe	Net Favorable[1] to U.S.	Favorable	Unfavorable	No Opinion
W.E. AVERAGE	6	42%	36%	22%
West Berlin	47	69	22	8
Copenhagen	13	41	28	31
Amsterdam	11	47	36	17
Milan	6	45	39	16
Helsinki	−3	35	38	27
Vienna	−4	32	36	32
Paris	−31	23	54	23
(Stockholm)				
Near East				
Athens	−25	18	43	39
New Delhi	−51	4	55	41
Far East				
Melbourne	50	68	18	14
Latin America				
Montevideo	10	26	16	58
Santiago	−11	28	39	33
(Mexico City)				
North America				
Toronto	52	72	20	8
N.Y./Chi./San Fran.	30	56	26	18

[1]"Net" equals "Favorable" minus "Unfavorable".

The Soviets reacted to American intervention in the Middle East with a violent propaganda offensive—Premier Nikita Khrushchev talked of turning the ships of the 6th Fleet into "modern coffins" (July 25). An exchange of unfriendly letters between the White House and the Kremlin led to an Eisenhower proposal that he and Khrushchev meet at a special summit meeting in the Security Council. The Russian Premier accepted but Far Eastern events required his presence in Peking (July 31–August 3). Then, as the situation in the Middle East cooled down—it became clear that nationalistic elements dominated the revolutionary government in Iraq—the United States lost interest in a special session of the Security Council and agreed to abandon the idea on August 5. The Soviets, for reasons of their own, called an emergency meeting of the United Nations General Assembly (August 8–21). Partly because the President appeared in person (August 13), while Khrushchev remained away, the meeting turned to the advantage of the United States. Eisenhower's address on the needs of the Middle East set the tone. A friendly exchange of letters between the President and Secretary General Dag Hammarskjold indicated the American role in the passage of a General Assembly Middle East resolution supported by the Administration (August 19). The resolution provided one more possibility of bringing peace to the Middle East. Two months later— almost as an after-thought—American troops completely withdrew from Lebanon (October 25). The President's final statement to his forces reviewed the events of the summer and fall.

Address by President Eisenhower to the United Nations General Assembly, August 13, 1958

[*Public Papers of the Presidents: 1958* (Washington, 1959), 606–16.]

It has been almost five years since I had the honor of addressing this Assembly. I then spoke of atomic power and urged that we should find the way by which the miraculous inventiveness of man should not be dedicated to his death but consecrated to his life. Since then great strides have been taken in the use of atomic energy for peaceful purposes. Tragically little has been done to eliminate the use of atomic and nuclear power for weapons purposes.

That is a danger.

That danger in turn gives rise to another danger—the danger that nations under aggressive leadership will seek to exploit man's horror of war by confronting the nations, particularly small nations, with an apparent choice between supine surrender, or war.

This tactic reappeared during the recent Near East crisis.

Some might call it "ballistic blackmail."

In most communities it is illegal to cry "fire" in a crowded assembly. Should it not be considered serious international misconduct to manufacture a general war scare in an effort to achieve local political aims?

Pressures such as these will never be successfully practiced against America, but they do create dangers which could affect each and every one of us. That is why I have asked for the privilege of again addressing you.

The immediate reason is two small countries—Lebanon and Jordan.

The cause is one of universal concern.

The lawful and freely elected Government of Lebanon, feeling itself endangered by civil strife fomented from without, sent the United States a desperate call for instant help. We responded to that call.

On the basis of that response an effort has been made to create a war hysteria. The impression is sought to be created that if small nations are assisted in their desire to survive, that endangers the peace.

This is truly an "upside down" portrayal. If it is made an international crime to help a small nation maintain its independence, then indeed the possibilities of conquest are unlimited. We will have nullified the provision of our Charter which recognizes the inherent right of collective self-defense. We will let loose forces that could generate great disasters.

The United Nations has, of course, a primary responsibility to maintain not only international peace but also "security." That is an important fact. But we must not evade a second fact, namely, that in the circumstances of the world since 1945, the United Nations has sometimes been blocked in its attempt to fulfill that function.

Respect for the liberty and freedom of all nations has always been a guiding principle of the United States. This respect has been consistently demonstrated by our unswerving adherence to the principles of the Charter, particularly in its opposition to aggression, direct or indirect. Sometimes we have made that demonstration in terms of collective measures called for by the United Nations. Sometimes we have done so pursuant to what the Charter calls "the inherent right of collective self-defense."

I recall the moments of clear danger we have faced since the end of the Second World War—Iran, Greece and Turkey, the Berlin blockade, Korea, the Straits of Taiwan.

A common principle guided the position of the United States on all of these occasions. That principle was that aggression, direct or indirect, must be checked before it gathered sufficient momentum to destroy us all—aggressor and defender alike.

It was this principle that was applied once again when the urgent appeals of the governments of Lebanon and Jordan were answered.

I would be less than candid if I did not tell you that the United States reserves, within the spirit of the Charter, the right to answer the legitimate appeal of any nation, particularly small nations.

I doubt that a single free government in all the world would willingly forego the right to ask for help if its sovereignty were imperiled.

But I must again emphasize that the United States seeks always to keep within the spirit of the Charter.

Thus when President Truman responded in 1947 to the urgent plea of Greece, the United States stipulated that our assistance would be withdrawn whenever the United Nations felt that its action could take the place of ours.

Similarly, when the United States responded to the urgent plea of Lebanon, we went at once to the Security Council and sought United Nations assistance for Lebanon so as to permit the withdrawal of United States forces.

United Nations action would have been taken, the United States forces already withdrawn, had it not been that two resolutions, one proposed by the United States, the other proposed by the Government of Japan, failed to pass because of one negative vote—a veto.

But nothing that I have said is to be construed as indicating that I regard the status quo as sacrosanct. Change is indeed the law of life and progress. But when change reflects the will of the people, then change can and should be brought about in peaceful ways.

In this context the United States respects the right of every Arab nation of the Near East to live in freedom without domination from any source, far or near.

In the same context, we believe that the Charter of the United Nations places on all of us certain solemn obligations. Without respect for each other's sovereignty and the exercise of great care in the means by which new patterns of international life are achieved, the projection of the peaceful vision of the Charter would become a mockery.

II

Let me turn now specifically to the problem of Lebanon.

When the United States military assistance began moving into Lebanon, I reported to the American people that we had immediately reacted to the plea of Lebanon because the situation was such that only prompt action would suffice.

I repeat to you the solemn pledge I then made: our assistance to Lebanon has but one single purpose—that is the purpose of the Charter and of such historic resolutions of the United Nations as the "Essentials for Peace" Resolution of 1949 and the "Peace through Deeds" Resolution of 1950. These denounce, as a form of aggression and as an international crime, the fomenting of civil strife in the interest of a foreign power.

We want to prevent that crime—or at least prevent its having fatal consequences. We have no other purpose whatsoever.

The United States troops will be totally withdrawn whenever this is requested by the duly constituted government of Lebanon or whenever, through action by the United Nations or otherwise, Lebanon is no longer exposed to the original danger.

It is my earnest hope that this Assembly, free of the veto, will consider how it can assure the continued independence and integrity of Lebanon, so that the political destiny of the Lebanese people will continue to lie in their own hands.

The United States Delegation will support measures to this end.

III

Another urgent problem is Jordan.

If we do not act promptly in Jordan a further dangerous crisis may result, for the method of indirect aggression discernible in Jordan may lead to conflicts endangering the peace.

We must recognize that peace in this area is fragile, and we must also recognize that the end of peace in Jordan could have consequences of a far-reaching nature. The United Nations has a particular responsibility in this matter, since it sponsored the Palestine Armistice Agreements upon which peace in the area rests and since it also sponsors the care of the Palestine refugees.

I hope this Assembly will be able to give expression to the interest of the United Nations in preserving the peace in Jordan.

IV

There is another matter which this Assembly should face in seeking to promote stability in the Near East. That is the question of inflammatory propaganda. The United Nations Assembly has on three occasions—in 1947, 1949 and 1950—passed resolutions designed to stop the projecting of irresponsible broadcasts from one nation into the homes of citizens of other nations, thereby "fomenting civil strife and subverting the will of the people in any State." We all know that these resolutions have recently been violated in many directions in the Near East.

If we, the United States, have been at fault we stand ready to be corrected.

I believe that this Assembly should reaffirm its enunciated policy and should consider means for monitoring the radio broadcasts directed across national frontiers in the troubled Near East area and for examining complaints from these nations which consider their national security jeopardized by external propaganda.

V

The countries of this area should also be freed from armed pressure and infiltration coming across their borders. When such interference threatens they should be able to get from the United Nations prompt and effective action to help safeguard their independence. This requires that adequate machinery be available to make the United Nations presence manifest in the area of trouble.

Therefore I believe this Assembly should take action looking toward the creation of a standby United Nations Peace Force. The need for such a Force in being is clearly demonstrated by recent events involving imminent danger to the integrity of two of our members.

I understand that this general subject is to be discussed at the 13th General Assembly and that our distinguished Secretary-General has taken an initiative in this matter. Recent events clearly demonstrate that this is a matter for urgent and positive action.

VI

I have proposed four areas of action for the consideration of the Assembly—in respect to Lebanon, Jordan, subversive propaganda and a standby United Nations force. These measures, basically, are designed to do one thing: to preserve the right of a nation and its people to determine their own destiny, consistent with the obligation to respect the rights of others.

This clearly applies to the great surge of Arab nationalism.

Let me state the position of my country unmistakably. The peoples of the Arab nations of the Near East clearly possess the right of determining and expressing their own destiny. Other nations should not interfere so long as this expression is found in ways compatible with international peace and security.

However, here as in other areas we have an opportunity to share in a great international task. That is the task of assisting the peoples of that area, under programs which they may desire, to make further progress toward the goals of human welfare they have set. Only on the basis of progressing economies can truly independent governments sustain themselves.

This is a real challenge to the Arab people and to us all.

To help the Arab countries fulfill these aspirations, here is what I propose:

First—that consultations be immediately undertaken by the Secretary-General with the Arab nations of the Near East to ascertain whether an agreement can be reached to establish an Arab development institution on a regional basis.

Second—that these consultations consider the composition and the possible functions of a regional Arab development institution, whose task would be to accelerate progress in such fields as industry, agriculture, water supply, health and education.

Third—other nations and private organizations which might be prepared to support this institution should also be consulted at an appropriate time.

Should the Arab States agree on the usefulness of such a soundly organized regional institution, and should they be prepared to support it with their own resources, the United States would also be prepared to support it.

The institution would be set up to provide loans to the Arab States as well as the technical assistance required in the formulation of development projects.

The institution should be governed by the Arab States themselves.

This proposal for a regional Arab development institution can, I believe, be realized on a basis which would attract international capital, both public and private.

I also believe that the best and quickest way to achieve the most desirable result would be for the Secretary-General to make two parallel approaches. First, to consult with the Arab States of the Near East to determine an area of agreement. Then to invite the International Bank for Reconstruction and Development, which has vast experience in this field, to make available its facilities for the planning of the organizational and operating techniques needed to establish the institution on a progressive course.

I hope it is clear that I am not suggesting a position of leadership for my own country in the work of creating such an institution. If this institution is to be a success, the function of leadership must belong to the Arab States themselves.

I would hope that high on the agenda of this institution would be action to meet one of the major challenges of the Near East, the great common shortage—water.

Much scientific and engineering work is already under way in the field of water development. For instance, atomic isotopes now permit us to chart the course of the great underground rivers. And new horizons are opening in the desalting of water. The ancient problem of water is on the threshold of solution. Energy, determination and science will carry it over that threshold.

Another great challenge facing the area is disease.

Already there is substantial effort among the peoples and governments of the Near East to conquer disease and disability. But much more remains to be done.

The United States is prepared to join with other governments and the World Health Organization in an all-out, joint attack on preventable disease in the Near East.

But to see the desert blossom again and preventable disease conquered is only a first step. As I look into the future I see the emergence of modern Arab States that would bring to this century contributions surpassing those we cannot forget from the past. We remember that Western arithmetic and algebra owe much to Arabic mathematicians and that much of the foundation of the world's medical science and astronomy was laid by Arab scholars. Above all, we remember that three of the world's great religions were born in the Near East.

But a true Arab renaissance can only develop in a healthy human setting. Material progress should not be an overriding objective in itself; but it is an important condition for achieving higher human, cultural and spiritual objectives.

But I repeat, if this vision of the modern Arab community is to come to life, the goals must be Arab goals.

VII

With the assistance of the United Nations, the countries of the Near East now have a unique opportunity to advance, in freedom, their security and their political and economic interests. If a plan for peace of the kind I am proposing can be carried forward, in a few short years we may be able to look back on the Lebanon and Jordan crises as the beginning of a great new era of Arab history.

But there is an important consideration which must remain in mind today and in the future.

If there is an end to external interference in the internal affairs of the Arab States of the Near East:—

If an adequate United Nations Peace Force is in existence ready for call by countries fearful for their security:—

If a regional development institution exists and is at work on the basic projects and programs designed to lift the living standards of the area, supported by friendly aid from abroad and governed by the Arab States themselves:—

Then with this good prospect, and indeed as a necessary condition for its fulfillment, I hope and believe that the nations of the area, intellectually and emotionally, will no longer feel the need to seek national security through spiralling military buildups which lead not only to economic impotence but to war.

Perhaps the nations involved in the 1948 hostilities may, as a first step, wish to call for a United Nations study of the flow of heavy armaments to those nations. My country would be glad to support the establishment of an appropriate United Nations body to examine this problem. This body would discuss it individually with these countries and see what arms control arrangements could be worked out under which the security of all these nations could be maintained more effectively than under a continued wasteful, dangerous competition in armaments. I recognize that any such arrangements must reflect these countries' own views.

VIII

I have tried to present to you the framework of a plan for peace in the Near East which would provide a setting of political order responsive to the rights of the people in each nation; which would avoid the dangers of a regional arms race; which would permit the peoples of the Near East to devote their energies wholeheartedly to the tasks of development and human progress in the widest sense.

It is important that the six elements of this program be viewed as a whole. They are:

(1) United Nations concern for Lebanon.

(2) United Nations measures to preserve peace in Jordan.

(3) An end to the fomenting from without of civil strife.

(4) A United Nations Peace Force.

(5) A regional economic development plan to assist and accelerate improvement in the living standards of the people in these Arab nations.

(6) Steps to avoid a new arms race spiral in the area.

To have solidity, the different elements of this plan for peace and progress should be considered and acted on together, as integral elements of a single concerted effort.

Therefore, I hope that this Assembly will seek simultaneously to set in motion measures that would create a climate of security in the Near East consonant with the principles of the United Nations Charter, and at the same time create the framework for a common effort to raise the standard of living of the Arab peoples.

IX

But the peoples of the Near East are not alone in their ambition for independence and development. We are living in a time when the whole world has become alive to the possibilities for modernizing their societies.

The American government has been steadily enlarging its allocations to foreign economic development in response to these worldwide hopes. We have joined in partnership with such groupings as the Organization of American States and the Colombo Plan; and we are working on methods to strengthen these regional arrangements. For example, in the case of the Organization of American States, we are consulting with our sister republics of this hemisphere to strengthen its role in economic development. And the government of the United States has not been alone in supporting development efforts. The British Commonwealth, the countries of Western Europe, and Japan have all made significant contributions.

But in many parts of the world both geography and wise economic planning favor national rather than regional development programs. The United States will, of course, continue its firm support of such national programs. Only where the desire for a regional approach is clearly manifested and where the advantage of regional over national is evident will the United States change to regional methods.

The United States is proud of the scope and variety of its development activities throughout the world. Those who know our history will realize that this is no sudden, new policy of my government. Ever since its birth, the United States has gladly shared its wealth with others. This it has done without thought of conquest or economic domination. After victory in two world wars and the expenditure of vast treasure there is no world map, either geographic or economic, on which anyone can find that the force of American arms or the power of the American Treasury has absorbed any foreign land or political or economic system. As we cherish our freedom, we believe in freedom for others.

X

The things I have talked about today are real and await our grasp. Within the Near East and within this Assembly are the forces of good sense, restraint, and wisdom to make, with time and patience, a framework of political order and of peace in that region.

But we also know that all these possibilities are shadowed, all our hopes are dimmed, by the fact of the arms race in nuclear weapons—a contest which drains off our best talents and vast resources, straining the nerves of all our peoples.

As I look out on this Assembly, with so many of you representing new nations, one thought above all impresses me.

The world that is being remade on our planet is going to be a world of many mature nations. As one after another of these new nations moves through the difficult transition to modernization and learns the methods of growth, from this travail new levels of prosperity and productivity will emerge.

This world of individual nations is not going to be controlled by any one power or group of powers. This world is not going to be committed to any one ideology.

Please believe me when I say that the dream of world domination by one power or of world conformity is an impossible dream.

The nature of today's weapons, the nature of modern communications, and the widening circle of new nations make it plain that we must, in the end, be a world community of open societies.

And the concept of the open society is the ultimate key to a system of arms control we can all trust.

We must, then, seek with new vigor, new initiative, the path to a peace based on the effective control of armaments, on economic advancement and on the freedom of all peoples to be ruled by governments of their choice. Only thus can we exercise the full capacity God has given us to enrich the lives of the individual human beings who are our ultimate concern, our responsibility and our strength.

In this memorable task there lies enough work and enough reward to satisfy the energies and ambitions of all leaders, everywhere.

Secretary General Dag Hammarskjold to President Eisenhower August 20, 1958

[Official File 116-SS-1, Eisenhower Papers.]

Dear Mr. President,

I am grateful for your letter of 15 August regarding the occasion of your address to the General Assembly.

I was glad that you were able once again to honor the Assembly with your presence and to bring a message which has been widely reflected in the debate.

After much negotiation it appears that the Assembly may be presented with a resolution that will meet with its general approval. I hope that with the steps that have been taken here and the follow-up that may be possible in the area, we may look forward to some improvement in the crisis spots of that area.

Again, you have my sincere thanks for your presence and your constructive address.

President Eisenhower to Secretary General Dag Hammarskjold August 26, 1958

[Official File 116-SS-1, Eisenhower Papers.]

Dear Mr. Secretary-General:

I appreciate your letter of August twentieth and your remarks about my address.

The decision taken by the General Assembly last week is a clear expression by the Members of the United Nations of their confidence in you. The United States shares that confidence.

Let me say also how deeply impressed I have been by your brilliant and tireless efforts in behalf of the peace of the world.

General Assembly Resolution on the Near East
August 19, 1958

[Department of State, *Bulletin,* XXXIX (September 15, 1958), 411–12.]

The General Assembly,

Having considered the item "Questions considered by the Security Council at its 838th meeting on 7 August 1958",

Noting the Charter aim that States should "practise tolerance and live together in peace with one another as good neighbours",

Noting that the Arab States have agreed, in the Pact of the League of Arab States to "strengthen the close relations and numerous ties which link the Arab States, and to support and stabilize these ties upon a basis of respect for the independence and sovereignty of these States, and to direct their efforts toward the common good of all the Arab countries, the improvement of their status, the security of their future and the realizaton of their aspirations and hopes",

Desiring to relieve international tension,

I

1. *Welcomes* the renewed assurances given by the Arab States to observe the provision of Article 8 of the Pact of the League of Arab States that "Each member State shall respect the systems of government established in the other member States and regard them as exclusive concerns of these States", and that "Each shall pledge to abstain from any action calculated to change established systems of government";

2. *Calls upon* all States Members of the United Nations to act strictly in accordance with the principles of mutual respect for each other's territorial integrity and sovereignty, of non-aggression, of strict non-interference in each other's internal affairs, and of equal and mutual benefit, and to ensure that their conduct by word and deed conforms to these principles;

II

Requests the Secretary-General to make forthwith, in consultation with the Governments concerned and in accordance with the Charter, and having in mind part I of this resolution, such practical arrangements as would adequately help in upholding the purposes and principles of the Charter in relation to Lebanon and Jordan in the present circumstances, and thereby facilitate the early withdrawal of the foreign troops from the two countries;

III

Invites the Secretary-General to continue his studies now under way and in this context to consult as appropriate with the Arab countries of the Near East with a view to possible assistance regarding an Arab development institution designed to further economic growth in these countries;

IV

1. *Requests* Member States to co-operate fully in carrying out this resolution;

2. *Invites* the Secretary-General to report hereunder, as appropriate, the first such report to be made not later than 30 September 1958.

Message from President Eisenhower to
United States Forces in Lebanon
October 18, 1958

[*Public Papers of the Presidents: 1958* (Washington, 1959), 756–57.]

This is the President.

Three months ago I spoke to you as you undertook the important task of helping Lebanon to maintain its independence. Your mission has now been performed.

You have written a new and honorable chapter in the history of America's dedication to freedom.

Let us recall what happened.

A small nation was imperiled by outside influences. In its moment of trial, Lebanon appealed to us for help. We promptly responded to meet the need. That need was met, and met peacefully. The United Nations also acted to strengthen the defense of Lebanon, and, as a result of your presence and of that action of the United Nations, the need is past and you are now withdrawing.

Two great lessons have been taught.

First, the United States is a friend to those who wish to live their own lives in freedom. We are not deterred by threats or abuse from giving needed help.

Second, the United States never seeks to turn the necessities of others into gains for itself.

I pledged to you, as you went forward, that as soon as the independence of Lebanon seemed secure, you would be immediately withdrawn.

That pledge is now being redeemed.

The United States has no aggressive ambitions. We have no desire to impose our will upon others. Just as we responded rapidly to the call for help, so we are responding rapidly to the ending of the need for help.

World order, and the independence of small nations everywhere, are more secure both because of your going to Lebanon and because of your now leaving Lebanon.

As you return to your regular duties, I express the pride of all America in the way you have performed your duties. You have conducted yourselves in an exemplary way that assured you a friendly reception from the Lebanese authorities and people. You have served a noble cause in the best tradition of American servicemen.

On behalf of the American people—thank you.

The Middle East returned to its usual state of "near war" in the months and years following the crisis of 1958. As the Eisenhower Administration drew to a close, a staff report indicated the continuing tensions in the area.

Memorandum from Assistant Special Counsel Phillip Areeda to President Eisenhower
July 29, 1960
[Official File 116-MM, Eisenhower Papers.]

For your consideration and transmittal to the Congress, the Secretary of State forwards a draft semi-annual Presidential report under the 1957 Joint Resolution concerning "Peace and Stability in the Middle East."

The report makes the following points:

(a) The Sino-Soviet bloc increased its aid to several Middle Eastern countries, notably the United Arab Republic (Aswan Dam), Yemen (port facilities), and Iraq (various).

(b) Conditions in the area remain relatively stable although the basic problems existing between Arab countries and Israel remain largely unresolved.

(c) The area continues its preoccupation with problems of economic development.

(d) Continued aid from the United States has helped materially in building the strength of these countries to resist communist pressures and has encouraged accelerated economic growth. The details are not stated in this unclassified report.

(e) United States contributions to support United Nations activities in the region have totaled $40.9 million through fiscal year 1960.

Your signature is recommended for the attached two letters of transmittal to the Congress.

5. THE FORMOSA RESOLUTION
AND THE QUEMOY-MATSU CRISIS

The situation in the Formosa Straits deteriorated markedly late in 1954. A mutual defense treaty between the United States and the Republic of China (March 3, 1955) did not still rumors of possible American efforts to "neutralize" Formosa, a position which had been proposed by European allies. Eisenhower, strongly believing the need for a clarifying statement, drafted a Special Message for Congress. Before the message reached the Hill, Minnesota Republican Representative Walter Judd, usually associated with a "hard line" on China policy, wired the President warning against the dangers of conciliating Communist China (January 22, 1955). Two days later, when the Special Message reached Congress, American intentions became clear. While holding out the possibilities for peaceful solutions, it could not be considered a "sell out." Congress acted swiftly, passing a resolution five days after the President's request. Both the Administration and Congress hoped that the wording would clarify United States policy over Formosa. Promptly, Eisenhower thanked Senator William Knowland for his assistance, and Sherman Adams assured Congressman Judd that American aims had not changed.

Telegram from Representative Walter Judd
to President Eisenhower
January 22, 1955
[Official File 168-B-1, Eisenhower Papers.]

MR. PRESIDENT: MAY I SUBMIT TWO SUGGESTIONS?

FIRST, IN ANY POLICY OR MESSAGE REGARDING FORMOSA I URGE THAT THE U.S.A. NOT NEUTRALIZE OR STERILIZE FORMOSA BUT ALLOW IT TO CONTINUE AS THREAT ON FLANK OF COMMUNIST CHINA TO DETER ITS MOVING FURTHER INTO SOUTH EAST ASIA. IT WAS PROTECTION OF THEIR FLANK BY THE SEVENTH FLEET IN TRUMAN'S ORDER OF 1950 THAT ASSURED COMMUNISTS THEY COULD INTERVENE IN KOREA WITH NO FEAR FROM THAT SOURCE. THEIR PRESENT

GOALS ARE NOT JUST FORMOSA BUT SOUTHEAST ASIA. TO
SUCCEED THEY MUST FIRST REDUCE FORMOSA OR GET US TO
REMOVE IT FROM ITS ROLE OF THORN IN THEIR SIDE. FOR US
TO IMPOSE A CEASE FIRE IN FORMOSA STRAITS WOULD BE
ALMOST AS USEFUL TO OUR ENEMIES AS ITS CONQUEST
WOULD BE AND MUCH CHEAPER AND SAFER FOR THEM. SUCH
A STERILIZATION OF FORMOSA WOULD BE MORE LIKELY TO
EXPAND AND EXTEND COMMUNIST HOSTILITIES IN ASIA
THAN TO LIMIT THEM.

SECOND, I URGE THAT RELATIVES OF PRISONERS NOT BE
SENT TO VISIT THEM. DO FAMILIES WANT JUST TO SEE THEIR
LOVES ONES OR TO HAVE THEM HOME? IF THE LATTER,
THEN LET THE COMMUNISTS KNOW THEIR TORTURE OF
RELATIVES WILL NOT AVAIL TO WEAKEN US. IF REDS INTEND
TO KILL OUR MEN OR HOLD THEM INDEFINITELY, THEY
COULD NEVER HAVE DISCLOSED THEIR EXISTENCE OR THE
SENTENCES IMPOSED. THEY HAVE HELD THEM FOR THIS DAY
WHEN THEY HOPE TO USE THEM TO SOFTEN AMERICA'S WILL
AND DIVERT ATTENTION FROM THEIR NEW AGGRESSIONS.
THEY WILL KEEP PRISONERS AS LONG AS CAN EXPLOIT THEM.
ONLY RESULT OF RELATIVES GOING TO SEE THE MEN WILL
BE TO DELAY THEIR RELEASE.

Special Message to the Congress by President Eisenhower on United States Policy for the Defense of Formosa January 24, 1955

[*Public Papers of the Presidents: 1955* (Washington, 1959), 207–11.]

To the Congress of the United States:

The most important objective of our nation's foreign policy is to safeguard the security of the United States by establishing and preserving a just
and honorable peace. In the Western Pacific, a situation is developing in
the Formosa Straits, that seriously imperils the peace and our security.

Since the end of Japanese hostilities in 1945, Formosa and the Pescadores
have been in the friendly hands of our loyal ally, the Republic of China.
We have recognized that it was important that these islands should remain
in friendly hands. In unfriendly hands, Formosa and the Pescadores would
seriously dislocate the existing, even if unstable, balance of moral, economic
and military forces upon which the peace of the Pacific depends. It would
create a breach in the island chain of the Western Pacific that constitutes,
for the United States and other free nations, the geographical backbone of

their security structure in that Ocean. In addition, this breach would interrupt North-South communications between other important elements of that barrier, and damage the economic life of countries friendly to us.

The United States and the friendly Government of the Republic of China, and indeed all the free nations, have a common interest that Formosa and the Pescadores should not fall into the control of aggressive Communist forces.

Influenced by such considerations, our government was prompt, when the Communists committed armed aggression in Korea in June 1950, to direct our Seventh Fleet to defend Formosa from possible invasion from the Communist mainland.

These considerations are still valid. The Seventh Fleet continues under Presidential directive to carry out that defensive mission. We also provide military and economic support to the Chinese Nationalist Government and we cooperate in every proper and feasible way with that Government in order to promote its security and stability. All of these military and related activities will be continued.

In addition, there was signed last December a Mutual Defense Treaty between this Government and the Republic of China covering Formosa and the neighboring Pescadores. It is a treaty of purely defensive character. That Treaty is now before the Senate of the United States.

Meanwhile Communist China has pursued a series of provocative political and military actions, establishing a pattern of aggressive purpose. That purpose, they proclaim, is the conquest of Formosa.

In September 1954 the Chinese Communists opened up heavy artillery fire upon Quemoy island, one of the natural approaches to Formosa, which had for several years been under the uncontested control of the Republic of China. Then came air attacks of mounting intensity against other free China islands, notably those in the vicinity of the Tachen group to the north of Formosa. One small island (Ichiang) was seized last week by air and amphibious operations after a gallant few fought bravely for days against overwhelming odds. There have been recent heavy air attacks and artillery fire against the main Tachen Islands themselves.

The Chinese Communists themselves assert that these attacks are a prelude to the conquest of Formosa. For example, after the fall of Ichiang, the Peiping Radio said that it showed a "determined will to fight for the liberation of Taiwan (Formosa). Our people will use all their strength to fulfill that task."

Clearly, this existing and developing situation poses a serious danger to the security of our country and of the entire Pacific area and indeed to the peace of the world. We believe that the situation is one for appropriate action of the United Nations under its charter, for the purpose of ending the present hostilities in that area. We would welcome assumption of such jurisdiction by that body.

Meanwhile, the situation has become sufficiently critical to impel me, without awaiting action by the United Nations, to ask the Congress to participate now, by specific resolution, in measures designed to improve the prospects for peace. These measures would contemplate the use of the armed forces of the United States if necessary to assure the security of Formosa and the Pescadores.

The actions that the United States must be ready to undertake are of various kinds. For example, we must be ready to assist the Republic of China to redeploy and consolidate its forces if it should so desire. Some of these forces are scattered throughout the smaller off-shore islands as a result of historical rather than military reasons directly related to defending Formosa. Because of the air situation in the area, withdrawals for the purpose of redeployment of Chinese Nationalist forces would be impractical without assistance of the armed forces of the United States.

Moreover, we must be alert to any concentration or employment of Chinese Communist forces obviously undertaken to facilitate attack upon Formosa, and be prepared to take appropriate military action.

I do not suggest that the United States enlarge its defensive obligations beyond Formosa and the Pescadores as provided by the Treaty now awaiting ratification. But unhappily, the danger of armed attack directed against that area compels us to take into account closely related localities and actions which, under current conditions, might determine the failure or the success of such an attack. The authority that may be accorded by the Congress would be used only in situations which are recognizable as parts of, or definite preliminaries to, an attack against the main positions of Formosa and the Pescadores.

Authority for some of the actions which might be required would be inherent in the authority of the Commander-in-Chief. Until Congress can act I would not hesitate, so far as my Constitutional powers extend, to take whatever emergency action might be forced upon us in order to protect the rights and security of the United States.

However, a suitable Congressional resolution would clearly and publicly establish the authority of the President as Commander-in-Chief to employ the armed forces of this nation promptly and effectively for the purposes indicated if in his judgment it became necessary. It would make clear the unified and serious intentions of our Government, our Congress and our people. Thus it will reduce the possibility that the Chinese Communists, misjudging our firm purpose and national unity, might be disposed to challenge the position of the United States, and precipitate a major crisis which even they would neither anticipate nor desire.

In the interest of peace, therefore, the United States must remove any doubt regarding our readiness to fight, if necessary, to preserve the vital stake of the free world in a free Formosa, and to engage in whatever operations may be required to carry out that purpose.

To make this plain requires not only Presidential action but also Congressional action. In a situation such as now confronts us, and under modern conditions of warfare, it would not be prudent to await the emergency before coming to the Congress. Then it might be too late. Already the warning signals are flying.

I believe that the threatening aspects of the present situation, if resolutely faced, may be temporary in character. Consequently, I recommend that the Resolution expire as soon as the President is able to report to the Congress that the peace and security of the area are reasonably assured by international conditions, resulting from United Nations action or otherwise.

Again I say that we would welcome action by the United Nations which might, in fact, bring an end to the active hostilities in the area. This critical situation has been created by the choice of the Chinese Communists, not by us. Their offensive military intent has been flaunted to the whole world by words and by deeds. Just as they created the situation, so they can end it if they so choose.

What we are now seeking is primarily to clarify present policy and to unite in its application. We are not establishing a new policy. Consequently, my recommendations do not call for an increase in the armed forces of the United States or any acceleration in military procurement or levels of defense production. If any unforeseen emergency arises requiring any change, I will communicate with the Congress. I hope, however, that the effect of an appropriate Congressional Resolution will be to calm the situation rather than to create further conflict.

One final point. The action I request is, of course, no substitute for the Treaty with the Republic of China which we have signed and which I have transmitted to the Senate. Indeed, present circumstances make it more than ever important that this basic agreement should be promptly brought into force, as a solemn evidence of our determination to stand fast in the agreed Treaty area and to thwart all attacks directed against it. If delay should make us appear indecisive in this basic respect, the pressures and dangers would surely mount.

Our purpose is peace. That cause will be served if, with your help, we demonstrate our unity and our determination. In all that we do we shall remain faithful to our obligations as a member of the United Nations to be ready to settle our international disputes by peaceful means in such a manner that international peace and security, and justice, are not endangered.

For the reasons outlined in this message, I respectfully request that the Congress take appropriate action to carry out the recommendations contained herein.

Joint Congressional Resolution Authorizing the President to Use United States Forces to Protect Formosa January 29, 1955

[Department of State, *American Foreign Policy, 1950–55: Basic Documents,* II (Washington, 1957), 2486–87.]

Whereas the primary purpose of the United States, in its relations with all other nations, is to develop and sustain a just and enduring peace for all; and

Whereas certain territories in the West Pacific under the jurisdiction of the Republic of China are now under armed attack, and threats and declarations have been and are being made by the Chinese Communists that such armed attack is in aid of and in preparation for armed attack on Formosa and the Pescadores,

Whereas such armed attack if continued would gravely endanger the peace and security of the West Pacific Area and particularly of Formosa and the Pescadores; and

Whereas the secure possession by friendly governments of the Western Pacific Island chain, of which Formosa is a part, is essential to the vital interests of the United States and all friendly nations in or bordering upon the Pacific Ocean; and

Whereas the President of the United States on January 6, 1955, submitted to the Senate for its advice and consent to ratification a Mutual Defense Treaty between the United States of America and the Republic of China, which recognizes that an armed attack in the West Pacific area directed against territories, therein described, in the region of Formosa and the Pescadores, would be dangerous to the peace and safety of the parties to the treaty: Therefore be it

Resolved by the Senate and House of Representatives of the United States of America in Congress assembled, That the President of the United States be and he hereby is authorized to employ the Armed Forces of the United States as he deems necessary for the specific purpose of securing and protecting Formosa and the Pescadores against armed attack, this authority to include the securing and protection of such related positions and territories of that area now in friendly hands and the taking of such other measures as he judges to be required or appropriate in assuring the defense of Formosa and the Pescadores.

This resolution shall expire when the President shall determine that the peace and security of the area is reasonably assured by international conditions created by action of the United Nations or otherwise, and shall so report to the Congress.

President Eisenhower to Senator William Knowland
January 31, 1955
[Official File 99-V, Eisenhower Papers.]

Dear Bill:

I can't tell you how much I appreciate your effective work of last week in connection with the Formosa Resolution. You did a splendid job and by your efforts demonstrated to the country a unity in the Legislative and Executive Branches that is encouraging and inspiring. I am profoundly grateful to you.

The Assistant to the President Sherman Adams
to Representative Walter Judd
February 1, 1955
[Official File 168-B-1, Eisenhower Papers.]

Dear Walt:

The President asked me to reply to your thoughtful telegram of January twenty-second concerning United States policy towards Formosa and possible visits by relatives of Americans imprisoned in Communist China.

I think you will agree that there was nothing in the President's message of January 24 calculated to bring about a neutralization or sterilization of Formosa. The President recognized that there were some outlying islands under the control of the Chinese Government which did not have great significance from the military standpoint and that some regrouping and consolidation of Chinese forces in the off-shore island positions might be desirable. However, such a move would be designed to strengthen the military posture of the Chinese Government; it would by no means diminish the capability of the Chinese Government to deal with any possible new aggression by the Chinese Communists.

The armed forces of the Government of the Republic of China have been systematically trained and equipped with American assistance, primarily for the defense of Formosa and the Pescadores, but they also constitute a significant element in the total free world forces available in the Pacific to oppose a fresh outbreak of Chinese Communist aggression, in whatever direction it might be launched. Communist aggression against Southeast Asia, or elsewhere, must be met by collective action of the free nations. It would be unthinkable to immobilize the armed forces of Free China in such a way as to prevent their participation in collective action against forces of the aggressor.

With regard to your suggestion as to possible visits of relatives to American prisoners in Communist China, Secretary Dulles, with the approval of the President, has notified the relatives that in view of the increasingly belligerent attitude and actions of the Chinese Communist regime in recent days, the Department has concluded that it would be imprudent at this time to issue passports valid for travel to Communist China to any American citizens. The State Department has also made it clear that the obligation of the Chinese Communist regime is to release the prisoners and permit them to return to their families and that this obligation is in no sense offset by the offer to allow relatives to visit prisoners.

>━●─○─●─○─●─○─●─○─●─○─●─○─●─○─●─○─●─○─●─○─●─○─●─○─●─○─●─○─●─○─●─○─●─●<

In April, 1955, following the Bandung [Indonesia] Conference, the Far Eastern crisis faded, only to reemerge during the summer of 1958. The heavy Communist Chinese bombardment of Quemoy and Matsu disrupted what appeared to be chances for a Khrushchev-Eisenhower summit. On September 4, Secretary Dulles reaffirmed the Administration position, purposely leaving vague what the American response would be in the event of an invasion of these major off-shore islands. Soon afterwards, the United States and Communist China agreed to resume discussions in Warsaw on September 15. However, many feared that the United States would be drawn into a war with Communist China over the "useless off-shore islands." On October 2, Eisenhower replied to Senator Theodore Francis Green, Chairman of the Senate Foreign Relations Committee, who had criticized the Admistration's Far Eastern policies. The President detailed his understanding of the issues involved. Although the Warsaw talks reduced tensions in the Formosa Straits, the Nationalist Chinese government felt distressed and letdown, thus necessitating a hurried trip to Taipei by Secretary Dulles (October 20–23) to reassure Chiang Kai-shek of the American commitment.

Statement by Secretary John Foster Dulles on the Formosa Crisis September 4, 1958

[*Public Papers of the Presidents: 1958* (Washington, 1959), 687–88.]

I have reviewed in detail with the President the serious situation which has resulted from aggressive Chinese Communist military actions in the Taiwan (Formosa) Straits area. The President has authorized me to make the following statement.

1. Neither Taiwan (Formosa) nor the islands of Quemoy and Matsu have ever been under the authority of the Chinese Communists. Since the end of the Second World War, a period of over 13 years, they have continuously been under the authority of Free China, that is, the Republic of China.

2. The United States is bound by treaty to help to defend Taiwan (Formosa) from armed attack and the President is authorized by Joint Resolution of the Congress to employ the armed forces of the United States for the securing and protecting of related positions such as Quemoy and Matsu.

3. Any attempt on the part of the Chinese Communists now to seize these positions or any of them would be a crude violation of the principles upon which world order is based, namely, that no country should use armed force to seize new territory.

4. The Chinese Communists have, for about 2 weeks, been subjecting Quemoy to heavy artillery bombardment and, by artillery fire and use of small naval craft, they have been harassing the regular supply of the civilian and military population of the Quemoys, which totals some 125 thousand persons. The official Peiping radio repeatedly announces the purpose of these military operations to be to take by armed force Taiwan (Formosa), as well as Quemoy and Matsu. In virtually every Peiping broadcast Taiwan (Formosa) and the offshore islands are linked as the objective of what is called the "Chinese Peoples Liberation Army."

5. Despite, however, what the Chinese Communists say, and so far have done, it is not yet certain that their purpose is in fact to make an all-out effort to conquer by force Taiwan (Formosa) and the offshore islands. Neither is it apparent that such efforts as are being made, or may be made, cannot be contained by the courageous, and purely defensive, efforts of the forces of the Republic of China, with such substantial logistical support as the United States is providing.

6. The Joint Resolution of Congress, above referred to, includes a finding to the effect that "the secure possession by friendly governments of the Western Pacific Island chain, of which Formosa is a part, is essential to the vital interests of the United States and all friendly nations in and bordering upon the Pacific Ocean." It further authorizes the President to employ the Armed Forces of the United States for the protection not only of Formosa but for "the securing and protection of such related positions and territories of that area now in friendly hands and the taking of such other measures as he judges to be required or appropriate in insuring the defense of Formosa." In view of the situation outlined in the preceding paragraph, the President has not yet made any finding under that Resolution that the employment of the Armed Forces of the United States is required or appropriate in insuring the defense of Formosa. The President would not, however, hesitate to make such a finding if he judged that the circumstances

made this necessary to accomplish the purposes of the Joint Resolution. In this connection, we have recognized that the securing and protecting of Quemoy and Matsu have increasingly become related to the defense of Taiwan (Formosa). This is indeed also recognized by the Chinese Communists. Military dispositions have been made by the United States so that a Presidential determination, if made, would be followed by action both timely and effective.

7. The President and I earnestly hope that the Chinese Communist regime will not again, as in the case of Korea, defy the basic principle upon which world order depends, namely, that armed force should not be used to achieve territorial ambitions. Any such naked use of force would pose an issue far transcending the offshore islands and even the security of Taiwan (Formosa). It would forecast a widespread use of force in the Far East which would endanger vital free world positions and the security of the United States. Acquiescence therein would threaten peace everywhere. We believe that the civilized world community will never condone overt military conquest as a legitimate instrument of policy.

8. The United States has not, however, abandoned hope that Peiping will stop short of defying the will of mankind for peace. This would not require it to abandon its claims, however ill-founded we may deem them to be. I recall that in the extended negotiations which the representatives of the United States and Chinese Communist regime conducted at Geneva between 1955 and 1958, a sustained effort was made by the United States to secure, with particular reference to the Taiwan area, a declaration of mutual and reciprocal renunciation of force, except in self-defense, which, however, would be without prejudice to the pursuit of policies by peaceful means. The Chinese Communists rejected any such declaration. We believe, however, that such a course of conduct constitutes the only civilized and acceptable procedure. The United States intends to follow that course, so far as it is concerned, unless and until the Chinese Communists, by their acts, leave us no choice but to react in defense of the principles to which all peace-loving governments are dedicated.

President Eisenhower to Senator Theodore Francis Green
October 2, 1958
[Official File 168-B-1, Eisenhower Papers.]

Dear Senator Green:

I acknowledge your letter of September twenty-ninth with reference to the situation in the Far East. I note that you are concerned that the United States might become involved in hostilities in defense of Quemoy and

Matsu; that it does not appear to you that Quemoy is vital to the defense of Formosa or the United States; that in such hostilities we would be without allies, and, finally, that military involvement in the defense of Quemoy would not command that support of the American people essential to successful military action.

Let me take up these points in order:

1. Neither you nor any other American need feel that the United States will be involved in military hostilities merely in defense of Quemoy or Matsu. I am quite aware of the fact that the Joint Resolution of Congress (January 29, 1955), which authorized the President to employ the armed forces of the United States in the Formosa area, authorized the securing and protection of such positions as Quemoy and Matsu only if the President judges that to be required or appropriate in assuring the defense of Formosa and the Pescadores.

I shall scrupulously observe that limitation contained in the Congressional authority granted me.

2. The Congressional Resolution had, of course, not merely negative but positive implications. I shall also observe these. I note that it does not appear to you that Quemoy is vital to the defense of Formosa or the United States. But the test which the Congress established was whether or not the defense of these positions was judged by the President to be required or appropriate in assuring the defense of Formosa. The Congressional Resolution conferring that responsibility on the President was adopted by almost unanimous vote of both Houses of the Congress. Since then the people of the United States reelected me to be that President. I shall, as President and Commander-in-Chief of the Armed Forces of the United States, exercise my lawful authority and judgment in discharging the responsibility thus laid upon me.

I welcome the opinions and counsel of others. But in the last analysis such opinions cannot legally replace my own.

The Chinese and Soviet Communist leaders assert, and have reason to believe, that if they can take Quemoy and Matsu by armed assault that will open the way for them to take Formosa and the Pescadores and, as they put it, "expel" the United States from the West Pacific and cause its Fleet to leave international waters and "go home."

I cannot dismiss these boastings as mere bluff. Certainly there is always the possibility that it may in certain contingencies, after taking account of all relevant facts, become necessary or appropriate for the defense of Formosa and the Pescadores also to take measures to secure and protect the related positions of Quemoy and Matsu.

I am striving to the best of my ability to avoid hostilities; to achieve a cease-fire, and a reasonable adjustment of the situation. You, I think, know my deep dedication to peace. It is second only to my dedication to the safety of the United States and its honorable discharge of obligations to its allies and to world order which have been assumed by constitutional process. We must not forget that the whole Formosa Straits situation is intimately connected with the security of the United States and the free world.

3. You say that in the event of hostilities we would be without allies "in fact or in heart." Of course, no nation other than the Republic of China has a treaty alliance with us in relation to the Formosa area. That is a well known fact—known to the Congress when it adopted the Formosa Joint Resolution and known to the Senate when it approved of our Treaty of Mutual Security with the Republic of China. But if you mean that the United States action in standing firm against armed Communist assault would not have the approval of our allies, then I believe that you are misinformed. Not only do I believe that our friends and allies would support the United States if hostilities should tragically, and against our will, be forced upon us, I believe that most of them would be appalled if the United States were spinelessly to retreat before the threat of Sino-Soviet armed aggression.

4. Finally, you state that even if the United States should become engaged in hostilities, there would not be "that support of the American people essential to successful military action."

With respect to those islands, I have often pointed out that the only way the United States could become involved in hostilities would be because of its firm stand against Communist attempts to gain their declared aims by force. I have also often said that firmness in supporting principle makes war less, rather than more, likely of occurrence.

I feel certain, beyond the shadow of a doubt, that if the United States became engaged in hostilities on account of the evil and aggressive assaults of the forces of Communism, the American people would unite as one to assure the success and triumph of our effort.

I deeply deplore the effect upon hostile forces of a statement that if we became engaged in battle, the United States would be defeated because of disunity at home. If that were believed, it would embolden our enemies and make almost inevitable the conflict which, I am sure, we both seek to avoid provided it can be avoided consistently with the honor and security of our country.

Though in this letter I have explained the facts and the principles that guide the government in dealing with the critical Formosa Straits situation, I cannot close without saying that our whole effort is now, and has always been, the preservation of a peace with honor and with justice. After all, this is the basic aspiration of all Americans, indeed of all peoples.

Inasmuch as there have been public reports on the essence of your letter, I feel I should make this reply public.

Statement by Secretary John Foster Dulles
on United States Commitment to Nationalist China
October 24, 1958
[Official File 168-B-1, Eisenhower Papers.]

I returned last night from three days in Taipei, Formosa. There we held consultations with the Government of the Republic of China pursuant to our Treaty of Mutual Defense. These consultations had been planned to occur during the period when the Chinese Communists had said they would not carry out their bombardments from the Mainland. However, while we were en route to Formosa, the Chinese Communists resumed firing on Quemoy in violation of their cease-fire pledge.

It is possible that the firing is more for psychological than for military purposes. Apparently the Communists desire to throw roadblocks in the way of stabilized tranquility. Last night the Chinese Communist official press agency boasted that "the United States has met with defeat in her original plot to use the Chinese temporary suspension of shelling Quemoy to promote a permanent cease-fire". The Communists seem to believe that they can best achieve domination of the Western Pacific if they perpetuate confusion and uncertainty and if they alternatively give hopes for peace and fears of war. They accompany their erratic action with intensive propaganda to the effect that if the people of Asia would unite to expel the United States from the Western Pacific, then all would be well.

We return confident that the Chinese Communists will not gain their ends either through their military efforts or their propaganda guile. Free China is resolute—its government, its armed forces and its people. All of the free countries of the Far East increasingly realize that Chinese Communism is a mortal danger. They are heartened by the manifest power of the United States and our stand against retreat in the face of armed aggression.

The will of the free peoples of Asia to resist Chinese Communism intrusions is, I judge, more solid than ever before.

While at Taipei I was again made aware, at first hand, that the dominant spirit within the Republic of China is not mere military defense but rather that of peacefully bringing freedom to all China. The Government realizes its responsibilities as the authentic custodian and defender of those honored cultural and spiritual values long identified with China. It believes that its mission is to bring about the restoration of freedom to the people on the Mainland and to do so, not by the use of force, but by conduct and example which will sustain the minds and hearts of the Mainland Chinese so that they are unconquerable.

I return convinced that the Government of Free China is prudent, resolute and dedicated to the peaceful achievement of its high mission as spokesman for the aspirations and traditions of China. . . .

Once more, the Far Eastern crisis cooled, although the intermittent bombardment of the off-shore islands by the Chinese Communists (always on odd days) punctuated the continuing tension. In June, 1960, Eisenhower visited Formosa and again pledged America to the cause of the Nationalist Chinese.

Joint Statement by President Eisenhower
and President Chiang Kai-shek
on Sino-American Friendship
June 19, 1960

[*Public Papers of the Presidents: 1960–61* (Washington, 1961), 509–11.]

At the invitation of President Chiang Kai-shek, President Dwight D. Eisenhower visited the Republic of China from June 18 to June 19, 1960. This historic journey of the President of the United States of America and the warmth and enthusiasm with which he was received by the Chinese people demonstrated anew the strong bonds of friendship between the two countries.

Both President Chiang and President Eisenhower welcomed the opportunity afforded them by this visit for an intimate exchange of views on various matters of common interest and concern, calling to mind that the two countries have always stood closely together as staunch allies in war as well as in peace. The talks between the two Chiefs of State were held in an atmosphere of utmost cordiality.

In the course of their discussions, the two Presidents reaffirmed the dedication of the two Governments to an untiring quest for peace with freedom and justice. They recognize that peace and security are indivisible and that justice among nations demands the freedom and dignity of all men in all lands.

Taking note of the continuing threat of Communist aggression against the free world in general and the Far Eastern free countries in particular, the two Presidents expressed full agreement on the vital necessity of achieving closer unity and strength among all free nations.

They pledged once again that both their Governments would continue to stand solidly behind the Sino-U. S. Mutual Defense Treaty in meeting the challenge posed by the Chinese Communists in this area. They deplored the outrageous and barbaric practice of the Chinese Communists in shelling and ruthlessly killing Chinese people on alternate days and noted that this practice emphasized the necessity for continued vigilance and firmness in the face of violence.

Discussions were also held on the importance of accelerating the economic expansion of the Republic of China in order to enhance the prosperity and well-being of its people. President Chiang explained the steps which his Government is taking to assure the early accomplishment of his goal. He expressed the appreciation of his Government and people for the valuable assistance which the United States of America has rendered to the Republic of China. President Eisenhower expressed the admiration of the American people for the progress achieved by the Republic of China in various fields in recent years and gave assurance of continuing United States assistance.

Finally, the two Presidents voiced their common determination that the two Governments should continue to dedicate themselves to the principles of the United Nations and devote their unremitting efforts to the intensifying of their cooperation and to the further strengthening of the traditional friendship between the Chinese and American peoples.

6. THE DEEPENING VIETNAM COMMITMENT

Immediately following the Geneva Conference the United States dispatched a team of agents (June 1, 1954) to carry out clandestine warfare against North Vietnam. This was done despite a Government declaration which promised not to disturb the Geneva accords. This secret operation (Saigon Military Mission), headed by Colonel Edward G. Lansdale, also had as a major objective the strengthening of Ngo Dinh Diem's position in South Vietnam. In the summer of the following year, Diem refused to begin negotiations—specified in the 1954 Geneva Accords—with the northern zone for elections to reunify the country. Later in the year he felt so confident of his position that he called for a referendum (October 23) to depose Bao Dai, Emperor of Vietnam (1932–45), whom the French had restored to power as a rival government to Ho Chi Minh in 1949. As the candidate of the new regime, Diem received 98.2 per cent of the 5,828,000 votes cast. Dai, who was languishing on the French Riviera, took little interest in the contest. The United States willingly accepted the new state of affairs.

Account of the Saigon Military Mission
June, 1954–April, 1955
[*The Pentagon Papers,* as quoted in *The New York Times,* July 5, 1971.]

I. Foreword

... This is the condensed account of one year in the operations of a "cold war" combat team, written by the team itself in the field, little by little in moments taken as the members could. The team is known as the Saigon Military Mission. The field is Vietnam. There are other teams in the field, American, French, British, Chinese, Vietnamese, Vietminh, and others. Each has its own story to tell. This is ours.

The Saigon Military Mission entered Vietnam on 1 June 1954 when its Chief arrived. However, this is the story of a team, and it wasn't until August 1954 that sufficient members arrived to constitute a team. So, this is mainly an account of the team's first year, from August 1954 to August 1955.

It was often a frustrating and perplexing year, up close. The Geneva Agreements signed on 21 July 1954 imposed restrictive rules upon all official Americans, including the Saigon Military Mission. An active and intelligent enemy made full use of legal rights to screen his activities in establishing his stay-behind organizations south of the 17th Parallel and in obtaining quick security north of that Parallel. The nation's economy and communications system were crippled by eight years of open war. The government, including its Army and other security forces, was in a painful transition from colonial to self rule, making it a year of hot-tempered incidents. Internal problems arose quickly to points where armed conflict was sought as the only solution. The enemy was frequently forgotten in the heavy atmosphere of suspicion, hatred, and jealousy.

The Saigon Military Mission received some blows from allies and the enemy in this atmosphere, as we worked to help stabilize the government and to beat the Geneva time-table of Communist takeover in the north. However, we did beat the time-table. The government did become stabilized. The Free Vietnamese are now becoming unified and learning how to cope with the Communist enemy. We are thankful that we had a chance to help in this work in a critical area of the world, to be positive and constructive in a year of doubt.

II. Mission

The Saigon Military Mission (SMM) was born in a Washington policy meeting early in 1954, when Dien Bien Phu was still holding out against the encircling Vietminh. The SMM was to enter into Vietnam quietly and assist the Vietnamese, rather than the French, in unconventional warfare. The French were to be kept as friendly allies in the process, as far as possible.

The broad mission for the team was to undertake paramilitary operations against the enemy and to wage political-psychological warfare. Later, after Geneva, the mission was modified to prepare the means for undertaking paramilitary operations in Communist areas rather than to wage unconventional warfare. . . .

III. Highlights of the Year

a. Early Days

The Saigon Military Mission (SMM) started on 1 June 1954, when its Chief, Colonel Edward G. Lansdale, USAF, arrived in Saigon with a small box of files and clothes and a borrowed typewriter, courtesy of an SA 16 flight set up for him by the 13th Air Force at Clark AFB. Lt-General John O'Daniel and Embassy Charge Rob McClintock had arranged for his appointment as Assistant Air Attache, since it was improper for U.S. officers at MAAG at that time to have advisory conferences with Vietnamese officers. Ambassador Heath had concurred already. There was no desk space for an office, no vehicle, no safe for files. He roomed with General O'Daniel, later moved to a small house rented by MAAG. Secret communications with Washington were provided through the Saigon station of CIA.

There was deepening gloom in Vietnam. Dien Bien Phu had fallen. The French were capitulating to the Vietminh at Geneva. The first night in Saigon, Vietminh saboteurs blew up large ammunition dumps at the airport, rocking Saigon throughout the night. General O'Daniel and Charge McClintock agreed that it was time to start taking positive action. O'Daniel paved the way for a quick first-hand survey of the situation throughout the country. McClintock paved the way for contacts with Vietnamese political leaders. Our Chief's reputation from the Philippines had preceded him. Hundreds of Vietnamese acquaintanceships were made quickly.

Working in close cooperation with George Hellyer, USIS Chief, a new psychological warfare campaign was devised for the Vietnamese Army and for the government in Hanoi. Shortly after, a refresher course in combat psywar was constructed and Vietnamese Army personnel were rushed through it. A similar course was initiated for the Ministry of Information. Rumor campaigns were added to the tactics and tried out in Hanoi. It was almost too late.

The first rumor campaign was to be a carefully planted story of a Chinese Communist regiment in Tonkin taking reprisals against a Vietminh village whose girls the Chinese had raped, recalling Chinese Nationalist troop behavior in 1945 and confirming Vietnamese fears of Chinese occupation under Vietminh rule; the story was to be planted by soldiers of the Vietnamese Armed Psywar Company in Hanoi dressed in civilian clothes. The troops received their instructions silently, dressed in civilian clothes, went on the mission, and failed to return. They had deserted to the Vietminh. Weeks later, Tonkinese told an excited story of the misbehavior of the Chinese Divisions in Vietminh territory. Investigated, it turned out to be the old rumor campaign, with Vietnamese embellishments.

There was political chaos. Prince Buu Loc no longer headed the government. Government ministries all but closed. The more volatile leaders of political groups were proposing a revolution, which included armed attacks on the French. Col. Jean Carbonel of the French Army proposed establishing a regime with Vietnamese (Nungs and others) known to him close to the Chinese border and asked for our backing. Our reply was that this was a policy decision to be made between the FEC top command and U.S. authorities.

Oscar Arellano, Junior Chamber International vice-president for Southeast Asia, stopped by for a visit with our Chief; an idea in this visit later grew into "Operation Brotherhood."

On 1 July, Major Lucien Conein arrived, as the second member of the team. He is a paramilitary specialist, well-known to the French for his help with French-operated maquis in Tonkin against the Japanese in 1945, the one American guerrilla fighter who had not been a member of the Patti Mission. He was assigned to MAAG for cover purposes. Arranged by Lt-Col

William Rosson, a meeting was held with Col Carbonel, Col Nguyen Van Vy, and the two SMM officers; Vy had seen his first combat in 1945 under Conein. Carbonel proposed establishing a maquis, to be kept as a secret between the four officers. SMM refused, learned later that Carbonel had kept the FEC Deuxieme Bureau informed. Shortly afterwards, at a Defense conference with General O'Daniel, our Chief had a chance to suggest Vy for a command in the North, making him a general. Secretary of State for Defense Le Ngoc Chan did so, Vy was grateful and remained so.

Ngo Dinh Diem arrived on 7 July, and within hours was in despair as the French forces withdrew from the Catholic provinces of Phat Diem and Nam Dinh in Tonkin. Catholic militia streamed north to Hanoi and Haiphong, their hearts filled with anger at French abandonment. The two SMM officers stopped a planned grenade attack by militia girls against French troops guarding a warehouse; the girls stated they had not eaten for three days; arrangements were made for Chinese merchants in Haiphong to feed them. Other militia attacks were stopped, including one against a withdrawing French artillery unit; the militia wanted the guns to stand and fight the Vietminh. The Tonkinese had hopes of American friendship and listened to the advice given them. Governor [name illegible] died, reportedly by poison. Tonkin's government changed as despair grew. On 21 July, the Geneva Agreement was signed. Tonkin was given to the Communists. Anti-Communists turned to SMM for help in establishing a resistance movement and several tentative initial arrangements were made.

Diem himself had reached a nadir of frustration, as his country disintegrated after the conference of foreigners. With the approval of Ambassador Heath and General O'Daniel, our Chief drew up a plan of overall governmental action and presented it to Diem, with Hellyer as interpreter. It called for fast constructive action and dynamic leadership. Although the plan was not adopted, it laid the foundation for a friendship which has lasted.

Oscar Arellano visited Saigon again. Major Charles T. R. Bohanan, a former team-mate in Philippine days, was in town. At an SMM conference with these two, "Operation Brotherhood" was born: volunteer medical teams of Free Asians to aid the Free Vietnamese who have few doctors of their own. Washington responded warmly to the idea. President Diem was visited; he issued an appeal to the Free World for help. The Junior Chamber International adopted the idea. SMM would monitor the operation quietly in the background.

President Diem had organized a Committee of Cabinet Ministers to handle the problem of refugees from the Communist North. The Committee system was a failure. No real plans had been made by the French or the Americans. After conferences with USOM (FOA) officials and with General O'Daniel, our Chief suggested to Ambassador Heath that he call a U.S. meeting to plan a single Vietnamese agency, under a Commissioner of Refugees to be appointed by President Diem, to run the Vietnamese refugee program and to provide a channel through which help could be given by the U.S., France, and other free nations. The meeting was called and the plan adopted, with MAAG under General O'Daniel in the coordinating role. Diem adopted the plan. The French pitched in enthusiastically to help. CAT asked SMM for help in obtaining a French contract for the refugee airlift, and got it. In return, CAT provided SMM with the means for secret air travel between the North and Saigon. . . .

b. *August 1954*

An agreement had been reached that the personnel ceiling of U.S. military personnel with MAAG would be frozen at the number present in Vietnam on the date of the cease-fire, under the terms of the Geneva Agreement. In South Vietnam this deadline was to be 11 August. It meant that SMM might have only two members present, unless action were taken. General O'Daniel agreed to the addition of ten SMM men under MAAG cover, plus any others in the Defense pipeline who arrived before the deadline. A call for help went out. Ten officers in Korea, Japan, and Okinawa were selected and were rushed to Vietnam.

SMM had one small MAAG house. Negotiations were started for other housing, but the new members of the team arrived before housing was ready and were crammed three and four to a hotel room for the first days. Meetings were held to assess the new members' abilities. None had had political-psychological warfare experience. Most were experienced in paramilitary and clandestine intelligence operations. Plans were made quickly, for time was running out in the north; already the Vietminh had started taking over secret control of Hanoi and other areas of Tonkin still held by French forces.

Major Conein was given responsibility for developing a paramilitary organization in the north, to be in position when the Vietminh took over. . . . [His] . . . team was moved north immediately as part of the MAAG staff working on the refugee problem. The team had headquarters in Hanoi, with a branch in Haiphong. Among cover duties, this team supervised the refugee flow for the Hanoi airlift organized by the French. One day, as a CAT C-46 finished loading, they saw a small child standing on the ground below the loading door. They shouted for the pilot to wait, picked the child up and shoved him into the aircraft, which then promptly taxied out for its takeoff in the constant air shuttle. A Vietnamese man and woman ran up to the team, asking what they had done with their small boy, whom they'd brought out to say good-bye to relatives. The chagrined team explained, finally talked the parents into going south to Free Vietnam, put them in the next aircraft to catch up with their son in Saigon. . . .

A second paramilitary team was formed to explore possibilities of organizing resistance against the Vietminh from bases in the south. This team consisted of Army Lt-Col Raymond Wittmayer, Army Major Fred Allen, and Army Lt Edward Williams. The latter was our only experienced counter-espionage officer and undertook double duties, including working with revolutionary political groups. Major Allen eventually was able to mount a Vietnamese paramilitary effort in Tonkin from the south, barely beating the Vietminh shutdown in Haiphong as his teams went in, trained and equipped for their assigned missions.

Navy Lt Edward Bain and Marine Captain Richard Smith were assigned as the support group for SMM. Actually, support for an effort such as SMM is a major operation in itself, running the gamut from the usual administrative and personnel functions to the intricate business of clandestine air, maritime, and land supply of paramilitary materiel. In effect, they became our official smugglers as well as paymasters, housing officers, transportation officers, warehousemen, file clerks, and mess officers. The work load was such that other team members frequently pitched in and helped.

c. September 1954

Highly-placed officials from Washington visited Saigon and, in private conversations, indicated that current estimates led to the conclusion that Vietnam probably would have to be written off as a loss. We admitted that prospects were gloomy, but were positive that there was still a fighting chance.

On 8 September, SMM officers visited Secretary of State for Defense Chan and walked into a tense situation in his office. Chan had just arrested Lt-Col Lan (G-6 of the Vietnamese Army) and Capt Giai (G-5 of the Army). Armed guards filled the room. We were told what had happened and assured that everything was all right by all three principals. Later, we discovered that Chan was alone and that the guards were Lt-Col Lan's commandos. Lan was charged with political terrorism (by his "action" squads) and Giai with anti-Diem propaganda (using G-5 leaflet, rumor, and broadcast facilities).

The arrest of Lan and Giai, who simply refused to consider themselves arrested, and of Lt Minh, officer in charge of the Army radio station which was guarded by Army troops, brought into the open a plot by the Army Chief of Staff, General Hinh, to overthrow the government. Hinh had hinted at such a plot to his American friends, using a silver cigarette box given him by Egypt's Naguib to carry the hint. SMM became thoroughly involved in the tense controversy which followed, due to our Chief's closeness to both President Diem and General Hinh. He had met the latter in the Philippines in 1952, was a friend of both Hinh's wife and favorite mistress. (The mistress was a pupil in a small English class conducted for mistresses of important personages, at their request. . . .)

While various U.S. officials including General O'Daniel and Foreign Service Officer Frank [name illegible] participated in U.S. attempts to heal the split between the President and his Army, Ambassador Heath asked us to make a major effort to end the controversy. This effort strained relations with Diem and never was successful, but did dampen Army enthusiasm for the plot. At one moment, when there was likelihood of an attack by armored vehicles on the Presidential Palace, SMM told Hinh bluntly that U.S. support most probably would stop in such an event. At the same time a group from the Presidential Guards asked for tactical advice on how to stop armored vehicles with the only weapons available to the Guards: carbines, rifles, and hand grenades. The advice, on tank traps and destruction with improvised weapons, must have sounded grim. The following morning, when the attack was to take place, we visited the Palace; not a guard was left on the grounds; President Diem was alone upstairs, calmly getting his work done.

As a result of the Hinh trouble, Diem started looking around for troops upon whom he could count. Some Tonkinese militia, refugees from the north, were assembled in Saigon close to the Palace. But they were insufficient for what he needed. Diem made an agreement with General Trinh Minh The, leader of some 3,000 Cao Dai dissidents in the vicinity of Tayninh, to give General The some needed financial support; The was to give armed support to the government if necessary and to provide a safehaven for the government if it had to flee. The's guerrillas, known as the Lien Minh, were strongly nationalist and were still fighting the Vietminh and the French. At Ambassador Heath's request, the U.S. secretly furnished Diem with funds for The, through the SMM. Shortly afterwards, an invitation came from The to visit him. Ambassador Heath approved the visit. . . .

The northern SMM team under Conein had organized a paramilitary group, (which we will disguise by the Vietnamese name of Binh) through the Northern Dai Viets, a political party with loyalties to Bao Dai. The group was to be trained and supported by the U.S. as patriotic Vietnamese, to come eventually under government control when the government was ready for such activities. Thirteen Binhs were quietly exfiltrated through the port of Haiphong, under the direction of Lt Andrews, and taken on the first stage of the journey to their training area by a U.S. Navy ship. This was the first of a series of helpful actions by Task Force 98, commanded by Admiral Sabin.

Another paramilitary group for Tonkin operations was being developed in Saigon through General Nguyen Van Vy. In September this group started shaping up fast, and the project was given to Major Allen. (We will give this group the Vietnamese name of Hao). . . .

Towards the end of the month, it was learned that the largest printing establishment in the north intended to remain in Hanoi and do business with the Vietminh. An attempt was made by SMM to destroy the modern presses, but Vietminh security agents already had moved into the plant and frustrated the attempt. This operation was under a Vietnamese patriot whom we shall call Trieu; his case officer was Capt Arundel. Earlier in the month they had engineered a black psywar strike in Hanoi: leaflets signed by the Vietminh instructing Tonkinese on how to behave for the Vietminh takeover of the Hanoi region in early October, including items about property, money reform, and a three-day holiday of workers upon takeover. The day following the distribution of these leaflets, refugee registration tripled. Two days later Vietminh currency was worth half the value prior to the leaflets. The Vietminh took to the radio to denounce the leaflets; the leaflets were so authentic in appearance that even most of the rank and file Vietminh were sure that the radio denunciations were a French trick.

The Hanoi psywar strike had other consequences. Binh had enlisted a high police official of Hanoi as part of his team, to effect the release from jail of any team members if arrested. The official at the last moment decided to assist in the leaflet distribution personally. Police officers spotted him, chased his vehicle through the empty Hanoi streets of early morning, finally opened fire on him and caught him. He was the only member of the group caught. He was held in prison as a Vietminh agent.

d. October 1954

Hanoi was evacuated on 9 October. The northern SMM team left with the last French troops, disturbed by what they had seen of the grim efficiency of the Vietminh in their takeover, the contrast between the silent march of the victorious Vietminh troops in their tennis shoes and the clanking armor of the well-equipped French whose Western tactics and equipment had failed against the Communist military-political-economic campaign.

The northern team had spent the last days of Hanoi in contaminating the oil supply of the bus company for a gradual wreckage of engines in the buses, in taking the first actions for delayed sabotage of the railroad (which required teamwork with a CIA special technical team in Japan who performed their part brilliantly), and in writing detailed notes of potential targets for future paramilitary operations (U.S. adherence to the Geneva Agreement prevented SMM from carrying out the active sabotage it desired to do against the power plant, water facilities, harbor, and bridge). The team had a bad moment when contaminating the oil. They had to work quickly at night, in an enclosed storage room. Fumes from the contaminant came close to knocking them out. Dizzy and weak-kneed, they masked their faces with handkerchiefs and completed the job.

Meanwhile, Polish and Russian ships had arrived in the south to transport southern Vietminh to Tonkin under the Geneva Agreement. This offered the opportunity for another black psywar strike. A leaflet was developed by Binh with the help of Capt Arundel, attributed to the Vietminh Resistance Committee. Among other items, it reassured the Vietminh they would be kept safe below decks from imperialist air and submarine attacks, and requested that warm clothing be brought; the warm clothing item would be coupled with a verbal rumor campaign that Vietminh were being sent into China as railroad laborers.

SMM had been busily developing G-5 of the Vietnamese Army for such psywar efforts. Under Arundel's direction, the First Armed Propaganda

Company printed the leaflets and distributed them, by soldiers in civilian clothes who penetrated into southern Vietminh zones on foot. (Distribution in Camau was made while columnist Joseph Alsop was on his visit there which led to his sensational, gloomy articles later; our soldier "Vietminh" failed in an attempt to get the leaflet into Alsop's hands in Camau; Alsop was never told this story). Intelligence reports and other later reports revealed that village and delegation committees complained about "deportation" to the north, after distribution of the leaflet. . . .

Contention between Diem and Hinh had become murderous. . . . Finally, we learned that Hinh was close to action; he had selected 26 October as the morning for an attack on the Presidential Palace. Hinh was counting heavily on Lt-Col Lan's special forces and on Captain Giai who was running Hinh's secret headquarters at Hinh's home. We invited these two officers to visit the Philippines, on the pretext that we were making an official trip, could take them along and open the way for them to see some inner workings of the fight against Filipino Communists which they probably would never see otherwise. Hinh reluctantly turned down his own invitation; he had had a memorable time of it on his last visit to Manila in 1952. Lt Col Lan was a French agent and the temptation to see behind-the-scenes was too much. He and Giai accompanied SMM officers on the MAAG C-47 which General O'Daniel instantly made available for theoperation. 26 October was spent in the Philippines. The attack on the palace didn't come off.

e. November 1954

General Lawton Collins arrived as Ambassador on 8 November. . . .

Collins, in his first press conference, made it plain that the U.S. was supporting President Diem. The new Ambassador applied pressure on General Hinh and on 29 November Hinh left for Paris. His other key conspirators followed.

Part of the SMM team became involved in staff work to back up the energetic campaign to save Vietnam which Collins pushed forward. Some SMM members were scattered around the Pacific, accompanying Vietnamese for secret training, obtaining and shipping supplies to be smuggled into north Vietnam and hidden there. In the Philippines, more support was being constructed to help SMM, in expediting the flow of supplies, and in creating Freedom Company, a non-profit Philippines corporation backed by President Magsaysay, which would supply Filipinos experienced in fighting the Communist Huks to help in Vietnam (or elsewhere). . . .

On 23 November, twenty-one selected Vietnamese agents and two cooks of our Hao paramilitary group were put aboard a Navy ship in the Saigon River, in daylight. They appeared as coolies, joined the coolie and refugee throng moving on and off ship, and disappeared one by one. It was brilliantly planned and executed, agents being picked up from unobtrusive assembly points throughout the metropolis. Lt Andrews made the plans and carried out the movement under the supervision of Major Allen. The ship took the Hao agents, in compartmented groups, to an overseas point, the first stage in a movement to a secret training area.

f. December 1954

. . . discussions between the U.S., Vietnamese and French had reached a point where it appeared that a military training mission using U.S. officers was in the immediate offing. General O'Daniel had a U.S.-French planning group working on the problem, under Col. Rosson. One paper they were developing was a plan for pacification of Vietminh and dissident areas; this paper was passed to SMM for its assistance with the drafting. SMM wrote much of the paper, changing the concept from the old rigid police controls of all areas to some of our concepts of winning over the population and instituting a classification of areas by the amount of trouble in each, the amount of control required, and fixing responsibilities between civil and military authorities. With a few changes, this was issued by President Diem on 31 December as the National Security Action (Pacification) Directive. . . .

There was still much disquiet in Vietnam, particularly among anti-Communist political groups who were not included in the government. SMM officers were contacted by a number of such groups who felt that they "would have to commit suicide in 1956" (the 1956 plebiscite promised in the 1954 Geneva agreement), when the Vietminh would surely take over against so weak a government. One group of farmers and milita in the south was talked out of migrating to Madagascar by SMM and staying on their farms. A number of these groups asked SMM for help in training personnel for eventual guerrilla warfare if the Vietminh won. Persons such as the then Minister of Defense and Trinh Minh The were among those loyal to the government who also requested such help. It was decided that a more basic guerrilla training program might be undertaken for such groups than was available at the secret training site to which we had sent the Binh and Hao groups. Plans were made with Major Bohanan and Mr. John C. Wachtel in the Philippines for a solution of this problem; the United States backed the development, through them, of a small Freedom Company training camp in a hidden valley on the Clark AFB reservation.

Till and Peg Durdin of the N.Y. Times, Hank Lieberman of the N.Y. Times, Homber Bigart of the N.Y. Herald-Tribune, John Mecklin of Life-Time, and John Roderick of Associated Press, have been warm friends of SMM and worked hard to penetrate the fabric of French propaganda and give the U.S. an objective account of events in Vietnam. The group met with us at times to analyze objectives and motives of propaganda known to them, meeting at their own request as U.S. citizens. These mature and responsible news correspondents performed a valuable service for their country. . . .

g. January 1955

The Vietminh long ago had adopted the Chinese Communist thought that the people are the water and the army is the fish. Vietminh relations with the mass of the population during the fighting had been exemplary, with a few exceptions; in contrast, the Vietnamese National Army had been like too many Asian armies, adept at cowing a population into feeding them, providing them with girls. SMM had been working on this problem from the beginning. Since the National Army was the only unit of government with a strong organization throughtout the country and with good communications, it was the key to stabilizing the situation quickly on a nation-wide basis. If Army and people could be brought together into a team, the first strong weapon against Communism could be forged.

The Vietminh were aware of this. We later learned that months before the signing of the Geneva Agreement they had been planning for action in the post-Geneva period; the National Army was to be the primary target for subversion efforts, it was given top priority by the Central Committee for operations against its enemy, and about 100 superior cadres were retrained for the operations and placed in the [words illegible] organization for the work, which commenced even before the agreement was signed. We didn't know it at the time, but this was SMM's major opponent, in a secret struggle for the National Army. . . .

General O'Daniel was anticipating the culmination of long negotiatons to permit U.S. training of the Vietnamese Armed Forces, against some resistance on the part of French groups. In January, negotiations were proceeding so well that General O'Daniel informally organized a combined U.S.-French training mission which eventually became known as the Training Relations & Instruction Mission (TRIM) under his command, but under the overall command of the top French commander, General Paul Ely.

The French had asked for top command of half the divisions in the TRIM staff. Their first priority was for command of the division supervising National Security Action by the Vietnamese, which could be developed into a continuation of strong French control of key elements of both Army and population. In conferences with Ambassador Collins and General O'Daniel, it was decided to transfer Colonel Lansdale from the Ambassador's staff to TRIM, to head the National Security division. Colonel Lansdale requested authority to coordinate all U.S. civil and military efforts in this National Security work. On 11 January, Ambassador Collins announced the change to the country team, and gave him authority to coordinate this work among all U.S. agencies in Vietnam. . . .

President Diem had continued requesting SMM help with the guard battalion for the Presidential Palace. We made arrangements with President Magsaysay in the Philippines and borrowed his senior aide and military advisor, Col. Napoleon Valeriano, who had a fine combat record against the Communist Huks and also had reorganized the Presidential Guard Battalion for Magsaysay. Valeriano, with three junior officers, arrived in January and went to work on Diem's guard battalion. Later, selected Vietnamese officers were trained with the Presidential Guards in Manila.

An efficient unit gradually emerged. Diem was warmly grateful for this help by Filipinos who also continuously taught our concept of loyalty and freedom.

The patriot we've named Trieu Dinh had been working on an almanac for popular sale, particularly in the northern cities and towns we could still reach. Noted Vietnamese astrologers were hired to write predictions about coming disasters to certain Vietminh leaders and undertakings, and to predict unity in the south. The work was carried out under the direction of Lt Phillips, based on our concept of the use of astrology for psywar in Southeast Asia. Copies of the almanac were shipped by air to Haiphong and then smuggled into Vietminh territory.

Dinh also had produced a Thomas Paine type series of essays on Vietnamese patriotism against the Communist Vietminh, under the guidance of Capt. Arundel. These essays were circulated among influential groups in Vietnam, earned front-page editorials in the leading daily newspaper in Saigon. Circulation increased with the publication of these essays. The publisher is known to SMM as The Dragon Lady and is a fine Vietnamese girl who has been the mistress of an anti-American French civilian. Despite anti-American remarks by her boy friend, we had helped her keep her paper from being closed by the government . . . and she found it profitable to heed our advice on the editorial content of her paper.

Arms and equipment for the Binh paramilitary team were being cached in the north in areas still free from the Vietminh. Personnel movements were covered by the flow of refugees. Haiphong was reminiscent of our own pioneer days as it was swamped with people whom it couldn't shelter. Living space and food were at a premium, nervous tension grew. It was a wild time for our northern team.

First supplies for the Hao paramilitary group started to arrive in Saigon. These shipments and the earlier ones for the Binh group were part of an efficient and effective air smuggling effort by the 581st [word illegible] Wing, U.S. Air Force, to support SMM, with help by CIA and Air Force personnel in both Okinawa and the Philippines. SMM officers frequently did coolie labor in manhandling tons of cargo, at times working throughout the night. . . . All . . . officers pitched in to help, as part of our "blood, sweat and tears". . . .

By 31 January, all operational equipment of the Binh paramilitary group had been trans-shipped to Haiphong from Saigon, mostly with the help of CAT, and the northern SMM team had it cached in operational sites. Security measures were tightened at the Haiphong airport and plans for bringing in the Hao equipment were changed from the air route to sea. Task Force 98, now 98.7 under command of Captain Frank, again was asked to give a helping hand and did so. . . .

. . . . Major Conein had briefed the members of the Binh paramilitary team and started them infiltrating into the north as individuals. The infiltration was carried out in careful stages over a 30 day period, a successful operation. The Binhs became normal citizens, carrying out every day civil pursuits, on the surface.

We had smuggled into Vietnam about eight and a half tons of supplies for the Hao paramilitary group. They included fourteen agent radios, 300 carbines, 90,000 rounds of carbine ammunition, 50 pistols, 10,000 rounds of pistol ammunition, and 300 pounds of explosives. Two and a half tons were delivered to the Hao agents in Tonkin, while the remainder was cached along the Red River by SMM, with the help of the Navy. . . .

j. April 1955
  . . . the Hao paramilitary team had finished its training at the secret training site and been flown by the Air Force to a holding site in the Philippines, where Major Allen and his officers briefed the paramilitary team. In mid-April, they were taken by the Navy to Haiphong, where they were gradually slipped ashore. Meanwhile, arms and other equipment including explosives were being flown into Saigon via our smuggling route, being readied for shipment north by the Navy task force handling refugees. The White team office gradually became an imposing munitions depot. Nightly shootings and bombings in restless Saigon caused us to give them dispersed storage behind thick walls as far as this one big house would permit. SMM personnel guarded the house night and day, for it also contained our major files other than the working file at our Command Post. All files were fixed for instant destruction, automatic weapons and hand grenades distributed to all personnel. It was a strange scene for new personnel just arriving. . . .

Haiphong was taken over by the Vietminh on 16 May. Our Binh and northern Hao teams were in place, completely equipped. It had taken a tremendous amount of hard work to beat the Geneva deadline, to locate, select, exfiltrate, train, infiltrate, equip the men of these two teams and have them in place, ready for actions required against the enemy. It would be a hard task to do openly, but this had to be kept secret from the Vietminh, the International Commission with its suspicious French and Poles and Indians, and even friendly Vietnamese. Movements of personnel and supplies had had to be over thousands of miles. . . .

State Department Report Recognizing Ngo Dinh Diem
as President of Vietnam
October 26, 1955
[Department of State, *American Foreign Policy, 1950–55: Basic Documents,* II (Washington, 1957), 2424–25.]

On October 26, the Government of Viet-Nam sent the following communication to the American Embassy at Saigon:

"The Ministry of Foreign Affairs has the honor to inform the United States Embassy that by referendum October 23 the Vietnamese people have pronounced themselves in favor of the deposition of Bao Dai and have recognized President Diem as Chief of State. It is hoped that the Government of the United States will continue as in the past to entertain diplomatic relations with the new Government of the State of Viet-Nam."

U. S. Ambassador G. Frederick Reinhardt, under instructions, has replied as follows:

"The Government of the United States looks forward to maintaining with the new Government of Viet-Nam the same cordial and friendly relations which have in the past so happily existed between the two governments."

The United States affirms its intention to maintain friendly relations with the Government of Viet-Nam. We are glad to see the evolution of orderly and effective democratic processes in an area of Southeast Asia which has been and continues to be threatened by Communist efforts to impose totalitarian control.

Diem, with American support, refused to arrange for the reunification election. Eisenhower continued to believe that Diem could create a stable non-communist nation in South Vietnam. On the first anniversary of Diem's election Eisenhower sent a congratulatory letter. The next spring Eisenhower accentuated American support by inviting Diem to Washington for a state visit. Their joint statement left little doubt of a growing commitment to Diem's South Vietnam.

President Eisenhower to President Ngo Dinh Diem
October 25, 1956
[*Public Papers of the Presidents: 1956* (Washington, 1958), 1019–20.]

Dear Mr. President:

The admiration with which I have watched the progress of the Republic of Viet-Nam during the past year prompts me to send to you the warmest congratulations of the American people on the occasion of the first anniversary of the Republic and upon the promulgation of the Vietnamese Constitution.

The American people have observed the remarkable struggle of the Vietnamese people during the past years to achieve and to maintain their independence. The successes of the Republic of Viet-Nam in thwarting the aggressive designs of Communism without, and in surmounting the most difficult obstacles within, have shown what can be achieved when a people rally to the cause of freedom.

We in America pray that those now still living in the enslaved part of your country may one day be united in peace under the free Republic of Viet-Nam.

The achievements of the Vietnamese people will long remain a source of inspiration to free peoples everywhere. As Viet-Nam enters this new period of national reconstruction and rehabilitation, my fellow countrymen and I are proud to be sharing some of the tasks which engage you.

May the Vietnamese people inspired by your dedicated leadership and the high principles of their democratic institutions, enjoy long years of prosperity in justice and in peace.

Joint Statement by President Eisenhower and President Ngo Dinh Diem on American-Vietnamese Friendship
May 12, 1957
[Public Papers of the Presidents: 1957 (Washington, 1958), 335–37.]

His Excellency Ngo Dinh Diem, President of the Republic of Viet-Nam, and President Eisenhower have held discussions during President Ngo Dinh Diem's state visit as the guest of President Eisenhower during May 8-10.

Their discussions have been supplemented by meetings between President Ngo Dinh Diem and his advisers and Secretary of State Dulles and other American officials. These meetings afforded the occasion for reaffirming close mutual friendship and support between the Republic of Viet-Nam and the United States. The two Presidents exchanged views on the promotion of peace and stability and the development and consolidation of freedom in Viet-Nam and in the Far East as a whole.

President Eisenhower complimented President Ngo Dinh Diem on the remarkable achievements of the Republic of Viet-Nam under the leadership of President Ngo Dinh Diem since he took office in July 1954. It was noted that in less than three years a chaotic situation resulting from years of war had been changed into one of progress and stability.

Nearly one million refugees who had fled from Communist tyranny in North Viet-Nam had been cared for and resettled in Free Viet-Nam.

Internal security had been effectively established.

A constitution had been promulgated and a national assembly elected.

Plans for agrarian reform have been launched, and a constructive program developed to meet long-range economic and social problems to promote higher living standards for the Vietnamese people.

President Ngo Dinh Diem reviewed with President Eisenhower the efforts and means of the Vietnamese Government to promote political stability and economic welfare in the Republic of Viet-Nam. President Eisenhower assured President Ngo Dinh Diem of the willingness of the United States to continue to offer effective assistance within the constitutional processes of the United States to meet these objectives.

President Eisenhower and President Ngo Dinh Diem looked forward to an end of the unhappy division of the Vietnamese people and confirmed the determination of the two Governments to work together to seek suitable means to bring about the peaceful unification of Viet-Nam in freedom in accordance with the purposes and principles of the United Nations Charter. It was noted with pleasure that the General Assembly of the United Nations by a large majority had found the Republic of Viet-Nam qualified for membership in the United Nations, which has been prevented by Soviet opposition.

President Eisenhower and President Ngo Dinh Diem noted in contrast the large build-up of Vietnamese Communist military forces in North Viet-Nam during the past two and one-half years, the harsh suppression of the revolts of the people of North Viet-Nam in seeking liberty, and their increasing hardships. While noting the apparent diminution during the last three years of Communist-inspired hostilities in Southeast Asia except in the Kingdom of Laos, President Eisenhower and President Ngo Dinh Diem expressed concern over continuing Communist subversive capabilities in this area and elsewhere. In particular, they agreed that the continued military build-up of the Chinese Communists, their refusal to renounce the use of force, and their unwillingness to subscribe to standards of conduct of civilized nations constitute a continuing threat to the safety of all free nations in Asia. To counter this threat, President Ngo Dinh Diem indicated his strong desire and his efforts to seek closer cooperation with the free countries of Asia.

Noting that the Republic of Viet-Nam is covered by Article IV of the Southeast Asia Collective Defense Treaty, President Eisenhower and President Ngo Dinh Diem agreed that aggression or subversion threatening the political independence of the Republic of Viet-Nam would be considered as endangering peace and stability. The just settlement of problems of the area by peaceful and legitimate means within the framework of the United Nations Charter will continue to be the mutual concern of both Governments. Finally, President Eisenhower and President Ngo Dinh Diem expressed the desire and determination of the two Governments to cooperate closely together for freedom and independence in the world.

As was only to be expected, the American effort to assist South Vietnam ran afoul of a body created at Geneva in 1954 to oversee the Accords. This organization, usually called the International Control Commission, was composed of representatives from Poland, India, and Canada. It received numerous complaints of violations from both sides. The following excerpts from the commission reports dealt with alleged South Vietnamese and American violations.

Seventh Interim Report of the International Commission for Supervision and Control in Vietnam
August 1, 1956–April 30, 1957

[Presented to Parliament by the Secretary of State for Foreign Affairs by Command of Her Majesty (London, 1957), 15 16.]

*   *   *

51. Many instances of arrival of military personnel and war materials in South Vietnam were reported by the Commission's teams and were stated by the Government of the Republic of Vietnam to be in transit. Some of the arrivals took place without advance notification. In some instances, during the period under report, the Commission was not notified about the exit, if any, of these war materials and military personnel and it was not in a position to say whether or not they left the country. The matter is being pursued.

52. During the period under report the Commission's fixed teams at Nha Trang and Tourane in South Vietnam reported that they were not allowed to control American military and other planes stated by the Government of the Republic of Vietnam to be United States Embassy planes. As directed by the Commission, its Legal Committee is examining whether, in exercise of immunities and privileges, diplomatic missions can introduce into Vietnam war material without repugnance to Article 17 of the Agreement . . .

55. In paragraph 63 of the Sixth Interim Report reference was made to the entry of an American Military Mission, called "TERM" (Temporary Equipment Recovery Mission), into South Vietnam in May, 1956. The Commission could not review the question after a lapse of three months, as originally decided, or carry out spot checks as no reply was received from the Government of the Republic of Vietnam until December, 1956. In this reply it was stated that TERM was expected to complete its task of cataloguing United States war material for eventual re-export from South Vietnam in a limited time and that before its withdrawal due intimation would be given, so that the Commission might exercise appropriate control. The Government of the Republic of Vietnam also agreed that the Commission might visit the installations where TERM personnel were carrying on

their activities. The strength of the Mission was stated not to exceed 350. The said Government did not comply with the Commission's request to furnish fortnightly reports regarding the activities of the Mission. The Commission informed the Government of the Republic of Vietnam in February, 1957, that it regarded this lapse with concern and asked for a report concerning the activities of TERM up to the end of January, 1957, and thereafter fortnightly reports to be sent expeditiously and without fail. It further asked to be informed when TERM would be completing its task and where TERM's activities were going on so that the Commission may decide where to send a mobile team for the purpose of ascertaining the activities of TERM. No reply has been received so far.

56. In paragraph 63 of the Sixth Interim Report a reference was made to the complaints of the P.A.V.N. High Command with regard to certain United States Military Missions in South Vietnam. During the period under review the Commission received a few more complaints and considered some of these. In one of these it was alleged that the existence of "MAAG" (Military Aid Advisory Group) and the introduction of United States military personnel were in effect a factual realisation of a military alliance between the Governments of the Republic of Vietnam and of the United States of America in contravention of Articles 16 and 19 and paragraphs 4 and 5 of the Final Declaration. In November, 1956, the Government of the Republic of Vietnam was asked to offer its specific comments on the allegations and also on certain enclosures to the letter of the P.A.V.N. High Command, in which it was stated that a military agreement had been concluded between the above two countries in February, 1955, and to furnish certain information regarding the status, purpose, original and present strength and the present activities of "MAAG." In February, 1957, the Commission received a letter from the Government of the Republic of Vietnam denying that the presence of "MAAG" constituted a violation of Articles 16 and 19 and stating that "MAAG" had started its activities in 1950 and that there had been no change in its activities, statute or structure and it had never exceeded its original strength and that there did not exist a formal or factual military alliance between the Governments of the Republic of Vietnam and of the United States of America. The matter is under consideration.

The P.A.V.N. High Command also alleged that two United States Military Missions—"TRIM" (Training Reorganisation Inspection Mission) and "CATO" (Combat Arms Training Organisation) founded in March, 1955, and in May, 1956, respectively, had come into existence in South Vietnam. The Commission asked in January, 1957, for the comments of the Government of the Republic of Vietnam. The reply is awaited.

In one of its complaints the P.A.V.N. High Command alleged a factual materialisation of a military alliance between the Government of the Republic of Vietnam and the member countries of "SEATO" (South-East

Asia Treaty Organisation) as military personnel, warships and jet planes of the said member countries participated in the National Day celebrations of South Vietnam on October 26, 1956. The Government of the Republic of Vietnam denied the factual materialisation of a military alliance with the "SEATO" Powers. The Commission viewed with concern the omission of the Government of the Republic of Vietnam to follow the procedures laid down by the Commission for the introduction of military missions and consequently concluded that it was not in a position to state whether and, if so, how far the provisions of Article 16 had been observed by the Government of the Republic of Vietnam and, whether or not, all or any of the war material in question had left South Vietnam. The Commission also concluded that the participation of foreign military personnel and war material in public celebrations of a ceremonial character did not necessarily prove the existence of a military alliance. The Commission has closed the case.

Eighth Interim Report of the International Commission for Supervision and Control in Vietnam
1958
[Presented to Parliament by the Secretary of State for Foreign Affairs by Command of Her Majesty; (London, 1958), II.]

*   *   *

30. In paragraph 56 of the Seventh Interim Report reference was made to the alleged factual materialisation of a military alliance between the Republic of Vietnam and the member countries of SEATO. A new complaint of the P.A.V.N. High Command concerning the presence of the representatives of the Republic of Vietnam at the SEATO Conference held at Manila in March, 1958, as observers has been sent to the Government of the Republic of Vietnam for comments.

31. In paragraphs 55 and 56 of the Seventh Interim Report, references were made to the American Military Missions called TERM (Temporary Equipment Recovery Mission), MAAG (Military Assistance Advisory Group), TRIM (Training Reorganisation and Inspection Mission) and CATO (Combat Arms Training Organisation).

32. The Government of the Republic of Vietnam submitted a report on TERM personnel up to September 30, 1957, and a statement of damaged or worn-out material of American origin shipped out of Vietnam up to May 31, 1957. Monthly reports asked for by the Commission have been submitted thereafter, though not on time, and no change in TERM personnel has been reported. The Government of the Republic of Vietnam furnished information about eight places where TERM is working, and the Commission decided to carry out spot checks in four of the eight places, and has

carried out these spot checks in three places. The reports of the Teams are under consideration. Regarding the question when this Mission, which is claimed to be temporary, would be completing its task and leaving Vietnam, the Government of the Republic of Vietnam has replied that it is impossible to forecast when TERM will cease its activities. The matter is under consideration.

As regards MAAG and other organisations referred to above, the Government of the Republic of Vietnam did not supply information on all the points requested by the Commission and the Commission expressed grave concern that all assistance and co-operation in this matter had not been offered in terms of Article 25 and asked the Mission in charge of relations with the Commission to supply the necessary information. The Canadian Delegation dissented from this decision citing Article 25 because it held that the essential information had already been supplied. Indian and Polish Delegations would like to point out that the Commission had unanimously decided earlier that the information furnished was inadequate and unsatisfactory and had expressed its concern over the non-receipt of a reply within the specified period and only then was Article 25 cited. A reply has since been received enclosing a copy of the Agreement of December 23, 1950, under which, according to the Party, MAAG operates and the reply is under consideration.

As time passed, most Americans remained totally unaware of the extent of the Vietnamese commitment. However, reports to the President kept him informed—and concerned—about the situation in Southeast Asia. The following excerpt from a 1959 commencement address by Eisenhower at Gettysburg College stressed the need for continued deep American involvement in that little known country.

Speech by President Eisenhower on Southeast Asia
Gettysburg, April 4, 1959

[*Public Papers of the Presidents: 1959* (Washington, 1960), 310–13.]

I shall not attempt to talk to you about education, but I shall speak of one vital purpose of education—the development of understanding—understanding, so that we may use with some measure of wisdom the knowledge we may have acquired, whether in school or out.

For no matter how much intellectual luggage we carry around in our heads, it becomes valuable only if we know how to use the information—only if we are able to relate one fact of a problem to the others do we truly understand them.

This is my subject today—the need for greater individual and collective understanding of some of the international facts of today's life. We need to understand our country's purpose and role in strengthening the world's free nations which, with us, see our concepts of freedom and human dignity threatened by atheistic dictatorship.

If through education—no matter how acquired—people develop understanding of basic issues, and so can distinguish between the common, long-term good of all, on the one hand, and convenient but shortsighted expediency on the other, they will support policies under which the nation will prosper. And if people should ever lack the discernment to understand, or the character to rise above their own selfish short-term interests, free government would become well nigh impossible to sustain. Such a government would be reduced to nothing more than a device which seeks merely to accommodate itself and the country's good to the bitter tugs-of-war of conflicting pressure groups. Disaster could eventually result.

Though the subject I have assigned myself is neither abstruse nor particularly difficult to comprehend, its importance to our national and individual lives is such that failure to marshal, to organize, and to analyze the facts pertaining to it could have for all of us consequences of the most serious character. We must study, think, and decide on the governmental program that we term "Mutual Security."

The true need and value of this program will be recognized by our people only if they can answer this question: "Why should America, at heavy and immediate sacrifice to herself, assist many other nations, particularly the less developed ones, in achieving greater moral, economic, and military strength?"

What are the facts?

The first and most important fact is the implacable and frequently expressed purpose of imperialistic communism to promote world revolution, destroy freedom, and communize the world.

Its methods are all-inclusive, ranging through the use of propaganda, political subversion, economic penetration, and the use or the threat of force.

The second fact is that our country is today spending an aggregate of about 47 billion dollars annually for the single purpose of preserving the nation's position and security in the world. This includes the costs of the Defense Department, the production of nuclear weapons, and mutual security. All three are mutually supporting and are blended into one program for our safety. The size of this cost conveys something of the entire program's importance—to the world and, indeed, to each of us.

And when I think of this importance to us, think of it in this one material figure, this cost annually for every single man, woman, and child of the entire nation is about 275 dollars a year.

The next fact we note is that since the Communist target is the world, every nation is comprehended in their campaign for domination. The weak and the most exposed stand in the most immediate danger.

Another fact, that we ignore to our peril, is that if aggression or subversion against the weaker of the free nations should achieve successive victories, communism would step-by-step overcome once free areas. The danger, even to the strongest, would become increasingly menacing.

Clearly, the self-interest of each free nation impels it to resist the loss to imperialistic communism of the freedom and independence of any other nation.

Freedom is truly indivisible.

To apply some of these truths to a particular case, let us consider, briefly, the country of Viet-Nam, and the importance to us of the security and progress of that country.

It is located, as you know, in the southeastern corner of Asia, exactly halfway round the world from Gettysburg College.

Viet-Nam is a country divided into two parts—like Korea and Germany. The southern half, with its twelve million people, is free, but poor. It is an under-developed country—its economy is weak—average individual income being less than $200 a year. The northern half has been turned over to communism. A line of demarcation running along the 17th parallel separates the two. To the north of this line stand several Communist divisions. These facts pose to South Viet-Nam two great tasks: self-defense and economic growth.

Understandably, the people of Viet-Nam want to make their country a thriving, self-sufficient member of the family of nations. This means economic expansion.

For Viet-Nam's economic growth, the acquisition of capital is vitally necessary. Now, the nation could create the capital needed for growth by stealing from the already meager rice bowls of its people and regimenting them into work battalions. This enslavement is the commune system— adopted by the new overlords of Red China. It would mean, of course, the loss of freedom within the country without any hostile outside action whatsoever.

Another way for Viet-Nam to get the necessary capital is through private investments from the outside, and through governmental loans and, where necessary, grants from other and more fortunately situated nations.

In either of these ways the economic problem of Viet-Nam could be solved. But only the second way can preserve freedom.

And there is still the other of Viet-Nam's great problems—how to support the military forces it needs without crushing its economy.

Because of the proximity of large Communist military formations in the North, Free Viet-Nam must maintain substantial numbers of men under arms. Moreover, while the government has shown real progress in cleaning out Communist guerillas, those remaining continue to be a disruptive influence in the nation's life.

Unassisted, Viet-Nam cannot at this time produce and support the military formations essential to it, or, equally important, the morale—the hope, the confidence, the pride—necessary to meet the dual threat of aggression from without and subversion within its borders.

Still another fact! Strategically, South Viet-Nam's capture by the Communists would bring their power several hundred miles into a hitherto free region. The remaining countries in Southeast Asia would be menaced by a great flanking movement. The freedom of twelve million people would be lost immediately, and that of 150 million others in adjacent lands would be seriously endangered. The loss of South Viet-Nam would set in motion a crumbling process that could, as it progressed, have grave consequences for us and for freedom.

Viet-Nam must have a reasonable degree of safety now—both for her people and for her property. Because of these facts, military as well as economic help is currently needed in Viet-Nam.

We reach the inescapable conclusion that our own national interests demand some help from us in sustaining in Viet-Nam the morale, the economic progress, and the military strength necessary to its continued existence in freedom.

Viet-Nam is just one example. One-third of the world's people face a similar challenge. All through Africa and Southern Asia people struggle to preserve liberty and improve their standards of living, to maintain their dignity as humans. It is imperative that they succeed.

But some uninformed Americans believe that we should turn our backs on these people, our friends. Our costs and taxes are very real, while the difficulties of other peoples often seem remote from us.

But the costs of continuous neglect of these problems would be far more than we must now bear—indeed more than we could afford. The added costs would be paid not only in vastly increased outlays of money, but in larger drafts of our youth into the Military Establishment, and in terms of increased danger to our own security and prosperity.

No matter what areas of Federal spending must be curtailed—and some should—our safety comes first. Since that safety is necessarily based upon a sound and thriving economy, its protection must equally engage our earnest attention.

Few people noticed that year-in and year-out messages from the United States continued to praise and bolster the South Vietnamese government. The President had expected that by 1960 a stable pro-Western nation would have emerged from the 1954 defeat.

President Eisenhower to President Ngo Dinh Diem
July 11, 1959

[*Public Papers of the Presidents: 1959* (Washington, 1960), 519.]

Dear Mr. President:

I extend to you my congratulations and sincere good wishes on the occasion of your fifth anniversary as national leader of Viet-Nam.

The world has watched with admiration the progress made by Viet-Nam in the five years since you assumed leadership. It is now a country strong in its determination to preserve its freedom and active in promoting the development of its economy. We in the United States are aware of your own indispensable role in bringing about this remarkable progress. It is a task in which we are proud to have been associated with you.

I wish you, Mr. President, and the people of the Republic of Viet-Nam, continued success in advancing toward your goal of a better life in freedom.

In the fall of 1960, American Ambassador to Saigon Elbridge Dubrow assessed the alternatives facing the United States in Vietnam. The Ambassador recommended that if President Diem was unable to regain support through political and social reforms, "it may become necessary for U.S. Government to begin consideration of alternative courses of action and leaders." The Ambassador's reports, among others, were used in preparing a national intelligence estimate for President Kennedy, an estimate which gave a bleak appraisal of the situation in Vietnam.

Cablegram from Ambassador to Saigon Elbridge Durbrow, to Secretary Christian Herter
Sept. 16, 1960

[*The Pentagon Papers,* as quoted in *The New York Times,* July 1, 1971.]

As indicated our 495 and 538 Diem regime confronted by two separate but related dangers. Danger from demonstrations or coup attempt in Saigon could occur earlier; likely to be predominantly non-Communistic in origin but Communists can be expected to endeavor infiltrate and exploit any such attempt. Even more serious danger is gradual Viet Cong extension of control over countryside which, if current Communists progress continues, would mean loss free Viet-nam to Communists. These two dangers are related because Communist successes in rural areas embolden them to extend their activities to Saigon and because non-Communist temptation to engage in demonstrations or coup is partly motivated by sincere desire prevent Communist take-over in Viet-nam.

Essentially [word illegible] sets of measures required to meet these two dangers. For Saigon danger essentially political and psychological measures required. For countryside danger security measures as well as political, psychological and economic measures needed. However both sets measures should be carried out simultaneously and to some extent individual steps will be aimed at both dangers.

Security recommendations have been made in our 539 and other messages, including formation internal security council, centralized intelligence, etc. This message therefore deals with our political and economic recommendations. I realize some measures I am recommending are drastic and would be most [word illegible] for an ambassador to make under normal circumstances. But conditions here are by no means normal. Diem government is in quite serious danger. Therefore, in my opinion prompt and even drastic action is called for. I am well aware that Diem has in past demonstrated astute judgment and has survived other serious crises. Possibly his judgment will prove superior to ours this time, but I believe nevertheless we have no alternative but to give him our best judgment of what we believe is required to preserve his government. While Diem obviously resented my frank talks earlier this year and will probably resent even more suggestions outlined below, he has apparently acted on some of our earlier suggestions and might act on at least some of the following.

1. I would propose have frank and friendly talk with Diem and explain our serious concern about present situation and his political position. I would tell him that, while matters I am raising deal primarily with internal affairs, I would like to talk to him frankly and try to be as helpful as I can be giving him the considered judgment of myself and some of his friends in Washington on appropriate measures to assist him in present serious situation. (Believe it best not indicate talking under instructions.) I would particularly stress desirability of actions to broaden and increase his [word illegible] support prior to 1961 presidential elections required by constitution before end April. I would propose following actions to President:

2. Psychological shock effect is required to take initiative from Communist propagandists as well as non-Communist oppositionists and convince population government taking effective measures to deal with present situation, otherwise we fear matters could get out of hand. To achieve that effect following suggested:

(A) Because of Vice President Tho's knowledge of south where Communist guerilla infiltration is increasing so rapidly would suggest that he be shifted from ministry national economy to ministry interior. (Diem has already made this suggestion but Vice President most reluctant take job.)

(B) It is important to remove any feeling within armed forces that favoritism and political considerations motivate promotions and assignments. Also vital in order deal effectively with Viet Cong threat that channels of command be followed both down and up. To assist in bringing about these changes in armed forces, I would suggest appointment of full-time minister national defense. (Thuan has indicated Diem has been thinking of giving Thuan defense job.)

(C) Rumors about Mr. and Mrs. Nhu are creating growing dissension within country and seriously damage political position of Diem government. Whether rumors true or false, politically important fact is that more and more people believe them to be true. Therefore, becoming increasingly clear that in interest Diem government some action should be taken. In analagous situation in other countries including US important, useful government personalities have had to be sacrificed for political reasons. I would suggest therefore that President might appoint Nhu to ambassadorship abroad.

D) Similarly Tran Kim Tuyen, Nhu's henchman and head of secret intelligence service, should be sent abroad in diplomatic capacity because of his growing identification in public mind with alleged secret police methods of repression and control.

(E) One or two cabinet ministers from opposition should be appointed to demonstrate Diem's desire to establish government of national union in fight against VC.

3. Make public announcement of disbandment of Can Lao party or at least its surfacing, with names and positions of all members made known publicly. Purpose this step would be to eliminate atmosphere of fear and suspicion and reduce public belief in favoritism and corruption, all of which party's semicovert status has given rise to.

4. Permit National Assembly wider legislative initiative and area of genuine debate and bestow on it authority to conduct, with appropriate publicity, public investigations of any department of government with right to question any official except President himself. This step would have three-fold purpose: (A) find some mechanism for dispelling through public investigation constantly generated rumors about government and its personalties; (B) provide people with avenue recourse against arbitrary actions by some government officials, (C) assuage some of intellectual opposition to government.

5. Require all government officials to declare publicly their property and financial holdings and give National Assembly authority to make public investigation of these declarations in effort dispel rumors of corruption

6. [Words illegible] of [words illegible] control over content of the Vietnamese publication [word illegible] magazines, radio, so that the [words illegible] to closing the gap between government and [words illegible] ideas from one to the other. To insure that the press would reflect, as well as lead, public opinion without becoming a means of

upsetting the entire GVN [word illegible], it should be held responsible to a self-imposed code of ethics or "canon" of press-conduct.

7. [Words illegible] to propaganda campaign about new 3-year development plan in effort convince people that government genuinely aims at [word illegible] their welfare. (This suggestion [word illegible] of course upon assessment of soundness of development plan, which has just reached us.)

8. Adopt following measures for immediate enhancement of peasant support of government: (A) establish mechanism for increasing price peasant will receive for paddy crop beginning to come on market in December, either by direct subsidization or establishment state purchasing mechanism; (B) institute modest payment for all corvee labor; (C) subsidize agroville families along same lines as land resettlement families until former on feet economically; (D) increase compensation paid to youth corps. If Diem asks how these measures are to be financed I shall suggest through increased taxes or increased deficit financing, and shall note that under certain circumstances reasonable deficit financing becomes a politically necessary measure for governments. I should add that using revenues for these fundamental and worthy purposes would be more effective than spending larger and larger sums on security forces, which, while they are essential and some additional funds for existing security forces may be required, are not complete answer to current problems.

9. Propose suggest to Diem that appropriate steps outlined above be announced dramatically in his annual state of union message to National Assembly in early October. Since Diem usually [word illegible] message in person this would have maximum effect, and I would recommend that it be broadcast live to country.

10. At [words illegible] on occasion fifth anniversary establishment Republic of Vietnam on October 26, it may become highly desirable for President Eisenhower to address a letter of continued support to Diem. Diem has undoubtedly noticed that Eisenhower letter recently delivered to Sihanouk. Not only for this reason, but also because it may become very important for us to give Diem continued reassurance of our support. Presidential letter which could be published here may prove to be very valuable.

Request any additional suggestions department may have and its approval for approach to Diem along lines paras 1 to 9.

We believe US should at this time support Diem as best available Vietnamese leader, but should recognize that overriding US objective is strongly anti-Communist Vietnamese government which can command loyal and enthusiastic support of widest possible segments of Vietnamese people, and is able to carry on effective fight against Communist guerillas. If Diem's position in country continues deteriorate as result failure adopt proper political, psychological economic and security measures, it may become necessary for US government to begin consideration alternative courses of action and leaders in order achieve our objective.

VI

*MODERN REPUBLICANISM
IN ACTION*

MODERN REPUBLICANISM IN ACTION

Introduction

Dwight Eisenhower's second Inaugural placed him among a select group of American Presidents who repeated the oath more than once. Since January 20, 1957, fell on a Sunday, he took the oath in private, and then went through the usual gala Inauguration ceremonies the following day. His Address contrasted sharply with the one he gave in 1953; he talked in conciliatory terms about the need for world peace. Friend and foe alike praised his call for understanding. But all in all, the dignity and majesty of the second Inaugural failed to confront the numerous problems faced by the President. Even as he spoke at the East Front of the Capitol, Administration officials revised drafts of a Special Message on the Middle East, a region made all the more dangerous by Israel's repeated refusals to withdraw from Egyptian territory. This and other perilous situations accentuated the problems of the Cold War, although domestic politics continued to follow traditional lines. Democratic congressional leaders generally approved of the Inaugural Address, even though they already had plans for domestic legislation that would run counter to Eisenhower's January 10 State of the Union Message. So did some Republicans.

The first clash between the President and the new Congress occurred over the Administration's proposed budget for the coming fiscal year. Largely because it would have set a record for peace-time spending, many Democrats called the budget extravagant, despite the fact that their plans would have increased it still further. On the other hand, numerous Old Guard Republicans wanted a massive cutback in federal expenditures. Within this context, the Congress commenced consideration of the 1958 budget. Eisenhower's desires for an expanded federal role revived the arguments that had raged for many years inside the Republican party, but which for the most part had been dormant since the 1952 election. Now, Old Guard Republicans conjured up visions of "hair-raising depressions" and other calamities that would result from "fiscal insanity." Aware of these considerations, Congress hassled over all appropriations and argued about the value of each federal program.

Even under the best of conditions, the 86th Congress would have presented many difficulties for the President. While a $72 billion budget finally passed, neither the "spenders" nor the "cutters" found pleasure in the results. Eisenhower, who did not get entirely what he wanted, believed that the nation had moved forward during 1957. However, when a recession struck the next year, both those who felt the Federal Government was doing too much and those who felt it was doing too little blamed national fiscal policies. Immediately the economic downturn became a political issue; many Democrats responded by advocating gigantic new programs, while Republicans generally adopted a "watch and wait" attitude. Above and beyond congressional reaction, the economic reversal became a national issue. Even though few feared another 1929, the decline gravely injured the Republican party. Optimistic predictions made during 1957 by GOP prognosticators were proven false in the fall of 1958. Again, an American political party tarred with the brush of recession could not win at the polls, as the Republicans suffered a disastrous defeat, second only to the debacle of 1936.

Before the overwhelmingly Democratic 87th Congress convened on January 7, 1959, pundits cited many reasons other than the recession for the staggering Republican loss. The most sensational issue involved The Assistant to the President Sherman Adams. His friendship with Bernard Goldfine, a New England textile manufacturer who had dealings with federal agencies, raised questions about the misuse of influence in high places. Adams very likely would have ridden out the storm, but many Republicans, especially members of the Old Guard, called for his dismissal. Ostensibly they reasoned that the "scandal" would hurt the party's chances even more than mounting unemployment. Yet, some observers believed that controversies over Adams' control of patronage constituted a more basic consideration. When Adams resigned on September 22, 1958, the Democrats called his decision an admission of wrongdoing and made even greater political capital out of the incident than expected. The affair offered support to Democratic charges that Eisenhower no longer worked full time as Chief Executive and that health factors prevented the man who had called for a government "clean as a hounds tooth" from knowing what was going on in the inner circles of his own Administration. Eisenhower's mild stroke on November 25, 1957, coupled with his frequent trips to the golf course, led many to believe that the "part-time President" accusations had a considerable degree of validity. Along the same lines, some observers noted that Eisenhower had failed to campaign energetically during 1958 on behalf of Republican candidates. Although such factors did hurt the party, an analysis of the 1958 election by the Republican National Committee focused the blame on pockets of unemployment. The results in Ohio seemed to validate this observation. There, a very large labor vote reacting to joblessness and a "right to work" amendment defeated the long-time Republican incumbent John Bricker, a staunch member of the Old Guard.

For the first time since he became President, Eisenhower faced a Congress overwhelmingly dominated by Democrats. For the previous four years small majorities had allowed the Democrats to organize Congress. Now, not only would they elect leaders but they would possess the power to override presidential vetoes—a situation that had not existed since 1867. Despite greater strains between Eisenhower and the 87th Congress, the relationship that had been established during his first term had changed only slightly, even though the Administration was compelled to compromise more often. For example, the President had to agree to statehood for Alaska (January 3, 1959), considered a Democratic stronghold, before Congress would admit Republican Hawaii to the Union (August 21, 1959). This compromise fulfilled long-promised action by both parties, which had been blocked for years by the political character of the two territories. When Congress drastically increased spending for education in the wake of the Soviet Union's launching of "Sputnik," Eisenhower agreed to the legislation while disagreeing with the spending level. Congress, in its turn, compromised by accepting more stringent controls on labor leaders than even many Democratic legislators desired. But the area in which the President and Congress disagreed most violently was military policy. When Democrats challenged the nation's defense posture, Eisenhower muted criticism by successfully advocating legislation calling for a reorganization of the Pentagon. The political implications, especially the "missle gap," would emerge as issues in the next election. While the problems over defense greatly distressed the President—especially because they involved his judgement in his field of special competence—an issue that was of even more annoyance to him was the Senate's refusal to confirm a Cabinet appointee. The nomination of Lewis Strauss as Secretary of Commerce appeared to Eisenhower as a normal presidential prerogative. When the upper house denied confirmation (June 19) for what the President believed totally partisan reasons (Strauss' acrimonious relationships with individual senators), Eisenhower said that politics had kept a great man's services from the nation. In many ways, the Senate's refusal to approve Strauss was the worst personal defeat the President suffered in his last two years, and it was symptomatic of a return to more partisan activities as the election of 1960 drew near.

During the final phase of the Administration, Eisenhower, under increasing Democratic attacks, reiterated in stronger terms the fiscal ideas that he had stressed in his 1952 campaign. The executive branch, in press releases and in public statements, emphasized balanced budgeting, self-liquidating projects, and strict limits on the scope of federal activities. No longer would programs like the interstate highways be justified without consideration of their expense; rather, such projects would be viewed purely in terms of their inflationary and deficit impact. The Administration had now run full course. In the last months, the values espoused in 1952 loomed somewhat larger than those of 1956.

1. THE GREAT BUDGET DEBATE

The 1957 State of the Union Message incorporated numerous proposals that fit into the broad scheme of Modern Republicanism. In many ways the President seemed bent on rallying the Congress to join him in embarking on a "new crusade."

State of the Union Message by President Eisenhower
January 10, 1957
[*Public Papers of the Presidents: 1957* (Washington, 1958), 17–30.]

To the Congress of the United States:

I appear before the Congress today to report on the State of the Union and the relationships of the Union to the other nations of the world. I come here, firmly convinced that at no time in the history of the Republic have circumstances more emphatically underscored the need, in all echelons of government, for vision and wisdom and resolution.

You meet in a season of stress that is testing the fitness of political systems and the validity of political philosophies. Each stress stems in part from causes peculiar to itself. But every stress is a reflection of a universal phenomenon.

In the world today, the surging and understandable tide of nationalism is marked by widespread revulsion and revolt against tyranny, injustice, inequality and poverty. As individuals, joined in a common hunger for freedom, men and women and even children pit their spirit against guns and tanks. On a larger scale, in an ever more persistent search for the self-respect of authentic sovereignty and the economic base on which national independence must rest, peoples sever old ties; seek new alliances; experiment—sometimes dangerously—in their struggle to satisfy these human aspirations.

Particularly, in the past year, this tide has changed the pattern of attitudes and thinking among millions. The changes already accomplished foreshadow a world transformed by the spirit of freedom. This is no faint and pious hope. The forces now at work in the minds and hearts of men will not be spent through many years. In the main, today's expressions of nationalism are, in spirit, echoes of our forefathers' struggle for independence.

This Republic cannot be aloof to these events heralding a new epoch in the affairs of mankind.

Our pledged word, our enlightened self-interest, our character as a Nation commit us to a high role in world affairs: a role of vigorous leadership, ready strength, sympathetic understanding.

The State of the Union, at the opening of the 85th Congress continues to vindicate the wisdom of the principles on which this Republic is founded. Proclaimed in the Constitution of the Nation and in many of our historic documents, and founded in devout religious convictions, these principles enunciate:

A vigilant regard for human liberty.

A wise concern for human welfare.

A ceaseless effort for human progress.

Fidelity to these principles, in our relations with other peoples, has won us new friendships and has increased our opportunity for service within the family of nations. The appeal of these principles is universal, lighting fires in the souls of men everywhere. We shall continue to uphold them, against those who deny them and in counselling with our friends.

At home, the application of these principles to the complex problems of our national life has brought us to an unprecedented peak in our economic prosperity and has exemplified in our way of life the enduring human values of mind and spirit.

Through the past four years these principles have guided the legislative programs submitted by the Administration to the Congress. As we attempt to apply them to current events, domestic and foreign, we must take into account the complex entity that is the United States of America; what endangers it; what can improve it.

The visible structure is our American economy itself. After more than a century and a half of constant expansion, it is still rich in a wide variety of natural resources. It is first among nations in its people's mastery of industrial skills. It is productive beyond our own needs of many foodstuffs and industrial products. It is rewarding to all our citizens in opportunity to earn and to advance in self-realization and in self-expression. It is fortunate in its wealth of educational and cultural and religious centers. It is vigorously dynamic in the limitless initiative and willingness to venture that characterize free enterprise. It is productive of a widely shared prosperity.

Our economy is strong, expanding, and fundamentally sound. But in any realistic appraisal, even the optimistic analyst will realize that in a prosperous period the principal threat to efficient functioning of a free enterprise system is inflation. We look back on four years of prosperous activities during which prices, the cost of living, have been relatively stable—that is, inflation has been held in check. But it is clear that the danger is always present, particularly if the government might become profligate in its expenditures or private groups might ignore all the possible results on our economy of unwise struggles for immediate gain.

This danger requires a firm resolution that the Federal Government shall utilize only a prudent share of the Nation's resources, that it shall live within its means, carefully measuring against need alternative proposals for expenditures.

Through the next four years, I shall continue to insist that the executive departments and agencies of Government search out additional ways to save money and manpower. I urge that the Congress be equally watchful in this matter.

We pledge the Government's share in guarding the integrity of the dollar. But the Government's efforts cannot be the entire campaign against inflation, the thief that can rob the individual of the value of the pension and social security he has earned during his productive life. For success, Government's efforts must be paralleled by the attitudes and actions of individual citizens.

I have often spoken of the purpose of this Administration to serve the national interest of 170 million people. The national interest must take precedence over temporary advantages which may be secured by particular groups at the expense of all the people.

In this regard I call on leaders in business and in labor to think well on their responsibility to the American people. With all elements of our society, they owe the Nation a vigilant guard againt the inflationary tendencies that are always at work in a dynamic economy operating at today's high levels. They can powerfully help counteract or accentuate such tendencies by their wage and price policies.

Business in its pricing policies should avoid unnecessary price increases especially at a time like the present when demand in so many areas presses hard on short supplies. A reasonable profit is essential to the new investments that provide more jobs in an expanding economy. But business leaders must, in the national interest, studiously avoid those price rises that are possible only because of vital or unusual needs of the whole nation.

If our economy is to remain healthy, increases in wages and other labor benefits, negotiated by labor and management, must be reasonably related to improvements in productivity. Such increases are beneficial, for they provide wage earners with greater purchasing power. Except where necessary to correct obvious injustices, wage increases that outrun productivity, however, are an inflationary factor. They make for higher prices for the public generally and impose a particular hardship on those whose welfare depends on the purchasing power of retirement income and savings. Wage negotiations should also take cognizance of the right of the public generally to share in the benefits of improvements in technology.

Freedom has been defined as the opportunity for self-discipline. This definition has a special application to the areas of wage and price policy in a free economy. Should we persistently fail to discipline ourselves, eventually there will be increasing pressure on government to redress the failure. By that process freedom will step by step disappear. No subject on the domestic scene should more attract the concern of the friends of American working men and women and of free business enterprise than the forces that threaten a steady depreciation of the value of our money.

Concerning developments in another vital sector of our economy—agriculture—I am gratified that the long slide in farm income has been halted and that further improvement is in prospect. This is heartening progress. Three tools that we have developed—improved surplus disposal, improved price support laws, and the soil bank—are working to reduce price-depressing government stocks of farm products. Our concern for the well-being of farm families demands that we constantly search for new ways by which they can share more fully in our unprecedented prosperity. Legislative recommendations in the field of agriculture are contained in the Budget Message.

Our soil, water, mineral, forest, fish, and wildlife resources are being conserved and improved more effectively. Their conservation and development are vital to the present and future strength of the Nation. But they must not be the concern of the Federal Government alone. State and local entities, and private enterprise should be encouraged to participate in such projects.

I would like to make special mention of programs for making the best uses of water, rapidly becoming our most precious natural resource, just as it can be, when neglected, a destroyer of both life and wealth. There has been prepared and published a comprehensive water report developed by a Cabinet Committee and relating to all phases of this particular problem.

In the light of this report, there are two things I believe we should keep constantly in mind. The first is that each of our great river valleys should be considered as a whole. Piecemeal operations within each lesser drainage area can be self-defeating or, at the very least, needlessly expensive. The second is that the domestic and industrial demands for water grow far more rapidly than does our population.

The whole matter of making the best use of each drop of water from the moment it touches our soil until it reaches the oceans, for such purposes as irrigation, flood control, power production, and domestic and industrial uses clearly demands the closest kind of cooperation and partnership between municipalities, States and the Federal Government. Through partnership of Federal, state and local authorities in these vast projects we can obtain the economy and efficiency of development and operation that springs from a lively sense of local responsibility.

Until such partnership is established on a proper and logical basis of sharing authority, responsibility and costs, our country will never have both the fully productive use of water that it so obviously needs and protection against disastrous flood.

If we fail in this, all the many tasks that need to be done in America could be accomplished only at an excessive cost, by the growth of a stifling bureaucracy, and eventually with a dangerous degree of centralized control over our national life.

In all domestic matters, I believe that the people of the United States will expect of us effective action to remedy past failure in meeting critical needs.

High priority should be given to the school construction bill. This will benefit children of all races throughout the country—and children of all races need schools now. A program designed to meet emergency needs for more classrooms should be enacted without delay. I am hopeful that this program can be enacted on its own merits, uncomplicated by provisions dealing with the complex problems of integration. I urge the people in all sections of the country to approach these problems with calm and reason, with mutual understanding and good will, and in the American tradition of deep respect for the orderly processes of law and justice.

I should say here that we have much reason to be proud of the progress our people are making in mutual understanding—the chief buttress of human and civil rights. Steadily we are moving closer to the goal of fair and equal treatment of citizens without regard to race or color. But unhappily much remains to be done.

Last year the Administration recommended to the Congress a four-point program to reinforce civil rights. That program included:

(1) creation of a bipartisan commission to investigate asserted violations of civil rights and to make recommendations;

(2) creation of a civil rights division in the Department of Justice in charge of an Assistant Attorney General;

(3) enactment by the Congress of new laws to aid in the enforcement of voting rights; and

(4) amendment of the laws so as to permit the Federal Government to seek from the civil courts preventive relief in civil rights cases.

I urge that the Congress enact this legislation.

Essential to the stable economic growth we seek is a system of well-adapted and efficient financial institutions. I believe the time has come to conduct a broad national inquiry into the nature, performance and adequacy of our financial system, both in terms of its direct service to the whole economy and in terms of its function as the mechanism through which monetary and credit policy takes effect. I believe the Congress should authorize the creation of a commission of able and qualified citizens to undertake this vital inquiry. Out of their findings and recommendations the Administration would develop and present to the Congress any legislative proposals that might be indicated for the purpose of improving our financial machinery.

In this message it seems unnecessary that I should repeat recommendations involving our domestic affairs that have been urged upon the Congress during the past four years, but which, in some instances, did not reach the stage of completely satisfactory legislation.

The Administration will, through future messages either directly from me or from heads of the departments and agencies, transmit to the Congress specific recommendations. These will involve our financial and fiscal affairs, our military and civil defenses; the administration of justice; our agricultural economy; our domestic and foreign commerce; the urgently needed increase in our postal rates; the development of our natural resources; our labor laws, including our labor-management relations legislation, and vital aspects of the health, education and welfare of our people. There will be special recommendations dealing with such subjects as atomic energy, the furthering of public works, the continued efforts to eliminate government competition with the businesses of tax-paying citizens.

A number of legislative recommendations will be mentioned specifically in my forthcoming Budget Message, which will reach you within the week. That message will also recommend such sums as are needed to implement the proposed action.

Turning to the international scene:

The existence of a strongly armed imperialistic dictatorship poses a continuing threat to the free world's and thus to our own Nation's security and peace. There are certain truths to be remembered here.

First, America alone and isolated cannot assure even its own security. We must be joined by the capability and resolution of nations that have proved themselves dependable defenders of freedom. Isolation from them invites war. Our security is also enhanced by the immeasurable interest that joins us with all peoples who believe that peace with justice must be preserved, that wars of aggression are crimes against humanity.

Another truth is that our survival in today's world requires modern, adequate, dependable military strength. Our Nation has made great strides in assuring a modern defense, so armed in new weapons, so deployed, so equipped, that today our security force is the most powerful in our peacetime history. It can punish heavily any enemy who undertakes to attack us. It is a major deterrent to war.

By our research and development more efficient weapons—some of amazing capabilities—are being constantly created. These vital efforts we shall continue. Yet we must not delude ourselves that safety necessarily increases as expenditures for military research or forces in being go up. Indeed, beyond a wise and reasonable level, which is always changing and is under constant study, money spent on arms may be money wasted on sterile metal or inflated costs, thereby weakening the very security and strength we seek.

National security requires far more than military power. Economic and moral factors play indispensable roles. Any program that endangers our economy could defeat us. Any weakening of our national will and resolution, any diminution of the vigor and initiative of our individual citizens, would strike a blow at the heart of our defenses.

The finest military establishment we can produce must work closely in cooperation with the forces of our friends. Our system of regional pacts, developed within the Charter of the United Nations, serves to increase both our own security and the security of other nations.

This system is still a recent introduction on the world scene. Its problems are many and difficult, because it insists on equality among its members and brings into association some nations traditionally divided. Repeatedly in recent months, the collapse of these regional alliances has been predicted. The strains upon them have been at times indeed severe. Despite these strains our regional alliances have proved durable and strong, and dire predictions of their disintegration have proved completely false.

With other free nations, we should vigorously prosecute measures that will promote mutual strength, prosperity and welfare within the free world. Strength is essentially a product of economic health and social well-being. Consequently, even as we continue our programs of military assistance, we must emphasize aid to our friends in building more productive economies and in better satisfying the natural demands of their people for progress. Thereby we shall move a long way toward a peaceful world.

A sound and safeguarded agreement for open skies, unarmed aerial sentinels, and reduced armament would provide a valuable contribution toward a durable peace in the years ahead. And we have been persistent in our effort to reach such an agreement. We are willing to enter any reliable agreement which would reverse the trend toward ever more devastating nuclear weapons; reciprocally provide against the possibility of surprise attack; mutually control the outer space missile and satellite development; and make feasible a lower level of armaments and armed forces and an easier burden of military expenditures. Our continuing negotiations in this field are a major part of our quest for a confident peace in this atomic age.

This quest requires as well a constructive attitude among all the nations of the free world toward expansion of trade and investment, that can give all of us opportunity to work out economic betterment.

An essential step in this field is the provision of an administrative agency to insure the orderly and proper operation of existing arrangements under which multilateral trade is now carried on. To that end I urge Congressional authorization for United States membership in the proposed Organization for Trade Cooperation, an action which will speed removal of discrimination against our export trade.

We welcome the efforts of a number of our European friends to achieve an integrated community to develop a common market. We likewise welcome their cooperative effort in the field of atomic energy.

To demonstrate once again our unalterable purpose to make of the atom a peaceful servant of humanity, I shortly shall ask the Congress to authorize full United States participation in the International Atomic Energy Agency.

World events have magnified both the responsibilities and the opportunities of the United States Information Agency. Just as, in recent months, the voice of communism has become more shaken and confused, the voice of truth must be more clearly heard. To enable our Information Agency to cope with these new responsibilities and opportunities, I am asking the Congress to increase appreciably the appropriations for this program and for legislation establishing a career service for the Agency's overseas foreign service officers.

The recent historic events in Hungary demand that all free nations share to the extent of their capabilities in the responsibility of granting asylum to victims of Communist persecution. I request the Congress promptly to enact legislation to regularize the status in the United States of Hungarian refugees brought here as parolees. I shall shortly recommend to the Congress by special message the changes in our immigration laws that I deem necessary in the light of our world responsibilities.

The cost of peace is something we must face boldly, fearlessly. Beyond money, it involves changes in attitudes, the renunciation of old prejudices, even the sacrifice of some seeming self-interest.

Only five days ago I expressed to you the grave concern of your Government over the threat of Soviet aggression in the Middle East. I asked for Congressional authorization to help counter this threat. I say again that this matter is of vital and immediate importance to the Nation's and the free world's security and peace. By our proposed programs in the Middle East, we hope to assist in establishing a climate in which constructive and long-term solutions to basic problems of the area may be sought.

From time to time, there will be presented to the Congress requests for other legislation in the broad field of international affairs. All requests will reflect the steadfast purpose of this Administration to pursue peace, based on justice. Although in some cases details will be new, the underlying purpose and objectives will remain the same.

All proposals made by the Administration in this field are based on the free world's unity. This unity may not be immediately obvious unless we examine link by link the chain of relationships that binds us to every area and to every nation. In spirit the free world is one because its people uphold the right of independent existence for all nations. I have already alluded to their economic interdependence. But their interdependence extends also into the field of security.

First of all, no reasonable man will question the absolute need for our American neighbors to be prosperous and secure. Their security and prosperity are inextricably bound to our own. And we are, of course, already joined with these neighbors by historic pledges.

Again, no reasonable man will deny that the freedom and prosperity and security of Western Europe are vital to our own prosperity and security. If the institutions, the skills, the manpower of its peoples were to fall under the domination of an aggressive imperialism, the violent change in the balance of world power and in the pattern of world commerce could not be fully compensated for by any American measures, military or economic.

But these people, whose economic strength is largely dependent on free and uninterrupted movement of oil from the Middle East, cannot prosper—indeed, their economies would be severely impaired—should that area be controlled by an enemy and the movement of oil be subject to its decisions.

Next, to the Eastward, are Asiatic and Far Eastern peoples, recently returned to independent control of their own affairs or now emerging into sovereign statehood. Their potential strength constitutes new assurance for stability and peace in the world—if they can retain their independence. Should they lose freedom and be dominated by an aggressor, the world-wide effects would imperil the security of the free world.

In short, the world has so shrunk that all free nations are our neighbors. Without cooperative neighbors, the United States cannot maintain its own security and welfare, because:

First, America's vital interests are world-wide, embracing both hemispheres and every continent.

Second, we have community of interest with every nation in the free world.

Third, interdependence of interests requires a decent respect for the rights and the peace of all peoples.

These principles motivate our actions within the United Nations. There, before all the world, by our loyalty to them, by our practice of them, let us strive to set a standard to which all who seek justice and who hunger for peace can rally.

May we at home, here at the Seat of Government, in all the cities and towns and farmlands of America, support these principles in a personal effort of dedication. Thereby each of us can help establish a secure world order in which opportunity for freedom and justice will be more widespread, and in which the resources now dissipated on the armaments of war can be released for the life and growth of all humanity.

When our forefathers prepared the immortal document that proclaimed our independence, they asserted that every individual is endowed by his Creator with certain inalienable rights. As we gaze back through history to that date, it is clear that our nation has striven to live up to this declaration, applying it to nations as well as to individuals.

Today we proudly assert that the government of the United States is still committed to this concept, both in its activities at home and abroad.

The purpose is Divine; the implementation is human.

Our country and its government have made mistakes—human mistakes. They have been of the head—not of the heart. And it is still true that the great concept of the dignity of all men, alike created in the image of the Almighty, has been the compass by which we have tried and are trying to steer our course.

So long as we continue by its guidance, there will be true progress in human affairs, both among ourselves and among those with whom we deal.

To achieve a more perfect fidelity to it, I submit, is a worthy ambition as we meet together in these first days of this, the first session of the 85th Congress.

The budget proposals for fiscal 1958 reflected Eisenhower's commitment to Modern Republicanism. In his budget summary he indicated that the Federal Government should spend $71.8 billion during the year beginning July 1, 1957. This constituted the largest peacetime budget ever presented to Congress.

Annual Presidential Budget Message
January 16, 1957
[*Public Papers of the Presidents: 1957* (Washington, 1958), 38–59.]

To the Congress of the United States:
I am presenting with this message my recommended budget for the United States Government for the fiscal year 1958, which begins next July 1.

This is the fourth budget which I have transmitted to the Congress.

In my first budget message—that for the fiscal year 1955—I emphasized the administration's determination to chart a course toward two important fiscal goals—balanced budgets and tax reductions.

Reductions in spending evidenced in the 1955 budget made possible a large tax reduction and tax reform program.

The 1956 budget was balanced.

The 1957 budget will be balanced.

A balanced budget is proposed for 1958.

I believe this policy of fiscal integrity has contributed significantly to the soundness of our Nation's economic growth and that it will continue to do so during the coming fiscal year.

Budget Totals

[Fiscal years. In billions]

	1956 actual	1957 estimate	1958 estimate
Budget receipts........................	$68.1	$70.6	$73.6
Budget expenditures.....................	66.5	68.9	71.8
Budget surplus.......................	1.6	1.7	1.8

This budget is for the first fiscal year of my second term in office. In making plans for the coming year, I have been guided by the following national objectives:

1. Peace, justice, and freedom for our own and other peoples;

2. Powerful armed forces to deter and, if need be, to defeat aggression;

3. A healthy and growing economy with prosperity widely shared;

4. Enhancement of individual opportunity and the well-being of all our people;

5. Wise conservation, development, and use of our great natural resources;

6. Fiscal integrity;

7. A well-balanced choice of programs at home and abroad; and

8. Increasing international trade and investment essential to the growth of the economies of the United States and the rest of the free world.

We have made considerable progress toward these goals. We will continue this progress in the years ahead.

Budget Policy

Today, almost 12 years after World War II, the United States has demonstrated that it is possible to sustain a high employment economy independent of war and continually unbalanced Federal budgets. Adjustments to changing economic circumstances have been and are being made successfully. Productivity and living conditions have improved. With sound public and private policies, the prospect for continued economic growth is bright.

Attainment of that goal is possible only with prudent management of the Government's fiscal affairs. Our Federal budget must contribute to the Nation's financial stability and to the preservation of the purchasing power of the dollar. Maintaining a sound dollar requires of us both self-discipline and courage. At a time like the present when the economy is operating at a very high rate and is subject to inflationary pressures, Government clearly should seek to alleviate rather than aggravate those pressures. Government can do its part. But business and labor leadership must earnestly cooperate—

or what Government can do in a free society at a time like this will *not* prevent inflation.

For the Government to do its part in the coming year, taxes must be retained at the present rates so that receipts will exceed budget expenditures and the public debt can be further reduced. The prospective budget surplus in the fiscal year 1958 will reinforce the restraining effect of present credit and monetary policies. The present situation also requires that less pressing expenditure programs must be held back and some meritorious proposals postponed.

Expenditure and appropriation policy.—While taking present economic conditions into consideration, the budget must also reflect the general responsibilities of a Government which will be serving 172 million people in the fiscal year 1958. In the face of continuing threats to world peace, our collective security must be strengthened through alert international policies and a strong defense. Progress toward greater equality of opportunity for all of our people as well as toward a balanced development and conservation of our national resources must go forward. Emphasis must continue upon promoting, through private enterprise, the development and productivity of our economy.

We must move forward in some areas of investment while we hold back in others. For example, the needs for schools, highways, and homes are so urgent that I am proposing to move ahead with programs to help our States, cities, and people undertake such construction at a prudent rate. However, in view of the present active competition for labor, materials, and equipment, I am not recommending some other desirable construction projects, and I have asked the head of each Federal agency to watch closely the timing of construction and to postpone work which can be appropriately put off until a later date.

New Authority to Incur Obligations
[Fiscal years. In billions]

	1956	1957	1958
Proposed for enactment in this session:			
Recommended at this time..............	....	....	$56.7
Proposed for later transmission:			
Under existing legislation..............	....	$0.8	(¹)
Under proposed legislation.............	....	.8	8.6
Total..............................	....	1.6	65.3
Enacted prior to this session:			
Current authorization..................	$53.8	60.7	....
Permanent authorization................	9.9	8.2	8.0
Total..............................	63.2	70.5	73.3

¹Less than 50 million dollars.

It is also important to hold to a minimum any increase in Government personnel in the coming period. I have directed the heads of the Federal agencies to give renewed emphasis to their efforts in this regard—efforts which have resulted in a net reduction of approximately 240,000 in the civilian work force during the past 4 years. Vacant positions are to be filled by new employment only if careful review by each agency has demonstrated that the positions cannot be abolished or filled by transfer. All proposals which might produce higher Federal payrolls in the future will be critically examined and evaluated.

Continuation of balanced budgets into the future requires that the total of new authority to incur obligations, as well as the budget expenditures for the year, should be less than the total of realistically anticipated budget receipts. This policy of controlling budget authorizations, which has been followed since the beginning of this administration, has helped us move from a budget deficit of 9.4 billion dollars in the fiscal year 1953 to balanced budgets in 1956, 1957, and 1958.

In this budget the total of new authority proposed for 1958 is 73.3 billion dollars, 279 million dollars less than estimated budget receipts. Of the total recommended new authority, specific action by this session of the Congress will be necessary for 65.3 billion dollars. Other new authority, such as that for paying interest on the public debt, will become available under previously enacted permanent authorizations.

The total amount of new obligational authority recommended for the fiscal year 1958 is 2.8 billion dollars greater than the present estimates for 1957. Budget expenditures are estimated to increase by 2.9 billion dollars to a total of 71.8 billion dollars in 1958. These estimates include my proposals for new legislation as well as present programs.

For both new obligational authority and expenditures, about seven-tenths of the estimated increase between 1957 and 1958 is for the military functions of the Department of Defense, reflecting the higher costs of producing, operating, and maintaining the complex new weapons and equipment being delivered in growing quantities to our defense establishment. Other major increases are for the Department of Health, Education, and Welfare, including my proposal for aiding school construction, and for the Atomic Energy Commission.

The figures contained in this budget for the fiscal years 1957 and 1958 are not precisely comparable to the actual figures for prior years. Under the provisions of legislation enacted last year, the financial transactions for the greatly expanded Federal-aid highway program are included in a self-liquidating trust fund and are not in the budget totals.

Revenue policy.—It is my firm belief that tax rates are still too high and that we should look forward to further tax reductions as soon as they can be accomplished within a sound budget policy. Reductions in tax rates would give relief to taxpayers and would also release funds for the activity and investment necessary for sustained economic growth through private initiative. However, the reduction of tax rates must give way under present circumstances to the cost of meeting our urgent national responsibilities.

For the present, therefore, I ask for continuation for another year of the existing excise tax rates on tobacco, liquor, and automobiles, which, under present law, would be reduced next April 1. I must also recommend that the present corporate tax rates be continued for another year. It would be neither fair nor appropriate to allow excise and corporate tax reductions to be made at a time when a general tax reduction cannot be undertaken.

In the area of taxation, I am especially interested in the problems of small business. Last August the Cabinet Committee on Small Business made a series of carefully considered recommendations in this field. Some relief in the tax burden affecting small business, as recommended by that Committee, which will give help with a minimum loss of revenue should have early consideration by the Congress. Any changes involving substantial loss of revenue should be considered at a later time when a general tax reduction is possible.

The present estimates of budget receipts for 1958 are based on the assumption that the Nation will continue to have a high level of business activity with increasing national income, and that the present tax rates will be continued. They are the best estimates we can make at this time, but, since they relate to a period 6 to 18 months away, significant changes may take place before the fiscal year 1958 is ended.

BUDGET RECEIPTS
[Fiscal years. In billions]

	1956 actual	1957 estimate	1958 estimate
Individual income taxes	$35.3	$38.5	$41.0
Corporation income taxes	21.3	21.4	22.0
Excise taxes[1]	10.0	9.2	8.9
Other taxes[1]	2.2	2.5	2.6
Miscellaneous receipts	3.0	3.0	3.3
Refunds of receipts (−)	−3.7	−3.9	−4.2
Total	68.1	70.6	73.6

[1] Net of transfers to trust funds.

Debt policy.—The budget surplus for the fiscal year 1956 of 1.6 billion dollars was used to reduce the public debt. This budget provides for further reductions in the public debt for the current fiscal year and for the fiscal year 1958.

The successive reductions in the debt from 1956 through 1958 are modest in relation to its total size. Nevertheless, I hope that these reductions, plus the collection of corporation tax payments on a more nearly current basis (as provided by the Internal Revenue Code of 1954), will make it unnecessary to ask the Congress again for a temporary increase in the legal limit of 275 billion dollars to cover seasonal borrowing during the coming fiscal year.

PUBLIC DEBT
[Fiscal years. In billions]

	1956 actual	1957 estimate	1958 estimate
Public debt at start of year................	$274.4	$272.8	$270.6
Change due to budget surplus (−)..........	−1.6	−1.7	−1.8
Change due to other factors................	(¹)	−.5	+.4
Public debt at close of year.............	272.8	270.6	269.2

¹Less than 50 million dollars.

The reduction in the public debt in the fiscal year 1957 is estimated to be larger than the budget surplus for that year, mainly because it is anticipated that some expenditures during the year can be financed by drawing down the amount of cash the Government has on hand.

For the fiscal year 1958, the reduction in the public debt will not be as much as the budget surplus. This situation results primarily from the fact that, in the aggregate, the trust funds are expected to draw down the amount of uninvested cash held for them by the Treasury.

Receipts from and payments to the public.—The restraint on inflationary pressures which will be exerted by the budget surplus in the fiscal year 1958 will be reinforced by net accumulations in the trust funds which the Government administers. These trust fund accumulations, such as those for highways and for old-age and survivors and disability insurance, are the excess of current receipts over current payments. They constitute reserves for future use which are invested in Government securities.

When the Government's budget transactions are consolidated with trust fund and other transactions to give a picture of the flow of money between the public and the Government as a whole, the receipts from the public are estimated to exceed payments to the public by 3 million dollars in the fiscal year 1958.

FEDERAL GOVERNMENT RECEIPTS FROM AND PAYMENTS TO THE PUBLIC
[Fiscal years. In billions]

	1956 actual	1957 estimate	1958 estimate
Receipts from the public..................	$77.1	$81.7	$85.9
Payments to the public...................	72.6	78.2	82.9
Excess of receipts from the public........	4.5	3.5	3.0

The decline between the fiscal years 1956 and 1957 in the excess of receipts from the public results mainly from the estimated withdrawal of cash from the Treasury by the International Monetary Fund in 1957. The cash payments are made as the Treasury redeems the notes which were part of the United States subscription to the Fund. This subscription was made in the fiscal year 1947 and is therefore not part of current budget expenditures.

The excess of receipts from the public is estimated to be still lower in 1958 mainly because of higher net payments from trust funds.

Budget Programs and Performance

By far the largest part of the budget for the coming fiscal year, 63 percent, will be devoted to maintaining and improving our own defenses and to strengthening the defenses and economies of other nations in the interest of collective security and world peace. Civil benefits will account for 24 percent of budget expenditures; interest, 10 percent; and all other operations, administration, and contingencies, 3 percent.

BUDGET EXPENDITURES BY PURPOSE

[Fiscal years. In billions]

	1956 actual	1957 estimate	1958 estimate
Protection, including collective security......	$42.4	$42.7	$45.3
Civil benefits............................	15.3	16.5	16.9
Interest.................................	6.8	7.3	7.4
Civil operations and administration..........	2.0	2.3	1.8
Allowance for contingencies...............	....	.2	.4
Total............................	66.5	68.9	71.8

Protection, including collective security.—As a simple matter of self-preservation, we must maintain our own strength and promote world stability by helping to build up the strength of friendly nations. At the same time, we must actively advance our other efforts for lasting peace and inform the world in all appropriate ways of our peaceful aims.

The new and more powerful weapons which are being delivered to our Armed Forces in increasing quantities and varieties are much more costly to produce, operate, and maintain than the weapons they are replacing. Furthermore, we are now engaged in the development of a whole new family of even more advanced weapons for all the services. Large expenditures will be required to bring these weapons into use. During the transition, we must continue to purchase enough of the current types to preserve our readiness until the effectiveness of the advanced weapons is demonstrated in tests. Despite these upward pressures on expenditures, future defense costs must be held to tolerable levels. Effective action must be taken to improve efficiency and to maintain a proper balance between expenditures for future military strength and expenditures for current readiness.

EXPENDITURES FOR PROTECTION, INCLUDING COLLECTIVE SECURITY

[Fiscal years. In billions]

	1956 actual	1957 estimate	1958 estimate
Major national security programs:			
Department of Defense—military functions	$35.8	$36.0	$38.0
Mutual security program—military.......	2.6	2.6	2.6
Atomic Energy Commission..............	1.7	1.9	2.3
Stockpiling and defense production expansion..	.6	.4	.4
Subtotal...........................	40.6	41.0	43.3
Related programs:			
Mutual security program—economic, technical, and other......................	1.6	1.5	1.8
United States Information Agency.........	.1	.1	.1
Federal Civil Defense Administration......	.1	.1	.1
Selective Service System.................	....	....	....
Subtotal...........................	1.8	1.7	2.0
Total.............................	42.4	42.7	45.3

The introduction of new equipment and weapons with vastly greater combat capability is also having a powerful impact on concepts of military strategy, tactics, and organization. The combat power of our divisions, wings, and warships has increased to such an extent that it is no longer valid to measure military power in terms of the number of such units.

I have given careful consideration to the many complex factors which enter into the development of a well-balanced military structure. I am convinced that the defense programs and funds for their support as recommended in this budget provide a wise and reasonable degree of protection for the Nation.

Our nuclear weapons and our ability to employ them constitute the most effective deterrent to an attack on the free nations. We shall continue to expand our nuclear arsenal until an agreement has been reached for reduction and regulation of armaments under safeguarded inspection guaranties.

At the same time, we are increasing the portion of the production of fissionable materials allocated to peaceful uses at home and abroad and we look forward to the day when all production may be used for peaceful purposes. This budget provides for increased effort on power reactor development and on new uses of atomic energy in biology, medicine, agriculture, and industry. It will also make possible greater sharing of our peaceful atomic energy developments with other nations through the atoms-for-peace program.

World events continue to demonstrate the value of our programs of mutual assistance. Continued assistance, both military and economic, to friendly nations will provide the essential margin beyond their own resources needed to support and strengthen their defenses and their economies. The intensified worldwide conflict of ideas also requires a further increase in our programs of international information.

EXPENDITURES FOR CIVIL BENEFITS

[Fiscal years. In billions]

	1956 actual	1957 estimate	1958 estimate
Additions to Federal assets................	$3.5	$3.0	$3.4
Long-range development..................	2.0	1.8	2.3
Current expense items...................	9.7	11.7	11.1
Total............................	15.3	16.5	16.9

Civil benefits.—During the past 4 years, the Government has acted affirmatively to advance the everyday well-being of our people by helping to improve their economic opportunities, helping to provide safeguards against economic and physical hazards, and helping to build needed public assets. The Government's leadership in assisting the people to satisfy their own needs has been so exercised that steady progress has taken place without paternalistic interference.

In the fiscal year 1958 we shall continue to move forward with many civil benefit programs already established by law.

To aid agriculture in its adjustments to new technologies and to changed world production and consumption patterns, the soil bank program will help reduce the production of surplus crops. Additional marketing research and service activities will develop new markets and new uses for our farm products. Watershed protection, aid to low-income farmers, and assistance in overcoming the problems of drought, wind erosion, and floods will be expanded.

The Federal Government is assisting the States and private enterprise to make major advances in our transportation system. Traffic control on our airways is being continually improved as new equipment is developed and becomes available. Orderly replacement by private shipping lines of the merchant ships built during World War II is underway. Through grants paid from the highway trust fund, the States, in partnership with the Federal Government, are beginning a 13-year program to complete construction of the Interstate Highway System.

Under the urban renewal program, which combines Federal, local, and private efforts, 41 urban renewal projects will have been completed by the close of the fiscal year 1958, and 531 more will be in various stages of planning or construction. Private financing of housing for military families, elderly families, cooperatives, and other groups having special difficulties in obtaining homes will be encouraged by special mortgage insurance and mortgage purchase programs.

Over the 3-year period, 1955 through 1957, nearly 400 new water-resource projects for flood control, navigation, irrigation, power, and water supply will have been started and about one-half of these projects will still be under construction in 1958. Because of the need for continued and orderly development of our resources, I recommend that construction be started at a modest rate in 1958 on some new projects for which planning is well advanced. Funds for initiating immediately the planning of new public works projects which the Congress is expected to authorize are also included in this budget.

Increased expenditures will be made for sound programs of health research and grants for hospitals, clinics, and diagnostic and rehabilitation centers.

Legislative recommendations for new civil benefits involving major expenditures are being confined to needs of the highest priority and will be discussed later in this message.

Interest.—Expenditures for interest are estimated to rise 100 million dollars to 7.4 billion dollars in the fiscal year 1958, despite reductions in the public debt in 1956, 1957, and 1958. The increase in interest charges is due to refinancing securities maturing during the coming year at the higher rates of interest which reflect the heavy demand for credit and capital throughout our prosperous economy.

Civil operations and administration.—Expenditures for the remaining operations of the Government are estimated to be 1.8 billion dollars in the fiscal year 1958, an amount 425 million dollars less than in 1957 and 185 million dollars less than in 1956. The decreases occur primarily because certain payments heretofore made by the Civil Service Commission and the Treasury Department will be charged to the appropriations of the several agencies in accordance with legislation enacted last year. These are the payments which the Government, as employer, makes to the civil service retirement fund and those which it makes for certified bills presented too late for payment in the regular way. This improved accounting procedure shows with greater accuracy the total cost of various agency programs and is responsible for part of the increase shown in the expenditures for protection and civil benefits.

Allowance for contingencies.—Sound budgeting requires that some general provision be made for contingencies which may arise in the coming period. This is especially important today, in view of uncertain world conditions. The Congress is not being asked to appropriate for purposes not known. This item makes allowance in the budget totals for probable future requests, including those to cover the cost of some legislative proposals for which the timing of expenditures is uncertain. As the needs arise, and as new legislation is passed, a specific request for funds will be made in each case. The amount allowed for expenditures is 400 million dollars, slightly over one-half of 1 percent of total budget expenditures estimated for 1958.

Management improvement.—The administration is constantly striving to improve the management of Government. Vigorous measures to increase efficiency have shown results in many Government operations.

In the Veterans Administration, for example, the staff in non-medical activities has been reduced by 10,000 in the past 4 years. Some of this reduction was made possible because of smaller numbers of insurance and readjustment payments, but most of the reduction in staff reflects better procedures, including extensive mechanization of operations.

In the overseas supply activities of the Department of Defense, new procedures employing faster communications and better transportation service have been established. These improved methods of supplying overseas units substantially reduce inventory requirements and thus save both capital investment and costs of handling.

In the Post Office Department, despite an 11 percent rise in the volume of mail in the 4 fiscal years 1954 through 1957, the average employment will have increased only a little more than 3 per cent. This is concrete evidence of the value of new methods, organization, and equipment.

After intensive reviews of their real property holdings, Government agencies over the past 3 fiscal years have transferred excess property costing over 131 million dollars to other agencies, thus reducing the volume of purchases needed by those agencies to meet new requirements. In addition, surplus real property worth 366 million dollars, including almost all of the Government-owned synthetic rubber plants, has been sold, thus putting most of this property on the tax rolls.

In accordance with the recommendations of the second Hoover Commission, an Office of Accounting has been established in the Bureau of the Budget to help the Federal agencies to improve further their financial management and, in that connection, to put into effect the principles of accrual accounting and cost-based budgeting approved in legislation enacted last year. Modern accrual accounting will make possible better management through improved information needed to control costs.

Legislative Program

This year I discussed only a few of the administration's legislative recommendations in the State of the Union message. Therefore, this part of the budget message is devoted to a discussion of other major proposals for legislation on which I recommend that the Congress take action during the present session. The legislative program is one on which the Congress and the executive agencies should be able to work together successfully.

In the course of the next few months the administration will recommend to the Congress a number of important legislative proposals. In the immediate future, I shall forward a message emphasizing the urgency of enactment of an adequate program of Federal aid for school construction, and a message on my proposals for amendment of our immigration laws. In connection with the administration's proposals on education, this budget provides for the start of a 4-year program of aid for school construction.

Two areas need earnest and prompt attention with a view to determining whether new national policies should be adopted in the light of reports and recommendations now pending in the Congress. These are numerous detailed recommendations of the second Hoover Commission which the committees were unable to consider prior to adjournment of the 84th Congress and the proposals made by the Advisory Committee on Transport Policy and Organization. Legislation to carry out the recommendations of the Committee was the subject of hearings during the last Congress. Because of the importance of strengthening our transportation system, these hearings should be completed in the present session. Proposals for legislation will again be submitted by the Secretary of Commerce.

Substantial budget increases are recommended for existing activities which will improve the health of the American people. The Congress is also urged to enact legislation under which the Federal Government can help the medical and dental schools to build more and better teaching, as well as research facilities to prevent the already acute shortage of trained medical manpower from becoming critical. It is also time to enact the necessary statutory basis for expansion and improvement of voluntary health insurance plans under which smaller insurance companies and nonprofit associations could pool their resources and experience.

In the welfare field, additional funds are likewise provided in the budget, and the Congress is urged to enact a new program of grants to the States to help fight juvenile delinquency.

In recent years, a succession of legislative enactments has moved a long way toward the goal of universal social security coverage, but there are a number of collateral steps which will add much to the meaning of our social security system as a whole. In part, these steps can be taken by budgetary action, for example, by giving particular attention to the needs of the rapidly increasing number of older persons in our society. Other steps will require legislation. First, the unemployment insurance system should be extended and improved. Similarly, congressional action is recommended to extend the Fair Labor Standards Act to additional workers. The Secretary of Labor will make recommendations on this act when hearings are held by the committees of the Congress. The Federal 8-hour laws should be revised and brought up to date and legislation should be enacted to assure equal pay for equal work. A modest program of grants under which the States can increase their efforts to improve occupational safety should be initiated. Likewise, legislation should be enacted to require the registration of employee pension and welfare funds to protect the interests of beneficiaries.

Of particular importance are recommendations to protect and foster the initiative of the small businessman. The Small Business Act should be extended. In order that small business may have better opportunity to secure adequate financing, issues of securities up to 500 thousand dollars should be exempted from the regular registration provisions of the Securities Act of 1933. Similarly, the Congress should enact legislation providing for notification to the Federal Government of proposed business mergers, and should amend the procedural provisions of the antitrust laws to facilitate their enforcement. Wage reporting for income tax and social security purposes should be consolidated and simplified. Other means of assisting small business will be discussed in the Economic Report.

I repeat my recommendation of last year for the prompt enactment of appropriate authority under which communities can be assisted in solving basic problems of persistent unemployment.

At the present time, I do not contemplate proposing an extensive program of personnel legislation comparable to the numerous constructive measures enacted in the last several years. Certain needed improvements in central personnel management are discussed in the general government section of my budget analysis. All of these measures deserve early attention and enactment by the Congress. In addition, the Secretary of Defense is now studying recommendations of his Advisory Committee on Professional and Technical Compensation. Any legislative recommendations growing out of the work of this committee respecting personnel policies and compensation systems of the military services will be presented at a later time.

We should not let another year go by without taking the necessary action to place the Post Office on a pay-as-you-go fiscal basis. The case for adjusting postal rates needs no further justification. It is supported by a vast majority of the general public as well as by most of the business community. The administration has demonstrated its capacity for improving the postal service, installing new and more efficient methods and equipment and cutting costs in accordance with good business practice. The Congress should take the further action needed to reduce the huge postal deficit. Then the further improvements needed in equipment and facilities can be made so that the American people may receive the mail service they deserve and have the right to expect.

Various agencies are being asked to review with the Congress the interest rates charged by the Government in connection with different kinds of loans, several of which have a fixed statutory maximum established when interest costs were much lower than today. It is desirable that there be more consistency and that more discretion be allowed in determining what going rates should be, dependent on the period of the loans and their conditions.

Recommendations concerned with proposed legislative changes in our housing laws will be found in the section of my budget analysis carrying the heading "Commerce and housing."

With respect to farm legislation, certain changes are being recommended in the corn program. Farmers who use all the wheat grown on their own farms for seed, feed, or food should be exempt from marketing quotas and penalties. The basic authority for disposal of surplus farm commodities for foreign currencies, title I of Public Law 480 of the 83d Congress, should be extended for 1 year and an additional 1 billion dollars of authorization for losses under this title should be provided. Legislation should also be enacted authorizing the barter of nonstrategic Government-owned agricultural surpluses to the nations of Eastern Europe.

The program of the administration in the field of natural resources is fully set forth in that section of the budget analysis. It will not be repeated here, except to indicate my continuing firm support of the necessary legislative action to enable Federal agencies to participate more fully with States, local governments, and private groups in the development of partnership resources projects. I urge once again the prompt enactment of legislation which will enable the Fryingpan-Arkansas multiple-purpose project to get underway in the fiscal year 1958.

I also recommend prompt action by the Congress to decide how the Niagara power project can best be developed.

In returning the Harris-Fulbright natural gas bill to the 84th Congress without my approval, I stated that legislation conforming to the basic objectives of that bill was needed. I am still of that opinion. It is essential that consumers of natural gas be protected. We must endeavor to make sure that there will be continued exploration and development of adequate field supplies of gas, and that producers' sales prices are arrived at fairly and competitively. In this way, and with authority vested in the Federal Power Commission to regulate interstate pipelines as to the price at which gas may be charged as an item of cost in fixing their rates, the price to the public will be fair. Legislation freeing gas producers from public utility-type regulation is essential if the incentives to find and develop new supplies of gas are to be preserved and sales of gas to interstate markets are not to be discouraged to the detriment of both consumers and producers, as well as the national interest.

The Congress is urged to carry out the proposals of the Judicial Conference for additional Federal judges. Also, when a district or circuit court judge who is the senior judge of the district or circuit becomes 70 and chooses not to retire, he should be relieved of his administrative duties. Furthermore, whenever a district court judge reaches 70 and chooses not to retire, the Congress should provide that upon certification by the Judicial

Conference of the need therefor, the President would be authorized to appoint an additional judge. When the judge who had reached 70 dies or retires, the vacancy thus created would not be filled.

Although it is not within my province to make any recommendation, I am deeply interested in the suggestion which has been made that the Congress should consider inviting the Chief Justice of the United States to address the Congress annually on the work of the judiciary and to present the recommendations of the Judicial Conference.

I recommend again that the Congress enact suitable legislation providing for home rule in the District of Columbia. Under any such system the citizens of the District should be authorized to elect local officials, to vote in Federal elections, and to have a delegate in the House of Representatives.

I also recommend the enactment of legislation admitting Hawaii into the Union as a State, and that, subject to area limitations and other safeguards for the conduct of defense activities so vitally necessary to our national security, statehood also be conferred upon Alaska.

The platforms of both major parties have advocated an amendment of the Constitution to insure equal rights for women. I believe that the Congress should make certain that women are not denied equal rights with men. Similarly, I believe that the Congress should propose a constitutional amendment lowering the voting age in Federal elections.

As has already been indicated in the State of the Union message, continuation of military and economic assistance to the free nations of the world is a keystone of the administration's efforts to promote peace, collective security, and well-being for all peoples. Essential complements of these assistance programs are steps to increase international trade and investment. Both can be materially advanced by taking the actions necessary to avoid unfair tax duplications on business conducted overseas and by the prompt enactment of legislation approving United States membership in the proposed Organization for Trade Cooperation. This administrative agency will greatly aid the orderly operation of existing arrangements governing multilateral trade to help prevent discrimination and restrictions against our foreign commerce.

Although necessity forces us to keep ever in mind the destructive power of nuclear weapons, it is equally essential that we keep in mind the firm determination of the United States to share the fruits of its efforts to develop the peaceful uses for atomic energy. Seventy-two nations have now signed the charter of the International Atomic Energy Agency, which was established under the auspices of the United Nations. Prompt action by the Congress is needed to authorize full participation by the United States in the work of this Agency. The United States has offered for distribution through this Agency 5,000 kilograms of fissionable uranium 235 out of the 20,000 kilograms previously offered for atomic research and power uses in other nations, as part of our atoms-for-peace program.

The analysis of the budget discusses present programs for veterans. A special message recommending changes needed in these programs will be transmitted to the Congress.

The remaining items to which special attention should be directed are (1) authorization to the President to make awards for distinguished civilian achievement, (2) establishment of a Federal Advisory Commission on the Arts, (3) acquisition and maintenance of an official residence for the Vice President, and (4) amendment of the Government Corporation Control Act to provide for budget and audit control over Government corporations which are authorized, directly or indirectly, to obtain or utilize Federal funds. It is also recommended that the Congress give further consideration to legislation which would place Government appropriations on an accrued expenditure basis.

The other proposals which are parts of the administration's legislative program are discussed in my analysis of the budget. The fact that they are not included in this summary presentation in no way detracts from their importance or the strength of my recommendation that they be considered and enacted by the Congress in its present session.

Analysis of the Budget

I am presenting my budgetary recommendations in greater detail under nine major program headings in the analysis of the budget which follows this message. The Economic Report will contain a further discussion of some of these proposals.

It is always difficult to make plans and forecast expenditures a year or more in advance. This is particularly true when historic events are taking place in Eastern Europe, when United Nations forces are deployed in the Middle East, when uncertainties abound in other parts of the world, and when in our own land economic change is continuous. This budget has taken into account present conditions and developments which today appear most likely at home and abroad. It provides funds for all necessary Government activities on a reasonable scale, and efforts will continue to be made by every executive department and agency to improve efficiency and to maintain expenditures well within the budget estimates. It is a carefully balanced budget—balanced in its receipts and expenditures, balanced in its choice of programs. I consider it well adapted to the needs of the present and the future.

The budget unleashed a flurry of criticism. The most publicized reaction came on January 15, 1957, when Secretary of the Treasury George Humphrey said, "If we don't reduce expenditures over a long period of time, I will predict that you will have a depression that will curl your hair." Unfortunately for the Administration, the press assumed that Humphrey meant that the budget under consideration would cause economic calamity. Eisenhower, speaking a few days later at a news conference, responded to several questions about the budget in general and Humphrey's remarks in particular.

Presidential News Conference
January 23, 1957

[*Public Papers of the Presidents: 1957* (Washington, 1958), 72–80.]

THE PRESIDENT: Please be seated.

Good morning, ladies and gentlemen. Are there any questions you would like to ask me?

QUESTION. Marvin L. Arrowsmith, *Associated Press:* Mr. President, the Secretary of the Treasury, Mr. Humphrey, said the other day that he feels the Administration's new budget is too high, that we are going to have a hair-curling depression if spending isn't cut, and he expressed the hope that Congress will be able to cut the budget.

Do you have any differences with him on those points?

THE PRESIDENT: Well, you have picked out two or three points that he made in a very long discussion.

Now, in the first place, you will recall there was a memorandum that was the basis of that discussion, a written memorandum, and that written memorandum I not only went over every word of it, I edited it, and it expresses my convictions very thoroughly.

Now, with the need for our Government to operate to the absolute limit of efficiency, I think there can be no question in the minds of any of us.

When he said a hair-curling depression, he wasn't talking about the immediate future. I know I am speaking correctly, because I have talked to him about it since. He is talking about long-term continuation of spending of the order of which we are now doing. He believes that that will prevent the accumulation of the necessary capital to produce jobs, and would bring about bad results.

What was the third point, Mr. Arrowsmith?

QUESTION. Mr. Arrowsmith: The third point was, he expressed the hope that Congress will be able to cut the budget in a proper way.

THE PRESIDENT: Yes.

Well, in my own instructions to the Cabinet and heads of all offices, I have told them that every place that there is a chance to save a dollar out of the money that we have budgeted and may be appropriated by the Congress, that will go on through the entire period.

You must remember that we start to make up these budgets well over two years in advance of the last day of their application, so you are doing a great deal of estimating.

As the process of appropriating this money goes on everybody that is examining the many details—and any of you that have looked at a budget know how many details are in it, there are literally thousands and thousands—anybody that is examining that seriously ought to find some place where he might save another dollar.

If they can, I think if Congress can, its committees, it is their duty to do it.

So with the thought behind the Secretary's statements I am in complete agreement, even though he made statements that I don't believe have a present and immediate application because, indeed, the outlook for the next few months in the economic field is very good indeed.

QUESTION. Richard L. Wilson, *Cowles Publications:* Mr. President, I would like to refer back, sir, to the difference in emphasis between you and Secretary Humphrey.

When you—before you first came into office, I believe you expressed the hope that the spending of the Government might be reduced to $60 billion a year. Now you are asking for, perhaps, $72 billion. Some predict that it may go up beyond that in later years. Does this represent any basic change in your approach to Government?

THE PRESIDENT: No, it doesn't, Mr. Wilson.

First of all, you must remember this: Mr. Humphrey, himself, said that this budget was the best budget the entire Government, after many months of work, could bring out. In other words, he approved this budget without qualifications, although he is hopeful, as I am, of saving money out of it.

Now, the $72 billions, there have been two things that have come along that have raised the budget above what I hoped it could be. First of all are a great many raises in expenditures for personnel, and when you consider that you have two and a half million in the civil service, and three million in the military services, all of those raises are very significant in your budget.

But, secondly, we have gone into this guided missile field which, up until four years ago, was almost neglected—not neglected, it just hadn't come to the fore. And the new B-52 type of airplane and everything of that kind has gone up so much in expense that without getting any more strength, but in merely improving the efficiency of every kind of warning system, every kind of piece of fighting equipment that you have on land and on the sea, and raises in pay, you have got more than the amount that you have discussed— the differences that you have got to account for.

QUESTION. Mr. Wilson: Wasn't it also a fact that in many of the domestic programs you have increased them, such as schools, and so on?

THE PRESIDENT: Well, of course, we are providing this year for the first of four years in the school building program. And I will say this: as long as the American people demand and, in my opinion, deserve the kind of services that this budget provides, we have got to spend this kind of money. And I do believe every time you reach such conclusion it becomes more incumbent upon everybody in the Federal service to look for ways to save money administratively, through eliminating duplication and that sort of thing, because I agree with Secretary Humphrey, while our proportion of the gross national product we are now taking is no greater than it was, say, in '54, the fact is this is an awful lot of money to take out of an economy when you are trying to get the accumulations that will provide for more expansion, for more jobs, and for more home-building and that sort of thing. It's a lot of money.

Many of the assaults on the 1958 budget came from members of the business community. A typical statement, which received wide attention, came from Ross Roy of Detroit, a conservative businessman.

Speech by Ross Roy on President Eisenhower's Proposed Budget February 9, 1957

[*Vital Speeches of the Day*, XXIII, no. 11 (March 15, 1957), 338–42.]*

The subject of my talk should be of interest to every citizen today in view of the Eisenhower Administration's budget for the 1958 fiscal year which calls for an expenditure of 71 billion, 800 million—nearly 72 billion dollars—an all-time high for a peacetime budget.

As you all know, there has been violent controversy over this budget. When it was first released, Secretary of the Treasury Humphrey predicted that, if taxing and spending are not *reduced* next year, we will be in for "a depression that will make your hair curl."

Then President Eisenhower, in a press conference on January 23, made the following statement: "As long as the American people demand and, in my opinion, deserve the kind of services that this budget provides, we have got to spend this kind of money."

*Reprinted with permission of *Vital Speeches of the Day*.

Last week, former President Hoover kept the controversy going. On February 4, he presided over the Third Annual Reorganization Conference of the Citizens Committee for the Hoover Report in Washington. At that conference, he was quoted as follows:

> Secretary Humphrey said that, unless we change some of our ways, we will see "a depression that will curl your hair." Mine has already been curled once— and I think I can detect the signs.

According to the Detroit Free Press of February 5, Hoover said:

> One sign of inflation is the current talk that we are having a new economic age, and the old economic laws are outmoded. Hoover said he had heard the same talk thirty years ago, when the inflation of the 1920s was building up the depression of the 1930s. 'Unless we curb inflation on its way up,' he said, 'Old man Economic Law will return with a full equipment of hair curlers'."

Hoover's statement was attacked the next day by some Democrat politicians, by Professor Sumner Slichter of Harvard, and by a few economics professors in Michigan. Here is Professor Slichter's amazing statement about the budget, as he was quoted in the Detroit Free Press of February 6:

> Of course, political pressures produce some expenditures that are pretty hard to justify. The government spends billions of dollars trying to persuade farmers to produce the wrong things. And it gives immense handouts to veterans that no one can justify. But not all the money spent on farm relief and veterans is wasted. The waste probably does not add up to 10 per cent of the total budget. Hence, if the waste were completely eliminated, the best we could hope for in lower taxes would be about a 10 per cent cut.

I can't see how anyone can toss off so lightly a 10 per cent cut in spending and taxes! 10 per cent of the proposed Eisenhower budget is over 7 billion dollars. This is actually more than the Federal government ever collected in total taxes in our entire history until the year 1941.

I agree with Senator Byrd, who says that Mr. Eisenhower's budget should be cut by "at least 5 billion dollars." It would be easy to cut it by 10 per cent, which would be over 7 billion dollars. In addition to a cut in defense expenditures, a cut can easily be made in so-called foreign aid, and the rest of the budget could be cut without sacrificing any of the government services which President Eisenhower says we're demanding.

Here's an example of waste in the Defense Department. I clipped this from the San Francisco News when I was there on business in January. The headline is "U. S.—Land Snafu Told."

> The Defense Department now wants to get rid of 1,056,083 acres of land on which it has spent $345 million for improvements—including golf courses, swimming pools, and clubs.
> At the same time, it was revealed today, it is asking for an additional 12.8 million acres of public land for use by the armed services.

" 'It makes your hair stand on end', said Chairman Clair Engle (D., Cal.), of the House Interior Committee. 'These are shocking figures. To sit down on these ranges and put in this expensive instrumentation and then have to pull up stakes . . . makes us wonder if there is any sense of responsibility over there in the (Defense) Department'."

It's difficult for me to understand the change which has taken place in President Eisenhower. On October 2, 1952, when he was a *candidate* for president, he said (speaking of the Democrats): "They say, 'You cannot cut taxes, you cannot end or minimize Korean losses. You cannot stop inflation . . . ' What kind of stuff is that—don't and can't? Of course, we can and will."

He followed up by cutting the proposed Truman budget for 1953 from a proposed $79 billion to $67,772,000,000—a cut of over 11 billion. During his '52 campaign, he promised that his fourth budget, that for the fiscal year of 1958, which we've been discussing, could be cut to approximately 60 billion. Instead, now he's proposing 71.8 billion, and, if this is spent, Mr. Eisenhower will have spent 339.4 billion in his first five years in office, as compared to Truman's expenditure of 262.7 billion in his last five years in office.

I believe that the time has come for a citizens' revolt against *high taxes* and a revolt against *big* Federal Government. I believe that most businessmen agree with me. I believe that the time has come when we as businessmen should be very vocal about our feelings.

But we can't be vocal about lower taxes and economy in our Federal Government if we're members of pressure groups which demand expenditures for pet projects. Here's what Hoover had to say about this: " . . . Most of the blame for unnecessary spending by the government could be traced to 'pressure groups' . . . There are probably more than a thousand of these pressure groups, working day and night, to get what they call 'theirs'. So far as I know, there is not a name among the registered lobbyists whose purpose is to *decrease* public expenditures."

As a businessman, I believe that I have always lived up to this code. I do *not* belong to any pressure group asking for theirs." I have never asked a Senator or Congressman to vote for a project that would call for increased spending and taxes and control over our daily lives.

I believe you can discern from all this that I regard the Federal Government as the worst offender in the area of *spending* and *taxes* and *inflation*. It surely is, for the Federal Government today takes nearly 70 per cent of our tax dollars. Only about 30 per cent goes for all state and local government combined.

I believe firmly that, unless we halt this trend to ever bigger Federal Government, we will eventually lose our freedom. We'll lose it in one of two ways:

First, we could lose it to Russia, and the Russians have told us how. They've said, in effect, "We'll just let Americans spend themselves into inflation and a depression, and then, when the collapse comes, it will be easy for us to take over."

Second, we could lose our freedom to a home-grown dictator when we reach a stage where the people themselves demand the strong man to bring order out of chaos—when they demand the "man on horseback," so to speak.

You might say, "It can't happen here," but all of history shows that it can happen to any nation. Here's how it could happen right here if we keep on the way we're going.

The budget is 72 billion now. If we citizens keep on demanding the services which Eisenhower says we deserve, the budget will keep on climbing—to 75 billion—80 billion—85 billion. Perhaps the Government can collect the necessary taxes for these increased budgets. But suppose we run into a recession or a depression. Then what do we do? Many people think that the Government should then spend *more*—should support the economy, so to speak, with a vast program of public works.

And then the national debt will get much larger, and interest on the debt will increase. Then we'll see inflation, the likes of which we've never seen in the United States—that's when we'll get the "hair curlers" that Secretary Humphrey and ex-President Hoover talked about.

We can't repudiate the national debt, for our entire bank structure would collapse. Don't forget that our banks hold the bonds which represent the debt. We can't repudiate the *interest* on the debt. Who is to say that some future Administration won't suggest printing more paper money—won't suggest devaluation of the dollar so as to lower this debt and its interest burden? Then we'll see the demand (not only in the United States but by other nations) that we submit temporarily to the strong man who will bring order out of chaos.

For the life of me, I don't see how we can spend ourselves into prosperity. If we can, we've really discovered something. If we can, why stop at *any* point in Government spending? Either we become *more* properous as the Government spends more or we become *less* prosperous. Which is it?

If we become *more* prosperous when the Federal Government spends more, why set a limit on the national debt at all? Pretty silly to limit it to 275 billion. Let her soar to 500 billion and we'll all be rich! Or to a trillion and we'll be even richer.

The fallacy in the "spend more" theory is that money isn't wealth. It's merely a means of exchange. Our wealth is in our production. We can't have more as a nation, or as individuals, than we produce.

President Eisenhower is asking for a bill in the new Congress which typifies this whole trend toward Federal Government domination of our daily lives. This is the so-called Federal-Aid-for-School-Construction Bill which would give $1,300,000,000 to the states for school construction, this to be distributed at the rate of $325,000,000 a year for the next four years.

Senator Morse says, however, that this isn't nearly enough and he's going to demand more. A Federal-Aid-to-Education Bill was defeated last year, as you know, chiefly because of the integration issue.

Here are the views of a former president of one of the oldest and largest universities in the United States on the subject of Federal Aid to Education:

> I would flatly oppose any grant by the Federal Government to all states in the union for educational purposes. Such a policy would create an ambition—almost a requirement—to spend money freely under the impulse of competition with other localities in the country. It would completly decry and defeat the watchful economy that comes about through *local* supervision over *local* expenditures of *local* revenues.

And in his letter to the House Sub-committee on Education, he concluded in this way:

> Very frankly, I firmly believe that the army of persons who urge greater and greater centralization of authority and greater and greater dependence upon the Federal Treasury are really more dangerous to our form of government than any external threat that can possibly be arrayed against us.

Now it may surprise you when I tell you *who* made these statements and *when* he made them. They were made by Mr. Eisenhower—when he was President of Columbia University in 1949.

Now, as President, Mr. Eisenhower has apparently changed his mind on this subject. Today he says that there will be no Federal control of education with his bill—or at least he doesn't *think* that there will be any under *his* administration.

The incongruous thing here is that the bill was defeated last year *because* of a threat of controls. Northern-Democrat members to the House insisted that there would be no Federal aid to states which did not accept integration in their schools. It's just silly to say that you'll ever have a disbursement of Federal funds without a measure of Federal control.

Every Federal-aid-to-education bill of recent years has contained some element of Federal control. Actually, the Supreme Court has ruled—in 1942—that the Government has the right to control that which it subsidizes.

Of course, there is no such thing as Federal aid—to education, or housing, or highways, or health or any other social segment of our economy. There is Federal *redistribution* of our tax money but not Federal aid. The Federal Government produces nothing. All it can do is *take* tax money from people in the states and give it *back* to people in the states.

How do we fare in Michigan on so-called Federal aid? We always lose because we'll always send more to Washington than we get back. We sent over 7 billion to Washington last year from the State of Michigan. This was over 10% of the total taxes collected by the Federal Government from *all* the states. Incidently, Michigan was second only to New York State in its total tax contribution to the Federal Government.

If this new budget were cut 10%, Michigan's share of the cut over 7 billion dollars would be over *700 million* dollars. This is nearly twice the total budget proposed for the State of Michigan for the coming year—411 million dollars.

We all know that if Congress were so minded, it would be *easy* to cut Federal Government expenses by 5%. A 5% reduction in our share of Federal expenses would be over 350 million dollars, nearly as much as our proposed total State budget for the coming year. Think what we could do with that much money in Michigan!

But let's get back to the subject of Federal aid to school construction. The February 8th issue of the magazine *U. S. News and World Report* carried a chart which indicated that the State of Michigan would be required to put up $16,233,000 annually in so-called "matching" funds to get back $12,102,-000 annually as a Federal grant for "aid" for Michigan schools.

Now here is exactly how all this works out. In 4 years, we would get about 48 million dollars from the Federal Government for "aid" for school construction if we promised to be good citizens and put up about 65 million in so-called "matching" funds. But here's what we send to Washington in order to get back the 48 million. As I said, Michigan citizens and businesses pay approximately 10% of all Federal Government taxes. That means that we will contribute 10% of the 1 billion 300 million which Mr. Eisenhower is asking for, or 130 million dollars—to get back 48 million dollars over a period of 4 years. There's just no other way to figure it.

One would think that if the purpose of the bill is to "equalize" educational opportunities in the states, the Federal aid would go *only* to the *poorer* states. But these Federal aid bills never work out that way. We are always made to think that *every*body gets *some*thing for nothing—a manifest impossibility.

The theory behind all this, of course, is that Federal aid will stimulate the states to spend more for education than they are now spending. That's why the National Education Association is so strongly for this bill. So-called Federal "grants" are usually on a basis where the state must meet some matching formula in order to get back the Federal funds which the state sends to Washington in the first place. *In other words, we bribe ourselves with our own money.*

The 12 million a year which we would get in Michigan under the proposed Federal Aid of School Construction bill is only a fraction of what we're *now* spending for school construction in Michigan. The 325 million a year for all the United States is only a fraction of what all the states are spending. Perhaps that's why, as you may have noted in this morning's Free Press, the Americans for Democratic Action have "urged enactment of a Federal school construction bill providing one billion dollars annually for new classrooms." This is more than three times what the Eisenhower administration wants to spend. As I said before, where does it all stop?

That brings up another subject. Should we be so naive as to think that this program will end in four years? Do Federal bureaus ever disband? Do people quit asking for things from Santa Claus? I repeat, we're being bribed with our own money.

All of us want our children to have the best education possible. We'll get the best education at the lowest cost when we keep the responsibility for education where it belongs—in the *home* and in the *community.* In my opinion, education is the last area in which we want any form of Federal subsidy and control.

One wonders at times how ridiculous we can get when we swallow this kind of a statement in connection with any kind of Federal aid—"state and local resources are inadequate for this problem." Actually, all resources are in the states and all production and wealth is in the states.

How ridiculous can we get when we ask for aid from a Federal Government which has a debt of 274 billion dollars while all the states combined have a debt of only 11 billion and many states have no indebtedness whatever? It's as if you sent $1,000 to a once-wealthy but now impoverished uncle so that he could send $800 back to you and you'd both feel better.

Now, I'd like to talk about what is really the gravest danger in this era of transferring state and local responsibility to the Federal Government—that's the absolute certainty that if we keep on the way we're going, we'll end up just as Rome did. There was a frightening example of this in a very typical American community just a few months ago. This is what is happening to our sense of individual responsibility.

Four times in the nine years before 1956, the citizens of Peoria, Illinois, refused in elections to raise their tax rate to support the schools. To quote an article by William T. Noble in the Detroit News of October 14, 1956:

> If voters on Nov. 6 don't approve a raise of $4 per $1,000 assessed valuation in taxes, Peoria's school children next Fall will be roaming the streets.
>
> The average Peorian however, insists he approves high-grade education for youth, but stoutly refuses to believe the schools actually will close.
>
> "The State of Illinois or the Federal government won't let that happen," said Peter Merkle, a painter, who heads the Peoria Taxpayers Association, reportedly a group that pops into existence immediately prior to any school tax election.

Now this story ended happily (or did it?) when the Peoria voters approved a $4 hike in their school tax rate in the November 6th election. But the virus which affected Peoria citizens was cured only temporarily. Actually the virus remains—in Peoria and in most other communities of the United States. The virus, the disease, is the creeping dependence upon

Washington on the part of the states, and the creeping dependence of local governments upon their state governments.

The virus that is draining us of our strength is the virus of indifference—the willingness to "Let George do it." It's the willingness to go to Washington, tin cup in hand, and ask for dollars which we've sent there in the first place.

The time has come for a revolt against the power to tax, which, as the famous Chief Justice Marshall said, is the power to destroy. The time has come for businessmen to demand economy in the government—to revolt against confiscatory taxes. I believe the revolt has started. A so-called liberal columnist mentions it in his column in one of our local papers of last Saturday. Speaking of it, he said:

> This business revolt has its ironies.
> In listening to businessmen, you will note that what they rant about is spending for social welfare ...
> Two things might be pointed out in this connection that are common knowledge to anyone who knows Washington.
> One is that money recommended in the Eisenhower budget for a social-welfare functions is comparatively negligible. . . The bulk of the budget—and this has been true for many years—is for the past wars and defense against possible future wars.

And then this columnist makes this amazing statement:

> Money for defense is the pot of gold that has kept business booming.

This is really interesting. If true, this columnist must believe we'd collapse if the threat of war with Russia were completely removed so that we could drastically cut defense expenditures. Or conversely, if what we're spending now is "The pot of gold that has kept business booming," why not spend *twice* as much and make business boom even more? This is all part and parcel of the "spend ourselves into prosperity" theory and if this is sound economics, we should have a new war every generation and have the *threat* of war *all* the time.

Like most so-called liberals, this columnist thinks it's terrible for businessmen to complain about anything; and that's typical of the attitude of too many people in this country. It's difficult to understand. All we do is employ the 66 million workers in the United States, withhold their taxes and send them to Washington, pay a corporation tax of 52% (if we're incorporated), and then take our dividends from the 48% that's left. As personal income, these are then taxed at regular income tax rates up to 91%.

Business produces *everything*—all the necessities and luxuries of life—but businessmen somehow are not supposed to be vocal about *anything*.

Now all of this brings me to the heart of my subject—"What can businessmen do to relieve the tax burden?" They can do a great deal if they want to do it.

There are 4¼ million businesses in the United States. At least 4 million of these would be classified as small businesses, employing less than 50 people. There are at least 150,000 small businesses in the State of Michigan, all of whom would benefit by a cut in Federal government spending and taxes. But how vocal are we businessmen about government spending? Let me quote from William McGaffin's column in the February 11 Free Press. He said:

> The folks back home want that record peacetime budget cut, to judge from the mail some members of Congress are getting.
>
> The volume of mail on the subject has varied considerably since the budget first came into the news.
>
> Senator Potter (R. Mich.), for instance, estimated recently he had received only about a dozen letters on it.
>
> Senator Lausche (D. O.), on the other hand, says he has had hundreds.

Isn't it rather astounding that Senator Potter has received only "about a dozen" letters on this subject?

Every businessman who feels as I do should write not only Senator Potter but Senator McNamara. And each of us should write our Congressman. In addition, I'm going to write Secretary Humphrey and Senator Byrd and encourage them to keep up the fight for national solvency and personal freedom.

Over and beyond this, there are many other things we can do. We can talk to our employees, our business associates, our friends and neighbors about this inflationary budget. We can suggest that they, too, write to their Senators and Congressmen demanding a cut in spending and taxes.

But we've got to do a lot more than that if we're going to make our voices heard. We've got to change our attitude toward politics in two ways—

One: We must become more interested in politics than we've ever been and we must be more vocal in our interest.

Two: We've got to be unselfish in our demands upon our representatives in Congress.

I have thought for many years that if we are eventually completely socialized in the United States, businessmen will contribute more to our downfall than any other group. One businessman who asks for government subsidy as a member of a pressure group does more to socialize us than a thousand of his employees.

Who are we in business to complain about the farm lobbies when we ask for protective tariffs for manufactured products?

Who are we to complain about government spending and taxes if we ask the government to spend money for a *local* pork-barrel project? Congressmen in such cases sneer at us and say that businessmen are for economy only when it's for the other fellow.

We'll get less spending and less taxes and more freedom only when we convince our political representatives that we're sincere and unselfish. It's imperative that we convince them that we don't want any advantages from government at the expense of some other group. We must convince them that we don't want the government to favor *any* group—labor leaders, farmers, or businessmen.

Let's remember what Hoover said about pressure groups, and let's remember that pressure groups consist of *individuals*. The remedy for all this is for each of us to accept *individual* responsibility—to accept *local* responsibility—to resist strong central government which has *always* been the enemy of personal freedom.

Let's remember the admonition of the great English statesman, Edmund Burke, who said: "The only thing necessary for the triumph of evil is for good men to do nothing."

As the controversy grew, the President reiterated his earlier suggestion that Congress take the lead in finding ways to cut the budget. When this topic arose at a March 13 press conference, his sharp answer reflected his reaction to a Democratic-sponsored House resolution of the previous day calling for the President to indicate the places and amounts where he thought cuts should be made.

Presidential News Conference
March 13, 1957
[*Public Papers of the Presidents: 1957* (Washington, 1958), 195.]

QUESTION. Mrs. May Craig, Portland, *Me. Press Herald:* Sir, in my experience, it is the first time that the President and the Secretary of the Treasury ever asked the Congress to cut their budget.

THE PRESIDENT: I didn't ask them to cut. I said if they could find places in that budget where their judgment disagreed with mine, and they were the final appropriating authority in this case, if they found such instances to go ahead and cut, and I would do my very best to get along with it.

I didn't say that I know where these places are except for the one I told you about, this budget deficit . . .

Congressional debate on the budget did not involve broad philosophical statements about spending. Rather, comments reflected particular members' views on pending appropriation bills. Congressman Clair Hoffman, a powerful Old Guard Republican from Michigan, touched on some objections to large spending in his rambling remarks about a federal library bill.

Speech by Congressman Clair Hoffman
on Federal Spending
March 29, 1967

[U.S., *Congressional Record*, 85th Cong., 1st Sess., 1957, CIII, Part 4, 4813–14.]

MR. CLAIR HOFFMAN (Rep., Mich.): Mr. Chairman, under permission previously granted to revise and extend my remarks, permit me to attempt to conclude at least a part of the argument which was in my mind when I arose to address the Committee.

As to other Members of the House, to me have come many letters, some requesting, some demanding, that I vote for the increased appropriation to carry on the library program. Usually, these letters have commended me for my economy record and have urgently requested, sometimes demanded, that the Congress reduce the budget.

Often the letters call attention to the huge public debt; to what the writers consider not only an exorbitant but a wasteful foreign-aid program: to the grievous tax burden which we have placed upon them.

It is obvious, as the President so well said at his last news conference, that there can be neither a reduction of the public debt nor a substantial cut in the budget nor a lessening of the tax burden if we are to continue many of the helpful and desirable programs which have been suggested either by the administration or by individual Members of Congress, but which are not necessary and which we cannot afford.

Listening to the debate on this bill during the last few days causes me to wonder how Washington, Franklin, and all the others who lived and distinguished themselves in those days were able to exist without the aid of the Departments of Labor, and Health, Education, and Welfare, and related agencies.

Yes, the Member from Michigan remembers that history tells us that, when Washington lost his teeth, all he was able to get to replace them were wooden substitutes. We recall that it is reported that, when he fell ill, the top physicians of those days bled him to death.

No one is suggesting that we, as a people or as individuals, make no effort to improve our situation, increase our advantages. On the other hand, in view of the record which has been made, it seems absurd to assume that we now cannot live, prosper, be happy, and contented, except as we grievously tax one segment of the population to support another.

Especially is this true when we know that, by so doing we actually hinder progress by taking away the incentive to work, practice thrift, so that the dollar we save can be used for expansion, new industries, the creation of more jobs.

To mind comes the example of Lincoln, who, we are told, at times lived miles from a school; who had but a half dozen books during his youth. He certainly had no electric light to aid him with his studies.

No one contends that we all are or can be Lincolns. But each of us can, if he so desires, get a worthwhile and sufficient education without any aid from the Federal Government.

Another angle of this program, one to which reference was previously made and called to the attention of the gentleman from North Carolina [Mr. Barden] was the kind and the quality of the books which it is almost certain will get into these libraries which, as he said, will be carried, through Federal aid, to the children who live on the back or side roads.

One of the very helpful acts of the good wife, with whom I have lived for more than 57 years, is to go to the Federal library each week, where she gets for me what are called "westerns."

Tired after a day's work on the floor and in the House; not enjoying golf, cocktail parties, or social events, my recreation is in part at least the reading of the westerns. They replace to some extent Jay Fenimore Cooper's Last of the Mohicans, The Prairie, Oak Openings, The Spy—yes, several others.

Zane Grey's novels long provided me with pleasure and a drowsiness which let me drift off for a peaceful rest and recuperation.

Recently, however, on several occasions, when the good wife was asked as to which of the westerns she had obtained from the library I should first read, she has suggested that I skip certain books because, as she said, "You won't care to read them." Without asking, I know to what she refers—this for the reason that, over the last few years, many of these otherwise worthwhile westerns, on page after page, have carried obscene, profane, and suggestive words, sentences, and paragraphs.

As to the suggestive passages, there might be a difference of opinion, but for the dirty, obscene, vulgar and profane language, there is no excuse.

Yet these books are in the public library. They are available to the young, those in formative state of mind, as well as to the older people who have sense enough to lay them aside or to disregard their content.

Public-spirited citizens of Michigan, parents and others, who were alarmed at the spread of youthful delinquency, through the action of thoughtful legislators, obtained the enactment of a State statute barring what was considered to be profane or obscene publications.

Just recently, the United States Supreme Court declared our Michigan statute unconstitutional because it violated the first amendment guaranteeing a free press and free speech.

My memory is that one of the reasons was that, even though the publications might be unsuitable or even unfit for youth to read, because free speech was a constitutional guaranty, the rights of adults under the first amendment could not be infringed, even though the purpose was to protect the youth of the land.

On the same theory it might be said that some of our criminal statutes might restrain youth but could not restrict the freedom of the adult.

The Court which rendered the decision referred to is the same Court which held that a slight beating on the picket line was excusable because, in the words of one of the Justices:

> The right of free speech cannot be denied by drawing from a trivial rough incident or a moment of animal exuberance the conclusion that otherwise peaceful picketing has the taint of force, [*Milk Wagon Drivers Union* v. *Meadowmoor Dairies* [312 U.S. 293].]

> It is the same Court, some may recall, which a few years ago held that an act passed by the Congress to outlaw racketeering applied only to racketeering by the Dillinger type of criminal—not to extortion which was an established union practice.

> True, as some may argue, we should first consider the interests of our own people before extending aid aggregating billions to other nations. But the argument that we should leave the attempt to reduce Federal expenditures until after consideration of the bill extending foreign aid is beside the point.

> We should cut the budget all along the line, until the total is within our ability to pay. In my judgment, the fact, if it be a fact, that foreign aid will be drastically cut is no reason for leaving larger than necessary amounts in our domestic programs or for going along with new programs however desirable, while the tax burden is so grievous, the interest-bearing debt so large.

As the spring wore on, the President's staff became increasingly concerned about the attacks on the budget. They drafted a set of guidelines designed to counter criticisms of the Administration's proposals.

Staff Memorandum on Criticism of the Proposed Budget
n.d.
[Official File 107-B, Eisenhower Papers.]

Serious concern has been expressed over two areas of attack on the Eisenhower Administration.

1. The attack on the proposed 1958 budget with the threat of major cuts and resultant crippling of the Administration's program.

2. The attack on the Administration itself, which is spearheaded by the charge that the Eisenhower Administration has adopted the "New Deal-Fair Deal" philosophy and uses the budget as evidence.

The Problem

How can these two attacks be met so that popular opinion will become more favorable toward the proposed 1958 budget, and so that the "New Deal" tag on the Administration will be replaced with better understanding of the President's true beliefs, policies and proposals?

Is Advertising the Answer?

The question has been raised as to whether or not an advertising campaign might be the solution to the problem.

Before answering that question it might be well to consider the current state of popular opinion.

It appears that there are three fairly general attitudes toward the proposed 1958 Budget.

1. *A feeling that the Budget is "just too big."*

It is the biggest peacetime budget in history. Public statements, even by its defenders, have acknowledged its bigness. Most importantly, people relate the size of the budget to lack of tax cuts . . . if there can be no cut in their taxes, the budget must be too big.

2. *A feeling that the Administration is not solidly behind its own budget.*

Statements by leaders in the Administration have implied more concern with the budget than defense of the budget. Attacks of opponents have been more frequent, more dramatic, more publicized than statements by proponents of the budget.

3. *As a result, a feeling of uneasiness about both the Budget and the Administration.*

People feel the technical details of the budget are over their heads. They are not clear as to the pros and cons. There also appears to be lack of understanding of the Administration's position, probably stemming from the approach "We'd like to cut the budget, but we don't see where or how it can be cut."

In light of these attitudes, the seriousness of the problem is obvious. And the solution to the problem is pointed out.

What is needed is to substitute clarity for confusion . . . to explain to the people clearly, simply, understandably, the facts behind the Budget and the facts of the Administration's beliefs and policies.

It is realized that many attempts to do just this have been and are being made. The present situation is evidence that they have not been successful.

It is our opinion that a newspaper advertising campaign would not be successful either.

The reasons for this opinion are as follows:

1. It is doubtful, considering the subject matter, that advertising would win very high readership, no matter how adroitly it was prepared and presented.

2. Regardless of who signed the advertising—whether it be "Citizens for Eisenhower-Nixon" or another group—there would not be the voice of authority that would command both attention and believability.

3. Even if such advertising could successfully present the facts about the budget, it could hardly serve as an authoritative voice of the Administration in explaining policies and practices. Hence, at best it could do only half the job.

4. An advertising campaign of the size needed would be costly. For example, just one full page advertisement in all newspapers with circulations of 50,000 and over would cost more than $250,000. The very act of such advertising with its obviously large expenditure of funds might well call forth criticism, especially from the opposition.

A Proposal

If an advertising campaign is not the answer to the problem, what is?

Let us restate the need: "To explain to the people clearly, simply, understandably, the facts behind the Budget and the facts of the Administration's beliefs and policies."

One way of meeting this need is suggested in the following plan. It is a 3-step plan.

Step 1—The Administration should decide upon a clear fixed policy—and agree to stick with it.

The importance of this as a first step cannot be overemphasized. The Administration must agree upon its own stand before it can hope to explain that stand to others.

In addition, a fixed policy will provide a rallying point for those supporting the Administration. It will make it difficult if not impossible for others to give lip-service support to the Administration while working against the Administration and its Budget. If they do not accept and support the agreed upon policy, they are obviously not supporters of the present Administration and will find it hard to masquerade as such.

Step 2—The President should make a clear cut statement, based on the agreed upon policy, explaining the Administration's beliefs and principles and showing how these are related to the proposed budget. This statement should be in the form of a televised talk with the people of the U. S. Its tone should be one of leadership and statesmanship—above the partisan political level that has marked much of the budget debate. For additional notes on this proposed talk see Appendix A.

Step 3—To achieve maximum effect from the President's talk, it should be followed immediately by speeches, talks and statements by leading members of the Administration and Party.

These follow-up speeches should take their cue from the President's speech. They should express the same basic policies and develop in detail the points covered in general by the President.

Such follow-up speeches should be *planned in advance,* speakers should be chosen, platforms selected, and speeches prepared before the President talks to the nation. Then after his talk the follow-up can go smoothly into operation according to the pre-planned schedule.

This plan would seem to have certain advantages and chances for success that are missing from any advertising campaign.

It establishes a definite, clear-cut administration policy, thus doing away with current confusion on the part of the public as to just where the Administration does stand, and what its feelings are about the Budget.

A Presidential talk will explain this policy and its meaning to the widest possible audience. It will do so with maximum impact and authority. It will have an effect in proportion to the people's liking and respect for the President.

The follow-up plan provides the essential element of repetition. Even a Presidential speech can be forgotten. Repetition of his main points by others—starting at the top level of the Administration and Party and continuing down to grass roots levels—should go far toward establishing in the minds of the people a better understanding of the Budget. It should also give people a clearer conception of the position of the Administration, and a realization of its deep and definite differences from the New Deal-Fair Deal philosophy.

Summary

A national advertising campaign is not recommended as a sound answer to the present situation.

Instead a 3-step plan is recommended, the steps being:
1. Agreement upon an administration policy with regard to the proposed budget.
2. Expression of that policy to the nation by the President.
3. Repetition of the agreed upon approach through a planned campaign of follow-up speakers.

Appendix A

Notes on the proposed Presidential television talk.

It is realized that the Budget is an extremely complicated subject. In addition, it deals with millions and billions of dollars, figures which have little meaning to an audience with five-thousand-dollar-a-year incomes, or less.

Therefore, every effort should be made to put the President's talk in words that can be grasped and understood by his audience. If the words and figures and ideas are simple and clear, then having the President talk face to face via television with the people of the country might be all that is required. However, some additional suggestions might prove helpful.

1. The use of simple, easy-to-follow charts could help to clarify the more difficult points of the talk.

2. The President might have other members of the Administration also take part in the talk. They might explain certain sections or details. This "team approach" could reinforce the feeling of Administration unity and agreement on policy.

3. The setting and staging of the talk should be carefully considered. For example, a globe or map might be a helpful prop when talking of mutual security problems.

4. The last part of the television time might be devoted to a question-and-answer period in which the President would be asked and would answer the questions about the Budget that average people might ask if they were present.

These suggestions may or may not be practical. They are offered chiefly to emphasize the importance of planning the Presidential talk so that it speaks to the people, simply, interestingly, and always in terms that they can understand.

On April 18, when the budget controversy threatened to disrupt the Administration's whole legislative program, the President wrote a long letter to Speaker of the House Sam Rayburn of Texas detailing his position on the issues involved.

President Eisenhower to Speaker Sam Rayburn
April 18, 1957

[*Public Papers of the Presidents: 1957* (Washington, 1958), 301–09.]

Dear Mr. Speaker:

I am sure many Members of the Congress are as gratified as I am to note the growing awareness of private citizens that the dollars spent by the Federal Government are in fact their own dollars, and that Federal benefits are not free but must be paid for out of taxes collected from the people. It is good to see this realization developing into a widespread insistence that

Federal activity be held to the minimum consistent with national needs. As this sentiment grows, our country will be strengthened in many ways.

The evident responsiveness of the Congress to this attitude I find equally encouraging. I assure you and your colleagues that the Executive Branch will continue to cooperate fully with Members of the Congress who work for sensible control of Federal spending.

In House Resolution 190 adopted last March, I noted the assertion that the public interest requires a "substantial reduction" in the 1958 budget and also the request that I advise the House where a reduction of that magnitude could best be made.

You will recall that last January, immediately after the budget was presented to the Congress, I requested the Director of the Bureau of the Budget to resurvey the expenditures of every Department and agency in an effort to find additional items that could properly be reduced. I have kept in close touch with those efforts. Some of the principal results are outlined in this letter.

You realize, of course, that the 1958 budget, as all Federal budgets, is in effect two budgets within one. One consists of requests for new spending authority to enable Federal agencies to obligate themselves to make expenditures sometime in the future. The other concerns the actual expenditures of the agencies in the next fiscal year. These expenditures will be made partly pursuant to spending authority granted in previous years and partly under new spending authority. For example, one-third of the total actual expenditures in the 1958 fiscal year will be made pursuant to spending authority granted not on the basis of the 1958 budget but on the basis of spending authority requested in earlier budgets. This problem I emphasize because of its importance in appraising the effect of cuts in new spending authority which, one might assume, will reduce the level of current spending but in fact may affect only future spending.

The House Resolution, for instance, does not distinguish between these two budgetary problems, so its call for a "substantial reduction," I assume, applies to both and contemplates the reduction of both by a considerable number of billions of dollars.

There are thousands of items in the budget, each an individual fiscal plan to carry forward a new program or a program previously authorized by the Congress. The preparation of these items begins long before the Congress acts, with the result that the budgetary process places a high premium on judgment and foresight. Because Departmental needs must be forecast a year or more in advance, no responsible official would realistically contend that every estimate for every item is precisely correct and could be changed only at the risk of serious public injury, or that the funds requested are certain to meet all future needs.

Nevertheless, painstaking efforts were made in preparing the budget to pare to the minimum all projected expenditures and programs, whether large or small. Estimates were substantially reduced before the Budget

Document was submitted to the Congress, and at my request a searching re-examination by all Departments and agencies has continued to go forward since that time in an effort to reduce expenditures whenever possible. I will later discuss possible reductions in new spending authority disclosed by these months of continuing review.

Before turning to budgetary specifics, however, I invite attention to certain general guidelines that, to the extent existing law permitted, were applied in formulating the 1958 budget. These may be helpful to the House in reaching its own budgetary decisions:

First, the Federal Government should undertake only essential activities that the people cannot sufficiently provide for themselves or obtain adequately through private voluntary action or local or State government. Both the Congress and the Executive Branch should adhere closely to this principle in the interest of sound, economical government.

Second, in times like these Government spending should be held below income in order to lead the way to further reductions in taxes and the public debt.

Third, all governmental expenditures should remain under close scrutiny in the interest of strict economy and, in the currently prevailing prosperity, to help relieve competing demands for economic resources.

Such guidelines have proved their practical worth. Today Federal civilian employees are almost a quarter of a million fewer than in January 1953. The $7.4 billion tax cut in 1954 has already saved our people almost $25 billion in taxes. For the first time in a quarter of a century we have in prospect three balanced budgets in a row. In fiscal year 1956 the surplus was $1.6 billion. It promises this fiscal year to be about the same size, and next year perhaps as much as $1.8 billion. If we hold to this course, we should have paid in these three years about $5 billion on the public debt, and the annual necessity to raise the statutory debt limit should have become a thing of the past.

By adhering to the same or similar guidelines, the House can help continue the progress already made.

Regarding the House appeal for guidance on specific budgetary items, I will comment first on the actual expenditures projected for next fiscal year and will later discuss possible reductions in new spending authority.

At the outset, we need to remind ourselves that, as in every household budget, all Federal expenditures are not equally subject to control. Many Federal expenditures are rigidly prescribed by law. Others are bills that simply have to be paid. In the 1958 fiscal year, such unavoidable expenditures will total about $17.6 billion, or 24 percent of all Federal expenditures. These funds must be spent for such items as veterans' pensions, public assistance, and the interest on the public debt. The "substantial reduction" called for by House Resolution 190 cannot be made in this part of the budget until and unless the Congress revises or repeals the governing laws.

In the second place, 63 percent of projected expenditures next fiscal year—some $45 billion—will support programs related to the protection of our country. Departmental estimates in this area were most carefully examined and prudently reduced before they were sent to the Congress. I foresee no early lessening of international tensions and dangers as would justify a significant downward revision in our defense and related programs. The fact is, as we carry forward our efforts for more peaceful world conditions, rapid technological advances in ships, aircraft, nuclear weapons, missiles and electronics press constantly for more, not fewer, Federal dollars. I most solemnly advise the House that in these times a cut of any appreciable consequence in current expenditures for national security and related programs would endanger our country and the peace of the world.

The remaining expenditures projected in the budget approximate $9 billion, 13 percent of the total. These support the rest of the Federal Government—such activities as public health, the various housing programs, all operations of most Executive Departments, the civil functions of the Corps of Engineers, the nationwide functions of the General Services Administration, the worldwide operations of the Department of State. Additional savings in such widely varied activities may well be found by the Executive Branch and the Congress. But a multi-billion-dollar reduction as evidently envisaged by the House Resolution would destroy or cripple many essential programs if concentrated in this limited area of the budget.

Thus, it is clear that a "substantial reduction" in Federal expenditures next fiscal year in keeping with House Resolution 190, whether in any one or a combination of these major segments of the budget, would weaken the nation's defenses, or cut back or eliminate programs now required by law or proposed in the public interest, or both. That forces the conclusion that a multi-billion-dollar reduction in 1958 expenditures can be accomplished only at the expense of the national safety and interest.

Turning now to requests for new spending authority, as distinguished from actual expenditures, we find a more promising outlook. Budgetary reviews since last January have disclosed the feasibility of postponing certain of these requests without serious damage to program levels. A number of the following actions, which I commend to the House, I have already suggested:

First, that new spending authority for the military assistance portion of the Mutual Security Program be reduced by $500 million. This reduction results mainly from the new management techniques through which lead-time financing has been reduced (notably for spare parts), maintenance support not justified by the rate of consumption of our allies has been eliminated, and items have been removed from grant aid which countries can now pay for themselves. If the funds previously appropriated are continued available, this reduction will not impair the operation of military forces of other countries at mutually agreed levels.

Second, that, by delaying less urgent projects, new spending authority for military public works be reduced by $200 million.

Third, that resulting from new projections of its operating rate and related financial requirements, the new spending authority for the Soil Bank Program be reduced by $254 million.

Fourth, that the investment of the Federal National Mortgage Association in special assistance functions be reduced from $250 million to $200 million, a reduction in new spending authority of $50 million.

Fifth, that the college housing authorization be reduced from $175 million to $150 million, a reduction in new spending authority of $25 million.

Sixth, that resulting from adjustments of construction schedules, the new spending authority of the Corps of Engineers be reduced by $13 million.

The House may wish to give attention to an additional item of $516 million requested for Army procurement and production. The existing authority, granted by the Congress during the Korean War, plus certain reimbursements received since then have made it unnecessary to request new spending authority for this purpose in recent years. Beginning in fiscal year 1959, the Army's need for such spending authority will recur. The $516 million item is requested now to enable the Army to phase efficiently into this new period and to ease the impact of this adjustment in fiscal year 1959. At the expense of efficient programming, the sum can be withheld if the House so chooses. Such action would, of course, increase by $516 million the large amount that will have to be authorized for Army procurement and production in fiscal year 1959.

Exclusive of the Army item just mentioned, but including a possible reduction of $300 million in the amount budgeted for contingent expenses, these reductions and postponements total $1.342 billion. Once again I remind the House that less than half of this reduction in new spending authority can be reflected in reductions in expenditures during the next fiscal year, and even a part of these expenditure reductions will have to be restored in the future. Such expenditure reductions as may result, however, will add to the $1.8 billion surplus already projected by the budget. Given continuation of healthy economic growth and of strict expenditure control, these figures combined will begin to lay a firm fiscal foundation for the time when we can be sufficiently assured that our income will so exceed our expenses as to justify a reasonable tax cut for every taxpayer while we continue to reduce the Government's debt.

I am, of course, aware of the cuts thus far proposed by the House. These will be absorbed wherever possible without serious injury to programs essential to the public interest. Where such cuts cannot be so absorbed, the Executive Branch must and will seek restoration of the needed funds. Some of the House "cuts" have involved large sums that the Executive Branch is compelled by law to pay. "Cuts" of that kind do not save money and must be later restored through supplemental appropriations unless the governing statutes are revised.

Aside from scrutinizing individual expenditures and reducing new spending authority as suggested above, I strongly urge the House also to improve the Federal budgetary situation by taking such steps as these, most of which I have urged before:

First—adjust postal rates as soon as possible to reduce and eventually eliminate the postal deficit.

Second—establish interest rates for Government loan programs that will induce private funds to participate in their financing and, at the least, require that such rates cover the borrowing costs of the Federal Government.

Third—provide user charges as, for instance, for the use of Federal airway facilities, that will relieve the general public of having to subsidize governmental services affording special benefits.

Fourth—require State financial participation in Federal disaster assistance programs.

Fifth—encourage State and local groups to engage in partnership with the Federal Government in major water resources development.

Sixth—reject new projects not approved by the Board of Engineers for Rivers and Harbors and not reviewed by all interested parties, including the affected States; provide where appropriate for more local participation in approved projects; and withhold authorization and construction of all but urgently needed projects.

Seventh—enact bills approved by the Administration to implement Hoover Commission recommendations, such as the authorization of appropriations on the basis of annual accrued expenditures and the extension of the Reorganization Act of 1949.

Eighth—establish procedures that will facilitate the return of surplus Federal land and other property to private, local or State use.

Ninth—before adopting unbudgeted programs, project the costs they would impose on the Federal budget in years ahead, and reappraise the necessity for and rate of implementation of each program.

And, tenth, to help assure continuing economy on the part of the Congress as well as the Executive Branch, take action that will grant the President the power now held by many State Governors to veto specific items in appropriations bills.

An improved budgetary situation and greater efficiency in our government will result from prompt approval of these recommendations by the Congress. All elements of the budget, meanwhile, will remain under searching examination by the Executive Branch in its continuing effort to find additional savings, large or small, that are possible under existing law. Any additional reductions found possible in new spending authority will be promptly reported in the usual way to the Senate and House of Representatives.

Finally, I repeat that as this effort to hold Federal costs and activities to the minimum proceeds sensibly in the Executive and Legislative Branches of our Federal Government, the public interest is bound to be well served.

>■━●━<

Some weeks later, on May 14, 1957, Eisenhower delivered a radio and television address to rally public support for the budget. Neither his letter to Rayburn nor his address quieted the opposition to his budget. However, the normal legislative process ultimately approved the vast majority of his proposals, and the budget for 1958 totaled almost the figure that he had originally suggested. As with previous Democratic Congresses, the President was able to negotiate a mutually agreeable settlement.

Address to the Nation by President Eisenhower on the Cost of Government May 14, 1957

[*Public Papers of the Presidents: 1957* (Washington, 1958), 341–52.]

My Fellow Citizens:

I should like to talk some facts with you tonight—about what happens to the tax dollars that you send to Washington.

I am speaking from the Presidential office here in the White House. In outward respects, this is quite an ordinary room. The furniture, the books, the telephones, even the paintings on the wall, are in no sense unusual.

But in one respect this room is unusual.

To this office—to the President, whoever he may be, there comes every day from all parts of the land and from all parts of the world a steady flow of dispatches, reports and visitors. They tell of the successes and the disappointments of our people in their efforts to help achieve peace with justice in the world. They tell, too, of the progress and difficulties in building a sturdy, prosperous and a just society here at home.

On the basis of this information, decisions, affecting all of us, have to be made every day. Because your President, aside from the Vice President, is the only governmental official chosen by a vote of all the people, he must make his decisions on the basis of what he thinks best for all the people. He cannot consider only a district, a state or a region in developing solutions to problems. He must always use the yardstick of the national interest.

It is from this overall viewpoint that I want to talk with you tonight about the cost of running your Government.

The budget now before Congress is huge; even though it represents a sharply smaller part of our national production than the first budget I submitted to the Congress four years ago. Since then we have sought unceasingly to make the taxpayer's dollar go further.

We have, for example, cut the government payroll by nearly 250,000 positions.

Taxes were cut in 1954 with savings so far of some 25 billion dollars to the American taxpayer.

The proposed budget is balanced—the third in a row.

The budget now under discussion represents carefully studied estimates of the cost of all the things the government is required by law to do or by what we believe to be necessary.

All of these things I have discussed with you many times. Indeed most of these national programs have been on the books for some years. There are no surprise proposals in this budget. It was made up under my personal direction by men and women who believe deeply in economy and efficiency in government. In the process some 13 billion dollars in departmental requests were eliminated.

Now when a budget is sent to Congress, it contains estimates of costs reaching 18 months into the future. So, as I have so frequently pointed out, these estimates cannot be exact to the very last dollar. That is why they are kept under constant examination in all Executive Departments—both before and after the Budget goes to the Congress. Many of these estimates are based upon formulas in laws passed by the Congress. They are as accurate as can be made based upon our experience in administering those laws. So, if the Congress should cut the estimates in this budget for things that are fixed by law, like veterans compensation and pensions, it should be clear that such cuts would not save money, because the actual costs, whatever they turn out to be must, by law, be paid.

I have often been asked how big our Federal budget ought to be. Now that question calls to mind a story about Abraham Lincoln. One day a man looking at him said, "Mr. Lincoln, how long should a man's legs be?" Well, he looked down at his rather long lanky legs and he said, "Well, they ought to be long enough to reach the ground."

Now that's not a very exact formula, but it has its point in this question. A budget, too, ought to reach the ground. The ground, in this case, is the essential national interest—and no more. That is the purpose of this budget.

No great reductions in it are possible unless Congress eliminates or curtails existing Federal programs, or unless all of us demand less service from the government, or unless we are willing to gamble with the safety of our country.

In this troubled world, our foremost national need is, of course, our own security. The overall cost is great, indeed—over 45 billion dollars in the budget now before the Congress. This is mainly what makes the budget so large—the costs of our present security and our quest for a just and lasting peace. There is no cut-rate price for security.

But before considering this heavy expenditure, let us look at the smaller, non-security costs we also have to pay. Including certain new activities important to America, this 26 billion dollar part of the budget meets the costs fixed by law, the routine jobs of government, and the domestic programs of service which our people have decided through the Congress to adopt.

In this 35% part of the budget, there are, first, the compulsory expenditures. We must pay the more than 7 billion dollars' interest on the national debt. Ours is not like the Soviet Government which recently told its people that it would no longer pay the interest on its government savings bonds.

Other programs are established by law, and the bulk of the expenditures under those laws is mandatory.

The largest among them provides 5 billion dollars for veterans' pensions, compensation, education, medical care, and other benefits.

Another large item of about 5 billion dollars is for agricultural programs: for price supports, the soil bank, land conservation, rural electrification, and other services of benefit to farmers.

The costs of these two great programs have tended to grow rather than to shrink over recent years.

In addition, about 3½ billion dollars is provided, as grants and loans to the states, to share the costs of such activities as administering unemployment compensation and the employment service. This sum assists the states in helping needy aged, the blind, the totally disabled and dependent children; promoting public health, sanitation, and the control of disease, as well as speeding slum clearance and urban renewal—an item which a committee of mayors recently urged me to support vigorously.

All these are programs long ago enacted by the Congress.

This part of the budget also provides funds for a new project which I have urged for two years to help overcome the acute shortage of schoolrooms in our country. The plan calls for a 4-year emergency program of schoolroom construction at a cost of 325 million dollars a year.

Now permit me a further word about this item. I deeply believe, as I am sure you do, that education is clearly a responsibility of state and local governments—and should remain so. But another truth is just as clear: during the depression, World War II, and the Korean conflict, our states and localities did not have the means and the opportunity to build enough classrooms to keep up with the increasing number of youngsters. This means that we need an emergency program to help states and localities build the schools our children must have. We must not continue to penalize our children and thereby the future of the nation.

We limit this aid to building; thus it will not result in Federal control of education. It is limited in scope to make sure that Federal help will go where it is needed most. Limited in time, it guarantees that Federal help will be temporary.

Now I have heard people say, and I am sure you have, that no Federal program can be temporary—that any activity begun in Washington will go on forever.

I reject that kind of talk.

I believe that Americans are responsible enough to do exactly what they want to do and then stop.

I support this program wholeheartedly because it is a get-in-and-get-out emergency plan solely to overcome a schoolroom deficit created by depression and by wars.

Now after meeting the costs of interest on the national debt, agriculture, veterans, and grants to the states, there remains in this non-security part of the budget about 5 billion dollars. This pays for everything else our Government expects to do next year.

It includes direct Federal expenditures related to labor and welfare—and for things like medical research. It includes the cost of conserving and developing our natural resources—improving the national parks, building dams and reservoirs, and protecting fish and wildlife.

It includes the weather bureau, disaster relief, the census, and subsidies for civil aviation and our merchant fleet.

It includes costs of the Congress and the courts, of law enforcement, and of tax collection.

Finally, it includes funds to cover the postal deficit, which will be more than half a billion dollars unless the Congress raises postal rates, as I have repeatedly urged. If the Congress acts, this cost will be borne by the users of the mails, thereby relieving the taxpayer of this burden.

In executing these programs we constantly stress economy and seek to avoid waste and duplication. In this endeavor we have had the benefit of the recommendation of two Hoover Commissions, the great portions of which have already been accepted and are in the process of being put into effect. Moreover, we postpone programs when we can. When we find it possible to revise cost estimates, we inform the Congress. In my letter of April 18th to the Speaker of the House of Representatives, I pointed out that we had been able to revise estimates of new spending authority downward by a possible 1.8 billion dollars, assuming Congressional cooperation.

While we shall insist on carrying out the Federal Government's proper role in meeting the needs of our growing economy and population, we shall not start any program that we do not believe necessary. We are determined to search out ways to save money and manpower so that government does not further add to the inflationary pressures on the economy.

If our people join us in this determination, we can look forward to sufficient excess of income over expenses to justify future tax reductions as we continue paying down on the public debt.

In all this we need the cooperation of the Congress and we need the help and understanding of every one of you. Almost every proposal for government aid or service has a number of citizens organized behind it. Usually each group wants the government to spend for its pet project, but to economize everywhere else. This is a good time to examine again the demands that each of us, our communities and our states, make upon the Federal Government. It is a time to limit those demands to what is necessary—and no more.

Turn with me now to the largest item in the budget—the defense of our country. There is where most of your tax dollars go.

As we survey the world in which we live, the first great concern of all of us is to make sure of the defense of our homes, our country and our way of life. The Communists have again and again announced their purpose of promoting revolution and of communizing the world by whatever means. It is important, and surely prudent, for us to understand the military strength the Communists maintain to help them achieve their purposes.

Now what is that strength today?

Without counting the Chinese Communists, the Soviets have the world's largest army. They have many times the number of submarines that Germany had when World War II began. They have atomic weapons and rockets and missiles. They have a large and growing air strength. They are competent in military technology and research. And all this is directed by a despotism which is fully capable of the supreme folly—that of unleashing these powerful forces if it should ever believe that it could—without destroying itself—succeed in destroying the free world.

One important purpose of our military arrangements is to convince others that if they start a general conflict they cannot escape their own destruction.

As I have said, the national defense item is by far the largest in our budget, but let us see just how large it is. The estimate just for our own military forces and our atomic development, together with a small amount for stockpiling critical and strategic materials, is almost 41 billion dollars. This does not, by any means, equal the full amount first recommended by our uniformed services. They wanted some 10 billion dollars more.

But I earnestly believe that this defense budget represents, in today's world, the proper dividing line between national danger on the one hand and excessive expenditure on the other. If it is materially cut, I believe the country would be taking a needless gamble. For myself, I have seen unwise military cuts before. I have more than once seen their terrible consequences. I am determined to do all I can to see that we do not follow that foolhardy road again.

Even after World War II had illustrated again the dangers of unpreparedness, our Armed Forces became so starved and depleted that by 1950 we had to withdraw our military strength from South Korea. That area was then declared to be outside our defense perimeter. The tragic results of that woeful weakness are too close to us to need recounting now to the families of America. But I say to you that I shall never agree to any program of false economy that would permit us to incur again that kind of risk to our country and to the lives of our citizens.

Good defense is not cheap defense.

The B-36 bomber, even though built after World War II, is already outmoded. Each one cost us about 3½ million dollars. Today's B-52 jet bomber costs 8 million dollars each.

Seven years ago, a fighter plane cost 300 thousand dollars. Today, one costs 1½ million dollars.

A submarine now costs twice as much as it did seven years ago.

Atomic energy costs four times as much as it did in 1950. Daily, munitions grow more complex, more powerful and more costly.

It is clear that unless we make some progress in our persistent efforts to secure an effective agreement to limit armaments, defense costs will tend to go up year by year, if we are to keep Communist forces from outstripping us.

Consequently, though our first responsibility is to maintain defenses adequate to keep the nation secure, we do not want, because of this cost, more military force than is necessary.

Judgments on the defense budget must reflect the stern fact that real military power can rest only on a sound economy. Only with a strong and thriving economy can we have the strength to protect our freedom. But since we maintain military forces as a matter of self-preservation, we must not recklessly reduce their power.

This dilemma presents hard decisions. But they are decisions that must be made by the President, as he presents his recommendations to the Congress. To this kind of problem I have devoted most of my life. I repeat my earnest belief that the estimate in the budget for our military forces, atomic energy and stockpiling—amounting to about 41 billion dollars—represents a defense program which is as nearly accurate, in present circumstances, as is humanly possible to make it.

To this defense total should properly be added—and will so be in the future—that part of our mutual security program which supplies arms and defense support to friendly countries in order to strengthen the military power of the free world. Expenditures for this purpose will amount next year to something over 3 billion dollars.

The costs in many of these friendly countries are low compared to ours, so this type of aid, even though moderate in amount, supplements their own efforts very effectively. This aid helps arm and maintain overseas: some five times as many active ground forces as the United States possesses; about twice as many naval combat ships; and about an equal number of planes. This aid is also a key factor in maintaining many of our vital military, naval and air bases abroad.

Without the military strength that this aid helps sustain overseas, we should have to add many more billions to our own defense spending, and have less security for our total effort.

Defense expenditures, for our own forces and our military assistance overseas, together with the domestic expenditures I have discussed, account for almost all—in fact, 98%—of the budget.

As we look at the whole range of the budget, there is only one hope of making the really great savings that we all want so much. That hope is to achieve an effective disarmament agreement with an easing of world tensions, so that the enormous sums we have to spend for our defense can be drastically reduced.

The savings we can hope to make in domestic programs are, at best, small by comparison. Of course, we could save material amounts if, by law, we abandoned or drastically cut back some of the larger programs. But in a world knowing real peace, we could save at least ten times as much in defense spending.

It is to hasten that day, as well as to enhance our security now, that the budget provides a moderate sum for waging peace.

This is a mission that military formations cannot, of themselves, accomplish. The entire free world military force merely puts a policeman on the corner to keep the robber out of our house and out of our neighborhood. It preserves from destruction what we already have.

But our Communist antagonists are resourceful and cunning. Their aggression is not limited to the use of force or the threat of its use. They are doing their best to take advantage of poverty and need in the developing nations, and so turn them against the free world. Success would enable them to win their long-sought goal of Communist encirclement of our country.

To meet the total threat, we, first of all—as I have pointed out—must sustain our defense preparations.

But we must do more.

We must wage peace aggressively through diplomatic efforts, through the economic and technical assistance part of the mutual security program, and through world-wide information activities to help bind the free world more firmly together. These efforts will cost about one billion dollars next year.

We wage peace on the diplomatic front through the efforts of the State Department to establish close ties with every other nation that values its independence and that recognizes the dignity of man.

We wage peace through the efforts of the United States Information Service to counteract the false propaganda spread by the Communists. We tell the truth about freedom and the rights of man and seek to win adherents to these concepts.

We wage peace through the mutual security program in another way. We help some nations in developing their own economies, so their people can be stronger partners in the defense of the free world against Communism.

Economic development is, of course, not a product for export from the United States or anywhere else. It is a homespun product, the product of a people's own work. Our opportunity is simply this: to help the peoples of these developing lands to help themselves. This we can do through sound technical assistance and, where necessary and unavailable from other sources, through loans and, at times, other kinds of financial aid. Within prudent limits, this practice is in their and our best interests.

On this subject I hope to talk with you again next week, but I assure you now that this billion dollar item is one of the most important to all of us in the entire budget.

I know that in these efforts to wage peace, all does not always go well. Weaknesses there are bound to be—troubles and disappointments as well.

But I never ordered a cease-fire in a battle because some of the ammunition misfired or went bad, or some commander—including myself—may have made a mistake.

We must always do better, but we must never stop in our battle for peace. We must keep everlastingly at this job—today the most important job in this entire world.

Our defense expenditures are to assure us the opportunity to wage peace; our expenditures for diplomatic work, economic and technical assistance and information services give us the means to wage peace. Together they cost 45 billion dollars—all but about a billion dollars of this for defense.

The rising costs of defense items account for more than 80 percent of the increase in next year's budget. These facts simply reflect the kind of world in which we are living.

The plain truth is that the price of peace is high.

That explains why taxes are high and why their further reduction has been delayed. It explains also why really big cuts in government spending depend on success in our efforts to wage peace.

The sacrifices demanded of each of us are great; but they are sacrifices of dollars for a peaceful world, not the sacrifices of our sons, our families, our homes and our cities to our own short-sightedness.

I believe that you are more secure in your homes tonight because of the effort and money our nation has put into these defense and related security programs. It is almost four years since an American fighting man has been killed in battle anywhere. Crises, great and small, we have had and will continue to have. Despite them, there has been an overall improvement in the prospects for keeping an honorable peace.

But I must say this to you: I can see no immediate relaxation of international tensions to provide the basis now for substantial reductions in these programs for preserving and waging peace. In fact, the gains we have already made impel us to press forward with no let-up.

If we do press forward—if we courageously bear these burdens of waging peace—I have every hope that, in God's good time success will crown our efforts. Then we shall know an easier and a better peace whose fruits will include a lightening of the spiritual and the material burdens we now must bear in order to gain it.

Thank you. Good night.

2. BENSON AND THE FARM PROGRAM

The whole "soil bank" proposal was based on the philosphy that Govern-
ment subsidies were the cause of farm surpluses rather than the result of
them. In addition, the farm surplus problem, with its price-depressing
effect, had become worse during Eisenhower's first three years in office.
Changes had been made in agricultural legislation to reduce the percentage
of parity paid in price support programs, but the basic surplus problem
remained. In the fall of 1955 Republican Senator Barry Goldwater of
Arizona wrote the President: "It is too early to come to any conclusion
because our program has not had a chance to prove itself and any thinking
farmer will realize that the Democratic approach would have been a
complete fiasco without the occurrence of two wars." The following year,*
the President proposed a new approach. He asked Congress (January 9,
1956) to enact a "soil bank" program to reduce the surplus. (Basically, the
"soil bank" would give discretion to the Secretary of Agriculture to set
payment rates for farmers who voluntarily took acres out of production.) In
April, a bill passed with a "soil bank" provision, although Democrats
restored the 90 per cent of parity principle to the legislation. This was
unacceptable to Eisenhower, as his veto message of April 16 clearly stated.
Congress reconsidered the farm program dilemma and finally passed an accep-
table bill, even though in his signing statement on May 28 Eisenhower not-
ed what he considered several serious weaknesses in the legislation.

Special Message to the Congress
by President Eisenhower on Agriculture
January 9, 1956
[*Public Papers of the Presidents: 1956* (Washington, 1958), 38–50.]

To the Congress of the United States:

In this Session no problem before the Congress demands more urgent
attention than the paradox facing our farm families. Although agriculture
is our basic industry, they find their prices and incomes depressed amid the

*Barry Goldwater to President Eisenhower, September 14, 1955, President's Personal
File 1010, Eisenhower Papers.

852

nation's greatest prosperity. For five years, their economy has declined. Unless corrected, these economic reversals are a direct threat to the well-being of all our people.

But more than prices and incomes are involved. In America, agriculture is more than an industry; it is a way of life. Throughout our history, the family farm has given strength and vitality to our entire social order. We must keep it healthy and vigorous.

Efforts toward this goal have been unremitting. Many new foundations of permanent value to all farm families have been laid in the past three years. Two years ago a new farm law was enacted, designed to gear agricultural production incentives to potential markets, thereby giving promise to our farm people of a stable and dependable future once the wartime inheritance of surpluses is removed from the farm economy. Loan programs have been substantially improved, enabling many more farmers to acquire family-sized farms and to improve their farms and homes. The benefits of Social Security protection have been extended to farm families. The return of the Farm Credit Administration to farmer control; expansion of soil conservation assistance and rural electrification and telephone programs; increased funds for research and extension work; initiation of new programs to aid low income farm families; adoption of tax provisions of benefit to farm people; increased storage facilities; upstream soil conservation programs; greatly expanded disposal activities for surplus farm products; strengthening our Department of Agriculture representation overseas in the interest of expanded markets—these and other advances have permanently reinforced the foundations of all agriculture.

Yet, beneficial though these advances are, persistent and critical farm problems require prompt Congressional action in this Session.

Remedies for these problems demand a clear understanding of their principal causes. These are:

First—production and market distortions, the result of war-time production incentives too long continued;

Second—current record livestock production and near-record crop harvests piled on top of previously accumulated carryovers;

Third—rising costs and high capital requirements.

In short, we have an over-supply of commodities which drives down prices as mounting costs force up from below. Thus is generated a severe price-cost squeeze from which our farm people, with the help of government, must be relieved.

We must free the farm economy from distortions rooted in wartime needs and thus enable our people in agriculture to achieve prosperity; in so doing they will help carry the nation's prosperity to still greater heights. The Administration and the Congress must move together to achieve this goal.

The requirements are clear. New means are needed to reduce surpluses and to widen markets. Costs must be cut and production must be better balanced with prospective needs.

The Main Problem—The Surplus

Of the many difficulties that aggravate the farm problem, mountainous surpluses overshadow everything else. Today's surpluses consist of commodities produced in a volume imperatively needed in wartime but unmarketable in peacetime at the same prices and in the same quantity.

The plain fact is that wartime production incentives were too long continued.

During the past three years, there has been no lack of effort to get rid of surplus stocks. Disposal efforts have been diligent and vigorous. Vast quantities have been moved—much of them given away. In the past three years we have found outlets for commodities in a value of more than four billion dollars—far more than in any comparable period in recent history.

But these disposal efforts have not been able to keep pace with the problem. For each bushel-equivalent sold, one and a half have replaced it in the stockpiles. Farmers, the intended beneficiaries of the support program, today find themselves in ever-growing danger from the mounting accumulations. Were it not for the government's bulging stocks, farmers would be getting far more for their products today.

Other consequences of past farm programs have been no less damaging. Both at home and abroad, markets have been lost. Foreign farm production has been increased. American exports have declined. Foreign products have been attracted to our shores.

Steadily this chain of events has lengthened. Our farmers have had to submit to drastic acreage controls that hamper efficient farm management. Even these controls have been self-defeating, because acres diverted from price-supported crops have been planted to other crops. These crops have been thrown into surplus and their prices have declined. Today, almost without regard to the livestock or crop he produces, nearly every farmer is adversely affected by our surpluses. The whole process, for instance, has contributed to the present plight of hog producers.

When three years ago this Administration assumed its responsibility in agriculture, work was begun immediately on what became the Agricultural Act of 1954. That Act was developed and passed with bipartisan support, as all our agricultural legislation should be.

The 1954 law brought realism into the use of the essential tool of price supports. It applied the principle of price flexibility to help keep commodity supplies in balance with markets. That principle is sound and essential to a well-rounded farm program. For two reasons, the 1954 law has not yet been able to make its potential contribution to solving our farm troubles. First, the law began to take hold only with the harvests of 1955; it has not yet had the opportunity to be effective. Second, the operation of the new law is smothered under surpluses amassed by the old program.

The attack on the surplus must go forward in full recognition of the fact that farm products are not actually marketed when delivered to and held by the government. A government warehouse is not a market. Even the most storable commodities cannot be added forever to government granaries, nor can they be indefinitely held. Ultimately the stockpiles must be used.

It is unthinkable to destroy food. Instead, we must move these stocks into domestic consumption or dispose of them abroad. Neither route under present conditions offers the results often expected. Surpluses moved domestically almost always compete directly with crops farmers are trying to sell. Moved abroad in quantities large enough to remedy present difficulties, they would shatter world prices and trade, injure our friends and undermine domestic prices as well.

To be sure, outlets for some of the surplus exist both at home and abroad. But experience has amply proved that neither the home nor foreign market can, under present conditions, readily absorb the tremendous stocks now depressing our agriculture.

Clearly new action is imperative. We must stop encouraging the production of surpluses. We must stop shifting acres from one crop to another, when such shifts result in new surpluses. Nor can crop problems be converted into millstones weighing down upon the producers of livestock.

Remedies are needed now, and it is up to the Administration and the Congress to provide them swiftly. As we seek to go forward, we must not go back to old programs that have failed utterly to protect farm families.

I recommend, therefore, the following nine-point program. I urge the Congress to pass this program with maximum speed, for delay can only aggravate and multiply the difficulties already sorely harassing millions of our rural people.

The Soil Bank

Our most pressing need today is to work off our surpluses so that our basic program of 1954 can succeed in gearing production to prospective markets at fair prices. A three-pronged attack is needed.

First, future production of crops in greatest surplus must be adjusted both to the accumulated stocks and to the potential markets.

Second, producers of other crops and of livestock must be relieved of excessive production from acreage diverted from surplus crops.

Third, lands poorly suited to tillage, now producing unneeded crops and subject to excessive wind and water erosion, must be retired from cultivation.

These essential adjustments can all be hastened through a Soil Bank Program. I recommend a Soil Bank of two parts.

The first is designed to meet the immediate need to reduce the crops in greatest over-supply. It may be called the Acreage Reserve Program.

The second part is a long-range attack to achieve better land use and protect farmers and ranchers from the effects of production on acres already diverted. It may be called the Conservation Reserve Program.

A. *The Acreage Reserve Program*

I recommend that the Congress consider a voluntary additional reduction in the acreage of certain crops which today are in serious surplus—wheat, cotton, corn and rice.

In considering the application of this program to each of these crops, the Congress will wish to accord special attention to their distinctive problems—notably in the case of corn—as set forth later in this Message.

I do not propose this program as a device to empty government warehouses so they may be filled again. There is, therefore, a basic corollary to the Acreage Reserve Program: in future years we must avoid, as a plague, farm programs that would encourage the building-up of new price-depressing surpluses.

What I here propose is essentially a deferred-production plan. As a necessary part of the voluntary acreage reduction, it is essential to protect the farmer's income. It would be grossly unfair to require farmers to bear the full burdens of this readjustment. Just as other readjustments from war were shouldered in considerable part by the nation as a whole, so should this.

In the case of wheat and cotton, for example, I look to a voluntary reduction equivalent to possibly one-fifth of the acreage otherwise permitted by allotments—perhaps 12 million acres of wheat and 3 million of cotton. It should be practical to include wheat already seeded if it is incorporated with the soil, as green manure, or by other accepted practices. This would make it possible for more farmers to enter the program immediately and thereby start at once to work down the surplus.

Administrative discretion is needed to assure that the rates of reduction in different areas are related to the supply and demand conditions for different grades and classes. The farmer's cooperation in this temporary program must not impair his historic acreage allotments. Rights of tenant farmers must be protected. I should expect the reduction in wheat and cotton plantings to continue for some 3 or 4 years, during which time these huge crop carry-overs should decline to normal levels.

In return for their voluntary participation in the Acreage Reserve Program cooperating farmers will be allocated certificates for commodities whose value will be based on the normal yields of the acres withheld in this Reserve. I recommend that these certificates be made available to cooperating farmers through their County Agricultural Stabilization Committees at normal harvest time for each crop. The certificates will be negotiable so farmers can convert them to cash. They will be redeemable by the Commodity Credit Corporation in cash, or in kind at specified rates.

I further recommend that the legislation provide that each participating farmer contract to refrain from cropping or grazing any land he puts in the Acreage Reserve.

By so reducing crop production, commodities now in government ownership can be used to supply market needs up to a proportionate amount.

Thus the bulging Commodity Credit Corporation stocks can be correspondingly worked down without depressing current market prices.

The program will operate in this way: A farmer, with an allotment of 100 acres of wheat, for example, may choose to plant only 80 acres and put the remaining 20 in the Acreage Reserve. His acreage allotment will not be affected. He will agree not to graze or harvest any crop from the 20 acres put into the reserve.

In return for this cooperation in the temporary acreage reduction program, he will receive a cashable certificate. The certificate will be equal to a percentage of the value of the crop he would have normally harvested from the 20 acres. This percentage will be set at an incentive level sufficiently high to assure success of the program.

This deferred production plan uses the surplus to reduce the surplus.

It will be financed with commodities already owned and paid for by the government. Time and shrinkage, storage and other costs are eroding away the present value of these stocks. Consequently, the real net cost to the government—taking these and other facts into consideration—will be substantially less than the apparent cost in payments made on certificates.

I emphasize that this program is specifically intended to provide an income to farmers while the essential adjustment in stocks is being accomplished.

There are many virtues in the plan.

It will help remove the crushing burden of surpluses, the essential precondition for the successful operation of a sound farm program.

It will reduce the massive and unproductive storage costs on government holdings—costs that are running about a million dollars a day.

It will provide an element of insurance since farmers are assured income from the reserve acres even in a year of crop failure.

It will ease apprehension among our friends abroad over our surplus-disposal program.

It will harmonize agricultural production with peacetime markets.

B. The Conservation Reserve

The second part of the Soil Bank—the Conservation Reserve Program—affects both today's surpluses and tomorrow's needs of our growing population.

Under the pressures of war and the production incentives continued in postwar years, large areas have come into cultivation which wise land use and sound conservation would have reserved to forage and trees.

In greater or lesser degree this problem exists throughout the nation. Continued cropping of these lands results, on the one hand, in wastage of soil and water resources, and on the other, in production of commodities now in surplus.

Today the nation does not need these acres in harvested crops.

We cannot accurately predict our country's food needs in the years ahead, except that they will steadily increase. We do know, however, that the sound course both for today and tomorrow is wisely to safeguard our precious heritage of food-producing resources so we may hand on an enriched legacy to future generations. The Conservation Reserve Program will contribute materially to that end.

Further, production from the acres today diverted from surplus crops is now seriously affecting other segments of our agriculture. The acreage of feed grains, notably oats, barley and grain sorghums, has been increased. The end product of this diversion has been greatly enlarged supplies of and lower prices for hogs, cattle and dairy and poultry products. Producers of fruit, vegetables, and other crops have been adversely affected. The proposed Conservation Reserve can also make a major contribution to solving this problem of diverted acres.

I propose that farmers be asked to contract voluntarily with the government to shift into forage, trees and water storage cultivated lands most needing conservation measures. Any farmer would be eligible to participate in this program regardless of the crop he produces or the area where his farm is located. I would hope that some 25 million acres would be brought into the Conservation Reserve.

Forest lands under good management are a constant and a renewable resource. One-third of our forest area is in farm woodlands. From this source can come a large share of the lumber, pulpwood and other forest products to meet the growing needs of our expanding economy. The Conservation Reserve can mean productive and protective tree cover for less productive lands now used for cultivated crops.

The government itself must encourage this transfer in order to achieve the advantages to the general welfare that will follow from improved resource use. I propose, therefore, that the government pay a fair share of the costs of establishing the conservation use, up to a specified per acre maximum that will vary by regions. The government's share will be sufficiently high to encourage broad participation and thus assure the success of the program. Further, as the farmer reorganizes his farm along these soil-conserving lines, I recommend that the government provide certain annual payments for a period of years related to the length of time needed to establish the new use of the land. The Congress will need to develop the basis and procedures for determining the amount of the payments. Here, as in the Acreage Reserve Program, I would not let the farmer's cooperation impair his historic acreage allotments.

The farmer, in turn, will agree that the acres put into this Conservation Reserve will be in addition to any land that he may put into the Acreage Reserve, and will represent a reduction in cropland cultivated. He will agree to carry out sound soil and water conservation on these acres, and to refrain from returning them to crop production and from grazing them for a specified period.

I urge the Congress to approve this program with the least possible delay so that a significant part of the desired 25 million acres can come into the program in 1956.

My estimate is that if the Congress acts in time, some 350 million dollars will be invested in the Conservation Reserve during the calendar year 1956, and a total of about a billion dollars over the next 3 years. Sums expended under this program will be in addition to the 250 million dollars provided for the Agricultural Conservation Program for the coming fiscal year.

In return the Conservation Reserve Program will bring these large rewards:

It will result in improved use of soil and water resources for the benefit of this and future generations.

It will increase our supply of much-needed farm-grown forest products.

It will help hold rain and snow where they fall and make possible more ponds and reservoirs on the farm.

It will reduce the undue stimulus to livestock production, and consequent low livestock prices, induced by feed-grain production on diverted acres.

It will similarly provide protection for producers of the many small-acreage crops whose markets are threatened by even a few diverted acres.

In combination with the Acreage Reserve Program for crops in surplus, the Conservation Reserve Program will help during the next several years to reduce the total volume of farm production and improve the balance among different farm commodities, both of which are important to a general improvement in farm prices.

Surplus Disposal

Production adjustments effected by the Soil Bank are needed to halt current additions to surpluses and to reduce stocks on hand. But additional relief must be obtained from the price-depressing influence of these huge carry-overs. In Public Law 480 the Congress has provided basic legislation for this purpose. The problem still exists, but not for lack of vigorous efforts to deal with it.

Surplus disposals have permitted substantial reductions in Commodity Credit Corporation stocks of butter, dried milk, cottonseed oil and meal, flaxseed and linseed oil and seeds. Surplus disposals by the Commodity Credit Corporation have risen from just over half a billion dollars in fiscal 1953 to more than 1.4 billion dollars in fiscal 1954, and to more than 2.1 billion dollars in fiscal 1955.

In the last fiscal year sales of government-owned price-supported commodities into the domestic market reached 403 million dollars. These were made with due care for the adverse effect they might have on prices received by farmers for current sales. Domestic donations to supply food for needy persons totaled an additional 196 million dollars. Overseas disposals, through barter and donations for constructive purposes, totaled 1.1 billion dollars. In spite of these vigorous efforts, the Commodity Credit Corporation investment in price-supported commodities increased by about one billion dollars during the fiscal year.

Because the problem continues to be so serious and stubborn, the Secretary of Agriculture is appointing an Agricultural Surplus Disposal Administrator who will report directly to the Secretary. The duties of the Administrator will relate to all activities of the Department associated with the utilization of Commodity Credit Corporation stocks and of our current abundant production.

Expanded opportunities will be sought to barter agricultural products, which deteriorate and are costly to store, for increased quantities of nonperishable strategic materials. Additional legislation may be needed in this field.

The bulk of price-supported commodities held by the government cannot now by law be sold into the domestic market except at prices equal to at least 105 percent of the support price plus carrying charges. This restriction has worked to the disadvantage of both farmers and the government by blocking sales that would clearly have been advantageous to both. I recommend legislation to permit, under proper safeguards, sales at not less than support levels plus carrying charges.

Present provisions of surplus disposal legislation permit export dispositions of government stocks to friendly nations only. Opportunities clearly to our interest may develop in the future to sell to countries excluded by this legislation. To enable us to realize on such opportunities I recommend repeal of section 304 of Public Law 480.

Strengthening Commodity Programs

Our frontal attack on the problems of surpluses, diverted acres, unbalanced production and unwise land use is carried in major part by the Soil Bank through the Acreage Reserve and the Conservation Reserve Programs.

These proposals are wholly in keeping with the fundamental principles of sound farm policy set forth in my special agricultural message of two years ago. In keeping with these principles the Administration:

(a) Whenever possible will continue to ease or eliminate controls over farmers; and

(b) For commodities on which price supports are discretionary, will continue to support these prices at the highest levels possible without accumulating new price-depressing surpluses.

In keeping with this latter principle, I am advised by the Secretary of Agriculture that, as a direct result of operation of various parts of our present farm program, the supply and demand conditions for soybeans and flaxseed are now such as to warrant an increase in the price support levels for these crops in 1956. The higher support levels will be announced shortly.

In respect to other commodity programs I submit the following specific suggestions.

Presidential Message on the Farm Bill Veto
April 16, 1956
[Public Papers of the Presidents: 1956 (Washington, 1958), 385–90.]

To the House of Representatives:

I am returning herewith, without my approval, H. R. 12, designated as the "Agricultural Act of 1956."

It is with intense disappointment and regret that I must take this action. I assure you my decision has been reached only after thorough consideration and searching my mind and my conscience. Our farm families are suffering reduced incomes. They had a right to expect workable and beneficial legislation to help solve their problems. This bill does not meet their needs.

I am disappointed at the long delays which this legislation encountered. My first special request in this session of the Congress was for prompt remedial farm legislation. A sound, constructive 9-point program to this end was submitted on January 9, with an urgent request for action. It was a program that came from the grassroots. Suggestions and criticisms from large numbers of farm people, in every type of agriculture, from every section of the country, were analyzed and used. It offered no magic panacea because, we can all agree, there is none. It did strike directly at the root of the low price-low income problem.

The problem is price-depressing surpluses. Excess stocks of certain farm commodities have mounted to market-destroying, price-depressing size as a result of war-time price incentives too long continued. Any forward-looking, sound program to meet the needs of farm people must remove the burden of these accumulations. They are depressing net farm income by many hundreds of millions of dollars a year.

H. R. 12 would not correct this situation. It would encourage more surpluses. It would do harm to every agricultural region of the country and also to the interests of consumers. Thus it fails to meet the test of being good for farmers and fair to all our people.

The bill is self-defeating. The Soil Bank proposal has been incorporated. This would be constructive, had it not been encumbered by contradictory provisions. The Soil Bank would provide an income incentive to farmers to reduce production temporarily so that surplus stocks might be reduced. Other provisions of this bill, however, would result in an equal or greater incentive to increase production and accumulate more surplus.

Among the provisions which make this bill unacceptable are: (1) the return to war-time rigid 90 percent of parity supports for the basic commodities; (2) dual parity for wheat, corn, cotton, and peanuts; (3) mandatory price supports for feed grains; (4) multiple-price plans for wheat and rice. The effect of these provisions would be to increase the amount of government control and further add to our price-depressing surpluses.

Specific objections relative to each of these provisions may be summarized as follows:

1. Price supports at war-time 90 percent of parity on basic crops were in effect in each year from 1944 through 1954. They were not responsible for the high commodity prices and high farm income of wartime and the immediate postwar years. Prices were then above support levels due to wartime inflation and the insatiable markets associated with war. Neither did 90 percent supports prevent prices from falling as postwar surplus stocks began to accumulate.

Price supports at wartime 90 percent on the six designated basic crops did encourage production of these crops relative to others. At the same time consumption was discouraged and the use of substitutes was stimulated. Market outlets shrank, and surplus accumulations mounted. Acreage controls had to be invoked, thereby rationing the right to produce. Wheat acreage was reduced from 79 to an allotment of 62 and then to the present 55 million acres. Cotton was cut from 25 to 20 and then on down to the present 17 million acres. These drastic reductions, forced by the application of the price support law, penalized many farmers directly by resulting in shrunken volume and uneconomic farming operations. In addition, acreage diverted from the basic crops shifted surplus problems into many other crops and livestock. Now almost every farmer is adversely affected, regardless of wheat crops or livestock he raises.

If wartime rigid 90 percent supports were the answer to the problem of our farm families, there would now be no problem.

Farm incomes have declined in every year except one between 1947 and 1954, and in all these years 90 percent supports were in effect.

Farmers are not intersted in price alone. What they really want for their families is more net income, which is affected by volume and costs as well as by price. The 90 percent of parity approach focuses on support price alone.

To return now to wartime 90 percent supports would be wrong. Production would be stimulated. Markets would be further destroyed, instead of expanded as must be done. More surplus would accumulate—and surpluses are price depressing. Regimentation by ever stricter production controls would be the end result.

It is inconceivable that we should ask farm families to go deeper into this self-defeating round of cause and effect.

2. The provision for dual parity would result in a permanent double standard of parity for determining price supports. Four crops would receive preferential treatment out of 160 products for which parity prices are figured. There is no justification in logic or in equity for such preferential treatment.

Particularly is this true because, under the working of the modernized parity formula enacted by the Congress, increasing the parity prices of some commodities automatically lowers the parity prices of all other commodities.

If parity prices for wheat, corn, cotton and peanuts are to be higher, then parity prices of the other products must be lower.

To whatever degree prices would be further artificially raised there would be a corresponding stimulus to production, more controls on farmers, reduced consumption, increased accumulations, and lower prices in the market. Such a device for parity manipulations could destroy the parity concept itself. It places a potent weapon in the hands of opponents of all price supports for farmers. We have no right to place the welfare of our farm families in such jeopardy.

3. The provision for mandatory supports on the feed grains would create more problems for farmers. The market for feed grains would shrink as livestock production would come to depend more on forage and less on grain. The flow of feed grains into government stocks would increase and production controls would necessarily be intensified. Price relationships between feed, livestock and livestock products would be distorted. Producers of feeder cattle, feeder lambs, and feeder pigs would be faced with downward pressure on prices. An imbalance would develop between feed crops and livestock products, with all its adverse consequences.

4. The multiple price plans for wheat and rice would have adverse effects upon producers of other crops, upon our relations with friendly foreign nations, and upon our consumers.

There are other serious defects in the bill, such as certain provisions found in the section dealing with the dairy industry. Still other features are administratively bad and would require the hiring of thousands of additional inspectors and enforcers.

I recognize that the restoration by H. R. 12 of wartime mandatory 90% price supports applies only to 1956 crops. This, in combination with other objectionable features of the bill, would put us back on the old road which has proved so harmful to farmers.

Bad as some provisions of this bill are, I would have signed it if in total it could be interpreted as sound and good for farmers and the nation.

After the most careful analysis I conclude that the bill is contradictory and self-defeating even as an emergency relief measure and it would lead to such serious consequences in additional surpluses and production controls as to further threaten the income and the welfare of our farm people.

Because the good features of the bill are combined with so much that would be detrimental to farmers' welfare, to sign it would be to retreat rather than advance toward a brighter future for our farm families.

We now have sound and forward-looking legislation in the Agricultural Act of 1954. Neither that Act, nor any other, can become fully effective so long as it is smothered under the vast surpluses that have accumulated. We imperatively need remedial legislation to remove this burden and enable the fundamentally sound program provided in the Act of 1954 to become workable. Such remedial measures were proposed in my message of January 9.

I am keenly mindful that the failure of the Congress to enact a good new farm bill can have unfavorable effects on farm income in 1956, unless prompt administrative efforts to offset them are made immediately. Particularly, the failure to enact a Soil Bank before planting time this year makes such administrative efforts imperative.

Consequently, we are going to take prompt and decisive administrative action to improve farm income now. I have conferred with the Secretary of Agriculture and the Administration is moving immediately on four major fronts:

1. In 1956, price supports on five of the basic crops—wheat, corn, cotton, rice and peanuts—will be set at a level of at least 82½% of parity. Tobacco will be supported as voted in the referendum in accordance with existing law.

Within this range of price support flexibility, the Administration intends to set minimum support levels that will result in a national average of:

Wheat at $2.00 a bushel

Corn at $1.50 a bushel

Rice at $4.50 per hundred pounds

A separate support for corn not under acreage control in the commercial corn area will be announced at an early date.

Price supports on cotton and peanuts have not yet been announced but will be at least 82½% of parity.

The Secretary of Agriculture will announce shortly the details of the new cotton export sales program.

2. For this year the support price of manufacturing milk will be increased to $3.25 per hundred pounds. The support price of butter fat will be increased to 58.6 cents a pound.

3. We will use Department of Agriculture funds, where assistance will be constructive, to strengthen the prices of perishable farm commodities. We will have well over $400 million for that purpose for the year beginning July 1.

These actions, the Administration will take immediately.

I now request Congress to pass a straight Soil Bank Bill as promptly as possible. It should be in operation before fall seeding for next year's crops. It is vital that we get the Soil Bank authorized in this session of the Congress. There is general agreement on it. I am ready to sign a sound Soil Bank Act as soon as Congress sends it to me. That can be accomplished in a very few days if the leadership in Congress will undertake the task.

This combined program of Administrative action and legislative enactment will begin now to improve the income and welfare of all our farm families.

Here is a challenge for both the Legislative and Executive branches of the Federal Government.

Statement by President Eisenhower
upon Signing the Agricultural Act of 1956
May 28, 1956

[*Public Papers of the Presidents: 1956* (Washington, 1958), 538–40.]

I have today approved the farm bill, H. R. 10875.

The heart of the bill is the soil bank. Its acreage reserve will help bring production of certain crops into balance with their markets. It will check current additions to our price-depressing, market-destroying surplus stocks of farm products. It is a concept rich with promise for improving our agricultural situation.

The conservation reserve feature of the soil bank can be the most significant advance in the conservation field in many years. It will result in improved use of our soil and water resources for the benefit of this and future generations. Together with the forestry provisions of the bill, it will increase our supply of much-needed forest products. It will help hold rain and snow where they fall and will heal with grass and trees the scars of erosion which now mar our countryside. It will make for better land use in those areas of the Great Plains which have experienced dust storms. It will reduce the stimulus to livestock production, induced by feed-grain output on acres diverted from wheat and cotton.

The delay in the bill's enactment, however, makes it virtually impossible to put the soil bank properly into effect in 1956 and I am disappointed that advance payments to farmers are not provided for.

Most of the harmful provisions of the previous farm bill have been deleted or have been substantially modified. Some of them still remain, however, and some new ones have been added.

Sections 202 and 203, which apply to cotton, are particularly unfortunate. This administration is committed to a policy of orderly disposal of agricultural surpluses abroad and a healthy expansion of international trade. This policy is in our national interest and serves to promote the strength of the free world. These two sections call for measures which could result in a serious setback to this policy.

Section 203 requires the Government to follow an inflexible program of cotton export sales with little regard to costs and without adequate regard to the far-reaching economic consequences at home and abroad. In order to avoid seriously disruptive effects, this section of the bill will have to be administered with extreme caution.

Section 202 intensifies further the restrictions already applied on imports of long-staple cotton at a time when domestic cotton of this type is fully competitive with foreign growths and domestic consumption is rising. The same section of the legislation requires the Government to export Commodity Credit Corporation stocks of extra long-staple cotton, a type which we normally do not sell abroad in significant quantities.

Section 204 authorizes the President to negotiate agreements to limit certain imports outside the procedures established by our Trade Agreements legislation. This section represents an undesirable complication in the field of foreign trade.

The effective operation of a two-price plan for rice is faced with several serious problems, which must be carefully evaluated before a decision is made as to whether to institute such a plan.

In freezing acreage allotments for rice and cotton for the next two years at the 1956 level the bill runs counter to the adjustment principle which underlies our basic agricultural legislation.

Despite the shortcomings of the bill, its advantages outweigh its harmful provisions. I am gratified with the constructive features it contains and I am hopeful that the Congress will review and repair its shortcomings.

In the wake of the 1956 election, Republican leaders showed concern over the farm vote. Secretary of Agriculture Ezra Taft Benson, whose belief in reducing Government controls had made him a controversial figure, participated in a frank discussion with Republican National Chairman Meade Alcorn about the overall farm problem.

Memorandum from Department of Agriculture Staff to Secretary Ezra Taft Benson
February 20, 1957
[Anderson Files, Eisenhower Papers.]

Some points the Secretary of Agriculture might wish to mention in his forthcoming discussion with Meade Alcorn:

1. The farm vote. It might be well to admit very frankly that Republican candidates lost a significant number of votes in many farm areas, particularly in the states west of the Mississippi. While drought was a complicating factor, basically it was the decline in farm prices and income over an extended period of years that hurt.

2. The farm outlook. While there was some improvement in farm prices and income during 1956, it would appear that we are still going to have serious problems with a number of farm commodities this year and in 1958.

3. Political activities. It might be well for the Secretary to offer his services in making political speeches as well as the services of his staff members who are excluded from the Hatch Act. The Chairman would no

doubt be interested in a review of the very heavy speaking schedules which the Secretary undertook in 1954 and 1956.

4. The trouble spots. The Chairman would unquestionably appreciate having the Secretary's judgment on the areas where we are likely to have problems in 1958 because of specific commodity problems. This might be the Midwest, with its corn-hog troubles and the Plains and Western states where wheat and cattle predominate. Some comment on Washington, Oregon and Idaho might also be appropriate and the Secretary is, of course, very familiar with this area.

5. Departmental programs and legislative needs. The Secretary might wish to review at least briefly what the Department is doing to eliminate surpluses and to bring production into better balance with current needs. Some discussion of necessary corn legislation would also seem to be in order.

Despite the "soil bank" and the considerable political attention given agriculture, the farm surplus grew. In January, 1958, Eisenhower sent Congress a Special Message on agriculture which proposed reducing surpluses by eliminating controls. The President's proposals were violently attacked by those who believed the federal role indispensable for agricultural stability. The Administration program had a great deal of trouble in Congress, but Eisenhower succeeded in obtaining an end to corn-acreage limitation and the "escalator clause."

Special Message to the Congress by President Eisenhower on Agriculture January 16, 1958

[*Public Papers of the Presidents: 1956* (Washington, 1958), 100–07.]

To the Congress of the United States:

The people of the United States are living in a world of rapid change. Developments both abroad and at home require re-emphasis in some of our efforts, redirection in others. This is true of defense, of education, of industry, and of labor. It is also true of agriculture.

The rapid changes taking place in agriculture are largely the result of a major breakthrough in agricultural science and technology. In recent years agriculture has been experiencing a veritable revolution in productivity.

A century ago, an American farm worker fed himself and three others. Today he feeds himself and 20 others. A century ago, our population was 82 per cent rural. Today it is only one third rural and only 12 per cent of our population actually live on farms.

Farm production per man-hour has doubled since 1940. There has been more change in agriculture within the lifetime of men now living than in the previous two thousand years.

Changes of such magnitude place great stress on our farm people and on the social, political and economic institutions which serve them. Far-reaching adjustments are being made which involve the lives and hopes of 20 million men, women and children on the farms of America.

The scientific revolution in agriculture is irreversible and is continuing. It cannot be avoided and it need not be feared. In recognition of this basic fact, we must find ways of utilizing more completely the abundance that our farm people are now able to produce; we must find ways of further expanding markets for this increased production, not only among our own citizens but among people all over the world who need the food and clothing we produce in such abundance. At the same time we must help our farm people to cope with the sometimes harsh consequences of their own unparalleled ability to produce, while preserving and strengthening free enterprise and the family farm.

Those who have fared best during the years of this agricultural revolution are the farmers on the 2,100,000 commercial farms that produce 90 per cent of the food and fiber that goes to market. Affected quite differently are the farmers on the 2,700,000 other farms that produce relatively little for sale. To them, the farm is primarily a place to live, with an opportunity to grow products for home use, for about three-fourths of their income is derived from off-farm sources.

Commercial family farms have their problems. So do small scale farmers, subsistence farmers and part-time farmers. The problems, however, are not always the same.

There is evidence that those farmers who produce the bulk of our farm products are meeting the problem of adjusting their operations to the changes now in progress. Moreover, there are other indications of strength in our farm economy.

Prices received by farmers on the average are running 3 per cent above those of a year ago.

During the last two years, farm net income has stabilized following several years of decline.

Farm real estate prices are at an all-time high, reflecting a basic optimism in the future earning power and security which farming and farm land ownership offer.

Three-fourths of our farms are owned by those who operate them, the highest percentage on record.

Total debt of our farm people equals only 11 per cent of total assets as compared with 19 per cent before World War II.

Exports of farm products, assisted by special government programs, reached an all-time high of 4.7 billion dollars during the year ending last June 30.

Surplus holdings of farm products in the hands of government appear to have passed their peak. Government investment in price supported commodities now stands at about seven billion dollars, one billion dollars below a year ago.

Substantial progress has been made in programs of education, research, conservation and other activities of proven merit. Work in all those areas has been substantially expanded.

With Government help, farm people, in the best American tradition, have gained bargaining power through their own farmer-owned and farmer-controlled cooperatives.

Yet key problems remain unresolved.

Rising production costs continue to limit net farm income. Prices of articles farmers buy more than doubled from 1939 to 1952. Since then they have risen 3 per cent. Prices received by farmers have not kept pace with their increased production costs. These are hard facts every farmer faces.

Moreover, acreage controls have failed to bring agricultural production into line, despite the severe restrictions they impose on the individual farmer's freedom to produce and to market his products. And unrealistic price support laws, some of which date back to the Agricultural Adjustment Act of 1938, result, as farmers now realize, in loss of markets.

Furthermore, there are large numbers of rural people who have not benefited from price supports. Nor have they benefited as they should from the great changes underway in agriculture. In fact, some have been put at a competitive disadvantage by the onrush of farm technology and other economic changes.

This is true not only in particular rural areas of low income, but for some people in almost every farm community. There are millions of rural people who, for reasons of small farms, poor soils, limited resources, age, inadequate credit, lack of education, poor health or insufficient managerial ability, have been unable to make the adjustments called for by modern technology.

Few of the dollars spent on agricultural programs have been of appreciable help to this group.

Price supports have scant meaning to a farmer with little to sell.

Reductions in acreage to support higher prices are contrary to the needs of a farmer whose production is already too small to give him a proper livelihood.

In my special agricultural message four years ago, I indicated that the Secretary of Agriculture would give attention to the problems peculiar to farm families with low incomes. As a result, the Rural Development Program was initiated. It is widening opportunities for those rural people on the lower rungs of the economic ladder.

For under-employed farmers who desire to continue in agriculture, the Rural Development Program, in cooperation with States and localities, offers research, education, supervised credit, and cost-sharing by the Federal Government in improving land, timber and water resources. Farm and home improvements are a major part of the program.

For those who wish to supplement or replace limited farm incomes with greater income from non-farm sources, there are being established vocational training programs in trades and skills. Additional industries are being established in farming areas where more employment and higher incomes are needed. Farm families which are interested are also being informed of job opportunities in other segments of the economy.

Though only about three years old, the Rural Development Program has already achieved much, and with the increased emphasis planned for the coming year, progress promises to be more rapid in the future.

Recommendations

Basic agricultural legislation now on the books was originally devised as an emergency effort to cope with a depression, then changed to help fight a war, and subsequently revised again in an effort to meet the needs of peace. It has not been adequately modified to deal with the effects of the technological revolution in agriculture. This must now be done.

It is essential that the following major steps be taken this year to improve the status of rural people in greatest need, to aid agricultural adjustment, provide more freedom, expand markets, and, thereby, to help raise farm family income.

First: The Conservation Reserve Program of the Soil Bank should be strengthened, and the Acreage Reserve Program terminated after the 1958 crop. The Conservation Reserve has shown promise in retiring marginal acres from crop production, in aiding the cause of conservation, and in taking whole farms out of production. The program is wholly voluntary and must remain so.

Because of its late enactment, the Acreage Reserve Program was hampered during 1956 in achieving production adjustment. And although the 1957 program succeeded in reducing wheat production by about 175 million bushels, cotton by 2 million bales, and corn by 220 million bushels below what it would otherwise have been, the number of farmers participating in 1958 is likely to be low, in part because of limitations that Congress imposed on the extent of participation by any one farm. So in the future the production adjustment acomplished by the Acreage Reserve is likely to be small.

We should now shift the emphasis of the Soil Bank away from the short-term Acreage Reserve, aimed at reducing surpluses of particular crops to the long-term Conservation Reserve, aimed at overall production adjustment.

This change will aid all farmers, especially the low-income farmer, who will, if he desires, be better able to retire his entire farm from production.

Expansion of the Conservation Reserve will be an effective instrument of adjustment only if it is accompanied by needed changes in price supports. It must not become merely a means of offsetting the production stimulus supplied by price supports held continually at incentive levels.

The Budget Message recommends a Conservation Reserve Program of $450 million for the 1959 calendar year.

Second: Authority to increase acreage allotments for cotton, wheat, rice, peanuts and tobacco should be provided. Under present legislation, acreage allotments and price supports for certain of the basic crops are determined by legal formulas. Under these formulas, allotments have already been cut sharply. Allotments for certain crops are likely to be reduced even further, despite growing evidence that acreage restrictions have not brought about needed adjustments.

Authority should be provided for the Secretary of Agriculture, in accordance with criteria which the Secretary will propose to the Congress, to increase allotments up to 50 per cent above the levels determined by existing formulas.

The law already specifies that the Secretary may provide price support at levels above those determined by formula, and this authority has been used. The law should also provide authority to increase acreage allotments when the statistical formula yields results clearly contrary to the general interest. But any acreage increases must be related to price adjustments which will permit the growth of markets necessary to absorb the increased production.

Such liberalization of acreage allotments as is possible would permit greater efficiency and higher incomes for small farmers who now are sharply restricted in the size of their operations.

Third: Acreage allotments for corn should be eliminated. The corn program has not worked. Huge surpluses have accumulated. As surpluses rise, present legislation provides that allotments must shrink. As allotments shrink, participation in the corn program dwindles. A year ago, 62 per cent of the corn farmers who voted in the referendum favored the elimination of corn acreage allotments. In 1957, only about 14 per cent of the corn production in the commercial corn area was eligible for the full price support. Thus, as allotments shrink, participation spirals downward, and price-depressing surpluses spiral upward.

Fourth: The escalator clauses in the basic law should be abolished. Provisions now in the law require that price supports be raised as soon as the surplus is reduced. This means that as one surplus is moved, incentives are automatically provided to build another. Until this basic law is changed, farm people can expect to be kept continually under the shadow of price-depressing surpluses.

The Soil Bank and surplus disposal programs have already cut deeply enough into our surplus to throw these escalator clauses into action to build more surpluses. Elimination of these escalator clauses is necessary if surplus disposal programs and the Soil Bank are to achieve their purpose.

Fifth: The overall range within which price supports may be provided should be substantially widened. Presently, price supports must be provided by rigid formula for cotton, wheat, corn, rice, peanuts, tobacco and dairy products between 75 and 90 per cent of parity. This range is too narrow to permit the growth of markets needed to absorb the production which, despite acreage controls, our farms appear certain to produce. Price supports for the above-named commodities should be determined administratively between 60 per cent and 90 per cent of parity, using the eight guidelines now provided by law for practically all other commodities. This needed change in price-support policy would open the door to market expansion, increased acreage allotments and greater freedom to produce.

For commodities like the feed grains, with respect to which the Secretary of Agriculture has had wide discretion in the past, price support has been offered at levels as high as could be justified under the criteria specified by law. This will be the Secretary's practice under the recommended legislation.

Sixth: Price supports for cotton should be based on the average quality of the crop. For cotton the law specifies that supports must be based on a grade that is far below the average quality. The law should be corrected to put cotton price supports on the same basis as for all other crops.

Seventh: The membership of the Commodity Credit Corporation Advisory Board should be enlarged and the Board's responsibilities increased. The recommended changes in determining acreage allotments and price support levels will make additional administrative discretion a necessity. To assist the Secretary of Agriculture in exercising this discretion, the bi-partisan Commodity Credit Corporation Advisory Board should be increased in number from five to seven. Members should be appointed by the President as at present, but with confirmation by the Senate. The Board should advise the Secretary regarding the establishing of price supports, determining of acreage allotments and related subjects.

Eighth: The Agricultural Trade Development and Assistance Act should be extended. This law is one of the major authorities for moving surplus commodities. The law should be extended for one year with an additional $1.5 billion authorized for sales for foreign currencies. But it must not, however, be allowed to become a device to postpone needed production and price adjustments. The extension should be limited to one year to give Congress the opportunity for annual review.

Ninth: Research efforts aimed at increasing industrial uses of farm products should be expanded. Our farms and forests are a major source of our raw materials. To a greater degree than at present, these raw materials can be used in industry, thereby broadening markets for our abundant farm products. New uses and new markets can be developed for our surplus crops. To bring this about, increased utilization research is needed and is proposed in the Budget Message. This will be moving in the direction recommended by the President's Commission on Increased Industrial Use of Agricultural Products.

In addition to the nine steps outlined here, the Congress should, as recommended in the Budget Message, (a) extend the National Wool Act, (b) continue the special school milk programs, (c) broaden the sources of funds for the Rural Electrification Administration, (d) require State participation in programs to relieve the effects of drought or other natural disaster, and (e) improve conservation accomplishment by restricting cost-sharing to those practices which achieve longer lasting conservation benefits.

These several recommendations constitute a Farm, Food and Fiber program which will assist our farmers to adjust to today's rapidly changing economy. It is a progress program that can make a substantial contribution to the well-being of America's farm families.

Neither the "soil bank" nor the Agriculture Act of 1958 solved the farm surplus problem. In fact, surpluses continued to grow. Secretary Benson strongly believed that the only solution to agriculture's problems was the "free market," where no restraints would be placed on and no protection given to farmers. In line with this view, the President prepared another Special Message, hoping that public pressure could be brought to bear on Congress. The President's staff drafted a national television address to be delivered when "the Special Message on agriculture goes up." As it turned out, however, the President never gave the proposed speech.

Congress did not pass the Administration's bill, but instead enacted legislation for specific crops. These laws—on wheat and tobacco—failed to meet the President's guidelines, so he vetoed them. The wheat bill veto (June 25) provides a good insight into his objections. As the Administration entered its final year, the surplus provided a greater problem than it had seven years before. An Eisenhower staff member expressed the exasperating circumstances in a letter to a friend. In it he said, "Thank goodness for one fellow who can dispose of his produce without government aid. You may have read that funds now invested in surplus are at an all time high."*

Draft of Proposed Speech for President Eisenhower
on Agriculture
January 28, 1959
[Official File 99-G-4, Eisenhower Papers.]

Good evening. I want to talk about a matter that concerns every American— our farm program and its relation to the food you eat and the taxes you pay.

*Clarence Francis to James Foster, January 12, 1960, Francis Files, Eisenhower Papers.

Today (or yesterday or whenever) I sent to the Congress a special message on agriculture. This message said, in effect, that the farm program we have had for so many years is outmoded and costly, and should be changed.

Our farm people have provided our country with the best diet ever enjoyed by any people at any time in the world's history. No other nation ever had such an abundant supply of such fine food. We are all grateful to our farm people for this dependable supply of wholesome, nutritious food and, I may add, for the fiber and other products that provide for our comfort and convenience. We will continue to increase our efforts to expand further the markets for our abundance.

Frankly, the country has done better in farm production than in farm legislation.

Government programs of price-support and production control were developed a quarter of a century ago in an effort to meet problems caused by the Great Depression. These programs were changed to stimulate production during the war. They have been only slightly modified since that time. We did make some small changes. They were in the right direction but they didn't go far enough.

On four separate occasions I have sent special messages to the Congress on this subject. The changes that were made were too few and too small to keep ahead of the scientific advance in agriculture.

The truth is that these old programs are not suited to present-day agriculture.

A program which dates back to the horse-and-buggy days isn't suited to gasoline-and-tractor farming.

So the government farm program has gotten into trouble.

Surpluses have built up. Markets have been lost. Controls have failed. Costs have risen.

Let me spell it out. This program is bankrupt.

Stocks of wheat are so great that if all wheat farmers took a year's vacation we would still have enough for all our needs. But our wheat farmers are not on vacation. They're coming up with another big crop.

While we pulled back our production of cotton, countries in Latin America and in the Mediterranean area have increased their acreage and taken over our markets.

Government has had to move in on agriculture and specify, crop by crop, what an individual farmer could grow.

Costs of these outmoded programs have risen to indefensible and dangerous levels.

I don't think the American people would begrudge these costs if they thought the problem was being solved. But obviously it's not being solved. We're not getting our money's worth.

The program doesn't help the small operator much, if it helps him any. The test is: "Who gets the money?" Of course, much of the money never goes to the farmers at all: it goes to the middlemen who store the products, and the government officials who do the paper work. A billion dollars a year, just to carry an unneeded inventory of wheat and corn and cotton and whatnot! Of the money which does go to farmers, the big operators get the biggest share. Half the farms, that is, the large ones, get ninety percent of the money. The other half, the small ones, get only ten percent of the money.

In all these difficulties, the farm people have my greatest sympathy. They have been smothered by surpluses and subjected to harsh controls by the failure of programs which often were not of their choosing. They are not to be blamed. They have responded to attractive mandatory support prices by increasing their production, just as anyone would.

There are produced, in the United States, some 250 farm commodities. The law has required that prices of twelve of these be supported at prescribed minimum levels. It is this requirement, together with the level of required support, that has created our farm surplus problems. Farmers who produce cattle, hogs, poultry, fruits, vegetables, and various other products the prices of which are not supported,—as well as those who produce crops the prices of which are supported at discretionary levels—have generally experienced growing markets rather than a build-up of stocks in warehouses.

I have recommended to the Congress that we make forthright changes in our farm price supports. If this is done, the surplus can be reduced, the costs cut, production controls relaxed and markets developed. Our farm people can make more of their own decisions. The Government can resume its proper function of promoting farm research, protecting soil and water resources, improving farm credit and so on. We would help build and stabilize markets, not price ourselves out of them.

The issue here is not a partisan one. The issue is whether or not the government's role with respect to agriculture is to be one that makes sense.

I think you want that program to make sense.

Thank you.

Special Message to the Congress by President Eisenhower on Agriculture January 29, 1959

[*Public Papers of the Presidents: 1959* (Washington, 1960), 146–51.]

To the Congress of the United States:

There are produced, in the United States, some 250 farm commodities. The law has required that prices of twelve of these be supported at prescribed minimum levels. It is this requirement, together with the level of required support, that has created our farm surplus problems. Farmers who produce cattle, hogs, poultry, fruits, vegetables, and various other products the prices of which are not supported—as well as those who produce crops the prices of which are supported at discretionary levels—have generally experienced growing markets rather than a build-up of stocks in warehouses.

Three of the twelve mandatory products (wheat, corn, and cotton) account for about eighty-five percent of the Federal inventory of price-supported commodities though they produce only twenty percent of the total cash farm income.

The price-support and production-control program has not worked.

1. *Most of the dollars are spent on the production of a relatively few large producers.*

Nearly a million and a half farms produce wheat. Ninety percent of the expenditures for price support on wheat result from production of about half of these farms—the largest ones.

Nearly a million farms produce cotton. Seventy-five percent of the expenditures for cotton price support result from production of about one-fourth of these farms—the largest ones.

For other supported crops, a similarly disproportionate share of the expenditure goes to the large producers.

For wheat, cotton, and rice producers who have allotments of one-hundred acres or more, the net budgetary expenditures per farm for the present fiscal year are approximately as follows:

	Per farm
Wheat	$7,000
Cotton	$10,000
Rice	$10,000

Though some presently unknown share of these expenditures will eventually be recovered through surplus disposal, the final cost of the operation will undoubtedly be impressively large.

Clearly, the existing price support program channels most of the dollars to those who store the surpluses and to relatively few producers of a few crops. It does little to help the farmers in greatest difficulty. For small operators the Rural Development Program approach, which helps develop additional sources of income, has clearly demonstrated that it is a far better alternative.

2. *The control program doesn't control.*

Mandatory supports are at a level which so stimulates new technology and the flow of capital into production as to offset, in large part, the control effort.

Despite acreage allotments and marketing quotas, despite a large soil bank program and despite massive surplus disposal, government investment in farm commodities will soon be at a new record high. On July 1, 1959, total government investment in farm commodities will total $9.1 billion.

Investment in commodities for which price support is mandatory will total $7.6 billion, of which $7.5 billion will consist of those crops designated by law as basic commodities: wheat, corn, cotton, rice, peanuts, and tobacco. And these stocks are increasing rather than diminishing.

We already hold such huge stocks of wheat that if not one bushel of the oncoming crop were harvested we would still have more than enough for domestic use, export sales, foreign donation and needed carry-over for an entire year.

3. *The program is excessively expensive.*

When the 1958 crops have come into Government ownership, the cost, in terms of storage, interest and other charges, of managing our inventory of supported crops, for which commercial markets do not exist at the support levels, will be running at a staggering rate, in excess of a billion dollars a year. Unless fundamental changes are made, this annual cost will rise.

This sum is approximately equal to the record amount being spent in fiscal 1960 by the Federal Government on all water resource projects in the United States including power, flood control, reclamation and improvement of rivers and harbors.

During the present fiscal year, the net budgetary outlay for programs for the stabilization of farm prices and farm income will be $5.4 billion. $4.3 billion of this is for commodities for which price supports are mandatory. While some unpredictable part of this outlay will be recovered in later years through sales for dollars, sales for foreign currency and through barter, the cost will be great, especially when compared with the net income of all farm operators in the United States, which in 1958 was $13 billion. Budgetary expenditures primarily for the support of farm prices and farm income are now equal to about forty percent of net farm income.

Not a bushel of wheat nor a pound of cotton presently is exported without direct cost to the Federal Treasury.

Heavy costs might be justifiable if they were temporary, if they were solving the problems of our farmers, and if they were leading to a better balance of supplies and markets. But unfortunately this is not true.

These difficulties are not to be attributed to any failure on the part of our farm people, who have done an outstanding job of producing efficiently. They have in fact responded to the price incentive as farm people—and other people—traditionally have.

Our farm families deserve programs that build markets. Instead they have programs that lose markets. This is because the overall standards for the programs that they have are outdated relationships that existed nearly half a century ago. This was before sixty percent of our present population was born.

At that time it took 106 man hours to grow and harvest one-hundred bushels of wheat. In recent years it has taken not 106 but 22. Since then the yield of wheat has doubled. Similar dramatic changes have occurred for other crops.

It is small wonder that a program developed many years ago to meet the problems of depression and war is ill-adapted to a time of prosperity, peace, and revolutionary changes in production.

The need to reduce the incentives for excess production has been explicit in the three special messages on agriculture which I have previously sent to the Congress. The point has repeatedly been made by the Secretary of Agriculture in his testimony and in his statements to the Congress. The Congress has moved in the right direction but by an insufficient amount. There has been a general tendency to underestimate the pace at which farm technology has been moving forward. Hence there has been a tendency to underestimate the production-inducing effect of the prescribed minimum price support levels.

Recommendation

I recommend that prices for those commodities subject to mandatory supports be related to a percentage of the average market price during the immediately preceding years. The appropriate percentage of the average market price should be discretionary with the Secretary of Agriculture at a level not less than seventy-five and not more than ninety percent of such average in accordance with the general guidelines set forth in the law. Growers of corn, our most valuable crop, have already chosen, by referendum vote, program changes which include supports based on such an average of market prices.

If, despite the onrush of science in agriculture, resulting in dramatic increases in yields per acre, the Congress still prefers to relate price supports to existing standards, the Secretary should be given discretion to establish the level in accordance with the guidelines now fixed by law for all commodities except those for which supports presently are mandatory.

Either of these changes would be constructive. The effect of either would be to reconcile the farm program with the facts of modern agriculture, to reduce the incentive for unrealistic production, to move in the direction of easing production controls, to permit the growth of commercial markets and to cut the cost of federal programs.

As we move to realistic farm programs, we must continue our vigorous efforts further to expand markets and find additional outlets for our farm products, both at home and abroad. In these efforts, there is an immediate and direct bearing on the cause of world peace. Food can be a powerful instrument for all the free world in building a durable peace. We and other surplus-producing nations must do our very best to make the fullest constructive use of our abundance of agricultural products to this end. These past four years our special export programs have provided friendly food-deficit nations with four billion dollars worth of farm products that we have in abundance. I am setting steps in motion to explore anew with other surplus-producing nations all practical means of utilizing the various agricultural surpluses of each in the interest of reinforcing peace and the well-being of friendly peoples throughout the world—in short, using food for peace.

Certain details regarding the needed changes in law, particularly with reference to wheat, are appended to this message in the form of a memorandum to me from the Secretary of Agriculture.

Difficulties of the present program should not drive us to programs which would involve us in even greater trouble. I refer to direct payment programs, which could soon make virtually all farm people dependent, for a large share of their income, upon annual appropriations from the Federal Treasury. I refer also to various multiple price programs, which would tax the American consumer so as to permit sale for feed and export at lower prices.

To assist the Congress in discharging its responsibility, the Administration stands ready, as always, to provide the appropriate Committees with studies, factual data and judgments. Continuation of the price support and production control programs in their present form would be intolerable.

I urge the Congress to deal promptly with this problem.

Presidential Message on the Wheat Program Veto
June 25, 1959

[Public Papers of the Presidents: 1959 (Washington, 1960), 476–77.]

To the Senate:

I am returning herewith, without my approval, S. 1968, a bill "To amend the Agricultural Act of 1949, as amended, the Agricultural Adjustment Act of 1938, as amended, and Public Law 74, Seventy-seventh Congress, as amended."

This bill seeks to enact temporary wheat legislation. It would require wheat producers to reduce their acreage by 25 percent and at the same time would provide for increases in price supports on wheat to 90 percent of parity.

On May 15 when I approved the Joint Resolution for extending the date for announcing the 1960 wheat acreage allotments and marketing quotas I said, "It is my hope that these additional two weeks will be used by the Congress to enact realistic and constructive—not stopgap—wheat legislation."

The proposed legislation embodied in H.R. 7246 is stopgap. It is not realistic. It is not constructive. It goes backward instead of forward. It is not in the interest of the wheat farmers of America.

The bill disregards the facts of modern agriculture. The history of acreage control programs—particularly in the case of wheat—reveals that they just do not control production. Under acreage controls in the 1954-58 period, acreage was reduced by over 25 percent but at the same time yield per acre was increased by about 30 percent. The same situation would be likely to happen in 1960 and 1961. The poorest acres would be retired from production and all the modern technology would be poured onto the remainder.

Hence the bill would probably increase, and in any event would not substantially decrease, the cost of the present excessively expensive wheat program now running at approximately $700 million a year.

In my January 29, 1959, special message on Agriculture, I recommended that price supports be related to a percentage of the average market price during the immediately preceding years. In this message I also stated that if in spite of the tremendous increases in yields per acre the Congress still preferred to relate price support to existing standards then the Secretary should have discretion in establishing support levels in accordance with guidelines now in the law.

Contrary to the recommendations I made, this bill prescribes for a sick patient another dose of what caused his illness. The proposed return to the discredited high, rigid price supports would hasten the complete collapse of the entire wheat program.

While the hour is late I feel that this Congress still has the opportunity to adopt realistic wheat legislation beneficial to all segments of our economy.

In 1954 the United States had supported a United Nations proposal specify-
ing that countries with an agricultural surplus sell for local currencies their
unneeded commodities to countries requiring additional food stuffs. Con-
gress enacted legislation to carry out this plan under the popular title of
Food for Peace. The Eisenhower Administration believed that this idea
represented a great boon to foreign policy objectives. By 1958 the program
had been generally successful. However, details of the impact of this and
other approaches needed clarification. The State Department assigned John
H. Davis to this task. Later, Secretary of Agriculture Benson forwarded to
Sherman Adams some of Davis' findings. In May, 1959, a Food for Peace
Conference met in Washington, D.C., and the President asked Benson to
restate the American commitment. By 1960, Food for Peace had become a
well-established part of American foreign policy. Details of the program
appeared from time to time in a "Fact Sheet."

Memorandum from Secretary Ezra Taft Benson
to The Assistant to the President Sherman Adams
April 29, 1958
[Official File 106-I-2, Eisenhower Papers.]

You are aware from our earlier discussions that John H. Davis, formerly
Assistant Secretary of Agriculture, has been engaged by the State Department to make a study of how U. S. farm surpluses can better serve American
foreign policy. A copy of the study is attached.

I

The first part of this study has been completed. The cogent findings are
these:

1. Our surplus production capacity in agriculture is likely to be of some duration.

2. Need for food in many countries outside the Soviet Bloc, above what
can be produced in these countries or bought with foreign exchange, is likely
to be large for some time to come. The maintenance of political stability in
these countries will probably require that some share of this need be met by
the United States.

3. This dual problem (our excess capacity and foreign need) can be
alleviated by a two-sided 5-year program:

   (a) Further adjustments in our programs for American agriculture,
       both administrative and legislative.
   (b) A Food-for-Peace program based on P. L. 480, gradually phased
       out as the receiving nations are assisted to raise their own produc-
       tion levels.

II

To adopt a program such as Davis recommends would involve little change from what we are now doing except that:

We would be *positive* instead of *negative:*

We would recognize that the problem is of *some duration* rather than *temporary;*

We would emphasize the *helpful foreign policy aspects* rather than to treat the operation as *iniquitous surplus disposal.*

III

The program proposed would have both advantages and disadvantages.

Advantages

1. Such an operation is likely to come into being in any case. The question is whether we give it leadership.

2. Such a step would maximize our greatest advantage over the Soviet Union. It would be agriculture's share in our foreign policy.

3. Properly handled, it would lift production and living levels in the free world.

4. Much credit would be reflected to this country for good stewardship of our scientific know-how, for our compassion for the world's needy and for our contribution to peace.

5. The farm policy focus would shift from the negative fight to reduce price supports to the more positive approach: "Use our abundance in the cause of peace."

6. Such a program may increase support for the President's legislative recommendations in the Agricultural Message of January 1958.

Disadvantages

1. If production levels in the recipient countries should fail to rise sufficiently, these countries would become dependent upon us for continuing help. We would have created a group of more or less permanent relief clients.

2. Unwisely handled, such a program could antagonize other agricultural exporting nations.

3. Such a program might easily become an excuse to further postpone needed changes in farm legislation.

4. Some people would object to spending so much American effort in behalf of other nations.

5. We might be accused of embracing a proposal favored by Senator Humphrey and others from the opposition camp.

IV

We have reviewed the proposal in the Department of Agriculture. While we are not now ready to advocate the program proposed, we consider that it merits consideration. It is my understanding that this also is the attitude of the State Department. Therefore, I propose the following steps:

1. The attitude of the President should be ascertained as to whether he considers the proposal deserving of serious consideration.

2. If the President is so inclined, the proposal should be reviewed by the various Departments in the Francis Committee on Agricultural Surplus Disposal, and in the Randall Commission on Foreign Economic Policy.

V

If the proposal receives approval in this review and if the White House approves, one or more of these steps could be taken:

1. The President could call an International Conference on Food for Peace. (A draft statement is attached, outlining what such a Conference might attempt.)

2. The Secretary of Agriculture could launch the proposal in a series of speeches.

3. The proposal could be made a part of the Administration's legislative program for 1959. (The actual legislative changes which would be required are not many. Public Law 480 in slightly modified form would be a suitable vehicle.)

I would be happy to confer with you on this matter as convenient.

President Eisenhower to Secretary Ezra Taft Benson
May 4, 1959
[Official File 106-I-2, Eisenhower Papers.]

Dear Mr. Secretary:

I should like to have you present the following message to visiting delegates to the Food for Peace conference which begins this evening:

"It gives me much pleasure to extend to you a cordial welcome, and to thank you for joining us in exploring anew the possibilities of more effectively using food abundance for peace.

It has long been an ideal of your countries and ours and of others as well, to alleviate hunger and to assist people of under-developed areas to achieve a more productive utilization of their resources. This assistance to them, coupled with realistic trade policies between them and us, leads to their economic independence, and to a mutually rewarding partnership in normal trade.

Far more has been done in recent years, in terms of practical helpfulness, than in any equal period in history. The countries represented at this conference have been among those in the forefront in this effort. It is encouraging to note that an attitude of understanding, which recognizes need, and an inclination toward practicality, which helps to meet it, have grown apace. It is fitting, therefore, that we now renew our efforts to give practical application to the ideals envisaged in the term Food for Peace.

Confident that your deliberation will contribute to world economic improvement, freedom and peace, I extend to you my appreciation and best wishes."

Food for Peace Fact Sheet
July, 1960
[Areeda Files, Eisenhower Papers.]

The term Food-for-Peace represents the concept that only with an adequate food supply can the world's people make the kind of progress that helps to assure peace.

The Food-for-Peace program supports the upward progress of the less developed part of the world. In practice, it calls for broad sharing of food resources by the "have" nations with the "have not" nations. This greater sharing of world food supplies has both utilitarian and humanitarian implications:

> It provides expanded outlets for the agricultural abundance of exporting countries;
> It strengthens the economic development efforts of recipient countries and helps them to achieve progress in a free and democratic way.

Food and peace have been closely linked in the minds of Americans for many years. After both World Wars, supplies from U. S. farms have helped to rehabilitate stricken areas. We have been the first to make massive quantities of agricultural supplies available as part of the energy requirements of Twentieth Century economic development. We have taken as a precept of our foreign policy that as long as we have the supplies to help, men shall not starve.

Today's Food-for-Peace program was announced by the President on January 29, 1959, when he said in a message to the Congress: "I am setting steps in motion to explore anew with other surplus-producing nations all practical means of utilizing the various agricultural surpluses of each in the interest of reinforcing peace and the well-being of friendly peoples through-out the world—in short, using food for peace."

Other friendly exporting nations have been invited to work with the U.S. under the Food-for-Peace concept to make maximum use of agricultural products in support of world peace and progress. A good beginning in this direction has been made with the establishing in 1959 of a 5-nation Wheat Utilization Committee—Argentina, Australia, Canada, France, and the United States, with the Food and Agriculture Organization of the United Nations as observer-adviser. As a recent accomplishment, the Committee has completed a joint study of opportunities for greater consumption of wheat in certain Far Eastern countries.

How the Program Works

The Food-for-Peace program is a supplement to the buying and selling for cash that accounts for most Free World distribution of farm products. Every effort is made to assure that the program does not displace cash transactions. Rather, it provides a means whereby a needy country may obtain farm products when—for reasons of dollar shortage—it lacks ability to buy in the cash market.

The Food-for-Peace program complements the world's commercial marketing system. Commercial marketing is regarded as the preferred way to distribute commodities. The problem is that only countries that have vigorous economies are able to be active in and benefit fully from the commercial marketing system. The Food-for-Peace program helps underdeveloped countries to meet some of their most pressing food import needs during their transitional period as they try to develop more vigorous economies and thereby become able to rely more fully on the traditional commercial market. During this development period the Food-for-Peace program adds to world trade, bringing a total movement of agricultural products that is greater than would be possible under cash transactions alone.

The chief United States instrument of the Food-for-Peace program is Public Law 480, the Agricultural Trade Development and Assistance Act of 1954, as amended. This is the major legislative authority of the U. S. for exporting surplus farm products outside the normal commercial channels of trade. It permits these types of special export activity: Sales of surplus agricultural commodities for foreign currencies, donations to foreign governments and needy people, barter for strategic and other foreign materials, and long term dollar credits to facilitate foreign buying of U. S. farm products. More than 100 countries and territories are participating or have participated in the program. In the 1959-60 year (ending June 30, 1960) shipments of U. S. farm products under special programs reached the following estimated totals, based on export market value:

U. S. agricultural exports: Amount under U. S. Government programs by type of program and amount sold for dollars, fiscal year 1960 (estimated).

Item	*Amount*
Government programs:	(Million dollars)
Public Law 480:	
Sales for foreign currency	825
Disaster relief	65
Donated to needy persons thru vol. agencies	110
Barter	150
Mutual Security:	
Sales for foreign currency	160
Total under Government programs	1,310
Sales for dollars	3,190
TOTAL U.S. FARM EXPORTS	4,500

Exports of U. S. agricultural products in fiscal year 1960 reached an estimated value of $4.5 billion. Of this amount, an estimated 71 percent was sales for dollars and 29 percent was exports under special Government programs, principally Public Law 480.

SALES FOR FOREIGN CURRENCIES: The largest component of the Public Law 480 program is Title I which provides for the sale of U. S. agricultural surpluses to needy countries with payment made in their own currencies. This program brings needy countries more supplies than they could afford to buy with their own limited dollar resources, thus helping to meet consumer needs. A substantial part of foreign currencies received by the U.S. is lent back to such countries, thus helping to finance their economic development.

Since the program's beginning in 1954, it has committed for export more than $5 billion worth of U. S. agricultural commodities (basis world market prices).

Agreements have been made under this authority with 38 countries, involving shipment of the following approximate quantities: 1,725 million bushels of wheat and wheat flour equivalent, 240 million bushels of feed grains, 4.5 million bales of cotton, 255 million pounds of dairy products, more than 4 billion pounds of fats and oils, 278 million pounds of tobacco, 63 million bags of rice, and smaller quantities of other commodities.

The largest single agreement under Title I was signed on May 4, 1960, between the United States and India. It provides for the sale to India over a four-year period of approximately 587 million bushels of U. S. wheat and 22 million bags of U. S. rice. One-fourth of the wheat and all of the rice may be used as food reserves. For these commodities, plus some ocean transportation cost, India will pay the U. S. $1,276 million in rupees. About 80 percent of the rupees will be made available to the Indian Government as loans and grants for economic development.

DONATIONS: Public Law 480 authorizes two types of donation programs. One involves direct grants of food to foreign governments to help meet famine or other need abroad. The other involves donations of food to indigents abroad through American voluntary agencies which, in turn, are responsible for the distribution overseas.

U. S. food grants to foreign governments to help meet disaster conditions abroad totaled $434 million (cost to U. S. Government) during the 5½ years ending December 31, 1959. During fiscal year 1960 disaster relief programs operated in 18 countries, including Morocco and Chile. In addition to disaster relief, such commodities have aided refugees, supported work relief programs, and helped school lunch programs.

U. S. food donations have been made through American voluntary agencies since 1950, having been originated in programs that preceded Public Law 480 (and greatly expanded under Public Law 480). Since 1950, well over 9 billion pounds of U. S. surplus commodities valued at over $1.5 billion (cost to U. S. Government) have been donated to foreign needy persons through 31 agencies, including the United Nations Children's Fund, operating in 109 countries and territories. Dairy products accounted for nearly 40 percent of the volume. At present 21 agencies have programs in 92 countries. Recipients of food assistance include maternal and child welfare centers, health centers, school lunch programs, needy families, refugees, and institutions for the aged, blind, orphans, etc. Commodities currently being donated are corn, corn meal, wheat, wheat flour, rice, and nonfat dry milk. Foods donated are identified as gifts of the American people.

BARTER: The barter program of Public Law 480 permits contracts between the Commodity Credit Corporation and private U. S. business firms to exchange CCC-owned agricultural commodities for strategic or other materials. The authority preceded but was broadened by Public Law 480. The value of barter exports from July 1954 through December 1959 totaled $1,140 million (export market value), involving wheat, cotton, corn, and other surplus commodities. In the past three years various precautions have been adopted to insure that barter transactions do not displace normal commercial exports.

LONG-TERM CREDIT: Late in 1959 the Congress added a new authority (Title IV) to Public Law 480 under which the U. S. may enter into agreements with friendly nations for delivery of surplus agricultural commodities for periods up to ten years. This would provide longer-term supply commitments for purchases of such commodities for consumption during periods of economic development. Meanwhile, the resources of such nations would be utilized more effectively for industrial and other economic development. Dollar payment for commodities delivered would be made in approximately equal annual amounts with interest, for periods of up to twenty years. This program is now in the pilot stage of implementation.

Mutual Benefit

The benefit of Public Law 480 to foreign recipients is obvious. From its beginning in 1954 through December 1959, export program commitments totaled $9.3 billion (CCC cost). This is approximately equal to half the value of the annual U. S. agricultural crop.

Appreciation was indicated following the recent Food-for-Peace agreement with India when its Hindustan Times commented editorially: "Outside the Marshall Plan, this program is the largest single act of aid from free world to free world. It is an unprecedented step undertaking to cover our food deficit for the next four years as well as to help build our buffer stock. American people have given India assurance they no longer need be under nagging fear of recurring food crises. Also, large amounts of rupee finance can be used to further development of the Third Plan. Indo-American political and economic relations are at an all-time high level of warmth and friendliness."

The United States receives two principal benefits from this program. One is the strengthening of U. S. foreign relationships. The other is the reduction of pressure from surpluses due to the additional export movement under Public Law 480.

Wheat is an example. The so-called surplus of U. S. wheat is approximately 1.4 billion bushels. Had there been no sales for foreign currency and had the same rate of production been maintained, existing carryover stocks of wheat could be twice their current size.

It has been noted that since 1954, approximately one-fourth of U. S. agricultural exports have been made under the Public Law 480 program. In 1959, the program accounted for three-fourths of U. S. vegetable oil exports, two-thirds of wheat exports, and over one-third of rice and cotton exports.

Some side benefits also accrue. For example, a portion of foreign currencies resulting from sales to other countries are used in promoting foreign sales for U. S. farm products in the dollar market. This work is being carried out in more than 50 countries in cooperation with U. S. private trade groups. This work helps to expand cash sales of U. S. farm products in the world market.

About 65 percent of the foreign currencies is being used to promote economic development in participating countries through loans and grants to these governments and loans to private U. S. and foreign business firms. About 7 percent is being used for military assistance grants to mutual security countries and the remainder pays U. S. expenses abroad and finances U. S. agency programs such as agricultural market development, State Department exchange programs, informational and scientific programs.

Further Sources of Information

Sales of U. S. farm surpluses
    for foreign currencies ....USDA/Foreign Agricultural Service
Donations for disaster
    relief ....International Cooperation Administration
Donations through U. S. voluntary
    agencies ....USDA/Agricultural Marketing Service and ICA
Barter ....USDA/Commodity Stabilization Service
Uses of foreign currencies ....ICA and USDA/FAS

Public Law 480

AN ACT to increase the consumption of United States agricultural commodities in foreign countries, to improve the foreign relations of the United States, and for other purposes.

Be it enacted by the Senate and House of Representatives of the United States of America in Congress assembled, That this Act may be cited as the "Agricultural Trade Development and Assistance Act of 1954."

SEC. 2: It is hereby declared to be the policy of Congress to expand international trade among the United States and friendly nations, to facilitate the convertibility of currency, to promote the economic stability of American agriculture and the national welfare, to make maximum efficient use of surplus agricultural commodities in furtherance of the foreign policy of the United States, and to stimulate and facilitate the expansion of foreign trade in agricultural commodities produced in the United States by providing a means whereby surplus agricultural commodities in excess of the usual marketings of such commodities may be sold through private trade channels, and foreign currencies accepted in payment therefor. It is further the policy to use foreign currencies which accrue to the United States under this Act to expand international trade, to encourage economic development, to purchase strategic materials, to pay United States obligations abroad, to promote collective strength, and to foster in other ways the foreign policy of the United States. (7 U.S.C. 1691)

3. THE ADMINISTRATION AND THE 1958 RECESSION

During the summer of 1957 economic indicators showed a fall in industrial production and a rise in unemployment. However, the cumulative effects of retrenchment did not become obvious until the end of the year. By January, 1958, the recession had taken center stage on the domestic scene. Inside the Administration, staff members pondered what actions should be taken, while people outside the Government also made far-ranging suggestions— from doing nothing to replaying Franklin Rossevelt's "Hundred Days." Eisenhower tended towards a policy of wait-and-watch, even though some members of his staff were terribly nervous about the economic situation. On January 23, 1958, Arthur Larson, a presidential speechwriter, sided with advisors who wanted to avoid discussion of the recession. The logic was that talking about economic reversals only made things worse.

Memorandum from Special Assistant Arthur Larson to The Assistant to the President Sherman Adams January 23, 1958

[Larson-Moos Files, Eisenhower Papers.]

After discussions with Saulnier and Hauge, I would recommend deferring a Presidential speech on the state of business until at least late March.

The principal reason is that the President's Economic Report has received widespread attention and says everything that could be said in a speech, and much more. A speech in the near future, therefore, would be an anticlimax.

The second reason is the one I mentioned the other day: it would be most unfortunate for a Presidential speech on the economy to be followed by a possible continued downward movement in the business cycle for perhaps two or three months.

By the middle of March, if the signs indicate an upturn in prospect, the President's speech could serve to catch the pendulum at the right point, and perhaps receive some credit for subsequent improvement. On the other hand, if the business situation should be more serious, presumably there would be some fresh actions to talk about. . . .

Throughout the whole economic downturn, Eisenhower remained convinced that the nation required no drastic measures. He responded to pleas for pump-priming, massive public works, and tax cuts with the same answer: they were unnecessary. However, while he wanted to avoid drastic actions, his economic statement of February 12, 1958, enumerated several contemplated anti-recession proposals.

Statement by President Eisenhower on the Economic Situation February 12, 1958

[*Public Papers of the Presidents: 1958* (Washington, 1959), 151–52.]

Yesterday the Departments of Labor and Commerce published figures for January on employment and unemployment. They indicate that the current falling off in the economy is sharper than usual for this time of year.

All of us are deeply concerned over the hardships that these figures record for the families of the additional breadwinners temporarily out of work, and those that have gone on a shortened work week. I know that we are concerned, too, with the loss of production involved and the pressure this puts on many businesses across the land. While these developments reflect important features of our present economic situation, they must be seen in perspective as we look ahead.

From the best advice I can get, and on my own study of the facts regularly placed before me, I believe that we have had most of our bad news on the unemployment front. I am convinced that we are not facing a prolonged downswing in activity. Every indication is that March will commence to see the start of a pickup in job opportunities. That should mark the beginning of the end of the downturn in our economy, provided we apply ourselves with confidence to the job ahead. As Americans we have a responsibility to work toward the early resumption of sound growth in our economy.

I have confidence in the recovery of our economy later this year for two reasons.

First, it is my conviction that the underlying forces of growth remain strong and undiminished. As a Nation, we must provide the needs of a population growing at a rate of three million a year. Billions of dollars are being spent every year on research and development that will mean new products and new jobs. Overseas economic development will provide growing markets for our resources. The future will belong, not to the faint-hearted, but to those who believe in it and prepare for it.

Second, the firm policy of the Government is to foster this recovery in every sound way. I am making sure that we will go forward on every practical avenue of action. Some steps have already been taken; others are under administrative review; still others are before Congress in the form of requests for legislation.

To dispel false impressions and to make clear the activities of this Administration in these fields, I am releasing today a Fact Paper setting forth programs and policies bearing on the current economic situation. They include action in recent months by the Federal Reserve System to ease credit, with dramatic results already achieved in a greater availability of credit and lower borrowing costs. Steps have been taken, going back to last August, to stimulate homebuilding, even though we were disappointed by the failure of the Congress to authorize interest rates that would attract mortgage money into many phases of home construction. They also include sharply stepped-up expenditures on the national highway building program, an increase in activity under the urban renewal program, and a sharp increase in the first half of this year in the rate at which defense procurement contracts will be placed with private industry.

These and other programs and proposals are outlined in the Fact Paper. If other measures are needed, I assure you they will be proposed—and in time. For example, for some time now the Administration has been engaged in systematic and comprehensive planning for expansion and modernization of public works and buildings, all of these useful public projects to be taken off the shelf when they could most appropriately be undertaken. Yesterday I directed the Postmaster General to present to the Congress a $2 billion program for modernization during the next 3-5 years of Post Office buildings and equipment throughout the country.

In all these matters of Government policy it is well to remember that with an economy as complex as ours, it is necessary not only to avoid the taking of wrong steps but confidently take the right ones. This we propose to do.

The "political" implications of the recession were obvious to everyone, and as frightening to Republicans as they were gratifying to Democrats. Republican National Chairman Meade Alcorn indicated his party's problems in a March 7, 1958, letter to Arthur Larson.

Republican National Chairman Meade Alcorn to Special Assistant Arthur Larson
March 7, 1958
[Larson-Moos Files, Eisenhower Papers.]

Dear Art:

George Gallup has made an interesting suggestion which I discussed with you on the telephone yesterday. As I understand it, it sums up about as follows:

Gallup believes that the intentions of a political party are sometimes more important to the people than what the Party has done in the past. For example, today Democrats are talking about what they intend to do or plan to do to fight recession, unemployment and so forth, while we Republicans reply that Democrats are trying to "talk us into a depression." Gallup believes that the situation requires immediate drastic affirmative action on the part of the Republican Party. He believes that our difficulty stems from the fact that in attacking the means employed by the Democrats some people get the mistaken notion that we are attacking the end. He believes that a major speech should be made, preferably by the President, not simply touching upon the subject but devoted entirely to the subject of pointing out that the Republican Party is today the Party which has the plans and has the intention and has the means with which to overcome all of the sources of recession, and that throughout its history it has, in fact, been the Party which has been directly identified with the interests, the hopes, the aspirations and the security of the greatest number of our people. Not only can the record be cited but even more dramatically the program of this Administration for providing jobs, for strengthening our economy, for broadening hopes for our people, etc., needs to be hit and hit very hard.

Despite hopeful predictions that the downward trend would "bottom out" in March of 1958, the economy did not show improvement during that month. The Administration had concluded that either a sizable tax cut or an accelerated public works program would be necessary if an upturn did not start shortly. The Council of Economic Advisors mainly advocated the tax cut proposal, which the Cabinet discussed seriously as late as May. The other major anti-recession weapon, while already in use to an extent, received a drastic boost by Congress through the enactment of a $1.6 billion public works authorization bill (June 25). The effectiveness of these schemes—taxes and public works—had received serious consideration inside the Administration. An April 30 memo by an economist to John Bragdon, Special Assistant for Public Works Planning, indicated some of the problems.

Memorandum of Economic Advisor Emmett Welch to Special Assistant John Bragdon April 30, 1958

[Bragdon Papers.]

This is in further reference to my memo of April 21 and your comments thereon. My memo of April 21 showed the timing of an individual income tax cut, and for the sake of simplicity assumed that the income tax cut would follow the timing of income tax withholdings. Actually, only about 2/3 of the total individual income tax is withheld. For the lower income levels the proportion withheld is much higher, nearly 100%. (I think Congress is more likely to enact a tax cut for the lower income groups than an across-the-board cut.) A large part of the individual income tax not withheld is paid quarterly on the basis of estimated tax liabilities. Therefore, the quarterly figures I have shown would not be changed by estimating withheld and other income tax liabilities separately. The monthly figures within quarters would be changed however.

An individual income tax cut can have about any timing that is desired. For example, while a tax cut of a given amount may be decided on for a year, it can all be taken in the early part of a year in the form of forgiven tax withholdings. Thus it may be decided to give a tax cut of $5 billion for the year and allow all of it by not making any tax withdrawals in the early part of the year. Many are advocating this.

If you want estimates of the various timings that would be possible for an individual income tax cut, I shall work them out. However, you can never even come close to the timing of a tax cut with public works, because you can have about any timing you want with a tax cut, whereas public works are subject to engineering and physical construction timing factors that cannot be greatly changed.

A cut in the corporate income tax would have a slower timing in terms of tax liability, than would an individual income tax cut. I did not work out the timing for a corporate income tax cut because it is generally agreed that a corporate income tax cut would not have much effect in stopping an economic downturn. During a recession plenty of credit and capital can be made available for business production and investment by monetary actions. Therefore, a cut in corporate income taxes will not, in itself, lead to increased spending or investment. It will merely lead to increased corporate assets or increased dividends. However, a reduction in corporate income taxes might indirectly have some recovery effects because of the psychological effects of the tax cut on business sentiment. Also, special forms of corporate tax cut such as allowing expenditures on research and development to be deducted from corporate taxable income might lead directly to increased business expenditures.

In order to arrive at the true effects of a tax cut vs. government expenditures, it is necessary to move away from the timing of the tax liability vs. the timing of the government expenditure to a comparison of the timing of the expenditures resulting from the two sources. This is implicit in your statement "Also, when the tax cut savings is realized, there is no assurance it will be spent instead of merely saved." This is the core of the problem. As I reported in my memo of April 29, the panel discussion on April 29 before the Joint Economic Committee brought out the fact that tax cuts received by low-income or unemployed families would be mostly spent—and quickly. As the income level increases, the proportion spent decreases and the rate of expenditure decreases. As indicated above, corporate income tax decreases in a recession (unless specialized) have very little effect on expenditures. Across-the-board tax decreases, therefore, lose some of their effectiveness. Income tax decreases concentrated in the lower income tax brackets or obtained by increased exemptions are most effective in a recession.

> *Note:* I clearly want to emphasize that there are changes in the tax structure to give greater incentive to long-run growth and development which I am very much in favor of. These are not recession measures, however.

There is a majority consensus among economists that to the extent that there is a need for increased government expenditures and to the extent they can be made quickly, they should be given preference to tax cuts as an anti-recession measure. There are also many economists who believe that even those public works which cannot be started immediately, should be undertaken in a capital goods recession such as the present, because we are faced with a slow recovery. Also because there is a long-run need for expanding public works as a base for economic growth. The significant point is that many economists are urging that some tax cuts be added to public works expenditures so as to start us on the road back quicker. There are a few die-hards who oppose increasing government expenditures under any circumstances, on the grounds that public expenditures are evil, per se.

Let me know if there are additional estimates or information on this subject that I can work up for you.

)━●━०━●━०━●━०━●━●━●━०━●━●━●━०━●━०━●━०━●━०━●━●━●━●━●━●━०━●━०━●━०━●━०━●━(

By July, 1958, the economy appeared to have finally "bottomed out." However, the Administration came under political attack for what it had or had not done. To counter, the White House staff drafted a summary designed to show that the Administration's anti-recession measures had been successful.

Memorandum of the White House Economic Staff on Anti-Recession Measures
July, 1958
[Larson-Moos Files, Eisenhower Papers.]

The Federal Government has taken positive action to combat the business downturn. Steps have already been taken to encourage housing by the reduction of down payments on FHA loans, and by permitting the inclusion of closing costs as a part of FHA down payments which, in effect, reduces the down payment further. In addition, we have released $177 million more funds for military housing and for building under other Federally-sponsored programs. We have also released $200 million of FHA purchase authority on low cost homes.

Credit easing action by the Federal Reserve System has been most dramatic. The discount rate paid by member banks on their borrowings from Federal Reserve is now 2¼%, as against 3½% last fall. This has been accompanied by an even greater falling-off of short-term interest rates in the market and a general easing up of bank credit. Long-term rates have also fallen rapidly, and partly as a result of this, the amount of new issues of securities by state and local governments is running 25% ahead of last year.

The Federal Reserve Board has also made more credit available by reducing reserve requirements on member banks by ½ of 1% and by cutting margin requirements on loans in the stock market from 70% to 50%.

The Defense Department incurred obligations for major procurement amounting to $6 billion in July–December 1957. Obligations for those purposes will total $10 billion in January–June 1958. That is an increase of $4 billion in six months—an annual rate of increase of $8 billion.

There has been a phenomenal increase in expenditures for military construction. During July–December 1957, military construction totaled only about $40 million a month. This total was up to $87 million in January, and will exceed $300 million a month for the remaining period of this fiscal year.

In addition, the military is doing everything possible in its renewed drive to see that more military procurement is placed through small businesses and through firms in areas where there is an adequate supply of available labor.

There has been an acceleration of civil public works projects which will result in the expenditure of nearly $200 million several months earlier than previously planned. This includes the Corps of Engineers, National Parks, and Indian Affairs, and hospitals, among other projects.

In addition, there are a great many programs in the January Budget which are now expanding significantly. Twice as many urban renewal projects will be under way in June 1959 than in June 1957. The highway program is expected to run at the rate of $1.8 billion in this fiscal year, and $2.4 billion in the fiscal year 1959 as compared with $1.0 billion in 1957. Thus a total of $2¼ billion more is being spent on highways in these two years than would have been spent at the 1957 rate.

There is a similar story to tell on civil public works. The 1957 rate of expenditures there amounted to $1.3 billion. The rate for 1958 is $1.7 billion, and for 1959 it is $2.0 billion. Thus over a billion dollars more is being put into these projects in 1958 and 1959 than if the 1957 rate had continued.

All of these programs are an active part of Federal spending *right now*.

In addition, I have not even mentioned our $2 billion post office modernization program, the proposal for extended unemployment insurance payments, the proposal for an additional $2.2 billion of Federal highway funds, $.2 billion additional funds for water resources projects, and various other proposals which I have made, but which the Congress has not yet acted upon.

>━●━o━●━o━●━o━●━o━●━o━●━o━●━o━●━o━●━o━●━o━●━o━●━o━●━o━●━o━●━o━●━o━●━o━●━(

Well after the recession had ended, John Bragdon's staff continued to investigate ways to maintain economic stability.

Memorandum of Economic Advisor Emmett Welch to Special Assistant John Bragdon
April 23, 1959
[Bragdon Papers.]

Recently, there has been considerable support (or at least, recognition) from unexpected sources for the premise that inadequate purchasing has been responsible for the recent recession, the slow-down in per capita growth in recent years, and the progressively increased under-utilization of resources.

It is clear that the increases in prices in recent years was not due to too many dollars chasing available goods. We had plenty of resources to have produced much more. We were investing heavily—which in itself always tends to support purchasing power. Nevertheless, inventories piled up and consumer debt increased sharply notwithstanding the fact we were producing well below our capacities.

Re clipping No. 1, note the emphasis on stimulating consumption in order to support production. Incidentally, there is no shortage of "wants" but of purchasing power. Marketing and advertising, while they do stimulate total wants as well as specific wants, do not create additional purchasing power to satisfy the wants. As a matter of fact, because of the inadequacy of purchasing power as compared with our ability to produce goods and services to satisfy wants, producers engage in competitive marketing and advertising in an attempt to divert the available purchasing power to their particular products and services. Progressively, price competition has been subordinated to the fringe benefits in the marketing process. (It is important to remember that purchasing power is increased by price declines, as well as by distributing more dollars).

Re clipping No. 2, it is significant to me that the Wallis statement emphasized the necessity of wages going up as much as productivity rather than that wages should rise no more than productivity.

━━━━━━━━━━━━━━━━━━━━━━━━━━━━━━━━━━━

Many Democrats elected in 1958 owed their victories to the recession, yet by the time Congress convened in January, 1959, the economy had practically recovered. Eisenhower's statement at the conclusion of the 1959 session stressed some of his difficulties with the new and heavily Democratic Congress.

Statement by President Eisenhower Following the Adjournment of Congress September 20, 1959

[*Public Papers of the Presidents: 1959* (Washington, 1960), 674–77.]

The 86th Congress, is now half over, with some needed gains accomplished, but with many disappointing failures. In the second session I shall continue doing my best to assure responsible government for the American people.

When this first session began eight months ago, a greatly increased Democratic majority arrived in Washington apparently convinced, first, that there was still a recession; second, that it was bound to get worse; third, that heavy Federal "pump-priming" was our only salvation; and fourth, that they were mandated by the American people swiftly to enact these huge spending programs into law.

As a result, last January the majority in Congress sponsored many schemes to plunge billions of dollars into Federal programs which I opposed as unwarranted or excessive.

The American public at once and emphatically stepped in. By letters, telegrams, telephone calls and personal visits to their Congressmen, the folks back home demanded a halt to excesses being advanced in Congress. Before the session had been underway two months, the public had forced the majority to shelve at least temporarily its more lavish proposals.

This was an historic turnabout. It is high tribute to the good sense and political vigor of our citizens. To me it is the most gratifying and most promising aspect of the work of the session just ended.

I feel much the same about the work of my fellow Republicans in this Congress. In both Houses they were powerfully led; they were unified; they had great fighting spirit; they rejected compromise on matters of principle. Therefore their influence upon majority decisions in Congress went far beyond their numerical strength. I think Americans generally feel as I do—that these Republican Senators and Congressmen well earned the Nation's plaudits for their performance this year.

I pay my respects to those among the political opposition without whose cooperation our efforts against extravagance and legislative excesses would have been in vain. These men, though subjected to severe party pressures, had the conviction and courage to stand up and be counted on issue after issue basic to the welfare of the Nation. Sincerely I congratulate them for their good work for America this session.

Next I acknowledge, as I have each year, my appreciation to those members of both parties who have approached in a bipartisan manner most of the matters important to the Nation's security and the conduct of foreign relations. To this standard of being Americans first and Democrats or Republicans second when the Nation's safety and world peace are involved, all of us must steadfastly adhere. I am gratified that so many have done so.

Some important features of the Administration's legislative program, submitted last January, were enacted into law.

We were able at last to take an important step toward labor reform. Here again I congratulate, most of all, the American people, for it was due to their outspoken indignation that ineffective legislation was set aside and that reasonably sturdy barriers were erected against abuses that for years have injured the cause of American labor.

Hawaiian Statehood also was a notable achievement—a great event that the American people have eagerly awaited many years.

The Congress initially refused to support the national highway program, except on the basis of piling up large additions to the already huge public debt. It is gratifying that the Congress finally agreed to a partial support of the program, but at a lower rate than I recommended.

There were disappointments, of course, as in all sessions. Foremost was the refusal to establish the necessary authority for sound management of the public debt. This refusal, by forcing the Treasury to rely exclusively on inflationary short-term borrowing, may reduce the contribution to price stability that a balanced budget helps to provide and could make most difficult the maintenance of confidence both at home and abroad in our determination to manage our financial affairs soundly. I am gratified, however, now to be able to reinvigorate our savings bonds program by bringing more equity to the millions of patriotic Americans who own and buy savings bonds.

Again the Congress refused to put our Postal Service on a self-sustaining basis.

Mutual security was deeply slashed, with potentially serious consequences for us all. I deplore the shortsightedness that this unfortunate action reveals. In these times especially, Americans are entitled to expect better of the Congress than this.

Nor can I fail to mention again my disappointment that the majority in Congress seems to find it so difficult to wean itself from the porkbarrel. It is somewhat short of inspiring to see the Congress so insistent upon mushrooming the huge public works expenditures already being made at record levels throughout America. This action and others of a similar nature taken this session will surely make the difficult budgetary situation still more acute. For years to come heavier burdens will be imposed upon the taxpaying public.

The Congress again failed to make a realistic approach to our serious agricultural problems. Not only are taxpayers everywhere rightly troubled over the enormous and constantly mounting costs of present programs, but also our farmers have been waiting quite long enough for effective remedies. They are entitled to sensible legislation that will allow them to plan confidently for a secure future, with reasonable assurance that their lives will be free of oppressive governmental restraint. It must be distressing to millions of our people that the best the Congress could bring itself to do in this session was to attempt a return to programs discredited long ago.

There have been claims that the Administration's Budget, submitted last January, was cut by the Congress. The Congress distorted the shape of the Budget in many respects—cutting where they should not have cut and adding, particularly in long-term items, vast sums that not only add to our financing difficulties but will also some day have to be paid by our grandchildren. Actually, the net effect of Congressional actions in this session is to increase, not decrease, Federal spending.

Finally, I remind everyone that the 86th Congress is only half over, and that it took an outspoken citizenry to divert it from its first purpose of having the Federal Government do new things it should not do—or more of the old than it should—at enormous cost to the public. The next session is only three months away. Should we again see extravagant proposals sponsored in the Congress, I shall continue to oppose them. I am confident of the continuing energetic support of the American people if such a struggle should develop. I believe that the American people can convert their gains for responsible government in this first session into a complete victory in the second.

4. THE SHERMAN ADAMS CONTROVERSY

Of greater personal concern to the President than the recession was the scandal that involved The Assistant to the President Sherman Adams. On June 16, 1958, a House Legislative Oversight Subcommittee, chaired by Democrat Oren Harris of Arkansas, disclosed that Adams might have had improper connections with Bernard Goldfine, a New England industrialist. In the following excerpts from the Subcommittee's hearings, Roger Robb, counsel for Goldfine, referred to favors his client bestowed on Adams. Later that day, two Subcommittee staff members, Robert Lishman, the chief counsel, and Francis McLaughlin, an investigator, engaged in a dramatic exchange that disclosed in greater detail the extent of the Adams-Goldfine relationship. These developments received nationwide attention.

House Hearing on Regulatory Commissions and Agencies
June 16, 1958

[U.S., Congress, House, Subcommittee of the Committee on Interstate and Foreign Commerce, *Hearings, Investigation of Regulatory Commissions and Agencies*, 85th Cong., 2nd Sess., 1958, 3465–69, 3484–88.]

*   *   *

THE CHAIRMAN (Oren Harris, Dem., Ark.): Mr. Robb, in the first place, you seem to base your request here on what happened at Boston last week. I think we might as well get the record straight on this proceeding here and the facts to start with in order that we can determine the proper procedure.

This committee has had staff members in Boston looking into these matters with reference to the administration of the laws of the Federal Communications Commission in connection with channel 5, the Federal Trade Commission in connection with the matter of proceedings before it, and the Securities and Exchange Commission in connection with matters over a long period of time before it.

There have been some accusations of the staff as to what it has done or failed to do, and I happen to know personally what the staff has been doing and what it has been trying to do, and I do not subscribe to the accusations that have been made.

I think the record ought to show that this staff has been carrying out instructions with which I, as chairman of the committee, am familiar, and some other members also.

That is No. 1.

No. 2, I think it should also be made very clear that the staff has been under instructions to get information that is pertinent, to this investigation and to the authority and responsibility of this committee. The staff has undertaken to get this information. The staff has also been under instructions to follow through with the information and reports it has had in order to determine whether or not such reports and information which it has are true.

It is the duty of our staff and this committee to endeavor to get all information, and then to determine whether or not it is pertinent to this investigation, carrying out the investigation from reports it has received.

The staff has endeavored to get those involved to cooperate in this, and there was nothing included and turned loose and reported in the newspapers in connection with any of this matter except general matters until those involved required this committee, by subpena, to exact from those involved the information that it feels it is entitled to have.

Because of that lack of cooperation, it was necessary for members of this committee to go to Boston in order to obtain information that the committee is entitled to have. Therefore, the committee does not feel that your reference to what happened in Boston last week is sufficient entitlement to your request here at the moment.

On the other hand, with respect to the matters relating to the subpena here, which the committee has requested and which the committee feels that it should have, with the information and explanation of the facts that we have, we feel it is as much our duty and responsibility to find out if records are untrue as it is if they are true, because what we are after are facts, and if we could have a little better cooperation of those involved I think we could eliminate some of the problems that have arisen here this morning.

If you feel that the information which is requested here by this subpena and which will be discussed in the committee would tend to in any way defame, degrade or incriminate any person, then it is my duty as chairman to present this to the committee for its consideration, as to whether or not it will be taken in executive session.

MR. ROGER ROBB: That is my request, Mr. Chairman, respectfully.

THE CHAIRMAN: You do state here, now, that such information, which has been requested and required to be brought to this committee by this subpena, if given to the committee, would tend to defame, degrade or incriminate some person? Do you feel that is true?

MR. ROBB: I base this request, Mr. Chairman, not only upon the information but upon the course of the hearings as I observed them in Boston.

The only way I know to predict the future is to look at the past.

THE CHAIRMAN: The Chair has already ruled on that, but the Chair is asking you the question now, Do you feel that any information that might be given in a public hearing in connection with this matter might tend to defame, degrade, or incriminate some person?

MR. ROBB: My opinion is, Mr. Chairman, that the way such information might well be used would tend to defame or degrade my clients and other persons.

THE CHAIRMAN: On that basis the Chair will be glad to entertain the request, and, consequently, we will ask the committee to meet at 1:30 this afternoon.

MR. CHARLES WOLVERTON (Dem., N.J.): Mr. Chairman, may I ask a question or two of the counsel?

THE CHAIRMAN: Yes.

MR. WOLVERTON: This rule to which you have referred says that any person who you have in mind might be defamed, degraded, or incriminated by any testimony that might be given today?

MR. ROBB: Let me make one thing crystal clear, Mr. Wolverton. I do not contend that this information would incriminate anybody. I do submit that it may well defame or degrade certain persons because of the way it might be handled.

The persons I specifically have in mind are the witness, Miss Paperman, and her employer, Mr. Bernard Goldfine. Those are the only persons for whom I have a right to speak.

MR. WOLVERTON: With respect to the witness who is present today, Miss Paperman, you do not contend that anything that she may be asked or may testify to would defame, degrade, or incriminate her?

MR. ROBB: I think it might well tend to defame or degrade her, yes, sir, because of the way it might be handled.

MR. WOLVERTON: Would you state in a general way what evidence you have in mind that would have that effect? I am sitting on this committee; I do not know what the evidence is, and I therefore am unable to judge whether it would defame, degrade, or incriminate any person, not knowing what the testimony will be. Evidently you do know because you made that statement.

MR. ROBB: I can state one thing specifically, Mr. Wolverton.

The subpena requires the witness to produce all records and so forth having to do with "expenditures made in behalf of all officials, employees, or representatives of the executive, legislative, and judicial branches of the Federal and State governments."

As the Congressman recalls, in Boston there was a statement made by counsel for the committee indicating that he contended there had been some corruption in that connection because one of Mr. Goldfine's companies had paid a hotel bill or paid for a room or rooms occupied by certain Members of Congress or the Senate and by Gov. Sherman Adams.

I think that statement made in Boston certainly tended to defame or degrade Mr. Goldfine and Miss Paperman. And, since we have here a subpena asking for those records, I anticipate similar statements and wild accusations might be made here. I think, if that is going to be done, it ought to be done in executive session.

THE CHAIRMAN: May I see the record?

You refer to what statement?

MR. ROBB: I think I could put my finger on it if the chairman would let me see it. It is the afternoon of the first day, and the opening statement, too. I have the opening statement.

THE CHAIRMAN: Was it on the 6th?

MR. ROBB: It was the first day, Mr. Chairman. I think it was on Thursday, Mr. Chairman. This seems to be Friday's, I think.

THE CHAIRMAN: We do not seem to have a copy up here.

MR. ROBB: I can refer to the statement, which stated this:

> Certain decisions reached and actions taken by the Federal Trade Commision and by the Securities and Exchange Commission appear from factual information in the files of the subcommittee to have been predicated upon mal-administration, inefficiency, and possibly even corruption. Some authenticated information in the files of the subcommittee indicates that these Commissions have been subjected to ex parte pressures by high Government officials in respect of the East Boston Co., the Boston Port Development Co., Northfield Mills, Inc., Strathmore Woolen Co.—

and so forth.

> There is evidence that certain high Federal officials have enjoyed, from the principal owner of such companies, unusually lavish and expensive hospitality. The subcommittee also has evidence that these high Federal officials received favors which would transgress the bounds of hospitality construed in the most lavish sense of the word. In some instances enforcement proceedings brought by the Federal agencies against certain of these companies have been withdrawn or watered down.

Then, tied up with that, Mr. Chairman, on Thursday, when I made an inquiry as to the pertinency of questions about certain checks, counsel stated, as I recall, that one of Mr. Goldfine's companies had paid bills for Gov. Sherman Adams at a hotel in Boston, clear implication or insinuation, Mr. Chairman, that was at some time in some way intended to influence or corrupt Gov. Sherman Adams.

THE CHAIRMAN: You can place your interpretation on what was said, but the facts speak for themselves. I think that the committee will develop all these facts to determine whether or not your interpretation is the correct one or if the facts speak themselves. You place that interpretation on this yourself.

All this committee is after and all Mr. Lishman was doing was simply stating facts. We, of course, certainly want to comply with the rules of the House, and will comply with them. That is our duty and responsibility, and, as chairman, I must so rule in connection with these decisions.

Mr. O'Hara.

MR. JAMES O'HARA (Dem., Mich.): Mr. Robb, is it your claim that the present witness would be involved if she was acting merely under the instructions of her employer, Mr. Goldfine, or that involved in her actions would be a defamation of her character?

MR. ROBB: I think so; yes, sir. Certainly Mr. Goldfine is involved in any such charges as we heard in Boston.

My only suggestion, gentlemen, is this:

If you are going to do these things, please let's do them in private so we can get these things thrashed out without having a lot of stuff in the newspapers which afterward blows up and proves not to be true.

I might say, Mr. Chairman, at this point that nobody has asked us these things in private, and nobody has asked Governor Adams about these matters in private. But we get this statement made in a public hearing which smears them both. We don't think that is fair, with all respect.

MR. WOLVERTON: Mr. Chairman, what I am interested in ascertaining is for whom counsel speaks.

MR. ROBB: I speak for Miss Paperman, and Mr. Goldfine, who is also my client.

MR. WOLVERTON: You made reference to Gov. Sherman Adams. Do you represent him?

MR. ROBB: No, sir; I do not. But any smear upon Governor Adams involving my client inevitably smears my clients, too.

MR. WOLVERTON: Who are your clients?

MR. ROBB: Miss Paperman and Mr. Goldfine.

MR. WOLVERTON: That is all?

MR. ROBB: At this time, sir. I always welcome more.

MR. WOLVERTON: I assume you are of the opinion that the efficiency you may show in representing those who have been mentioned may bring additional representations to you. Is that right?

THE CHAIRMAN: The committee will meet at 1:30 this afternoon to determine this request.

Mr. Lishman?

MR. ROBERT LISHMAN: I would like to add a brief statement.

For some weeks the staff of the subcommittee, as the members know, attempted to work out an arrangement with the Pilgrim Bank in Boston whereby members of the staff, in cooperation with bank officials, would obtain pertinent information from the bank's records.

The bank was under a subpena. In answer to this subpena, there came to Washington its vice president and counsel and another bank official, and they brought with them two very large ledgers containing material which the committee desired. We could have insisted that these bank records be left here in Washington for examination by the committee staff to weed out the pertinent information which is necessary for the purpose of this investigation.

The bank officials and counsel stated that it would disrupt the business of the bank if it were handled that way. They gave us a letter in which they agreed that if we would allow them to bring the books back to Boston on the very same day, they would immediately compile the pertinent information for us and then permit the committee staff members to go on the bank premises and verify whether or not the information furnished by the bank itself was correct, complete, and accurate.

This proceeding was arranged not only to accommodate the bank in its business but also to preserve in confidence the material the committee desired until, at the appropriate time in the context of its investigation of the three Federal agencies involved, it would become necessary to make public such information.

After we had made this arrangement with the bank, we were informed by the bank officials that Mr. Goldfine had come to the bank, threatened them with loss of business and a possible lawsuit, and they could not live up to this cooperative arrangement which was designed to preserve the privacy of these records until it was necessary to present them in a public hearing.

When we were faced with this situation, the committee had no alternative but to request that these records be supplied.

In the proceedings in Boston we were met continuously with the refusals to answer on the grounds that the information we sought was not relevant.

We submit that with regard to the SEC it was a period of nearly 8 years in which two of the companies involved filed no annual reports with the Commission, although the company was a registered company.

Whether this failure of the Commission to have these reports filed was due to an oversight on their part or a deficiency in the law, or possibly outside, improper pressure is one of the facets of relevancy concerning which we desire these records.

I submit that this entire situation would never have arisen if the bank had been permitted by Mr. Goldfine to live up to its arrangement with the committee whereby the privacy of these records would have been preserved. . . .

MR. LISHMAN: What did these allegations made to the subcommittee consist of?

MR. FRANCIS MCLAUGHLIN: With reference to the Securities and Exchange Commission in the matters pending before it and in which Mr. Goldfine had an interest, it was alleged that Mr. Goldfine was able to obtain this treatment only because of his close friendship with Sherman Adams, Assistant to the President of the United States.

MR. LISHMAN: And with respect to the Federal Trade Commission, are you familiar with what those allegations consisted of?

MR. MCLAUGHLIN: Yes, sir.

MR. LISHMAN: Will you please state them?

MR. MCLAUGHLIN: That he was able to obtain the treatment that he did at the Federal Trade Commission also because of his friendship with Sherman Adams, the Assistant to the President of the United States.

THE CHAIRMAN: Who made these allegations?

MR. MCLAUGHLIN: Sir, the allegations, in part, were made by Mr. John Fox of Boston, Mass., and also in the course of the investigation information was obtained from employees at the Federal Trade Commission who were present at the time of a conversation between Mr. Goldfine and Mr. Sherman Adams in a telephone conversation.

MR. LISHMAN: Now, Mr. McLaughlin, did you undertake to verify whether these allegations had any substance?

MR. MCLAUGHLIN: Yes, sir, I did.

MR. LISHMAN: Will you describe some of the steps that you took to verify the accuracy of these allegations?

MR. MCLAUGHLIN: Yes, sir.

On May 7, I believe it was, this year, I served a subpena upon the manager of the Sheraton-Plaza Hotel in Boston, Mass. This subpena called for all records, books, registrations, papers, correspondence, and other writings pertaining to any and all accounts in the name of Bernard Goldfine, individual or otherwise, including, without limitation, reservations made, room assignments, payments for rooms, meals, refreshments, entertainment, and other services during the period January 1, 1952, to date, and to any and all accounts in the name of any and all of the following companies: Foxcroft Realty Trust Co., Georges River Woolen Co., Goldfine Investment Trust, Lebandale Mills, Lebanon Woolen Mills, Linconshire, Ltd., George Mabbett & Sons, Northfield Mills, Puritan Mills, Strathmore Commodities, Strathmore Realty Co., Strathmore Silks, Strathmore Woolen Co., Wilton Woolen Co., Mascoma Mills.

MR. LISHMAN: Were Northfield Mills and Strathmore Mills two companies that were involved by the Federal Trade Commission?

MR. MCLAUGHLIN: They were, sir.

MR. LISHMAN: Did the Sheraton-Plaza honor this subpena?

MR. MCLAUGHLIN: In part, sir.

MR. LISHMAN: And in the part that has been honored, did the Sheraton-Plaza supply you with documentary evidence that Gov. Sherman Adams had been entertained and his expenses paid for by Mr. Bernard Goldfine and one of these companies?

MR. MCLAUGHLIN: Yes, sir; they did.

MR. LISHMAN: Would you please read into the record the documentary proof that you secured in this respect from the Sheraton-Plaza Hotel?

MR. MCLAUGHLIN: Yes, sir.

I have here what is called a guest ledger card submitted in response to the subpena by the Sheraton-Plaza Corp. It bears the number CD 27344. The guest is registered as Governor and Mrs. Sherman Adams, of Washington, D.C. It covers the period November 24, through November 26, 1955, and the balance due on November 26, 1955 was $220.56.

The guest ledger folio, in addition to bearing the name of Governor and Mrs. Sherman Adams as guests, has typed in under the remarks "Charge the complete bill to Bernard Goldfine."

THE CHAIRMAN: Mr. Moulder.

MR. MOULDER: Was the bill paid by Mr. Goldfine?

MR. MCLAUGHLIN: According to the records at the Sheraton-Plaza, it was, sir.

MR. LISHMAN: One of the items subpenaed from Miss Paperman is a canceled check to verify this payment which has been reported to us by the hotel. The relevancy, I think, is apparent.

MR. WILLIAMS: Was this payment made by Mr. Goldfine, personally, or by one of the corporations?

MR. MCLAUGHLIN: That is what we are endeavoring to find out, sir. It is charged to Mr. Bernard Goldfine, and it is my understanding from interviewing employees of the hotel that all charges to Bernard Goldfine are charged to the account of Strathmore Woolen Co.

I have a guest folio ledger card, No. CD 33123, registered guest, Governor and Mrs. Sherman Adams, covering the period December 27 and 28, 1955, and the balance due on December 28, 1955, was $151.11. Under the column "Remarks" on the guest folio ledger is "Entire bill to be charged to Mr. Bernard Goldfine."

I also have registration CD 33113 covering the same period, December 27 and 28, 1955. The guest registered is Sarah Adams, Lincoln, N.H., in the amount of $9.39. And under "Remarks" is "Charge entire bill to Bernard Goldfine.

I have guest folio card CD 48296, listed as guests Mr. and Mrs. Sherman Adams. The suite was 65D.

Did you want me to mention the price of the suite in the other?

MR. LISHMAN: I think it is advisable to show that there were quarters that were being paid for.

MR. MCLAUGHLIN: Yes, sir.

The suite with reference to CD 27344 is $37 per room. The same with the second guest ledger I referred to, CD 33123.

MR. MOULDER: What was it?

MR. MCLAUGHLIN: $37, sir, per room.

MR. MOULDER: How many rooms?

MR. MCLAUGHLIN: It was a suite, and, as I understand it, a suite consists of rooms 523 and 525.

This is guest folio card CD 48296, Mr. and Mrs. Sherman Adams. The suite is 65D. It covers the period March 10 to March 12, 1956. The total amount is $164.00, and under "Remarks" is stated "Charge entire bill to Bernard Goldfine."

Guest folio card CD 58161; the guests, Governor and Mrs. Sherman Adams, The White House, Washington, D.C. It covers the period April 24 and April 25, 1956. The suite was for $65 per day. The total is $187.85, and under "Remarks" it reads "Entire bill to Bernard Goldfine."

I have a registration card, No. CE 65773, which bears the notation "Entire bill to B. Goldfine." The guests are registered as Mr. and Mrs. Sherman Adams of Lincoln, N.H.

The guest folio card bearing the same number, CE 65773, reflects that the suite was $50 per day. The total bill for the end of this period, March 8–9, 1957, was $170.36. Under "Remarks"—"Entire bill to Bernard Goldfine."

Next is the guest registration card CE 82981, "Charge entire bill to B. Goldfine." Name: Sherman Adams, City, Washington, D.C. The costs for this one room was $50. The total cost on the guest ledger card was $50. It was the only charge, was for the room.

Under the transfer to city ledger is the remark "Bernard Goldfine, Strathmore Woolen."

I have guest registration CE 84386, Mr. and Mrs. Sherman Adams, Lincoln, N.H.

MR. LISHMAN: Mr. Witness, may I interrupt?

MR. MCLAUGHLIN: Yes, sir.

MR. LISHMAN: On the account for $187.85 is there a notation on there that you haven't read?

MR. MCLAUGHLIN: $187, did you say?

MR. LISHMAN: Yes, sir. Is there one there with Strathmore Woolen Mills on it?

MR. MCLAUGHLIN: All of these under "Remarks" state "Entire bill to Bernard Goldfine."

On guest ledger card CE 82981 under the column "Transfer to city ledger," which is a standard reading on the form, it says "Bernard Goldfine, Strathmore Woolen." But the guest is Mr. Sherman Adams.

MR. LISHMAN: What is the amount of that?

MR. MCLAUGHLIN: $50.

On the guest registration card CE 84386, Mr. and Mrs. Sherman Adams, Lincoln, N.H. The guest folio card, the same number, covers the period June 7–8, 1957. The amount is $106.83, and under "Remarks" is "Charge to B. Goldfine."

Guest registration card CE 26289 bears the notation "Complete bill, Bernard Goldfine." Guests are registered as Mr. and Mrs. Sherman Adams, 2400 Tilden Street NW., Washington, D.C. The suite was $50 a day.

The total for the period September 21 through September 26 is $361.13. Under "Remarks" is "Complete bill to Bernard Goldfine."

Guest registration card CF 11000. Name: Mr. and Mrs. Sherman Adams, Washington, D.C. It bears the notation "Entire bill to Bernard Goldfine."

The guest ledger card covering the period December 6 to December 8, 1957, is in the total amount of $161.27. Under "Remarks" is "Entire bill to Mr. Bernard Goldfine."

Guest registration card No. CF 42130, Mr. and Mrs. Sherman Adams, Washington, D.C. It bears the notation—I can't read it all, but it says "Charge to account of Bernard Goldfine."

The guest folio card for the period May 5 and May 6, 1958, which was the day before I served the subpena on the hotel, showed a total of $59.46, and contains the remark "Entire bill to Bernard Goldfine."

I have other registration cards, but no guest folios.

MR. LISHMAN: On Mr. Sherman Adams?

MR. MCLAUGHLIN: Yes, sir.

MR. LISHMAN: Will you read those into the record?

THE CHAIRMAN: Mr. Lishman, I did not hear your last question of the witness.

MR. MCLAUGHLIN: I made the comment, sir, that I have other guest registration cards, but I do not have the guest folio card which contains the charges, and this registration is in the name of Mr. and Mrs. Sherman Adams, 2400 Tilden Street, Washington, D.C., No. C 5575, and the date stamped on it appears to be March 14, 1954.

The final one, C-61050, Gov. Sherman Adams and Mrs. Sherman Adams, "Charge entire bill to Bernard Goldfine," which also was noted on the other registration card. It is December 21, 1954.

I have attempted to arrange these in chronological order. The first one I read was for 1955, in which they forwarded a guest folio card, but these registrations are for 1954 apparently, and we do not have the amount of charges on those two particular registrations.

THE CHAIRMAN: Is that all of this witness?

MR. LISHMAN: No, sir. We have one or two more items.

Mr. McLaughlin, in the course of your inquiry did you ascertain that there were registrations at the Sheraton-Plaza wherein it appears that Mr. Adams was a guest but not registered?

MR. MCLAUGHLIN: Yes, sir.

MR. LISHMAN: And was a guest apparently of Mr. Goldfine?

MR. MCLAUGHLIN: Yes, sir.

MR. LISHMAN: Will you please state what documentary evidence you have as to that, and will you read that documentary evidence into the record?

MR. MCLAUGHLIN: In examining the accounts at the Sheraton-Plaza I noticed that there was an entry for $315.70 for registration in the name of Mr. Bernard Goldfine himself. There was supposed to be one person staying in the suite.

It appears to me to be unusual inasmuch as Mr. Bernard Goldfine resides not too far from the Sheraton-Plaza in Boston, and it was for a period of 4 days. So I called for and examined with Mr. O'Hara of the staff the microfilm records substantiating the charges as they appear in the guest ledger card. In so doing I examined the various expenses, and I came across one room-service ticket of November 21, 1956, which is charged on the guest ledger card. That is in the amount of $1.25. The room-service card, No. 46932, waiter No. 156, states to the effect that room 423, which was the suite engaged and in which Mr. Bernard Goldfine held the registration, was served with ice and four glasses. The charge was $1, and there was a tip of 25 cents to the waiter. At the bottom of the ticket is the signature "S. Adams," which is crossed out, but is legible on the room-service ticket, and Bernard Goldfine is written in above, which led me to believe that Mr. Adams may have been the guest in fact.

I went back to the guest folio ledger and I noted the last entry was to room 421; the suite being registered for was 423 and 425. We then went through the microfilm records and ascertained that room 421 was occupied by Mr. Samuel Adams of Hanover, N.H.

It is my understanding that Governor Adams' son was a student at Dartmouth.

MR. LISHMAN: And that bill was charged to whom?

MR. MCLAUGHLIN: That bill was charged to Mr. Bernard Goldfine since the registration was in Mr. Goldfine's name.

MR. LISHMAN: Did you ascertain whether or not Mr. Bernard Goldfine or any of the companies which he controls regularly maintains a suite at the Sheraton-Plaza Hotel?

MR. MCLAUGHLIN: That question was specifically asked at the Sheraton-Plaza, and Mr. Goldfine does not maintain a regular suite nor has he in the past and that each and every entry here is a separate item charged to him.

MR. LISHMAN: Now, Mr. Chairman, we have further evidence which would establish the relevancy of the material which has been subpenaed from Miss Paperman, but I believe we have already stated sufficient for the record to justify the conclusion that it is pertinent and relevant to this subcommittee to have the canceled checks evidencing the completeness of the payments which are shown in the record of the Sheraton-Plaza Hotel. . . .

Almost immediately, Sherman Adams wrote a letter explaining his conduct. The following day, June 17, refusing to stand on the traditional separation of powers prerogatives, Adams made a dramatic appearance before the Subcommittee. Interrogated at length, Adams parried questions and never admitted anything more than a lack of "prudence."

House Hearing on Regulatory Commissions and Agencies June 17, 1958

[U.S., Congress, House, Subcommittee of the Committee on Interstate and Foreign Commerce, *Hearings, Investigation of Regulatory Commissions and Agencies,* 85th Cong., 2nd Sess., 1958, 3718–23, 3738–40.]

* * *

MR. LISHMAN: Mr. Chairman, I have a few questions to ask Mr. Adams concerning his letter of June 12, 1958, to you as chairman. They will be confined to ascertaining whether or not, as a result of Mr. Adams' calls and arrangements for appointments for Mr. Goldfine resulted in Mr. Goldfine receiving certain information that an ordinary citizen who had gone to that agency could not have received under the Federal statute involved and under the rules and regulations of that particular Commission.

Now, Mr. Adams, we all agree that this is and should be a Government of laws and not of men, is that correct?

MR. ADAMS: That is correct.

MR. LISHMAN: We all agree that the independent administrative commissions of this Government should administer the law without fear or favor, intelligently, efficiently, and without being subjected to outside representation.

We agree on that, do we?

MR. ADAMS: Mr. Counsel, on that question, I touched on that question in the statement which I made. It is a close question. I look back on the system which over the years has placed upon the people in the executive department the duties, as I see them, of making contacts, yes, with independent agencies, but there is a difference, and I have pointed that out, between simply making an inquiry or an appointment, and suggesting that the official in any particular agency perform any act or refrain from performing any act in respect to the matter at hand.

That, Mr. Counsel, I have never done.

MR. LISHMAN: Well, inadvertently or not, I want to call your attention to certain facts which I will draw no conclusion from. On June 12, in your June 12th letter, you state:

> Late in 1953 Mr. Goldfine gave me a letter he had received from the Federal Trade Commission's Wool Labeling Division and asked me what had prompted it. I called the Chairman of the Federal Trade Commission, Mr. Edward F. Howrey, on the telephone, and asked if the information Mr.

Goldfine desired could be made available to him. As a result of this call, Mr. Howrey prepared a short memorandum which I passed along to Mr. Goldfine.

A copy of Mr. Howrey's memorandum is enclosed. About a month later, before sending the Howrey memorandum to central files, my secretary called Mr. Howrey's office to inquire whether or not the matter was still current. She was informed that 2 weeks previously the company had agreed in writing to comply in every respect with the requirements of the Wool Labeling Act and that hence the matter was closed.

That is a correct quotation from your June 12th letter.

Again on page 2 of your letter, you state, and this time I will not quote. That some time in 1956 Mr. Goldfine, during a conversation with you, complained about the actions of the Securities and Exchange Commission in what he called the east Boston case. You say that he never asked you to do anything, but that you requested special counsel to find out what it was about, and that then he in turn called the General Counsel of the Securities and Exchange Commission for this information and reported back to you.

Now, I would like to ask: After you received this report from the Special Counsel, did you pass that information on to Mr. Goldfine?

MR. ADAMS: Not to my recollection.

MR. LISHMAN: Did you discuss the information you had obtained with Mr. Goldfine?

MR. ADAMS: Not to my recollection.

MR. LISHMAN: Did you discuss it with any representative of Mr. Goldfine?

MR. ADAMS: Not to my recollection.

MR. LISHMAN: As a matter of fact, do you know whether or not the General Counsel of the SEC came to the Office of the Special Counsel of the President and brought with him certain file material from the SEC?

MR. ADAMS: I do not. I have no knowledge of such occasion.

MR. LISHMAN: Now I would like to call your attention to the fact that in the memorandum dated January 4, 1954, from Chairman Howrey of the Federal Trade Commission to you, the statement is made, among others:

> On November 3, 1953, Einiger Mills lodged a complaint against Robert Lawrence, Inc., a Boston coat manufacturer, operating under the trade name of Leopold Morse, which was using Northfield fabrication labeled 90-percent wool, 10-percent vicuna. According to our wool division, this letter was inaccurate for the reason that the fabric contained nylon fabrication.

In the concluding paragraph of this memorandum to you from Mr. Howrey:

> Mr. Hannah advises me that if Northfield will give adequate assurances that all their labeling will be corrected, the case can be closed on what we call a voluntary cooperative basis.

Now I should like to call to your attention, Mr. Adams, and inquire, as to whether or not you knew at the time you made this request of Mr. Howrey as to what had prompted the action against Mr. Goldfine and his companies, that there was in effect under the rules and regulations of the Federal Trade Commission Act, a rule which reads as follows: And it is Rule 1.115 of the Rules of Practice, Procedures, and Organization, part 1, subpart (b), and it reads as follows:

> Confidentiality of applications. It has always been and now is strict Commission policy not to publish or divulge the name of an applicant or a complaining party.

Were you familiar with this rule of the Commission when you inquired of Mr. Howrey what had prompted its proceedings against Mr. Goldfine and his company?

MR. ADAMS: I was not.

MR. LISHMAN: Could Mr. Goldfine personally have gone down there and found out the name of the company complaining against him at that time under that rule?

MR. ADAMS: In my opinion, Mr. Counsel, I would say this: This was entirely a routine matter so far as I was concerned, and follows a routine practice which is part and parcel of practically our daily duties. When we get an inquiry in respect to any particular case it is the normal procedure to send that to the responsible person in the agency involved without comment.

In this case I made no reference to the merits of the case. I knew nothing about the merits of the case. I did not intend to advise myself about the merits of the case. All that I ever did in that particular matter was to send the inquiry to the man who was responsible as Chairman of the Commission for a reply.

Now, Mr. Counsel, I simply asked him for whatever information I could pass along to the person who inquired of me, a question which is in the record, and that was all that I had to do with the matter.

MR. LISHMAN: Mr. Adams, your letter states that Mr. Goldfine asked you what had prompted the investigation at the FTC, and that you called Mr. Howrey to ask him to supply you with what had prompted this investigation. Is that correct? If it isn't correct I would like to have it straightened out.

MR. ADAMS: Well, that obviously was what prompted the letter. To me, it was an inquiry for information. The only thing I ever asked Mr. Howrey for was information.

MR. LISHMAN: The statement has been made that, as a result of your phone call to Mr. Howrey and the memorandum you received, Mr. Goldfine got no other treatment than any ordinary citizen would have gotten.

I have read you Mr. Howrey's memorandum in which he discloses to you the name of the complainant in the case, which was prohibited under the rules of the Commission as being confidential. And he also told you in his memorandum, which is also prohibited by law from being revealed under section 15, United States Code, section 50, that—

> Mr. Hannah advises me that if Northfield will give adequate assurances that all their labeling will be corrected, the case can be closed on what we call a voluntary cooperative basis.

It seems to me that the record is clear that Mr. Goldfine advertently or inadvertently did get a preferred treatment in that he was receiving information from an independent regulatory commission to which he was not entitled either under the law or its own regulations.

MR. ADAMS: Now, so far as I am concerned, Mr. Lishman, the information that he got was supplied by a responsible official in an independent agency. And again, so far as I am concerned, I repeat I made no special request of any kind whatsoever.

I am unfamiliar, as I have said, in respect to the rules, regulations or the statute that covered these proceedings. I never attempted to advise myself concerning those rules and regulations.

So far as the information that he got, I had assumed quite obviously that what he got he was entitled to under the routine of the procedures in the agency itself.

MR. LISHMAN: I will state to you, Mr. Adams, that yesterday Mr. Howrey was a witness, and he testified that the memorandum he sent to you he did not consider official Trade Commission business, that it was a personal memorandum; no copy of it was ever left in the files of the Commission. And it seems to me that under the law and the regulations of the Federal Trade Commission in that memorandum he has personally divulged to you information which was passed on to Mr. Bernard Goldfine contrary to the statute and to the applicable rules of the Commission relating to confidential matter, and in that respect I will state for the record that on occasions when this subcommittee has attempted to find out the names of complainants against others than Mr. Goldfine at the Commission, they have been met with this rule of confidentiality, and, under protest in some instances, the information has been supplied on the basis that it would be kept extremely confidential and for the use of the committee only.

Now there was no such caveat in Mr. Howrey's memorandum to you. Is that correct?

MR. ADAMS: I don't recall if there was.

MR. LISHMAN: I will show it to you (handing document to witness).

Do you know at the time when special counsel received the information from the Securities and Exchange Commission that the material in question was not part of a public record?

MR. ADAMS: I'm sorry. Are you referring to the FTC matter?

MR. LISHMAN: No. The SEC now, the Securities and Exchange Commission.

MR. ADAMS: Exactly what material are you referring to?

MR. LISHMAN: We are informed that Mr. Meeker brought with him a file containing information as to the East Boston Co., and that Mr. Morgan asked Mr. Meeker for a rundown on the Commission's case against the East Boston Co. If I am wrong on this information I certainly want to have it corrected.

MR. ADAMS: So far as I have any recollection, I have never seen that file and have no knowledge of it.

MR. LISHMAN: Again I want to call attention that this was something in which it would appear—and it will be developed—that under the rules and regulations of the Securities and Exchange Act of 1934, Mr. Goldfine would not have been entitled to know what is in this file under rule 244 of the rules of the Commission. So again, and on this point the record will be developed later, it would appear that Mr. Goldfine had received preferential treatment in the sense that with this Commission, as in the case of the Federal Trade Commission, he was able to have information passed to him which was in the files made confidential by law and by the Commission regulations.

I have no further questions.

MR. ADAMS: Mr. Lishman, may I say that this appears to me to be an unwarranted assumption on your part.

As far as I have any knowledge—and I haven't consulted counsel on this question—I have no knowledge that Mr. Goldfine had any access to any information contained in that memorandum whatever.

MR. LISHMAN: Mr. Adams, your letter to the chairman of June 12, and I will quote it, first about the Federal Trade—

MR. ADAMS: I am not talking about the Federal Trade. I am talking about the SEC. With respect to the Federal Trade Commission, let me repeat again, that it is routine practice, of myself and my associates in the White House staff, to make inquiries concerning questions which are posed to us about matters in the regulatory agencies.

We received this information, and we had no knowledge, so far as I am concerned, and I believe that also applies to my associates, we had no knowledge whatever that the information that is given to us is restricted unless the reports which we get so state.

To the best of my knowledge, as I recall the situation, there was never any condition attached to this.

MR. LISHMAN: Mr. Adams, for what purpose did you arrange to have the SEC case against East Boston run down if it was not to get this information for Mr. Goldfine?

MR. ADAMS: Simply because I received a complaint and I inquired about the complaint I received. When I was told that this involved a matter of noncompliance in a certain respect, there was nothing that I did or my counsel did, or anyone else in the White House staff did, to the best of my knowledge and belief about it at all, nor did we make any report thereon.

MR. LISHMAN: Did you ever discuss the SEC case with Senators Payne and Cotton?

MR. ADAMS: I think there was some discussion about that at one time, but so far as I am concerned, it was a casual discussion, and there was no discussion with respect to the handling of those cases, to the best of my recollection.

MR. LISHMAN: I will conclude with this statement:

As counsel to this subcommittee, I have endeavored to conduct it in a fair and impartial manner, but you can well understand, in view of the prominence of the characters involved, that sometimes this duty has been an extremely difficult one.

I have never made any personal accusations with respect to any person, unless and until we have had conclusive evidence with respect to the matter.

I hope you will understand that that will continue to be the position of this counsel.

MR. ADAMS: If I may, and this is repetitive, it is in connection with these two matters that I, for my part, have never attempted to influence or to request or in any other way to bring about any decision in behalf of Mr. Goldfine or anybody else with respect to any matters before independent agencies.

MR. LISHMAN: Thank you, Mr. Adams.

THE CHAIRMAN: Mr. Flynt?

MR. JOHN FLYNT (Dem., Ga.): Governor Adams, do you believe that an average citizen requesting the information which you requested of Mr. Howrey could have received it?

MR. ADAMS: Yes, I do.

May I say, Mr. Flynt, in that connection, that I think the average citizen obviously would have to demonstrate that he had a legitimate problem that came before that agency, that particular agency, and that that agency quite obviously had a duty to perform in acquainting him with the matter under discussion.

Obviously, we are not talking about irrelevant matters or capricious matters. We are talking about matters that have to do with legitimate business of these agencies themselves.

MR. FLYNT: Governor Adams, do you know, of your own knowledge, whether Mr. Goldfine was represented by legal counsel in the matter then pending before the Federal Trade Commission?

MR. ADAMS: My assumption is that he was.

MR. FLYNT: That he was. Do you know now, or did you know at the time of your inquiry, what action, if any, his attorney or counsel of record had already taken to procure the information which you sought?

MR. ADAMS: Not definitely, no, sir.

MR. FLYNT: Do you know now?

MR. ADAMS: I do not.

MR. FLYNT: You do not.

Is it routine for you and other members of the White House staff to inquire as to the status of the matters which are in what is termed, the adjudicatory stage as contrasted with a legislative proceeding or quasi-legislative proceeding before one of the administrative agencies?

MR. ADAMS: Mr. Flynt, that is a rather technical question, as you can understand, because it might not be known to us in exactly what stage that particular inquiry was when we received an inquiry.

I would say it is routine when we receive a request for information as to case status to make inquiry about that case status.

MR. FLYNT: As to the status of the case then pending before a regulatory body?

MR. ADAMS: Well, quite obviously, before a regulatory body, because we are concerned here with regulatory bodies. I assume that your question relates to inquiries which we have about cases pending before regulatory bodies.

MR. FLYNT: That is correct.

Now, I did not mean for that question to be routine, because I phrased it as nearly as I could from one of the answers that you gave to the committee counsel, when, as I hastily wrote it down, you said, "It is routine for me and my staff to inquire from regulatory bodies when requests are made of us," or "when inquiries were made of us," I think were your words.

MR. ADAMS: As to case status.

MR. FLYNT: Do you realize that a member of a regulatory body might attach a great deal more significance to a call from you than they would from a party litigant, from a party under investigation, from a counsel for such a party, or from a Member of this or the other body of Congress?

MR. ADAMS: Mr. Flynt, I think that poses a very appropriate question. Perhaps here that the manner under which the White House staff operates is a result of a rather long history of routine, whether that is wise or not I would consider subject to consideration by your committee.

However, there is a very fine line of distinction which has to be drawn, it seems to me, between a question which I am sure you consider legitimate and proper, and a question that you might say overstepped the bounds of propriety and that might result in a regulatory agency being perhaps unduly impressed with the interest displayed in such a question.

That, I might add, is something that I think is a very proper question for the committee of which you are a member to consider. . . .

THE CHAIRMAN: Governor, back to the other matter which we left.

The other item was before the Securities and Exchange Commission when for a period of 8 years Mr. Goldfine, for some reason, disagreed with what others thought he should do in complying with the law. You stated in your letter to me last week that you had a staff member make an inquiry as to the status of that case in the Securities and Exchange Commission. I assume that you also know that that matter was settled by what some call a partial compliance—I think filing the reports of 1 or 2 years—and with the payment of the cost to the Commission over the period of years that the case had been before it. Or did you know about that?

MR. ADAMS: Mr. Chairman, I am unfamiliar with the details of this case, and I would not be able to testify in respect to the matters which you bring up.

THE CHAIRMAN: You just merely made the inquiry because it was brought to your attention?

MR. ADAMS: That is correct.

THE CHAIRMAN: Did Mr. Goldfine bring it to your attention himself personally?

MR. ADAMS: I think he did on one occasion, and I think his counsel—

THE CHAIRMAN: He did not advise you when he brought it to your attention that he had failed to file his reports as the law requires?

MR. ADAMS: He did not go into the details of the extent of his failure to file a report, which I later came to know was required by the Commission. And, as I say, I made no examination of the details of this and did not base my judgment at all, in respect to the inquiry which I asked counsel to make, on any such failure to observe the technicalities of the statute.

THE CHAIRMAN: In view of these incidents and the long-time relationship that existed between you and Mr. Goldfine and the position that you occupy, do you think, Governor Adams, that in these instances that you overstepped the bounds of propriety?

MR. ADAMS: Mr. Chairman, that is a fair question, and I should like to answer it in as much candor as I know you would answer it if you sat here where I sit at the present time.

As I look in retrospect over my own activities and the activities of my associates in the staff of the President, I came to the conclusion, some 2 years ago, as I recall it, that there could very likely be, as a result of an instance similar to this—and there were many instances when we received these inquiries and that I called—I think it is all right, Mr. Chairman, if I testify to this committee that I called my staff together and we counseled together on this point, and that I think that since that time, Mr. Chairman, sensitive to the implications that might accrue from instances such as you have related, that it was desirable for the staff of the President of the United States to refrain from doing anything which might possibly lead to any question such as you have posed.

Now, Mr. Chairman, I have no excuses to offer. I did not come up here to make apology to you or this committee. But there again, if there were any errors here, as I have already stated, they were errors, in respect to these matters, perhaps of inexperience and I do not wish to testify that I am a fledgling in this business of politics. Nevertheless, I think, to repeat, that there are lessons to be learned, and I think perhaps somewhat more prudence would undoubtedly have perhaps obviated some of the questions that have come before your committee, and I cannot wholly disagree with the implications contained in your question.

THE CHAIRMAN: Did you read the editorial in the Washington Post a few days ago? I believe it was Thursday of last week. It was entitled "The Unwritten Letter."

MR. ADAMS: Mr. Chairman, I am an avid reader of the Washington Post.

THE CHAIRMAN: I am sure the Washington Post will be pleased to hear that.

This "Unwritten Letter," just the very thing we are talking about here, said, among other things—and this is what they said the letter should contain:

> Notwithstanding the knowledge that I intended no wrong, although in fact no intervention of mine altered the course of the Government toward Mr. Goldfine, I am convinced that in these matters I was mistaken.

Would you say that was a fair statement?

MR. ADAMS: Mr. Chairman, I will say this, that if I had the decisions now before me to make I believe I would have acted a little more prudently.

THE CHAIRMAN: When you made the decision from the experience that you had, was that about the time the President made his statement at the news conference in which he said, and I quote:

> If anyone ever comes to any part of this Government claiming some privilege for even as low as an introduction to an official he wants to meet, on the basis that he is a part of my family or my friends, that he has any connection with the White House, he is to be thrown out instantly. I cannot believe that anybody on my staff would ever be guilty of anything indiscreet, but if ever anything came to my attention of that kind, any part of this Government, that individual would be gone.

That was the time when there were a lot of reports about people seeking favors and so forth, about 2 years ago.

I assume from what has been said here in this discussion that you, as many of us, if not indeed all of us, learn from the hard road of experience about how to handle these tremendous and important problems.

Governor Adams, again let me thank you for your appearance here today and your very frank statements in helping to clear up the truth and the facts which we only seek.

We have sympathy for anyone who serves in the position you hold, with the tremendous responsibility that is yours.

MR. ADAMS: Thank you, Mr. Chairman.

THE CHAIRMAN: Mr. O'Hara.

MR. O'HARA: Governor, permit me to personally express my thanks for your appearance here this morning before the committee. Having the highest regard for your character, your honesty, and your integrity, I assure you that I am personally grateful that you have appeared here this morning.

Thank you very much.

MR. ADAMS: Thank you.

On June 18, Eisenhower used a press conference to state formally his support for and faith in Sherman Adams.

Presidential News Conference
June 18, 1958

[*Public Papers of the Presidents: 1958* (Washington, 1959), 478–81.]

THE PRESIDENT: Good morning. Please sit down.

Ladies and gentlemen, this morning I want to start off with two or three announcements, the first of which I have dictated, because I want to give it to you exactly as I intend it.

I showed this to Mr. Hagerty, who is just now having it mimeographed in order, if you are interested, that you can have the exact wording, rather than an abbreviated version.

[*Reading*] The intense publicity lately surrounding the name of Sherman Adams makes it desirable, even necessary, that I start this conference with an expression of my own views about the matter.

First, as a result of this entire incident, all of us in America should have been made aware of one truth—this is that a gift is not necessarily a bribe. One is evil, the other is a tangible expression of friendship.

Almost without exception, everybody seeking public office accepts political contributions. These are gifts to further a political career. Yet we do not make a generality that these gifts are intended to color the later official votes, recommendations, and actions of the recipients.

In the general case, this whole activity is understood, accepted, and approved.

The circumstances surrounding the innocent receipt by a public official of any gift are therefore important, so that the public may clearly distinguish between innocent and guilty action.

Among these circumstances are the character and reputation of the individual, the record of his subsequent actions, and evidence of intent or lack of intent to exert undue influence.

Anyone who knows Sherman Adams has never had any doubt of his personal integrity and honesty. No one has believed that he could be bought; but there is a feeling or belief that he was not sufficiently alert in making certain that the gifts, of which he was the recipient, could be so misinterpreted as to be considered as attempts to influence his political actions. To that extent he has been, as he stated yesterday, "imprudent."

Now, the utmost in prudence must necessarily be observed by everyone attached to the White House because of the possible effect of any slightest inquiry, suggestion, or observation emanating from this office and reaching any other part of the Government. Carelessness must be avoided.

My own conclusions of this entire episode are as follows:

I believe that the presentation made by Governor Adams to the congressional committee yesterday truthfully represents the pertinent facts. I personally like Governor Adams. I admire his abilities. I respect him because of his personal and official integrity. I need him.

Admitting the lack of that careful prudence in this incident that Governor Adams yesterday referred to, I believe with my whole heart that he is an invaluable public servant doing a difficult job efficiently, honestly, and tirelessly.

Now, ladies and gentlemen, so far as I am concerned, this is all that I can, all that I shall, say. [*Ends reading*]

If there are any questions from any part of this body, they will go to Mr. Hagerty and not to me.

I am ready for questions.

QUESTION. Marvin L. Arrowsmith, *Associated Press:* Mr. President, I don't know whether this transgresses your embargo or not, but some Republicans running for re-election say they are going to have difficulty facing the voters on the Adams-Goldfine issue in the light of this administration's 1952 attacks on the so-called mess in Washington.

Do you care to comment on those Republican views?

THE PRESIDENT: No, I think not, Mr. Arrowsmith.

I have given you my statement. It is what I believe is demanded and expected and needed in the circumstances.

QUESTION. Edward P. Morgan, *American Broadcasting Company:* Mr. President, this question has not to do with Mr. Adams but Government procedure possibly regarding Mr. Goldfine. May I state it to see whether it falls within or without your embargo?

In past instances, Mr. President, when difficulties of this kind have come up regarding propriety, you have stated, you have indicated strongly that one of the most important matters is to get the facts out.

House investigators say that to them one of the most important matters is how Mr. Goldfine viewed this relationship with people in the Government, and that the only way they can really find this out, is to whether he claimed as business deductions the gifts he made on his income tax. Apparently the only way they can get the income tax returns is by a special presidential order through the Department of Justice.

If you were so asked, would you be inclined to make such an order?

THE PRESIDENT: Well, I think I would consult the Attorney General and precedents in like cases.

I have nothing else to say, because I don't know anything further about it. It's a question that has come suddenly, and I have no other way of answering it. . . .

Despite the President's press conference statement, the Adams affair became a highly publicized controversy, complete with grave political implications for the Republican party. Democrats, sensing a new "mess in Washington," increased their demands for Adams' removal. Eisenhower asked Vice President Nixon to check on Republican congressional attitudes. The general consensus was that Adams should resign to avoid giving the Democrats an issue in the fall. Despite this reaction, and buttressed by privately obtained derogatory information about Goldfine's business activities, the President declined to take action. Apparently, he remained convinced that the attacks were overwhelmingly partisan, that Democrats wanted to make political hay, and that Old Guard Republicans wanted to get Adams for alleged mistreatment. The President and Adams might have ridden out the storm had it not been for the early September election in Maine. There, Republican Senator Frederick Payne, who had admitted dealings with Goldfine, suffered a crushing defeat. This loss in a predominately Republican state convinced the President that Adams would have to go. On September 22, Adams handed in his resignation, which Eisenhower quickly accepted. A few hours later, Adams went on national radio and television to explain his actions.

President Eisenhower to
The Assistant to the President Sherman Adams
September 22, 1958
[*Public Papers of the Presidents: 1958* (Washington, 1959), 704–05.]

Dear Sherman:

I deeply deplore the circumstances that have decided you to resign as The Assistant to the President.

Your selfless and tireless devotion to the work of the White House and to me personally has been universally recognized. In discharging the responsibilities of your vitally important post, with no hope of reward other than your own satisfaction in knowing that you have served your country well, your total dedication to the nation's welfare has been of the highest possible order.

Your performance has been brilliant; the public has been the beneficiary of your unselfish work. After our six years of intimate association you have, as you have had throughout, my complete trust, confidence and respect.

I accept your resignation with sadness. You will be sorely missed by your colleagues on the staff and by the departments and agencies of the government, with which you have worked so efficiently.

With warm regard and highest esteem,

Address by The Assistant to the President Sherman Adams
on the Reasons for his Resignation
September 22, 1958
[*The New York Times,* September 23, 1958.]

Ladies and Gentlemen:

Since last June, a spirited controversy has taken place in which I, Sherman Adams, Assistant to the President, have found myself cast in the principal role.

This controversy has, at times, unfortunately displaced public consideration of much more important and far-reaching problems that directly affect the welfare of our country and its people.

It is quite probable that a great many of you now listening to me have expressed, some time in the course of this controversy and as private citizens, your views on this matter.

It seems to me that nearly everyone active in public life in one capacity or another has done so. I am here tonight to express mine.

Several months ago, a committee of the House of Representatives started hearings designed to elicit information as to whether or not any person or persons had exerted improper influence upon the regulatory agencies of the Government.

In the course of the hearings I testified before that committee. The sworn testimony that I then gave together with that of every responsible official of whom the committee made inquiry clearly established that I had never influenced nor attempted to influence any agency or any officer or employee of any agency in any case, decision or matter whatsoever.

Despite the fact that this testimony is wholly undisputed, a calculated and contrived effort has nevertheless been made to attack and to discredit me. As part of this effort the committee received completely irresponsible testimony and without conscience gave ear to rumor, innuendo and even unsubstantiated gossip.

A campaign of villification by those who seek personal advantage by my removal from public life has continued up to this very moment.

These efforts, it is now clear, have been intended to destroy me and so doing, to embarrass the Administration and the President of the United States.

Now an easy and an obvious way to bring such an attack to an end is to remove the target. There were those who thought I should resign because they felt I had been imprudent in not perceiving the interpretation that could be placed upon my exchanging gifts with a friend, even of some fifteen years' standing.

I am sure that many of you have wondered why I have not chosen that course; why, at the very beginning of the controversy, I did not immediately resign.

Well, I would like to tell you why.

First, it is not, nor has it ever been, my nature to run in the face of adversity. And in many years of public service, nearly twenty now, I have never once done so.

Second, since I have done no wrong, my resigning could have been construed as an admission that I had, in the atmosphere which has surrounded the controversy.

Third, when a man has been afforded the privilege that has been mine of serving a great American, a great humanitarian and a great President, when a man has come to understand the selflessness and the dedication with which that President has served all of our people regardless of race, creed, religious or political persuasion, it poses a decision, as I am sure you can readily appreciate, which is difficult in the extreme to make.

Against my distaste for giving any grounds whatever to the charge of retreating under fire, against my desire to complete my duty during the remaining two years of the term for which President Eisenhower was elected, I must give full consideration to the effect of my continuing presence on the public scene.

Under the circumstances, and in light of the events of the past three months in which I have been made to be directly concerned, I just ask myself whether my retention in office might conceivably delay or retard, even in small degree, the achievement of those goals of President Eisenhower which yet are ahead.

Another factor that I feel I must consider is whether the retention of my services might possibly diminish the chances which my party has of regaining control of the Congress in the November elections.

Within the past few days I have reached a decision.

Early this morning I flew from Washington to the President's vacation headquarters at Newport, R.I. I conferred with him and in the course of that conference I have tendered my resignation.

This he has accepted, to be effective as soon as an orderly transition can be arranged for the assumption of my duties and responsibilities.

This action of mine is final and unqualified. It is not open to reconsideration.

It is my steadfast belief that the principles and the programs for which Dwight Eisenhower stands serve the best interests of our country and, indeed, the people of the free world. They deserve to be strengthened through the support of everyone of us.

I believe that I can now best serve my President and contribute to the support of his objectives by the course that I have undertaken to follow.

I am now about to retire after nearly six years in the position in which I have served with pride, in which I have given my best efforts to hold with honor.

Now nearly twenty years of public service come to a close. But I can say that it has brought a depth of satisfaction that will always be with me.

Good night.

Nine days after the resignation, the President made clear in response to a press conference question that the White House could run without Adams.

Presidential News Conference
October 1, 1958
[*Public Papers of the Presidents: 1958* (Washington, 1959), 716–17.]

QUESTION. Edward P. Morgan, *American Broadcasting Company:* Mr. President, in the past you have made it very clear that you, yourself, make all the final decisions in the White House, but—

THE PRESIDENT: If I didn't, wouldn't there have been chaos? [*Laughter*]

QUESTION. Mr. Morgan: Conceded, sir.

In view of the vital role, as expressed by yourself, that Governor Adams has played in the White House staff, and he is now leaving, do you have any idea of changing the emphasis of the staff work in the White House in such a way that you, yourself, would participate more in the preliminaries to those decisions?

THE PRESIDENT: Let's get a little background.

General Persons will be sworn in as The Assistant to the President very early in the week. Now, the staff will have to be organized under him, and he has been very familiar with the methods that I, as a commander and now as President, have used over a great many years. Frankly, I think they have been fairly successful. . . .

The President must know the general purpose of everything that is going on, the general problem that is there, whether or not it is being solved or the solution is going ahead according to principles in which he believes and which he has promulgated; and, finally, he must say "yes" or "no."

Now, I will tell you, while we don't in the White House have large, big staff conferences with every last subordinate present, the constant meetings in my office of the important staff leaders are, I think, much more frequent than they ever were in any military organization that I have known.

Now, with respect to the diffusion, what I shall do is this—and I think here is a place that I probably have been guilty of not making some things clear: I shall probably issue a memorandum or a type of organization which will show all the American people, if they are interested, exactly the channels through which these questions come up, who are the individuals that I will hold responsible for studying them first, and then what individuals will come to me to argue them. Frequently the staff officer will say, "All right, Agriculture believes this"; somebody else, "Labor believes that." I'm sort of on this side, but bring them both in, and then we have it out. And then the decision is made that way.

But I will put out that information to prevent any misunderstanding of exactly what we are doing.

5. THE 1958 ELECTION DISASTER

In June, 1957, in the midst of nationwide prosperity, the leaders of the Republican party predicted major gains in the next year's congressional elections. After a series of regional meetings, they sent Eisenhower an optimistic report about the party's chances.

Meade Alcorn, Bertha Adkins, Andrew Schoepell, and Richard Simpson to President Eisenhower
June 4, 1957
[Price-Stambaugh Files, Eisenhower Papers.]

Dear Mr. President:

We are submitting herewith the reports on the six Regional Conferences held this spring at Omaha, April 12–13; Providence, April 26–27; Salt Lake City, May 3–4; Louisville, May 10–11; Cincinnati, May 17–18, and Trenton, May 24–25.

As you know, these conferences were sponsored jointly by the Republican National, Senatorial and Congressional Committees. In all, 47 States and the District of Columbia participated.

Looking at the conferences from an overall basis, we are encouraged by the following:

1. The conferences have provided a much-needed forum for Republican leaders to air their opinions on the issues of the day. This discussion has cleared the atmosphere and the publicity on it has served a good purpose.

2. They have brought national, regional and state leaders of the Party together on common grounds and permitted all of us to become better acquainted with each other as individuals and with each other's problems.

3. They have served to focus attention on the importance of electing a Republican House and Senate next year and we are happy to report that the campaign is actively under way in the states and districts. This is the earliest nation-wide beginning of a Congressional campaign in either party's history.

4. There has been a marked improvement in team spirit and your own declared intention of working vigorously in the '58 election has given Party morale a tremendous boost. The country is becoming increasingly aware of the difficulties you face in dealing with a Democrat-controlled Congress.

5. We find that the Republican organization on a national basis is the same that led to your big victory in 1956. It is strong and eager to work. The self-examination we've been through has been constructive and beneficial. While there are various differences of opinion within the party, the overall accomplishments of your Administration in achieving unparalleled prosperity under conditions of peace is a record which makes every Republican proud.

Probably the most important result of the conferences was the work of Committee No. 5, which permitted the heads of the national committees to go over each and every Congressional race in the country with the state leaders and assess the chances of victory. We had detailed discussions on candidates, party finances, organization strengths and weaknesses, and detailed appraisal of the opposition. An interesting sidelight is the fact that the backbone of the Republican Party's organization is women power and that the Young Republican movement is vigorous and effective in many parts of the country.

Based on what the state leaders told us, the Republican Party may expect to win control of the House, but the fight for control of the Senate will be close, and our job is most difficult and depends on many factors. They also told us we can pick up several of the governorship races in 1957 and 1958. It should be emphasized these estimates are given 18 months before Election.

The Regional Conferences are to be followed by state and district conferences this fall and next spring, and we hope to keep in close touch with these to watch how sentiment changes and how the campaign develops.

We believe the conferences were a huge success, and feel we are on the road to a victory for '58.

Summary of Six Regional Reports
Committee on Prospects for 1957–58

The participants representing each of the States conferred with the national leaders in closed sessions for a candid review of each State's prospects in the forthcoming 1957–58 elections.

The following is a summary of what *they, the Republican leaders in each State,* reported to us:

Governors

At stake in the 1957–58 elections:	35
Of which we now hold:	13
We were told we may expect to win:	20
Net gain:	7

U.S. Senator

Seats at stake in 1958:	32
Of which we now hold:	21
We were told we may expect to win:	21
and that there was an outside chance of winning:	3 others
Net gain:	0

As of today, the Senate race is very close and many factors may enter the picture between now and the campaign next year.

House of Representatives

Seats at stake in 1958:	435
Of which we now hold:	200
We were told we may expect to win:	219
And have a chance to pick up 8 additional seats in the South, depending on how effectively the Republican drive in the South develops.	
Net gain:	19

Thus, we were told we could win control of the House.

Summary of Six Regional Reports
Committees on Republican Goals

At the six Republican Regional Conferences, Committees on Republican Goals in each instance devoted a major portion of their round-table discussions to items of national interest, such as Federal fiscal policies and the budget, Federal aid to education, civil rights, foreign policy (with particular emphasis upon mutual security programs), agriculture and labor.

At some of the meetings, area problems received considerable attention—tariff policies at Providence and to a lesser degree at Trenton. Minerals policies and reclamation overshadowed even the budget at Salt Lake City.

There was a strong thread of conservatism through all of the discussions and the reports. This was most pronounced at Cincinnati and perhaps least at Providence.

Summarized briefly, here are the general attitudes reflected in the Committee III reports at the six meetings:

Federal Fiscal Policies

While the budget was discussed in detail at each of the six meetings, related items such as tax reduction and monetary policies received attention at some but not all of the conferences.

Omaha reported "decided dissatisfaction" with the size of the budget and expressed "unanimous opinion" that it could be cut. Commended were the President's economic policies leading to "stabilization of the dollar."

Salt Lake City emphasized the need for the President to present the issues involved in the budget to the people "not by way of defense of this budget, but by way of explanation . . . that peace and the lives of American military personnel cannot be measured in terms of money."

Providence said "the cost of peace is high . . . We know that the budget is big but we cannot allow weariness with taxes to induce us to settle for less than full international security." Endorsed were Administration efforts in stabilizing the dollar and the "tight money policy."

Louisville recommended careful scrutiny of the budget "with an eye toward further reductions—including items concerning Federal grants to states and foreign aid." The report said, "The people of the South want an immediate reduction in taxes," as well as "a substantial reduction in the national debt." Commended was the President's announcement that he would speak on the budget.

Cincinnati reported "widespread dissatisfaction with the budget jeopardizes Republican chances in the 1958 and 1960 elections." Applauded were the "fiscal integrity of our Government," the halt of deficit spending, reduction of the national debt and the tax cut of 1954.

Trenton endorsed "strongly" the President's request for item veto authority. The report noted criticism not so much of the "size of the budget as from the manner of its public presentation." The need for Administration teamwork was noted.

Federal Aid to Education

There was probably more sharp disagreement with the Administration on this than on any other question. Except at Providence, where the classroom construction program was endorsed, and at Salt Lake, where state and local responsibility was stressed in general terms, there was either unanimous or strong majority opinion expressed against even such limited Federal assistance in the field of education. The consensus was that a construction program would lead to further Federal participation and eventually to Federal control.

Civil Rights

Strong support for the Administration civil rights program was evident at Omaha, Providence, Cincinnati and Trenton. The Salt Lake meeting reported no civil rights problems in the area. At Louisville, a policy of "moderation" was urged, as was "preservation of the constitutional right of trial by jury."

Mutual Assistance—Foreign Aid—Foreign Policy

Omaha favored foreign economic aid "only insofar as it implements our national defense and advances our national interests and the preservation of world peace." The leadership shown by the President and his Administration in maintaining peace was highly praised.

Providence reaffirmed "our faith and confidence in the President's mutual security program."

Salt Lake City said "foreign aid is presently a necessity" and urged continuance of Administration efforts to eliminate "wasteful and unnecessary expenses and excess personnel."

Louisville reported general feeling in the South that "foreign aid appropriations are higher than they should be" but urged continued efforts toward "helping other countries help themselves." The report advocated a "vigorous program" to acquaint the public with the "successes of our foreign policy."

Cincinnati reported people are "largely uninformed as to the specific contents and reasons for much of the aid program and therefore question its present scope and costs." Pride was expressed in U. S. military posture and in the conduct of foreign affairs.

Trenton endorsed "in full" the President's statement on mutual security and urged further public education concerning the need for foreign assistance programs.

Agriculture

In general, there was far more support than criticism voiced in connection with the Administration's farm policies at all six meetings. Some complaints concerning the wheat program were expressed in the Salt Lake report.

The Soil Bank was specifically commended at Omaha, Salt Lake City and Providence. Louisville praised Administration efforts to meet the farm problem and expressed hope for an early return to "natural laws of supply and demand." Cincinnati noted "confidence . . . in the principles advocated by Secretary Benson," adding there still remain "serious problems . . . especially in obtaining for farm families a fair share of the national income." Trenton went on record supporting the President's proposal of last year that dollar limitations be placed upon the size of price support assistance to individual farmers in order to keep programs "within their purpose."

One political conclusion with respect to agriculture was reached at the Salt Lake meeting: "There is real need to tell and sell the Administration's story in the field of agriculture. We should encourage more active Republican organization work among farmers and an expanded public relations effort beamed at farm families."

Labor

Cincinnati expressed approval of the Administration's "hands-off policy in labor and management disputes" and called for safeguards against "abuses which certain labor leaders have perpetrated on their own people."

Trenton urged Republican sponsorship of legislation to protect union funds and to protect union members from the "dictatorial and autocratic powers exercised by a few labor leaders."

Tariffs

Providence pointed to the impact of imports on New England's textile and jewelry industries and urged the creation of a special commission to study methods of aiding "small industries, particularly in distressed areas."

Louisville requested review of tariff policies "with a view toward increased protection of the textile industry and other Southern industries . . . "

Trenton supported the "general principles of the Administration in fostering world trade" and expressed satisfaction with the President's order increasing wool tariffs.

Salt Lake City recommended that the 1934 Trade Agreements Act be permitted to expire in June 1958.

Minerals

Salt Lake City favored development of a long-range minerals policy, as did *Louisville*.

Postal Rates

Cincinnati favored the Administration postal rate increases.

Leadership

Trenton pointed to the need for the Republican Party to "provide a reservoir of attractive candidates for future political campaigns both at the state and national levels." It was suggested that the President, with the advice of state Republican leaders, could appoint to important Federal positions "Republicans who could then, after achieving experience, competence and recognition, go on to run successfully for public office."

Summary of Six Regional Reports
Committees on Democrat Weaknesses

The basic weaknesses of the Democrat Party can be listed in order of importance as follows:

I. *Factionalism*

    a. North vs. South split based on states rights and civil rights.

    b. Liberal vs. Conservative. This is true in every state to some degree; it is often interpreted as Labor vs. Other Force.

    c. Political or personality splits; such as the McKinney-Skillen fight in Indiana; Kennedy-Furcolo in Massachusetts; Talmadge-anti-Talmadge in Georgia. Some of these splits are based on differences in philosophy, but they are principally personality conflicts.

II. *Defection of Negro and Nationality Groups*

The reports tend to indicate that the party in power, by its executive authority, has an increasing appeal to these people. The peaceful liberation policies of the Administration are tending to split the nationality groups from the Democrats and advances in civil rights have a similar effect with the Negroes. Widely shared prosperity further contributes to this defection.

III. *Failure to Recognize Women's and Youth Groups*

The Democrat women and the Young Democrats in almost every state are expending the majority of their efforts in a fight for basic recognition.

IV. *Labor*

The disclosures of the McClellan Committee, which tend to lessen the influence of Labor bosses, may be recognized in most states as building rank and file revolts evident in the Eisenhower vote in 1952 and 1956. Overdependence on Labor funds tends to augment the splits noted in Point I.

V. *Failure of New-Face Governors to Live Up to Publicly-Expressed Goals of Democrat High Command*

For example, Muskie ran on a platform of new industry for Maine. Maine's total industry, however, has not increased. The inexperience of Leader of Pennsylvania has led to weak appointments and the Pardon Board scandals. Meyner of New Jersey has failed to meet the state's principal problems; aid to education and industrial water. These problems are larger now than when he took office.

Conclusion

There was an absolute consensus of opinion by the six regions of the value of continuing this activity of defining the weaknesses of our Democrat opponents. To this end it was suggested that the Truth Squad and the Answer Desk be reactivated; that this research material could be released through state campaign headquarters and through national headquarters, particularly when Congress is not in session.

Summary of Six Regional Reports
Committees on Republican Organization

A consensus of the views of these six districts can be summarized as follows:

I. *Good Organization*

It is agreed that the key to good organization rests entirely on a foundation of effective door-to-door work. To this end, the committees recommend:

A. *Training:*

    1. The county and state leadership has direct responsibility for a continued program of training sessions for precinct workers.

    2. National, state and county leaders must establish a similar set of tools for precinct workers. These would include manuals, training aids and schools.

    3. Employed professional directors are needed at the state and county level to assist and supervise volunteers.

B. *Work Planning*

To be effective a volunteer must receive specific instructions. Leadership on the state and county level has the responsibility not only to plan the campaign but to list the actual tasks necessary to the execution of the plan. The result of this listing would be that each worker would then have a part in the overall plan. This would further enable leadership to enlighten the volunteer as to the importance of his responsibility.

C. *Recognition*

    1. Building leadership: Essential to good leadership is the degree of prestige and recognition built into the leading positions at all levels of the party. The failure to recognize local leadership in patronage matters tends to destroy all of these factors. It is recommended, therefore, that all political appointments originate with the leaders in the area of residence. A further problem in the area is demonstrated by the following quote: "A good many guys and gals are good politicians until they are elected or appointed—when they become statesmen."

    2. Recognition of affiliated groups: Particular emphasis should be placed on the contributions of the National Federation of Republican Women and the Young Republicans. This calls for increased recognition of their efforts and results. It has been suggested that

the presidents of these groups be made ex officio members of the state committees. This call for recognition is based on these organizations' unique ability as recruiting and educating forces within the party. It is recommended that particular stress be put on the following three programs:

a. The Young Republican recruit program under which a young person is assigned as an aide or non-voting alternate to each member of the central committee at every level.

b. The Republican Women's Federation program, "Welcome Neighbor," which provides a splendid service, especially to newcomers in the community.

c. The plan whereby a young person is assigned as an administrative aide to each candidate.

3. The committee urges the further broadening of the party base by inclusion of groups such as labor, nationalities, farmers, veterans and professional associations, and to use participation and legislation as a continuing program for these groups.

4. It is recommended that polls and surveys be conducted periodically in the precinct, not only to reflect the thinking of the individual voter but also to give recognition. Results should be transmitted to the next higher levels of leadership.

5. The use of letters and certificates by present Governmental and party leaders is recommended as a means of recognition.

II. *Good Programming*

It is recommended that a continuing strategy and policy committee be maintained—representative of all segments of the political party—including nominated candidates, office holders and party officials. This committee would set the over-all policy and campaign strategy for the total Republican effort, and would act as a unifying force between all elements of the party.

III. *Good Candidates*

To make sure we have a Republican candidate for each partisan office, procedure should be set up designed: (1) to study all available candidates, (2) if no satisfactory candidate is available, to seek out and draft a candidate, and (3) to encourage candidates to conduct their primary campaigns in such a manner that all Republicans may unite behind the person selected by the people as the nominee of the party.

It has been said that the official party machinery should refrain from the selection and encouragement of candidates, since it is the organization's function to support and elect the Republican candidates selected by the people at the direct primary. There can be no criticism of volunteers who seek and support the finest possible candidates. On the other hand, someone must see to it that we nominate inspiring candidates who truly represent Republican objectives and who have the intestinal fortitude to stand up and be counted, the personality and ability to be elected and to deserve such election, and the ability to campaign and speak vigorously. If the Republican Party is to win or even deserve to win in 1958, the securing of outstanding candidates for every partisan office is an absolute essential and, if no one else is going to do the job, the official party must get in and do it.

IV. *Good Communications*

There is a continuing need to improve communications between every level of the party organization. There must exist a clear understanding of the common objectives as well as the methods of operation by all Republicans, from the National Chairman to the newest Republican recruit.

State and national officers within a state should accept responsibility for an organized, continuing program of contact with county and local officers. This program would enable state leaders to create enthusiasm among local workers and to check local organizations on effectiveness of organization, a common programming and the development of good candidates.

Newsletters and other regular means of communication should be employed. These letters, whether originated by members of Congress, national headquarters or state headquarters, must carry specific facts, both legislative and executive, and convincing reasons for the electorate to support the Republican Party. "Straight From the Shoulder," it is felt, should be continued, as a means of supplying these "fighting facts" to all levels. It is suggested that materials sent from the National Committee, Young Republicans, and Women's Federation be reviewed in order to avoid duplication and excessive mailings. It is further recommended that national headquarters accept more responsibility for assisting the state and local committees in the development of news and public relations. It is recommended that each state central committee establish a permanent headquarters and that this office should be staffed with a full-time, paid executive director and/or public relations expert.

V. *Good Financing*

Adequate financing is necessary in order to achieve support of the party program and its candidates. Therefore, it is recommended that the base of financial participation be further broadened, not only to insure adequate financing but also to create party responsibility.

Three plans are recommended to the National Finance Committee for consideration for purposes of augmenting its regular finance operations:

1. Salute Dinners, to be a nation-wide fund-raising, one-day affair tied together by a national, closed-circuit television broadcast. It is suggested that the dinners take place on a significant Republican date early in 1958.

2. The Finance Committee is urged to promote an annual Neighbor-to-Neighbor campaign and fund-raising program to be held throughout the country in the fall of 1957.

3. All states are urged to supply immediate and adequate financing to all levels of party activity.

Summary of Six Regional Reports
Committees on Formulation of State, Congressional
District, or County Conferences

As a follow-up to the regional conferences, a series of state and district conferences are planned. Committees were appointed to look into this subject and the following is a summary of their recommendations.

I. *State Conferences* (under sponsorship of Republican State Committee)

    A. Time—Fall of 1957 (September, October, November)

    B. Purpose of the State Conference is to conduct "fact-finding sessions" or "Let the people speak" before the Committee in the following fields:

        1. Agriculture
        2. Civil Rights
        3. Conservation and Natural Resources
        4. Education
        5. Foreign Affairs and National Defense
        6. Human Welfare
        7. Industry
        8. Labor
        9. Small Business
       10. State Issues

11. Taxation and Fiscal Policy
12. Veterans Affairs

C. Organizations to be invited:
   Labor groups
   Agricultural Organizations
      Farm Bureau
      Grange
      Farmers' Unions
   Business and Management Organizations
      Chamber of Commerce
      Association of Manufacturers
   Medical Associations
   Educational Associations
   Service Clubs
      Kiwanis
      Rotary
      Lions
      Exchange
   Veterans Organizations
   Women's Organizations
      League of Women Voters
      Business and Professional Women
      Federated Womens Clubs
   Newspaper Publishers

II. *Congressional District and County Conferences*

A. Purpose and Functions of Conferences: Fact-finding sessions on local, state and national issues (Conferences to be patterned on proposals for the state conferences except insofar as local circumstances may require some changes).

B. Time (March, April, May 1958)

III. *Problem of organization of State, County, and Congressional Conferences to be left to discretion of State and local leaders. Considerable flexibility of organizational meetings allowable due to peculiarities of State and its political units.*

IV. *Conferences to be conducted by State Chairman, assisted by Vice Chairman in conjunction with National Committee members, State Finance Chairman, NFRW President, Chairman of State YR organization, and any other state-recognized organizations or leaders decided upon by existing Republican authorities.*

V. *Follow-up on Conferences*

A. The summation of results of State Conferences to be forwarded to the Chairmen of the three National Committees and also to President Eisenhower.

B. The summation of results of Congressional District and County Conferences to be forwarded to Republican State Committee and other Statewide officials of the Party.

Even after the Recession of 1958 and the Adams Affair, the President still expected a 1958 Republican victory. In a letter to retiring Minority Leader William Knowland of California he indicated this belief.

President Eisenhower to Senator William Knowland
August 25, 1958
[*Public Papers of the Presidents: 1958* (Washington, 1959), 638.]

Dear Bill:

You will be leaving shortly to return to California, there to wage a political campaign on behalf of a philosophy of government in which we both believe.

Before you go, I want to tell you how grateful I am for your tireless efforts as Senate Majority Leader and then as Senate Minority Leader. In both of these capacities you demonstrated the characteristics of leadership, of integrity, and devotion in the service of the Nation.

The people of this country owe you a debt of gratitude for your contribution to good government and for helping maintain peace in the world. I am certain that the people of California are aware of your admirable qualifications, fine character, and dedication to duty, and would want to utilize your services as Governor of that great State.

I am well aware of the political sacrifice that you have made in continuing to discharge your responsibilities so faithfully during the past several weeks. For this I am especially grateful.

You take with you my best wishes and those of Mrs. Eisenhower for a successful campaign, and our affection for both you and Helen.

By late October the President had come close to accepting the inevitability of defeat, as his brief birthday letter to House Minority Leader Joseph Martin of Massachusetts disclosed.

President Eisenhower to Representative Joseph Martin
October 29, 1958
[President's Personal File 297, Eisenhower Papers.]

Dear Joe:

I am definitely not one of the gloom-and-doom boys, but to be on the safe side I am glad that your birthday anniversary is the day *before* election.

At any rate, I do want to assure you of my felicitations and good wishes and, as always, my warm personal regard,

>────o─●─o─●─o─●─o─●─o─●─o─●─o─●─o─●─o─●─o─●─o─●─o─●─o─●─o─●─o─●─o─●─o─●─o─●─o─●<

Following the 1958 Republican defeat, Eisenhower wrote a series of letters intended to console defeated candidates. The President's correspondence always indicated the nation's loss; defeated candidates responded differently, as the letters that follow illustrate.

President Eisenhower to Senator John Bricker
November 5, 1958
[Official File 138-A-9-C, Eisenhower Papers.]

Dear John:

I am deeply distressed by the outcome in Ohio. Though I know the results are a great personal disappointment to you, the Senate and the Nation suffer by far the greater loss in your leaving. I for one will keenly feel your absence.

Senator William Knowland to President Eisenhower
November 12, 1958
[President's Personal File 851, Eisenhower Papers.]

Dear Mr. President:

Your letter of November 7 has been received and is greatly appreciated.

I do not regret having raised the issues I did or having made the fight. It may help alert the people of California and the Nation to some of the fundamental issues facing us and some of the dangers ahead.

In case you did not see the full text of the same, I am enclosing a copy of my election night statement, together with a copy of my telegram of congratulations to Governor-Elect Brown.

I expect to be in Washington at the end of this month and will look forward to seeing you at that time.

One of the most pleasant recollections I shall carry away as a result of thirteen years in the United States Senate has been my association with you during the 1952 campaign tour and in the six years that have passed since then.

Senator John Bricker to President Eisenhower
November 26, 1958
[Official File 138-A-9-C, Eisenhower Papers.]

Dear Mr. President:

I received your gracious and kind telegram in regard to my defeat in Ohio.

I could have withstood the trend and everything else had it not been for the right-to-work amendment which the Chamber of Commerce insisted on putting on the ballot. I pleaded with them not to do so, but they thought they knew more about public sentiment than I did and I have been dealing in the field for thirty years.

I wish that I might have been with you for the next two years so that I could help here and there, but people in the State didn't see fit to make it so. The right-to-work amendment brought out between 400,000 and 500,000 votes on the other side, most of whom did not know or care who was elected to the Senate and were directed by Cope to vote against me. I had wanted to quit as you well remember but I would like to have done it voluntarily.

After the Chamber of Commerce determined to put the right-to-work issue on the ballot I would have gotten off the ticket then if I could have done so with any honor. I talked to Ray Bliss about it and he was against it.

But you know I wish for you the very best of health and success. I hope that we can revive the fundamental principles of conservatism in this country, the only avenue for saving the Republic and the liberties of our people.

In the aftermath of the election disaster, the Republican National Committee compiled a detailed summary of the results.

Summary of the Results of the 1958 Election
[Files of the Republican National Committee, 1932 65.]

In 1958 the Republican Party suffered a severe defeat. Not since 1936 have there been fewer Republicans in the House of Representatives, fewer Republican governors or fewer Republicans in state legislative bodies.

House of Representatives

The nationwide vote for Republican candidates for the House of Representatives was 19.8 million, 43.7 per cent of the vote reported cast for the House. This was 5.7 million votes less than the Democratic candidates polled. The Republican vote was 150,000 below that of 1954; the Democrat vote was 3,200,000 more than that of four years earlier.

153 Republicans and 283 Democrats were elected to the House. Compared with the outcome of the 1956 elections, this is a net loss of 48 seats. 49 Districts which elected Republicans in 1956 reversed themselves in 1958 whereas only one district (the 9th Minnesota) replaced a Democrat with a Republican.

Senate

Of 36 Senate seats filled by election in 1958 (including Alaska's two new seats), Republicans won 8 (Arizona, Delaware, Maryland, Nebraska, New York, North Dakota, Pennsylvania, Vermont). 13 Republican-held seats were lost to Democrats (California, Connecticut, Indiana, Maine, Michigan, Minnesota, Nevada, New Jersey, Ohio, Utah, West Virginia (2), and Wyoming). No switches from Democrat to Republican took place as a result of the election. In the Senate in the 86th Congress there are 34 Republicans, 64 Democrats.

State Elections

Of 34 gubernatorial races in 1958, the Republicans won eight, four of them (Arizona, New York, Oregon, and Rhode Island) in states previously held by Democrats.

Democrats won 26 contests, nine of them in states previously held by Republicans (California, Maryland, Nebraska, Nevada, New Mexico, Ohio, South Dakota, Wisconsin, Wyoming). In 1959 there are 14 Republican governors and 35 Democrats.

In contests for state legislative bodies, Republicans had a net loss of 686 seats.

Interpretation

To interpret the mood of the voters in 1958 is beyond the scope of this study. It may be of interest, however, to note the interpretations which have been made by others whose opinions deserve a respectful hearing.

Samuel Lubell, who has been taking the voters' pulse for many years, ascribed the Republican misfortune to four factors: recession, failure to control inflation, a widespread loss of confidence in the President, and the drive to outlaw the union shop through right-to-work laws.

The American Institute of Public Opinion (the Gallup Poll) offered seven reasons for the outcome of the election:

1. The "image" of the Republican Party as the party of wealth and big business.
2. The preponderance of voters of Democrat inclination.
3. Loss of confidence in the ability of the Republicans to handle the major problems.
4. The lopsided Democrat vote in Southern states.
5. A decrease in the popularity of the President.
6. Harder work by Democrats in the precincts.
7. The loss of support among independent voters.

It can be readily seen that some of these "reasons" do not explain much.

More revealing are certain other Gallup findings. The following are the issues which people regarded as most important in the spring of 1958 and at election time, according to this poll:

October 1958	*Spring 1958*
1. Struggle with Communism; keeping the peace.	1. Unemployment
2. Integration	2. Keeping the Peace
3. High cost of living	3. Sputnik, Space
4. Unemployment	4. Integration

According to Gallup, 63 per cent of the voters felt that the Democrats could best handle what they considered the most important problem of 1958.

On one aspect of the problem which the voters regarded as most important shortly before the election, Gallup found a sharp drop in confidence in the Republican Party. He gave the following report on the response to the question "which party is best able to keep the United States out of war."

Party Best Able to Keep U.S. Out of War

	Rep.	Dem.	No Difference	No Opinion
Oct. 1956	42	17	20	21
June 1957	45	19	17	19
May 1958	30	24	31	15
Aug. 1958	26	24	30	20

Finally, Gallup reported that the major defections from Republican ranks took place between November 1957 and May 1958, when the percentage of voters desiring a Republican Congress dropped from 47 to 42. This was the time of Sputnik and the most severe phase of the short-lived recession.

Whereas Lubell emphasizes domestic problems in his interpretation of the election, the American Institute of Public Opinion seems to stress international affairs.

Recession

It seems clear that unemployment in the course of the economic downturn of 1957 58 was a factor of some importance in Republican losses.

A presumption that such was the case arises from the mere fact that 38 of the 49 House districts which switched from Republican to Democrat in 1958 contained one or more areas of substantial labor surplus one month before the election.

*Smaller Labor Market Areas** Election returns from 47 smaller labor market areas with substantial unemployment located within these districts which switched parties have been studied. In 44 of these 47 areas, there was a decline of the Republican percentage of the vote. In 35 areas the decline was greater than the national average. In 31 of the 47, the decline was greater than the decrease in the Republican percentage in the state as a whole. In 20 of the 47 areas, the Republican percentage of the vote was more than 10 points below that of 1954.

For example, in Kansas the Republican percentage of the Congressional vote statewide slipped 7.1 points from the 1954 level. But in areas of heavy unemployment, the percentage point decrease was much greater. In the Parsons labor market area (for example) it dropped 11.7 points; in the Independence-Coffeyville area the drop was 15.6 points. In Schenectady County, New York, the decline was 16.3 percentage points whereas in New York State as a whole, it was only 1.2 points.

Major Labor Market Areas

The news from areas with heavy unemployment was not uniformly bad.

*The Department of Labor distinguishes two types of areas in reporting on unemployment: Major labor market areas and smaller labor market areas. Differences in Republican fortunes in the two justify giving separate treatment to each.

Although losses preponderate and many of the losses were drastic, there were surplus labor areas in which gains were made.

The following table shows the change in the Republican percentage of the Congressional vote between 1954 and 1958 in the major labor market areas in which unemployment exceeded 9 per cent of the labor force in October 1958.

Change in Republican Percentage of the Congressional Vote in Major Labor Market Areas With Heavy Unemployment[1]

		Pct. Pt. Loss			Pct. Pt. Gain
Conn.	Bridgeport (City and 4 neighboring towns)	−12.2	Conn.	New Britain (City and 1 neighboring town)	+0.3
	Waterbury (City)	−9.0	Mich.	Flint	+1.9
Ind.	Evansville	−10.4		Lansing	+7.2
	Ft. Wayne	−12.1		Muskegon	+2.6
	South Bend	−7.4		Saginaw	+0.1
Mich.	Detroit (6 C.D.'s)	−5.0	Wis.	Superior	+13.8
	Grand Rapids	−0.2	N. Y.	Buffalo (42d C.D.)	+1.3
Minn.	Duluth	−3.8	Pa.	Altoona	+8.0
N. Y.	Buffalo (40th C.D.)	−0.1		Erie	+3.6
	Buffalo (41st C.D.)	−13.4		Johnstown	+5.0
	Utica — Rome	−9.3		Pittsburgh	+1.1
Ohio	Canton	−0.2	Tenn.	Knoxville	+10.4
	Lorain — Elyria	−0.1	W. Va.	Wheeling	+7.2
	Youngstown	−4.8			
	Steubenville	−12.7			
Pa.	Scranton	−1.5			
	Wilkes-Barre	−10.8			
R. I.	Providence	−1.8			
W. Va.	Huntington-Ashland (entire labor mkt area)	−7.2			
	Charleston	−5.3			

It is noteworthy that in Michigan and Pennsylvania—perhaps the hardest hit states—many areas of heavy unemployment returned increased Republican margins over 1954.

[1]Unless otherwise noted, the vote used for this table was the vote of the county in which the city is located.

In general, it is clear that there was a more consistent pattern of Republican losses in smaller labor market areas suffering from heavy unemployment than there was in the major labor market areas. Nevertheless, losses in both types were frequent enough to establish the fact that recession played a part in the 1958 defeat.

6. LEGISLATIVE RESPONSES TO FOREIGN AND DOMESTIC PRESSURES

The overall tone of the 1958 State of the Union Message clearly reflected the increasing pressures that had been brought to bear on the President. His statement was sober and serious. Indeed, he seemed to reflect annoyance at recent criticisms of his Administration. Although some of the momentum was gone from his avowed Modern Republicanism, several domestic proposals received strong support.

State of the Union Message by President Eisenhower
January 9, 1958
[*Public Papers of the Presidents: 1958* (Washington, 1959), 2–15.]

Mr. President, Mr. Speaker, Members of the 85th Congress:

It is again my high privilege to extend personal greetings to the members of the 85th Congress.

All of us realize that, as this new session begins, many Americans are troubled about recent world developments which they believe may threaten our nation's safety. Honest men differ in their appraisal of America's material and intellectual strength, and the dangers that confront us. But all know these dangers are real.

The purpose of this message is to outline the measures that can give the American people a confidence—just as real—in their own security.

I am not here to justify the past, gloss over the problems of the present, or propose easy solutions for the future.

I am here to state what I believe to be right and what I believe to be wrong; and to propose action for correcting what I think wrong!

I

There are two tasks confronting us that so far outweigh all others that I shall devote this year's message entirely to them.

The first is to ensure our safety through strength.

As to our strength, I have repeatedly voiced this conviction: We now have a broadly based and efficient defensive strength, including a great deterrent

948

power, which is, for the present, our main guarantee against war; but, unless we act wisely and promptly, we could lose that capacity to deter attack or defend ourselves.

My profoundest conviction is that the American people will say, as one man: No matter what the exertions or sacrifices, we shall maintain that necessary strength!

But we could make no more tragic mistake than merely to concentrate on military strength.

For if we did only this, the future would hold nothing for the world but an Age of Terror.

And so our second task is to do the constructive work of building a genuine peace. We must never become so preoccupied with our desire for military strength that we neglect those areas of economic development, trade, diplomacy, education, ideas and principles where the foundations of real peace must be laid.

II

The threat to our safety, and to the hope of a peaceful world can be simply stated. It is communist imperialism.

This threat is not something imagined by critics of the Soviets. Soviet spokesmen, from the beginning, have publicly and frequently declared their aim to expand their power, one way or another, throughout the world.

The threat has become increasingly serious as this expansionist aim has been reinforced by an advancing industrial, military and scientific establishment.

But what makes the Soviet threat unique in history is its all-inclusiveness. Every human activity is pressed into service as a weapon of expansion. Trade, economic development, military power, arts, science, education, the whole world of ideas—all are harnessed to this same chariot of expansion.

The Soviets are, in short, waging total cold war.

The only answer to a regime that wages total cold war is to wage total peace.

This means bringing to bear every asset of our personal and national lives upon the task of building the conditions in which security and peace can grow.

III

Among our assets, let us first briefly glance at our military power.

Military power serves the cause of security by making prohibitive the cost of any aggressive attack.

It serves the cause of peace by holding up a shield behind which the patient constructive work of peace can go on.

But it can serve neither cause if we make either of two mistakes. The one would be to overestimate our strength, and thus neglect crucially important actions in the period just ahead. The other would be to underestimate our strength. Thereby we might be tempted to become irresolute in our foreign relations, to dishearten our friends, and to lose our national poise and perspective in approaching the complex problems ahead.

Any orderly balance-sheet of military strength must be in two parts. The first is the position as of today. The second is the position in the period ahead.

As of today: our defensive shield comprehends a vast complex of ground, sea, and air units, superbly equipped and strategically deployed around the world. The most powerful deterrent to war in the world today lies in the retaliatory power of our Strategic Air Command and the aircraft of our Navy. They present to any potential attacker who would unleash war upon the world the prospect of virtual annihilation of his own country.

Even if we assume a surprise attack on our bases, with a marked reduction in our striking power, our bombers would immediately be on their way in sufficient strength to accomplish this mission of retaliation. Every informed government knows this. It is no secret.

Since the Korean Armistice, the American people have spent $225 billion in maintaining and strengthening this overall defensive shield.

This is the position as of today.

Now as to the period ahead: Every part of our military establishment must and will be equipped to do its defensive job with the most modern weapons and methods. But it is particularly important to our planning that we make a candid estimate of the effect of long-range ballistic missiles on the present deterrent power I have described.

At this moment, the consensus of opinion is that we are probably somewhat behind the Soviets in some areas of long-range ballistic missile development. But it is my conviction, based on close study of all relevant intelligence, that if we make the necessary effort, we will have the missiles, in the needed quantity and in time, to sustain and strengthen the deterrent power of our increasingly efficient bombers. One encouraging fact evidencing this ability is the rate of progress we have achieved since we began to concentrate on these missiles.

The intermediate ballistic missiles, Thor and Jupiter, have already been ordered into production. The parallel progress in the intercontinental ballistic missile effort will be advanced by our plans for acceleration. The development of the submarine-based Polaris missile system has progressed so well that its future procurement schedules are being moved forward markedly.

When it is remembered that our country has concentrated on the development of ballistic missiles for only about a third as long as the Soviets, these achievements show a rate of progress that speaks for itself. Only a brief time back, we were spending at the rate of only about one million dollars a year on long range ballistic missiles. In 1957 we spent more than one billion dollars on the Atlas, Titan, Thor, Jupiter, and Polaris programs alone.

But I repeat, gratifying though this rate of progress is, we must still do more!

Our real problem, then, is not our strength today; it is rather the vital necessity of action today to ensure our strength tomorrow.

What I have just said applies to our strength as a single country. But we are not alone. I have returned from the recent NATO meeting with renewed conviction that, because we are a part of a world-wide community of free and peaceful nations, our own security is immeasurably increased.

By contrast, the Soviet Union has surrounded itself with captive and sullen nations. Like a crack in the crust of an uneasily sleeping volcano, the Hungarian uprising revealed the depth and intensity of the patriotic longing for liberty that still burns within these countries.

The world thinks of us as a country which is strong, but which will never start a war. The world also thinks of us as a land which has never enslaved anyone and which is animated by humane ideals. This friendship, based on common ideals, is one of our greatest sources of strength.

It cements into a cohesive security arrangement the aggregate of the spiritual, military and economic strength of all those nations which, with us, are allied by treaties and agreements.

Up to this point, I have talked solely about our military strength to deter a possible future war.

I now want to talk about the strength we need to win a different kind of war—one that has already been launched against us.

It is the massive economic offensive that has been mounted by the communist imperialists against free nations.

The communist imperialist regimes have for some time been largely frustrated in their attempts at expansion based directly on force. As a result, they have begun to concentrate heavily on economic penetration, particularly of newly-developing countries, as a preliminary to political domination.

This non-military drive, if underestimated, could defeat the free world regardless of our military strength. This danger is all the greater precisely because many of us fail or refuse to recognize it. Thus, some people may be tempted to finance our extra military effort by cutting economic assistance. But at the very time when the economic threat is assuming menacing proportions, to fail to strengthen our own effort would be nothing less than reckless folly!

Admittedly, most of us did not anticipate the psychological impact upon the world of the launching of the first earth satellite. Let us not make the same kind of mistake in another field, by failing to anticipate the much more serious impact of the Soviet economic offensive.

As with our military potential, our economic assets are more than equal to the task. Our independent farmers produce an abundance of food and fibre. Our free workers are versatile, intelligent, and hard-working. Our businessmen are imaginative and resourceful. The productivity, the adaptability of the American economy is the solid foundation-stone of our security structure.

We have just concluded another prosperous year. Our output was once more the greatest in the nation's history. In the latter part of the year, some decline in employment and output occurred, following the exceptionally rapid expansion of recent years. In a free economy, reflecting as it does the independent judgments of millions of people, growth typically moves forward unevenly. But the basic forces of growth remain unimpaired. There are solid grounds for confidence that economic growth will be resumed without an extended interruption. Moreover, the Federal Government, constantly alert to signs of weakening in any part of our economy, always stands ready, with its full power, to take any appropriate further action to promote renewed business expansion.

If our history teaches us anything, it is this lesson: so far as the economic potential of our nation is concerned, the believers in the future of America have always been the realists.

I count myself as one of this company.

Our long-range problem, then, is not the stamina of our enormous engine of production. Our problem is to make sure that we use these vast economic forces confidently and creatively, not only in direct military defense efforts, but likewise in our foreign policy, through such activities as mutual economic aid and foreign trade.

In much the same way, we have tremendous potential resources on other non-military fronts to help in countering the Soviet threat: education, science, research, and, not least, the ideas and principles by which we live. And in all these cases the task ahead is to bring these resources more sharply to bear upon the new tasks of security and peace in a swiftly-changing world.

IV

There are many items in the Administration's program, of a kind frequently included in a State of the Union Message, with which I am not dealing today. They are important to us and to our prosperity. But I am reserving them for treatment in separate communications because of my purpose today of speaking only about matters bearing directly upon our security and peace.

I now place before you an outline of action designed to focus our resources upon the two tasks of security and peace.

In this special category I list eight items requiring action. They are not merely desirable. They are imperative.

1. Defense Reorganization

The first need is to assure ourselves that military organization facilitates rather than hinders the functioning of the military establishment in maintaining the security of the nation.

Since World War II, the purpose of achieving maximum organizational efficiency in a modern defense establishment has several times occasioned action by the Congress and by the Executive.

The advent of revolutionary new devices, bringing with them the problem of overall continental defense, creates new difficulties, reminiscent of those attending the advent of the airplane half a century ago.

Some of the important new weapons which technology has produced do not fit into any existing service pattern. They cut across all services, involve all services, and transcend all services, at every stage from development to operation. In some instances they defy classification according to branch of service.

Unfortunately, the uncertainties resulting from such a situation, and the jurisdictional disputes attending upon it, tend to bewilder and confuse the public and create the impression that service differences are damaging the national interest.

Let us proudly remember that the members of the Armed Forces give their basic allegiance solely to the United States. Of that fact all of us are certain. But pride of service and mistaken zeal in promoting particular doctrine has more than once occasioned the kind of difficulty of which I have just spoken.

I am not attempting today to pass judgment on the charge of harmful service rivalries. But one thing is sure. Whatever they are, America wants them stopped.

Recently I have had under special study the never-ending problem of efficient organization, complicated as it is by new weapons. Soon my conclusions will be finalized. I shall promptly take such Executive action as is necessary and, in a separate message, I shall present appropriate recommendations to the Congress.

Meanwhile, without anticipating the detailed form that a reorganization should take, I can state its main lines in terms of objectives:

A major purpose of military organization is to achieve real unity in the Defense establishment in all the principal features of military activities. Of all these, one of the most important to our nation's security is strategic planning and control. This work must be done under unified direction.

The defense structure must be one which, as a whole, can assume, with top efficiency and without friction, the defense of America. The Defense establishment must therefore plan for a better integration of its defensive resources, particularly with respect to the newer weapons now building and under development. These obviously require full coordination in their development, production and use. Good organization can help assure this coordination.

In recognition of the need for single control in some of our most advanced development projects, the Secretary of Defense has already decided to concentrate into one organization all the anti-missile and satellite technology undertaken within the Department of Defense.

Another requirement of military organization is a clear subordination of the military services to duly constituted civilian authority. This control must be real; not merely on the surface.

Next there must be assurance that an excessive number of compartments in organization will not create costly and confusing compartments in our scientific and industrial effort.

Finally, to end inter-service disputes requires clear organization and decisive central direction, supported by the unstinted cooperation of every individual in the defense establishment, civilian and military.

2. *Accelerated Defense Effort*

The second major action item is the acceleration of the defense effort in particular areas affected by the fast pace of scientific and technological advance.

Some of the points at which improved and increased effort are most essential are these:

We must have sure warning in case of attack. The improvement of warning equipment is becoming increasingly important as we approach the period when long-range missiles will come into use.

We must protect and disperse our striking forces and increase their readiness for instant reaction. This means more base facilities and standby crews.

We must maintain deterrent retaliatory power. This means, among other things, stepped-up long range missile programs; accelerated programs for other effective missile systems; and, for some years, more advanced aircraft.

We must maintain freedom of the seas. This means nuclear submarines and cruisers; improved anti-submarine weapons; missile ships; and the like.

We must maintain all necessary types of mobile forces to deal with local conflicts, should there be need. This means further improvements in equipment, mobility, tactics and fire power.

Through increases in pay and incentive, we must maintain in the armed forces the skilled manpower modern military forces require.

We must be forward-looking in our research and development to anticipate and achieve the unimagined weapons of the future.

With these and other improvements, we intend to assure that our vigilance, power, and technical excellence keep abreast of any realistic threat we face.

3. *Mutual Aid*

Third: We must continue to strengthen our mutual security efforts.

Most people now realize that our programs of military aid and defense support are an integral part of our own defense effort. If the foundations of the Free World structure were progressively allowed to crumble under the pressure of communist imperialism, the entire house of freedom would be in danger of collapse.

As for the mutual economic assistance program, the benefit to us is threefold. First, the countries receiving this aid become bulwarks against communist encroachment as their military defenses and economies are strengthened. Nations that are conscious of a steady improvement in their industry, education, health and standard of living are not apt to fall prey to the blandishments of communist imperialists.

Second, these countries are helped to reach the point where mutually profitable trade can expand between them and us.

Third, the mutual confidence that comes from working together on constructive projects creates an atmosphere in which real understanding and peace can flourish.

To help bring these multiple benefits, our economic aid effort should be made more effective.

In proposals for future economic aid, I am stressing a greater use of repayable loans, through the Development Loan Fund, through funds generated by sale of surplus farm products, and through the Export-Import Bank.

While some increase in Government funds will be required, it remains our objective to encourage shifting to the use of private capital sources as rapidly as possible.

One great obstacle to the economic aid program in the past has been, not a rational argument against it on the merits, but a catchword: "give-away program."

The real fact is that no investment we make in our own security and peace can pay us greater dividends than necessary amounts of economic aid to friendly nations.

This is no "give-away."

Let's stick to facts!

We cannot afford to have one of our most essential security programs shot down with a slogan!

4. Mutual Trade

Fourth: Both in our national interest, and in the interest of world peace, we must have a five-year extension of the Trade Agreements Act with broadened authority to negotiate.

World trade supports a significant segment of American industry and agriculture. It provides employment for four and one-half million American workers. It helps supply our ever increasing demand for raw materials. It provides the opportunity for American free enterprise to develop on a worldwide scale. It strengthens our friends and increases their desire to be friends. World trade helps to lay the groundwork for peace by making all free nations of the world stronger and more self-reliant.

America is today the world's greatest trading nation. If we use this great asset wisely to meet the expanding demands of the world, we shall not only provide future opportunities for our own business, agriculture, and labor, but in the process strengthen our security posture and other prospects for a prosperous, harmonious world.

As President McKinley said, as long ago as 1901: "Isolation is no longer possible or desirable. . . . The period of exclusiveness is past."

5. Scientific Cooperation With Our Allies

Fifth: It is of the highest importance that the Congress enact the necessary legislation to enable us to exchange appropriate scientific and technical information with friendly countries as part of our effort to achieve effective scientific cooperation.

It is wasteful in the extreme for friendly allies to consume talent and money in solving problems that their friends have already solved—all because of artificial barriers to sharing. We cannot afford to cut ourselves off from the brilliant talents and minds of scientists in friendly countries. The task ahead will be hard enough without handcuffs of our own making.

The groundwork for this kind of cooperation has already been laid in discussions among NATO countries. Promptness in following through with legislation will be the best possible evidence of American unity of purpose in cooperating with our friends.

6. Education And Research

Sixth: In the area of education and research, I recommend a balanced program to improve our resources, involving an investment of about a billion dollars over a four year period. This involves new activities by the Department of Health, Education and Welfare designed principally to encourage improved teaching quality and student opportunities in the interests of national security. It also provides a five-fold increase in sums available to the National Science Foundation for its special activities in stimulating and improving science education.

Scrupulous attention has been paid to maintaining local control of educational policy, spurring the maximum amount of local effort, and to avoiding undue stress on the physical sciences at the expense of other branches of learning.

In the field of research, I am asking for substantial increases in basic research funds, including a doubling of the funds available to the National Science Foundation for this purpose.

But federal action can do only a part of the job. In both education and research, redoubled exertions will be necessary on the part of all Americans if we are to rise to the demands of our times. This means hard work on the part of state and local governments, private industry, schools and colleges, private organizations and foundations, teachers, parents, and—perhaps most important of all—the student himself, with his bag of books and his homework.

With this kind of all-inclusive campaign, I have no doubt that we can create the intellectual capital we need for the years ahead, invest it in the right places—and do all this, not as regimented pawns, but as free men and women!

7. Spending And Saving

Seventh: To provide for this extra effort for security, we must apply stern tests of priority to other expenditures, both military and civilian.

This extra effort involves, most immediately, the need for a supplemental defense appropriation of $1.3 billion for fiscal year 1958.

In the 1959 budget, increased expenditures for missiles, nuclear ships, atomic energy, research and development, science and education, a special contingency fund to deal with possible new technological discoveries, and increases in pay and incentives to obtain and retain competent manpower add up to a total increase over the comparable figures in the 1957 budget of about $4 billion.

I believe that, in spite of these necessary increases, we should strive to finance the 1959 security effort out of expected revenues. While we now believe that expected revenues and expenditures will roughly balance, our real purpose will be to achieve adequate security, but always with the utmost regard for efficiency and careful management.

This purpose will require the cooperation of Congress in making careful analysis of estimates presented, reducing expenditure on less essential military programs and installations, postponing some new civilian programs, transferring some to the states, and curtailing or eliminating others.

Such related matters as the national debt ceiling and tax revenues will be dealt with in later messages.

8. Works of Peace

My last call for action is not primarily addressed to the Congress and people of the United States. Rather, it is a message from the people of the United States to all other peoples, especially those of the Soviet Union.

This is the spirit of what we would like to say:

"In the last analysis, there is only one solution to the grim problems that lie ahead. The world must stop the present plunge toward more and more destructive weapons of war, and turn the corner that will start our steps firmly on the path toward lasting peace.

"Our greatest hope for success lies in a universal fact: the people of the world, as people, have always wanted peace and want peace now.

"The problem, then, is to find a way of translating this universal desire into action.

"This will require more than words of peace. It requires works of peace."

Now, may I try to give you some concrete examples of the kind of works of peace that might make a beginning in the new direction.

For a start our people should learn to know each other better. Recent negotiations in Washington have provided a basis in principle for greater freedom of communication and exchange of people. I urge the Soviet government to cooperate in turning principle into practice by prompt and tangible actions that will break down the unnatural barriers that have blocked the flow of thought and understanding between our people.

Another kind of work of peace is cooperation on projects of human welfare. For example, we now have it within our power to eradicate from the face of the earth that age-old scourge of mankind: malaria. We are embarking with other nations in an all-out five-year campaign to blot out this curse forever. We invite the Soviets to join with us in this great work of humanity.

Indeed, we would be willing to pool our efforts with the Soviets in other campaigns against the diseases that are the common enemy of all mortals— such as cancer and heart disease.

If people can get together on such projects, is it not possible that we could then go on to a full-scale cooperative program of Science for Peace?

We have as a guide and inspiration the success of our Atoms-for-Peace proposal, which in only a few years, under United Nations auspices, became a reality in the International Atomic Energy Agency.

A program of Science for Peace might provide a means of funneling into one place the results of research from scientists everywhere and from there making it available to all parts of the world.

There is almost no limit to the human betterment that could result from such cooperation. Hunger and disease could increasingly be driven from the earth. The age-old dream of a good life for all could, at long last, be translated into reality.

But of all the works of peace, none is more needed now than a real first step toward disarmament.

Last August the United Nations General Assembly, by an overwhelming vote, approved a disarmament plan that we and our allies sincerely believed to be fair and practical. The Soviets have rejected both the plan, and the negotiating procedure set up by the United Nations. As a result, negotiation on this supremely important issue is now at a standstill.

But the world cannot afford to stand still on disarmament! We must never give up the search for a basis of agreement.

Our allies from time to time develop differing ideas on how to proceed. We must concert these convictions among ourselves. Thereafter, any reasonable proposal that holds promise for disarmament and reduction of tension must be heard, discussed, and, if possible, negotiated.

But a disarmament proposal, to hold real promise, must at the minimum have one feature: reliable means to ensure compliance by all. It takes actions and demonstrated integrity on both sides to create and sustain confidence. And confidence in a genuine disarmament agreement is vital, not only to the signers of the agreement, but also to the millions of people all over the world who are weary of tensions and armaments.

I say once more, to all peoples, that we will always go the extra mile with anyone on earth if it will bring us nearer a genuine peace.

Conclusion

These, then, are the ways in which we must funnel our energies more efficiently into the task of advancing security and peace.

These actions demand and expect two things of the American people: sacrifice, and a high degree of understanding. For sacrifice to be effective it must be intelligent. Sacrifice must be made for the right purpose and in the right place—even if that place happens to come close to home!

After all, it is no good demanding sacrifice in general terms one day, and the next day, for local reasons, opposing the elimination of some unneeded federal facility.

It is pointless to condemn federal spending in general, and the next moment condemn just as strongly an effort to reduce the particular federal grant that touches one's own interest.

And it makes no sense whatever to spend additional billions on military strength to deter a potential danger, and then, by cutting aid and trade programs, let the world succumb to a present danger in economic guise.

My friends of the Congress: The world is waiting to see how wisely and decisively a free representative government will now act.

I believe that this Congress possesses and will display the wisdom promptly to do its part in translating into law the actions demanded by our nation's interests. But, to make law effective, our kind of government needs the full voluntary support of millions of Americans for these actions.

I am fully confident that the response of the Congress and of the American people will make this time of test a time of honor. Mankind then will see more clearly than ever that the future belongs, not to the concept of the regimented atheistic state, but to the people—the God-fearing, peace-loving people of all the world.

The proposed budget for fiscal 1959 provided another dramatic example of a response to outside pressure. Eisenhower's major concern for the new budget involved increased expenditures for defense. Domestic matters received little attention.

Annual Presidential Budget Message
January 13, 1958

[*Public Papers of the Presidents: 1958* (Washington, 1959), 17–24.]

To the Congress of the United States:

The budget for the fiscal year 1959 which I am transmitting with this message reflects the swiftly moving character of the time in which we live. It is clearly a time of growing opportunity as technology and science almost daily open wholly new vistas to all mankind. Yet it is also a time of growing danger. The progress of the Soviets in long range missiles and other offensive weapons, together with their continuing rejection of a workable disarmament, compels us to increase certain of our defense activities which we have only recently expanded many fold.

We know that we are sturdy today in the many strengths that keep the peace. This budget reflects our determination to remain so in the future.

This budget reflects another determination—that of adhering to those principles of governmental and fiscal soundness that have always guided this administration—economy in expenditures, efficiency in operations, promotion of growth and stability in a free-enterprise economy, a vigorous Federal-State system, concern for human well-being, priority of national security over lesser needs, revenues adequate to cover expenditures and permit debt reduction during periods of high business activity, and revision and reduction of taxes when possible.

To meet the responsibilities imposed on us by world conditions and by the fiscal principles to which we adhere, the budget for 1959 contains recommendations to provide:

1. An immediate increase for 1958 of $1.3 billion in spending authority for the Department of Defense, and a further increase of $2.5 billion in 1959 over 1958, to be applied principally to accelerate missile procurement, to strengthen our nuclear retaliatory power, and to spur military research and development programs;

2. A resulting increase of $2.8 billion in estimated 1959 expenditures over 1957 for missiles, nuclear armed or powered ships, atomic energy, research and development, science and education, plus a further provision of $0.5 billion for defense purposes, if needed; in addition, authority to transfer up to $2 billion between military appropriations, in order to take prompt advantage of new developments;

3. A decrease of $1.5 billion in 1959 expenditures below 1957 for other military arms and equipment and aircraft of declining importance, in favor of the newer weapons;

4. Curtailments, revisions, or eliminations of certain present civil programs, and deferments of previously recommended new programs, in order to restrain nonmilitary spending in 1959 and to provide the basis for budgetary savings of several billion dollars annually within a few years;

5. Continuation of present tax rates to help achieve a balanced budget in 1959.

I believe that this budget adequately provides for our Federal responsibilities in the year ahead.

The estimated budget totals for the current fiscal year and for the fiscal year 1959 are compared with actual results of earlier years in the following table:

Budget Totals

[Fiscal years. In billions]

	1956 actual	1957 actual	1958 estimate	1959 estimate
Budget receipts	$68.1	$71.0	$72.4	$74.4
Budget expenditures	66.5	69.4	72.8	73.9
Budget surplus (+) or deficit (−)	+1.6	+1.6	−.4	+.5
New obligational authority	63.2	70.2	¹74.4	72.5

¹Includes $6.6 billion of anticipated supplemental requests.

DEFENSE, SCIENCE, AND THE BUDGET.—Americans are determined to maintain our ability to deter war and to repel and decisively counter any possible attack. Today we possess military superiority over any potential aggressor or aggressors. Every American should clearly understand that the vast defense programs undertaken during the past several years have greatly advanced our military preparedness and developed and harnessed impressive new scientific achievements. We have sharply increased the numbers of scientists and engineers assigned to top priority defense programs. We have expanded many fold the expenditures for the development of missiles, both defensive and counteroffensive. We have accelerated development of advanced guidance systems, new fuels, and heat-resistant materials. We have greatly enlarged our network of warning devices and communications.

Our longer-range ballistic missile development, in particular, has long had the highest national priority. The result is striking. Whereas in 1953 we spent only $1 million on these programs, we spent $1 billion in 1957 and will spend more in 1958 and still more in 1959.

Our defenses are strong today, both as a deterrent to war and for use as a crushing response to any attack. Now our concern is for the future. Certain elements of our defense program have reached the point where they can be further accelerated. I will transmit to the Congress, immediately, a supplemental appropriation request of $1.3 billion for the Department of Defense for the fiscal year 1958. Further increases in new obligational authority are requested for the fiscal year 1959. The recommended authority for the military functions of the Department of Defense is $39.1 billion, which is $0.6 billion more than was requested in last year's budget for 1958 and $3.8 billion more than the amount the Congress has thus far enacted for 1958. Spending for military functions of the Department of Defense in 1959 is estimated to total $39.8 billion.

The development of longer-range ballistic missiles, construction of missile sites and detection systems, and other missile programs including guided missile ships will be substantially augmented. The total expenditures for missile research, development and procurement, for guided missile ships, and for missile-related construction will be $4.3 billion in 1958 and $5.3 billion in 1959, compared with $3 billion spent in 1957, $1.7 billion in 1956, and $1.2 billion in 1955. Commencing in 1958, we will procure a number of new missiles which have been recently developed and have now become operational.

As an indispensable part of our efforts to maintain an adequate defense, the budget recommendations for 1959 call for continued contributions to the efforts of free world nations to promote the collective defense and economic growth. The Soviet threat to freedom is far more than military power alone. Poverty and ignorance, and the despair, fear, and unrest that flow from them, have always been enemies to liberty. The Communists well know this and unceasingly exploit these factors to extend their influence and control. This Soviet economic assault on freedom is rapidly growing. Conquest by this route is no less menacing to us and other free nations than conquest by military force. We must, accordingly, vigorously advance our programs to assist other peoples in their efforts to remove poverty and ignorance. As we succeed in these military and economic efforts, our own freedom and security are strengthened, and the prospects for peace are improved.

Scientific and research efforts throughout the Nation must be expanded. This is a task not only for the Government but also for private industry, foundations, and educational institutions. The Government, on its part, will increase its efforts in this area. Supplemental appropriations for 1958 will be requested for the National Advisory Committee for Aeronautics and the National Science Foundation, as well as the Department of Defense. For 1959, new programs to promote education in science are being recommended and basic research activities are being generally expanded.

CHANGES IN EMPHASIS.—Total Government expenditures (1) for all procurement to equip our forces and those of our allies with weapons, ships, planes, and missiles, (2) for atomic energy, and (3) for all scientific research and education will be approximately $21.1 billion in 1958 and $21.6 billion in 1959, compared with $20.5 billion in 1957.

Within these totals for procurement and science, we have gradually but substantially changed our emphasis. This administration's continuing attention in recent years to new concepts of defense is shown by the fact that more than 75% of the total funds for procurement in the 1959 budget and 1958 supplemental requests is programed for new types of equipment which had not been developed in the fiscal year 1955 or were not being bought in production quantities in that year—the first full year following the Korean conflict. In 1953, missiles alone took less than 2 cents of each dollar spent for major procurement; in 1957, missiles took about 15 cents of every procurement dollar; and in 1959 will take about 24 cents.

The greatly increased firepower of modern weapons and the continuing increase in efficiency permit a further reduction in the numbers of military personnel. Procurement of older types of weapons and equipment is also being reduced. Other defense expenditures will be reduced by closing installations that are outmoded or are of limited use, and by rightening maintenance standards, procurement practices, and supply management.

BUDGET AUTHORIZATIONS AND EXPENDITURES.—As a result of the increases in our key protection programs recommended in this budget for the current fiscal year and the coming fiscal year, total new obligational authority and budget expenditures for each of these years will be larger than in 1957— even though it is recommended that certain other programs, both defense and civil, be retarded or reduced.

Total appropriations and other forms of new obligational authority recommended for the fiscal year 1959 amount to $72.5 billion. This is $4.7 billion more than has been enacted for 1958 and $2.3 billion more than for 1957. In addition, $6.6 billion of supplemental authorizations are estimated for the current year, 1958, for the Department of Defense, Commodity Credit Corporation, Export-Import Bank, and other agencies.

Budget expenditures in the fiscal year 1959 are estimated to be $73.9 billion. This is $1.1 billion more than now estimated for 1958 and $4.5 billion more than in 1957.

Not all of the obligational authority enacted for a fiscal year is spent in the same year. Amounts of authority enacted in prior years but which have not yet been spent and are carried forward from one fiscal year to the next are called unexpended balances. These balances are not cash on hand, but represent authority to draw on future receipts of the Treasury in order to pay bills.

The total balances of appropriations to be carried forward at the end of the fiscal year 1959 are estimated to be $39.9 billion. Of this amount 78% will have been obligated; that is, already committed.

The largest part of the unexpended balances of appropriations is in the Department of Defense, reflecting the long time which necessarily elapses between the placing of orders for complex military equipment and delivery and final payment. It is estimated that $32.1 billion will be carried forward by that Department at the end of 1959, of which $24.4 billion will have been obligated.

BUDGET RECEIPTS.— Although higher than in previous years, the current estimate of receipts for the fiscal year 1958 is somewhat smaller than earlier expectations, reflecting readjustments currently taking place in our economy following the rapid growth of the past several years. It now appears that 1958 budget receipts will not exceed $72.4 billion, although they will be well above 1957 receipts of $71 billion. A combination of increased defense expenditures and decreased receipts in the revised estimates for the current fiscal year results in an estimated budget deficit of $0.4 billion.

There are strong grounds to support my confidence that the expansion of our economy will soon be resumed, bringing higher levels of receipts with present tax rates. The acceleration of defense efforts already under way, the increasing pace of activity in a number of programs involving State and local as well as Federal expenditures, the rapid pace of technological advance and its application by American industry, the expanding needs and desires of our growing population, and Government policies designed to facilitate the resumption of growth are among the major factors that justify this confidence. While there are many uncertainties in forecasting results 18 months in advance, our best estimate at this time of budget receipts for 1959 is $74.4 billion. This would produce a balanced budget with a surplus of $0.5 billion in 1959.

[Editorial note: At this point in the budget message appears a diagram entitled "Source of Budget Receipts—Fiscal Year 1959 Estimate (Net of Refunds). The diagram shows the expected yield of various taxes as follows:

EXPECTED YIELD OF VARIOUS TAXES

Tax	Percent of total
Individual income	52
Corporation income	27
Excise	13
Other	8
	100

With relatively minor exceptions, present tax rates have not been changed since 1954 when a program of tax reduction and reform was enacted, saving taxpayers nearly $7.5 billion annually. If the Congress follows my recommendations, I believe that we shall be able to do what is required for our defense efforts and meet the basic needs of our domestic programs without an increase in tax rates. To maintain present rates, I recommend that tax rates on corporation income and certain excises, which under existing law are scheduled for reduction next July 1, be extended for another year.

We shall continue our efforts to assure that no one can avoid paying his fair share of the country's total high tax burden. Pending legislation (H.R. 8381), which was developed jointly by the Treasury Department and the House Committee on Ways and Means to remove unintended tax benefits and hardships, should be enacted with a few modifications. The Treasury Department will continue to review the operation of the tax laws and make recommendations for such additional changes as are needed to close loopholes.

There are certain technical tax revisions which will give substantial benefits to small business, with a minimum loss of revenue and with no changes in tax rates. These revisions will be set forth in the Economic Report. They are based on the work of the Cabinet Committee on Small Business.

DEBT LIMIT.— A debt limitation serves as a proper reminder of the importance of operating economically in discharging the responsibilities placed by the Constitution and the statutes on the executive branch. However, the present limit of $275 billion is too restrictive in view of rising defense expenditures and of the need for more flexibility to permit efficient and economical debt management.

Therefore, I will recommend that the present limit be revised upward temporarily through the fiscal year 1959. There should be an adequate margin to take care of any unexpected developments and to give the Treasury some much-needed flexibility in conducting its financing during this coming period.

TRUST FUNDS.—The total budget expenditures and receipts discussed thus far exclude funds held in trust by the Government. Budget totals are important indicators of fiscal policy and are a major determinant of changes in the public debt. However, to measure more fully the scope of all Federal Government activities and their impact on the national economy it is necessary to consider the trust funds as well as the budget funds.

In the fiscal year 1959, the expenditures of the trust funds will rise by an estimated $1.2 billion, compared with an increase of only $0.2 billion in their receipts. Payments for the highway program are estimated to increase $0.6 billion to $2.5 billion and benefits under the old-age and survivors insurance program will also increase $0.6 billion to $8.7 billion. These payments will help contribute to economic stability during the coming period and will also aid in the long-run growth of the economy.

TRUST FUNDS

[Fiscal years. In billions]

	1957 actual	1958 estimate	1959 estimate
Trust receipts	$14.4	$16.4	$16.6
Trust expenditures	13.0	15.2	16.4
Trust accumulations	1.4	1.2	0.3

RECEIPTS FROM AND PAYMENTS TO THE PUBLIC.—A consolidation of budget and trust funds which eliminates interfund payments and noncash transactions shows that the total Federal payments to the public in the fiscal year 1959 will be $1.8 billion more than in 1958. Payments to the public in 1959 will be $0.6 billion less than receipts from the public.

FEDERAL GOVERNMENT RECEIPTS FROM AND PAYMENTS TO THE PUBLIC

[Fiscal years. In billions]

	1957 actual	1958 estimate	1959 estimate
Receipts from the public	$82.1	$85.1	$87.3
Payments to the public	80.0	84.9	86.7
Excess of receipts over payments	2.1	0.2	0.6

When the 2nd Session of the 85th Congress convened on January 7, 1958, the White House remained optimistic about the chance of passing new programs. A series of Legislative Notes detailed the Administration's plans. Some of the proposals became law, others did not. Significant legislative achievements included: changes in the tariff; federal loans to assist state unemployment compensation systems; and a reorganization of the Pentagon. Two other legislative enactments provided case studies of the kinds of foreign and domestic pressures that required Administration attention and congressional response. The National Defense Education Act of 1958 demonstrated the American reaction to Sputnik. The Labor-Management Reporting and Disclosure Act of 1959 followed exposés of corruption in several trade unions.

Legislative Notes II
January 6, 1958
[Persons Files, Eisenhower Papers.]

Foreign Policy. Senate Foreign Relations Committee in executive session Thursday will hear Secretary Dulles report on the NATO meeting in Paris. Some Democratic Senators are urging the Committee to conduct an overall study of American foreign policy in light of the Russian satellite and missile development.

2. *Highways.* Senate Public Works Subcommittee will begin hearings January 8 on the status of the Federal highway program with testimony from Commerce Secretary Weeks and Federal Highway Administrator Tallamy. Chairman Gore (D-Tenn.) said the Subcommittee will review the progress made on the highway program and "will be particularly interested in the recent allocation of additional mileage to the interstate system and . . . the desirability of authorizing further mileage additions at this time."

3. *Education.* In a statement to be released tonight, the Council of Basic Education said that the President's new aid to education proposal fails to meet the real problem in the Nation's schools. While the plan has much to recommend it, its administration would be in the hands of those professional educators who, by use of the "soft" theory of education, are responsible for our present educational difficulties. The great need, it states, is for a thorough reappraisal of educational principles to give us a needed ideological and philosophical base before it can be decided what kind and how much financial aid is needed.

4. *Labor.* Senators McClellan (D-Ark.) and Ives (R-N.Y.) said they hope Congress this year will pass legislation to curb evils exposed in the Senate Rackets Committee. Sen. Potter (R-Mich.) said that all signs point to enactment of new laws to police union welfare funds. Sen. Ives, who soon will introduce several labor bills, said he opposes any legislation to put unions under the anti-trust laws.

5. *Rivers and Harbors.* Rep. Brooks (D-La.) president of the National Rivers and Harbors Congress, said he believes that the 1959 budget should include $1 billion for rivers and harbors development. He indicated that foreign aid should be cut if necessary to finance the water development program.

6. *Missiles.* The Senate Armed Services Preparedness Subcommittee, in executive session today, heard R. Adm. Rickover discuss the Navy's atomic submarine program. In his testimony he made the following statements: he listed as major problems training and the procurement of competent personnel who are willing to accept responsibility; his organization has been on a war basis for several years and the principal factor in the success of the nuclear sub was that he was left alone; too many projects are hampered by red tape—trained people are hounded by conferences and committees and a continued demand for justification of what they are doing; and there must be a clear line of authority with someone having power to make decisions and to stick to them.

Adm. Rickover is continuing in afternoon session and will be followed by Maj. Gen. Medaris, Dr. Martin, and Lt. Gen. Gavin who will be questioned as to the reasons for his resignation as Army Research Chief.

The Committee will hear Navy witnesses Wednesday morning and on Thursday, Mr. Nelson Rockefeller will testify.

Tomorrow morning there will be a caucus of Democratic Senators for a defense briefing and Republican Senators will be briefed tomorrow afternoon.

The launching of the first earth satellite by the Soviets on October 4, 1957, dispelled a myth among many Americans that Russian technology was vastly inferior to that of the free world. After the first shock of Sputnik had subsided, Congress and the President realized that scientific education in the United States needed rapid improvement. The Department of Health, Education, and Welfare had long advocated a federal program of scholarships and loans for college students, but opposition to additional federal aid to education had stymied action. Now, the external pressure of Soviet achievements improved the chances of favorable congressional consideration. While the furor over Sputnik aided the legislative efforts, a Republican National Committee staff member feared an overreaction by the public.

Memorandum from Robert Humphreys to The Assistant to the President Sherman Adams January 2, 1958

[Larson-Moos Files, Eisenhower Papers.]

Concerning our telephone conversation of December 31: In the present state of affairs we need two things—

1. Some words that can see service for a few months ahead.
2. Reassurance.

In the last several days I have noticed the columnists and editorial writers are beginning to take a little saner tack but I would suggest it would be helpful if some language something like the following could be agreed to, to implement point 1:

> To some people calamity is always welcome. They seize on setbacks in the broad march of progress and shout "Fire!" These promoters of panic do immeasurable harm, not only to our international relations but to our domestic peace of mind. This Administration is not going to be swayed by them in its determination to maintain a sane balance between our military security on the one hand, and our moral and economic security on the other.

Point 2 could be implemented with a number of facts but here is one that impresses me:

> There is nothing new nor revolutionary in scientific achievement by the Russian people. They have historically, since the days of Catherine the Great, made substantial contributions to scientific research and discovery. For nearly 200 years before the advent of Communism the Russian Imperial Academy of Science stood in great eminence in the scientific world. Every American high school student has heard of Mendeleyev and Pavlov because of their important work in chemistry and physiology respectively. Lobachevsky, Chebicker, Mechnikov, Klaus, Lenz and Lomonosov are only a few of the

Russians whose names are written indelibly into the records of scientific progress. All of these scientists were the products of basic Russian ingenuity in scientific fields and all of them did their work long before the Communists seized control of Russia.

Even Communism could not dampen this Russian aptitude for research and discovery—it has only guided it into more materialistic channels.

Of course the Russian people have continued to make impressive strides scientifically and they undoubtedly will do so in the future. No nation has a monopoly on scientific brains and no nation should have. We should not forget that there is scarcely a nation on the face of the earth whose scientists have not produced important results at one time or another.

I understand there was a book published in 1952—"Science and Intellectual Freedom in Russia" by Lazar Volin—by the American Association for the Advancement of Science which does a very good job on pre-Communist science.

>⬤–○–(

On January 27, 1958, the President sent a Special Message to Congress requesting a broad new program to bolster American science.

Special Message to the Congress
from President Eisenhower on Education
January 27, 1958

[*Public Papers of the Presidents: 1958* (Washington, 1959), 127 32.]

To the Congress of the United States:

Education best fulfills its high purpose when responsibility for education is kept close to the people it serves—when it is rooted in the home, nurtured in the community, and sustained by a rich variety of public, private, and individual resources. The bond linking home and school and community— the responsiveness of each to the needs of the others—is a precious asset of American education.

This bond must be strengthened, not weakened, as American education faces new responsibilities in the cause of freedom. For the increased support our educational system now requires, we must look primarily to citizens and parents acting in their own communities, school boards and city councils, teachers, principals, school superintendents, State boards of education and State legislatures, trustees and faculties of private institutions.

Because of the national security interest in the quality and scope of our educational system in the years immediately ahead, however, the Federal

Government must also undertake to play an emergency role. The Administration is therefore recommending certain emergency Federal actions to encourage and assist greater effort in specific areas of national concern. These recommendations place principal emphasis on our national security requirements.

Our immediate national security aims—to continue to strengthen our armed forces and improve the weapons at their command—can be furthered only by the efforts of individuals whose training is already far advanced. But if we are to maintain our position of leadership, we must see to it that today's young people are prepared to contribute the maximum to our future progress. Because of the growing importance of science and technology, we must necessarily give special—but by no means exclusive—attention to education in science and engineering.

The Secretary of Health, Education, and Welfare and the Director of the National Science Foundation have recommended to me a comprehensive and interrelated program to deal with this problem. Such program contemplates a major expansion of the education activities now carried on by the National Science Foundation, and the establishment of new programs in the Department of Health, Education, and Welfare. I have approved their recommendations, and commend them to the Congress as the Administration program in the field of education. This is a temporary program and should not be considered as a permanent Federal responsibility.

Programs of the National Science Foundation

The Programs of the National Science Foundation designed to foster science education were developed in cooperation with the scientific community under the guidance of the distinguished members of the National Science Board. They have come to be recognized by the educational and scientific communities as among the most significant contributions currently being made to the improvement of science education in the United States.

The Administration has recommended a five-fold increase in appropriations for the scientific education activities of the National Science Foundation. These increased appropriations will enable the Foundation, through its various programs, to assist in laying a firmer base for the education of our future scientists. More immediately, these programs will help supply additional highly competent scientists and engineers vitally needed by the country at this time.

1. *Improvement of the subject-matter knowledge of science and mathematics teachers.*

First, the Administration is recommending an increase in funds to support institutes sponsored by the Foundation for the supplementary training of science and mathematics teachers and a somewhat larger increase to support teacher fellowships. This will provide additional study opportunities to enable more science and mathematics teachers in our schools and colleges to improve their fundamental knowledge and through improved teaching techniques, stimulate the interest and imagination of more students in these important subjects.

2. *Improvement of course content.*

Second, the Administration is recommending an increase in funds to enable the Foundation to stimulate the improvement of the content of science courses at all levels of our educational system. The efforts of even the most dedicated and competent teachers will not be effective if the curricula and materials with which they work are out-of-date or poorly conceived.

3. *Encouragement of science as a career.*

Third, the Administration is proposing an expansion of the Foundation's programs for encouraging able students to consider science as a career. Good teaching and properly designed courses are important factors in this regard, but there are other ways in which interest in these fields may be awakened and nurtured. The Foundation has already developed a series of programs directly focused on the problem of interesting individual students in science careers, and these programs should be expanded.

4. *Graduate fellowships.*

Fourth, the Administration is recommending an increase in the Foundation's graduate fellowship program. The enlarged program will make it possible for additional competent students to obtain better training for productive and creative scientific effort.

5. *Expansion of other programs.*

The Administration is recommending that funds be provided to enable the Foundation to initiate several new programs which will provide fellowship support for secondary school science teachers (during the summer months), for graduate students who serve during the school year as teaching assistants, and for individuals who wish to obtain additional education so that they may become high school science and mathematics teachers.

Programs of the Department of Health, Education, and Welfare

The education programs of the National Science Foundation deal exclusively with science education and operate mainly through scientific societies and science departments of colleges and universities. There is, however, an emergency and temporary need for certain additional Federal programs to strengthen general education, and also for certain Federal programs to strengthen science education in our State and local school systems. The Administration is recommending legislation authorizing these additional programs in the Department of Health, Education, and Welfare for a four-year period only.

1. *Reducing the waste of talent.*

High-quality professional personnel in science, engineering, teaching, languages, and other critical fields are necessary to our national security effort. Each year, nevertheless, many young people drop out of high school before graduation. Many able high school graduates do not go on to college. This represents a waste of needed talent. Much of this waste could be avoided if the aptitudes of these young people were identified and they were encouraged toward the fullest development of their abilities.

The Administration proposes, therefore, that the Congress authorize:

(a) Matching grants to the States to encourage improved State and local testing programs to identify the potential abilities of students at an early stage in their education.

(b) Matching grants to the States to encourage the strengthening of local counseling and guidance services, so that more able students will be encouraged to stay in high school, to put more effort into their academic work, and to prepare for higher education. The program also would provide for grants of funds to colleges and universities to permit them to establish training institutes to improve the qualifications of counseling and guidance personnel.

(c) A program of Federal scholarships for able high school graduates who lack adequate financial means to go to college. The Administration recommends approximately 10,000 new scholarships annually, reaching a total of 40,000 in the fourth year, to be closely coordinated with the testing and counseling programs. Scholarships should be allotted among the States on an equitable basis and awarded by State agencies on the basis of ability and need. Although it should not be compulsory for students to pursue a specific course of study in order to qualify, reasonable preference should be given to students with good preparation or high aptitude in science or mathematics.

2. *Strengthening the teaching of science and mathematics.*

National security requires that prompt action be taken to improve and expand the teaching of science and mathematics. Federal matching funds can help to stimulate the organization of programs to advance the teaching of these subjects in the public schools.

The Administration therefore recommends that the Congress authorize Federal grants to the States, on a matching basis, for this purpose. These funds would be used, in the discretion of the States and the local school systems, either to help employ additional qualified science and mathematics teachers, to help purchase laboratory equipment and other materials, to supplement salaries of qualified science and mathematics teachers, or for other related programs.

3. *Increasing the supply of college teachers.*

To help assure a more adequate supply of trained college teachers, so crucial in the development of tomorrow's leaders, the Administration recommends that the Congress authorize the Department of Health, Education, and Welfare to provide:

(a) Graduate fellowships to encourage more students to prepare for college teaching careers. Fellows would be nominated by higher educational institutions.

(b) Federal grants, on a matching basis, to institutions of higher education to assist in expanding their graduate school capacity. Funds would be used, in the discretion of the institution itself, either for salaries or teaching materials.

4. *Improving foreign language teaching.*

Knowledge of foreign languages is particularly important today in the light of America's responsibilities of leadership in the free world. And yet the American people generally are deficient in foreign languages, particularly those of the emerging nations in Asia, Africa, and the Near East. It is important to our national security that such deficiencies be promptly overcome. The Administration therefore recommends that the Department of Health, Education, and Welfare be authorized to provide a four-year program for:

(a) Support of special centers in colleges and universities to provide instruction in foreign languages which are important today but which are not now commonly taught in the United States.

(b) Support of institutes for those who are already teaching foreign languages in our schools and colleges. These institutes would give training to improve the quality and effectiveness of foreign language teaching.

5. *Strengthening the Office of Education.*

More information about our educational system on a national basis is essential to the progress of American education. The United States Office of Education is the principal source of such data.

Much of the information compiled by the Office of Education must originate with State educational agencies. The Administration therefore recommends that the Office of Education be authorized to make grants to State educational agencies for improving the collection of statistical data about the status and progress of education.

This emergency program stems from national need, and its fruits will bear directly on national security. The method of accomplishment is sound:

the keystone is State, local, and private effort; the Federal role is to assist—not to control or supplant—those efforts.

The Administration urges prompt enactment of these recommendations in the essential interest of national security.

<hr/>

When the House Committee on Education and Labor conducted hearings, Dr. Wernher von Braun, the Director, Development Operations Division, Army Ballistic Missile Agency, who had been involved in Germany's World War II rocket program, gave testimony stressing the international pressures that required better education in science. Although there was no doubt that Congress would pass a law, the specific provisions caused considerable debate and required several compromises. The final measure, which Eisenhower signed on September 2, 1958, included provisions for federal loans to students as well as over 5,000 graduate fellowships and grants to improve the teaching of science, mathematics, and foreign languages.

Statement by Dr. Wernher von Braun
on Scientific Education
March 14, 1958

[U.S., Congress, House, Subcommittee of the Committee on Education and Labor, Scholarship and Loan Program, 85th Cong., 2nd Sess., 1958, 1308–11.]

MR. WERNHER VON BRAUN: Mr. Chairman, and members of the committee: The Communists' threat to the free world extends far beyond armies and politics. It involves every aspect of our way of life: Religion, economics, industry, science, technology, and education.

If we recall the generally low technological status which the Soviets evidenced during World War II, and evaluate the tremendous physical damage inflicted upon Soviet industry by the war, it becomes frighteningly clear that their rate of progress in those areas which they have carefully selected for maximum effort greatly exceeds ours. The choice they have made between tools of power and consumer goods is obvious.

The real peril lies in enormous momentum they have built up in a dynamic program to attain supremacy in science and technology. The state-controlled educational system is turning out competent engineers and scientists in greater numbers than ours. It is upon this broad foundation that the Russian is waging his campaign for world domination—not upon the gleanings derived from picking the brains of captive, foreign scientists as many still seem to believe. The Soviets have grasped the significance of man's imminent conquest of space and have moved far along the road in that direction. Clearly, we must accelerate our effort in several areas at a rate calculated to overtake and surpass the Russian advantage because the loss of this race inevitably would cost us all we treasure—our freedom itself.

While the primary concern must be with national defense, I would emphasize the point again that superiority in weaponry alone—if we can attain and maintain it—is not sufficient. We are faced with a challenge that can only be overcome by the united will and effort of free peoples in every phase of our civilization.

It is my understanding that the members of this committee want my views on scientific education generally as it relates to national defense. It is my conviction that the problem, as I have stated, cannot be dealt with exclusively in terms of weapons which are usually considered the outward manifestation of our defense posture, when placed at the disposal of adequate and well-trained forces in being.

Modern defense programs, such as the long-range rocket systems, ballistic and guided missiles, supersonic aircraft, radar detection systems, antiaircraft and antimissile defenses, are the most complex and the most costly, I suppose, in the history of man. Their development involves all the physical sciences, the most advanced technology, abstruse mathematics and new levels of industrial engineering and production.

The efficient operation and effective maintenance of such devices require a new kind of soldier, who may one day be memorialized as the man with the slide rule — a 20th century counterpart of the musket-bearing farmer.

For these reasons alone, it is vital to the national interest that we increase the output of scientific and technical personnel so that the input of trained manpower in the Government, industry, research institutions, college and public school classrooms, and the Armed Forces will be of sufficient quality and quantity to meet the requirements of the technological revolution which we are currently experiencing.

I would state the problem in these words:

First: We must recruit more young people into scientific and technical careers.

Second: We must make these careers more attractive to induce more young people to select them.

Third: This involves inspiration, at home as well as in school; competent teachers, adequate laboratories and libraries, assistance to those who require it to finance undergraduate study at least, provision of fellowships or other stipends, to encourage graduate study.

It would seem a decision must be made as to whether we can expand our scientific, mathematic, and language curricula within the existing course structure; whether it is advisable to establish technical schools apart from those secondary schools offering various courses of study; whether to revise our offerings, particularly in the secondary schools, to eliminate some of the more enjoyable in favor of the more demanding mental disciplines.

These questions must be answered in each community because it is very much in the American tradition that the provision of public education is strictly the concern of the school district in the administration of the program. It is also, of course, the Nation's concern that schools and faculties and necessary impediments should be adequate to meet the needs not of today only, but of the world in which the student will live 5, 10, and more years from now. It is preparation for tomorrow which is the fundamental requirement underlying our approach to free and universal education, and it is upon the adequacy of that preparation that we must evaluate the performance of our system.

I believe it is entirely proper and in keeping with the democratic tradition for the Federal Government through the responsible agency to furnish necessary assistance for the support of an adequate educational system. We have for some years supported our farm economy by large sums of money appropriated for the control of crops. It seems to me that it makes little sense to overlook the most important crop of all; namely, the minds of our children.

If the Federal Government can properly assist the States in the provision of an adequate highway system for national defense, it can and should assist the educational enterprise whose health and vitality are vital to our democracy. I know there has been Federal aid, running into substantial figures, furnished to schools and colleges. There obviously must be more, in one form or another, if we are to prepare our children for the future. If we fail in that, we fail them and ourselves.

I am sure that the concrete evidence of congressional interest in this situation and the plain determination to do something about it will materially contribute to a practical solution. If it will aid your efforts, the following suggestions are offered—admittedly, I am not a professional educator, so these might be considered a layman's opinions:

1. The plans to stimulate teacher interest in summer courses and extension studies are sound, but what about the utilization of the vacation periods by the students we want to interest in the sciences and mathematics and languages? Many towns and cities conduct summer schools for the upper grades and high schools for makeup purposes, or purely social or recreational programs. Certainly a boy or girl seriously interested in basic preparation would welcome the opportunity to continue physics, chemistry, trigonometry, or allied courses and thus advance his understanding of them.

2. Youth can hardly be blamed for turning to the more glamorous attractions during school years. Scarcely a newspaper in this country does not boast of one or more sports pages; radio and television coverage of athletics is in like proportion. But do you see any science page, or mathematics page? Do you hear any reports of scientific or technical competitions? The task of putting things in proper proportion is not exclusively the responsibility of the youngsters. What about the service clubs and the parents groups who promote football dinners, basketball soirees, and

the like? These are healthy expressions of adult interest—but they ought to be balanced with some recognition of and attention to the fundamental disciplines which are musts for tomorrow's citizens.

3. Some attention should be paid to evaluating the formulas by which Federal and State aid to local school districts are apportioned. I believe a common measure is average daily attendance. In effect, this tells the school administrator that if you want to get the maximum amount from the State capitol, it's your job to keep attendance at its peak. Is this perhaps an explanation for the snap courses, or other inducements to persuade the disinterested, uninspired teen-ager to linger on when perhaps his own best interests would be served by releasing him to find a job? A more realistic formula needs to be found which would more accurately measure the value of the school's services to the community.

4. Why not admit interested teenagers to adult classes in their areas of greatest interest? Many districts sponsor evening schools in order to extend their services to the older generation. If a boy wants to get more math, more science than he can handle in the normal school day, why stop him from taking as big a bite as he wishes?

5. I think we must guard against any tendency to measure whatever program the Congress and administration adopt in terms of numbers. Whether we are talking about numbers of students, numbers of fellowships, numbers of teachers, or numbers of any other factor. Let's face it—we are outnumbered by the Communist world. Our chief reliance must be placed upon the quality of our effort and the quality of its product.

6. There is a wholesome concern for guidance and counseling aspects of school administration. We must keep in mind, however, that attempting to guide or counsel a student when he is about to leave secondary school is rather a belated effort. If his aptitudes indicate scientific, mathematical, or linguistic ability, the time to find it out and advise him and his parents is at as early a date in his preparatory years as possible. Then only is it possible to shape his course of study, within the limits of the school's offering, in the right direction. There is little to be gained by telling the 1958 high school graduate that he could and should have studied science, if he has failed to acquire the basic preparation essential for admission to college or university.

7. More attention is being paid to uncovering individual abilities and to encouraging outstanding students. Why not extend this to the teacher as well, and find some appropriate way to reward those performing exemplary service in the more difficult studies, instead of adhering to the rigid salary guides which reward mediocrity equally with superiority.

8. Fundamental to all of this is the need to bring parents to full realization of the impact of science and technology upon this and succeeding generations. Once that has been achieved, their influence will be felt where it can be of greatest value—in the home and in the community which governs the school.

I have appreciated this opportunity of appearing before the committee and shall be happy to answer any questions you may have.

Please bear in mind again that I am working under the handicap that I have no background whatsoever as an educator, so whatever I can say is a layman's opinion.

〉◀━〇━〇◀━〇◀━〇◀━〇◀〇◀〇◀━〇◀〇◀〇◀━〇◀━〇◀〇◀〇◀〇◀〇◀〇◀━〇◀━〇◀━〇◀〇◀━〇◀━〇◀━〇━〇◀〈

Even though the National Defense Education Act of 1958 increased the federal role in education, some high Administration officials still opposed federal aid to education. In 1960, when Congress debated a new bill, which included funds for school construction, Secretary of Agriculture Ezra Taft Benson wrote to the President outlining strenuous opposition. Eisenhower's reply, in which he thanked the Secretary for his interest, did not indicate that the Administration would reverse its position.

Secretary Ezra Taft Benson to President Eisenhower
May 26, 1960
[Official File 99-B, Eisenhower Papers.]

Dear Mr. President:

I was very much disturbed to read in the Wall Street Journal this morning an article indicating that "Vice President Nixon apparently has sold the Eisenhower Administration on accepting a Democratic Federal Aid to Education Bill with certain modifications." I sincerely hope this is not so.

You know, of course, how I feel about the question of Federal aid to education. I have indicated many times that the consequences of an injudicious increase in Federal aid to education would be Federal control, the impairment of free inquiry and the extinction of many independent and church-related colleges.

We must continue to guard against Federal control of education. You, yourself, said in your special message to the Congress in January 1956 "The responsibility for public education rests with the States and local communities. Federal action which infringes upon this principle is alien to our system. But our history has demonstrated that the Federal Government, in the interest of the whole people, can should help with certain problems of nationwide scope and concern when States and communities—acting independently—cannot solve the full problem or solve it rapidly enough."

The program for Federal aid to education currently proposed may not appear to contemplate a high degree of Federal financing and decision making. But you know, as I do, that "once the camel gets his nose under the tent" there is no telling how far he will go.

I cannot too strongly urge that we continue to guard against the proposed shift of responsibility in education to the Federal government.

Republicans had long been concerned about the misuse of power by labor unions. The merger in December, 1955, of the AF of L-CIO raised the possibilities of strong political action by the new organization. The Presidents reaction to the creation of the AF of L-CIO stressed that trade unions should be democratic. In ·a letter to the President, Republican Senator Barry Goldwater of Arizona expressed a conservative's view of the situation. Eisenhower's friendly response dodged the questions raised.

Senator Barry Goldwater to President Eisenhower
January 6, 1956
[Official File 102-B-3, Eisenhower Papers.]

Dear Mr. President:

Although this is late, I still want to thank you for your stand in favor of the political freedoms of the individual, in your talk to the AFL-CIO merger meeting.

You rang a clear note, consistent with the Republican position of true liberalism, when you said that "the rights of minorities holding differing social, economic and political views must be scrupulously protected and their views accurately reflected."

I am happy to agree wholeheartedly with your position, which should definitely be the position of the Republican Party, as a whole.

President Eisenhower to Senator Barry Goldwater
January 10, 1956
[Official File 102-B-3, Eisenhower Papers.]

Dear Barry:

I am glad to have your reaction to my statement to the AF of L-CIO meeting and especially to see the emphasis in your letter on a point that every one of us can usefully stress—that historically a liberal system has been one which accords maximum freedom to the individual. One of the greatest political distortions in our history took place when "liberalism" became identified in the public mind with an ever growing, ever more powerful central government. I hope we are making progress in dispelling that dangerous illusion.

Thanks, too, for your kind reference to me. I value it especially from you.

><del>—o—o—o—o—o—o—o—o—o—o—o—o—o—o—o—o—o—o—o—o—</del><

During 1958 a special Senate committee, chaired by Democratic Senator John McClellan of Arkansas, disclosed that some unions, in particular the Teamsters, had misused pension and welfare funds. The behavior at the hearings by the union's top officials shocked the American people and led to a Special Message by the President requesting labor reforms.

Special Message to the Congress from President Eisenhower on Labor-Management Relations January 28, 1959

[*Public Papers of the Presidents: 1959* (Washington, 1960), 143–45.]

To the Congress of the United States:

In the State of the Union Message on January ninth, I reported again to the Congress on the need for enactment of effective Federal legislation designed:

To safeguard workers' funds in union treasuries against misuse of any kind whatsoever.

To protect the rights and freedoms of individual union members, including the basic right to free and secret election of officers.

To advance true and responsible collective bargaining.

To protect the public and innocent third parties from unfair and coercive practices such as boycotting and blackmail picketing.

There is submitted herewith for the consideration of the Congress a 20-point program which will eliminate abuses demonstrated by the hearings of the McClellan Committee, protect the public interest and insure the rights and economic freedoms of millions of American workers.

Complete and effective labor-management legislation, not a piecemeal program, is essential to assure the American public that true, responsible collective bargaining can be carried on with full protection to the rights and freedoms of workers and with adequate guarantees of the public interest.

These recommendations, when adopted, should do much to eliminate those abuses and improper practices which, I am firmly convinced, the American public expects and believes will be corrected through legislative action. Equally important, they will do so without imposing arbitrary restrictions or punitive measures on the legitimate activities of honest labor and management officials.

I recommend legislation—

1. To require all unions to file detailed annual reports with the Department of Labor and furnish information to their members with respect to their financial operations. These reports would be open to the public, including union members.

2. To require all unions to file with the Department of Labor, as public information, copies of their constitutions and bylaws and information as to their organization and procedures, which would be required to include provisions, which are observed, meeting minimum standards for periodic secret ballot elections of officers, for the removal of officers, and for the imposition of supervisory control over the affairs of subordinate bodies.

3. To require all unions to keep proper records on the matters required to be reported, open to examination by Government representatives and to permit union members, subject to reasonable conditions and upon request, to see and examine these records.

4. To require unions, union officers and agents, and employers to report and keep proper records with respect to any payments, transactions, or investments which create conflicts of interests or have as their objective the interference with the statutory rights of individual union members and employees.

5. To require that union officers hold and administer union funds and property solely for the benefit of the union members and for furthering the purpose of the union and to make this duty enforceable in any court in a suit for an accounting by the union or by members.

6. To require that unions observe minimum standards for the conduct of the elections of officers, including in addition to periodic elections, the right of members to vote in secret without restraint or coercion and upon due notice, uniform opportunity for all members to be candidates, procedures to ensure an accurate tabulation of votes, a ban upon the use of union or employer funds to promote candidacies for union office, and requiring constitutions and bylaws to contain detailed statements of election procedures and compliance with such procedures.

7. To require unions to observe minimum standards and to conform to the appropriate provisions of their constitution and bylaws in exercising supervisory control over the affairs of subordinate bodies; such control should be limited in purpose to correcting corruption, or the disregard of democratic procedures or other practices detrimental to the rights of the members in the subordinate body, and assuring the performance of duties as a bargaining representative.

8. To place the administration of this legislation in the Secretary of Labor and to provide him with appropriate and adequate authority to issue regulations, investigate, subpoena witnesses and records, bring court action to compel compliance and to correct violations, and institute administrative procedures leading to decisions and orders, which would be subject to judicial review, necessary to effectuate the purposes of the legislation.

9. To prescribe criminal penalties for wilful violations of the Act, for concealment or destruction of records required to be kept, for bribery between employers and employee representatives, for improper payments by employers or their representatives to employees or employee representatives, for embezzlement of union funds, and for false entries or destruction of union books and records.

10. To preserve for union members any present remedies under State or Federal laws, in addition to those provided under this legislation.

11. To amend the secondary boycott provisions of the National Labor Relations Act so as to cover the direct coercion of employers to cease or agree to cease doing business with other persons; union pressures directed against secondary employers not otherwise subject to the Act; and inducements of individual employees to refuse to perform services with the object of forcing their employers to stop doing business with others; and to make clear that secondary activity is permitted against an employer performing "farmed-out struck work" and, under certain circumstances, against secondary employers engaged in work at a common construction site with the primary employer.

12. To make it illegal for a union, by picketing, to coerce an employer to recognize it as the bargaining representative of his employees or his employees to accept or designate it as their representative where the employer has recognized in accordance with law another labor organization, or where a representation election has been conducted within the last preceding 12 months, or where it cannot be demonstrated that there is a sufficient showing of interest on the part of the employees in being represented by the picketing union or where the picketing has continued for a reasonable period of time without the desires of the employees being determined by a representation election; and to provide speedy and effective enforcement measures.

For seven months following the President's message on labor-management relations, Congress failed to act. Then, on August 6, 1959, Eisenhower delivered a national radio and television address in which he demanded congressional passage of the Administration's bill.

National TV and Radio Address by President Eisenhower on Labor Union Reform
August 6, 1959
[McCabe Files, Eisenhower Papers.]

My Fellow Americans:

I want to speak to you tonight about an issue of great importance to every man, every woman and every child in this nation. It is above any partisan political consideration. It affects every American, regardless of occupation, regardless of political affiliation.

I speak of labor reform legislation.

In these few minutes I hope to place before you some salient facts affecting this matter so that all of us may more fully understand what is at stake.

This nation needs a law to meet the kind of racketeering, corruption, and abuses of power disclosed in many instances by the Senate Investigating Committee headed by Senator McClellan. For two years, I have advocated such a law.

For many months, newspapers have carried extensive accounts of racketeering and corruption in labor-management matters. Many of you have actually witnessed disclosures of this corruption on television in your own homes. It is a national disgrace.

The legislation we need has nothing to do with wages—or strikes—or problems we normally face when employers and employees disagree. Nor am I talking of any new approach to collective bargaining. Nor about any new labor-management philosophy. I am talking solely about a reform law—a law to protect the American people from the gangsters, racketeers, and other corrupt elements who have invaded the labor-management field.

You know, a great deal is being said and written about this subject. We hear one bill called a "weak" bill—another, a "strong" bill—and so on. The American people are not interested in adjectives—or in labels. They are interested in a law which will eliminate the abuses.

I want only effective protection from gangsters and crooks for the people of America—for the men and women who labor with their hands, their minds, their energies, to make America a better place for themselves and for their families.

We all know that only a small minority of individuals among unions and employers are involved in corrupt activities. We know that the vast numbers of employers and union officials are honest, and deplore corruption as much as you and I deplore it.

But any corrupt minority is too large.

The damage that such a minority does to working men and women, and to the American public cannot be tolerated.

After all—employers and unions operate in this field under the sanction and protection of Federal law. The people very properly look to their government to pass effective laws to stop abuses.

To date, legislation to correct these deplorable conditions has not been enacted. Meanwhile, the evidence of abuses has continued to mount before Congressional Committees. Chief among the abuses from which Americans need protection are the oppressive practices of coercion.

Take a company in the average American town—your town. A union official comes in to the office, presents the company with a proposed labor contract, and demands that the company either sign or be picketed. The company refuses, because its employees don't want to join that union. And remember, the law definitely gives employees the right to have or not to have a union—clearly a basic American right of choice.

Now what happens? The union official carries out the threat and puts a picket line outside the plant—to drive away customers—to cut off deliveries. In short, to force the employees into a union they do not want. This is one example of what has been called blackmail picketing. It is unfair and unjust. This could force the company out of business and result in the loss of all the jobs in the plant.

I want that sort of thing stopped. So does America.

Take another company—let us say, a furniture manufacturer. The employees vote against joining a particular union. Instead of picketing the furniture plant itself, unscrupulous organizing officials, in this case, use another scheme. They picket the stores which sell the furniture this plant manufactures. The purpose is to prevent those stores from handling that furniture.

How can anyone justify this kind of pressure against stores which are not involved in any dispute. They are innocent bystanders. This kind of action is designed to make the stores bring pressure on the furniture plant and its employees—to force those employees into a union they do not want. This is an example of a "secondary boycott."

I want that sort of thing stopped. So does America.

The blackmail picket line and the secondary boycott cannot possibly help the working men and women of America.

Another important problem is that of the so-called "No-Man's-Land." Under existing law, the States have practically no authority over labor cases, according to Supreme Court decision.

Here is a typical example of what can happen in this situation. A labor dispute occurs at a small plant. The union—or the employer—goes to the Federal Labor Board. The Board says the case is too small for Federal action—because it has only a small effect on interstate commerce. Then, the union, or the employer, goes to State officials, but they can't do anything because the States have no authority. That leaves the worker and his employer in this "No-Man's-Land"—cut off from Federal or State help.

What is the result? The disputing parties have no recourse to law. So, all too often, the dispute is "settled"—if we can use such a word—by force, with a test of strength between them, with damage to one or both, and to the community.

I want the "No-Man's-Land" abolished, because I believe that small unions and small businessmen have rights, just as everyone else. I want to give the States authority to deal with cases the Federal Board cannot and should not handle and, by all means, we must not bring every case to the Federal level, as some have proposed. In this kind of situation the States can act more promptly and more effectively than can the Federal Government.

Now any reform bill worthy of the name must also protect the individual rights of union members—within their unions. It must assure them of fair elections. It must assure them of honest handling of their money—money made up by dues often collected under auspices of Federal law. It must also give to the government effective authority to investigate and enforce these provisions. Unless it does these things—and deals effectively with the problems of coercive picketing, boycotting, and the "No-Man's-Land"—it is not a reform bill at all.

Now let us examine what Congress has done so far this year. Has its action measured up to the minimum requirements I have outlined to protect the American people? I regret to say that, as yet, the answer is no—definitely no.

The bill which passed the Senate in April is not effective. It does not deal with or curb the picketing or boycotting practices I have described. And while it purports to deal with the "No-Man's-Land," it gives no real relief.

In the House of Representatives, the Labor Committee bill is even less effective than the Senate bill. It, too, fails to deal with picketing and boycotting practices I have described. Its provisions relating to the "No-Man's-Land" go precisely in the wrong direction. And it actually exempts about 70% of all unions from reporting on their finances. It even removes criminal penalties against those who violate the rights of union members.

Neither the Senate bill nor the House Committee bill will really curb the abuses the American people want to see corrected.

However, Congress need not limit itself to such a choice.

The Administration bill is still before the Congress. There is also before the House a bi-partisan bill jointly sponsored by two Members of the House Labor Committee—Mr. Landrum of Georgia, a Democrat, and Mr. Griffin of Michigan, a Republican. The Landrum-Griffin bill is a good start toward a real labor reform bill, containing many of the corrective provisions I have urged.

Again I emphasize: Labor reform is not a partisan matter. Further, I don't come before you in any partisan sense. I am not a candidate for office. In this or other issues, I do not seek the support of any special interests. I am only trying to make sure that American workers and the public get the kind of protection that Americans deserve.

Nearly one hundred years ago Abraham Lincoln in his memorable Address spoke of the sacrifices made so that, in his words: "government of the people, by the people, for the people, shall not perish from the earth." That was the question he posed to our nation in his generation.

In our lives and actions, the people of America, in private and public sectors, daily face millions of choices with this continuing question always in the background.

As the Congress prepares to vote on labor reform, this great question is still, as always, with us. In the basic sense, the issue is: Shall the people govern? If they do not, crooks and racketeers could prevail.

This business of government—including this question of labor reform—is your business. It is every citizen's business.

Americans want reform legislation which will be truly effective. It is my earnest hope that Congress will be fully responsive to an overwhelming national demand.

Thank you, and Good Night.

The President's personal intervention effectively rallied public opinion behind his labor-management proposals. Within a week, the House passed a bill that included a "bill of rights" for union members and a requirement that union officers report to the Government on the handling of pension and welfare funds. Eisenhower continued his campaign for the bill by thanking the House for its action. Favorable Senate action followed within days and the President signed the legislation on September 14, 1958. Despite the howls of labor leaders, the law, popularly known as the Landrum-Griffin Act, represented a great personal triumph for Eisenhower.

Statement by President Eisenhower Following the Adoption by the House of the Landrum-Griffin Labor Bill
August 13, 1959
[*Public Papers of the Presidents: 1959* (Washington, 1960), 583–84.]

With, I am sure, millions of Americans I applaud the House of Representatives for its vote today in support of the Landrum-Griffin Labor Reform Bill which would deal effectively with the abuses disclosed by the McClellan Committee. I congratulate all those who voted in support of this legislation.

This action gives cause for real hope that the Congress will ultimately pass a good Labor Reform Bill.

7. STATEHOOD FOR ALASKA AND HAWAII

For many years the platforms of both the Republican and Democratic parties had advocated the admission of Hawaii and Alaska as states. In fact, statehood bills had been introduced repeatedly in Congress for the two territories. In 1952 the Republican platform repeated its endorsement. However, statehood for either territory did not have a high place on the new Administration's priority list. Residents of the two territories objected to the delay. Ernest Gruening, a Democrat appointed Governor of the Alaska Territory, took exception to an Esienhower press conference statement early in 1953 and restated the territory's case.

Governor Ernest Gruening to President Eisenhower
March 12, 1953
[General File 17-M-4, Eisenhower Papers.]

Dear Mr. President:

I hope you will not consider it presumptuous of me to take issue with your statement on Alaska statehood if your press interview of February 25 was correctly quoted in The New York Times of February 26. Replying to Barnet Nover, of The Denver Post, the following comment was attributed to you:

> He believed the Republican platform says that the Alaska situation will be studied to make a determination as to whether or not statehood should be recommended and granted.

The Republican platform was explicit. It favored statehood for Alaska "under an equitable enabling act." This is a reference to the contention made by certain Senators that the bill presented in the last Congress was not sufficiently generous and that it left Alaska a sort of vassal of federal executive agencies. Needless to say, those of us who have been battling for Alaskan statehood for some years felt that that was as generous an act as Congress would approve, and welcomed statehood on that basis as infinitely preferable to the continuation of the inferior and retarding status of territoriality. Certainly no one in Alaska would object to a more generous bill! Therefore, it seems to me the platform clearly commits the present administration to work out an "equitable bill" and recommend its passage.

Every Congressional committee to which Alaskan statehood has been presented in the last four years has rendered a do-pass verdict. That included the House Committee on Public Lands to which the Alaskan statehood bill was referred in the 80th (Republican) Congress.

Certainly the 1952 Republican platform raised no doubts and offered the nation the promise of an "equitable" act to make Alaska a state. Now that Hawaii is going in—a cause for rejoicing for all believers in democracy—I hope you will give Alaskan statehood a nod in line with your fine pronouncement concerning both Hawaii and Alaska in Denver three years ago.

>—o—o—o—o—o—o—o—o—o—o—o—o—o—o—o—o—o—o—o—o—o—<

While both parties supported statehood for the two territories, Democrats and Republicans disagreed over which should enter the Union first. Republicans wanted Hawaii, which had consistently voted for the GOP, while Democrats favored Alaska, traditionally a stronghold of their party. Thus, during the 83rd Congress the House—under Republican control—passed an enabling act for Hawaii. When the bill reached the Senate in 1954, Democrat Clinton Anderson of New Mexico led a fight to add Alaskan statehood to the measure. The success of Anderson's motion forced Republicans to accept the fact that they could not get Hawaii into the Union without adding Alaska. Republican Hugh Butler of Nebraska, Chairman of the Committee on the Interior and Insular Affairs, spelled out the political ramifications in a letter to Majority Leader William Knowland of California, a copy of which was sent to the White House. Butler added an additional note for the President indicating what had to be done to obtain congressional action. Anderson's proposal passed the Senate (April 1, 1954) but failed in the House (July 26). Apparently, a bill that joined the two territories could not succeed in the House, given the partisan and racial opposition which a duel proposal evoked.

Senator Hugh Butler to President Eisenhower
March 12, 1954
[General File 17-M-4, Eisenhower Papers.]

Dear Mr. President:

Enclosed is a copy of a letter I have this day written to the Honorable William F. Knowland, Majority Leader, with respect to our Party's position and future course of action on the combined Hawaii and Alaska Statehood measures.

I have expressed myself candidly and frankly, Mr. President, on what I believe to have been a weakness in our position prior to yesterday's vote on the Anderson joinder motion, and have made what I hope are clear-cut recommendations respecting our course of action with respect to the combined bill.

)━0━0━0━0━0━0━0━0━0━0━0━0━0━0━0━0━0━0━0━0━0━0━0━0━(

Senator Hugh Butler to Senator William Knowland
March 12, 1954
[General File 17-M-4, Eisenhower Papers.]

Dear Bill:

I know you are as disappointed as I at the result of yesterday's vote on the Anderson motion to join Alaska to the Hawaii Statehood bill. While I am disappointed, deeply disappointed, I am not surprised. You will recall that I predicted the result at our meeting last Monday at the White House, when I asserted that if the joinder motion carried, I would support the combined measure.

The obvious question that presents itself is: Where do the Senate Republicans and the Administration go from here on the Statehood issue? In my opinion, all of us, including the President, must face that fact that whether we like it or not we will have to take Alaska or not get Statehood for Hawaii at all.

I wish very much that the President had taken a clear stand, one way or the other, prior to yesterday's vote. The statement attributed to him in Denver in 1950, which as far as I can ascertain he has never denied nor repudiated, in support of Statehood for both Territories, could have been used to our advantage. Had the President reaffirmed that position, indicating the Alaska bill would be signed, if passed, then there would have been much less reason for Senator Anderson and those of his supporters who sincerely want statehood for both Territories to try to join them. Had the President's alleged support for Alaska been denied or repudiated, indicating a veto of Alaska statehood, there might also have been less support for joinder.

However, the important thing now is that we Republicans take the right course of action from this point. My own considered opinion is that we should clearly and unequivocally support the combined measure. A statement from the President to that effect, even now, would be of substantial help. If a filibuster develops, we should publicly call upon the so-called "liberal" Democrats—those who voted to join with the idea of helping Alaska—to help us break it by holding round-the-clock sessions or even invoking cloture.

Such clear-cut action would not only enable us to salvage much of what we have lost with respect to Republican strength in Hawaii, but it would greatly strengthen the Party's position in Alaska. It would be very helpful, politically, with respect to the country as a whole. For I am convinced that the majority of Americans do favor statehood for both Territories.

Both as Chairman of the Committee and as an individual Senator, I have made my own position very clear. After my personal visit to Alaska last summer, I am convinced the Territory is ready for Statehood, under the right kind of an enabling act. The bill the Committee worked out is that kind of bill. Many residents of Alaska who formerly opposed statehood have confirmed my own judgment in this respect.

I am sending a copy of this letter to the White House and would appreciate your views on my recommendation as to our Party's course of action.

＊＊＊＊＊＊＊＊＊＊＊＊＊＊＊＊＊＊＊＊＊＊＊

In 1955 Alaskans, ignoring suggestions to partition the territory before statehood and taking an optimistic view of congressional action, called a constitutional convention on November 8. After serious deliberations, a delegate to the convention wrote to a friend connected with the Republican National Committee about the struggle for statehood. The letter was considered important enough to be sent on to the White House.

Barrie White, Jr. to Chauncey Robbins
January 2, 1956
[General File 17-M-4, Eisenhower Papers.]

Dear Chauncey:

Have been intending to write you for many moons, but something always delays me. As you may know, our last legislature provided for a Constitutional Convention to be held prior to the passage of a Statehood enabling act, at our own expense. I was elected a delegate, to my great delight, and we have been in session at the University of Alaska, Fairbanks, since November 8. We are currently home to "hold hearings," reconvene next Wednesday. I am sure the session will last the maximum time, until Feb. 5.

So I am still very much in the thick of the Statehood fight, although retired as president of Operation Statehood last fall. My purpose in writing is to pass on some observations I have made, for what they may be worth. As you know, I am a Republican, but have not been active politically and because of my position with Operation Statehood have often been included in—or on the fringe of—conversations I might not otherwise have heard.

To sketch in briefly the background of my remarks: In Denver in 1950, Eisenhower made a very strong statement in favor of Statehood for Alaska. In '52 our elections here went overwhelmingly Republican, followed by a Republican victory nationally. Next, to Alaskans dismay, we find the administration dragging its feet on Alaska Statehood, while pumping enthusiastically for Hawaii. Alaskans find the Secretary of the Interior, and the administration in general, disinterested in doing much of anything at all for Alaska.

While Alaska's right to and readiness for Statehood become crystal clear, and national support rises to new and overwhelming proportions, the administration becomes increasingly vague and contradictory on the subject. At the peak of hopefulness, Alaskans charter a plane and fly to Washington to see Interior Department officials, Congressmen and, if possible, the President. The Secretary sees fit to absent himself from town, while throughout his department, the Bureau of the Budget, and from key Congressmen we get a runaround. The President is unable to give us any assurances of his support, with only a vague mention of "problems." The Director of the Division of Islands and Territories is caught in some highly inappropriate remarks made during a cocktail party at his house, which are subsequently published throughout Alaska.

When the going gets a little tougher, then the administration starts referring vaguely to "military problems" in granting Statehood to Alaska, problems every Alaskan recognizes as phony or easily capable of solution.

Next the Secretary of the Interior shows up in Alaska, visibly anxious to meet with Operation Statehood, among others. At this meeting he makes his now famous remarks, while referring to us as "you Democrats," about Alaskans not being ladies and gentlemen—all before any of us say a word to him. He goes on creating havoc throughout his Alaskan tour.

So with the stage all set—far better than they could have done it themselves—the Democrats start showing up, Stevenson, Kefauver and Paul Butler among others. Oil is poured upon the troubled waters. To no one's surprise, Alaska goes overwhelmingly Democratic in '54.

So much for the background. My observation, made over many months, is this. I see a good deal of evidence that a careful record is being compiled. A record that goes back to Taft's arrival in Seattle many years ago as a Statehood advocate and his departure as an opponent. One that includes sources and reasons behind campaign contributions made throughout the northwest; the forces at play in the appointment of Governor Heintzleman;

who has the ear of the President re Alaskan matters, etc. If I am correct, all this will be condensed and popularized in the mink coat style and used forcefully next fall. Statehood by itself, for all its rightness, makes dull politicking; but everyone can get their teeth into mysterious changes in policy, deals and skullduggery.

And Alaskans, of course, can't help but go along. Our Constitution will be written and presented to Congress at this session. Moreover there is a move within the Convention to provide by ordinance for electing our two Senators and a Representative at the next election and sending them back to Washington demanding their seats. (Tennessee, Michigan, Oregon and California used this method to obtain Statehood.) There is a move afoot to center the Statehood battle on colonialism—which of course the refusal to grant Statehood is, in a sense—to gain the attention of the rest of the world. There is increasing talk, if these moves fail, of banding together and refusing to pay our Federal income taxes. In other words, Alaskans are fast losing patience and will go along with anything which will popularize and publicize their plight.

Of course what I say must be interpreted in the light of my desire to see Alaska get Statehood, but I think I can also view it objectively. I've always felt it is a situation where the administration has everything to gain and nothing to lose by adopting a constructive attitude. It is becoming a situation where the reverse can hurt substantially.

Whether or not Knowland made his recent visit for personal reasons, it is a fact he said all the right things and made many friends. This kind of approach, leading to a positive stand on the part of the administration for Statehood, could I am sure recover all that has been lost. I don't know what Knowland has accomplished if anything with the President since his return, but I've got my fingers crossed. I do have minutes of a meeting a few of us had with him at the University, and Daphne has the minutes of a meeting in Anchorage, and he certainly went all out. I'm willing to believe his sincerity unless proven wrong.

I've been trying to walk the narrow line between betraying confidences on the one hand, and get across to someone I hope can do something about it — someone I can confide in — how serious the situation is on the other. Its seriousness to the future of Republicanism in Alaska has long been obvious — I fully believe the time has come when the seriousness goes far beyond our borders.

I don't imagine you have anything less than 27 telephones ringing at the moment, so my apologies for the length of this chat. I'll not elongate it with an account of our doings, but Daphne and I still are hoping for a visit. I needn't wish you an eventful '56, but may it be prosperous and full of victories!

The Alaskans approved a Constitution on April 24, 1956, and in October elected senators and representatives to serve in the United States Congress. This ploy, which gave the proposed Alaskan delegation the nickname "Tennessee delegation" — after a strategy employed successfully over 150 years earlier — was designed to force federal action by showing a readiness for statehood. When the Alaskan delegation arrived in Washington, "Senator-elect" Gruening again pleaded the territory's case to the President. Possibly because of the unusual approach used by the Alaskans, the White House indicated that statehood would not be considered under any such pressure.

Governor Ernest Gruening, William Egan and Ralph Rivers to President Eisenhower
January 2, 1957
[General File 17-M-4, Eisenhower Papers.]

Dear Mr. President:

In the October 9 Alaskan general election the undersigned were elected by the voters of Alaska to present the case for Alaskan statehood to the Administration and to the Congress, and in consonance with both national party platforms to seek immediate admission of Alaska as the 49th state.

Through a representative of the Alaska Statehood Committee, John B. Adams, a written request was made to the White House on December 20th through Mr. Bernard Shanley for an appointment January 2nd for the undersigned to pay a courtesy call on the President to present a memorial from the People of Alaska and to discuss appropriate measures to assure immediate Statehood for Alaska. We are informed your busy schedule precludes an appointment today and that you have requested Secretary Seaton to meet with us today.

So that we may keep the people of Alaska advised of our progress on their mandate we would appreciate advice on the earliest date we will have the honor of seeing you in person and also an estimate of what date you will transmit to Congress the new Alaska State Constitution which Governor B. Frank Heintzleman forwarded to you last June.

Please also accept our sincere wishes for good health in this New Year for you and your family, for peace and progress for our Nation and for your strongest possible recommendations in your State of the Union message for legislation to admit Alaska as a State of the Union immediately.

Your early reply will be appreciated in care of Alaska Delegate E. L. Bartlett, House Office Building.

Assistant to the President Jack Anderson
to Ernest Gruening
January 5, 1957
[General File 17-M-4, Eisenhower Papers.]

Dear Mr. Gruening:

The President wishes me to thank you and Mr. Egan and Mr. Rivers for your joint letter of January second. He also appreciates receiving the memorial from the good people of Alaska urging statehood for Alaska.

You asked in your letter for an estimated date when the President will transmit to Congress the new Alaskan State Constitution which Governor Heintzleman has already forwarded to the Chief Executive. The proposed Constitution and the entire question of Alaskan statehood is now undergoing close study and review in the Department of the Interior. When these studies have been completed appropriate recommendations will be made to the President.

The President's schedule is particularly heavy at this time of the year, and for that reason it is virtually impossible to designate any time now when you might see him personally. When we can see the light, your request for an appointment will be called to the President's attention.

The President appreciates your good wishes for himself and family in this new year.

On April 12, 1957, Democratic Senator Frank Church of Idaho, a member of the Committee on Interior and Insular Affairs, wrote the President about the difficulties faced by advocates of both Alaskan and Hawaiian admittance. The White House reiterated what had become a standard position.

Senator Frank Church to President Eisenhower
April 12, 1957
[General File 17-M-4, Eisenhower Papers.]

Mr. President:

On November 23, 1956, shortly following my election to the United States Senate, I wrote to you concerning a highly important bipartisan matter, our foreign policy. In that letter, I pledged my support, within the full limits of my convictions, to your efforts to keep the peace, and I have already had occasion, by vote in the Senate, to honor that pledge.

Today, I feel obliged to write you about another vital bipartisan matter, statehood for Hawaii and Alaska. The platforms of both the Democratic and Republican Parties have long supported statehood for the two territories, and the cause has your personal endorsement. Yet, for reasons quite apart from the merits of the cause, I am fearful that statehood for both Hawaii and Alaska will once again fail of enactment in the Congress, unless you actively undertake to support your endorsement with the full potential of your high office.

As a member of the Senate Committee on Interior and Insular Affairs, I have participated in the hearings, recently concluded, on the statehood bills. I am also a co-sponsor of these bills. The evidence presented at the hearings makes the case for statehood so compelling that our continued failure to grant it will soon be regarded as a denial of the very tradition that has made our country strong and great. As measured by every historic test, the people of Hawaii and Alaska have qualified for statehood for many years. Again and again, they have petitioned the Congress, but each time to no avail. Now, at the outset of your second term as President, they come once more to seek their rights, and they need your help.

It is clear, from past years, that your endorsement of statehood alone will not suffice. But it is my conviction, as well as that of many other advocates of statehood in the Congress, that if you will personally undertake to champion the cause of statehood for Hawaii and Alaska, and give the pending bills your determined and persistent support, both bills will pass, and statehood will be won in this session of the Congress.

That you will take up this fight, and assert the needed leadership that only a President can give, is the earnest hope of the great host of American citizens in Hawaii and Alaska, who ask only that they be granted the elemental rights for which we once fought a revolution, and long regarded as the prerogatives of free men.

Assistant to the President Jack Anderson
to Senator Frank Church
April 18, 1957
[General File 17-M-4, Eisenhower Papers.]

Dear Senator Church:

On behalf of the President, I have been asked to reply to your April 12th letter respecting statehood for Hawaii and Alaska. That the President and the Administration aggressively support statehood for both these Territories is clearly revealed by the Republican Party Platform, by the Administration's legislative program set forth in the President's Budget Message, by the President's press conference statements and by remarks of the Republican leadership following meetings with the President at the White House. Moreover, Administration witnesses have pursued this same policy in presenting testimony to the Congressional Committees dealing with these important measures.

You may rest assured that the President's position regarding statehood for both Alaska and Hawaii remains unchanged and that the Administration will continue to strive for their statehood.

Whatever the reason, the 1957 effort to create two new states failed. By 1958 a general consensus had developed that in order to get Hawaiian statehood Alaska's admission to the Union would have to come first. This compromise pleased Democrats more than Republicans, but assured that Hawaii would follow quickly, because the non-contiguous issue would be laid to rest. Following this concept, the House acted favorably on an Alaskan statehood bill on May 28, 1958. Church's letter to the President and the White House reply show the compromise proceedings in action.

Senator Frank Church to President Eisenhower
May 21, 1958
[General File 17-M-4, Eisenhower Papers.]

Mr. President:

Statehood for Alaska is a part of the platform of the Republican Party as it is of the Democratic Party. Secretary of Interior Fred A. Seaton, a member of your official family, has effectively and forthrightly worked for statehood legislation and has reflected great credit upon your Administration in these efforts.

On April 12, 1957, I wrote you about statehood, stating my fear that "unless you actively undertake to support your endorsement with the full potential of your high office" statehood would fail.

A bill to admit Alaska to the Union is now the pending business of the House of Representatives. I am disturbed to note that the leadership of your party in that body has not supported your position with respect to taking up this bill, and I fear now, as I feared in April, 1957, that your determined and persistent support is requisite for success of this struggle.

I hope that the American citizens in Alaska, so long denied statehood, may receive this support now. Next week may be too late.

Assistant to the President Jack Anderson
to Senator Frank Church
May 22, 1958
[General File 17-M-4, Eisenhower Papers.]

Dear Senator Church:

It is a pleasure to acknowledge, on behalf of the President, your May 21st letter in further regard to statehood for Alaska. You know, of course, of yesterday's action in the House which brought this measure to the Floor for debate. The President is gratified that the merits of the pending bill are now having the full consideration of the House membership. I assure you that the President continues to stand squarely behind the 1956 Platform statement in support of Alaskan statehood.

On June 30, 1958, the Senate passed a statehood bill for Alaska by a wide margin, 64 to 20, and sent the bill to the President. The comments on the legislation by the executive agency most directly concerned, the Department of the Interior, detailed its position.

Secretary Fred Seaton
to Budget Director Maurice Stans
July 1, 1958
[Bill Files, Records Office, Bureau of the Budget.]

Dear Mr. Stans:

This report contains our views on the enrolled bill, H. R. 7999, "To provide for the admission of the State of Alaska into the Union."

We strongly recommend that this enrolled bill be approved by the President.

Approval of this measure would permit Alaska to be admitted into the Union as the forty-ninth State, upon the taking of certain prescribed steps, without further Congressional action, and the Constitution of the State of Alaska, which was approved by a vote of the people of Alaska on April 24, 1956, would be accepted as the Constitution of the new State.

The justifications for the grant of statehood to Alaska have been given many times, and it would seem that they need not be repeated here in detail. This Administration has supported statehood for Alaska, and has taken the position that all of the Territory of Alaska should become the State of Alaska, subject to special powers in the President with respect to national defense in this area. H. R. 7999 would grant statehood to all of the Territory of Alaska and section 10 of the enrolled bill makes specific provision for the President to create special national defense withdrawals over which the Federal Government may exercise exclusive jurisdiction in an area north and west of a geographical line described therein. In our opinion the bill thus satisfies these two conditions in the Administration's long-announced position on Alaska statehood.

The bill would provide grants of substantial amounts of land and other property to the new State. Certain lands and property would be immediately turned over to the State of Alaska so that the Government programs, in connection with which they are used, may be taken over by the State as a normal State function without interruption. In addition, provision is made for the grant of 103,350,000 acres of Federally owned land to the State of Alaska to be selected by the State within twenty-five years after the date of admission. Of this amount of land, 400,000 acres of vacant and unappropriated lands within national forests and 400,000 acres of vacant, unappropriated and unreserved public lands are to be selected from lands adjacent to established communities or suitable for prospective community centers and recreational areas. In addition, the State of Alaska would be authorized to select 102,550,000 acres of land from the remaining vacant, unappropriated, and unreserved public lands in Alaska. None of the public lands to be selected by the State may be within the area which is subject to special national defense withdrawal under section 10 without the approval of the President or his designated representative. It is our view that these grants of land and property will give substantial assurance that the new State will have the ability to sustain itself during its early formative years and to perform the functions and services a State is normally called upon and expected to perform.

The provisions of section 10 relating to special national defense withdrawals in the northern and western area of Alaska are designed to implement the conduct of defense activities necessary to our national security. It ought to be noted once again that such a withdrawal created by Presidential proclamation would vest exclusive Federal jurisdiction over an area, in order that the President could freely take any action necessary to protect the Nation. At the same time, however, residents within the withdrawn area would continue to have the right to vote in all Federal, State, and local elections; the functions of any municipalities and school districts within the withdrawn area would continue to be performed by those subdivisions; and the right to serve civil or criminal processes would be reserved. The authority granted to the President is similar to that which is now available to the Federal Government in twenty-five States pursuant to their Constitutions or special statutory enactments.

The bill contains provisions regarding the procedures to be followed in accomplishing the transfer to a status of statehood from a territorial status which are believed to be adequate and necessary. Section 8 would require a referendum on propositions designed to record the views of the people of Alaska on (1) their desires for the immediate admission of Alaska into the Union as a State, (2) their acceptance of the boundaries of the State as they are provided for in H. R. 7999, and (3) their consent to the provisions of the bill relating to the reservation of rights or powers to the United States and the terms or conditions of the grants of lands or other property to the State. If the vote of the majority of the electors on any one of the propositions shall not be in the affirmative, the provisions of H. R. 7999 would be ineffectual.

There are necessary provisions in the bill with regard to the continued force and effect of Territorial laws until and unless changed by the State legislature, and the application of Federal laws which are applicable generally within all the State. Similarly, requisite provision is made for the creation of a Federal district court for the proposed State, the termination of the jurisdiction of the District Court for the Territory of Alaska, the continuation of lawsuits, the succession of courts, and the satisfaction of rights of litigants in suits before such courts.

In all, we are convinced that the bill contains adequate provisions for the satisfactory transfer of governmental functions from the Territory to the State, for the safeguard of the rights and liberties of the people in the area, and for the protection of the interests and security of the United States.

Specific mention should be made of the provision contained in section 6(e) which reserves to the Federal Government the administration of the fish and wildlife resources of Alaska until the beginning of the first calendar year following the expiration of ninety legislative days after the Secretary of the Interior certifies to the Congress that the legislature of the State of Alaska has made adequate provisions for the administration, management, and conservation of these resources in the national interest. We would prefer that this provision not appear in the statehood bill. In our view this function, as all functions normally vested in States, should be immediately vested in the State of Alaska. However, we believe that any objection to this single provision is far outweighed by the overwhelming national interest in the grant of statehood to Alaska as the bill would otherwise provide.

Section 7 contains a provision directing the President to certify the enactment of the statehood measure to the Governor of Alaska no later than

July 3, 1958. As you know, we have taken the position that this provision is directory, and not mandatory; that the primary objective of this section is that official notification be sent to the Governor of Alaska upon enactment of the measure; and that the intent of the section would not be defeated if such notification is given after July 3. However, we do urge that the President approve the enrolled bill and give the required notification to the Governor of Alaska at as early a time as possible in order to demonstrate to the people of Alaska and of the entire Nation that the proposed new State will be unhesitatingly welcomed into the Union.

>━●━○━●━○━●━●━○━●━○━○━●━○━●━○━●━○━●━○━●━○━●━○━●━○━●━◄

On July 7, 1958, the President signed a bill providing for Alaskan statehood. In his introductory remarks, heard over national radio and television, he indicated his satisfaction.

Statement by President Eisenhower on Alaskan Statehood
July 7, 1958
[Bill Files, Records Office, Bureau of the Budget.]

I have today approved H. R. 7999, to provide for the admission of the State of Alaska into the Union.

While I am pleased with the action of Congress admitting Alaska, I am extremely disturbed over reports that no action is contemplated by the current Congress on pending legislation to admit Hawaii as a State. My messages to Congress urging enactment of statehood legislation have particularly referred to the qualifications of Hawaii, as well as Alaska, and I personally believe that Hawaii is qualified for statehood equally with Alaska. The thousands of loyal, patriotic Americans in Hawaii who suffered the ravages of World War II with us and who experienced that first disastrous attack upon Pearl Harbor must not be forgotten.

Pursuant to section 10 of the Alaska Statehood Act, I am authorized to make special national defense withdrawals to assure that the defense requirements of our Nation are adequately protected. I have requested the Secretary of Defense to review our defense needs in Alaska, and to make recommendations to me with respect to the extent to which the authority vested in me by section 10 of the Act should be exercised.

━●━○━●━○━●━○━●━○━●━●━○━●━○━●━●━○━●━○━●━○━●━○━●━○━●━○━c

Action followed swiftly on Hawaii. In the next session of Congress an enabling bill quickly moved through the House (March 12, 1959) and the Senate (March 11), despite some last ditch efforts to create a commonwealth on the Puerto Rican style rather than a state. Long-term opposition based on the island's racial composition and the "communist-dominated" longshoreman's union crumbled before Administration pressure. One example of the White House effort was Secretary of the Interior Seaton's letter of February 4 to the Senate committee considering the bill.

Secretary Fred Seaton to Senator James Murray
February 4, 1959
[U.S., Congress, 85th Cong., 1st Sess., Senate Report 80, 24–25.]

Dear Senator Murray:

This will reply to your request for the views of this Department on S. 50, providing for the admission of the Territory of Hawaii into the Union.

We urge the enactment of Hawaii admission legislation. We shall be glad to assist the committee in any way it may desire in connection with the technical language of the bill.

Now that the admission of Alaska as a State in the Union is a fact, we believe that the prompt admission of Hawaii, our only remaining incorporated Territory, will represent a timely addition to this Nation's complement of States. Furthermore, the admission of Hawaii will fulfill a solemn obligation on the part of the United States to the people of Hawaii—first expressed in the treaty of annexation in 1898.

The bill provides for the admission of Hawaii into the Union as a State, and prescribes the procedure to be followed for that purpose. It properly recognizes the actions already taken by the government and the people of the Territory to form and adopt a State constitution, and ratifies those actions.

With the admission into the Union of Alaska, many of the objections formerly argued against the admission of Hawaii are no longer applicable. The opposition to admission of noncontiguous areas, for example, is obviously outdated. In fact, Hawaii is in every way as well-qualified for statehood as is Alaska.

Hawaii is truly American in every aspect of its life. Its people have been citizens of the United States since 1900; they have no other loyalty. They have lived under the same laws, paid the same taxes, and enjoyed the same constitutional guarantees as other Americans for over half a century. The Americanism of the people of Hawaii goes beyond mere legal conformity. Hawaii is pervaded by American ideals and practices in its civic organizations and private charities, in its educational system and its athletics, in its press and radio, and in its way of living generally.

While a substantial proportion of Hawaii's people are of racial extractions originating in a distant continent, we believe there are no finer patriots in the Nation—as was proved by the kind of service given by Hawaii's sons during World War II and the Korean conflict.

Hawaii has also met every objective test of fitness for statehood. The civilian population of Hawaii for 1958 was estimated by the Census Bureau to be 578,000. Although recent figures on military population cannot be revealed for security reasons, it seems likely that the military population in 1958 amounted to about 59,000, the same figure as for 1957, thus giving Hawaii a total of 637,000 for 1958.

Thus, Hawaii's population exceeds that of the following 6 States: New Hampshire, 584,000; Delaware, 454,000; Vermont, 372,000; Wyoming, 320,-000; Nevada, 267,000; and Alaska, 214,000.

In recent years Federal internal revenue collections in Hawaii have generally exceeded those in 10 of the present States. In fiscal 1958 such collections in Hawaii amounted to $166,306,000, which were greater than the collections in New Hampshire, Vermont, North Dakota, South Dakota, Montana, Idaho, Wyoming, New Mexico, Nevada, or Alaska.

The Hawaiian Tax Commissioner has estimated the islands' gross Territorial product for 1958 at the impressive total of $2,109,890,000.

For many years the people of Hawaii have exercised self-government in a manner that demonstrates their firm adherence to the ideals of free government. The Hawaiian economy is well developed and prosperous. It can easily support the slight additional expense to the Hawaiian taxpayer that will result from statehood.

The Territory of Hawaii has repeatedly petitioned for statehood, and 8 years ago adopted a State constitution which was ratified overwhelmingly by the voters. The constitution evidences a sound and mature grasp of governmental problems.

President Eisenhower has repeatedly recommended statehood for Hawaii. In opening his state of the Union address of January 9, the President said: "May I voice the hope that before my term of office is ended I shall have the opportunity and great satisfaction of seeing the 50th star in our national flag." And in his budget message to the 86th Congress, the President stated: "I again recommend that the Congress enact legislation to admit Hawaii into the Union as a State, and to grant home rule to the District of Columbia. It would be unconscionable if either of these actions were delayed any longer."

We appreciate this opportunity to again express our views on this important subject. And we stand ready to aid your committee, in any manner, to assure early consideration by the Congress of the petition of the people of Hawaii for admission of Hawaii into our Union. As a matter of simple justice, the prompt admission of Hawaii, our last incorporated Territory, should be accomplished as soon as possible.

The Bureau of the Budget has advised that there is no objection to the submission of this report to your committee.

Following quick passage of the bill by Congress, the Secretary of the Interior again reiterated to the White House the reasons for Hawaiian statehood.

Secretary Fred Seaton
to Budget Director Maurice Stans
March 17, 1959
[Bill Files, Records Office, Bureau of the Budget.]

Dear Mr. Stans:

This is to confirm the position of this Department as expressed in a telephone conversation on March 13 between representatives of this Department and of your Bureau on the enrolled bill, S. 50, "To provide for the admission of the State of Hawaii into the Union."

We strongly recommend that this enrolled bill be approved by the President.

Approval of this measure would permit Hawaii to be admitted into the Union as the fiftieth State, upon the taking of certain prescribed steps, without further Congressional action, and the Constitution of the State of Hawaii, which was approved by a vote of the people of Hawaii on November 7, 1950, would be accepted as the Constitution of the new State.

The numerous justifications for the grant of Statehood to Hawaii have been given many times and it would seem that they need not be repeated here in every detail. This Administration consistently has urged statehood for Hawaii. The admission of Hawaii will fulfill a solemn obligation on the part of the United States to the people of Hawaii—first expressed in the treaty of Annexation in 1898.

Hawaii has met every objective test of fitness for Statehood. Its people have been citizens of the United States since 1900; they have no other loyalty. They have lived under the same laws, paid the same taxes, and enjoyed nearly the same constitutional guarantees as other Americans for over a half century. For many years, the people of Hawaii have exercised self-government in a manner that demonstrates their firm adherence to the ideals of free government. The Hawaiian economy is well-developed and prosperous. But Americanism of the people of Hawaii goes beyond mere legal conformity and economic ability. Hawaii is pervaded by American ideals and practices in its civic organizations and private charities, in its educational system and its athletics, in its press and radio, and in its way of living generally.

Therefore, we urge that the President approve the enrolled bill and give the required notification to the Governor of Hawaii, as soon as is practicable, in order to demonstrate to the people of Hawaii and the entire Nation that the proposed new State will be welcomed unhesitatingly into the Union.

On March 18, 1959, Eisenhower signed the legislation, informed the Bureau of the Budget of its duties in the transition of Hawaii from territory to statehood, and wrote the territorial governor of the action. Ironically, in the first Presidential election (1960) in which the two new states participated, "Republican" Hawaii went Democratic and "Democratic" Alaska voted Republican.

Statement by President Eisenhower on Hawaiian Statehood
March 18, 1959
[Bill Files, Records Office, Bureau of the Budget.]

It has given me great satisfaction to sign the Act providing for the admission of Hawaii into the Union.

Since my inauguration in 1953 I have consistently urged that this legislation be enacted, so the action of the Congress so early in this session is most gratifying.

Under this legislation, the citizens of Hawaii will soon decide whether their Islands shall become our fiftieth State. In so doing, they will demonstrate anew to the world the vitality of the principles of freedom and self-determination—the principles upon which this Nation was founded 172 years ago.

President Eisenhower to Budget Director Maurice Stans
March 18, 1959
[Bill Files, Records Office, Bureau of the Budget.]

Dear Mr. Stans:

In view of the imminent admission of the State of Hawaii into the Union, it is essential that the Federal Government promptly initiate a careful study of the effects of statehood and develop a systematic and coordinated program for effecting an orderly transition from territorial status to statehood.

I believe that the Bureau of the Budget should assume leadership for Executive Branch action in this area, beyond the regular responsibilities of the Department of the Interior, as it has done, at my request, in the case of Alaska statehood. Therefore, I am asking you, with the cooperation of the interested departments and agencies, to undertake the task of reviewing the implications of Hawaii statehood, developing a comprehensive plan for accomplishing the transition, and presenting to me recommendations for dealing with any matters requiring my attention.

President Eisenhower to Governor William Quinn
March 18, 1959
[Bill Files, Records Office, Bureau of the Budget.]

Dear Governor Quinn:

In accordance with the provisions of Section 6 of Public Law 86-3, I am very happy to certify to you the fact that I approved the law today, March 18, 1959.

As you start the procedure that will, I hope, result in the admission of Hawaii into the Union as a State on equal footing with the other States, you and the people of Hawaii have my very best wishes.

8. THE STRAUSS NOMINATION

On July 14, 1958, Dwight Eisenhower bestowed on Admiral Lewis L. Strauss, the retiring Chairman of the Atomic Energy Commission, a Medal of Freedom, and at the same time appointed him to the new post of Special Assistant to Promote Peaceful Use of the Atom. The President said: "Lewis, we have met here this morning to mark the passing of a distinguished public servant from one office into another." Strauss served only a few months in his new post. On October 24, he received a recess appointment as Secretary of Commerce. Despite rumors that Strauss had requested that he not be reappointed to the AEC because of animosities between him and Senator Clinton Anderson, the Chairman of the Joint Congressional Committee on Atomic Energy, the President gambled that the Senate would approve the Admiral for the new post. The Senate, however, delayed consideration of the appointment until March, 1959, and then held hearings lasting almost two months. Senator Anderson, during the committee proceedings, raised questions about Strauss' qualifications.

Senate Hearing on the Nomination of Lewis Strauss
May 4, 1959

[U.S., Congress, Senate, Committee on Interstate and Foreign Commerce, *Hearings, Nomination of Lewis L. Strauss*, 86th Cong., 1st Sess., 1959, 508–11.]

MR. CLINTON ANDERSON (Dem., N.M.): First of all, I would require a complete financial statement. Such a requirement is no reflection upon anybody, but has been proved to be a sensible procedure when nominations are made for positions of responsibility.

Senator Byrd, chairman of the Finance Committee, of which I am a member, requires these statements almost routinely. We had before us not long ago on the Finance Committee several Treasury nominations, and each nominee submitted a list of stocks and bond holdings and other investments. When John Graham and Jack Floberg were nominated to the AEC, the Joint Committee on Atomic Energy required complete financial statements from both of them and they were supplied without question.

The present Chairman of the AEC was required by the White House to submit a full financial statement, and that statement was later supplied—I believe through the White House—to me as chairman of the Joint Committee. When the statement was first submitted, it was discussed by Mr. McCone, Senator Knowland, Senator Hickenlooper, and me prior to the time that Mr. McCone's name was even submitted to the Congress.

It was the basis of questions during his examination before the Joint Committee. After consultations, he rearranged his personal affairs and placed certain stocks in trust during such time as he might serve the Government. All this is in the nature of the proper procedure before any possibility can arise of a conflict of interests. The mere fact that no complete statement has ever been required from Mr. Strauss should not relieve him from the responsibility of filing one now.

I therefore suggest that you obtain from Mr. Strauss a financial statement. This financial statement, of course, would cover not only his direct holdings but any indirect devices by which he owns or participates in the control of financial undertakings, such as the Flumen Corp. named in the St. Louis Post-Dispatch of November 2, 1958, as being headed by the admiral's brother, L. Z. M. Strauss, but with the admiral himself a stockholder in it.

It would naturally include also the Lewis and Rosa Strauss Foundation, merely because this foundation has been making gifts to people associated with Admiral Strauss in his work. It would not include any trust accounts which Mrs. Strauss might have from her father or the son might have from his grandfather, but the Flumen Corp. could be quite different from these.

I frankly do not know if personal financial interests have influenced in any degree Mr. Strauss' activities in the atomic energy field and in the field of government generally. However, the committee might want to look at the allegations in the story carried by the St. Louis Post-Dispatch to which I alluded before. I quote from the St. Louis Post-Dispatch story:

> When he was with the Rockefellers, Strauss figured in a bitterly contested legal battle over Eastern Air Lines acquisition of Colonial Airlines. The Civil Aeronautics Board approved the transaction as being in the public interest, but it held that Eastern had violated the act because purchasers within its influence had acquired control by Colonial before getting CAB approval by buying 110,000 shares of Colonial stock.
>
> Among these purchasers were Laurence S. Rockefeller who bought 27,200 shares, and a Strauss family trust, which bought 16,000 shares the same day. The trust, called the Flumen Corp., was headed by Strauss' brother, L. Z. M. Strauss, and Lewis Strauss was a stockholder in it.

There is, of course, the celebrated Dixon-Yates affair which Mr. Strauss quarterbacked for the banking and private utility interests in their assault on a successful Government power program. When I discuss that, I will devote more time to what I regard as the deception practiced upon the Congress and the country than on other points, but the committee may want to remember the enormous coverage given that contract during more than a year and devote its own time to it accordingly.

I should pause there to say, Mr. Chairman, that I know people will say that this business of giving a financial statement in complete detail is an unusual and onerous thing. I only say that when I paid $50,000 for a 5 percent interest in a radio and television station, I was required to file a financial statement that showed every stock I owned anywhere in the world and what my income had been. And that was published in every newspaper that wanted to publish it, including my hometown newspaper.

Now, if it is important that you get a financial statement from a man in order to let him buy a 5 percent interest in a radio station, why isn't it important to find out something about the man who directs the Department of Commerce?

Strauss, the Congress, and the Joint Committee

I now come to the matter of Mr. Strauss' relationship with the Joint Committee and his various deliberate efforts to avoid keeping the Joint Committee fully and currently informed on key matters in accordance with law:

Section 202 of the Atomic Energy Act of 1954 provides in relevant part as follows:

> The Commission shall keep the Joint Committee fully and currently informed of all its activities. . . .

The extensive legislative history of the 1954 amendments makes clear that the word "all" was added to emphasize the complete obligation of the Commission and its chairman to keep the committee informed of their activities. It was directly aimed at Mr. Strauss who had already in 1954 violated the law in carrying out his obligations.

In hearings before the Joint Committee on June 3, 1954, on amendments to the 1946 act at pages 672, 673, Chairman Cole had the following exchange with Mr. Strauss:

> Chairman COLE. Mr. Strauss, I wanted to ask you with reference to a section of existing law. Section 15 of the present law, subparagraph B, says:
> "The Commission"—meaning the Atomic Energy Commission—"shall keep the joint committee fully and currently informed with respect to the Commission's activities."
> My interpretation of that sentence and that responsibility imposed on the Commission is all inclusive with respect to the Commission's activities, with the possible exception of those areas where the Commission's activities may be related or connected in some way with national defense war plans. In all other lesser areas it is my view that is a statutory obligation of the Commission to keep this committee informed on all of its activities.
> Mr. STRAUSS. That is the view of the witness, and any respect in which I have failed to do so—that would be dereliction.

Chairman COLE. You will agree there have been instances recently in which the word "promptly" has certainly been violated.

Chairman COLE. I will express it differently. You will agree there have been recent instances where that principle has been resisted, where the Commission has resisted informing the committee on matters which the committee requested of the Commission?

Now, my purpose in bringing that out is at this time to write into the bill language which may be even stronger than what is in there now and I do not know what stronger language could be used than to say it is the duty of the Commission to keep the Joint Committee fully and currently informed on all the Commission's activities.

Mr. STRAUSS. Would you accept the change in wording, Mr. Chairman, that instead of resisting, it has been delayed? I do not believe there is anything which the Joint Committee had requested that the Commission has failed to comply with. Nor in respect to such information as crosses the desk of the Chairman has there been any delay in furnishing, as a matter of fact.

Chairman COLE. It may not be in your memory, but it certainly is within mine, that for the first time within the history of this committee it was necessary for the committee to adopt a formal resolution to get information from the Commission.

Mr. STRAUSS. I am aware of that.

Chairman COLE. You may not call that resistance, but I do.

In reporting out the 1954 amendments, the Joint Committee in Senate Report No. 1699 accompanying the bill had the following to say about the section 202 obligation:

The Commission and the Department of Defense are required to keep the Joint Committee fully and currently informed with respect to all atomic energy matters. It is the intent of Congress that the Joint Committee be informed while matters are pending, rather than after action has been taken. All Government agencies are required to furnish any information relating to atomic energy requested by the Joint Committee. . . .

Despite this legislative history of section 202, as amended, and the fact that the President signed the law, there were repeated instances where Mr. Strauss did not keep the Joint Committee fully and currently informed on important matters. His technique was to deluge the committee with considerable numbers of individual letters, and reports. But on key questions he would hold out important information until its disclosure would serve his purposes, or sometimes until the Joint Committee got wind of something and forced his hand.

A typical practice was to send up a letter with a press release after hours or on a Friday night or weekend, so that he could get his story out without comment by Joint Committee members.

I am listing below a few examples of deliberate nondisclosure of significant information until its release suited his purpose or was forced by the Joint Committee:

1. 1954–55 in the Dixon-Yates controversy he held out, through the device of executive privilege, considerable information.

2. In 1956, Mr. Strauss issued a press statement on Thursday evening, July 19, for immediate release on the results of current weapons tests. This release was the first significant public announcement of the so-called clean bomb. Yet the Joint Committee and its chairman had no advance notice of this information and its release. Chairman Strauss had an alibi that the AEC congressional liaison had tried to get in touch with our staff and staff director after regular business hours—at 6:40 P.M. that evening—but that our offices were closed.

Joint Committee records show, however, that the office was open until 6:30 P.M. during the period that AEC was notifying the press and other offices. Mr. Strauss must have posted a watchman at our door to permit his office to deliver the information 5 minutes after the office closed.

Mr. Strauss also alibied that AEC had tried to reach me at that time at home, but that I was unavailable. As a matter of fact, I was attending a well publicized dinner in honor of Senator Walter George. (The chronology of these events was discussed in great detail in a committee meeting on July 23, 1956 at transcript pp. 142–161.)

So the result was that Mr. Strauss stole a march in his ill-starred effort to persuade the people of this country and the world that the "clean bomb" is "humanitarian." As you know, the effort fell flat and has been allowed to die on the vine by the present administration.

3. In 1956, Mr. Strauss also held out important information on another matter—namely, AEC plans to transfer secret blueprints of the *Nautilus* submarine to the British even though there were still doubts as to British security procedures in the wake of the Klaus Fuchs case. In our hearings in 1958 on the amendments to the 1954 act to permit exchange of military information and material with allies, at pages 513 and 519, there appears Mr. Strauss' chronology of these events, and also one by the Joint Committee. You should compare them.

A December 11, 1957, letter from Strauss to the White House illustrated the differences that existed between the AEC Chairman and Senator Anderson.

AEC Chairman Lewis Strauss
to Press Secretary James Hagerty
December 11, 1957
[Official File 108-G, Eisenhower Papers.]

The Russians have announced the launching of a nuclear powered surface ship (an icebreaker). The following facts may be of some use in this connection.

Two years and 8 months ago the President stated that high priority should be assigned to the project of building a nuclear powered merchant ship (April 9, 1955). The AEC requested that funds for its construction be included in the legislation for the forthcoming fiscal year and several bills were introduced. The measure was defeated in the Senate by a vote of 42 to 41 after a bitter attack in which Senator Anderson, then Chairman of the Joint Committee, stated, "What then are the merits of the proposed ship? Would it be good propaganda? Would it convince anyone of our peaceful intentions? I think not. This ship is supposed to sail into foreign ports as a smokestackless wonder, convincing all who see her that we are using atomic energy for peaceful purposes."

On the floor of the House, Representative Holifield led the attack on the proposal as "premature" and "uneconomical."

Finally on July 23, 1956, conferees of both Houses reported on measures which had been favorably adopted but over a year had been lost since the initial proposal by the President.

On July 25, 1956, Senator Anderson on the Senate floor stated, "It would be far better to take an additional year's time for redesign and development work in order to move clearly forward, and to hasten the day of wide-spread application of nuclear power by the American merchant marine." Senator Anderson has now in a letter to the President dated December 5 spoken patronizingly of the greater recognition by the Executive Branch of the "Soviet challenge." As much or more than anyone, he failed to recognize the challenge and delayed us in beating them to this demonstration.

When the nomination reached the Senate floor on March 17, 1959—amidst great nationwide publicity—a three-month heated debate ensued. Democratic opposition to Strauss emerged when Senator Estes Kefauver of Tennessee raised anew Strauss' alleged non-cooperation during the Monopoly Subcommittee investigation of the 1951 Dixon-Yates controversy. To be sure, the Admiral had his defenders, as the following remarks by Republican Senator Jacob Javits of New York indicate, but the final vote on June 19, 1959, rejected Strauss' appointment 49 to 46. The Senate action reflected more a widespread dislike of Strauss than it did any desire to embarrass the Administration.

Senate Speech by Jacob Javits
on the Nomination of Lewis Strauss
June 18, 1959

[U.S., *Congressional Record*, 86th Cong., 1st Sess., 1959, CV, Part 9, 11206–08.]

MR. JACOB JAVITS (Rep., N.Y.). Mr. President, as I said, again Mr. Strauss disclosed his humanity as the Director of the Memorial Hospital in New

York. There it became his tragic duty to tell our illustrious colleague, Robert Taft, that his illness was to be fatal. I think this is rather illustrative not only of the humanity of the man but of his integrity, rather than a lack of integrity. Think of the kind of decency, the kind of character, the dignity—indeed, the kind of love of man for his fellow man—involved when one man has to tell another, especially another whose own career was so illustrious as that of Bob Taft, such sad news. Senator Taft was then the leader in the Senate on the Republican side. Mr. Strauss had to tell him he had only a number of months to live. The mere fact that Mr. Strauss was chosen by the doctors or by his fellow directors at Memorial Hospital to do this again indicates what I have said before.

How is it that this man, considered to be a man of the highest probity, of the greatest integrity, of the most distinguished personality and standing, as evidenced by all the actions which have occurred in his life, suddenly becomes a man who cannot be trusted, who lacks integrity and whose nomination to be a Cabinet officer should be denied? Again, I say, Mr. President, it is just outside reason and outside human experience.

Mr. President, to continue, after the outbreak of World War II, Mr. Strauss, being a Navy Reserve officer, was ordered to active duty in February 1941. I point out that that was long before Pearl Harbor. It was almost a full year before Pearl Harbor.

In the Bureau of Ordnance, where he served, he originated the "E" pennant for civilian contractors. As I said when I began, I had a considerable amount of contact with Mr. Strauss in the Bureau of Ordnance because I was then in the Chemical Corps myself and had a very close relationship with the Navy's Bureau of Ordnance in connection with work in which both Mr. Strauss and I were engaged. I was then a lieutenant colonel in the Chemical Corps for the combined Chiefs of Staff.

Incidentally, Mr. President, I know of my own personal knowledge that Mr. Strauss held within his own grasp not only the highest order of authority in the Navy—and I ask Senators to remember he was a Reserve officer and not an Annapolis graduate—but he also held the highest confidence in terms of the knowledge he was allowed to possess as an officer of the Navy. This is one other aspect of an honored life lived in an aura of the greatest credit and the greatest integrity, which we are suddenly asked to believe has completely changed and reversed itself and become unworthy of trust.

Incidentally, this is one of the things which nobody is denying to Mr. Strauss. He originated the "E" pennant for civilian contractors, which was a great morale builder during World War II.

Mr. President, it amuses me that the very extended hearing got to the point of minutia, as is evident when one reads the transcript, considering the fact that Mr. Strauss was not claiming credit for being responsible for the H-bomb development, but that he was entitled only to a little bit of the credit and was not entitled to all the credit; and that Mr. Strauss was not claiming all the credit for a detection system with regard to atomic explosions by which in 1949 we first detected that the Soviet Union had exploded an atom bomb, and that he was not entitled to all the credit but was only entitled to a little bit of the credit.

Mr. President, it seems to me that anybody who was entitled to only a little bit of the credit for events of that character is certainly worthy of praise. If I were entitled to a little bit of the credit for having developed the detection system which detected the first Russian atomic explosion, or if I were entitled to a little bit of the credit, just a small percentage of the credit, for the foresight of pushing forward the American development of the H-bomb, I would consider I was one of the most honored citizens in the United States of America.

Mr. President, I assure Senators that I would not haggle about whether I were given all the credit or just a little bit of the credit. It seems to me that we as Senators of the United States ought to be very grateful for men who are entitled even to a little bit of the credit for such elements of our national survival as that and we should be a little more gracious about it than to suggest that he is claiming too much credit.

In any case, Mr. President, with respect to the "E" award, nobody argues about that. Apparently Mr. Strauss did originate the idea for the "E" pennant, which was a great morale builder during World War II. He coordinated the Navy's inspection of weapons production, and he represented the Navy in the interdepartmental committee on atomic energy.

Those are pretty high-class jobs, Mr. President. This is in my opinion the Navy's way of saying that Mr. Strauss is a pretty high-class man.

Secretary of the Navy Forrestal made Strauss his special assistant. When he left the Navy after 4 years of active duty with the rank of rear admiral, he had been awarded the Legion of Merit with gold star in lieu of a second award, and the Distinguished Service Medal with an oak leaf cluster in lieu of a third award.

This seems to me to have been a pretty illustrious naval career, especially for a Reserve officer.

Mr. Strauss had hardly returned to civilian life when President Truman nominated him as a member of the Atomic Energy Commission.

I should like to digress at this point for a minute, Mr. President, because I must say that the effort to dress up the opposition to the nomination of Mr. Strauss as being based on a lack of competence, it seems to me, really collapses in the face of that kind of fact. I think this only goes further to confirm the postulate of my argument that Mr. Strauss is being tried on the issue of integrity and not on the issue of competence.

It is almost inconceivable that Mr. Strauss could be incompetent, since he served all through World War II as one of the principal officers for ordnance in the Navy, right under the gaze of Harry Truman's Joint Supervisory Committee, which was the reason why Harry Truman became a candidate for Vice President on the Democratic ticket, since he had done such a splendid job in the Senate on the committee which was supervising our war effort and our war operations.

It is inconceivable that if President Truman had the remotest notion that Strauss, who was immediately under his gaze as one of the main officers of the Navy in ordnance, was a man who lacked competence and integrity, he would have named him as one of the members of the new Atomic Energy Commission. Obviously, again, we have a white light on the situation so far as the estimate of Strauss' capability and integrity is concerned.

Again I come to the question of credit. Admiral Strauss was at least one of those mainly responsible—although there are those who say that he claims too much credit—for the establishment of a detection system for atomic explosions. As I stated a moment ago, this was the system which, in 1949, confirmed Russia's possession of the atomic bomb.

Also, in the same way, he is at least one of those in high places who urged that the United States begin immediately the production of a hydrogen bomb, and he had an important responsibility in forwarding our hydrogen bomb program. Here, too, there are those who say that he claims too much credit.

Let us assume that he does. Let us assume that that is a serious fault, a grave mistake. But it does not represent any lack of integrity. Neither does it represent a situation in which a man has not rendered great service to the country. I repeat, a little credit in connection with such colossal events as determined the very survival of the United States as the main force for freedom in the world would certainly entitle such a man to commend himself to the Senate of the United States, rather than to have such a circumstance used as a term of deprecation or criticism of his qualifications for high public office.

Mind you, the indictment is that he claimed too much credit. No one denies that he is entitled to some of the credit. In my opinion, some of the credit in such matters entitles him to be commended to us and entitles him to the gratitude of the United States.

When Mr. Strauss retired to private life after serving more than 4 years as a member of the Atomic Energy Commission, where President Truman had him under his view, and where he could observe him all the time, Admiral Strauss wanted to know what President Truman thought about him. I am sure that President Truman knew that Strauss was a Republican. That was no secret from him. President Truman offered Strauss a position as a member of the Federal Reserve Board, but Strauss chose to go back to his private concerns and became financial officer for the Rockefeller brothers.

Three years later he was recalled to Washington. Although he had supported Senator Robert Taft in opposition to Mr. Eisenhower as a candidate for the Republican nomination for the Presidency, it was President Eisenhower who appointed Admiral Strauss as Chairman of the Atomic Energy Commission, and who, since his retirement as Chairman of the Commission, appointed him last October as Secretary of Commerce.

We should have before us the facts as to the honors which have been awarded to this man by our own and by foreign governments and by institutions of higher learning. I have pointed out that he has been awarded the Legion of Merit with gold star awarded by the Navy in lieu of a second award, and the Distinguished Service Medal with an oak leaf cluster awarded by the Army. He has been made an officer of the Legion of Honor by France and a grand officer of the Order of Leopold of Belgium, and has received a number of other decorations and awards from foreign governments. He was awarded the Medal of Freedom by President Eisenhower in July of 1958. He has received 23 honorary degrees from colleges and universities in the United States and other countries.

I think that is a pretty fair score. I doubt very much if one could get very far beyond the fingers of one hand in numbering the citizens of the United States who have been similarly honored. I am not aware of the exact census, but I think this company is a pretty select one. Let those of us who are to vote on the question of confirmation of Mr. Strauss' nomination think for a moment about the effect upon governments which have decorated Strauss— the Government of France, the Government of Belgium, and of other governments; let us think about the effect upon the faculties; student bodies, and bodies of alumni of the schools and universities which have awarded him honorary degrees; and the effect upon the congregation and temple which he headed in such a distinguished manner for so many years, if we turn down his nomination. I think this should be a very heavy burden upon the conscience of every Senator who proposes to take action in this case which would place Strauss in a most unfortunate light.

Mr. Strauss is president of the board of trustees of the Institute for Advanced Study at Princeton. I should like to point out that after Dr. J. Robert Oppenheimer had lost his security clearance Mr. Strauss voted to retain him as director of the Institute for Advanced Study. To those who might suggest, notwithstanding the facts in the record as to participation by Mr. Strauss in Dr. Oppenheimer's loss of clearance, that this was an act of contrition, I should like to say that Mr. Strauss also retained Dr. Oppenheimer as head of a committee to make awards to scientists from the Lewis and Rosa Strauss memorial fund, which is Mr. Strauss' own charitable foundation.

I think that is a very interesting point. I am not passing judgment; I am not trying to pose as a supercensor, but it is said that what was done with regard to Strauss in the committee, and various aspects of the testimony against Strauss, were attributable to the Oppenheimer case. I shall not pass judgment on that question, but certainly Dr. Oppenheimer himself must have had a judgment. At least, he must have had a judgment that Strauss was acting as an honest man, that Strauss was at least a man of personal integrity and character. If he had thought, for example, that Strauss was a man who lacked character and integrity, that he was a man who could not be trusted, that he was a very slippery fellow, do any of my colleagues believe that a man of Dr. Oppenheimer's character would have continued his association with Strauss? I am here to testify to Dr. Oppenheimer's character, whatever may have been charged with respect to security indiscretions. He is a great character. He is an outstanding scientist not only in the United States but in the world. Is it conceivable that such a man would have allowed himself to remain associated with the personal charity of Strauss if he had thought that in the proceedings on security clearance Strauss had shown any lack of character or integrity? He might have disagreed with him. He would not be half the man he is if he did not disagree with him. But obviously he had no reservations about the honesty of his purpose or the integrity of his decisions.

I think that is a very revealing and important thing. When I read the biography of Strauss, and the intimate details of which I was not aware, this particular incident had a very profound effect on me.

The President, who had thought Strauss should have been confirmed in "three minutes," felt strongly enough about the "courage" of the 14 Democrats who voted for confirmation to send each a letter of appreciation. The response of one senator showed how difficult the vote had been.

President Eisenhower to Senator Albert Gore
June 19, 1959
[Official File 99-V, Eisenhower Papers.]

Dear Senator Gore:

I cannot fail to recognize the courage, wisdom and spirit of fairness you demonstrated in the vote on the confirmation of Lewis Strauss.

I am grateful.

Senator Albert Gore to President Eisenhower
June 19, 1959
[Official File 99-V, Eisenhower Papers.]

Dear Mr. President:

Your generous letter has just been received and I thank you.

As you know, this was not an easy vote for me. You may be sure, though, that I would not change it if I could.

First of all, I respected your choice for your own official family, not that the President has unlimited Constitutional rights in this regard, but because the traditional latitude and tolerance in Cabinet appointments is at the very heart of responsibility and accountability of the Chief Executive in our system.

Also, considering our history and precedents, I was apprehensive that rejection would be interpreted abroad as a rebuff and a blow to the prestige of the United States Presidency at a critical time. This I am sure will be overcome.

Finally, this seemed to me to be a time to give a man, beset from all sides, a little benefit of doubt and, if necessary, as in my case, a little forgiveness for human error.

On the same day that the Senate acted, the President issued a statement expressing his feelings about the "disgraceful fight against confirming Lewis Strauss as Secretary of Commerce."

Statement by President Eisenhower
on the Rejection of the Nomination of Lewis Strauss
June 19, 1959

[*Public Papers of the Presidents: 1959* (Washington, 1960), 472.]

Last night the Senate refused to confirm the nomination as Secretary of Commerce of Lewis Strauss—a man who in war and in peace has served his Nation loyally, honorably and effectively, under four different Presidents.

I am losing a truly valuable associate in the business of government. More than this—if the Nation is to be denied the right to have as public servants in responsible positions men of his proven character, ability and integrity, then indeed it is the American people who are the losers through this sad episode.

9. APPREHENSIONS OVER FISCAL PROGRAMS

With the overwhelming Democratic victory in November, 1958, it was inevitable that the new Congress would put great pressure on the President to accept massive anti-recession spending programs. Eisenhower's mood was more optimistic than it had been a year earlier, but he strongly warned against fiscal excesses when he said: "We must examine every item of governmental expense critically. To do otherwise would betray our nation's future. Thrift is one of the characteristics that has made this nation great. Why should we ignore it now?"

State of the Union Message by President Eisenhower
January 9, 1959
[*Public Papers of the Presidents: 1959* (Washington, 1960), 5–18.]

Mr. President, Mr. Speaker, Members of the 86th Congress, my fellow citizens:

This is the moment when Congress and the Executive annually begin their cooperative work to build a better America.

One basic purpose unites us: To promote strength and security, side by side with liberty and opportunity.

As we meet today, in the 170th year of the Republic, our Nation must continue to provide—as all other free governments have had to do throughout time—a satisfactory answer to a question as old as history. It is: Can Government based upon liberty and the God-given rights of man, permanently endure when ceaselessly challenged by a dictatorship, hostile to our mode of life, and controlling an economic and military power of great and growing strength?

For us the answer has always been found, and is still found in the devotion, the vision, the courage and the fortitude of our people.

Moreover, this challenge we face, not as a single powerful nation, but as one that has in recent decades reached a position of recognized leadership in the Free World.

We have arrived at this position of leadership in an era of remarkable productivity and growth. It is also a time when man's power of mass destruction has reached fearful proportions.

Possession of such capabilities helps create world suspicion and tension. We, on our part, know that we seek only a just peace for all, with aggressive designs against no one. Yet we realize that there is uneasiness in the world because of a belief on the part of peoples that through arrogance, miscalculation or fear of attack, catastrophic war could be launched. Keeping the peace in today's world more than ever calls for the utmost in the nation's resolution, wisdom, steadiness and unremitting effort.

We cannot build peace through desire alone. Moreover, we have learned the bitter lesson that international agreements, historically considered by us as sacred, are regarded in Communist doctrine and in practice to be mere scraps of paper. The most recent proof of their disdain of international obligations, solemnly undertaken, is their announced intention to abandon their responsibilities respecting Berlin.

As a consequence, we can have no confidence in any treaty to which Communists are a party except where such a treaty provides within itself for self-enforcing mechanisms. Indeed, the demonstrated disregard of the Communists of their own pledges is one of the greatest obstacles to success in substituting the Rule of Law for rule by force.

Yet step by step we must strengthen the institutions of peace—a peace that rests upon justice—a peace that depends upon a deep knowledge and clear understanding by all peoples of the cause and consequences of possible failure in this great purpose.

I

To achieve this peace we seek to prevent war at any place and in any dimension. If, despite our best efforts, a local dispute should flare into armed hostilities, the next problem would be to keep the conflict from spreading, and so compromising freedom. In support of these objectives we maintain forces of great power and flexibility.

Our formidable air striking forces are a powerful deterrent to general war. Large and growing portions of these units can depart from their bases in a matter of minutes.

Similar forces are included in our naval fleets.

Ground and other tactical formations can move with swiftness and precision, when requested by friendly and responsible governments, to help curb threatened aggression. The stabilizing influence of this capacity has been dramatically demonstrated more than once over the past year.

Our military and related scientific progress has been highly gratifying.

Great strides have been made in the development of ballistic missiles. Intermediate range missiles are now being deployed in operational units.

The Atlas intercontinental ballistic missile program has been marked by rapid development as evidenced by recent successful tests. Missile training units have been established and launching sites are far along in construction.

New aircraft that fly at twice the speed of sound are entering our squadrons.

We have successfully placed five satellites in orbit, which have gathered information of scientific importance never before available. Our latest satellite illustrates our steady advance in rocketry and foreshadows new developments in world-wide communications.

Warning systems constantly improve.

Our atomic submarines have shattered endurance records and made historic voyages under the North Polar Sea.

A major segment of our national scientific and engineering community is working intensively to achieve new and greater developments. Advance in military technology requires adequate financing but, of course, even more, it requires talent and time.

All this is given only as a matter of history; as a record of our progress in space and ballistic missile fields in no more than four years of intensive effort. At the same time we clearly recognize that some of the recent Soviet accomplishments in this particular technology are indeed brilliant.

Under the law enacted last year the Department of Defense is being reorganized to give the Secretary of Defense full authority over the military establishment. Greater efficiency, more cohesive effort and speedier reaction to emergencies are among the many advantages we are already noting from these changes.

These few highlights point up our steady military gains. We are rightfully gratified by the achievements they represent. But we must remember that these imposing armaments are purchased at great cost.

National Security programs account for nearly sixty percent of the entire Federal budget for this coming fiscal year.

Modern weapons are exceedingly expensive.

The overall cost of introducing ATLAS into our armed forces will average $35 million per missile on the firing line.

This year we are investing an aggregate of close to $7 billion in missile programs alone.

Other billions go for research, development, test and evaluation of new weapons systems.

Our latest atomic submarines will cost $50 million each, while some special types will cost three times as much.

We are now ordering fighter aircraft which are priced at fifty times as much as the fighters of World War II.

We are buying certain bombers that cost their weight in gold.

These sums are tremendous, even when compared with the marvelous resiliency and capacity of our economy.

Such expenditures demand both balance and perspective in our planning for defense. At every turn, we must weigh, judge and select. Needless duplication of weapons and forces must be avoided.

We must guard against feverish building of vast armaments to meet glibly predicted moments of so-called "maximum peril." The threat we face is not sporadic or dated: It is continuous. Hence we must not be swayed in our calculations either by groundless fear or by complacency. We must avoid extremes, for vacillation between extremes is inefficient, costly, and destructive of morale. In these days of unceasing technological advance, we must plan our defense expenditures systematically and with care, fully recognizing that obsolescence compels the never-ending replacement of older weapons with new ones.

The defense budget for the coming year has been planned on the basis of these principles and considerations. Over these many months I have personally participated in its development.

The aim is a sensible posture of defense. The secondary aim is increased efficiency and avoidance of waste. Both are achieved by this budgetary plan.

Working by these guide lines I believe with all my heart that America can be as sure of the strength and efficiency of her armed forces as she is of their loyalty. I am equally sure that the nation will thus avoid useless expenditures which, in the name of security, might tend to undermine the economy and, therefore, the nation's safety.

Our own vast strength is only a part of that required for dependable security. Because of this we have joined with nearly 50 other nations in collective security arrangements. In these common undertakings each nation is expected to contribute what it can in sharing the heavy load. Each supplies part of a strategic deployment to protect the forward boundaries of freedom.

Constantly we seek new ways to make more effective our contribution to this system of collective security. Recently I have asked a Committee of eminent Americans of both parties to re-appraise our military assistance programs and the relative emphasis which should be placed on military and economic aid.

I am hopeful that preliminary recommendations of this Committee will be available in time to assist in shaping the Mutual Security program for the coming fiscal year.

Any survey of the free world's defense structure cannot fail to impart a feeling of regret that so much of our effort and resources must be devoted to armaments. At Geneva and elsewhere we continue to seek technical and other agreements that may help to open up, with some promise, the issues of international disarmament. America will never give up hope that eventually all nations can, with mutual confidence, drastically reduce these non-productive expenditures.

II

The material foundation of our national safety is a strong and expanding economy. This we have—and this we must maintain. Only with such an economy can we be secure and simultaneously provide for the well-being of our people.

A year ago the nation was experiencing a decline in employment and output. Today that recession is fading into history, and this without gigantic, hastily-improvised public works projects or untimely tax reductions. A healthy and vigorous recovery has been under way since last May. New homes are being built at the highest rate in several years. Retail sales are at peak levels. Personal income is at an all-time high.

The marked forward thrust of our economy reaffirms our confidence in competitive enterprise. But—clearly—wisdom and prudence in both the public and private sectors of the economy are always necessary.

Our outlook is this: 1960 commitments for our armed forces, the Atomic Energy Commission and Military Assistance exceed 47 billion dollars. In the foreseeable future they are not likely to be significantly lower. With an annual population increase of three million, other governmental costs are bound to mount.

After we have provided wisely for our military strength, we must judge how to allocate our remaining government resources most effectively to promote our well-being and economic growth.

Federal programs that will benefit all citizens are moving forward.

Next year we will be spending increased amounts on health programs;
  on Federal assistance to science and education;
  on the development of the nation's water resources;
  on the renewal of urban areas;
  and on our vast system of Federal-aid highways.

Each of these additional outlays is being made necessary by the surging growth of America.

Let me illustrate. Responsive to this growth, Federal grants and long-term loans to assist 14 major types of capital improvements in our cities will total over 2 billion dollars in 1960—double the expenditure of two years ago. The major responsibility for development in these fields rests in the localities, even though the Federal Government will continue to do its proper part in meeting the genuine needs of a burgeoning population.

But the progress of our economy can more than match the growth of our needs. We need only to act wisely and confidently.

Here, I hope you will permit me to digress long enough to express something that is much on my mind.

The basic question facing us today is more than mere survival—the military defense of national life and territory. It is the preservation of a *way* of life.

We must meet the world challenge and at the same time permit no stagnation in America.

Unless we *progress*, we *regress*.

We can successfully sustain security and remain true to our heritage of freedom if we clearly visualize the tasks ahead and set out to perform them with resolution and fervor. We must first define these tasks and then understand what we must do to perform them.

If progress is to be steady we must have long-term guides extending far ahead, certainly five, possibly even ten years. They must reflect the knowledge that before the end of five years we will have a population of over 190 million. They must be goals that stand high, and so inspire every citizen to climb always toward mounting levels of moral, intellectual and material strength. Every advance toward them must stir pride in individual and national achievements.

To define these goals, I intend to mobilize help from every available source.

We need more than politically ordained national objectives to challenge the best efforts of free men and women. A group of selfless and devoted individuals, outside of government, could effectively participate in making the necessary appraisal of the potentials of our future. The result would be establishment of national goals that would not only spur us on to our finest efforts, but would meet the stern test of practicality.

The Committee I plan will comprise educators and representatives of labor, management, finance, the professions and every other kind of useful activity.

Such a study would update and supplement, in the light of continuous changes in our society and its economy, the monumental work of the Committee on Recent Social Trends which was appointed in 1931 by President Hoover. Its report has stood the test of time and has had a beneficial influence on national development. The new Committee would be concerned, among other things, with the acceleration of our economy's growth and the living standards of our people, their health and education, their better assurance of life and liberty and their greater opportunities. It would also be concerned with methods to meet such goals and what levels of government—Local, State, or Federal—might or should be particularly concerned.

As one example, consider our schools, operated under the authority of local communities and states. In their capacity and in their quality they conform to no recognizable standards. In some places facilities are ample, in others meager. Pay of teachers ranges between wide limits, from the adequate to the shameful. As would be expected, quality of teaching varies just as widely. But to our teachers we commit the most valuable possession of the nation and of the family—our children.

We must have teachers of competence. To obtain and hold them we need standards. We need a National Goal. Once established I am certain that public opinion would compel steady progress toward its accomplishment.

Such studies would be helpful, I believe, to government at all levels and to all individuals. The goals so established could help us see our current needs in perspective. They will spur progress.

We do not forget, of course, that our nation's progress and fiscal integrity are interdependent and inseparable. We can afford everything we clearly need, but we cannot afford one cent of waste. We must examine every item of governmental expense critically. To do otherwise would betray our nation's future. Thrift is one of the characteristics that has made this nation great. Why should we ignore it now?

We must avoid any contribution to inflationary processes, which could disrupt sound growth in our economy.

Prices have displayed a welcome stability in recent months and, if we are wise and resolute, we will not tolerate inflation in the years to come. But history makes clear the risks inherent in any failure to deal firmly with the basic causes of inflation. Two of the most important of these causes are the wage-price spiral and continued deficit financing.

Inflation would reduce job opportunities, price us out of world markets, shrink the value of savings and penalize the thrift so essential to finance a growing economy.

Inflation is not a Robin Hood, taking from the rich to give to the poor. Rather, it deals most cruelly with those who can least protect themselves. It strikes hardest those millions of our citizens whose incomes do not quickly rise with the cost of living. When prices soar, the pensioner and the widow see their security undermined, the man of thrift sees his savings melt away; the white collar worker, the minister, and the teacher see their standards of living dragged down.

Inflation can be prevented. But this demands statesmanship on the part of business and labor leaders and of government at all levels.

We must encourage the self-discipline, the restraint necessary to curb the wage-price spiral and we must meet current costs from current revenue.

To minimize the danger of future soaring prices and to keep our economy sound and expanding, I shall present to the Congress certain proposals.

First, I shall submit a balanced budget for the next year, a year expected to be the most prosperous in our history. It is a realistic budget with wholly attainable objectives.

If we cannot live within our means during such a time of rising prosperity, the hope for fiscal integrity will fade. If we persist in living beyond our means, we make it difficult for every family in our land to balance its own household budget. But to live within our means would be a tangible demonstration of the self-discipline needed to assure a stable dollar.

The Constitution entrusts the Executive with many functions, but the Congress—and the Congress alone—has the power of the purse. Ultimately upon Congress rests responsibility for determining the scope and amount of Federal spending.

By working together, the Congress and the Executive can keep a balance between income and outgo. If this is done there is real hope that we can look forward to a time in the foreseeable future when needed tax reforms can be accomplished.

In this hope, I am requesting the Secretary of the Treasury to prepare appropriate proposals for revising, at the proper time, our tax structure, to remove inequities and to enhance incentives for all Americans to work, to save, and to invest. Such recommendations will be made as soon as our fiscal condition permits. These prospects will be brightened if 1960 expenditures do not exceed the levels recommended.

Second, I shall recommend to the Congress that the Chief Executive be given the responsibility either to approve or to veto specific items in appropriations and authorization bills.[1] This would save tax dollars.

Third, to reduce Federal operations in an area where private enterprise can do the job, I shall recommend legislation for greater flexibility in extending Federal credit, and in improving the procedures under which private credits are insured or guaranteed. Present practices have needlessly added large sums to Federal expenditures.

Fourth, action is required to make more effective use of the large Federal expenditures for agriculture and to achieve greater fiscal control in this area.

Outlays of the Department of Agriculture for the current fiscal year for the support of farm prices on a very few farm products will exceed five billion dollars. That is a sum equal to approximately two-fifths of the net income of all farm operators in the entire United States.

By the end of this fiscal year it is estimated that there will be in Government hands surplus farm products worth about nine billion dollars. And by July 1, 1959, Government expenditures for storage, interest, and handling of its agricultural inventory will reach a rate of one billion dollars a year.

---

[1]At this point the message, as recorded from the floor and printed in the Congressional Record, shows the following interpolation: I assure you gentlemen that I know this recommendation has been made time and again by every President that has appeared in this hall for many years, but I say this, it still is one of the most important corrections that could be made in our annual expenditure program, because this would save tax dollars. [Applause]

This level of expenditure for farm products could be made willingly for a temporary period if it were leading to a sound solution of the problem. But unfortunately this is not true. We need new legislation.

In the past I have sent messages to the Congress requesting greater freedom for our farmers to manage their own farms and greater freedom for markets to reflect the wishes of producers and consumers. Legislative changes that followed were appropriate in direction but did not go far enough.

The situation calls for prompt and forthright action. Recommendation for action will be contained in a message to be transmitted to the Congress shortly.

These fiscal and related actions will help create an environment of price stability for economic growth. However, certain additional measures are needed.

I shall ask Congress to amend the Employment Act of 1946 to make it clear that Government intends to use all appropriate means to protect the buying power of the dollar.

I am establishing a continuing Cabinet group on Price Stability for Economic Growth to study governmental and private policies affecting costs, prices, and economic growth. It will strive also to build a better public understanding of the conditions necessary for maintaining growth and price stability.

Studies are being undertaken to improve our information on prices, wages, and productivity.

I believe all citizens in all walks of life will support this program of action to accelerate economic growth and promote price stability.

III

I take up next certain aspects of our international situation and our programs to strengthen it.

America's security can be assured only within a world community of strong, stable, independent nations, in which the concepts of freedom, justice and human dignity can flourish.

There can be no such thing as Fortress America. If ever we were reduced to the isolation implied by that term, we would occupy a prison, not a fortress. The question whether we can afford to help other nations that want to defend their freedom but cannot fully do so from their own means, has only one answer: we can and we must, we have been doing so since 1947.

Our foreign policy has long been dedicated to building a permanent and just peace.

During the past six years our free world security arrangements have been bolstered and the bonds of freedom have been more closely knit. Our friends in Western Europe are experiencing new internal vitality, and are increasingly more able to resist external threats.

Over the years the world has come to understand clearly that it is our firm policy not to countenance aggression. In Lebanon, Taiwan, and Berlin—our stand has been clear, right, and expressive of the determined will of a united people.

Acting with other free nations we have undertaken the solemn obligation to defend the people of free Berlin against any effort to destroy their freedom. In the meantime we shall constantly seek meaningful agreements to settle this and other problems, knowing full well that not only the integrity of a single city, but the hope of all free peoples is at stake.

We need, likewise, to continue helping to build the economic base so essential to the Free World's stability and strength.

The International Monetary Fund and the World Bank have both fully proven their worth as instruments of international financial cooperation. Their Executive Directors have recommended an increase in each member country's subscription. I am requesting the Congress for immediate approval of our share of these increases.

We are now negotiating with representatives of the twenty Latin American Republics for the creation of an inter-American financial institution. Its purpose would be to join all the American Republics in a common institution which would promote and finance development in Latin America, and make more effective the use of capital from the World Bank, the Export-Import Bank, and private sources.

Private enterprise continues to make major contributions to economic development in all parts of the world. But we have not yet marshalled the full potential of American business for this task, particularly in countries which have recently attained their independence. I shall present to this Congress a program designed to encourage greater participation by private enterprise in economic development abroad.

Further, all of us know that to advance the cause of freedom we must do much more than help build sound economies. The spiritual, intellectual, and physical strength of people throughout the world will in the last analysis determine their willingness and their ability to resist Communism.

To give a single illustration of our many efforts in these fields: We have been a participant in the effort that has been made over the past few years against one of the great scourges of mankind—disease. Through the Mutual Security program public health officials are being trained by American universities to serve in less developed countries. We are engaged in intensive malaria eradication projects in many parts of the world. America's major successes in our own country prove the feasibility of success everywhere.

By these and other means we shall continue and expand our campaign against the afflictions that now bring needless suffering and death to so many of the world's people. We wish to be part of a great shared effort toward the triumph of health.

IV

America is best described by one word, freedom.

If we hope to strengthen freedom in the world we must be ever mindful of how our own conduct reacts elsewhere. No nation has ever been so floodlighted by world opinion as the United States is today. Everything we do is carefully scrutinized by other peoples throughout the world. The bad is seen along with the good.

Because we are human we err. But as free men we are also responsible for correcting the errors and imperfections of our ways.

Last January I made comprehensive recommendations to the Congress for legislation in the labor-management field. To my disappointment, Congress failed to act. The McClellan Committee disclosures of corruption, racketeering, and abuse of trust and power in labor-management affairs have aroused America and amazed other peoples. They emphasize the need for improved local law enforcement and the enactment of effective Federal legislation to protect the public interest and to insure the rights and economic freedoms of millions of American workers. Half-hearted measures will not do. I shall recommend prompt enactment of legislation designed:

To safeguard workers' funds in union treasuries against misuse of any kind whatsoever.

To protect the rights and freedoms of individual union members, including the basic right to free and secret elections of officers.

To advance true and responsible collective bargaining.

To protect the public and innocent third parties from unfair and coercive practices such as boycotting and blackmail picketing.

The workers and the public must have these vital protections.

In other areas of human rights—freedom from discrimination in voting, in public education, in access to jobs, and in other respects—the world is likewise watching our conduct.

The image of America abroad is not improved when school children, through closing of some of our schools and through no fault of their own, are deprived of their opportunity for an education.

The government of a free people has no purpose more noble than to work for the maximum realization of equality of opportunity under law. This is not the sole responsibility of any one branch of our government. The judicial arm, which has the ultimate authority for interpreting the Constitution, has held that certain state laws and practices discriminate upon racial grounds and are unconstitutional. Whenever the supremacy of the Constitution of the United States is challenged I shall continue to take every action necessary to uphold it.

One of the fundamental concepts of our constitutional system is that it guarantees to every individual, regardless of race, religion, or national origin, the equal protection of the laws. Those of us who are privileged to hold public office have a solemn obligation to make meaningful this inspiring objective. We can fulfill that obligation by our leadership in teaching, persuading, demonstrating, and in enforcing the law.

We are making noticeable progress in the field of civil rights—we are moving forward toward achievement of equality of opportunity for all people everywhere in the United States. In the interest of the nation and of each of its citizens, that progress must continue.

Legislative proposals of the Administration in this field will be submitted to the Congress early in the session. All of us should help to make clear that the government is united in the common purpose of giving support to the law and the decisions of the Courts.

By moving steadily toward the goal of greater freedom under law, for our own people, we shall be the better prepared to work for the cause of freedom under law throughout the world.

All peoples are sorely tired of the fear, destruction, and the waste of war. As never before, the world knows the human and material costs of war and seeks to replace force with a genuine rule of law among nations.

It is my purpose to intensify efforts during the coming two years in seeking ways to supplement the procedures of the United Nations and other bodies with similar objectives, to the end that the rule of law may replace the rule of force in the affairs of nations. Measures toward this end will be proposed later, including a re-examination of our own relation to the International Court of Justice.

Finally—let us remind ourselves that Marxist scripture is not new; it is not the gospel of the future. Its basic objective is dictatorship, old as history. What *is* new is the shining prospect that man can build a world where all can live in dignity.

We seek victory—not over any nation or people—but over the ancient enemies of us all; victory over ignorance, poverty, disease, and human degradation wherever they may be found.

We march in the noblest of causes—human freedom.

If we make ourselves worthy of America's ideals, if we do not forget that our nation was founded on the premise that all men are creatures of God's making, the world will come to know that it is free men who carry forward the true promise of human progress and dignity.

The proposed budget for fiscal 1960 reflected the same kind of conservative economic policy contained in Eisenhower's State of the Union Address. As originally presented, expenditures for 1960 were to be almost $4 billion less than the previous year.

Annual Presidential Budget Message
January 19, 1959
[*Public Papers of the Presidents: 1959* (Washington, 1960), 36–43.]

To the Congress of the United States:

The situation we face today as a Nation differs significantly from that of a year ago. We are now entering a period of national prosperity and high employment. This is a time for the Government to conduct itself so as best to help the Nation move forward strongly and confidently in economic and social progress at home, while fulfilling our responsibilities abroad. The budget of the United States for the fiscal year 1960, transmitted herewith, will effectively and responsibly carry out the Government's role in dealing with the problems and the opportunities of the period ahead.

This budget proposes to increase our military effectiveness, to enhance domestic wellbeing, to help friendly nations to foster their development, to preserve fiscal soundness, and to encourage economic growth and stability, not only in the fiscal year 1960 but in the years beyond. And it clearly shows that these things can be done within our income.

We cannot, of course, undertake to satisfy all proposals for Government spending. But as we choose which ones the Government should accept, we must always remember that freedom and the long-run strength of our economy are prerequisite to attainment of our national goals. Otherwise, we cannot, for long, meet the imperatives of individual freedom, national security, and the many other necessary responsibilities of Government. In short, this budget fits the conditions of today because:

1. IT IS A BALANCED BUDGET.—My recommendations call for an approximate equality between revenues and expenditures, with a small surplus.

2. IT IS A RESPONSIBLE BUDGET.—By avoiding a deficit, it will help prevent further increases in the cost of living and the hidden and unfair tax that inflation imposes on personal savings and incomes.

3. IT IS A CONFIDENT BUDGET.—It anticipates, in a rapidly advancing economy, increases in revenues without new general taxes, and counts upon the unity and good judgment of the American people in supporting a level of government activity which such revenues will make possible.

4. IT IS A POSITIVE BUDGET.—It responds to national needs, with due regard to urgencies and priorities, without being either extravagant or unduly limiting.

5. IT IS AN ATTAINABLE BUDGET.—Its proposals are realistic and can be achieved with the cooperation of the Congress.

Any budget is a financial plan. The budget for the Government is proposed by the President, but it is acted upon by the Congress which has the duty under the Constitution to authorize and appropriate for expenditures. Therefore, responsibility for the Government's finances is a shared one. Achievement of the plan set forth in this budget from here on depends upon congressional response, popular support, and developments in our economy and in the world.

Future Budget Outlook

The actions we take now on the 1960 budget will affect the fiscal outlook for many years to come. This budget was prepared in the light of the following general prospects for Government finances for the next few years.

Growth of revenues.—Our Nation's population and labor force will continue to increase. The output per hour of work on our farms and in our factories can also be expected to grow as it has in the past. With sustained economic expansion, with employment of our people and resources at high levels, and with continued technological advance, the value of total national production and income will be substantially larger in the future than it is today.

Economic growth generates higher personal incomes and business profits. Under our graduated income tax system, with present tax rates, budget receipts should grow even faster than national income, although the rise in receipts certainly will not be uniform from year to year. Also, some tax reforms and downward tax adjustments will be essential in future years to help maintain and strengthen the incentives for continued economic growth. With a balance in our finances in 1960, we can look forward to tax reduction in the reasonably foreseeable future. In the long run, taxes should be so arranged that in periods of prosperity some annual provision is made for debt reduction, even though at a modest rate.

Control of expenditures.—The estimated 1960 expenditures, while $3.9 billion less than in 1959, will still be $12.4 billion higher than in 1955, an average increase of almost $2.5 billion a year. These figures emphasize that if we are to succeed in keeping total expenditures under control in the coming years we must recognize certain hard facts.

First, defense spending will remain extremely large as long as we must maintain military readiness in an era of world trouble and unrest. Until there is a significant and secure easing of world tensions, the actions by the Department of Defense to realign forces, close unneeded installations, and cut back outmoded weapons will achieve only relatively small expenditure reductions. Keeping our military structure capable and ready to meet any threat means that we must continue to strengthen our defenses. It is but a reflection of the world in which we live to stress again the fact that modern weapons are complex and costly to develop, costly to procure, and costly to operate and maintain.

Second, without one single new action by the Congress to authorize additional projects or programs, Government outlays for some of our major activities are certain to keep on rising for several years after 1960 because of commitments made in the past. For example, commitments for urban renewal capital grants have exceeded net expenditures by about $200 million or more for each of the last 3 years. Money to meet these commitments will be paid out in the years immediately ahead. Similarly, continued construction of the many water resources projects underway throughout the country will raise expenditures for these programs in the next 2 years beyond the current record amount.

Moreover, inescapable demands resulting from new technology and the growth of our Nation, and new requirements resulting from the changing nature of our society, will generate Federal expenditures in future years. As a matter of national policy we must, for example, make our airways measure up to the operational and safety needs of the jet age. We must not forget that a rapidly growing population creates virtually automatic increases in many Federal responsibilities.

Fiscal soundness and progress.—Both domestic and defense needs require that we keep our financial house in order. This means that we must adhere to two policies:

First, we must review all government activities as a part of the continuing budgetary process from year to year. Changing circumstances will inevitably offer opportunities for economies in a variety of existing Federal programs. If we do not make such reviews and act forthrightly on their findings, the combination of old commitments and new authorizations for new or enlarged Federal responsibilities could swell expenditures unnecessarily and inconsistently. Consonant with this policy of review, reductions have been recommended in this budget for 1960 appropriations which will affect expenditures not only in that year but also in later years. Furthermore, this budget contains proposals to modify certain activities and institute certain charges for special services. These recommendations are practicable and sound. They should be enacted.

Second, we must examine new programs and proposals with a critical eye. Desirability alone is not a sound criterion for adding to Federal responsibilities. The impact today and tomorrow on the entire Nation must be carefully assessed.

Our economy will continue to grow vigorously. This growth will produce additional Federal revenues, but it will not produce them without limit. We cannot take our resources for granted and we cannot spend them indiscriminately. We must deal with new conditions as they arise. We must choose what the Federal Government will do and how it will do it. If the choice is responsibly made, reductions obtained through economies and the rising revenues accompanying economic growth will produce surpluses which can be used to lessen the burden of taxes, meet the cost of essential new Government services, and reduce the public debt. The proposals in this budget have been formulated with these long-run objectives in mind.

Budget Totals

Budget expenditures are proposed to be held to $77 billion in fiscal 1960, which is $3.9 billion less than the estimated 1959 level of $80.9 billion.

With continued vigorous economic recovery, and with the relatively few new tax adjustments proposed herein, budget receipts in fiscal 1960 are expected to reach a total of $77.1 billion, an increase of $9.1 billion over fiscal 1959.

Thus a very modest surplus of about $0.1 billion is estimated for 1960, compared with a recession-induced deficit of $12.9 billion in the current fiscal year. This estimated balance assumes enactment of recommendations for extending present excises and corporation income taxes scheduled for reduction under existing law, for some new tax legislation to remove inequities and loopholes, for increased charges for special services, and for reductions in some current programs. It also assumes that certain programs can be made self-financing by stepping up the sale of portfolio assets.

Financing of the $12.9 billion budget deficit for the current fiscal year will increase the public debt to $285 billion by June 30, 1959, $2 billion in excess of the present permanent debt limit. With a balanced budget in 1960, a $285 billion debt is indicated also for June 30, 1960. On the basis of these estimates, it will be necessary to renew the request made during the past session of Congress for a permanent debt ceiling of $285 billion and, further, to seek an increase in the temporary debt ceiling sufficient to cover heavy borrowing requirements during the first half of the fiscal year 1960, borrowings which would be repaid before June 30, 1960.

The new authority to incur obligations recommended for fiscal 1960 is $76.8 billion, which is slightly less than the estimates for expenditures and for receipts. Further reductions in new obligational authority can be attained in 1961 by the Congress enacting my recommendations for program modifications.

BUDGET TOTALS

[Fiscal years. In billions]

	1957 actual	1958 actual	1959 estimate	1960 estimate
Budget receipts......................	$71.0	$69.1	$68.0	$77.1
Budget expenditures..................	69.4	71.9	80.9	77.0
Budget surplus (+) or deficit (−).....	+1.6	−2.8	−12.9	+0.1
New obligational authority............	70.2	76.3	82.4	76.8

[1] Includes $8.7 billion of anticipated supplemental requests.

A consolidation of budget and trust fund transactions on a cash basis shows that the total Federal receipts from the public in fiscal 1960 are expected to exceed payments to the public by $0.6 billion. This figure exceeds the budget surplus in 1960 mainly because (1) cash payments of interest on redeemed savings bonds are less than the accrued interest included in budget expenditures and (2) trust fund receipts exceed trust fund expenditures.

FEDERAL GOVERNMENT RECEIPTS FROM AND PAYMENTS TO THE PUBLIC

[Fiscal years. In billions]

	1957 actual	1958 actual	1959 estimate	1960 estimate
Receipts from the public...............	$82.1	$81.9	$81.7	$93.5
Payments to the public................	80.0	83.4	94.9	92.9
Excess of receipts over payments.......	2.1	. . . . .	. . . . .	0.6
Excess of payments over receipts.......	. . . . .	1.5	13.2	. . . . .

Budget Receipts

Extension of present tax rates.—The budget outlook for 1960 makes it essential to extend present tax rates on corporation profits and certain excise taxes another year beyond their present expiration date of June 30, 1959.

Development of a more equitable tax system.—Considerable progress was made last year in removing unintended benefits and hardships from the tax laws. Continued attention is necessary in this area. As the budget permits, additional reforms should be undertaken to increase the fairness of the tax system, to reduce the tax restraints on incentives to work and invest, and wherever feasible to simplify the laws. I hope that the committees of the Congress will work with the Treasury Department in preparing further adjustments of our tax laws for the future.

I urge the Congress to take action now on certain specific changes to maintain or increase revenues and to make the laws more equitable. The Treasury Department has recently proposed an equitable plan for taxing the income of life insurance companies. Specific proposals for corrective amendments of the laws on taxation of cooperatives will be transmitted to the Congress shortly. The Treasury will also recommend an amendment specifying the treatment processes which shall be considered mining for the purpose of computing percentage depletion in the case of mineral products. This amendment, prompted by court decisions, is designed to prevent an unintended extension of percentage depletion allowances to the sales price of finished products; a similar recommendation with respect to cement and clay products was made to the Congress last year.

Other changes in tax rates.—In order to make highway-related taxes support our vast highway expenditures, excises on motor fuels need to be increased 1½ cents a gallon to 4½ cents. These receipts will go into the highway trust fund and preserve the pay-as-we-go principle, so that contributions from general tax funds to build Federal aid highways will not be necessary.

At the same time, to help defray the rising costs of operating the Federal airways, receipts from excises on aviation gasoline should be retained in general budget receipts rather than transferred to the highway trust fund. The estimates of budget and trust fund receipts from excise taxes reflect such proposed action. They also include a proposal to have users of the Federal airways pay a greater share of costs through increased rates on aviation gasoline and a new tax on jet fuels. These taxes, like the highway gasoline tax, should be 4½ cents per gallon. I believe it fair and sound that such taxes be reflected in the rates of transportation paid by the passengers and shippers.

BUDGET RECEIPTS

[Fiscal years. In billions]

	1958 actual	1959 estimate	1960 estimate
Individual income taxes	$34.7	$36.9	$40.7
Corporation income taxes	20.1	17.0	21.5
Excise taxes	8.6	8.5	8.9
All other receipts	5.7	5.6	6.0
Total	69.1	68.0	77.1

As part of my proposals referred to later in this message to return responsibility for certain Federal programs to the States—in this instance, responsibility for vocational education and for waste treatment facilities—Federal excise taxes on local telephone service should be revised effective July 1, 1960, to allow limited credits for telephone taxes paid to the States.

Revenues.—The resurgence of our economy has been stronger than was assumed in the budget estimates that were published last September. Consequently, budget receipts for the fiscal year 1959 are now expected to total $68 billion instead of the $67 billion estimated at that time.

The estimate of $77.1 billion in receipts for 1960 is contingent on enactment of the tax recommendations mentioned earlier. Of this estimate, approximtely $76.5 billion reflects the increases in receipts under present tax rates and present tax sources while $0.6 billion is from new taxes and increased nontax sources.

The anticipated rate of recovery of revenues in fiscal 1960 may be compared with the experience of the fiscal years 1955 and 1956, which reflect the recovery from the recession of the calendar year 1954. After adjusting for comparability in corporate tax payment dates, the increase in revenues from 1955 to 1956 was more than the increase estimated in this budget. With similar forces of economic recovery at work today, I have confidence that our revenue estimate is sound and will be attained.

>━•━0━•━0━•━0━•━0━•━0━•━0━•━0━•━0━•━0━•━0━•━0━•━0━•<

A specific example of the Administration's apprehension over excessive spending involved the Federal-aid Highway Act of 1956, in which the Federal Government had financed 90 per cent of the cost for an interstate system. An indication of the growing uneasiness about spending appeared in a draft memorandum of General John Bragdon, Special Assistant for Public Works Planning. Although he ignored the 1958 recession, it was, nevertheless, a major reason for the growing federal deficit.

Memorandum of Special Assistant John Bragdon to Economic Advisor Raymond Saulnier November 20, 1958
[Bragdon Papers.]

Attached is a memorandum dealing with *"immediate* user" charges on the Interstate Highway System. I would like to submit this to the President. The "brief study" indicated therein should require only a few weeks so that any legislation which might be considered advisable could be submitted at the opening of Congress.

May I discuss this with you at an early date in order to give any further explanation needed and receive your comments?

*   *   *

Memorandum

The President has on numerous occasions expressed his liking for self-liquidating programs.

In the public works fields there is lack of balance and equity of treatment in the different fields of transportation with respect to Federal subsidies and direct user charges. Tabulation A attached illustrates this. I believe it would be feasible to institute these charges in two fields, namely, navigation and interstate highways. In the case of navigation, a study is under way by the

Department of Commerce on the feasibility of imposing direct user charges. No comment is therefore made at this time except to note that the traffic on our inland waterways was 232 billion ton-miles in 1957 and in our ports 1,132 million tons. Even a small charge would bring appreciable revenue and would help to balance present inequities.

With respect to highways, the Highway Act of 1956, Public Law 627 made a declaration of policy that if the total receipts of the trust funds are less than the total expenditures from such funds or if the distribution of the tax burden among classes using Federal highways is not equitable, Congress could enact legislation to correct these.

I believe the tax burden to build up the highway fund is inequitable in that the users of our 3½ million miles of streets and highways are *all* called upon to pay for 41,000 miles of super highways, which is only 1.2% of all roads, and which many never use. An *"immediate* user" charge would correct this.

It is a fact that receipts are less than expenditures. It is also a fact that the terrific cost of $35 billion in ten years creates a present imbalance in the public works field. For every 14¢ of Federal aid to all other public works programs, 100¢ is being spent on Federal aid highways. This great inroad into the total tax potential can be totally or largely eliminated if *immediate* user charges are substituted for the present gasoline excise tax.

There are attached three tables made up of figures furnished by the Bureau of Public Roads in May of 1955, in connection with the study then being made of the feasibility of toll roads in accordance with Section 13 of the Highway Act of 1954. These figures were based on a traffic count survey by the Bureau of Public Roads and were never published. They indicate that under the then existing conditions 30,800 miles of the Interstate System could have been feasibly financed by tolls. This was the total mileage then estimated as requiring construction to meet Bureau of Public Roads' standards. While these tabulations are three years old, it is believed that they are fundamentally still valid, if adjusted to present costs and under analogous assumptions.

I recommend that a brief study be initiated at once by the Department of Commerce in the pattern of that suggested by the attached tables, but adjusted to present costs and estimated increments of traffic density *without* new field traffic counts, and with revised assumptions as to toll charges. It is suggested that the study be completed by December 30, 1958.

I recommend that an ad hoc committee be formed to consist of the Secretary of Commerce, Secretary of Treasury, Director of the Budget, Chairman of the Council of Economic Advisers, and Coordinator of Public Works Planning to advise with respect to the study and consider its results.

The President's actions during his last two years in office reflected his deep concern over increased federal spending. In a November, 1958, press conference, he chided those who he felt wanted to solve every problem by federal spending. The next year his fears of financial irresponsibility increased, and he vetoed a housing bill (July 7) purely on cost considerations. On July 2, 1959, he spelled out clearly his apprehensions about the controversial highway program.

President Eisenhower to Special Assistant John Bragdon
July 2, 1959
[Bragdon Papers.]

Dear General Bragdon:

The Federal-aid Highway Act of 1956 provided for a sharply accelerated roads program, established a time limit for completing the National System of Interstate and Defense Highways, committed the Federal Government to the completion of a 40,000-mile system irrespective of cost, increased the Federal share for Interstate projects to 90% and established a "pay-as-you-go" system for funding Federal-aid payments. Questions have arisen as to (1) whether present policies of routing will achieve most economically the purposes sought; (2) whether design standards are greater than needed; and (3) whether needs justify a system of the magnitude currently planned. The cost of the system has increased from the $25 billion anticipated when the legislation was under consideration to a 1958 estimate of $36 billion, and is almost certain to increase substantially above this under present highway policies.

A broad review of the Federal highway program should be initiated to:

1. Reexamine policies, methods, and standards now in effect in order to ascertain their effectiveness in achieving basic national objectives. This reexamination should cover, but not be limited to, intra-metropolitan area routing including ingress and egress, interchanges, grade separations, frontage roads, traffic lanes, utility relocations, and engineering design.

2. Delineate Federal responsibility as distinguished from State and local responsibility in financing, planning, and supervising the highway program.

3. Determine the means for improving coordination between planning for Federal-aid highways and State-local planning, especially urban planning.

4. Develop recommendations covering the legislative and administrative action required to redirect the program as indicated in 1, 2, and

3, in a manner that will (a) minimize the Federal cost of the highway program, and (b) assure financing these costs from the Trust Fund on a self-sustaining basis.

In this study priority should be given to those aspects of the problem where maximum savings can be effected. As specific conclusions and recommendations are developed, I expect them to be implemented, after appropriate clearances, without waiting for the final report to be completed.

The scope and method for carrying on this study should be developed jointly by you, the Director of the Bureau of the Budget and the Department of Commerce. However, in view of your assigned duties in the area of public works planning, I want you to assume responsibility for carrying out this broad study of the highway program. It will, of course, be necessary to consult on a continuing basis with the Bureau of the Budget in order that the study and the final recommendation are consistent with overall budgetary, legislative, and management policies of the Federal Government.

In view of the importance of this study it is my wish that you give this project highest priority in your work program.

You should also coordinate this work with the Secretary of Commerce who will furnish you such assistance and data as may be necessary.

I am addressing letters to the Secretary of Commerce and the Director of the Bureau of the Budget regarding this study as well as a separate study to be undertaken under the direction of the Budget Bureau on the immediate problem of avoiding appropriations from the general fund to meet impending deficits in 1960 and 1961 in the Highway Trust Fund.

The interstate highway system became the focal point of the budget discussions. Since the program had become the greatest public works project in United States history, budget cutters naturally focused on it as a prime target for reduced spending. The possibility of road building financed by tolls, although rejected earlier, received continued analysis. The Bureau of Public Roads carried out a study of this sort for General Bragdon in December of 1959.

E. L. Armstrong to John Allen, Jr.
December 23, 1959
[Bragdon Papers.]

The attached report has been prepared in response to Mr. B. H. Lindman's November 6, 1959 memorandum to Mr. Normann on the basis of an understanding that this memorandum constitutes an official directive from General Bragdon for whom Mr. Lindman serves as a consultant.

Because the time that would have been required to make the complete toll-road feasibility study necessary to meet the requirements of the memorandum was not available to General Bragdon's group, it was necessary to "streamline" it to a considerable extent. This was handled through negotiation with Mr. Lindman, and we believe he understands that the information given in the attached report is all that can be developed meaningfully from the data at hand.

Mr. Lindman's memorandum suggests that legislation which would permit the States to incorporate portions of the Interstate System as State toll roads would afford a new source of revenue to the Government. Certain inducements to encourage the States to elect this plan are offered.

Legislation already in effect permits the incorporation of existing toll roads into the Interstate System under certain terms and conditions which do accomplish a reduction in the overall financial burden of the Federal Government, and virtually all of the toll roads now in existence which meet the terms of the legislation have already been so incorporated. Tolls continue to be collected on these projects for their maintenance and amortization. Had these toll roads not been incorporated into the system it would have been necessary to increase the estimated costs of the Interstate System to the Federal Government and the States by an estimated $2.5 billion.

It is possible under the legislation for a State desiring to do so to construct additional sections of the Interstate System as toll facilities, and in so doing the present estimated cost of completing the system to be financed by the Highway Trust Fund would be correspondingly reduced. There are some sections of the Interstate System now being planned and constructed with funds other than those provided by the Highway Trust Fund, and these are shown in the estimate of cost included in the report submitted by the Secretary of Commerce to the 85th Congress and printed as House Document No. 300. On page 5 of that report in Table B it is indicated that $1,940,474,000 of constructional work will be provided with financing other than from the Highway Trust Fund. Any State which so desires can, in addition, construct bridges on its portion of the Interstate System without availing itself of the funds provided from the Highway Trust Fund. I do not know of any State, however, which is now proposing to do this except in the instances referred to in the report mentioned above.

The entire matter of feasibility of toll road financing was carefully investigated pursuant to Congressional directive and reported by the Secretary of Commerce to the 84th Congress as House Document 139 of the 84th Congress.

Because of the type of traffic service required to be rendered by the Interstate System and the necessity to integrate it completely with all highway needs which are being supplied by other highway systems, there is serious question as to the practicability of the toll method on a majority of the mileage of the Interstate System. I believe that the preferred method of financing is along the lines now in effect, supplemented by tolls, wherever feasible as was suggested by the President in his transmittal of the Clay Committee Report to the Congress in 1955.

It is difficult to see how the States could be induced to adopt a toll financing plan which would relieve the Trust Fund of the Federal Government's share of the construction cost while other States retained the present 30 percent participation. Data submitted by the States in connection with the Section 210 study show that 80 percent of the passenger car travel on the Interstate System, exclusive of the portions on which tolls are now being collected, is by vehicles registered within the State in which the travel occurs. If a State adopted the plan, the cost of amortizing the bonds would be largely met by tolls collected from the residents of that State. At the same time those residents would be contributing, through the gas tax, to the Federal share of the cost of free Interstate System roads in other States.

There may be special situations where the proposal for toll financing would have merit. It is difficult to see, however, how the proposal would have sufficient appeal to contribute, in any important degree, to the solution of the Interstate System financing problem.

Eisenhower's fiscal philosophy did not change during his last year in office. His veto of the Area Redevelopment Bill on May 13, 1960, reflected his belief that the legislation "would squander the federal taxpayers' money."

Statement by President Eisenhower Explaining his Veto of the Area Redevelopment Bill
May 13, 1960

[*Public Papers of the Presidents: 1960* (Washington, 1961), 417-20.]

To the Senate of the United States:

I return herewith, without my approval, S. 722, the Area Redevelopment Bill.

For five consecutive years I have urged the Congress to enact sound area assistance legislation. On repeated occasions I have clearly outlined standards for the kind of program that is needed and that I would gladly approve.

In 1958 I vetoed a bill because it departed greatly from those standards. In 1959, despite my renewed urging, no area assistance bill was passed by the Congress.

Now in 1960, another election year, a new bill is before me that contains certain features which I find even more objectionable than those I found unacceptable in the 1958 bill.

The people of the relatively few communities of chronic unemployment— who want to share in the general prosperity—are, after five years, properly becoming increasingly impatient and are rightfully desirous of constructive action. The need is for truly sound and helpful legislation on which the Congress and the Executive can agree. There is still time and I willingly pledge once again my wholehearted cooperation in obtaining such a law.

S. 722 is seriously defective in six major respects which are summarized immediately below and discussed in detail thereafter.

1. S. 722 would squander the federal taxpayers' money where there is only temporary economic difficulty, curable without the special federal assistance provided in the bill. In consequence, communities in genuine need would receive less federal help for industrial development projects than under the Administration's proposal.

2. Essential local, State and private initiative would be materially inhibited by the excessive federal participation that S. 722 would authorize.

3. Federal financing of plant machinery and equipment is unwise and unnecessary and therefore wasteful of money that otherwise could be of real help.

4. The federal loan assistance which S. 722 would provide for the construction of sewers, water mains, access roads and other public facilities is

unnecessary because such assistance is already available under an existing Government program. Outright grants for such a purpose, a provision of S. 722, are wholly inappropriate.

5. The provisions for federal loans for the construction of industrial buildings in rural areas are incongruous and unnecessary.

6. The creation of a new federal agency is not needed and would actually delay initiation of the new program for many months.

I

The most striking defect of S. 722 is that it would make eligible for federal assistance areas that don't need it—thus providing less help for communities in genuine need than would the Administration's proposal. S. 722, as opposed to the Administration bill, would more than double the number of eligible communities competing for federal participation in loans for the construction or refurbishing of plants for industrial use—the main objective of both bills. Communities experiencing only temporary economic difficulty would accordingly be made eligible under S. 722 and the dissipation of federal help among them would deprive communities afflicted with truly chronic unemployment of the full measure of assistance they so desperately desire and which the Administration bill would give them.

II

Lasting solutions to the problems of chronic unemployment can only be forthcoming if local citizens—the people most immediately concerned—take the lead in planning and financing them. The principal objective is to develop new industry. The Federal Government can and should help, but the major role in the undertaking must be the local community's. Neither money alone, nor the Federal Government alone, can do the job. The States also must help, and many are, but in many instances and in many ways they could do much more.

Under S. 722, however, financing of industrial development projects by the Federal Government—limited to 35% under the Administration's proposal—could go as high as 65%, local community participation could be as low as 10% and private financing as little as 5%. Furthermore, although S. 722 conditions this assistance on approval by a local economic development organization, if no such organization exists one can be appointed from Washington.

III

S. 722 would authorize federal loans for the acquisition of machinery and equipment to manufacturers locating in eligible areas. Loans for machinery and equipment are unnecessary, unwise and costly. Much more money would be required and unnecessarily spent, much less money would find its way into truly helpful projects, and manufacturers would be subsidized unnecessarily vis-a-vis their competitors.

IV

S. 722 would authorize further unnecessary spending by providing both loans and grants—up to 100% of the cost—for the construction of access roads, sewers, water mains and other local public facilities.

Grants for local public facilities far exceed any appropriate federal responsibility. Even though relatively modest at the start, they would set predictably expensive and discriminatory precedents.

With regard to loans for such purposes, exemption from federal income taxes makes it possible today for local communities in almost every case to borrow on reasonable terms from private sources. Whenever such financing is difficult to obtain, the need can be filled by the existing Public Facility Loan Program of the Housing and Home Finance Agency—a program which S. 722 would needlessly duplicate and for which an additional $100 million authorization has already been requested.

V

S. 722 would make a minimum of 600 rural counties eligible for federal loans for the construction of industrial buildings in such areas. The Rural Development Program and the Small Business Administration are already contributing greatly to the economic improvement of low income rural areas. Increasing the impact of these two activities, particularly the Rural Development Program, is a preferable course.

VI

Finally, S. 722 would also create a new federal agency and would, in consequence, mean many unnecessary additions to the federal payroll and a considerable delay in the program before the new agency could be staffed and functioning effectively. None of this is necessary, for all that needs to be done can be done—much better and immediately—by the existing Department of Commerce.

Again, I strongly urge the Congress to enact new legislation at this session—but without those features of S. 722 that I find objectionable. I would, however, accept the eligibility criteria set forth in the bill that first passed the Senate even though these criteria are broader than those contained in the Administration bill.

Moreover, during the process of developing a new bill, I would hope that in other areas of past differences solutions could be found satisfactory to both the Congress and the Executive.

My profound hope is that sound, new legislation will be promptly enacted. If it is, our communities of chronic unemployment will be only the immediate beneficiaries. A tone will have been set that would hold forth, for the remainder of the session, the hope of sound and rewarding legislation in other vital areas—mutual security, wheat, sugar, minimum wage, interest rates, revenue measures, medical care for the aged and aid to education to mention but a few.

Only this result can truly serve the finest and best interests of all our people.

VII

THE CRISIS OVER CIVIL RIGHTS

THE CRISIS OVER CIVIL RIGHTS

Introduction

During the immediate postwar years, President Truman desegregated the armed forces, appointed a committee to study racial problems, proposed a fair employment practices commission, and supported anti-lynching legislation. In 1948 he ran on the strongest civil rights plank in recent history. Yet, during the ensuing four years Congress failed to implement Truman's civil rights goals. By 1952 civil rights pressure groups forced both parties to draft platforms supporting racial equality. During the course of the campaign, both Stevenson and Eisenhower spoke about the need for legal equality—but in general terms. Neither party considered the "black vote" crucial to victory.

Although the President's personal views on civil rights prior to 1952 were generally unknown beyond the fact that he had integrated several combat units during World War II, his Administration saw important advances in the movement for equality for all under law. While his bid for the Presidency received support from numerous Southern advocates of segregation, Eisenhower's position remained throughout the campaign consistent with his party's platform. The Great Crusade did not emphasize civil rights, though people generally believed that Eisenhower was in favor of racial equality. Ironically, it was Eisenhower, certainly no civil rights activist, who was in the White House when the "black revolution" began. The President's 1953 Inaugural Address stressed foreign affairs as the most important issue before the nation, but before his first Administration had ended, the civil rights struggle overshadowed all other issues.

On February 2, 1953, in his first State of the Union Message Eisenhower stated that he considered a primary goal of his Administration "the attainment of equal opportunity for all." In concrete terms he proposed "to use whatever authority exists in the office of the President to end segregation in the District of Columbia, including the Federal Government, and any

1049

segregation of the armed forces." Newspaper headlines tended to stress that part of his Message regarding the "unleashing" of Chiang Kai-shek, while ignoring the civil rights pronouncements. Over the next several months the White House moved quietly and effectively to end segregation in the nation's capital. On October 26, 1953, for example, the Secretary of Labor announced that contracts made by the District of Columbia would contain clauses barring racial discrimination in employment. Eisenhower thought that his goals for the District could best be accomplished without undue fanfare. Republican efforts to revive the party in the South may also have been a factor in the decision to avoid maximum civil rights publicity. Indeed, desegregation of veterans hospitals, Southern naval yards, and other scattered federal installations proceeded very quietly. Nonetheless, they did proceed, and by the time of the 1956 campaign the Republicans could boast of impressive civil rights achievements. Few, however, paid much attention to these claims, which were credited to election year politics.

The Administration also tried to make political capital out of the 1953 appointment of Earl Warren to the Supreme Court by declaring, as Eisenhower said in a letter to industrialist H. L. Hunt, its intentions "to restore the Court to the position of prestige it formerly held." Warren, governor of California at the time of his selection, had been a major force in the GOP for many years. Twice he had won both the Democratic and Republican nominations for the highest office in his native state. He served as governor from 1943 to 1953. In 1948 he had run as the Republican vice presidential nominee, and in 1952 he had been an "alternate" possibility for his party's presidential nomination in the event that Eisenhower and Robert Taft deadlocked. Warren's stature made him a serious contender for a high position under a Republican Administration, and when Chief Justice Fred Vinson died unexpectedly on September 8, 1953, Warren immediately became a potential replacement. Moreover, Eisenhower wanted a man of national reputation for the Court. Although Warren fulfilled that requirement, his judicial experience was limited to having been Attorney General of California (1939-43). Despite this drawback, his nomination met with negligible opposition, despite a petty fight in the Senate Judiciary Committee which had nothing to do with Warren's qualifications. Once cleared, he quickly received Senate confirmation. Warren's views on civil rights—a hallmark of his Court tenure—elicited little comment.

Even before Warren took his oath of office on October 5, 1953, the Supreme Court had under consideration a series of cases dealing with segregation in public schools. In November, Attorney General Herbert Brownell advised the Court that he believed that school segregation violated the 14th Amendment. Eisenhower was fully aware of Brownell's position and made no objection. For several months, with a minimum of publicity, the Court considered the legal aspects of school integration. Then, on May 17, 1954, the Court voted unanimously in the case of *Brown* v. *Board of*

Education of Topeka that segregation on the basis of race violated the Constitution. Over the next year the Court elaborated on the ruling, tried to establish the principle of a "prompt and reasonable start" on integration, and required acceptance "with all deliberate speed." The action overturned the "separate but equal" concept established in *Plessy* v. *Ferguson* (1896) which had long been applied to public education. Eisenhower consistently refused to express his approval of the Supreme Court's rejection of segregated schooling, but he moved quickly to implement the decision in the District of Columbia. Although he declined to make a public endorsement, basing his refusal on the separation of powers doctrine, the President recorded in his memoirs: "I definitely agreed with the unanimous decision."

With the Brown decision, the Supreme Court suddenly became a major instrument in effecting social change. At the time of the decision, however, most Americans, including Eisenhower, failed to recognize that a civil rights revolution had begun. Many white Southerners, however, saw the new trend as a threat to the "Southern way of life" and organized citizens' councils to resist further desegregation. The Court ruling, even though it involved only public schools, created a rallying point for segregationists, who feared an extension of integration to other activities. To maintain white supremacy, extremists often resorted to economic harassment, disfranchisement, and occasional violence. These obstructionist tactics deeply concerned the President. His response was federal action.

Eisenhower viewed the problem of southern blacks on two levels: public segregation and the right to vote. In 1956 he concluded that, as a first step, the Federal Government should act promptly to protect black voting rights. His legislative proposal passed the House (July 23) but failed to overcome a Southern filibuster in the Senate. The next year, following his reelection, an even more intensified effort by the President finally bore results. In August, 1957, Congress passed the first major voting rights legislation since Reconstruction. Although compromises seriously marred the enforcement of this 1957 act, its passage nevertheless was a milestone in the struggle for racial equality. Moreover, Eisenhower's ability to dramatize publicly the issue for several months increased pressure on Congress for enactment. The law required strengthening in 1960 because officials in several southern states had found ways to skirt congressional intent. In the final analysis, while the aims remained small, the portent for future federal involvement was large.

It was one thing to outlaw racial voting restrictions and another to integrate schools. *Brown* v. *Board of Education* initially involved only a small number of students but, sooner or later, a serious confrontation seemed inevitable. It occurred in September, 1957, when Arkansas Governor Orval Faubus used the National Guard to defy federal court instructions to admit black students to Central High School in Little Rock. The governor's stand precipitated a major constitutional crisis, which caused Eisenhower to send federal troops to Little Rock to enforce the integration order (September 24). Federal power triumphed in spite of Faubus' opposition, and the Federal Government's interpretation of the Constitution remained supreme.

The Eisenhower Administration, building on foundations laid by Franklin Roosevelt and Harry Truman, continued the progress towards the goal of equality for all. The 1950's saw considerable achievements in the legal aspects of integration, but despite the gains, black voters continued to identify with the Democratic party. In 1960, John Kennedy easily swept the black vote.

1. MINORITY GROUP POLITICS

For all practical purposes minority group politics in 1952 meant an attempt to win as much as possible of the Jewish vote. Traditionally, a sizable majority of American Jews voted Democratic. Although President Harry Truman's recognition of Israel in 1948 had bolstered this allegiance, Republican strategists believed that Eisenhower could make inroads into the Jewish vote. During the campaign, the Eisenhower staff showed concern about matters of interest to the Jewish Community, wrote friendly letters to Jewish supporters and contributors, and sought support by establishing a "Jewish Division." Despite Eisenhower's sweeping victory, there was no indication of any significant change from the way a vast majority of American Jews had voted in the past.

Governor Sherman Adams to Maxwell Abbell
September 28, 1952
[Official File 144-B-3, Eisenhower Papers.]

Dear Mr. Abbell:

I am very glad you wrote me in some detail concerning the attitude of Jewish voters generally and particularly with reference to the McCarran Act and continuance of aid to Israel. I have turned this letter over where it will do the most good with a recommendation that your suggestions should be followed up much along the lines you mention and in the very near future.

Your continued interest is very greatly appreciated and your expression of good wishes has been passed along to General Eisenhower. He sends his best regards to you and Mrs. Abbell.

I also wish to thank you for your further contribution from you and Mrs. Abbell. You may be sure it is deeply appreciated.

Bernard Katzen to Governor Sherman Adams
October 28, 1952
[Official File 144-B-3, Eisenhower Papers.]

As far as publicity is concerned about the meeting of Zionist Leaders and Stevenson, I feel that it is important that the General make every effort to meet up with the Jewish leaders that we are having luncheon with tomorrow at the Roosevelt. Although it didn't get too much publicity—publicity being confined to page 16 of the Tribune and a small item in the Times, page 25—yet the Yiddish paper had a front page picture and four column spread and other publicity in Yiddish papers.

The meeting tomorrow is for leaders of Jewish Division of the National campaign. If the General can't make it, he certainly ought to send a telegram, stating whether or not it can be released to the press. If he can't come, perhaps you could. Of course, it's up to you but even two minutes would have a good counteracting effect.

Soon after taking office, Eisenhower faced the problem of how to answer Americans who questioned the Government's position, or lack of position, on anti-Semitism in communist nations. The following correspondence indicated how the President's staff handled the situation. Rather than dwell on the alienation of the Arab world, the reply emphasized America's concern for minorities everywhere.

Presidential Advisor Bernard Shanley to
Reverend Harry Emerson Fosdick
March 11, 1953
[Official File 144-B-3, Eisenhower Papers.]

Dear Dr. Fosdick:

The telegram which Mr. William A. Aiken and fifty other American citizens, including yourself, addressed to the President on February 19, 1953, has been referred to me for reply. In the absence of an identifying address for Mr. William A. Aiken, I am writing to you with reference to the protest made against the anti-Jewish activities now being carried on by the Soviet

Union and other Eastern European Governments and expressing concern that the United States in taking action to combat these persecutions will not act in such a manner as to alienate the Arab States adjacent to Israel and the entire Moslem world.

The views and proposals of your group relate to problems which are now of deep concern to the United States Government. I assure you they will receive consideration along with studies which have been prepared on this subject to assist the officials of our Government in this matter.

The United States Government regards the recent acts of the Soviet Union and its satellite states against those of the Jewish faith as additional manifestations of the inhuman policy which has been pursued toward most minority groups living within the confines of these totalitarian regimes. During the past years the Free World has witnessed the actions of the Soviet dominated states directed at different times to the persecution of the Greek Orthodox congregations, the imprisonment of Roman Catholic prelates, the oppression of Moslem communities, and the harassing of Protestant leaders and churches. The present wave of persecutions is the most recent of a long series.

In a recent letter congratulating the American Jewish Committee upon the celebration of its forty-sixth anniversary, the President expressed the deep concern with which the United States Government views the recent attacks on civil and religious liberty in Eastern Europe.

You are doubtless aware of the passage by the Senate on February 27 of Senate Resolution 84 which condemns not only the recent violations against those of the Jewish faith, but also the vicious and inhuman campaigns conducted against the other minority groups referred to above. The United States Government will give the fullest publicity to this resolution in the Free World and to the peoples behind the Iron Curtain.

In accordance with this resolution, the United States Government intends to take measures to insure that these persecutions of minority groups by the Soviet Union and its satellite states will be fully discussed in the present General Assembly of the United Nations.

During Eisenhower's first four years in office, domestic Jewish issues were, at least from the Republican political point of view, closely tied to consider-ations about Israel. The Administration received numerous communica-tions from anti-Zionists, but it viewed the Zionist position as representative of American Jewish thought. When Soviet influence increased in the Middle East, and Arab countries became more hostile toward the West, the United States almost automatically viewed Israel as a bulwark against the spread of communism. Thus, American support for Israel served a foreign policy objective and at the same time aided the Republican party. The 1956 Republican platform was very clear on this issue. The election, which took place in the midst of the Suez conflict, showed a marked in-crease in Jewish support for Eisenhower. This may have reflected his policies toward Israel, but it may also have indicated his general popularity with all Americans.

Republican Platform Statement on Israel
1956

We recognize the existence of a major threat to international peace in the Near East. We support a policy of impartial friendship for the peoples of the Arab states and Israel to promote a peaceful settlement of the causes of tension in that area, including the human problem of the Palestine-Arab refugees.

Progress toward a just settlement of the tragic conflict between the Jewish State and the Arab nations in Palestine was upset by the Soviet Bloc sales of arms to Arab countries. But prospects of peace have now been reinforced by the mission to Palestine of the United Nations Secretary General upon the initiative of the United States.

We regard the preservation of Israel as an important tenet of American foreign policy. We are determined that the integrity of an independent Jewish State shall be maintained. We shall support the independence of Israel against armed aggression. The best hope for peace in the Middle East lies in the United Nations. We pledge our continued efforts to eliminate the obstacles to a lasting peace in this area.

2. DESEGREGATION OF WASHINGTON, D.C.

During the 1952 campaign, Eisenhower did not emphasize the Republican platform's civil rights planks. Immediately upon taking office, however, he set in motion plans to desegregate the District of Columbia. The following correspondence demonstrates the high priority given this effort. Merlyn Pitzele was Chairman of the New York State Board of Mediation.

Merlyn Pitzele to President Eisenhower
January 27, 1953
[Official File 71-V, Eisenhower Papers.]

Dear Mr. President:

You told me, when we discussed the matter in the Commodore Hotel before your Inauguration, that you wanted me to think out for you what you might do as President—without legislation or Executive Order—to abate racial discrimination in the District of Columbia.

I am now ready to bring to you a set of simple proposals which have been arrived at as the result of study, discussion, and considerable thought.

I would like to bring them in, set them before you on paper, and brief you on the subject in what need not be at all a lengthy session.

Appointment Secretary Thomas Stephens
to Merlyn Pitzele
January 28, 1953
[Official File 71-V, Eisenhower Papers.]

Dear Mel:

With reference to your letter to the President and regarding which we spoke yesterday, when do you think you will be back in Washington again—or when would it be convenient for you to come and visit with the President regarding the matter of racial segregation in the District of Columbia? As far as our calendar is concerned, the President could see you at 2:30 P.M. next Thursday, February 5th, and I will keep this time for you awaiting your confirmation or refusal.

A major stumbling block to the desegregation of the District involved the refusal of many restaurants to serve blacks. Prior to the Eisenhower Administration, a case had been brought against the Thompson restaurant chain. The action, based on Reconstruction legislation, was quashed by both municipal and appellate courts. However, the Supreme Court reversed the decision on June 8, 1953, after Attorney General Herbert Brownell had argued for the Federal Government in favor of the case. Brownell's appearance, which may or may not have influenced the Court, reaffirmed the Administration's position on civil rights.

District of Columbia v. John R. Thompson Co.
June 8, 1953
[344 U. S. 102]

MR. JUSTICE DOUGLAS delivered the opinion of the Court.

This is a criminal proceeding prosecuted by information against respondent for refusal to serve certain members of the Negro race at one of its restaurants in the District of Columbia solely on account of the race and color of those persons. The information is in four counts, the first charging a violation of the Act of the Legislative Assembly of the District of Columbia, June 20, 1872, and the others charging violations of the Act of the Legislative Assembly of the District of Columbia, June 26, 1873, L.Dist.-Col.1871–1873, pp. 65, 116. Each Act makes it a crime to discriminate against a person on account of race or color or to refuse service to him on that ground.

The Municipal Court quashed the information on the ground that the 1872 and 1873 Acts had been repealed by implication on the enactment by Congress of the Organic Act of June 11, 1878, 20 Stat. 102. On appeal the Municipal Court of Appeals held that the 1872 and 1873 Acts were valid when enacted, that the former Act insofar as it applies to restaurants, had been repealed, but that the latter Act was still in effect. It therefore affirmed the Municipal Court insofar as it dismissed the count based on the 1872 Act and reversed the Municipal Court on the other counts. 81 A.2d 249. On cross-appeal, the Court of Appeals held that the 1872 and 1873 Acts were unenforceable and that the entire information should be dismissed. 92 U. S. App. D.C.—, 203 F.2d 579. The case is here on certiorari.

I

The history of congressional legislation dealing with the District of Columbia begins with the Act of July 16, 1790, 1 Stat. 130, by which the District was established as the permanent seat of the Government of the United States. We need not review for the purposes of this case the variety of congressional enactments pertaining to the management of the affairs of the District between that date and 1871. It is with the Organic Act of February 21, 1871, 16 Stat. 419, that we are particularly concerned.

That Act created a government by the name of the District of Columbia, constituted it "a body corporate for municipal purposes" with all of the powers of a municipal corporation "not inconsistent with the Constitution and laws of the United States and the provisions of this act", and gave it jurisdiction over all the territory within the limits of the District. § 1. The Act vested "legislative power and authority" in a Legislative Assembly consisting of a Council and a House of Delegates, members of the Council to be appointed by the President with the advice and consent of the Senate and members of the House of Delegates to be elected by male citizens residing in the District §§ 5, 7. The act provided, with exceptions not material here, that "the legislative power of the District shall extend to all rightful subjects of legislation within said District, consistent with the Constitution of the United States and the provisions of this act". § 18. All acts of the Legislative Assembly were made subject at all times "to repeal or modification" by Congress. § 18. And it was provided that nothing in the Act should be construed to deprive Congress of "the power of legislation" over the District "in as ample manner as if this law had not been enacted." § 18. Executive power was vested in a governor appointed by the President by and with the advice of the Senate. § 2. And it was provided that the District should have in the House of Representatives an elected delegate having the same rights and privileges as those of delegates from federal territories. § 34.

This government (which was short-lived) was characterized by the Court as a "territorial government." Eckloff v. District of Columbia, 135 U. S. 240, 241, 10 S.Ct. 752, 34 L.Ed. 120. The analogy is an apt one. The grant to the Legislative Assembly by § 18 of legislative power which extends "to all rightful subjects of legislation" is substantially identical with the grant of legislative power to territorial governments which reads: "The legislative power of every Territory shall extend to all rightful subjects of legislation not inconsistent with the Constitution and laws of the United States." R.S. § 1851.

The power of Congress over the District and its power over the Territories are phrased in very similar language in the Constitution. Article I, § 8, cl. 17 of the Constitution provides that "The Congress shall have Power . . . To exercise exclusive Legislation in all Cases whatsoever, over such District (not exceeding ten Miles square) as may, by Cession of particular States, and the Acceptance of Congress, become the Seat of the Government of the United States". Article IV, § 3, cl. 2 of the Constitution grants Congress authority over territories in the following words:

> The Congress shall have Power to dispose of and make all needful Rules and Regulations respecting the Territory or other Property belonging to the United States . . .

[1] The power of Congress to delegate legislative power to a territory is well settled. Simms v. Simms, 175 U. S. 162, 168, 20 S.Ct. 58, 60, 44 L.Ed. 115; Binns v. United States, 194 U. S. 486, 491, 24 S.Ct. 816, 817, 48 L.Ed. 1087; Christianson v. King County, 239 U. S. 356, 365, 36 S.Ct. 114, 118, 60 L.Ed. 327. The power which Congress constitutionally may delegate to a territory (subject of course to "the right of Congress to revise, alter, and revoke," Hornbuckle v. Toombs, 18 Wall. 648, 655, 21 L.Ed. 966, covers all matters "which, within the limits of a state, are regulated by the laws of the state only." Simms v. Simms, supra, 175 U. S. at page 168, 20 S.Ct. at page 60.

The power of Congress to grant self-government to the District of Columbia under Art. I, § 8, cl. 17 of the Constitution would seem to be as great as its authority to do so in the case of territories. But a majority of the judges of the Court of Appeals held that Congress had the constitutional authority to delegate "municipal" but not "general" legislative powers and that the Acts of 1872 and 1873, being in the nature of civil rights legislation, fell in the latter group and were for Congress alone to enact. In reaching that conclusion the Court of Appeals relied upon two decisions of the Court, Stoutenburgh v. Hennick, 129 U. S. 141, 9 S.Ct. 256, 32 L.Ed. 637, and Metropolitan R. Co. v. District of Columbia, 132 U. S. 1, 10 S.Ct. 19, 33 L.Ed. 231. The first of these cases involved an act of the Legislative Assembly of the District imposing a license tax on businesses within the District. The Court held, following Robbins v. Taxing District of Shelby County, 120 U. S. 489, 7 S.Ct. 592, 30 L.Ed. 694, that it could not be constitutionally applied to a representative of a Maryland company soliciting orders in the District of Columbia. The result would have been the same, as the Robbins case indicates, had a state rather than the District enacted such a law. So, while it is true that the Court spoke of the authority of Congress to delegate to the District the power to prescribe "local regulation" but not "general legislation," those words in the setting of the case suggest no more than the difference between local matters on the one hand and national matters, such as interstate commerce, on the other.

The second of these cases, Metropolitan R. Co. v. District of Columbia, 132 U. S. 1, 10 S.Ct. 19, 33 L.Ed. 231, presented the question of the capacity of the District of Columbia to sue. The Court held that it might do so, noting that while the District was "a separate political community", its sovereign power was lodged in the Congress. "The subordinate legislative powers of a municipal character, which have been or may be lodged in the city corporations, or in the District corporation, do not make those bodies sovereign. Crimes committed in the District are not crimes against the District, but against the United States. Therefore, while the District may, in a sense, be called a state, it is such in a very qualified sense." 132 U. S. at page 9, 10 S.Ct. at page 22. But there is no suggestion in that case that Congress lacks the authority under the Constitution to delegate the powers of home rule to the District.

[2, 3] The power of Congress over the District of Columbia relates not only to "national power" but to "all the powers of legislation which may be exercised by a state in dealing with its affairs". Atlantic Cleaners & Dyers v. United States, 286 U. S. 427, 435, 52 S.Ct. 607, 609, 76 L.Ed. 1204. And see Stoutenburgh v. Hennick, supra, 129 U. S. at page 147, 9 S.Ct. 256. There is no reason why a state, if it so chooses, may not fashion its basic law so as to grant home rule or self-government to its municipal corporations. The Court in Barnes v. District of Columbia, 91 U. S. 540, 544, 23 L.Ed. 440, in construing the Organic Act of February 21, 1871, the one with which we are presently concerned, stated:

> A municipal corporation, in the exercise of all of its duties, including those most strictly local or internal, is but a department of the State. The legislature may give it all the powers such a being is capable of receiving, making it a miniature State within its locality.

[4] This is the theory which underlies the constitutional provisions of some states allowing cities to have home rule. So it is that decision after decision has held that the delegated power of municipalities is as broad as the police power of the state, except as that power may be restricted by terms of the grant or by the state constitution. See McQuillin, The Law of Municipal Corporations (3d ed. 1949), § 16.02 et seq. And certainly so far as the Federal Constitution is concerned there is no doubt that legislation which prohibits discrimination on the basis of race in the use of facilities serving a public function is within the police power of the states. See Railway Mail Ass'n v. Corsi, 326 U. S. 88, 93-94, 65 S.Ct. 1483, 1487, 89 L.Ed. 2072; Bob-Lo Excursion Co. v. People of,State of Michigan, 333 U. S. 28, 34, 68 S.Ct. 358, 361, 92 L.Ed. 455. It would seem then that on the analogy of the delegation of powers of self-government and home rule both to municipalities and to territories there is no constitutional barrier to the delegation by Congress to the District of Columbia of full legislative power, subject of course to constitutional limitations to which all lawmaking is subservient and subject also to the power of Congress at any time to revise, alter, or revoke the authority granted.

[5] There is, however, a suggestion that the power of Congress "To exercise exclusive Legislation" granted by Art. I, § 8, cl. 17 of the Constitution is nondelegable because it is "exclusive." But it is clear from the history of the provision that the word "exclusive" was employed to eliminate any possibility that the legislative power of Congress over the District was to be concurrent with that of the ceding states. See The Federalist, No. 43; Elliott's Debates, pp. 432-433; 2 Story, Commentaries (4th ed. 1873), § 1218. Madison summed up the need for an "exclusive" power in the Congress as follows:

> Let me remark, if not already remarked, that there must be a cession, by particular states, of the district to Congress, and that the states may settle the

terms of the cession. The states may make what stipulation they please in it, and, if they apprehend any danger, they may refuse it altogether. How could the general government be guarded from the undue influence of particular states, or from insults, without such exclusive power?

See Elliott's, op. cit., supra, p. 433.

[6, 7] We conclude that the Congress had the authority under Art. I, § 8, cl. 17 of the Constitution to delegate its lawmaking authority to the Legislative Assembly of the municipal corporation which was created by the Organic Act of 1871 and that the "rightful subjects of legislation" within the meaning of § 18 of that Act was as broad as the police power of a state so as to include a law prohibiting discriminations against Negroes by the owners and managers of restaurants in the District of Columbia.

II

[8–10] The Acts of 1872 and 1873 survived, we think, all subsequent changes in the government of the District of Columbia and remain today a part of the governing body of laws applicable to the District. The Legislative Assembly was abolished by the Act of June 20, 1874, 18 Stat. 116. That Act provided that the District should be governed by a Commission. §2. The Revised Statutes relating to the District of Columbia, approved June 20, 1874, kept in full force the prior laws and ordinances "not inconsistent with this chapter, and except as modified or repealed by Congress or the legislative assembly of the District". § 91. Those Acts were followed by the present Organic Act of the District of Columbia approved June 11, 1878, 20 Stat. 102, which provides that "all laws now in force relating to the District of Columbia not inconsistent with the provisions of this act shall remain in full force and effect." § 1. We find nothing in the 1874 Act nor in the 1878 Act inconsistent with the Acts here in question. And we find no other intervening act which would effect a repeal of them. Nor is there any suggestion in the briefs or oral argument that the acts of 1872 and 1873, presently litigated, did not survive the Acts of 1874 and 1878. It indeed appears the Acts of 1874 and 1878 precluded the repeal of these anti-discrimination laws except by an Act of Congress. As Metropolitan R. Co. v. District of Columbia, supra, 132 U. S. at page 7, 10 S.Ct. at page 22 says the "legislative powers" of the District ceased with the Organic Act and thereafter municipal government was confined "to mere administration."

The Commissioners by the Joint Resolution of February 26, 1892, 27 Stat. 394, were vested with local legislative power as respects "reasonable and usual police regulations". But there is no suggestion that their power to make local ordinances was ever exercised to supplant these anti-discrimination laws of the Legislative Assembly with new and different ordinances. Rather the argument is that the 1872 and 1873 Acts were repealed by the Code of 1901, 31 Stat. 1189. Section 1636 of that Code provides in part:

All acts and parts of acts of the general assembly of the State of Maryland general and permanent in their nature, all like acts and parts of acts of the legislative assembly of the District of Columbia, and all like acts and parts of acts of Congress applying solely to the District of Columbia in force in said District on the day of the passage of this act are hereby repealed, except: ...

Third. Acts and parts of acts relating to the organization of the District government, or to its obligations, or the powers or duties of the Commissioners of the District of Columbia, or their subordinates or employees, or to police regulations, and generally all acts and parts of acts relating to municipal affairs only, including those regulating the charges of public-service corporations. ...

[11, 12] The Court of Appeals held that these anti-discrimination laws were "general and permanent" legislation within the meaning of § 1636 and repealed by it, not being saved by the exceptions. The Department of Justice presents an elaborate argument, based on the legislative history of the 1901 Code, to the effect that the anti-discrimination laws here involved were not "general and permanent" laws within the meaning of § 1636. But the lines of analysis presented are quite shadowy; and we find it difficult not to agree that the 1872 and 1873 Acts were "general and permanent" as contrasted to statutes which are private, special, or temporary. That is the sense in which we believe the words "general and permanent" were used in the Code. We conclude, however, that they were saved from repeal by the *Third* exception clause quoted above.

It is our view that these anti-discrimination laws governing restaurants in the District are "police regulations" and acts "relating to municipal affairs" within the meaning of the *Third* exception in § 1636. The Court of Appeals in United States v. Cella, 37 App.D.C. 433, 435, in construing an Act providing that prosecutions for violations of penal statutes "in the nature of police or municipal regulations" should be in the name of the District, said,

A municipal ordinance or police regulation is peculiarly applicable to the inhabitants of a particular place; in other words, it is local in character.

The laws which require equal service to all who eat in restaurants in the District are as local in character as laws regulating public health, schools, streets, and parks. In Johnson v. District of Columbia, 30 App.D.C. 520, the Court of Appeals held that an Act of the Legislative Assembly prohibiting cruelty to animals was a police regulation saved from repeal by the *Third* exception to § 1636. The court said it was legislation "in the interest of peace and order" and conducive "to the morals and general welfare of the community." 30 App.D.C. at page 522. Regulation of public eating and drinking establishments in the District has been delegated by Congress to the municipal government from the very beginning. In terms of the history of the District of Columbia there is indeed no subject of legislation more firmly identified with local affairs than the regulation of restaurants.

[13–15] There remains for consideration only whether the Acts of 1872 and 1873 were abandoned or repealed as a result of non-use and administrative practice. There was one view in the Court of Appeals that these laws are presently unenforceable for that reason. We do not agree. The failure of the executive branch to enforce a law does not result in its modification or repeal. See Louisville & N. R. Co. v. United States, 282 U. S. 740, 759, 51 S.Ct. 297, 304, 75 L.Ed. 672; United States v. Morton Salt Co., 338 U. S. 632, 647, 648, 70 S.Ct. 357, 366, 94 L.Ed. 401. The repeal of laws is as much a legislative function as their enactment.

Congress has had the power to repeal the 1872 and 1873 Acts from the dates of their passage by the Legislative Assembly. But as we have seen, it has not done so.

Congress also has had the authority to delegate to a municipal government for the District the power to pass laws which would alter or repeal the Acts of the Legislative Assembly. As we have seen, the Organic Act of the District of Columbia approved June 11, 1878, withdrew legislative powers from the municipal government. In 1892 the Commissioners were given legislative power as respects "reasonable and usual police regulations". That legislative authority could have been employed to repeal the Acts of 1872 and 1873. See Stevens v. Stoutenburgh, 8 App.D.C. 513. For as we have noted, regulations of restaurants is a matter plainly within the scope of police regulation. But the Commissioners passed no ordinances dealing with the rights of Negroes in the restaurants of the District. It is argued that their power to do so was withdrawn by Congress in the Code of 1901. It is pointed out that the Code of 1901 kept in force the acts, ordinances, and regulations not repealed; and from that the conclusion is drawn that only Congress could thereafter amend or repeal these enactments of the Legislative Assembly.

We find it unnecessary to resolve that question. For even if we assume that after the Code of 1901 the Commissioners had the authority to replace these anti-discrimination laws with other ones, we find no indication that they ever did so. Certainly no ordinance was enacted which purported to repeal or modify those laws or which, by providing a different measure of a restaurant owner's duty, established a standard in conflict with that provided by the Legislative Assembly.

But it is said that the licensing authority of the Commissioners over restaurants has been employed for 75 years without regard to the equal service requirements of the 1872 and 1873 Acts, that no licenses have been forfeited for violations of those Acts, and that the licensing authority of the Commissioners has been employed in effect to repeal or set aside the provisions of those Acts. But those regulations are health, safety, and sanitary measures. They do not purport to be a complete codification of ordinances regulating restaurants. They contain neither a requirement that Negroes be segregated nor that Negroes be treated without discrimination.

The case therefore appears to us no different than one where the executive department neglects or refuses to enforce a requirement long prescribed by the legislature.

It would be a more troublesome case if the 1872 and 1873 Acts were licensing laws which through the years had been modified and changed under the legislative authority of the Commissioners. But these Acts do not provide any machinery for the granting and revocation of licenses. They are *regulatory* laws prescribing in terms of civil rights the duties of restaurant owners to members of the public. Upon conviction for violating their provisions, penalties are imposed. There is a fine and in addition a forfeiture of license without right of renewal for a year. But these Acts, unlike the sanitary requirements laid upon restaurants, do not prescribe conditions for the issuance of a license. Like the regulation of wages and hours of work, the employment of minors, and the requirement that restaurants have flameproof draperies, these laws merely *regulate* a licensed business. Therefore, the exercise of the *licensing* authority of the Commissioners could not modify, alter, or repeal these laws. Nor can we discover any other legislative force which has removed them from the existing body of law.

[16] Cases of hardship are put where criminal laws so long in disuse as to be no longer known to exist are enforced against innocent parties. But that condition does not bear on the continuing validity of the law; it is only an ameliorating factor in enforcement.

We have said that the Acts of 1872 and 1873 survived the intervening changes in the government of the District of Columbia and are presently enforceable. We would speak more accurately if we said that the 1873 Act survived. For there is a subsidiary question, which we do not reach and which will be open on remand of the case to the Court of Appeals, whether the 1872 Act under which the first count of the information is laid was repealed by the 1873 Act. On that we express no opinion.

Reversed.

MR. JUSTICE JACKSON took no part in the consideration or decision of this case.

On November 25, 1953, Samuel Spencer, President, Board of Commissioners of the District of Columbia, reported to Eisenhower on the progress that had been made in desegregating Washington. The President's response was indicative of his concern in this matter.

District of Columbia Commissioner Samuel Spencer to President Eisenhower
November 25, 1953
[Official File 71-V, Eisenhower Papers.]

My dear Mr. President:

In your State of the Union message delivered on February 2, 1953, you stated that you would "use whatever authority exists in the office of the President to end segregation in the District of Columbia."

Since that time several notable advances have been made toward that objective. Firstly, as a result of the decision of the United States Supreme Court in the Thompson Restaurant case last June, negroes have since that time been free to eat in all restaurants and hotels in the District of Columbia. I am happy to report that this result has been achieved quietly and without incident. Secondly, for several months substantially all the movie theatres in the District of Columbia have freely admitted negroes by voluntary action. Thirdly, the National Capital Housing Authority last June adopted a policy of integration and has been progressively opening its public housing projects until at the present time there are only three which are not integrated or in the process of integration. Fourthly, a few weeks ago the District Government issued an order that its contracts would henceforth contain a clause requiring that contractors should not discriminate in employment practices. This clause is similar to that used in the contracts of the federal government.

Another step forward has now been taken by the Board of Commissioners. An order has been issued today stating that it is the policy of the District Government, throughout all the departments, agencies, and instrumentalities under the administrative supervision of the Commissioners, that all personnel actions shall be based on merit and fitness, and that there shall be no discrimination because of race, creed, or color in such matters. The order further sets forth a policy of non-discrimination and non-segregation with respect to the use of governmental institutions, facilities and services. The order is effective immediately except in a few special situations to which it will be extended as rapidly as conditions permit. The order sets up grievance procedures and provides for reports by department heads.

This order brings the policy of the District Government into accord with that of the federal government. I believe that it constitutes an important milestone in reaching the objective which you stated in your State of the Union message.

President Eisenhower
to District of Columbia Commissioner Samuel Spencer
December 20, 1953
[Official File 71-V, Eisenhower Papers.]

Dear Mr. Spencer:

When I returned to my office this morning, I found your letter of November twenty-fifth. I had, of course, previously seen the newspaper accounts of the progress you have made toward ending racial discrimination in the District of Columbia. Because the District is an area of exclusive Federal jurisdiction, I deem this progress to be of special significance. My congratulations!

On March 10, 1954, at an NAACP conference, Eisenhower reiterated the Administration's position on civil rights, and what had been accomplished in Washington, D.C.

Speech by President Eisenhower on Civil Rights
March 10, 1954
[*Public Papers of the Presidents: 1954* (Washington, 1960), 310–11.]

Ladies and gentlemen:

From time to time the President of the United States has the privilege of appearing before a body of Americans assembled here in Washington to extend to them greetings on behalf of the administration and of the Federal Government here located.

And certainly, more often than not, he also has the privilege of extending felicitations and well wishes in the prosecution of their work.

It is the last part of this statement that I want to refer to for a moment. My welcome to you is warm and sincere, but I should like also to take your time to talk about the good wishes that I extend for the prosecution of your work.

I believe most sincerely in the statement of Lincoln that this nation was dedicated to the proposition that all men are created equal. I believe with the writers of the Declaration of Independence that men are endowed by their Creator with certain rights. And furthermore, I believe that the vast majority, the great mass of Americans want to make those concepts a living reality in their lives.

I was talking only a few minutes ago with some of your leaders in the anteroom just off this hall. I had a chance to express my belief that all of us can take inspiration from this one thought: the great faith of the American people taken in the mass.

There are vociferous minorities. There are people who, for selfish or for fearful reasons, do not fully live up to the concepts held and so eloquently stated by our Founding Fathers—or by Lincoln. But, by and large, the mass of America wants to be decent, and good, and just.

Our people do not want to make differentiations among people based upon inconsequential matters of nature involving color and race.

Admitting quickly—even if sadly—that the ideals of those people have not been reached, let us still remember this: this same thing is true of everything we do in life. Ideals are really never reached by imperfect humans. But the striving for them makes better both the great body we are trying to affect and ourselves.

And so—and I hope, my dear friends, that doesn't sound like a sermon—I am merely trying to state my beliefs as fully and as frankly as I know how to do. But I believe that this struggle, this one that in your case now has gone on for, lo, these many decades, is producing results on the part of the administration.

I stated my own personal views many times before the election. I have tried to state them since. Wherever Federal authority clearly extends, I will do the utmost that lies within my power to bring into living reality this expression of equality among all men.

By no means do I come here to make a political statement or to outline for you what has been done. But I do submit that in the two areas that I spoke about in the campaign, definite progress has been made. It is in the areas of all the armed services and where their territories and functions and activities extend, and right here in the District of Columbia. With respect to these, I expressed certain convictions and determinations. Not in all cases have the full results been achieved. But we are still trying. I know of no other slogan that is so good for all of us as once we have determined upon and visualized a worthy ideal, to keep on trying with all that is in us.

I wish for each of you an enjoyable time in this Capital. I hope that you, aside from the fruitfulness of your work, have the satisfaction of seeing something around this town that you will carry back with really fond memories. I hope that you will find something just outside of the beauty of the buildings and the niceness of nature.

For all of you—good luck and goodbye.

On March 5, 1956, at a civil rights leadership meeting held in Washington, Congressman Hugh Scott of Pennsylvania defended the Administration's civil rights record in a manner that brought praise from a White House staff member.

Cabinet Secretary Maxwell Rabb
to The Assistant to the President Sherman Adams
March 6, 1956
[Official File 102-B-3, Eisenhower Papers.]

Hugh Scott went into a very difficult situation since it is estimated that three-fourths of the people attending the Conference are Democrats. However, from all reports which have reached me, he did an excellent job of presenting the Administration's case and he bested Mr. Butler in the discussion.

Mr. Scott gave his address first and he gave a reasoned statement, stressing the Administration's achievements. He expressed the necessity for bipartisan cooperation and effort on this. Mr. Butler then replied with a demagogic speech, tearing into the Administration as having no record in civil rights. When he finished, Arnold Aronson asked Scott if he wanted to offer a rebuttal and Scott accepted. This infuriated Butler who said that this was "not in the contract" and that he did not want to enter into a debate on this with a proxy.

When Scott spoke, he started out by asking, "Would you people be meeting here in the Willard if this conference had been held before 1953?" and the audience thundered back, "No!." He got the same response when he asked if they would be eating in the Washington restaurants if the meeting had been held four years ago. And then he asked, "What about Senator Eastland, Mr. Butler?" The audience then took up the question and interrupted Butler's remarks with the call several times.

It seems to me that this entire meeting points up one thing which we must not overlook and that is that this is a subject of the most intense interest to the people who were represented there. Civil Rights will have more than academic importance in the next election; it will be a crusading issue for millions of Americans.

During the 1956 campaign the Republicans actively sought black votes. Campaign documents claimed numerous civil rights firsts for the Eisenhower Administration. While exaggerated in places, there was no denying that progress had been made. There was also no denying that the desegregation of Washington helped Republicans increase their share of the black vote.

Campaign Literature on the Civil Rights Accomplishments of the Eisenhower Administration
1956
[Morrow Files, Eisenhower Papers.]

As Republicans this Administration does not want to take away from any person or organization any of the things they have done to help gain our Civil Rights.

Each Civil Rights advance should be put in its proper category, so that no one can take credit for what he did not do. In the Thompson Restaurant case in Washington, D.C., Mrs. Mary Church Terrell and Rev. William Jernigan, two magnificent crusaders, brought about that victory. Neither Democrats nor Republicans can take credit for it.

The school decision of May 17, 1954, was the result of tireless work by the NAACP after a long and bitter court fight. So neither Democrats nor Republicans can claim credit for that.

But we *do* want full credit for opening up the theaters, hotels and other places of amusement in Washington, D.C. We *do* want credit for integrating the fire department in Washington, D.C. We *do* want credit for the successful desegregation of the schools in the District of Columbia.

We *do* want credit for the May 3rd ruling of the District of Columbia Commissioners banning segregation in all places of amusement throughout the District of Columbia. This act was described by the Washington Post as follows: "The action was a second major step in the desegregation of the city's licensed establishments, comparing in import with the Supreme Court's ruling in the Thompson Restaurant case, against race discrimination in eating places here in June 1953!" This means that all bowling alleys and other licensed places of amusement are open to all.

We also want most of the credit for Air Force, Army, Marines and Navy, reporting segregation entirely eliminated in the past three years.

We *do* want credit for ending segregation at West Point.

We *do* want credit for ending segregation in Veterans' hospitals.

We *do* want credit for ending school segregation on all but two installations on Federal Property.

We *do* want credit for the improved operation of the Committee on Government Employment Policy resulting in the upgrading of thousands of employees in 1955; three hundred Negroes were made supervisors in the Post Office alone. On one atomic energy installation in the South, Negro employees have gone up from 84 to over 500 and white collar corkers from 1 to 25.

We *do* want credit for setting up a new Government Contract Committee in 1953, putting Vice-President Richard Nixon in charge with the following results: White collar jobs for Negroes are now available in these industries for the first time:

(a) Packing Houses.

(b) Public Utilities.

(c) Federal Reserve System.

(d) Chemical industry—placed 25 to 30.

(e) Eliminated two types of contracts in the Oil industry. White workers received higher pay than colored in the South.

(f) We have been instrumental in having a special aircraft training program for Negroes in the aircraft industry where they were not used at all.

We *do* want credit for the Capital Transit Company in Washington, D.C. employing Negro bus and trolley operators.

We *do* want credit for the Washington, D.C. Board of Commissioners' enforcement of the 85-year-old anti-discrimination laws in all places of public accommodations, ending a 75-year lapse in enforcement.

We *do* want credit for the Police Commissioner in the District of Columbia, ordering Metropolitan Police Boys' Clubs to stop using Government facilities on a segregated basis.

We *do* want credit for stopping the Bureau of Indian Affairs from negotiating a contract with Mississippi omitting the standard non-discrimination clause.

We *do* want credit for getting 308 new jobs for Negroes in Government above $6,000 ranging from auditor-in-charge to an Assistant Secretary of Labor.

We *do* want credit for having pulled one of the outstanding diplomatic coups of all times. Three rulers of darker nations were the official guests of President and Mrs. Eisenhower in less than one year. They were Emperor Haille Selassie of Ethiopia, President William V. S. Tubman of Liberia, and President Paul Magliore of Haiti.

We *do* want credit for opening up the White House to Negroes for all types of social events from lawn parties to State dinners for the first time in history.

We *do* want credit for the magnificent Civil Rights program sent to Congress by Attorney General Herbert Brownell.

This proposal asks action by the Congress on legislation to provide for a bipartisan commission on Civil Rights which will have 6 members appointed by the President—with no more than three from the same political party. The Commission will have the authority to hold public hearings in order to point up the extent of responsibility of the Federal Government and state under our constitutional system.

The Attorney General has also proposed to the Congress that the Civil Rights section of the Department of Justice be removed from under the Criminal Division and set up under an Assistant Attorney General appointed by the President.

He has also urged three changes in the "right to vote" law:

First, addition of a section which will prevent anyone from threatening, intimidating, or coercing an individual in the exercise of his right to vote, whether claiming to act under authority of law or not, in any election, general, special or primary, concerning candidates for federal office.

Second, authorization to the Attorney General to bring injunction or other Civil proceedings on behalf of the United States or the aggrieved person in any case covered by the law.

Third, elimination of the requirement that all state administrative and judicial remedies must be exhausted before access can be had to the federal courts.

This program has been endorsed by the NAACP and other National groups both religious and fraternal.

These words of Dwight D. Eisenhower, our leader, express our position in this day of stress:

"People are made in the image of God. They are divinely endowed with aspirations and talents. Their destiny reflects their divine origin. Therefore, the Republican Party must be inspired by a concern that comprehends *every American;* that sets up no walls of birth or creed or party; that ranks all men and women of decency and good will *equal in their dignity.*"

3. THE WARREN APPOINTMENT

In 1953 the future of the civil rights movement depended to a great extent upon then upcoming Supreme Court decisions. Yet hardly anyone discussed prospective members of the Court in terms of their views on desegregation. During the first few months of the Eisenhower Administration there appeared little likelihood of an imminent vacancy—none of the Justices had indicated a desire to retire and none were in poor health. Then, on September 8, 1953, Chief Justice Fred Vinson was struck with a fatal heart attack. For the first time in 20 years a GOP President had the opportunity to make a Supreme Court appointment. As Eisenhower considered possible candidates, he received advice from many quarters. One letter came from Texas oil millionaire H. L. Hunt.

H. L. Hunt to President Eisenhower
September 17, 1953
Official File 100-A, Eisenhower Papers.]

Dear President Eisenhower:

I wish to present a point of view regarding the highly important appointments coming up.

Our nation cannot survive unless the important positions are filled by persons absolutely loyal to their country and highly intolerant of everyone whose loyalty can be questioned by any reasonable person. If actions which smack of possible disloyalty must be excused as dumbness it makes little difference as far as the nation's welfare if the official is disloyal or only dumb.

For many years the Liberals and men of small stature have dominated the Supreme Court. This has been true to such an extent that the Court has failed to command the confidence of the public, become subject to open criticism and fallen into disrepute. As a start to correcting this situation the vacant post should be filled with a forthright Conservative and a man with sufficient stature to command public confidence from the time of his appointment. If the new Justice were to be a Republican who cannot be accused of Socialist tendencies his appointment would be a start toward balancing the political complexion of the Court.

Appointees of unquestioned loyalty will be particularly welcome at this time. The Jenner Committee Report disclosing the open treason which has prevailed is being widely read. The *Dallas News, Houston Chronicle,* and many other papers are running it in 22 daily installments. Senator McCarthy's "methods" are meeting a much higher percent approval than formerly—now 78 percent.

There are more Democrats than Republicans and unless there are clear cut issues between the two parties the Republicans are apt to lose their majority in the Senate and Lower House. Governor Stevenson for the Democrats is finding faults with the critics of Communists at home. The Republicans for the safety of the nation should defend the anti-Communists and I believe a clear cut division on this issue would afford the best possible campaign material for the Republicans.

A vast majority are as anxious for you to turn in a great Administration as you yourself are. Best wishes,

President Eisenhower to H. L. Hunt
September 24, 1953
[Official File 100-A, Eisenhower Papers.]

Dear Mr. Hunt:

Thank you for your recent letter. I am glad to have your views of the various matters you discuss.

As far as the Supreme Court appointment is concerned, I am determined to do my part to restore the Court to the position of prestige it formerly held in the eyes of the American people.

The President was under great pressure to nominate a Republican who would please a broad segment of the party as well as the general public. Eisenhower's desire to add a nationally known figure precluded several noted jurists. Moreover, consideration of a sitting Associate Justice was complicated by the fact that they were all Democratic appointees. For many reasons, Governor Earl Warren became the President's choice—a choice that must have delighted Senator William Knowland, who had recommended the California governor in a letter written from overseas a few days before the appointment. The President's reply to Knowland came after the appointment had been made.

Senator William Knowland to President Eisenhower
September 25, 1953
[Official File 100-A, Eisenhower Papers.]

Dear Mr. President:

At 0600 this morning I take off for Kabal, Afghanistan. On Sunday I leave for Cairo, London and Washington. On or about October 2nd I will call Tom Stephens for an appointment. To date I have been highly pleased by the quality and devotion to the national interest of our Ambassadors in the countries I have visited.

From this distance and with the limited news reports available I am not in a position to know all the facts relative to the vacancy created by the death of Chief Justice Vinson. I sincerely hope that the name of Governor Earl Warren is being considered. I feel certain that his legal background as Attorney General of California and his administrative experiences are qualifications for the Supreme Court.

It is quite possible that you may be considering moving one of the present Associate Justices up to take the place of the late Chief Justice in which event there would be another appointment to be made.

Having known Earl Warren for more than thirty years I can testify to his integrity, devotion to public duty, great ability and his maturity of judgement.

These things I would have said in person if I was there to say them. Since both plane travel and life itself is a bit uncertain I wanted to bring these views of mine to your attention while the matter was under consideration.

Please give my best regards to your wife. I hope both of you enjoyed your visit to Colorado.

President Eisenhower to Senator William Knowland
October 6, 1953
[Official File 100-A, Eisenhower Papers.]

Dear Bill:

While I realize that your brief visit to my office took place after I had received your note sent from Karachi, I cannot refrain from expressing again my complete agreement with the estimate you give of Earl Warren's qualifications for the position of Chief Justice. Needless to say, I am delighted that my choice for that important post coincided with yours.

Before making a final decision, Eisenhower sent Attorney General Herbert Brownell on a secret trip to Sacramento to meet with Warren. While the President admired Warren's philosophy, he wanted the evaluation of a "qualified lawyer." Brownell reported favorably, despite press stories that his real purpose in going to California was to convince Warren to take an Assossiate Justiceship after one of the sitting Justices was elevated to Chief Justice. On September 30, 1953, the President announced the appointment. Governor Warren heard about his nomination at the same time as did most Americans. Eisenhower's answer to the governor's wire expressed satisfaction.

Governor Earl Warren to President Eisenhower
September 30, 1953
[Official File 100-A, Eisenhower Papers.]

DEAR MR. PRESIDENT: YOUR DESIGNATION OF ME TO BE CHIEF JUSTICE OF THE SUPREME COURT HAS JUST BEEN AN-NOUNCED OVER THE AIR WITH FULL APPRECIATION OF YOUR CONFIDENCE AND OF THE RESPONSIBILITY IMPOSED I GRATEFULLY AND HUMBLY ACCEPT YOU MAY BE SURE THAT I WILL DO MY BEST TO INTERPRET THE CONSTITUTION FAIRLY AND TO DEFEND IT FAITHFULLY AGAINST EVERY ENCROACHMENT.

President Eisenhower to Governor Earl Warren
September 30, 1953
[Official File 100-A, Eisenhower Papers.]

Thank you very much for your fine telegram. As you already know, I reached the decision to make you Chief Justice because of my deep conviction that you are uniquely qualified to serve our country in that highly important post. Please remember me kindly to your family.

Public response to the Warren appointment was minimal. Gossip that Eisenhower had acted to pay off a political debt was ill-founded. He felt that he owed nothing politically to the California governor. White House staff member Arthur Minnich summarized this and other reactions to the appointment in a memorandum. David Lawrence, editor of U. S. News and World Report *and a well-known Old Guard Republican, wrote a nationally syndicated column criticizing the appointment. Fulton Lewis, Jr., a radio commentator on a national network who had long opposed New Deal ideology, also criticized Warren. Of more interest than the nature of the opposition, however, was the limited volume of the response.*

Memorandum from Presidential Assistant Arthur Minnich
to President Eisenhower
October 13, 1953
[Official File 100-A, Eisenhower Papers.]

In regard to the unfavorable mail concerning Governor Warren's appointment as Chief Justice, the most frequent criticism was that Governor Warren lacked prior judicial experience. Many writers voiced admiration for Governor Warren's integrity, but believed an eminent jurist should have been chosen.

The other frequent criticism was that the appointment was dictated by politics.

Random criticisms charged him with a "New Deal" philosophy, a middle-of-the-road position, and a failure in California.

Many of the letters seem inspired by the David Lawrence editorial and a Fulton Lewis broadcast. There were more lawyers who commented than any other single profession.

Criticism came from all over the United States, although California writers had a plurality.

Total—85 unfavorable, 31 favorable.

4. THE 1957 CIVIL RIGHTS ACT

Although the Eisenhower Administration had progressed on a few civil rights issues, the executive branch had not attempted to obtain any legislation prior to 1956. Indeed, some Republicans had tried to minimize publicity about the accomplishments which had been made. This reflected the sensitive nature of the topic as well as GOP efforts to strengthen the party in the South. However, by 1955 national concern had reached a point where the Administration came under increasing pressure to act. In response to a report sent him by Val Washington, Director of Minorities for the Republican National Committee, the President's response testified not only to a personal concern for the rights of blacks, but also to the growing political importance of civil rights. Washington, who had long been one of the few blacks holding an important post in the Republican National Committee, suddenly found himself in a position where his views received considerable attention. Another mark of increasing Administration interest was the appointment of a black, E. Frederic Morrow, to the White House staff. Morrow, who had traveled with and worked for Eisenhower in the 1952 campaign, had waited more than two years for the appointment that made him the first black American to serve as a presidential assistant. While Morrow's main duties did not involve civil rights—he had no desire to be "the black man in the White House"—he naturally felt deeply about the subject. Following the lynching of a black teenager from Chicago in Mississippi on August 31, 1955, and the subsequent acquittal of the accused men, Morrow wrote a memorandum expressing his thoughts on the case and other matters. Near the end of 1955 a lower echelon staff member, Joseph Douglass, compiled a program to improve "relations with the Negro group." All the concerns expressed by such men as Washington, Morrow, and Douglass pointed in one direction—national civil rights legislation.

President Eisenhower to Val Washington
August 1, 1955
[Official File 142-A, Eisenhower Papers.]

Dear Val:

Naturally, every report on the fulfillment in this Administration of Republican pledges made in the campaign of 1952 gives me a great deal of satisfaction. In a special sense, however, your letter on the complete realization of fourteen points presented to the Negro voters of the Nation during that campaign is particularly heartening and gratifying. You relate an achievement which emphatically proves that the unity of the American people is neither a mere political platitude nor a purely philosophical concept.

As Americans, we believe in the equal dignity of all our people, whatever their racial origin or background may be; in their equal right to freedom and opportunity and the benefits of our common citizenship. Now, during this Administration, we have advanced far—on every front of our daily life—the factual application of our belief. We have demonstrated a dynamic loyalty to the principles on which the Republic is founded.

All of us realize that much must still be done. All of us, whatever our position or our party may be, must still work tirelessly toward the goal of a stronger and more warmly human unity. But all of us have reason for just pride in the tremendous advances of the past thirty months. The credit should be widely shared.

You, and millions of others like you, have contributed greatly by an outstanding devotion to the Republic and by unfaltering service to it; thereby, the esteem, the respect of your fellow citizens has been earned. The Republican Party has been firm in its insistence that there can be only one class of citizenship and has been effective in its practice of this conviction; thereby it has proved itself, in our day, a vigorous and productive champion of the ideals and purposes of Lincoln.

But I am sure, the major credit must go to the people of the United States. Their sense of fair play, their recognition that all our citizens are bound in a common destiny, their spiritual faith in the dignity of all men under God—these deeply rooted characteristics of the American people are the ultimate source of the achievement reported by you.

My thanks are yours for the report you have made. My best wishes to you and to all associated with you on the Committee and in the field.

Presidential Assistant E. Frederic Morrow
to Cabinet Secretary Maxwell Rabb
November 29, 1955
[Morrow Files, Eisenhower Papers.]

I served more than eight years as Field Secretary of the National Association for the Advancement of Colored People, and during that period faced every manner of problem that comes within the realm of race relations. Therefore, I am especially alert to racial conditions and situations that will eventually affect the welfare of the country, and which will particularly bring headaches and possibly severe criticism to the Administration. It is for these reasons alone that I presume to present my considered judgment on a dangerous situation that is now affecting the country.

The killing of the young Negro, Emmett Till, in Mississippi this fall, has received official attention from this Administration through the Office of the Attorney General. Under normal circumstances, this would be enough to satisfy most people, that the police arm of the Federal Government was alert to all situations where possible Federal laws have been violated. However, this particular situation is so fraught with emotion because of the circumstances under which the crime was committed, and the fact that the victim was a youngster, that normal methods of dealing with the usual case of crime are not completely acceptable to all of the interested parties.

There are visible indications that we are on the verge of a dangerous racial conflagration in the Southern section of the country. My official duties in the past few months have taken me to the deep South, to the Middle West, and throughout the Eastern seaboard, and the one theme on the lips and in the minds of all Negroes is the injustice of the Till matter, and the fact that nothing can be done to effect justice in this case. The warning signs in the South are all too clear; the harrassed Negro is sullen, bitter, and talking strongly of retaliation whenever future situations dictate.

Mass meetings are being held by the scores across the country, and are attended by thousands of people who want to hear the story from the mother of the boy or other witnesses. The Till case is a subject of unceasing publicity in the press, and the subject of numerous Sunday sermons in the pulpits of the land. An example of the passion that this case has generated was indicated to me in Youngstown a few weeks ago, when I attended services at a prominent church, and heard the well-educated minister of the congregation state that "we Negroes lynch too easily and we must learn to resist with everything in our power if we would put a stop to this barbarous custom."

It is a well-known fact that Negroes in Mississippi have formed an underground and are determined to protect themselves by methods that, if used, can only lead to further terror and bloodshed.

On the other hand, a frightening power has been built in Mississippi by the anti-desegregation White Citizens Councils, and their principal method is one of economic terrorism. These Councils are fanning out throughout the South, and they have created a climate of fear and terrorism that holds the entire area in a vise.

As a member of the White House Staff, I am sitting in the middle of this, and I have been accused of being cowardly for not bringing this situation to the attention of the Administration, and requesting the President to make some kind of observation on this unwholesome problem. My mail has been heavy and angry, and wherever I go, people have expressed disappointment that no word has come from the White House deploring this situation. I always point out, of course, that our Attorney General has followed this situation with interest and skill and that he will act when and if Federal laws are violated. But this does not still the protestations. There is a clamor for some kind of statement from the White House that will indicate the Administration is aware of, and condemns with vigor, any kind of racist activity in the United States.

I feel the time has come when it might be advisable for Governor Adams or Vice President Nixon to invite to Washington a dozen of the prominent Negro leaders in the country and sit down with them and exchange views on this very dangerous problem. It will not be a matter of committing the Administration to any action it cannot take, but it will be a demonstration to the whole country that the responsible leaders, white and Negro, have a deep concern about this situation, and wish to sit down and talk about it intelligently and dispassionately. There is precedent for this kind of meeting, for, in my lifetime, it happened several times with Presidents Hoover, Roosevelt and Truman. Meetings of this kind always have a steadying effect upon responsible Negro leaders for they are able to go through the country and assure Negro citizens that the head of the nation is concerned about their welfare and will utilize the prestige of his office to prevail upon all to exercise common sense and common decency in dealing with the problem. By the same token, it notifies any racist element that the Administration frowns upon their un-American tactics, and will use the Office of the Attorney General to bring to justice any infractions of Federal laws.

I would be happy to sit down and work out a list of invitees for such a meeting, and I feel that time is of the essence.

Memorandum from Staff Assistant Joseph Douglass to Cabinet Secretary Maxwell Rabb
December 22, 1955
[Morrow Files, Eisenhower Papers.]

I am writing this memorandum to set forth my views as to possible steps to be taken in reference to your observations and those made by the group in our recent meeting in reference to the question of minority group relationships.

My personal views are first that it would be unwise to discredit or ignore the findings of the Gallup Poll. Second, I concur that optimum relations with the Negro group have not been achieved despite the record of accomplishments and the genuine effort and will on the part of the Administration to help improve matters. Third, I do believe that matters can be improved.

Analysis of Problems

In seeking to analyze the present state of affairs, I think the situation can be reduced to basic causes of (1) the rather "objective" non-aggressive approach which has been employed by the Administration, (2) the absence of a clearly systematic plan of approach in this area, (3) the minimum utilization of spokesmen on the subject, (4) the absence of planned rebuttal to critics, (5) failure to capitalize fully on opportunities, and (6) failure to develop and stimulate leadership significantly at State and local levels.

There may be other causes such as stereotypes which have developed as to the identification of the other group with the "problems of the common man", and the fact that so called national "leaders" of the group over the past few years have been identified with the other group in advisory and consultative capacities. It is my confirmed opinion that none of these difficulties is insurmountable and that the record can be gotten across and confidence inspired.

Explanation of Above

(1) *Non-aggressive approach.* The idea has been permitted to grow that the Administration moves quietly but solidly and that no issue is made of objective progress. Whereas this is commendable, some horn-blowing is necessary to show what is being done and future hopes and plans.

(2) *Absence of Clearly Systematic Plan.* Perhaps two or three objectives need to be clearly identified in the public's view as what the Administration will seek to accomplish. Despite efforts, developments cannot occur after which the record of past achievements is heralded. Plans have to be developed as to current efforts for future developments as well.

Good progress has been made in so called "top" appointments but there is the great middle where progress is slow. (The great middle is where most Negroes had jobs under a war-inflated economy in government and industry.)

(3) *Minimum Utilization of Spokesmen.* More efforts have to be made to get minority spokesmen before the public both with Negro groups and with other groups. More spokesmen generally should include the record of progress in their remarks.

(4) *Planned Rebuttal to Critics.* When attacks are made publicly they should be answered in the same medium. (Without answers, people tend to believe that the attacks made are true.)

(5) *Failure to Capitalize on Opportunities.* The group is seeking status and much of its status is received vicariously so that Bunche et al become heroes. As much as possible in events of national importance, significant roles should be played by Negroes—(introduction of speakers—meet the press—sessions—Vice-President's conference—one of principal speakers, etc.).

(6) *Failure to Develop and Stimulate Leadership at Local Levels.* In order for the local leaders to have status, opportunities must be provided for

them to come to Washington, to be consulted and to have a part in developments. (Nearly 40 Negro representatives after being invited were nearly excluded as observers at the White House Conference on Education. While here there were no Administration efforts to have them invited to a group meeting honoring them, etc., or opportunity provided other than on a random basis to present their observations or evaluation of the conference.)

Elements Of A Suggested Plan

I propose that efforts should be made to move forward in several areas to accomplish the desired objectives as follows:
(1) *Taking the offensive Role in Civil Rights*
    A. Many more press releases about the record.
    B. Placing more people in the field at meetings of organizations.
    C. Exposing the voting records of opponents to civil rights measures.
    D. Counteracting immediately with rebuttals critical statements in the press.
    E. Increased prominence to work of Negro appointees as a group and in their individual roles.
    F. Stepped-up introduction of Administration bills on civil rights.
    G. Interpret efforts as not being politically motivated.
(2) *Seeking to have the President and Vice-President take Strong Stands on the Issues*
    A. State of the Union Message.
    B. Possibility of a special message on progress.
    C. Establishment of large informal advisory group on intergroup matters (representative of all minorities) with possibility of a national conference.
    D. President and Vice-President to call in officials for brief chats.
(3) *Provision of Greater Opportunities for Negro Press to have Conferences with Cabinet Members and other Officials*
    Numerous opportunities present themselves where members of the Negro Press could be invited such as at a conference in Agriculture on Low Income Families.
(4) *Providing Opportunities for Minority Members to Play more Vital Roles in National, State and Local Meetings*
    Note: An example, no Negro was included on the program as a speaker at the recent White House Conference on Education.
(5) *Have Fairly Regular Meetings of the Across-Government Negro Appointed Group to Help Identify Problems and Map Strategy*
(6) Others?

Expected Results

Among the results an approach of this kind could (1) show clearly where the Administration stands; (2) make clear to the least informed the progressive record of achievement; (3) discredit criticisms levelled at the Administration; (4) point up the unresolved issues and approaches being made to their solution; (5) expose the voting record of the other group; (6) expand opportunities of participation by minority persons and hence the identification of these persons with the large problems of the day; (7) develop an improved press; and (8) re-assure dubious members of the Administration that efforts being made are productive of good results in the interest of an improved and stronger Nation.

Mechanics

I feel that in order for the approaches employed to bear the most productive fruit, there should be central coordination and close liaison among representatives of all of the Departments, the White House, and the National Committee.

Meetings of the type held on December 20 should be as frequent as necessary in order to maintain required liaison, develop added plans and to evaluate progress.

In his 1956 State of the Union Message Eisenhower said: "It is disturbing that in some localities allegations persist that Negro citizens are being deprived of their right to vote and are likewise being subjected to unwarranted economic pressures. I recommend that the substance of these charges be thoroughly examined by a bipartisan commission created by the Congress." An Administration-backed bill was introduced in Congress early in 1956. In March, Eisenhower decided to throw the full weight of the Administration behind the legislation. During hearings before a House committee, the Attorney General presented a defense of the proposed measure. The testimony was considered important enough to warrant a "Cabinet Paper-Privileged" classification.

Cabinet Paper-Privileged on Civil Rights
April 10, 1956
[Morrow Files, Eisenhower Papers.]

The Cabinet

The Civil Rights Program—
Letter and Statement by the Attorney General

The attached approved paper, and its appendix, are circulated for the information of the Cabinet.

The approved paper is the letter which was sent on April 9, 1956 by the Attorney General to the Vice President and to the Speaker of the House, and released to the press on the same day.

This letter was approved by the President subsequent to the Cabinet meeting of March 23, 1956.

As an appendix to the letter, there is also circulated a copy of the Attorney General's statement on the civil rights program, given on Tuesday April 10, 1956 before the House Judiciary Committee.

Maxwell M. Rabb
Secretary to the Cabinet

STATEMENT BY THE ATTORNEY GENERAL ON LEGISLATIVE PROPOSALS FOR THE CREATION OF A CIVIL RIGHTS COMMISSION, THE CREATION OF A CIVIL RIGHTS DIVISION IN THE DEPARTMENT OF JUSTICE AND FOR THE AMENDMENT OF THE VOTING AND CIVIL RIGHTS STATUTES IN CERTAIN RESPECTS INCLUDING THE ADDITION TO BOTH OF PROVISIONS FOR THEIR ENFORCEMENT BY CIVIL REMEDIES IN THE DEPARTMENT OF JUSTICE.

BEFORE HOUSE JUDICIARY COMMITTEE
TUESDAY, APRIL 10, 1956 AT 10:00 A.M.

In his State of the Union Message, President Eisenhower said that his administration would recommend to the Congress a program to advance the efforts of the Government, within the area of Federal responsibility, to the end that every person may be judged and measured by what he is, rather than by his color, race or religion. Recently I transmitted to the Speaker of this House and to the President of the Senate our proposals on this subject. I am grateful for the opportunity to appear before this Committee to discuss these proposals and to comment, as well, upon other proposals relating to this same subject which are already pending before this Committee.

My letters to the Speaker of the House and to the President of the Senate recommend Congressional legislation on four matters: First, creation of the Bipartisan Commission on Civil Rights recommended by the President in his State of the Union Message; second, creation of an additional office of Assistant Attorney General to head a new Civil Rights Division in the Department of Justice; third, amendment of existing statutes to give further protection to the right to vote and to add civil remedies in the Department of Justice for their enforcement; and fourth, amendment of other civil rights laws to include the addition of civil remedies in the Department of Justice for their enforcement.

I. Civil Rights Commission.

In recommending the creation of a bipartisan civil rights commission, President Eisenhower said in his State of the Union Message:

> It is disturbing that in some localities allegations persist that Negro citizens are being deprived of their right to vote and are likewise being subjected to unwarranted economic pressures. I recommend that the substance of these charges be thoroughly examined by a bipartisan commission created by the Congress.

A bill detailing the Commission proposal was submitted with my letters to the Speaker of the House and the President of the Senate. It provides that the Commission shall have six members, appointed by the President with the advice and consent of the Senate. No more than three shall be from the same political party. The Commission shall be temporary, expiring two years from the effective date of the statute, unless extended by Congress. It will have authority to subpoena witnesses, take testimony under oath and request necessary data from any executive department or agency. It may be required to make interim reports pending completion of a comprehensive final report containing findings and recommendations.

The Commission will have authority to hold public hearings. It will investigate the allegations that certain citizens of the United States are being deprived of their right to vote or are being subjected to unwarranted economic pressures by reason of their color, race, religion or national origin. It will study and collect information concerning economic, social and legal developments constituting a denial of equal protection of the laws. It will appraise the laws and policies of the Federal Government with respect to equal protection of the laws under the federal constitution.

The need for more knowledge and greater understanding of these most complex and difficult problems is manifest. A full scale public study of them conducted over a two-year period by a competent bipartisan commission, such as is recommended by the President, will tend to unite responsible people of good will in common effort to solve these problems. Such a study will bring clearer definition of the constitutional boundaries between Federal and State governments and will insure that remedial proposals are within the appropriate areas of Federal and State responsibility. Through greater public understanding of these matters the Commission may chart a course of progress to guide the nation in the years ahead.

For a study such as that proposed by the President, the authority to hold public hearings, to subpoena witnesses, to take testimony under oath and to request necessary data from executive departments and agencies is obviously essential. No agency in the Executive Branch of Government has the legal authority to exercise such powers in a study of matters relating to civil rights.

II. Civil Rights Division in the Department of Justice.

In 1939 the present Civil Rights Section was created in the Criminal Division of the Department of Justice. Its function and purpose has been to direct, supervise and conduct criminal prosecutions of violations of the federal constitution and laws guaranteeing civil rights to individuals. As long as its activities were confined to the enforcement of criminal laws it was logical that it should be a section of the Criminal Division.

Recently, however, the Justice Department has been obliged to engage in activity in the civil rights field which is non-criminal in character. An example is the recent participation of the Department, as amicus curiae, in a civil suit to prevent by injunction unlawful interference with the efforts of the school board at Hoxie, Arkansas, to eliminate racial discrimination in the school in conformity with the Supreme Court's decision. The non-criminal activity of the Department in the civil rights field is constantly increasing in importance as well as in amount. If my recommendations, discussed subsequently, for legislation to provide civil remedies in the Department of Justice for the enforcement of voting and other civil rights are followed, the Department's duties and activities in the civil courts will increase even more rapidly than in the past.

It is essential that all the Department's civil rights activity, both criminal and non-criminal, be consolidated in a single organization, but it is not appropriate that an organization with important civil as well as criminal functions should be administered as a part of the Criminal Division.

Consequently, I most earnestly recommend that the appointment of a new assistant attorney general be authorized by the Congress in order to permit the proper consolidation and organization of the Department's civil and criminal activities in the area of civil rights into a division of the Department and under the direction of a highly qualified lawyer with the status of an assistant attorney general. A draft of legislation to effect this result was transmitted with my letters to the Speaker of the House and the President of the Senate.

III. Amendments to Give Greater Protection to the Right to Vote and to Provide Civil Remedies in the Department of Justice for their Enforcement.

The right to vote is one of our most precious rights. It is the cornerstone of our form of government and affords protection for our other rights. It must be zealously safeguarded.

Article I, Sections 2 and 4, of the Constitution place in the Congress the power and the duty to protect by appropriate laws elections for office under the Government of the United States. With respect to elections for state and local office, the Fifteenth Amendment to the Constitution provides that the right of citizens of the United States to vote shall not be denied or abridged by the United States or by any state on account of race, color, or previous condition of servitude. And the Fourteenth Amendment prohibits any state from making or enforcing laws which abridge the privileges and immunities of citizens of the United States and from denying to any person the equal protection of the laws. The courts have held that these prohibitions operate against election laws which discriminate on account of race, color, religion or national origin.

To implement these provisions of the Constitution Congress passed many years ago a voting statute, 42 U.S.C. 1971, which provides that all citizens shall be entitled and allowed to vote at all elections, state or federal, without distinction based upon race or color. It was the duty of Congress under the Constitution and its amendments to pass legislation giving full protection to the right to vote and undoubtedly it was the intent of Congress to provide such protection by passing 42 U.S.C. 1971.

However, in the years since its enactment, a number of serious defects in the statute have become plainly apparent, most of them having been pointed out in judicial decisions. The most obvious defect in the law is that it does not protect the voters in federal elections from unlawful interference with their voting rights by private persons. It applies only to those who act "under color of law," which means to public officials. The activities of private persons and organizations designed to disfranchise voters in federal or state elections on account of race or color are not covered by the present wording of 42 U.S.C. 1971 and the statute fails, therefore, to afford voters the full protection from discrimination contemplated and guaranteed by the Constitution and its amendments.

Section 1971 of Title 42, United States Code, is clearly defective in another important respect. It fails to lodge in the Attorney General any authority to invoke civil remedies for enforcement of voting rights and is particularly lacking in any provision authorizing the Attorney General to apply to the courts for preventive relief against violation of voting rights. We think this is a major defect. The ultimate goal of the Constitution and of Congress is the safeguarding of the free exercise of the voting right, acknowledging the legitimate power of the states to prescribe necessary and fair voting qualifications. Civil proceedings by the Attorney General to forestall illegal interference and denial of the right to vote would be far more effective in achieving this goal than the private suits for damages presently authorized by the statute or the criminal proceedings authorized under other laws which can never be instituted until after the harm is done.

Consequently, I think that Congress should now recognize that in order to properly execute the Constitution and its amendments, and in order to perfect the intended application of the statute, Section 1971 of Title 42, United States Code, should be amended by:

First, the addition of a section which will prevent anyone, whether acting under color of law or not, from threatening, intimidating or coercing an individual in his right to vote in any election, general, special or primary, concerning candidates for federal office.

Second, authorization to the Attorney General to bring civil proceedings on behalf of the United States or any aggrieved person for preventive or other civil relief in any case covered by the statute.

Third, express provision that all state administrative and judicial remedies need not be first exhausted before resort to the federal courts.

IV. Amendment of Other Civil Rights Laws to Include the Addition of Civil Remedies in the Department of Justice for their Enforcement.

In attempting to achieve the constitutional goal of respect for and observance of the civil rights of individuals, it has been, in my opinion, a mistake for the Congress to have relied so heavily upon the criminal law and to have made so little use of the more flexible and often more practical and effective processes of the civil courts. Although the Attorney General, under present statutes, can prosecute after violations of the civil rights laws have occurred, he cannot seek preventive relief in the courts when violations are threatened or, in spite of an occasional arrest or prosecution, are persistently repeated.

Criminal prosecution can never begin until after the harm is done and it can never be invoked to forestall a violation of civil rights no matter how obvious the threat of violation may be. Moreover, criminal prosecution for civil rights violations, when they involve state or local officials as they often do, stir up an immense amount of ill feeling in the community and inevitably tend to cause very bad relations between state and local officials on the one hand and the federal officials responsible for the investigation and prosecution on the other. A great deal of this could be avoided if the Congress would authorize the Attorney General to seek preventive and other appropriate relief from the civil courts in civil rights cases.

Let me illustrate:

In 1952, several Negro citizens of a certain county in Mississippi submitted affidavits to us alleging that because of their race the Registrar of Voters refused to register them. Although the Mississippi statutes at that time required only that an applicant be able to read and write the Constitution, these affidavits alleged that the Registrar demanded that the Negro citizens answer such questions as "What is due process of law?" "How many bubbles in a bar of soap?", etc. Those submitting affidavits included college graduates, teachers and businessmen yet none of them, according to the Registrar, could meet the voting requirements. If the Attorney General had the power to invoke the injunctive process, the Registrar could have been ordered to stop these discriminatory practices and qualify these citizens according to Mississippi law.

Another illustration:

The United States Supreme Court recently reversed the conviction of a Negro sentenced to death by a state court because of a showing that Negroes had been systematically excluded from the panels of the grand and petit juries that had indicted and tried him. In so doing the Supreme Court stated that according to the undisputed evidence in the record before it systematic discrimination against Negroes in the selection of jury panels had persisted for many years past in the county where the case had been tried. In its opinion the Court mentioned parenthetically but pointedly that such discrimination was a denial of equal protection of the laws and it would follow that it was a violation of the federal civil rights laws.

Accordingly, the Department of Justice had no alternative except to institute an investigation to determine whether in the selection of jury panels in the county in question the civil rights laws of the United States were being violated, as suggested by the record before the Supreme Court. The mere institution of this inquiry aroused a storm of indignation in the county and state in question. This is understandable since, if such violations were continuing, the only course open to the Government was criminal prosecution of those responsible. That might well have meant the indictment in the federal court of the local court attaches and others responsible under the circumstances.

Fortunately the Department was never faced with so difficult and disagreeable a duty. The investigation showed that, whatever the practice may have been during the earlier years with which the Supreme Court's record was concerned, in recent years there had been no discrimination against Negroes in the selection of juries in that county.

Supposing, however, that on investigation, the facts had proved otherwise. The necessarily resulting prosecution would have stirred up such dissension and ill will in the community and in the state that it might well have done more harm than good. Such unfortunate collisions in the criminal courts between federal and state officials can be avoided if the Congress would authorize the Attorney General to apply to the civil courts for preventive relief in civil rights cases. In such a civil proceeding the facts can be determined, the rights of the parties adjudicated and future violations of the law prevented by order of the court without having to subject state officials to the indignity, hazards and personal expense of a criminal prosecution in the courts of the United States.

Congress could authorize the Attorney General to seek civil remedies in the civil courts for the enforcement of civil rights by a simple amendment to Section 1985 of Title 42, United States Code. That statute presently authorizes civil suits by private persons who are injured by acts done in furtherance of a conspiracy to do any of the following things: (1) to prevent officers from performing their duties; (2) to obstruct justice; (3) to deprive persons of their rights to the equal protection of the laws and equal privileges under the laws.

A subsection could be added to that statute to give authority to the Attorney General to institute a civil action for redress or preventive relief whenever any persons have engaged or are about to engage in any acts or practices which would give rise to a cause of action under the present provisions of the law.

Such an amendment would provide a procedure for enforcement of civil rights which in my opinion would be far simpler, more flexible, more reasonable and more effective than the criminal sanctions which are the only remedy now available.

V. Comment on Other Proposals Relating to Civil Rights Now Pending Before this Committee.

There must certainly be grave doubt as to whether it is wise to propose at the present time any further extension of the criminal law into the extraordinarily sensitive and delicate area of civil rights. Because of this doubt and because of my conviction previously expressed as to the importance of civil remedies in this field, the Department of Justice is not proposing at this time any amendments to sections 241 and 242 of Title 18, United States Code, which are the two principal criminal statutes intended for the protection of civil rights. Whether the present moment is appropriate for such legislation is, of course, a question for the Congress to determine.

Nevertheless, it must be conceded that all question of timeliness aside and considered strictly from a law enforcement point of view both statutes have defects. I have observed that H.R. 627 would amend them both and, if they are to be amended, I have a few comments and suggestions to offer.

First: Section 241 of Title 18, United States Code, makes it unlawful for two or more persons to conspire "to injure, oppress, threaten or intimidate any citizen in the free exercise or enjoyment of any right or privilege secured to him by the Constitution or laws of the United States, or because of his having so exercised the same." The statute fails to penalize such injury, oppression, threats or intimidation when committed by a single individual, which not infrequently occurs. This should be corrected.

Second: The word "citizen" now appearing in the statute should be changed to "person" and the words "right or privilege secured to him by the Constitution" should be changed to "right, privilege or immunity secured or protected by the Constitution." The purpose of the suggested changes is to protect more completely the interests guaranteed to all persons by the 14th and 15th Amendments.

Third: The penalty in ordinary cases should be left as it is, a misdemeanor, but more substantial penalties should be provided for unlawful conduct prohibited by this statute which results in maiming or death.

The amendment of Section 242 of Title 18 would be so extraordinarily complicated that I do not recommend that it be attempted at the present time. In the case of *Screws* vs. *U.S.* 325 U.S. 91 the statute was upheld by a closely divided court only because of the construction placed by the court upon the word "willfully" as it appears in the statute. Yet it is the construction placed upon that word by the Supreme Court that causes the most serious practical difficulties in enforcement and other amendments would be of little avail without changing the word "willfully." However, to make the change would seriously jeopardize once more the constitutionality of the entire statute. Consequently, it is recommended that amendments should not be attempted at the present time.

———————————————————————————

The 1956 Civil Rights bill passed the House on July 23 but failed in the Senate. As the legislation approached a vote in the House Rules Committee, Republican legislators and members of the executive branch displayed keen interest. Congressman Hugh Scott of Pennsylvania wrote to Maxwell Rabb about the bill's course through Congress. Rabb's memorandum to Bryce Harlow attested to the high priority that civil rights matters had obtained.

Representative Hugh Scott to Cabinet Secretary Maxwell Rabb
June 19, 1956
[Official File 142-A, Eisenhower Papers.]

Dear Max:

The R. N. C. have asked me to address the National Convention of the NAACP at San Francisco on the evening of June 29. I have a series of commitments for that weekend but they seem to feel that this meeting is important—I do too—and if it is okay at your end, I will somehow work myself out of these commitments and hit for the Coast.

Parenthetically, I can make a much better speech if I can say that *all* Republicans on the Rules Committee voted solidly to report out the Civil Rights bill. Such action would dramatically highlight the four–four division on the Democratic side.

Memorandum from Cabinet Secretary Maxwell Rabb
to Special Assistant Bryce Harlow
June 20, 1956
[Official File 142-A, Eisenhower Papers.]

Hugh Scott is taking a very difficult assignment of addressing the National Convention of the NAACP in California on June 29th. It is important that we have a top-flight representative there, and he has revised his whole program to do this.

(1) If you run into him on the Hill, it will be most helpful if you could tell him that we, in the White House, have been made aware of this fact and appreciate what he has done.

(2) Hugh also makes the point about Leo Allen's vote on the civil rights bill. He feels that if there is full Republican Rules Committee support on the civil rights bill, it will give impact to his speech and also spike the anticipated Democratic defense that the civil rights bill was blocked with Republican support.

N.B. I see where Leo Allen went with the Republicans on the Committee: That is very good.

MAX—WILL DO. GOOD IDEA. BH.

Eisenhower's 1956 election mandate strengthened his position with regard to civil rights legislation. In his January 10, 1957, State of the Union Message, the President reiterated his request for a civil rights bill, and in the ensuing weeks he pressured Republican congressional leaders to pass one without delay. The White House tried to keep legislators as fully informed as possible. One part of this effort was a "Fact Paper" distributed in March of 1957.

The Administration and Civil Rights—Fact Paper
March 27, 1957
[Morrow Files, Eisenhower Papers.]

President Eisenhower, in his 1957 State of the Union Message reemphasized that we in this nation have much reason to be gratified at the progress our people are making in mutual understanding.

He reiterated that we are steadily moving closer to the goal of fair and equal treatment of all citizens without regard to race or color. The President observed, however, that "unhappily, much remains to be done." As a substantial step toward achieving this goal he urged passage of the following:

   I. Creation of a bipartisan commission to investigate asserted violations of law in the field of civil rights, especially involving the right to vote, and to make recommendations;

  II. Creation of a civil rights division in the Department of Justice in charge of a Presidentially appointed Assistant Attorney General;

 III. Enactment by the Congress of new laws to aid in the enforcement of voting rights;

  IV. Amendment of the laws so as to permit the Federal Government to seek from the civil courts preventive relief in civil rights cases.

I. *CIVIL RIGHTS COMMISSION*—In recommending originally in 1956 the creation of a bipartisan civil rights commission, President Eisenhower said: "It is disturbing that in some localities allegations persist that Negro citizens are being deprived of their right to vote and are likewise being subjected to unwarranted economic pressures. I recommend that the substance of these charges be thoroughly examined by a bipartisan commission created by the Congress."

Above and beyond the need for improving the legal remedies for dealing with specific civil rights violations is the need for greater knowledge and understanding of all of the complex problems involved. The bipartisan Executive Commission would be a temporary body designed to obtain information and not a continuing agency.

II. *CIVIL RIGHTS DIVISION IN THE DEPARTMENT OF JUSTICE*—At present the Civil Rights Section of the Department of Justice is one of a number of sections located within the Criminal Division. The protection of civil rights guaranteed by the Constitution is a governmental responsibility of first importance. More emphasis should be on civil law remedies, and the civil rights enforcement activities of the Department of Justice should not, therefore, be confined to the Criminal Division.

III. *AMENDMENTS TO GIVE GREATER PROTECTION TO THE RIGHT TO VOTE AND TO PROVIDE CIVIL REMEDIES IN THE DEPARTMENT OF JUSTICE FOR THEIR ENFORCEMENT*—The right to vote is the one right, perhaps more than any other, upon which all other constitutional rights depend for their effective protection.

The major defect has been the failure of Congress thus far to specifically authorize the Attorney General to invoke civil powers and remedies to supplement the existing authority for Federal criminal prosecution. Criminal prosecutions of course cannot be instituted until after the harm actually has been done. Yet no amount of criminal punishment can rectify the harm which the national interest suffers when citizens are illegally kept from the polls. What is needed is to lodge power in the Department of Justice to proceed in civil suits in which the problem can often be solved in advance of the election.

The proposed legislation would: (1) Prevent anyone from threatening, intimidating, or coercing an individual in the exercise of his right to vote in any election for federal office. (2) Authorize the Attorney General to bring injunction or other civil proceedings on behalf of the United States or an aggrieved person. (3) Eliminate the requirement that all state administrative and judicial remedies must be exhausted before access can be had to the federal court.

IV. *AMENDMENT OF OTHER CIVIL RIGHTS LAWS TO INCLUDE THE ADDITION OF CIVIL REMEDIES FOR THEIR ENFORCEMENT*—In attempting to achieve the constitutional goal of the observance of civil rights, the Administration feels that it has been a mistake for the Congress to have relied so heavily upon the criminal law and to have made so little use of the more flexible and often more effective processes of the civil courts. Just as in the voting field (III above) the Attorney General can now prosecute after violations of the civil rights laws have occurred. However, he cannot seek preventive relief in the courts when violations are threatened or persistently repeated.

Congress could authorize the Attorney General to seek civil remedies in the civil courts for the enforcement of civil rights by a simple amendment. Existing statute authorizes civil suits by private persons who are injured by acts done in furtherance of a conspiracy to do many of the following things: (1) To prevent officers from performing their duties; (2) to obstruct justice; (3) to deprive persons of their rights to the equal protection of the laws and equal privileges under the laws.

A subsection could be added to that statute to give authority to the Attorney General to institute a civil action for redress or preventive relief whenever any persons have engaged or are about to engage in acts which would give rise to a cause of action under the present provisions of the law. Such an amendment would provide a procedure for enforcement of civil rights which would be simpler and more effective than the criminal sanctions which are the only remedy now available.

On June 18, 1957, the Administration bill passed the House of Representatives by a margin of better than 2 to 1. When the bill reached the Senate, a successful parliamentary maneuver saved it from cosignment to the Senate Judiciary Committee and almost certain death. Southern opponents, in an attempt to further cloud the issue, then proposed a national referendum on the legislation. This scheme, like other delaying tactics, failed, and debate to consider the bill commenced on July 8. One of the opening salvos from the South was fired by North Carolina's Democratic Senator Sam Ervin. A constitutional lawyer, Ervin attacked the bill as a subversion of traditional legal safeguards.

Senate Speech by Sam Ervin on Civil Rights
July 8, 1957

[U. S., *Congressional Record*, 85th Cong., 1st Sess., 1957, CIII, Part 8, 10991–94.]

MR. SAM ERVIN (Dem., N.C.): Mr. President, I rise in opposition to the motion of the able and distinguished minority leader. I do this because I know that the greatest blessing which could befall the United States at this particular time would be for further action on the civil-rights bill to be postponed until Congress reconvenes in January. If such postponement were had, it would afford the President, the Senate, the American bench and bar, and the American people an opportunity to discover what a queer concoction of constitutional and legal sins masquerades under the beguiling name of civil rights in this cunningly conceived and deviously worded bill.

At a news conference several weeks ago, a reporter put to President Eisenhower, who is not a lawyer, a question relating to the provisions of the civil rights bill. The President gave the reporter a characteristically honest answer. He said he did not understand what he called the legal quirks in the bill. The President made a somewhat similar confession at his news conference last week when he stated that he had been reading the bill and did not understand all of its language.

I have repeatedly asserted during recent weeks that President Eisenhower would not favor the civil-rights bill if he understood its provisions and implications.

I knew that President Eisenhower did not understand the legal quirks in the civil rights bill. Had he done so, he would never have described it as a moderate legislative proposal.

I based my assertion that President Eisenhower would not favor the civil-rights bill if he understood its provisions and implications upon this abiding conviction: President Eisenhower is an honest man, and he meant exactly what he said when he declared, in substance, at New Orleans on October 13, 1952, and at Houston on October 14, 1952, that he deplored and would always resist Federal encroachment upon the rights and affairs of the States and that an all-powerful Washington bureaucracy will rob us one by one of the whole bundle of our liberties unless we preserve to our States, our counties, and our hometowns the power to administer affairs which are primarily local in nature.

As one who has spent the major portion of his days and energies in the study of constitutional and legal principles, I can readily appreciate why President Eisenhower or any other person finds it difficult to understand the legal quirks in the civil rights bill.

Incidentally, the term "legal quirk" is fittingly used in connection with the bill. According to the dictionary, a "quirk" is a deviation from the regular course.

The civil-rights bill is certainly a deviation from the regular course. It is so conceived and so worded as to conceal rather than reveal its provisions and implications. Consequently, no one can obtain any reliable notion as to the significance of the legal quirks in the bill simply by reading it. To do this, one must spend weeks studying constitutional and legal history, legal rules, equitable principles, Congressional enactments, and court decisions.

When one studies the civil-rights bill in the light of these things, he discovers that its provisions and implications are utterly repugnant to the American constitutional and legal systems.

I oppose the civil-rights bill. My opposition to it does not arise out of any matter of race. As a member of the school board in my hometown and as a representative from my county in the North Carolina Legislature, I have always done everything within my power to secure adequate educational opportunity for all of North Carolina's children of all races. As a lawyer, legislator, and judge, I have always done everything within my power to make it certain that all men stand equal before the law. As a private citizen and public official, I have always maintained that all qualified citizens of all races are entitled to vote.

I oppose the civil rights bill simply because I love our constitutional and legal systems, and desire above all things to preserve them for the benefit of all Americans of all races and all generations.

I know from my study of the civil-rights bill that this will not be done if the bill or any substantial provisions in it are enacted into law. Diligent efforts are made to present the bill in the guise of a meritorious and mild bill.

It is said, for example, that the bill is simply designed to secure voting rights for Negroes in Southern States. I am going to say this bluntly, and I will say it plainly, so that he who runs may read and not err in so doing: There is not a scintilla of truth in the oft-repeated assertion that the bill is simply designed to secure voting rights to Negroes in Southern States. The bill proposes to confer upon the Attorney General of the United States the power to bring suit to suppress any of the practices specified in section 1985, title 42, of the United States Code. This section contains three subsections, and each of these subsections has many clauses. I call attention to one clause alone. It contains a provision authorizing the Attorney General to bring suit at the expense of the taxpayers in the name of the United States in cases where there are any conspiracies threatening or consummated to deprive any person of the equal protection of the law under the 14th amendment.

Under that clause alone the Attorney General can bring suit in behalf of any citizens of any race, any aliens of any race, and any private corporations within the territorial jurisdiction of the United States upon the allegation that they have been discriminated against by any statute of any State or any application of State law to them on the part of any State or local officials. When we consider the fact that the term "State law" includes ordinances of municipalities, we get some idea of the breadth of the power which the Attorney General would have under this one clause.

Mr. President, I hold in my hand volume 16A of Corpus Juris Secundum. I invite the attention of the Senate to the provisions of pages 269 to 536, inclusive, of this volume. These 240 pages are required merely to state in the most general way the number of subjects concerning which the Attorney General could litigate, at the expense of private taxpayers, on behalf of citizens, aliens, and private corporations under this one clause of subsection 3, section 1985, title 42 of the United States Code.

The Attorney General, under part III of the proposed law, would be empowered to bring literally hundreds upon hundreds of different types of cases, in addition to cases to secure voting rights and to compel the integration of public schools. Mr. President, in every one of those cases the President would have the authority, under section 1993, of title 42, to call out the Army, the Navy, or the militia to enforce the decrees entered in any one of those hundreds upon hundreds of cases.

The civil-rights bill is, in truth, as drastic and indefensible a legislative proposal as was ever submitted to any legislative body in this country.

When all is said, it is not surprising that this is so. The bill is presented to Congress at a time when never-ending agitation on racial subjects by both designing and sincere men impairs our national sanity, and diminishes in substantial measure the capacity of our public men to see the United States steady and to see it whole.

The bill is based on the strange thesis that the best way to promote the civil rights of some Americans is to rob other Americans of civil rights equally as precious and to reduce the supposedly sovereign States to meaningless zeros on the Nation's map.

The only reason advanced by the proponents of the bill for urging its enactment is, in essence, an insulting and insupportable indictment of a whole people. They say that southern officials and southern people are generally faithless to their oaths as public officers and jurors, and for that reason can be justifiably denied the right to invoke for their protection in courts of justice the constitutional and legal safeguards erected in times past by the Founding Fathers and Congress to protect all Americans from governmental tyranny.

When all is said, the bill, if enacted, would make the constitutional and legal status of Southern State officials and southern local officials inferior to that of murderers, rapists, counterfeiters, smugglers, dope peddlers, and parties to the Communist conspiracy.

Congress would do well to pause and ponder this indisputable fact: The provisions of the bill are far broader than the reasons assigned for urging its enactment. I say to my friends who champion the bill that if these provisions can be used today to make legal pariahs and second-class litigants out of southerners involved in civil-right cases, they can be used with equal facility tomorrow to reduce other Americans involved in countless other cases to the like status.

The drastic provisions of the bill are even more surprising than the thesis of its proponents or the reason given by them for urging its enactment. They ignore the primary lesson taught by history, that is, that no man is fit to be trusted with unlimited governmental power.

If the bill should be enacted by Congress and successfully run the constitutional gauntlet, it would vest in a single fallible human being; namely, the temporary occupant of the Office of Attorney General, regardless of his character or qualifications, autocratic, and despotic powers, which have no counterpart in American history, and which are repugnant to the basic concepts underlying and supporting the American constitutional and legal systems.

When one studies the bill, he finds, to his utter consternation, that it undertakes to delegate to the Attorney General of the United States the power, at his uncontrolled election, to nullify State statutes prescribing administrative remedies duly enacted by State legislatures in the undoubted exercise of the legislative powers reserved to the States by the 10th amendment. If that provision of the bill can be sustained from the standpoint of the Constitution, then our Constitution has become a rope of sand, affording no protection to the States or the people of the Nation.

Our ancestors appraised at its full value the everlasting truth embodied in Daniel Webster's assertion that "whatever government is not a government of laws is a despotism, let it be called what it may."

Consequently, they based the governmental and legal systems of America upon these fundamental concepts:

First, that our Government should be a government by law and not a government by men—a government in which laws should have authority over men, not men over laws.

Second, that our courts should administer equal and exact justice according to certain and uniform laws applying in like manner to all men in like situations.

Parts III and IV of the civil-rights bill provide, in substance, that "the Attorney General may institute for the United States, or in the name of the United States," a new civil action or proceeding to enforce or vindicate certain supposed civil rights of private citizens.

By these words, the bill proposes to do these two things: First, to establish a new procedure for the enforcement or vindication of certain supposed civil rights of private persons at the expense of the taxpayers; and second, to confer upon one fallible human being, namely, the temporary occupant of the office of Attorney General, whoever he may be, the despotic power to grant the benefit of the new procedure to some persons and to withhold it from others.

The proposed law is not to be operative at all unless the Attorney General, acting either with or without reason, so wills. This is not government by law. This is not even government by men. This is government by the whim and caprice of the Attorney General.

It is to be noted, moreover, that the new procedure to be authorized by the bill is to be used for and against such persons only as the Attorney General may select. This being true, the bill is utterly repugnant to the fundamental concept that courts are created to administer equal and exact justice in compliance with certain and uniform laws applying in like manner to all men in like circumstances.

When all is said on this phase of the matter, Congress is asked to enact the civil-rights bill as a public law, and, at the same time, to make the public law the private possession of the temporary occupant of the office of the Attorney General, whoever he may be. The bill does not give civil rights to anybody. It does not give anybody any rights, except the Attorney General of the United States; and it says that he is to have complete authority over the law.

I am somewhat surprised that some of my Democratic colleagues show a disposition to place so much confidence in the occupant of the office of Attorney General. I am unwilling to repose so much confidence in any human being who ever trod earth's surface. I would never vote to pass a public law and make it the private possession of the occupant of any office, especially in the case of an office whose occupant is ordinarily appointed to it because of his political acumen rather than his legal ability.

If one is to understand the laws and institutions of today, he must know the events of yesterday which gave them birth. For this reason, I deem it necessary to consider the origins of relevant constitutional and legal safeguards.

The founders of our Government were wise men.

They knew that tyranny uses the forms of law to crush those who oppose her will.

They knew that the right of trial by jury is the best security of the people against governmental oppression.

They knew that the surest test of a witness is had when he is confronted on cross-examination by counsel for the adverse party.

They knew the history of the long struggle of the English people to secure and preserve such basic legal safeguards as the right of trial by jury and the right to confront and cross-examine adverse witnesses.

They knew the history of the repeated efforts of tyrannical kings and subservient parliaments to deprive the English people of the benefit of such legal safeguards.

They knew the history of the Court of Star Chamber, and rightly deducted from it "that the rights and liberties of the people will not long survive in any country where the administration of the law is committed exclusively to a caste endowed with boundless discretion and a long term of office, no matter how learned, able, and honest its members may be."

They knew the history of Chief Justice Jeffreys and his bloody assizes, and rightly inferred from it that tyranny on the bench is as objectionable as tyranny on the throne.

They knew that it is abhorrent to justice to punish any man twice for the same offense.

They knew that in 1764 and 1765 the British Parliament, at the instigation of King George III and his ministers, enacted the Sugar Act, the Stamp Act, and other measures, whereby they deprived American colonists of the right of trial by jury in cases arising under the revenue and trade laws by a device astoundingly similar to that invoked by the civil-rights bill, namely, "by extending beyond its ancient limits the jurisdiction of the courts of admiralty" in which trial by jury was not available.

They knew that the Stamp Act Congress, which was attended by delegates from nine of the Thirteen Colonies, forthwith met in New York, and adopted the Colonial Declaration of Rights of October 19, 1765, condemning this action of Parliament on the ground "that trial by jury is the inherent and invaluable right of every British subject in these Colonies."

They knew that in 1768 the British Parliament, at the urging of King George III and his ministers, enacted the statute known as 8 George III, chapter 22, whereby they deprived American colonists of the right of trial by jury in cases arising under the laws relating to trade and revenue by a repetition of the device resembling that invoked by the civil-rights bill, namely, "by extending beyond their ancient limits the powers of the courts of admiralty" in which trial by jury was not available.

They knew that the First Continental Congress adopted the Declaration of October 14, 1774, denouncing this action of the British Parliament on the ground that American colonists were entitled to the common law of England, and more especially to the great and inestimable privilege of being tried by their peers of the vicinage according to the course of that law.

They knew that the Declaration of Independence assigned the fact that American colonists had been deprived in many cases of the benefits of trial by jury as one of the injuries and usurpations requiring the American colonists to dissolve their political bands with England.

They knew that tranquillity was not to be always anticipated in a republic; that strife would rise between classes and sections, and even civil war might come; and that in such times judges themselves might not be safely trusted in criminal cases, especially in prosecutions for political offenses, where the whole power of the executive is arrayed against the accused party.

The knew that what was done in the past might be attempted in the future, and that troublous times would arise, when rulers and people would become restive under restraint, and seek by sharp and decisive methods to accomplish ends deemed just and proper and that the principles of constitutional liberty would be in peril, unless established by irrepealable law.

They knew that the best part of the inheritance of America from England was the right of trial by jury, both in criminal cases and in suits at common law. For these reasons, the founders of our Government enshrined these guaranties in the Constitution:

That "the trial of all crimes, except in cases of impeachment, shall be by jury."—article III, section 2.

That "no person shall be held to answer for a capital, or otherwise infamous offense, unless on a presentment or indictment of a grand jury, except in cases arising in the land or naval forces, or in the militia, when in actual service in time of war or public danger; nor shall any person be subject for the same offense to be twice put in jeopardy of life or limb"—amendment 5.

That "in all criminal prosecutions, the accused shall enjoy the right to a speedy and public trial, by an impartial jury of the State and district wherein the crime shall have been committed . . . and to be informed of the nature and cause of the accusation; to be confronted with the witnesses against him; to have compulsory process for obtaining witnesses in his favor, and to have the assistance of counsel for his defense"—amendment 6.

That "in suits at common law, where the value in controversy shall exceed $20, the right of trial by jury shall be preserved"—amendment 7.

Americans in general and Senators in particular will do well to pause and ponder the statement made a few days ago by a great Pennsylvania lawyer, David F. Maxwell, the retiring president of the American Bar Association, before the State bar of Texas, in an accurate and eloquent answer to the charge that trial by jury is an outmoded, time-consuming process which can be replaced by more efficient legal procedure. After pointing out the truth that a group of average citizens sitting as jurors can mete out more even justice than can the most competent and experienced judge, Mr. Maxwell said:

> Let us in this country take warning; the jury alone is able to function as the thin wedge of reserved power that separates our system of law from the monolithic, totalitarian despotism behind the Iron and Bamboo Curtains.

At the time of the ratification of the Constitution, courts of equity existed in the several States, either in conjunction with, or independent of, the courts of law. The basis of the jurisdiction then exercised by courts of equity, which historically function without juries, was the protection of private rights of property.

In stating that courts of equity historically function without juries, I do not overlook the circumstance that the chancellor or judge of such a court has discretionary authority to call an advisory jury to his aid. An advisory jury is not a jury, however, in the real sense of the term, because the chancellor or judge is at liberty to reject its verdict and act solely on his own findings.

In some of the cases cognizable by them at the time of the ratification of the Constitution, courts of equity used restraining orders and temporary and permanent injunctions. The role of the restraining order and the temporary injunction was to preserve the status quo in respect to property in dispute until the conflicting claims to it could be determined in a trial on the merits, and the role of the permanent injunction was to secure the enjoyment of the property by the person adjudged its owner in the trial on the merits. Restraining orders and injunctions did not issue to inhibit criminal acts except in cases where such acts threatened irreparable injury to property rights.

In urging the ratification of the Constitution, Alexander Hamilton made a statement, which appears in esssay No. 80, in the Federalist, concerning the jurisdiction of courts of equity at that time. The statement reads as follows:

> It has also been asked, what need of the word "equity"? What equitable causes can grow out of the Constitution and laws of the United States? There is hardly a subject of litigation between individuals, which may not involve those ingredients of fraud, accident, trust, or hardship, which would render the matter an object of equitable rather than of legal jurisdiction, as the distinction is known and established in several of the States. It is the peculiar province, for instance, of a court of equity to relieve against what are called hard bargains: these are contracts in which, though there may have been no direct fraud or deceit, sufficient to invalidate them in a court of law, yet there may have been some undue and unconscionable advantage taken of the necessities or misfortunes of one of the parties, which a court of equity would not tolerate. In such cases, where foreigners were concerned on either side, it would be impossible for the Federal judicatories to do justice without an equitable as well as a legal jurisdiction. Agreements to convey lands claimed under the grants of different States, may afford another example of the necessity of an equitable jurisdiction in the Federal courts. This reasoning may not be so palpable in those States where the formal and technical distinction between law and equity is not maintained, as in this State, where it is exemplified by every day's practice.

I read Alexander Hamilton's statement concerning equity jurisdiction as it existed at the time of the ratification of the Constitution, to point out the fact that all claims that this bill provides for a customary use of equity process, is wholly without foundation in fact as well as in equity.

Courts of equity punished disobedience to restraining orders and injunctions by fines or imprisonment in proceedings for contempt conducted by chancellors or judges without juries.

It seems appropriate to note at this point changes occurring in the field of equity since the ratification of the Constitution. Since that time many States have extended the right of trial by jury to issues of fact arising in actions of an equitable nature. As this has not been done on the Federal level, actions of an equitable nature are still triable on the merits by judges without juries in district courts of the United States.

Beginning with the Interstate Commerce Commission Act of 1887, Congress has adopted 28 statutes creating new public rights and corresponding new public wrongs. The new public rights are enforcible by injunctive process as rights of the United States in its capacity as a sovereign nation in actions brought by the United States or specified Federal officials or agencies. The new public wrongs are punishable in the manner prescribed by law for other crimes. A painstaking analysis makes it obvious that each of the 28 statutes is clearly distinguishable from the civil-rights bill. In consequence, I refrain from further comment upon them.

The injunctive process is susceptible to abuse. This is particularly true when its use is extended beyond its ancient limits to the field occupied by criminal law.

Some of the objections to the use of the injunctive process in this field are well stated by a legal writer in these words:

> The objections to criminal equity are that it deprives defendant of his jury trial; that it deprives him of the protection of the higher burden of proof required in criminal prosecutions; that after imprisonment and fine for violation of an equity injunction, defendant may be subjected under the criminal law to punishment for the same acts; that it substitutes for the definite penalties fixed by the legislature whatever punishment for contempt a particular judge may see fit to exact; that it is often no more than an attempt to overcome by circumvention the supposed shortcomings of jurors; and that it may result, or induce the public to believe that it results, in the arbitrary exercise of power or in government by injuction. (43 C. J. S., Injunctions, sec. 150.)

Happily, the use of the injunctive process was confined in large measure to its ancient limits during the first century of our national existence.

Unhappily, however, its susceptibility to abuse was clearly revealed at the end of that period, when courts of equity, acting on the allegations of employers that such action was necessary to protect their property rights from irreparable injury, converted the extraordinary writ of injunction to ordinary and wholesale use to defeat the efforts of labor to secure fair wages and reasonable working conditions.

The most shameful story in the judicial annals of America was written during the ensuing years, when courts of equity robbed labor of its right to trial by jury, its right to freedom of the press, and its right to freedom of speech by substituting government by injunction for government by law.

Space and time preclude a review of the numerous episodes in this shameful story. Consequently we must content ourselves with calling attention to only one of them—the one recorded in the case of *Gompers* v. *the United States* (233 U. S. 604).

In that case Samuel Gompers, one of the wisest and most patriotic labor leaders of America of all time, was charged with contempt of court because of his alleged disobedience to an injunction issued by a Federal court of the District of Columbia on the application of Bucks Stove & Range Co., which undertook to defeat by the injunctive process the demands of its striking employees for better working conditions.

A Federal judge sitting without a jury adjudged Gompers guilty of contempt and sentenced him to jail for disobedience of the injunction because he had truthfully stated orally and in print that no law compelled his hearers and readers to buy a stove manufactured by Bucks Stove & Range Co.

Gompers managed to escape actual service of the jail sentence merely because the Supreme Court held on his appeal that the contempt proceedings had not been initiated within 3 years after the violations alleged, and in consequence the trial judge had lost his power to punish Gompers for contempt under the 3-year statute of limitations.

The abuse of the injunctive and contempt processes in industrial controversies prompted Congress to enact in 1914 as a section of the Clayton Act a statutory provision extending the right of trial by jury under certain circumstances to respondents in proceedings to punish violations of injunctions as indirect contempts of court. An indirect contempt is one committed outside the presence of the court.

This statutory provision is now embodied in somewhat altered phraseology in sections 402 and 3691 of title 13 of the United States Code. . . .

During the Senate debate, rumors spread across the country that the Administration planned to weaken the bill in order to assure the passage of some sort of legislation. On July 12, E. Frederic Morrow advised Sherman Adams that the Administration should stand fast.

Memorandum from Presidential Assistant E. Frederic Morrow to The Assistant to the President Sherman Adams
July 12, 1957
[Morrow Files, Eisenhower Papers.]

This note is not intended to be presumptuous, but informative.

Negro citizens are alarmed over reports that the Administration will "soften" the requirements of the Administration bill on Civil Rights before Congress. The general feeling is that this is a very definite retreat from the Platform of the Administration and the attitude on Civil Rights it has maintained since California. Negroes are primarily concerned with and in Civil Rights legislation, so they would rather have no legislation at all than to have a watered-down version that would merely be giving lip service to democratic ideals.

The rapid manner in which the bill went through the House and the forthright way in which Senator Knowland got the bill before the Senate had the Administration and the Republican Party well on the way toward regaining the confidence and the votes of Negro voters in this country.

However, in the last few days the talk of Administration capitulation to the South has resulted in a complete turnabout in feeling and attitude by Negro leadership.

Any weakening of the Administration bill will make it very difficult for any speaker to appear before Negro audiences in this country in an appeal for support in 1958 and 1960. It is my personal feeling that up till now the Republicans have maintained a strong moral position that win, lose or draw would have resulted in a new strength and new admiration on the part of millions of American voters. As it stands now we are not only threatened with loss of this high moral position, but also with possible loss of the legislation and thousands of potential votes.

⊢━◦━━◦

The Administration and Republican senators did indeed stand fast, as the President's statement of July 16 noted.

Statement by President Eisenhower on the Objectives of the Civil Rights Bill
July 16, 1957
[*Public Papers of the Presidents: 1957* (Washington, 1958), 545.]

I am gratified that the Senate, by a vote of 71 to 18 has now made H. R. 6127 the pending business before that body.

This legislation seeks to accomplish these four simple objectives:

1. To protect the constitutional right of all citizens to vote regardless of race or color. In this connection we seek to uphold the traditional authority of the Federal courts to enforce their orders. This means that a jury trial should not be interposed in contempt of court cases growing out of violations of such orders.

2. To provide a reasonable program of assistance in efforts to protect other constitutional rights of our citizens.

3. To establish a bi-partisan Presidential commission to study and recommend any further appropriate steps to protect these constitutional rights.

4. To authorize an additional Assistant Attorney General to administer the legal responsibilities of the Federal Government involving civil rights.

The details of language changes are a legislative matter. I would hope, however, that the Senate, in whatever clarification it may determine to make, will keep the measure an effective piece of legislation to carry out these four objectives—each one of which is consistent with simple justice and equality afforded to every citizen under the Constitution of the United States.

I hope that Senate action on this measure will be accomplished at this session without undue delay.

‒‒‒

Despite some success, the legislation was in grave danger of being either amended to death or entirely defeated. Val Washington's July 18 letter to Eisenhower reflected the gloomy mood that prevailed among the measure's supporters.

Val Washington to President Eisenhower
July 18, 1957
[Morrow Files, Eisenhower Papers.]

Dear Mr. President:

I did not feel until today that it was necessary to write you about this unfortunate Civil Rights fiasco which is in the headlines of every paper throughout the World.

At the outset, let me say that your Civil Rights Bill is a very moderate one, so what is there to compromise? It does nothing more than call for protective measures guaranteeing all of the rights due any citizen under the Constitution of the United States and the Supreme Court decisions.

Most certainly if the southern opponents of the bill do not intend to continue taking advantage of and ignoring the Civil Rights of Negroes, there is nothing in any of the four points which they could possibly resent either in language or fact.

I am not a radical or extremist, but as a Negro I have always sought and demanded my rights within the orderly processes of the law. I shall continue to do so. There are many of us who have worked and patiently waited years for a Republican regime willing to change unlawful traditions which rob us of our rights as first-class citizens. We knew that in you we had a leader who would, when given an opportunity, rectify the flagrant injustices and inequities by which we have been penalized. This situation has existed for years through no fault of our own.

I refuse to believe that you would ever compromise any basic right because of pressures from those so prejudiced that they wish to continue humiliating loyal citizens. We have a right to share and share alike in all that is a part of the American way of life—the sweet as well as the bitter. I know you will not let us down.

>●━●━○━○━○━○━●━○━○━○━○━○━○━●━○━○━○━●━●━●━○━●━○━●━●━●━●━○━●━<

In sharp contrast to Washington's letter was one sent the President by former South Carolina Governor James Byrnes, one of the South's most prominent segregationist leaders. Byrnes' comments which went beyond the constitutional issues, brought a quick and precise answer from Eisenhower.

Former Governor James Byrnes to President Eisenhower
July 17, 1957
[Official File 102-B-3, Eisenhower Papers.]

Dear Mr. President:
I think you will agree I have not burdened you with unsolicited advice. I write you now only because of the statement you were quoted as having made at your press conference that you did not fully understand some of the language of the civil rights bill; and further, because of your statement issued yesterday that the pending legislation should permit courts to preserve their traditional right to enforce their orders.

As early as last September, in addressing the Vermont Bar Association, I warned that upon information received from a source regarded by me as reliable, an effort would be made by the Department of Justice to circumvent the laws of the United States so as to permit a Judge to imprison a citizen charged with contempt of court without granting the defendant the right of trial by a jury. The statute specifically provides for a jury trial for any person charged with criminal contempt of court whenever the act complained of constitutes not only a violation of the court order, but the criminal law either of the United States or a state *UNLESS* the United States government is a party to the suit in which the injunction is issued.

This year in Illinois and in Ohio, in addressing those State Bar Associations, I noted that I had not been wrong in my prediction; that in Clinton, Tennessee, in a suit between several citizens and county school officials, which had been pending for more than a year, sixteen persons had been arrested, charged with contempt of court for violation of a court order, enjoining interference with the administration of the school. The alleged interference was an attack by one of the group against a citizen who had escorted Negro children to the school. Since the United States was not a party to the suit, the defendants clearly were entitled to a jury trial because the alleged offense was a violation of state laws.

In order to circumvent the law of the United States, the Department of Justice, through the District Attorney in Tennessee, petitioned the court last January to make the United States a party to the suit. The petition was granted. It was evident the sole purpose of intervention was to evade the statute and deny defendants a jury trial. Many editors and columnists in and out of the South, protested against this circumvention. Someone realized they could not explain or defend such conduct and a department official announced that the government would not oppose the motion of the defendants for a jury trial.

This history justifies the statement of Senator Russell as to what may be expected of the department if the civil rights bill should be passed without provision for a jury trial. In your statement you refer to the "traditional right" of a court to enforce its orders. The question in Tennessee was not whether the court would follow tradition, but whether it would follow the law of the United States. The Attorney General, recognizing that under the present law he could not deny to a defendant the right of trial by a jury, now seeks by the provisions of the civil rights bill to change the law. He seeks the authority to bring an action in the name of the United States against a citizen whenever he believes that citizen has violated the law or threatens to violate the law. He will then ask for an injunction against the citizen and for an alleged violation he will seek a conviction by a judge instead of a jury. That is too much power to vest in any Attorney General. You may believe Mr. Brownell would not abuse the power but he will not be Attorney General forever. Power should never be vested in any individual on the theory it will not be exercised.

The only excuse offered by the Attorney General for refusing a citizen the constitutional right of trial by a jury, is that "juries in the South would not convict." That is an insult to the men and women of the South. You appoint Judges, but the appointments are made from a list recommended by the Attorney General. If any of the District Judges now in office aspire to the Circuit Court of Appeals or the Supreme Court, that ambition will be gratified only if the Department of Justice makes a favorable recommendation. If any one said the Attorney General wants the right to arrest a citizen and have him tried by a Judge because the Judge can receive judicial promotion only upon the recommendation of the Attorney General, I would think it an insult to the Attorney General and the Judges. It is equally insulting to fifty million people in the Southern States to say there cannot be found honest men and women to serve on juries in the United States Courts.

You submitted your political fortunes to the people of the Southern States and they have shown great confidence in you. I hope you will show some confidence in them. With all good wishes . . .

President Eisenhower to James Byrnes
July 23, 1957

[Official File 102-B-3, Eisenhower Papers.]

Dear Governor Byrnes:

Your letter, just received, expresses sentiments shared by others who have written about the Civil Rights legislation. Time and time again in press conferences I have pointed out that the practice of segregating educational facilities was authorized by the law of the land, under Supreme Court ruling, from 1896 to 1954. Under that ruling, I have also explained, customs were established in certain sections of our country which were repudiated and declared illegal by the Supreme Court ruling of 1954, a ruling concerning which I had no more advance notice than did you or any other individual citizen.

It was my purpose, thereafter, in considering the responsibilities of the Executive Department, to provide a moderate approach to a difficult problem and to make haste slowly in seeking to meet it. Certainly there has been no intent on my part to recommend punitive legislation. Both of us know full well that in a government such as ours, primary reliance for law enforcement has to be upon general acceptance of legislation and voluntary compliance with it. I believe that in the question under discussion there are moral values as well as legal requirements to be considered; moreover, I am aware that emotions are deeply stirred on both sides.

The specific point you wrote me about—the jury trial—is essentially a legal matter. But as I read your letter, it seems to me that what you are really objecting to is the giving of authority to the Attorney General to institute civil actions. The pending legislation, however, was conceived under the theory that the whole public has an interest in protection of the right, for example, to vote—that the Attorney General should be given authority to enforce this public right by civil action, just as he now has authority to enforce it by criminal prosecution.

It seems to me that the public interest in the protection of voting rights is at least as great as the public interest in the maintenance of minimum wages, or in the truthfulness of financial and other statements in connection with securities sales, or in the shipment in interstate commerce of contraband oil. In all of these instances—and there are many more that could be cited—the Attorney General is authorized to bring suits to enjoin violations of the law (for which criminal penalties are also provided), and violations of such injunctions are tried without a jury. It seems to me that the right to vote is more important in our way of life than are the regulations cited above.

Certainly I never said—and I have no recollection of the Attorney General ever having said—that "juries in the South will not convict." But I don't see how we can provide for a jury trial in this legislation and leave the rest of the great body of Federal law covered by the rule of no jury trial.

With regard to a press conference statement of mine that I "did not fully understand some of the language of the bill," I was referring to conflicting legal opinions that had been given me regarding Section III. One of these opinions was that the authority sought would be clearly circumscribed and limited by other existing laws; the other opinion was that the authority could, in ambitious hands, be expanded to constitute a virtual police state procedure. As I stated at the beginning of this letter, the last thing I desire is to persecute anyone.

I note you expressed hope that I should show confidence in the people of the South. I am compelled to wonder why you have to express such a thought as nothing more than a hope. Many of my dearest friends are in that region, I spent a not inconsiderable part of my life in the South or in border states, and, moreover, this question of assuring the civil rights of all citizens does *not* apply exclusively to the southern areas.

I do not feel that I need yield to anyone in my respect for the sentiments, convictions, and character of the average American, no matter where he may happen to dwell.

I would appreciate it if you would convey my warm greetings to Mrs. Byrnes and, of course, best wishes to yourself.

By the end of the first week in August the Senate had seriously weakened the bill by passing an amendment permitting jury trials in contempt cases. Val Washington's anger at this turn of events led to a public letter that denounced Senate Majority Leader Lyndon Johnson's role in the proceedings. In the following days the House refused to accept the Senate's version of the bill, which had passed on August 7. In the midst of great pressure from the White House, strong public statements from civil rights organizations, and sincere efforts on the part of many congressmen to get the best bill possible, behind-the-scenes negotiations sought an acceptable compromise. Senator Johnson broke the logjam by obtaining significant Southern support to allow jury trials only under certain circumstances in contempt situations arising from voting rights proceedings. This cleared the way for quick action, and despite a slight delay from a last ditch Southern filibuster, the President signed the bill on September 9. There was no signing statement, however, because of the Little Rock crisis.

Val Washington to Senator Lyndon Johnson
August 6, 1957

[Morrow Files, Eisenhower Papers.]

Dear Senator Johnson:

In reading the morning papers I notice that you have attacked Vice President Nixon for expressing his honest conviction about the failure of the Senate to concur with the House and the President in formulating a decent and fair Civil Rights Bill.

This Bill, which was meant to protect the voting rights of many millions of Negroes in Southern states and to guarantee their rights under the 14th Amendment of the Constitution, was emasculated by the adroit handling of you with the aid of other Democrat leaders.

To accuse Vice President Nixon of playing politics certainly is not in good taste coming from you. Your record is one of continuous voting against all Civil Rights during your terms in both the House and the Senate.

On this particular piece of legislation you registered these unfriendly votes: (1) On June 20 you voted to send the Bill to the Judiciary Committee headed by Senator Eastland. In his hands it would have died without ever having been considered. (2) On July 16 you voted again (on Senator Wayne Morse's motion) to send it to the Judiciary Committee which would not have acted on it. (3) On July 24 you voted to strike Part 3 of the Bill. This would have allowed Negroes to enjoy the same civil rights of all other American citizens under the 14th Amendment to the Constitution. (4) On August 1 you voted for Trial by Jury in voting rights cases which would automatically eliminate any chance for Negroes to be protected in most Southern states.

If a Southern jury would not convict confessed kidnappers of Emmett Till after he was found murdered, why would they convict an election official for refusing to give a Negro his right of suffrage?

Friday, August 2, shortly after midnight, one of the blackest days in American history was recorded for Negroes and other dark races, not only in the United States, but around the world.

For over 80 years there has not been one civil rights bill seriously considered by the United States Senate. After over 50 years of earnest effort on the part of Negroes and their friends we finally had our day before that great democratic body, the United States Senate.

Even though we have fought and died in every war in defense of our country, paid taxes for support of government institutions and have honored all other responsibilities expected of citizens, the Senate yielded to the dictates of 11 Southern states. These are the same states which kept Negroes enslaved for nearly 250 years. It was the same section of the country where the controlling politicians still try to operate under slave day philosophy that a Negro has no right a white man has to respect.

As a result of the 3 weeks deliberation in the Senate 5 million Negroes, or over 30 per cent of the population of these 11 states will still be deprived of their right to vote, in this, the greatest democracy in the world. The right to vote without coercion and humiliation would have been a very small concession to these millions of loyal Americans in their many years of struggle for first-class citizenship.

If the Senate had passed the Eisenhower Civil Rights Bill as the House did, it could have been pointed to as a beacon which would have cast its light over all the world. It would have been a signal to all darker races to rally to the cause of democracy and stand up against efforts to communize the world.

In the Senate, the drum beaters for democracy and constitutional government have been weighed in the balance and found wanting. They have joined in the greatest mockery and travesty on justice debated in the Senate in the past 80 years.

At the bar of world opinion the United States has lost one of the greatest sales points of a democracy for the recruiting of new advocates—Equality for all its citizens regardless of Race, Creed, Color or National Origin.

Since you have been so persistent in your anti-civil rights attitude, one would have to be suspect of your supposed change of heart. I am positive, Senator that neither you, nor any of your Southern colleagues would vote for this Bill unless you know it is meaningless and ineffective.

Most certainly the Vice President need not apologize for being disappointed in the Senate's action because his feeling is shared by many millions of Americans.

Interest in the new Civil Rights Commission came from varied sources. Samuel Lubell, a noted political analyst, displayed his concern in the following letter.

Samuel Lubell to Cabinet Secretary Maxwell Rabb
October 31, 1957
[Morrow Files, Eisenhower Papers.]

Dear Max,

Thought you'd be interested in the new Opinion Reporting Workshop which we're setting up at the Columbia School of Journalism. We're announcing it this week-end. The enclosed paper is a memorandum that was used around Columbia University to explain the project.

It's too bad we couldn't get Foundation support for that study I proposed of how people in the South feel about desegregation. If it had gone through we would have had our work done just about when Little Rock hit. Think how valuable it would be now to know what specific measures of gradual desegregation would command the greatest support in the South and among what groups.

As a matter of fact the study should still be made. Some weeks ago, as you probably know, I wrote Mr. Brownell suggesting that the new Civil Rights Commission that is to be named be assigned the job of developing a program of compliance with the court through gradual desegregation on a basis that would serve as a rallying ground for all the forces of law and order in the country. I won't go into the reasons for such an action since I assume that my letter to Mr. Brownell, or its contents, got to your attention. He wrote me that he was going to pass on my thoughts to the White House staff people dealing with the problem.

Anyway whether the fact-finding is done by and for this Civil Rights Commission or independently, it should be done. The best time to get into the field would be this spring so the survey could be finished in time for its impact on the next school year.

Although great hopes had been raised by the passage of the 1957 Civil Rights Act, the Civil Rights Commission, like any other new organization, had to solve many mundane problems.

Second Meeting of the Civil Rights Commission
January 10, 1958
[Morrow Files, Eisenhower Papers.]

Decisions

Space—The seventh floor of 726 Jackson Place will be taken over and used by the Commission after its renovation.

Travel Reimbursement—Commission members will be paid $12 per day for expenses and will also receive $50 per day when actually employed on the business of the Commission. This $50 per day can be claimed when all or any part of a day has been spent in actual work of the commission, whether at home, in transit or at the office.

Personnel—Mr. Price of the White House and Mr. Brasser of the Civil Service Commission will meet on Tuesday, Jan. 14, to discuss office personnel.

Staff Director—The names of Messrs. Baine, Kintner and Johnson were sent to the White House for confirmation and action. After a Staff Director has been decided upon, other staff members will be considered.

Purpose of the Commission—All members of the Commission agreed that: the first order was to carry out the Public Law in, 1. restoring the franchise to all American citizens, Negro, Puerto Rican, Mexican, etc., and, 2, to fulfill the second and third clauses of the Law. It was also decided to set up task forces, and committees in communities all over America and work with local outstanding citizens to overcome local tensions.

The second meeting of the President's Commission on Civil Rights came to order at approximately 9:30 a.m., January 10, 1958. President Eisenhower has designated Dean Storey as Vice Chairman of the Commission.

Mr. Douglas R. Price and Mr. Gerald Morgan, both of the White House, sat in on this meeting for the purpose of making helpful suggestions to the Commission.

The following discussion took place: *Travel*—Forms were distributed to all members of the Commission, and Mr. Price explained to the members how reimbursement for official travel was obtained.

Space—Mr. Price informed the Commission that at the present time, the entire seventh floor of 726 Jackson Place was vacant, and this space consisted of two suites, or ten rooms in all. He also informed the Commission that there would be additional space available in the future on the first floor, the mezzanine and the sixth floors. Chairman Hannah suggested using the seventh floor, and instructed Mr. Price to go ahead and make the necessary arrangements to renovate the space.

Personnel—Mr. Price suggested that Mr. Brasser from the Civil Service Commission go over proposed plans with Chairman Hannah. He informed the Commission that all employees except attorneys, who would be considered under Schedule A, had to be Civil Service employees. It was decided at the last meeting that a Staff Director would be necessary. Dr. Hannah mentioned borrowing a temporary Staff Director from some government agency until a permanent Director could be obtained. Mr. Price suggested that Mrs. Arth, of the State Department, take over the position temporarily. Dean Storey suggested approaching Mr. Brasser with reference to borrowing a man from the Civil Service Commission with the understanding that if he was liked, they would retain him permanently. Dr. Hannah asked Mr. Price to investigate this area. Mr. Price will meet with Mr. Brasser on Tuesday.

Dean Storey suggested going ahead on a temporary basis with Mrs. Arth. He also suggested renovating the 7th floor as soon as possible.

Gov. Carlton mentioned the matter of time with compensation. Mr. Price explained that expenses will be paid from the time left home, while the $50 per day may be obtained only when actual time is spent on official business. Mr. Price will get a definite determination on this. Dean Storey advanced the theory that it is pretty much left up to the individual.

Gov. Battle asked for the possible date of confirmation by the Senate on their appointments. Gov. Battle felt that definite commitments should not be made until confirmation had been received. Mr. Morgan felt that nomination would probably go up today or Tuesday. Dr. Hannah will sound out Sen. Eastland on this. Dr. Hannah thanked Mr. Price for his services to the Commission, and Mr. Price left.

Staff Director—At the last meeting, three men were decided on by the members of the Commission for the job of Staff Director. They were Ryan, Malone, and Littleton. However, none of these men have been able to accept the position of Staff Director.

At this point, much discussion ensued as to another list of possible names to be sent to the President for the position of Staff Director. The three names decided on, and agreed upon by all members of the Commission were: Charles Baine, Attorney at law, Earle W. Kintner of the Federal Trade Commission, and Walter R. Johnson, past Attorney General from Nebraska.

These men were chosen for their reputations, for their views on the Civil Rights question, for their ability to work hard and do the job at hand. Other names considered were: Wallace H. Savage, Elliott Richardson, William Rodgers, Dean Henry Brandis, Dean Fordham, Mr. Crawford, Mr.

James Moore, Mr. Coburn, Mr. Powell, Mr. Richards, Mr. Harry Ransom, Dean Ribble, Dean Coffman.

Purpose of the Commission—Father Hesburgh stressed the importance of assembling all the facts in this matter, in order to bring about an understanding of the problem at hand. Dr. Hannah agreed with Fr. Hesburgh's theory. Gov. Battle was impressed with the theory of taking up the voting privilege and working on that. Gov. Carlton said that while restoring the franchise was of prime importance, it was also necessary to establish good will. Sec. Wilkins stressed carrying out the responsibilities defined in the Public Law (85-315). Sec. Wilkins also advocated the making of recommendations and a report, and the forming of local committees. He thinks the Commission is going to have some hearings, in some communities, in order to get at the facts. Dr. Hannah agreed with the Sec. Father Hesburgh suggested that the Commission find out about the good work that is being done. Dean Storey felt that there were two definite things the Commission can do under the terms of the act. 1. Restore the voting rights to all Americans, and 2. constitute advisory committees. Dean Storey also suggested the use of task forces to help the Commission. It was decided that committees would be set up in only selected areas, but not necessarily all in the South. Dean Storey reminded the Commission members that the responsibilities of the Commission take in the Civil Rights of all Americans, such as Puerto Ricans, Mexicans, etc., as well as those of the colored race.

Agreed: To fulfill No. 1 of the Public law of the Civil Rights Commission. To carry out the mandate of Nos. 2 and 3. Meeting adjourned at approximately 3:50 P.M.

5. FEDERAL INTERVENTION IN THE LITTLE ROCK DESEGREGATION CRISIS

As early as 1955 the Little Rock School Board had submitted a plan for gradual school intergration which the federal courts approved. This proposal called for desegregation to begin at the high school level with the 1957 fall term. Since some school districts in Arkansas had already been peacefully integrated, almost all elected officials in Little Rock supported the plan, and few people expected serious difficulties. The state's Democratic governor, Orval Faubus, had a reputation as a "liberal" on the race issue and had not objected to any previous desegregation orders. Then, shortly before school opened for the fall term, a group of white parents asked an Arkansas state court to delay integration. Surprisingly, Governor Faubus testified on behalf of the plaintiffs and warned that racial mixing in Little Rock schools would result in violence. While the state court asked for a delay (August 29), a federal court rejected this position (August 30) and issued an order prohibiting any persons from disrupting "the opening of the integrated high school in the Little Rock School District on September 3." Faubus countered by mobilizing the Arkansas National Guard to bar black students (September 2). On the morning of September 3 a token contingent of nine black students were turned away by bayonet from Little Rock Central High School. The school, located on the edge of a racially changing residential neighborhood, was the most prestigious in Little Rock. At this early stage of the controversy no one knew exactly what the Federal Government would do. Back in mid-July Eisenhower had told the press about the unlikeliness of using federal force to integrate schools. Possibly reporters recalled this remark when they questioned him about the crisis.

Presidential News Conference
July 17, 1957

[*Public Papers of the Presidents: 1957* (Washington, 1958), 546.]

QUESTION. Merriman Smith, *United Press:* Mr. President, since you have had an opportunity to discuss your civil rights program with Attorney General Brownell, are you aware that under laws dating back to the

Reconstruction era, that you now have the authority to use military force to put through the school integration in the South, and are you aware, too, sir, that part 3 of your current bill carries this forward from the Reconstruction era?

THE PRESIDENT: Well, first of all, lawyers have differed about some of these authorities of which you speak, but I have been informed by various lawyers that that power does exist. But I want to say this: I can't imagine any set of circumstances that would ever induce me to send Federal troops into a Federal court and into any area to enforce the orders of a Federal court, because I believe that common sense of America will never require it.

Now, there may be that kind of authority resting somewhere, but certainly I am not seeking any additional authority of that kind, and I would never believe that it would be a wise thing to do in this country. . . .

Presidential News Conference
September 3, 1957

[*Public Papers of the Presidents: 1957* (Washington, 1958), 640–41, 648.]

QUESTION. Merriman Smith, *United Press:* Mr. President, over quite a wide section of the South today and this week, children are going back to school under difficult circumstances, in places where integration is being attempted for the first time.

We have a case in Arkansas this morning where the Governor has ordered State troops around a school that a Federal court had ordered integrated. I just wonder what you think of this situation.

THE PRESIDENT: Well, first, to say "what you think about it" is sort of a broad subject that you are giving me.

Actually, this particular incident came to my attention the first thing this morning. I have been in contact with the Attorney General's office. They are taking a look at it. They are going to find out exactly what has happened, and discuss this with the Federal judge. As of this moment, I cannot say anything further about the particular point, because that is all I know about it.

Now, time and again a number of people—I, among them—have argued that you cannot change people's hearts merely by laws. Laws presumably express the conscience of a nation and its determination or will to do something. But the laws here are to be executed gradually, according to the dictum of the Supreme Court, and I understand that the plan worked out by the school board of Little Rock was approved by the district judge. I believe it is a ten-year plan.

Now there seems to have been a road block thrown in the way of that plan, and the next decision will have to be by the lawyers and jurists.

*   *   *

QUESTION. Anthony Lewis, *The New York Times:* As to school integration, Mr. President, do you have any plans to take a personal part in the problem this fall, for example, by speaking on it or getting in touch with Governor Faubus of Arkansas?

THE PRESIDENT: My speaking will be always on this subject, as I have always done, urging Americans to recognize what America is, the concepts on which it is based, and to do their part so far as they possibly can to bring about the kind of America that was visualized by our forebears. Now, it is for this reason, because I know this is a slow process. The Supreme Court in its decision of '54 pointed out the emotional difficulties that would be encountered by Negroes if given equal but separate schools, and I think probably their reasoning was correct, at least I have no quarrel with it.

But there are very strong emotions on the other side, people that see a picture of a mongrelization of the race, they call it. They are very strong emotions, and we are going to whip this thing in the long run by Americans being true to themselves and not merely by law . . .

Since the federal courts had ordered the Little Rock School Board to integrate the local schools, the board immediately asked that it not be cited for contempt because of the governor's action. On September 3 a federal judge, after hearing testimony, reiterated the order for desegregation. The next day the court requested help from other federal agencies in its investigations. Faubus now feared that he might be arrested for contempt. He hurriedly sent a long telegram to the President. It received a quick reply. Faubus then responded in what seemed a conciliatory manner.

Governor Orval Faubus to President Eisenhower
September 4, 1957
[Official File 142-A-5-A, Eisenhower Papers.]

MR. PRESIDENT:

I WAS ONE OF THE SOLDIERS OF YOUR COMMAND IN WORLD WAR TWO. I SPENT 300 DAYS OF COMBAT WITH AN INFANTRY DIVISION DEFENDING OUR COUNTRY, ITS PEOPLE AND THEIR RIGHTS ON THE BATTLEFIELDS OF FIVE NATIONS.

THE QUESTION IN ISSUE AT LITTLE ROCK AT THIS MOMENT IS NOT INTEGRATION VS. SEGREGATION. PEACEFUL

INTEGRATION HAS BEEN ACCOMPLISHED FOR SOME TIME IN THE UNIVERSITY OF ARKANSAS, STATE SUPPORTED COLLEGES AND A NUMBER OF PUBLIC SCHOOLS. THIS WEEK PEACEFUL INTEGRATION WAS ACCOMPLISHED IN THREE MORE OF OUR LARGEST PUBLIC SCHOOLS—FORT SMITH, VAN BUREN, OZARK. IT IS IMPOSSIBLE TO INTEGRATE SOME OF OUR SCHOOLS AT THIS TIME WITHOUT VIOLENCE. THE SUPREME COURT RECOGNIZED THAT CONDITIONS IN EACH COMMUNITY MUST BE CONSIDERED AND I HAVE IN-TERPRETED YOUR PUBLIC STATEMENTS TO INDICATE THAT YOU ARE IN AGREEMENT WITH THIS PREMISE.

THE QUESTION NOW IS WHETHER OR NOT THE HEAD OF A SOVEREIGN STATE CAN EXERCISE HIS CONSTITUTIONAL POWERS AND DISCRETION IN MAINTAINING PEACE AND GOOD ORDER WITHIN HIS JURISDICTION, BEING ACCOUNT-ABLE TO HIS OWN CONSCIENCE AND TO HIS OWN PEOPLE.

CERTAIN UNITS OF THE NATIONAL GUARD HAVE BEEN PLACED ON DUTY TO PRESERVE THE PEACE AND GOOD OR-DER OF THIS COMMUNITY. YOU—AS A MILITARY MAN—KNOW THAT THE COMMANDER MUST HAVE THE AUTHORITY AND THE DISCRETION TO TAKE THE NECESSARY STEPS WAR-RANTED BY THE SITUATION WITH WHICH HE MUST DEAL.

I AM RELIABLY INFORMED THAT FEDERAL AUTHORITIES IN LITTLE ROCK HAVE THIS DAY BEEN DISCUSSING PLANS TO TAKE INTO CUSTODY, BY FORCE, THE HEAD OF A SOVEREIGN STATE. THIS WOULD BE IN COMPLETE DISREGARD OF THE CONSTITUTIONAL GUARANTEES OF THE SEPARATION AND INDEPENDENCE OF THE THREE BRANCHES OF GOVERNMENT AND THE RIGHTS AND POWERS OF A STATE. AS THE DULY ELECTED GOVERNOR AND REPRESENTATIVE OF THE PEOPLE OF ARKANSAS I CAN NO MORE SURRENDER THESE RIGHTS THAN YOU COULD SURRENDER THE RIGHTS OF THE DULY ELECTED CHIEF EXECUTIVE OF OUR NATION. TO DO SO WOULD SET A PRECEDENT THAT WOULD JEOPARDIZE THE RIGHTS AND POWERS OF THE GOVERNOR OF ANY STATE.

I MUST FOLLOW THE PRECEDENT SET BY YOU AS A CHIEF EXECUTIVE WHEN YOU DECLINED TO HAVE YOUR ADMINIS-TRATIVE AIDS SUMMONED TO TESTIFY BEFORE A CONGRES-SIONAL COMMITTEE.

I HAVE STRONG REASONS TO BELIEVE THAT THE TELE-PHONE LINES TO THE ARKANSAS EXECUTIVE MANSION HAVE BEEN TAPPED—I SUSPECT THE FEDERAL AGENTS. THE SITUA-TION IN LITTLE ROCK AND ARKANSAS GROWS MORE EX-PLOSIVE BY THE HOUR. THIS IS CAUSED FOR THE MOST PART

BY THE MISUNDERSTANDING OF OUR PROBLEMS BY A FEDERAL JUDGE WHO DECREED "IMMEDIATE" INTEGRATION OF THE PUBLIC SCHOOLS OF LITTLE ROCK WITHOUT HEARING ANY EVIDENCE WHATSOEVER AS TO THE CONDITIONS NOW EXISTING IN THIS COMMUNITY. THE SITUATION IS FURTHER AGGRAVATED BY THE IMPENDING UNWARRANTED INTERFERENCE OF FEDERAL AGENTS. IF THESE ACTIONS CONTINUE, OR IF MY EXECUTIVE AUTHORITY AS GOVERNOR TO MAINTAIN THE PEACE IS BREACHED, THEN I CAN NO LONGER BE RESPONSIBLE FOR THE RESULTS. THE INJURY TO PERSONS AND PROPERTY THAT WOULD BE CAUSED—THE BLOOD THAT MAY BE SHED, WILL BE ON THE HANDS OF THE FEDERAL GOVERNMENT AND ITS AGENTS. THE SPLENDID PROGRESS WE HAVE MADE IN ARKANSAS FOR THE PAST FEW YEARS TOWARD MEETING OUR PROBLEMS OF RACE RELATIONSHIP WILL HAVE BEEN COMPLETELY AND UTTERLY DESTROYED. MANY EXPRESSIONS OF FAIRNESS AND UNDERSTANDING HAVE COME FROM YOU REGARDING THE PROBLEMS OF THE SOUTH AND OF THE NATION. AS GOVERNOR OF ARKANSAS I APPEAL TO YOU TO USE YOUR GOOD OFFICES TO MODIFY THE EXTREME STAND AND STOP THE UNWARRANTED INTERFERENCE OF FEDERAL AGENTS IN THIS AREA SO THAT WE MAY AGAIN ENJOY DOMESTIC TRANQUILITY AND CONTINUE IN OUR PURSUIT OF IDEAL RELATIONS BETWEEN THE RACES.

TIME IS THE ESSENCE OF THE SITUATION WITH WHICH I AM CONFRONTED—MAY I HAVE THE ASSURANCE OF YOUR UNDERSTANDING AND COOPERATION?

President Eisenhower to Governor Orval Faubus
September 5, 1957
[Official File 142-A-5-A, Eisenhower Papers.]

Your telegram received requesting my assurance of understanding of and cooperation in the course of action you have taken on school integration recommended by the Little Rock School Board and ordered by the United States District Court pursuant to the mandate of the United States Supreme Court.

When I became President, I took an oath to support and defend the Constitution of the United States. The only assurance I can give you is that the Federal Constitution will be upheld by me by every legal means at my command.

There is no basis of fact to the statements you make in your telegram that Federal authorities have been considering taking you into custody or that telephone lines to your Executive Mansion have been tapped by any agency of the Federal Government.

At the request of Judge Davies, the Department of Justice is presently collecting facts as to interference with or failure to comply with the District Court's order. You and other state officials—as well as the National Guard which, of course, is uniformed, armed and partially sustained by the Government—will, I am sure, give full cooperation to the United States District Court.

Governor Orval Faubus to President Eisenhower
September 6, 1957
[Official File 142-A-5-A, Eisenhower Papers.]

MR PRESIDENT.

THANK YOU FOR YOUR TELEGRAM IN REPLY TO MY APPEAL FOR YOUR UNDERSTANDING AND COOPERATION IN CONNECTION WITH MY EFFORTS TO PRESERVE THE PUBLIC PEACE AND GOOD ORDER IN THIS COMMUNITY. I HAVE NOTIFIED THE UNITED STATES DISTRICT ATTORNEY AND THE F.B.I. THAT MY PERSONAL COUNSEL, WILLIAM J. SMITH, AND THE DIRECTOR OF ARKANSAS STATE POLICE, HERMAN LINDSEY, ARE AVAILABLE TO DISCUSS CERTAIN EVIDENCE UPON WHICH I ACTED TO PRESERVE THE PUBLIC PEACE. I SHALL COOPERATE IN UPHOLDING THE CONSTITUTION OF ARKANSAS AND THE NATION

While black students remained barred from Little Rock Central High, many people tried to mediate what was rapidly becoming a major constitutional confrontation between state and federal power. Democratic Congressman Brooks Hays, whose district included Little Rock, sought to act as a "go between" for Eisenhower and Faubus. Hays' efforts culminated in a September 14 conference at Newport, Rhode Island, where Eisenhower was resting after Congress had adjourned. In a telegram requesting the meeting, Faubus departed from a previously agreed upon text by adding that he would "comply with the order . . . consistent with my responsibilities under the Constitution of the United States and that of Arkansas." This addition disturbed the Attorney General, who thought that the governor should have mentioned only federal responsibilities. However, the President met with Faubus—despite still another telegram in which the governor called Newport "your vacation headquarters." On the surface, the conference went fairly well, as the final statements by both parties seemed to indicate.

Statement by President Eisenhower Following a Meeting with Governor Orval Faubus
September 14, 1957

[*Public Papers of the Presidents: 1957* (Washington, 1958), 674–75.]

At the request of Governor Faubus of Arkansas I met with him this morning in a constructive discussion regarding the carrying out of the orders of the Federal Court in the matter of the high schools of Little Rock.

The Governor stated his intention to respect the decisions of the United States District Court and to give his full cooperation in carrying out his responsibilities in respect to these decisions. In so doing, I recognize the inescapable responsibility resting upon the Governor to preserve law and order in his state.

I am gratified by his constructive and cooperative attitude at our meeting. I have assured the Governor of the cooperation of Federal officials. I was pleased to hear from the Governor of the progress already made in the elimination of segregation in other activities in the State of Arkansas.

I am sure it is the desire of the Governor not only to observe the supreme law of the land but to use the influence of his office in orderly progress of the plans which are already the subject of the order of the Court.

NOTE: The President's statement was released at the U.S. Naval Base, Newport, R.I. This release also included a statement by Governor Faubus, issued at Providence the same day. The Governor referred to "friendly and constructive discussion of the problem" with the President, and felt that his trip to Newport had been worthwhile. Among other things Governor Faubus stated "I have assured the President of my desire to cooperate with him in carrying out the duties resting upon both of us under the Federal Constitution. In addition, I must harmonize my actions under the Constitution of Arkansas with the requirements of the Constitution of the United States."

Following the Newport meeting Faubus returned home, kept the Arkansas National Guard at the high school, and continued to confer with Hays. Finally, after the federal court issued an injunction directing Faubus to stop interfering with integration of the school (September 20), he removed his forces, requested black parents to keep their children away, and asked for restraint by the people of Little Rock. He then left the state to attend the Southern Governor's Conference. Mayor Woodrow Wilson Mann of Little Rock announced that the school would open with local police maintaining order. However, on Monday morning, September 23, a howling mob overwhelmed the police. The mayor then sent an urgent telegram to the President requesting assistance.

Mayor Woodrow Mann to President Eisenhower
September 23, 1957
[Official File 142-A-5-A, Eisenhower Papers.]

THE PRESIDENT.

THE CITY POLICE, TOGETHER WITH THE STATE POLICE, MADE A VALIANT EFFORT TO CONTROL THE MOB TODAY AT CENTRAL HIGH SCHOOL. IN THE FINAL ANALYSIS, IT WAS DEEMED ADVISABLE BY THE OFFICER ON THE GROUND AND IN CHARGE TO HAVE THE COLORED CHILDREN REMOVED TO THEIR HOMES FOR SAFETY PURPOSES.

THE MOB THAT GATHERED WAS NO SPONTANEOUS ASSEMBLY. IT WAS AGITATED, AROUSED, AND ASSEMBLED BY A CONCERTED PLAN OF ACTION.

ONE OF THE PRINCIPAL AGITATORS IN THE CROWD WAS A MAN BY THE NAME OF JIMMY KARAM, WHO IS A POLITICAL AND SOCIAL INTIMATE OF GOVERNOR FAUBUS, AND WHOSE WIFE IS NOW WITH GOVERNOR'S PARTY AT THE SOUTHERN GOVERNOR'S CONFERENCE. KARAM HAS A LONG RECORD OF EXPERIENCE IN STRIKE-BREAKING, AND OTHER ACTIVITIES SUCH AS HE ENGAGED IN TODAY.

THE MANNER IN WHICH THE MOB WAS FORMED AND ITS ACTION, TOGETHER WITH THE PRESENCE OF JIMMY KARAM, LEADS TO THE INEVITABLE CONCLUSION THAT GOVERNOR FAUBUS AT LEAST WAS COGNIZANT OF WHAT WAS GOING TO TAKE PLACE.

DETAILED INFORMATION ON THE EVENTS OF THE DAY WILL BE TURNED OVER TO THE JUSTICE DEPARTMENT FOR SUCH ACTION AS THE FEDERAL GOVERNMENT DEEMS APPROPRIATE.

IF THE JUSTICE DEPARTMENT DESIRES TO ENFORCE THE
ORDERS OF THE FEDERAL COURT IN REGARD TO INTE-
GRATION IN THIS CITY, THE CITY POLICE WILL BE AVAIL-
ABLE TO LEND SUCH SUPPORT AS YOU MAY REQUIRE.

I AM NOT MAKING THIS WIRE PUBLIC. THIS IS FOR YOUR
INFORMATION AND FOR THE JUSTICE DEPARTMENT TO USE
AS IT CONSIDERS NECESSARY.

*In a critical meeting at Newport held late in the day on September 23, the
President pondered his course of action. Formal minutes were not kept for
the conference, but notes were made. Some of them, written by E. Frederic
Morrow, recorded what was happening; others were in the form of questions and answers presented to those present. For this reason the notes do
not form a connected narrative about policies being planned. Yet a number
of highlights stand out. The President realized the seriousness of the situation, but was reluctant to use federal force. Late in the evening, he issued a
proclamation instructing those involved to follow the court orders. He also
released a short statement.*

Notes of Presidential Advisor E. Frederic Morrow
on the Little Rock Crisis
September 23, 1957
[Morrow Files, Eisenhower Papers.]*

*E. Frederic Morrow material is reprinted with Mr. Morrow's permission.

Presidential Proclamation 3204
September 23, 1957
[*Federal Register,* XXII, No. 186 (September 25, 1957), 7628.]

Whereas certain persons in the State of Arkansas, individually and in unlawful assemblages, combinations, and conspiracies, have wilfully obstructed the enforcement of orders of the United States District Court for the Eastern District of Arkansas with respect to matters relating to enrollment and attendance at public schools, particularly at Central High School, located in Little Rock School District, Little Rock, Arkansas; and

Whereas such wilful obstruction of justice hinders the execution of the laws of that State and of the United States, and makes it impracticable to enforce such laws by the ordinary course of judicial proceedings; and

Whereas such obstruction of justice constitutes a denial of the equal protection of the laws secured by the Constitution of the United States and impedes the course of justice under those laws:

Now, therefore, I, Dwight D. Eisenhower, President of the United States, under and by virtue of the authority vested in me by the Constitution and statutes of the United States, including Chapter 15 of Title 10 of the United States Code, particularly sections 332, 333 and 334 thereof, do command all persons engaged in such obstruction of justice to cease and desist therefrom, and to disperse forthwith.

In witness whereof, I have hereunto set my hand and caused the Seal of the United States of America to be affixed.

Done at the City of Newport, Rhode Island this twenty-third day of September in the year of our Lord Nineteen hundred and fifty-seven and of the Independence of the United States of America the one hundred and eighty-second.

Statement by President Eisenhower on the Little Rock Crisis
September 23, 1957
[Morrow Files, Eisenhower Papers.]

I WANT TO MAKE SEVERAL THINGS VERY CLEAR IN CONNECTION WITH THE DISGRACEFUL OCCURRENCES OF TODAY AT CENTRAL HIGH SCHOOL IN THE CITY OF LITTLE ROCK. THEY ARE:

1. THE FEDERAL LAW AND ORDERS OF A UNITED STATES DISTRICT COURT IMPLEMENTING THAT LAW CAN NOT BE FLOUTED WITH IMPUNITY BY ANY INDIVIDUAL OR ANY MOB OF EXTREMISTS.

2. I WILL USE THE FULL POWER OF THE UNITED STATES
INCLUDING WHATEVER FORCE MAY BE NECESSARY TO PRE-
VENT ANY OBSTRUCTION OF THE LAW AND TO CARRY OUT
THE ORDERS OF THE FEDERAL COURT.

3. OF COURSE EVERY RIGHT THINKING CITIZEN WILL HOPE
THAT THE AMERICAN SENSE OF JUSTICE AND FAIR PLAY WILL
PREVAIL IN THIS CASE. IT WILL BE A SAD DAY FOR THIS
COUNTRY—BOTH AT HOME AND ABROAD—IF SCHOOL CHIL-
DREN CAN SAFELY ATTEND THEIR CLASSES ONLY UNDER
ARMED GUARDS.

4. I REPEAT MY EXPRESSED CONFIDENCE THAT THE CITI-
ZENS OF LITTLE ROCK AND OF ARKANSAS WILL RESPECT THE
LAW AND WILL NOT COUNTENANCE VIOLATIONS OF LAW AND
ORDER BY EXTREMISTS.

---

*On the morning of September 24, widespread disorders occurred through-
out Little Rock. Shortly after 9:00 A.M., Mayor Mann telegraphed the
President about the mounting disorder.*

Mayor Woodrow Mann to President Eisenhower
September 24, 1957
[Official File 142-A-5-A, Eisenhower Papers.]

PRESIDENT DWIGHT D. EISENHOWER:
THE IMMEDIATE NEED FOR FEDERAL TROOPS IS URGENT.
THE MOB IS MUCH LARGER IN NUMBERS AT 8AM THAN AT
ANY TIME YESTERDAY PEOPLE ARE CONVERGING ON THE
SCENE FROM ALL DIRECTIONS MOB IS ARMED AND ENGAGING
IN FISTICUFFS AND OTHER ACTS OF VIOLENCE. SITUATION IS
OUT OF CONTROL AND POLICE CANNOT DISPERSE THE MOB I
AM PLEADING TO YOU AS PRESIDENT OF THE UNITED STATES
IN THE INTEREST OF HUMANITY LAW AND ORDER AND BE-
CAUSE OF DEMOCRACY WORLD WIDE TO PROVIDE THE NECES-
SARY FEDERAL TROOPS WITHIN SEVERAL HOURS. ACTION BY
YOU WILL RESTORE PEACE AND ORDER AND COMPLIANCE
WITH YOUR PROCLAMATION.

It was at this time that Eisenhower decided to intervene. Various staff notes recorded the Administration's plans.

Notes of Presidential Advisor E. Frederic Morrow
on the Little Rock Crisis
September 24, 1957
[Morrow Files, Eisenhower Papers.]

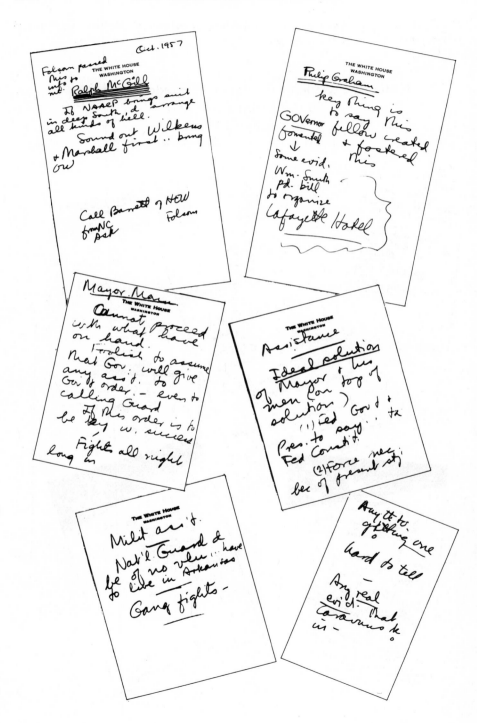

The President flew back to Washington from Newport on September 24. At 8:07 P.M., Eastern time, he issued Executive Order 10730, which sent United States troops to Little Rock to restore order and integrate the school. He then explained his action on national radio and television. The Federal Government had found it necessary to intervene with United States forces in the internal affairs of Arkansas, despite the strong desire of everyone involved to avoid this action.

Executive Order 10730
September 24, 1957
[*Federal Register*, XXII, No. 186 (September 25, 1957), 7628.]

Whereas on September 23, 1957, I issued Proclamation No. 3204 reading in part as follows:

Whereas certain persons in the State of Arkansas, individually and in unlawful assemblages, combinations, and conspiracies, have wilfully obstructed the enforcement of orders of the United States District Court for the Eastern District of Arkansas with respect to matters relating to enrollment and attendance at public schools, particularly at Central High School, located in Little Rock School District, Little Rock, Arkansas; and

Whereas such wilful obstruction of justice hinders the execution of the laws of that State and of the United States, and makes it impracticable to enforce such laws by the ordinary course of judicial proceedings; and

Whereas such obstruction of justice constitutes a denial of the equal protection of the laws secured by the Constitution of the United States and impedes the course of justice under those laws:

"*Now, therefore, I, Dwight D. Eisenhower,* President of the United States, under and by virtue of the authority vested in me by the Constitution and Statutes of the United States, including Chapter 15 of Title 10 of the United States Code, particularly sections 332, 333 and 334 thereof, do command all persons engaged in such obstruction of justice to cease and desist therefrom, and to disperse forthwith;" and

Whereas the command contained in that Proclamation has not been obeyed and wilful obstruction of enforcement of said court orders still exists and threatens to continue:

Now, therefore, by virtue of the authority vested in me by the Constitution and Statutes of the United States, including Chapter 15 of Title 10, particularly sections 332, 333 and 334 thereof, and section 301 of Title 3 of the United States Code, it is hereby ordered as follows:

Section 1. I hereby authorize and direct the Secretary of Defense to order into the active military service of the United States as he may deem appropriate to carry out the purposes of this Order, any or all of the units of the National Guard of the United States and of the Air National Guard of the United States within the State of Arkansas to serve in the active military service of the United States for an indefinite period and until relieved by appropriate orders.

Sec. 2. The Secretary of Defense is authorized and directed to take all appropriate steps to enforce any orders of the United States District Court for the Eastern District of Arkansas for the removal of obstruction of justice in the State of Arkansas with respect to matters relating to enrollment and attendance at public schools in the Little Rock School District, Little Rock, Arkansas. In carrying out the provisions of this section, the Secretary of Defense is authorized to use the units, and members thereof, ordered into the active military service of the United States pursuant to Section 1 of this Order.

Sec. 3. In furtherance of the enforcement of the aforementioned orders of the United States District Court for the Eastern District of Arkansas, the Secretary of Defense is authorized to use such of the armed forces of the United States as he may deem necessary.

Sec. 4. The Secretary of Defense is authorized to delegate to the Secretary of the Army or the Secretary of the Air Force, or both, any of the authority conferred upon him by this Order.

Many Southerners violently opposed the President's decision. Among these was Senator Richard Russell of Georgia, who had been the "Southern candidate" at the 1956 Democratic National Convention. Russell's letter harshly criticized the action. Eisenhower's response—coming after the restoration of order in Little Rock and the integration of Central High School (September 25)—recounted the constitutional basis for the sending of federal troops.

President Eisenhower to Senator Richard Russell
September 27, 1957
[Official File 142-A-5-A, Eisenhower Papers.]

The Honorable Richard B. Russell

Few times in my life have I felt as saddened as when the obligations of my office required me to order the use of force within a state to carry out the decisions of a Federal Court. My conviction is that had the police powers of the State of Arkansas been utilized not to frustrate the orders of the Court but to support them, the ensuing violence and open disrespect for the law and the Federal Judiciary would never have occurred. The Arkansas National Guard could have handled the situation with ease had it been instructed to do so. As a matter of fact, had the integration of Central High School been permitted to take place without the intervention of the National Guard, there is little doubt that the process would have gone along quite as smoothly and quietly as it has in other Arkansas communities. When a State, by seeking to frustrate the orders of a Federal Court, encourages mobs of extremists to flout the orders of a Federal Court, and when a State refuses to utilize its police powers to protect against mobs persons who are peaceably exercising their right under the Constitution as defined in such Court orders, the oath of office of the President requires that he take action to give that protection. Failure to act in such a case would be tantamount to acquiescence in anarchy and the dissolution of the union.

I must say that I completely fail to comprehend your comparison of our troops to Hitler's storm troopers. In one case military power was used to further the ambitions and purposes of a ruthless dictator; in the other to preserve the institutions of free government.

You allege certain wrong-doings on the part of individual soldiers at Little Rock. The Secretary of the Army will assemble the facts and report them directly to you.

Strong support for Eisenhower's intervention came from many quarters, including the American black community. The Reverend Doctor Martin Luther King, Jr., who had recently received national attention as the leader of a bus boycott in Montgomery, Alabama, congratulated the President on behalf of the Southern Christian Leadership Conference. The President sent a personal response thanking Dr. King.

Reverend Martin Luther King, Jr., to President Eisenhower
September 25, 1957
[Official File 142-A-5-A, Eisenhower Papers.]

THE PRESIDENT

I WISH TO EXPRESS MY SINCERE SUPPORT FOR THE STAND YOU HAVE TAKEN TO RESTORE LAW AND ORDER IN LITTLE ROCK, ARKANSAS. IN THE LONG RUN, JUSTICE FINALLY MUST

SPRING FROM A NEW MORAL CLIMATE. YET SPIRITUAL FORC-
ES CANNOT EMERGE IN A SITUATION OF MOB VIOLENCE.

YOU SHOULD KNOW THAT THE OVERWHELMING MAJORITY
OF SOUTHERNERS, NEGRO AND WHITE STAND FIRMLY BE-
HIND YOUR RESOLUTE ACTION. THE PEN OF HISTORY WILL
RECORD THAT EVEN THE SMALL AND CONFUSED MINORITY
THAT OPPOSE INTEGRATION WITH VIOLENCE WILL LIVE TO
SEE THAT YOUR ACTION HAS BEEN OF GREAT BENEFIT TO
OUR NATION AND TO THE CHRISTIAN TRADITIONS OF FAIR
PLAY AND BROTHERHOOD.

President Eisenhower to Reverend Martin Luther King, Jr.
October 7, 1957
[Official File 142-A-5-A, Eisenhower Papers.]

PERSONAL

Dear Mr. King:
Thank you for sending me your comments regarding the necessity of the
decision I had to make in the difficult Arkansas situation. I appreciated
your thoughtful expression of the basic and compelling factors involved.

I share your confidence that Americans everywhere remain devoted to our
tradition of adherence to orderly processes of law.

---

*The Little Rock crisis had political implications. The White House staff
suggested that the President respond to a grassroots reaction from a
Michigan man and write a friendly letter to Thurgood Marshall, the
General Council of the NAACP.*

Memorandum from Cabinet Secretary Maxwell Rabb
to Presidential Secretary Ann Whitman
October 21, 1957
[Official File 142-A-5-A, Eisenhower Papers.]

Attached hereto is a letter I received from Thurgood Marshall, General
Counsel of the NAACP, enclosing a typical "grassroots" reaction to the
President's recent actions.

In my opinion, a Presidential acknowledgment in this instance could have a great deal of value. While I am on the best of terms with Thurgood, notes from the President to him and to his correspondent will have him purring like a cat. It may well be that I will have to call on him, as I have in the past, to desist from taking some action that will rock the boat so far as the country is concerned. This will help.

I am attaching a suggested draft together with a draft for Thurgood. He, incidentally, has wired several times with respect to the Little Rock incident and has not been given a personal response—in each case it was considered but deemed unnecessary.

NAACP Counsel Thurgood Marshall to Cabinet Secretary Maxwell Rabb
October 17, 1957
[Official File 142-A-5-A, Eisenhower Papers.]

Dear Max:

Of the letters of one kind or another we have received recently, for some reason which I cannot explain, this post card appears to be very important as an expression of grassroots approval of the stand taken by President Eisenhower.

I thought you might want it and perhaps it would be good for the President to see it. At anyrate, here it is.

Philip Thomas to NAACP Counsel Thurgood Marshall
October 11, 1957
[Official File 142-A-5-A, Eisenhower Papers.]

My Dear Mr. Marshall: 10-11-57
Route 2-Box 166
Dear Sir; Thanks for your statement in the git of Oct 10-57.
I agree with you wholeheartedly on the Republican votes.
Mr. Eisenhower has made a stand, my (God) Watch over him and his family. (Thanks) you sir;
Philip Thomas

President Eisenhower to Philip Thomas
October 23, 1957
[Official File 142-A-5-A, Eisenhower Papers.]

Dear Mr. Thomas:

Mr. Thurgood Marshall was kind enough to send me the card he recently received from you.

It was encouraging to read your comments and I deeply appreciated your thoughtful prayer for me and the members of my family.

President Eisenhower to NAACP Counsel Thurgood Marshall
October 23, 1957
[Official File 142-A-5-A, Eisenhower Papers.]

Dear Mr. Marshall:

Mr. Rabb has shown me the card from Mr. Philip Thomas which you kindly forwarded. Its contents were of great interest and for your information I am enclosing a copy of the letter I have sent to Mr. Thomas.

The trouble you have taken to bring this message to my attention is very much appreciated.

The United States Army left Little Rock on November 27, 1957, and until the end of the school year the following spring, federalized units of the Arkansas National Guard patrolled Little Rock Central High School. The school's integration did not resolve all problems. Before the withdrawal of federal forces, Val Washington, head of the Minorities Division of the Republican National Committee, wrote the Administration about various difficulties that had arisen. Mrs. Daisy Bates was a leader of the local NAACP. General Walton Walker commanded the United States Army units. Although Walker in later years became associated with right-wing activities, at Little Rock he gave no indication of his political affiliation.

Val Washington to Cabinet Secretary Maxwell Rabb
November 14, 1957

[Official File 142-A-5-A, Eisenhower Papers.]

I have been very disturbed this week because of unfavorable reports from Little Rock.

Is there any reason why General Walker should not have liaison with civilians like Daisy Bates for the purpose of getting direct information? As you know, Mrs. Bates is the one person the Negro students look to for guidance. I believe if she could talk to someone immediately after the children report to her, many misunderstandings and fears that crop up would be eliminated.

Apparently the Negro community has no idea when troops are to be withdrawn or where to contact 101 in order to get immediate relief when disturbances arise. Of course you realize that the National Guard, lacking the necessary experience and maybe suffering from some prejudice because they are Arkansans, do not have the same effect on the general populace as the Federal troops.

I am most disturbed about the report of two days ago that between 1 and 1:30 in the afternoon, Thomas Jefferson, one of the Negro students, was knocked unconscious in the hall. At the time there were only two National Guardsmen stationed on each floor and none of the 101 troops. The true story was not given to the childrens' parents until after 4:30 in the afternoon. Upon learning of the incident Mrs. Bates checked for authenticity and attempted to reach General Walker. She was always stopped by some Captain or some underling who said he would pass the information on to higher authority. She was, therefore, stopped cold but became so upset she called me. Before talking to me she had talked to Harry Ashmore, Editor of the Gazette, because he has been friendly throughout this period of disturbance. He evidently had some knowledge of the incident when Mrs. Bates talked to him because his paper had written a story on it. About 8:30 that night, Captain Branyan of the 101 called and wanted to know why the information was given to the Negro papers and not to them. Mrs. Bates was very upset with this remark because she had been trying in vain to convey information to them ever since their arrival in Little Rock.

The young man who slipped up behind Thomas Jefferson and knocked him out is named Hugh Williams. However, no one was willing to admit having seen Williams hit Jefferson. Yesterday a Captain of 101 went to the school and Hugh Williams was called into the principal's office. He admitted having attacked Jefferson and was suspended for three days.

It is Mrs. Bates' belief that between 1,500 and 1,700 of the white students are willing to accept integration. There are only 75 to 100 who cause all of the trouble. This small group is so well organized and coached that they are more effective than the larger group. Certainly, besides enforcing the law, some guidance should be given the nearly 1,700 students who want to do the right thing.

From all indications the Negro children are very determined and do not intend to leave the school. Some way should be found to give them assurance that they are well protected at all times and we sincerely intend to stand behind them and uphold the law if it takes one day or eternity. The Administration has done a terrific job. There is no reason why we should lose face because of a few outlaws.

On October 25, 1957, Governor Faubus telegraphed the President. It was answered by the Secretary of the Army.

Governor Orval Faubus to President Eisenhower
October 25, 1957
[Official File 142-A-5-A, Eisenhower Papers.]

THE PRESIDENT.
THE ANNOUNCED PLAN OF GENERAL WALKER, COMMANDER OF THE LITTLE ROCK OCCUPATIONAL FORCES, TO SCREEN ARKANSAS NATIONAL GUARDSMEN AND SELECT ON AN INDIVIDUAL BASIS THOSE TO BE RETAINED IN THE FEDERAL ARMY IS NOTHING MORE THAN A CLEVER SCHEME TO CIRCUMVENT THE SELECTIVE SERVICE LAW AND DRAFT CITI-

ZENS OF ARKANSAS INTO THE FEDERAL ARMY CONTRARY
TO THE PLAN APPROVED BY CONGRESS FOR PEACE TIME COM-
PULSORY SERVICE.

CONGRESS HAS PROVIDED A WAY THROUGH THE SELECTIVE
SERVICE LAW TO FURNISH THE U.S. MILITARY WITH ALL
NEEDED MANPOWER. THIS ACT OF CONGRESS IS THE LAW OF
THE LAND. MEMBERS OF THE NATIONAL GUARD ARE CITIZEN
SOLDIERS WHO HAVE VOLUNTEERED FOR TRAINING AND A
STATE OF READINESS TO SERVE OUR COUNTRY AS FEDERAL
SOLDIERS IN TIME OF WAR. THE PRESENT USE OF GUARDSMEN
IN ARKANSAS IS A VIOLATION OF THEIR RIGHTS AND A
BREACH OF FAITH WITH THEM ON THE PART OF THE FEDER-
AL GOVERNMENT. UNLESS THIS SCHEME IS ABANDONED
IMMEDIATELY IT WILL JEOPARDIZE OR DESTROY THE MO-
RALE OF MEMBERS OF THE NATIONAL GUARD THROUGHOUT
THE NATION.

FOR THE ABOVE REASONS I DEMAND THAT THE NATIONAL
GUARDSMEN STILL FEDERALIZED IN ARKANSAS BE RE-
TURNED IMMEDIATELY TO THEIR FORMER STATUS OF
ARKANSAS CITIZEN SOLDIERS.

TODAY I AM WIRING SENATOR RUSSELL, CHAIRMAN OF THE
SENATE ARMED SERVICES COMMITTEE, URGING THAT HIS
COMMITTEE INVESTIGATE THIS FLAGRANT AND UNWAR-
RANTED EVASION OF THE SELECTIVE SERVICE LAW ENACTED
BY THE CONGRESS.

Secretary Wilber Brucker to Governor Orval Faubus
October 26, 1957
[Official File 142-A-5-A, Eisenhower Papers.]

Dear Governor Faubus:

This letter replies to your telegram of 25 October 1957 to both the
President of the United States and myself.

As the purpose of the Universal Military Training and Service Act (Title
50, United States Code, App. 451) is entirely different from those contained
in the law (Title 10, United States Code, Section 332, 333 and 334) under
which the Arkansas National Guard was called into Federal service, you
must be fully aware that your allegations are not correct in law or in fact.

I am replying to your letter with reluctance in view of your malicious
disrespect in referring to General Walker as "Commander of the Little
Rock Occupational Forces."

VIII

PERSONAL DIPLOMACY

PERSONAL DIPLOMACY

Introduction

During the last two years of Dwight Eisenhower's Presidency, the threat of international communism dominated American foreign policy. Although the Administration still considered the Soviet Union the chief Cold War antagonist, there were several indications that a softening of this attitude was developing. John Foster Dulles' death on May 24, 1959, ended an era in the State Department, and Dwight Eisenhower, for all practical purposes, became his own Secretary of State. Such points of controversy as Berlin, the Middle East, Formosa and the offshore islands, and Indochina remained, but at least the President and the Soviet leaders were beginning to explore ways to reduce tensions. By mid-1959 Premier Nikita Khrushchev could pay a friendly visit to the United States (September 15–27) and in turn could invite President Eisenhower to the Soviet Union. It became clear that while the goals of both sides remained the same, new channels of communication had been opened. It became equally clear that when Dwight Eisenhower left office on January 20, 1961, the possibilities of a major war had receded.

The massive 1958 Democratic congressional victories precipitated a barrage of criticism aimed at the President's conduct of foreign affairs and at the Administration's national defense policies. Democrats repeatedly focused on the volatile defense issue and charged the existence of a "missile gap," citing Soviet space achievements as evidence for their accusations. Furthermore, the Democrats said that the President had failed to modernize American weapons systems and that his obsession with "fiscal responsibility" had undermined the nation's defense. Although the President vehemently refuted the accusations, many observers felt that the Democratic assault did hurt the Republican party. Eisenhower muted some of his critics by reorganizing the Department of Defense, but he steadfastly refused to accept the existence of a "missile gap." Despite this, some Republican leaders feared that the issue would emerge with dramatic force during the 1960 campaign.

The President's new emphasis on personal diplomacy also opened the Administration to criticism. Some Democrats said that Eisenhower was attempting to mute serious foreign policy issues by substituting personality for policy. When Eisenhower was received with great acclaim overseas, Democrats tended to downgrade the significance; on the other hand, when Vice President Richard Nixon met with hostile receptions, they argued that America's prestige had declined. Eisenhower, however, sincerely believed that his world trips improved both the image of the United States and the chances for peace. Given the rapidly changing nature of the Cold War, it now seemed to him as important to visit Caracas and Kabul as Paris and Geneva.

Eisenhower was especially concerned with Latin America. Fears generated by the experience in Guatemala had heightened his desire to create a climate designed to prevent any more pro-communist governments. At first, the Administration had sought to foster economic growth and stability through private investment. While this may have been fiscally sound, it revived bitter memories of Dollar Diplomacy. As the decade progressed, Latin America became increasingly unstable; a series of coups, strikes, and riots reflected the failure of both the Administration policy and the incumbent Latin American governments to restore order. In an attempt to improve relations, Vice President Nixon visited several Latin American nations in the spring of 1958. Numerous unfriendly incidents, which culminated when Venezuelan mobs threatened Nixon's life, marred the good will visit. Upon his return, the Vice President, despite the antagonism encountered on his trip, proposed a crash program to aid the area. But before any significant changes could even be planned, a dramatic event occurred in Cuba.

On January 1, 1959, Fidel Castro ousted the long-time Cuban strongman Fulgencio Batista. Castro's triumph created confusion among American policy planners. Some saw a new Simon Bolivar, others a petty dictator, and still others a Cuban Karl Marx. As Castro consolidated his power, the United States quickly implemented an already expanded aid program with the establishment of the Inter-American Development Bank (August 7). Within months, the flow of American aid improved relations with almost every Latin American country except Cuba. In fact, during February, 1960, Eisenhower visited "our friends to the south" without untoward incident. Here, the Administration's use of personal diplomacy seemed to be successful, although traditional friendship with Cuba continued to deteriorate. By the end of Eisenhower's second term, diplomatic relations had been broken and secret plans had been made to overthrow Castro.

By the beginning of 1960, personal diplomacy had proven a valid approach to the conduct of foreign policy. Eisenhower looked forward to a May summit conference in Paris and to a triumphant journey through the Soviet Union. These events would end his Administration on a splendid note; he might not end the Cold War, but he would most likely succeed in his desire to alleviate world tensions. Then, on May Day, 1960, an American

U–2 spy plane was shot down deep inside the Soviet Union. This startling event—coming on the eve of the Paris Conference—diverted Soviet-American relations away from meaningful dialogue and into an acrimonious debate. It disrupted the proceedings at Paris, led to the cancellation of Eisenhower's Soviet trip, and rekindled Cold War tensions. Even though the President's plans had been disrupted, his staff quickly made alternate arrangements for an extended tour of the Far East (June 12–25). Although most of the Pacific travels went well, riots by Japanese leftist groups forced Eisenhower to change his itinerary. He ended his last overseas trip where he had started almost eight years earlier—in Korea.

1. THE DEATH OF JOHN FOSTER DULLES

John Foster Dulles was a powerful and self-assured Secretary of State. His close working and personal relationship with Dwight Eisenhower was often likened to that which existed between George Washington and Alexander Hamilton. When Dulles was stricken with cancer in the fall of 1956, Eisenhower's distress was profound. He visited Dulles in the hospital almost daily and fretted in private over the possibility of losing so close an associate and friend. By June, 1957, Dulles had apparently recovered and had fully resumed his duties. That year also marked the Secretary's 50th year in the foreign service. The President used the occasion to write a warm personal letter.

President Eisenhower to Secretary John Foster Dulles
June 15, 1957
[President's Personal File 359, Eisenhower Papers.]

Dear Foster:

I am told that today marks the fiftieth year since you first began your service in the field of foreign affairs, when you served as secretary on the Chinese delegation to the second Peace Conference at The Hague. Apparently, your associates of that early date clearly recognized your ability to carry heavy responsibilities, for heavy they must have been for a young man of nineteen.

In any event, through that experience you were committed to the waging of peace, and your name has been prominently associated with many of the International Conferences, since that date, which have had as their purpose the development of world stability and peace based on justice. In those years of enriching experience, you have gone on to ever increasing responsibility in the field of public service to which you have dedicated yourself, and have established a reputation for meeting every new assignment and challenge with wisdom, imagination and vigor.

My personal appreciation of your extraordinary ability in the field of international relations has constantly grown since you became Secretary of State in 1953.

Your statesmanship has been demonstrated in countless negotiations and conferences of international import. The beneficial results of your labors can never be accurately measured, but such accomplishments as the conclusion of the Austrian Peace Treaty, the formulation and adoption of the Caracas Resolution against Communist infiltration into this Hemisphere, the development of the Southeast Asia Treaty Organization, the Formosa Declaration of 1955, and the Doctrine for the Middle East which the Congress recently approved, bear witness to your competence as our country's chief representative in global relations.

Recitation of these few instances serves at least to give some hint of the broad basis on which rests my personal and official gratitude to you. I am quite certain that as this Administration joins those which are viewed from long historical perspective, your accomplishments will establish you as one of the greatest of our Secretaries of State.

Nevertheless, at this moment, the future must occupy both you and me more than can the past. In extending to you my felicitations on a half century of fruitful service to your country, I also express my profound hope that the nation shall have the benefit of your experience and wisdom for many years to come.

Early in 1959 Secretary Dulles entered the hospital to undergo surgery for a hernia. At a press conference shortly thereafter, the President was asked about the illness, and his response implied the great trust he placed in the Secretary. Four days later came the announcement that Dulles' cancer had recurred. Eisenhower, at a February 18 press conference, responded dolefully to a question about a successor.

Presidential News Conference
February 10, 1959
[*Public Papers of the Presidents: 1959* (Washington, 1960), 178.]

*   *   *

QUESTION. Peter Lisagor, *Chicago Daily News:* In view of Mr. Dulles' leave, do you plan to devote more of your own time and energy to the conduct of foreign affairs?

THE PRESIDENT: Well, if I do, something else is going to suffer because I don't know of anything that I give as much time to, every week and every day, as I do to foreign affairs. Actually, I don't know of any Cabinet officer that I give half the time to that I do to Secretary Dulles; and if I go into any more personal conduct of the thing, then I am going to have to neglect a few other departments, that's sure. . . .

Presidential News Conference
February 18, 1959

[*Public Papers of the Presidents: 1959* (Washington, 1960), 191–92.]

QUESTION. Merriman Smith, *United Press International:* Mr. President, in recent days there have been at least two reports concerning Secretary Dulles; one, that he tried to resign and you refused to consider it, and then there have been other published reports, apparently emanating from Capitol Hill, that you have been sounding out certain Republicans on what you might do in event that it became necessary to select a successor to Mr. Dulles.

Now, in the light, against the background of these two reports, I wonder if you could discuss with us the Secretary's condition and how you view his future.

THE PRESIDENT: Well, I want to start off with a little reminiscing.

I once told General Marshall that there was a certain corps commander in the United States that I wanted to get over into Europe right away; I needed him and there was a corps needed such a man with such qualifications. I got a telegram saying, well, sure, he is a very fine man, but he is so crippled out in Walter Reed that the doctors won't assure you that he can move around. And I said, you send the man and I will send him to battle in a litter, because he can do better that way than most people I know. Now, I feel this way about Secretary Dulles. The doctors have assured me there is nothing in his disease that is going to touch his heart and his head, and that is what we want.

I am constitutionally responsible for conducting the foreign affairs of the United States, and the man who has been my closest associate, certainly my principal assistant, and on whom all the responsibility for details has been resting, my closest friend and confidante in this whole business, is Secretary Dulles. I know of no man—in my knowledge—in the world that has equaled his wisdom and his knowledge in this whole complicated business.

Therefore, as long as Secretary Dulles believes that he is in shape to carry on, he is exactly the person I want.

So far as his offer to resign, I must tell you this is no new thing. His dedication and his selflessness is so great that from the very first day he came into this office, he has constantly said, "If ever, Mr. President, I become for you either a political or a national liability, remember you have my resignation always, to be accepted at your pleasure."

Well, now, of course, this has been his attitude. There has never been a specific statement ever that he wants to resign, because to be saying that would mean that he was ready to lay down his duties and responsibilities that he believes to be so important.

And so, I just say to you again, as long as he is ready to carry on, he is the man I want. And I have not discussed with anyone the possibility of his successor. . . .

For a time Dulles appeared on the road to recovery. A trip to Florida, during which he seemed in good spirits, raised hopes that his malignancy had been arrested. The optimism was short-lived; he returned to Washington a dying man. On April 15, 1959, the President, while vacationing in Augusta, Georgia, was informed that Dulles could not continue. The next day he received a formal resignation.

Presidential News Conference
April 15, 1959

[*Public Papers of the Presidents: 1959* (Washington, 1959), 327–28.]

THE PRESIDENT: What I have to say concerns Secretary Dulles.

QUESTION: What was that, Mr. President?

THE PRESIDENT: It concerns Secretary Dulles. I had a conversation this morning with him, and in view of the findings the doctors have made—yesterday—and which were not yet reported when I met him day before yesterday, he has definitely made up his mind to submit his resignation.

The formal letter of resignation will reach me in a day or so. I will then reply to it.

I want to make one or two things clear. The findings are not of the kind, so far as I am aware, that make him helpless. He is, nevertheless, incapacitated, so far as carrying on the administrative burdens of the office, as well as doing the thinking for it over there.

QUESTION: You say he is absolutely incapacitated?

THE PRESIDENT: I am saying incapacitated for carrying on the administrative load, in addition to assisting the making of policy. So I have asked him to remain as my consultant, and I will appoint him to some office that makes it possible for him to be useful both to the State Department and to me; because I think all of you know my opinion of Secretary Dulles. I personally believe he has filled his office with greater distinction and greater ability than any other man our country has known. He is a man of tremendous character and courage, intelligence and wisdom. Therefore my determination to keep him close where he can be useful, both to the State Department and to me and indeed in considering everything that may affect our foreign relations, I think is a very wise and proper thing to do.

With respect to a possible successor, no final decision has been made, and I will let you people know as quickly as this is practicable.

Now I believe there is no other particular additional information that I can provide, but if there are any questions on this particular subject, I would be glad to entertain any of them.

QUESTION: One thing, Mr. President, is there anything that you would care to say as to the effect of this necessary action on the coming meeting of the foreign ministers?

THE PRESIDENT: Well, yes; I think I should say something about it. As you know, both Foster and I have kept in close communication on this matter. He has developed a team over in the State Department of which he is very proud and in which he has great confidence. And we believe that whatever the decision is, that there will be no damage to the, you might say, effectiveness of our presentations in the next conference.

QUESTION: Would you expect the Secretary's successor to come from within the Government?

THE PRESIDENT: I wouldn't want to say so at the moment.

QUESTION: Mr. President, does this mean that Mr. Herter will attend both the April 29 and May 11 foreign ministers conferences as our representative?

THE PRESIDENT: I would say this: no matter who the appointee is, yes. He would be going to both, no matter who the successor. He would be going almost as a matter of necessity, I think, because he is familiar with it.

QUESTION: Mr. President, does this mean that the Secretary will become a member of the White House staff and not a State Department employee then?

THE PRESIDENT: I haven't even thought of the exact status, but it will be on a consultative basis. As you know, in each department, and for me, there are allowed certain consultants, but he will be there on that basis. And this, by the way, is something that I know that he wants to do, as well as knowing that I want him to do it.

QUESTION: Mr. President, can you give us an idea when you might be able to make up your mind about his successor?

THE PRESIDENT: Well, I can just say this: it will not be long delayed. It will be a matter of days. . . .

Secretary John Foster Dulles to President Eisenhower
April 15, 1959

[*Public Papers of the Presidents: 1959* (Washington, 1960), 330.]

Dear Mr. President:

It is apparent to me that I shall not be well enough soon enough to continue to serve as Secretary of State. Accordingly, I tender my resignation to be effective at your convenience.

I am deeply grateful for the opportunities and responsibilities you have given me.

I was brought up in the belief that this nation of ours was not merely a self-serving society but was founded with a mission to help build a world where liberty and justice would prevail. Today that concept faces a formidable and ruthless challenge from International Communism. This has made it manifestly difficult to adhere steadfastly to our national idealism and national mission and at the same time avoid the awful catastrophe of war. You have given inspiring leadership in this essential task and it has been a deep satisfaction to me to have been intimately associated with you in these matters.

If I can, in a more limited capacity, continue to serve, I shall be happy to do so.

Faithfully yours,
John Foster Dulles

President Eisenhower to Secretary John Foster Dulles
April 16, 1959

[*Public Papers of the Presidents: 1959* (Washington, 1960), 329–30.]

Dear Foster:

I accept, with deepest personal regret and only because I have no alternative, your resignation as Secretary of State, effective upon the qualification of your successor.

In so doing, I can but repeat what the vast outpouring of affection and admiration from the entire free world has told you. You have, with the talents you so abundantly possess and with your exemplary integrity of character, employed your rich heritage as well as your unique experience in handling our relations with other countries. You have been a staunch bulwark of our nation against the machinations of Imperialistic Communism. You have won to the side of the free world countless peoples, and inspired in them renewed courage and determination to fight for freedom and principle. As a statesman of world stature you have set a record in the stewardship of our foreign relations that stands clear and strong for all to see.

By this letter I request you to serve in the future, to whatever extent your health will permit, as a consultant to me and the State Department in international affairs. I know that all Americans join me in the fervent hope that you will thus be able to continue the important contributions that only you can make toward a just peace in the world.

The President received letters from all over the world concerning John Foster Dulles' illness. Typical was the warm message from French Foreign Minister Jules Moch.

Foreign Minister Jules Moch to President Eisenhower
April 20, 1959
[President's Personal File 359, Eisenhower Papers.]

My dear Mr. President:

You have been spared nothing during your Presidency, either physical suffering or mental anguish.

When my wife and I read that you had to resign yourself to an acceptance of John Foster Dulles' resignation, we understood how sad you and Mrs. Eisenhower must have been.

Allow me to express our admiration for the courage, stoicism, and sense of duty of the man who was your closest associate and to say how deeply we share your sorrow. Already, when after his first operation, he came to London to strengthen the American Delegation to the Sub-Committee on Disarmament—presided over by our friend Harold E. Stassen—the French Delegation understood the lofty example of good citizenship which the Secretary of State was then giving. May the rest he has been obliged to take on doctors' orders enable him to recover his health. May you keep a friend whose invaluable loyalty has never faltered.

Please give our regards to Mrs. Eisenhower and accept, my dear Mr. President, the assurance of our heartfelt sympathy.

President Eisenhower to Foreign Minister Jules Moch
April 30, 1959
[President's Personal File 359, Eisenhower Papers.]

Dear Jules:

Thank you for your characteristically understanding note about the illness of Foster Dulles. There are few men of such stature in this world of ours, and it is a great sorrow for his friends everywhere that he is no longer able to carry on the heavy responsibilities that he has discharged with such distinction, skill and courage.

With gratitude to you and your wife for your thoughtfulness in writing, and warm personal regard,

Dulles' health failed steadily and on May 24, 1959, President Eisenhower had the sad responsibility of issuing the death announcement.

White House Press Release
May 24, 1959
[President's Personal File 359, Eisenhower Papers.]

John Foster Dulles is dead. A lifetime of labor for world peace has ended. His countrymen and all who believe in justice and the rule of law grieve at the passing from the earthly scene of one of the truly great men of our time.

Throughout his life, and particularly during his eventful six years as Secretary of State, his courage, his wisdom, and his friendly understanding were devoted to bettering relations among nations. He was a foe only to tyranny.

Because he believed in the dignity of men and in their brotherhood under God, he was an ardent supporter of their deepest hopes and aspirations. From his life and work, humanity will, in the years to come, gain renewed inspiration to work ever harder for the attainment of the goal of peace with justice. In the pursuit of that goal, he ignored every personal cost and sacrifice, however great.

We, who were privileged to work with him, have lost a dear and close friend as all Americans have lost a champion of freedom. United, we extend to Mrs. Dulles, to her children and to all members of the Dulles family our prayers and deepest sympathy, and the assurance that in our memories will live affection, respect and admiration for John Foster Dulles.

2. THE GIRARD CASE

All United States military detachments stationed in friendly nations fall under Status of Forces treaties. These agreements determine the conditions under which American servicemen can be tried by foreign courts. In January, 1957, an American soldier, William Girard, killed a Japanese woman at an American military base. Later, Girard was turned over to Japanese officials for trial in keeping with the United States-Japan Status of Forces treaty. Mainly because Girard was on active duty at the time of the killing, his case became a cause célèbre, *and by May it had evolved into a matter of deep national interest. At a May 22 press conference, the President indicated that the matter was under official review. A week later, a Cabinet committee, refusing to bow to public opinion, decided that the Girard case should remain under Japanese jurisdiction, and on June 3, at a bipartisan meeting with congressional leaders, the President announced his stand and accepted the possibility of negative repercussions. Typical of many critics' views about the Status of Forces Treaty was the position expressed by Democratic Congressman W. R. Poage. The President's reply explained the Administration's position.*

Bipartisan Meeting
June 3, 1957
[Official File 328, Eisenhower Papers.]

6:30 P.M. MONDAY, JUNE 3, 1957

BIPARTISAN MEETING— (Girard Case)
(Off the Record—Enter S. E. Gate for appointment in the Mansion)

Senator Lyndon Johnson
Senator William F. Knowland

Speaker Sam Rayburn
Congressman Joseph Martin, Jr.

Meeting broke up about 7:30 P.M.

In addition to the above:
The President
General Persons
Mr. Harlow

Representative W. R. Poage to President Eisenhower
June 5, 1957
[Official File 328, Eisenhower Papers.]

Dear Mr. President:

The American people cannot understand your decision to surrender serviceman Girard to Japanese authorities. We understand that it is claimed that he was acting beyond the scope of his orders. Possibly this is so, but surely he didn't happen to be at this target range by accident. He was there because someone, acting under your authority as Commander in Chief of the Armed Forces, had ordered him to be there. If, however, there be any doubt about whether this man was acting pursuant to his duty or in violation thereof, it seems clear to me that the courts of the United States—not of Japan—should try this question of fact before surrendering him to some foreign power.

I recognize the importance of maintaining friendly relations with foreign nations and I realize that every nation properly insists on the right to try those who are accused of crime in their lands, but this does not carry with it the right to try a soldier of the United States who is performing a duty as such. I fear that this action is going to set in motion a chain of circumstances and resentment which is going to make it far more difficult to maintain our far-flung military outposts around the world.

Mr. President, I lay no claim to knowledge of either military affairs or statecraft, but I have observed the action of legislative bodies for a number of years. I think it is entirely probable that unless you make some very firm and unequivocal statement assuring the American people and American servicemen that there will be no repetition of this kind of surrender to foreign public opinion that American public opinion will understandably force a very substantial reduction in our military security abroad.

President Eisenhower to Representative W. R. Poage
June 5, 1957
[Official File 328, Eisenhower Papers.]

Dear Mr. Poage:

As indicated by your June 5 letter, the protection of the rights of our soldiers overseas is a duty our Government can neither lightly regard nor casually handle without serious consequences for our soldiers and our nation as well. Equally true, our soldiers are stationed abroad as part of our Government's duty to undergird our international efforts and as a projection of our own defense. The consequence is that those twin goals are unavoidably intermeshed in every such matter as the Girard situation when it becomes gravely significant either to ourselves or to a friendly power.

As regards the Girard matter, the State-Defense statement to the press relates the circumstances as thoroughly as can be done at this time without possible prejudice to the cause of this soldier in legal proceedings. I am satisfied both that he will have a fair trial, with his every right fully protected, and that proceeding as our nation has in this instance is warranted by the considerations set forth in the public release.

Your concern, as well as the motivation of your letter, I appreciate deeply. These matters I have worked closely with over the years, here and abroad. You are entirely correct that they are fraught with possibilities of great importance to our country and the cause of world peace.

The political repercussions that the President had been warned about in the Girard case soon appeared. In early July, 1957, Congress debated House Joint Resolution 16, which would have revised Status of Forces treaties so that only American courts could try United States servicemen accused of crimes. Later in the month the President wrote to Minority Leader Joseph Martin of Massachusetts expressing Administration opposition to the resolution. Girard's mild treatment by the Japanese—he received a three-year suspended sentence—defused the situation and led to the defeat of the resolution (July 17).

President Eisenhower to Representative Joseph Martin, Jr.
July 20, 1957
[Official File 116-H-3, Eisenhower Papers.]

Dear Joe:

I welcome the opportunity to reply to your request for comment as to the effect of the enactment of legislation having the purposes of House Joint Resolution 16 upon the status of our forces overseas.

In my judgment, the passage of any such legislation by the Congress would gravely threaten our security, alienate our friends, and give aid and comfort to those who want to destroy our way of life.

No longer does anyone suggest that we can safely withdraw behind the boundaries of a "fortress America". Yet this would be the ultimate effect of enacting this resolution. I can think of no recent legislative proposal which would so threaten the essential security of the United States.

Our troops are not overseas for the purpose of making war. Nor are they stationed around the world today merely for the protection of the lands where they happen to be located. They are there as allies to help maintain world peace so essential to the safety and the welfare of the United States.

We cannot demand—indeed we should not ask—that for us alone our allies in the struggle to maintain world peace should grant extraterritoriality and completely surrender their rights of sovereignty over criminal offenses committed in their lands. It must be remembered that the Congress in World War II in considering this issue as to allied troops in the United States was unwilling to relinquish our sovereignty under such circumstances.

This has been no partisan political matter in the United States. The NATO Status of Forces Agreement which crystallized these concepts was negotiated and signed in 1951 under the previous Administration. It was approved by the Senate by vote of 72 to 15 during this Administration. Such resolutions as H.J.Res. 16 have been previously rejected under the strongest sort of bipartisan leadership.

Although under international law each of our allies has full jurisdiction over criminal offenses committed within its borders, this rule has been qualified to our advantage in such agreements as the NATO Status of Forces Treaty. The United States is given primary jurisdiction where the offense is committed by a serviceman against another member of the United States forces, its civilian component, or a dependent, or against their property. Also, the United States is given primary jurisdiction where the offense arises out of an act done in the performance of official duty, whether it occurs on base or off base.

It has been, is, and so far as I can foresee will be our policy not to waive the primary United States right to try where the "performance of duty" matter is clear. As a matter of fact, no waiver of primary United States right to try has ever been given where that matter was clear.

Naturally, we are all directly concerned with protecting the best interests of our military forces. During my entire adult life I have been concerned with the welfare of the troops under my command, and I can assure you that the officers who are now in direct command of our armed forces share this concern and are watchful that every man in those forces be accorded fair treatment at all times and under all circumstances.

We have done our very best to insure that every member of our armed forces who is charged with a criminal offense abroad receives a fair trial and thus far, I believe, we have been successful in this.

Our display of confidence in the laws and courts of other nations through our status of forces agreements has produced a high degree of cooperation from these other nations. On a worldwide basis our allies in the first three and one-half years of the operation of such agreements have waived their undisputed primary jurisdiction in over sixty-five percent of the cases in which they had the primary right to try an alleged offender who was a member of our military establishment overseas. Japan has been particularly cooperative, since in this same period Japan has waived its primary jurisdiction to try in over ninety-six percent of the cases in which they had such right.

I regard as equally unfortunate any attempt to add the substance of H. J. Res. 16 as an amendment to any other measure, because such action would be gravely prejudicial to our national security.

For these reasons I feel most strongly that the passage of any legislation having the purposes of H. J. Res. 16 would be most hurtful to our national interests and to our aim of maintaining in the world the principles of peace and freedom. In our own interest, we need to continue to forge the bonds of understanding among the free nations.

3. UNITED STATES AND CUBA

On January 1, 1959, after several years of revolutionary activity against the Batista regime, Fidel Castro assumed power in Cuba. Although he had been depicted as a Robin Hood by some American reporters, the United States took a wary look at the guerrilla leader before formally recognizing his new government. On January 7, the State Department explained United States policy.

United States Recognizes New Government of Cuba
January 7, 1959
[Department of State, *Bulletin*, XL (January 26, 1959), 128.]

The U.S. Embassy at Havana on January 7 informed the Foreign Minister of Cuba, Roberto Daniel Agramonte Pichardo, that the U.S. Government had recognized the new Government of Cuba. The following note was delivered to the Cuban Foreign Minister by Ambassador Earl E. T. Smith.

I have been instructed by my Government to inform Your Excellency that, having noted with satisfaction the assurances given by the new Government of Cuba of its intention to comply with the international obligations and agreements of Cuba, the Government of the United States is pleased to recognize the Government under the Presidency of Dr. Manuel Urrutia Lleo, as the provisional Government of the Republic of Cuba.

At the same time the Government of the United States expresses the sincere good will of the Government and people of the United States toward the new Government and the people of Cuba.

Explanation of United States Policy Toward Cuba
January 15, 1959
[Department of State, *Bulletin*, XI (February 2, 1959), 162-63.]

Recent statements in the Cuban and American press critical of United States policy in Cuba and of Ambassador [Earl E. T.] Smith reflect a widespread lack of understanding of what United States policy toward Cuba has been.

The policy of the United States with respect to the Cuban revolution has been strictly one of nonintervention in Cuban domestic affairs, and the Ambassador's role has conformed always to this policy. Much as the American people, being free themselves, would have liked to have seen a free democratic system in Cuba, the United States Government was pledged in agreements with its sister republics to a course of nonintervention. Like all the other American Republics, the United States maintained normal diplomatic relations with the Batista government. Under established inter-American policy this did not imply judgment in favor of the domestic policy of that government or against the revolutionary forces. From the time when it became evident that Cuba was undergoing a revolution which had the support of a large segment of the population, the United States demonstrated its determination to avoid all possible involvement in Cuba's internal conflict by suspending all sales and shipments of combat arms to the Batista government. This action coincided with the renewed suspension of constitutional guaranties by the Batista government following a 46-day period during which the suspension had been lifted following the appeal of the United States Government through its Ambassador.

The United States military missions to Cuba were established in 1950 and '51 pursuant to agreements between the United States and Cuba, negotiated with the Prio government. These agreements had as their sole purpose cooperation in the common defense of Cuba and the United States, and of the hemisphere as a whole. The function of the missions was to lend technical advice, facilitate access to United States technical military experience, arrange for the admissions of Cubans to United States service schools and academies, and facilitate the procurement of equipment and arms as recommended by the missions for common defense as described above. Similar United States missions are maintained in 19 of the other American Republics. In utilizing for the purpose of putting down the Cuban revolution any part of the equipment that had been provided under the agreement prior to the arms suspension or the small unit that had been previously trained and constituted expressly for the common defense, the government of Batista acted in disregard of the agreement and over the reiterated objections of the United States. No napalm was sold or otherwise provided by the United States for use against the Cuban revolutionaries. Eight napalm bombs were sold in 1955 for demonstration purposes. This sale was approved prior to the existence of the recent revolution in Cuba. By agreement between the Departments of State and Defense, none has been supplied to Cuba since. As for the missions themselves, they had no contact whatever with any military operations against the revolutionaries. They trained no personnel for this purpose. No mission personnel were present at any time in the zones of operation. Therefore, the charge that the United States supplied arms for Batista's operations against the rebels or that the missions assisted these operations in any way is completely false.

><><><><><><><><><><><><><><><><><><><><><><><><><

With Castro in power Cuban-American relations began to deteriorate almost immediately. The Cuban government permitted the Communist party to operate openly, indulged in violently anti-American speeches, and carried out numerous executions of political foes. President Eisenhower became suspicious that Castro himself might be a communist, despite reassuring reports by the CIA. When the American Society of Newspaper Editors invited Castro to speak in Washington in April, Eisenhower considered refusing him a visa. Technically, he could not enter the country under a diplomatic passport because he held no constitutional office. Although this idea was ultimately dropped, the President refused to meet with Castro. However, after Castro gave a moderate speech to the editors (April 17), Vice President Richard Nixon arranged a conference with the Cuban leader (April 19). The public reports of the three-hour meeting suggested that the two men had communicated amiably. A secret Nixon memorandum to the President, however, showed a far different evaluation. The document remains classified but Nixon recorded his feelings in a magazine article.

Richard Nixon's Summary of Meeting with Fidel Castro
April 19, 1959*

[*Readers Digest*, LXXXV, No. 511 (November 1964), 283–84.]

On April 19, 1959, I met for the first and only time the man who was to be the major foreign-policy issue of the 1960 Presidential campaign. . . .

The man, of course, was Fidel Castro. It is safe to say that no other individual in the world has created such a conflict of opinion in the United States. Many foreign-policy experts strongly support Sen. J. William Fulbright's view that Castro is merely "a nuisance but not a grave threat to the United States." The opposing view, which I share, is that Castro is a dangerous threat to our peace and security—and that we cannot tolerate the presence of his communist regime 90 miles from our shores. The primary

*Reprinted with permission of the *Readers Digest*.

evidence which caused me to reach this conclusion was provided by Castro himself in the conversation I had with him more than five years ago.

It was a Sunday afternoon, and there was nothing I wanted less to do than to go down to my Capitol office for a meeting with the new Cuban dictator. But there were special circumstances which prompted me to schedule the appointment.

Castro had come to power in Cuba a little more than three months before. He was now in Washington at the invitation of the American Society of Newspaper Editors. Because his visit was unofficial, and because he had been making violent anti-American statements, President Eisenhower had declined to see him.

Since I had had considerable experience in dealing with Latin American problems and because they thought some special treatment might change Castro's unfriendly attitude, our ambassador to Cuba, Philip Bonsal, and Secretary of State Christian Herter urged me to meet with him. I agreed, on the condition that the two of us would talk alone, without members of his staff or mine present, and that there should be no photographs taken or other attempts made to exploit our conference for publicity purposes. It seemed to me that until he demonstrated some intention of modifying his anti-American stand he should not be accorded the same treatment I would give to other visiting foreign officials.

Apart from the beard and the battle-fatigue uniform which are now his trademarks, Castro was one of the most striking foreign officials I met during my eight years as Vice President. As I told President Eisenhower later, he seemed to have that indefinable quality which, for good or evil, makes a leader of men.

He had a compelling, intense voice, sparkling black eyes, and he radiated vitality. After $3\frac{1}{2}$ hours of discussion I summed up my impressions in this way—he looked like a revolutionary, talked like an idealistic college professor and reacted like a communist. He was intelligent, shrewd, at times eloquent. He gave an *appearance* of sincerity, but what he said followed a pattern all too familiar to me. I had had conversations with many communist leaders abroad and in the United States. The answers to questions came back almost parrotlike from them, as they now did from Castro.

Q. Why don't you have free elections?

A. The people of Cuba don't want free elections; they produce bad government.

Q. Why don't you give fair trials to those whom you charge oppose the revolution?

A. The people of Cuba don't want them to have fair trials. They want them shot as quickly as possible.

Q. Aren't you afraid the communists in your government will eventually take it over?

A. I am not afraid of the communists; I can handle them.

I made no headway in attempting to convince him that international communism is more than just an economic and political idea and that its agents are dangerously effective in their ability to grasp power and to set up dictatorships.

At the conclusion of our conference I wrote a four-page secret memorandum, and sent copies to President Eisenhower, Secretary Herter and Allen Dulles, head of the Central Intelligence Agency. My conclusion was, "Castro is either incredibly naïve about communism or is under communist discipline. . . .

>━●━0━●━0━●━0━●━0━●━0━●━0━●━0━●━0━●━0━●━0━●━0━●━0━●━0━●━0━●━0━●━0━●━<

On May 17, 1959, Cuba passed an agrarian reform law which affected the holdings of many wealthy Americans. The United States viewed the new law with alarm and voiced official protest.

United States Informs Cuba of Views on Agrarian Reform Law June 11, 1959

[Department of State, *Bulletin,* XL (June 29, 1959), 958–59.]

The Department of State instructed the American Ambassador at Havana, Philip W. Bonsal, to deliver to the Cuban Minister of State, Roberto Agramonte, on June 11 a note stating certain views of the U.S. Government on the Cuban Agrarian Reform Law. The substance of the note is as follows.

I have the honor to refer to the Cuban Agrarian Reform Law, the text of which was published in the extraordinary special edition of the *Official Gazette* of June 3. This law, which is now being given detailed study by my Government, deals with matters of deep and legitimate interest to the United States consumers of Cuban products and to United States investors in Cuba.

Preliminary published drafts of this legislation have already given rise to such exchanges of views as those held in Washington on May 27 between Ambassador Dihigo and Assistant Secretary Rubottom and on June 1 between Your Excellency and the undersigned. As stated by the representatives of the United States in both these conversations, the Government of the United States understands and is sympathetic to the objectives which the Government of Cuba is presumed to be seeking to attain through this law. Various United States programs of technical cooperation and assistance in the agricultural field undertaken with other countries of this hemisphere and elsewhere have aimed at the same goal of encouraging greater agricultural production, new crops, and crop diversification so as to raise the standard of living of the inhabitants of rural areas and thereby contribute to the overall economic growth of those countries. The Government of the United States recognizes that soundly conceived and executed programs for rural betterment, including land reform in certain areas, can contribute to a higher standard of living, political stability, and social progress. In various international bodies over the past years my Government's position on this subject has been consistent and unequivocal.

At the same time it is evident that a widespread redistribution of land in a manner which might have serious adverse effects on productivity could prove harmful to the general economy and tend to discourage desirable private and public investment in both agriculture and industry. From the viewpoint of the interests of consumers in the United States of Cuban products and of private United States investors, present and prospective, in Cuba, it is the confident hope of the Government of the United States that agrarian reform in Cuba will be so carried out as not to impair or reduce but rather to increase the productivity of the Cuban economy.

The United States recognizes that under international law a state has the right to take property within its jurisdiction for public purposes in the absence of treaty provisions or other agreement to the contrary; however, this right is coupled with the corresponding obligation on the part of a state that such taking will be accompanied by payment of prompt, adequate, and effective compensation. United States citizens have invested in agricultural and other enterprises in Cuba for many years. This investment has been made under several Cuban Constitutions, all of which contained provisions for due compensation in case of expropriation, including the Cuban Constitution of 1940 which provided that should property be expropriated by the state there must be prior payment of the proper indemnification in cash, in the amount judicially determined.

The wording of the Cuban agrarian law gives serious concern to the Government of the United States with regard to the adequacy of the provision for compensation to its citizens whose property may be expropriated. In view of the many occasions in the past in which consultation on problems affecting both countries has proved mutually beneficial I regret that to date the Government of Cuba has found no opportunity to hear the views of those United States investors in Cuba whose interest would appear to be adversely affected.

Many of these United States interests have been a part of the Cuban economy over a long period of time. They have contributed to the progress and expansion of that economy. So far as the Department of State is aware they have complied with their obligations under Cuban law. It is respectfully suggested to Your Excellency that they are entitled to considerate treatment because they are actually and potentially constructive factors in the expanding Cuban economy which, it is understood, Your Excellency's Government seeks to achieve.

Because of the traditional friendly relations and these economic ties between our two countries, Your Excellency will, I am sure, appreciate and understand the hope of the United States Government that it may be possible to hold further exchanges of views from time to time as required on the effects of the Agrarian Reform Law on matters which are of deep mutual concern to our two governments.

By the fall of 1959 Eisenhower had begun to consider various actions to counter Castro's increasingly anti-American position. However, in public he remained noncommittal.

Presidential News Conference
October 28, 1959
[*Public Papers of the Presidents: 1959* (Washington, 1960), 751.]

QUESTION. Edward T. Folliard, *Washington Post:* Mr. President, do you want to comment on the behavior of Fidel Castro? What do you suppose, sir, is eating him?

THE PRESIDENT: Actually, I went over very carefully with the Secretary of State the statement that he made about the charges that have been made by Mr. Castro and our reply to it. I think that is about as full an answer as I can make at this time. I have no idea of discussing possible motivation of a man, what he is really doing, and certainly I am not qualified to go into such abstruse and difficult subjects as that.

I do feel this: here is a country that you would believe, on the basis of our history, would be one of our real friends. The whole history—first of our intervention in 1898, our making and helping set up Cuban independence, the second time we had to go in and did the same thing to make sure that they were on a sound basis, the trade concessions we have made and the very close relationships that have existed most of the time with them—would seem to make it a puzzling matter to figure out just exactly why the Cubans and the Cuban Government would be so unhappy when, after all, their principal market is right here, their best market. You would think they would want good relationships. I don't know exactly what the difficulty is. . . .

In the first weeks of 1960, the Administration reconsidered its official position toward Cuba. On January 26, a formal policy statement reiterated the American commitment to nonintervention. However, Eisenhower did decide on a trip to South America which he hoped would help counter Castro's growing hemispheric influence. The President understood, of course, that in the eyes of many Latin Americans Castro was a hero, and upon his return he ordered the CIA "to organize the training of Cuban exiles, mainly in Guatemala, against a possible future day when they might return to their homeland." Thus events were set into motion that would culminate in the 1961 Bay of Pigs invasion.

Statement by President Eisenhower
on United States Policy Toward Cuba
January 26, 1960
[*Public Papers of the Presidents: 1960–61* (Washington, 1961), 134–36.]

Secretary Herter and I have been giving careful consideration to the problem of relations between the Governments of the United States and Cuba. Ambassador Bonsal, who is currently in Washington, shared in our discussions. We have been, for many months, deeply concerned and perplexed at the steady deterioration of those relations reflected especially by recent public statements by Prime Minister Castro of Cuba, as well as by statements in official publicity organs of the Cuban Government. These statements contain unwarranted attacks on our Government and on our leading officials. These attacks involve serious charges none of which, however, has been the subject of formal representations by the Government of Cuba to our Government. We believe these charges to be totally unfounded.

We have prepared a re-statement of our policy toward Cuba, a country with whose people the people of the United States have enjoyed and expect to continue to enjoy a firm and mutually beneficial friendship.

The United States Government adheres strictly to the policy of nonintervention in the domestic affairs of other countries, including Cuba. This policy is incorporated in our treaty commitments as a member of the Organization of American States.

Second, the United States Government has consistently endeavored to prevent illegal acts in territory under its jurisdiction directed against other governments. United States law enforcement agencies have been increasingly successful in the prevention of such acts. The United States record in this respect compares very favorably with that of Cuba from whose territory a number of invasions directed against other countries have departed during the past year, in several cases attended with serious loss of life and property damage in the territory of those other countries. The United States authorities will continue to enforce United States laws, including those which reflect commitments under Inter-American treaties, and hope that other governments will act similarly. Our Government has repeatedly indicated that it will welcome any information from the Cuban Government or from other governments regarding incidents occurring within their jurisdiction or notice, which would be of assistance to our law enforcement agencies in this respect.

Third, the United States Government views with increasing concern the tendency of spokesmen of the Cuban Government, including Prime Minister Castro, to create the illusion of aggressive acts and conspiratorial activities aimed at the Cuban Government and attributed to United States officials or agencies. The promotion of unfounded illusions of this kind can hardly facilitate the development, in the real interest of the two peoples, of relations of understanding and confidence between their governments. The United States Government regrets that its earnest efforts over the past year to establish a basis for such understanding and confidence have not been reciprocated.

Fourth, the United States Government, of course, recognizes the right of the Cuban Government and people in the exercise of their national sovereignty to undertake those social, economic and political reforms which, with due regard for their obligations under international law, they may think desirable. This position has frequently been stated and it reflects a real understanding of and sympathy with the ideals and aspirations of the Cuban people. Similarly, the United States Government and people will continue to assert and to defend, in the exercise of their own sovereignty, their legitimate interests.

Fifth, the United States Government believes that its citizens have made constructive contributions to the economies of other countries by means of their investments and their work in those countries and that such contributions, taking into account changing conditions, can continue on a mutually satisfactory basis. The United States Government will continue to bring to the attention of the Cuban Government any instances in which the rights of its citizens under Cuban law and under international law have been disregarded and in which redress under Cuban law is apparently unavailable or denied. In this connection it is the hope of the United States Government that differences of opinion between the two governments in matters recognized under international law as subject to diplomatic negotiations will be resolved through such negotiations. In the event that disagreements between the two governments concerning this matter should persist, it would be the intention of the United States Government to seek solutions through other appropriate international procedures.

The above points seem to me to furnish reasonable bases for a workable and satisfactory relationship between our two sovereign countries. I should like only to add that the United States Government has confidence in the ability of the Cuban people to recognize and defeat the intrigues of international communism which are aimed at destroying democratic institutions in Cuba and the traditional and mutually beneficial friendship between the Cuban and American peoples.

In February, 1960, the Soviet Union agreed to buy 1,000,000 tons of Cuban sugar at the world price. The Soviets also lent Castro money and promised to provide him with certain military equipment. All this, plus Castro's continued attacks on the United States, led to a presidential request that American purchases of Cuban sugar be reduced (July 6). For many decades the United States had guaranteed to buy much of the Cuban sugar crop at prices well above the world level.

Statement by President Eisenhower upon Signing Bill Relating to the Cuban Sugar Quota
July 6, 1960

[*Public Papers of the Presidents: 1960–61* (Washington, 1961), 562–63.]

I have today approved legislation enacted by the Congress which authorizes the President to determine Cuba's sugar quota for the balance of calendar year 1960 and for the three-month period ending March 31, 1961. In conformity with this legislation I have signed a proclamation which, in the national interest, establishes the Cuban sugar quota for the balance of 1960 at 39,752 short tons, plus the sugar certified for entry prior to July 3, 1960. This represents a reduction of 700,000 short tons from the original 1960 Cuban quota of 3,119,655 short tons.

This deficit will be filled by purchases from other free world suppliers.

The importance of the United States Government's action relating to sugar quota legislation makes it desirable, I believe, to set forth the reasons which led the Congress to authorize and the Executive to take this action in the national interest.

Normally about one-third of our total sugar supply comes from Cuba. Despite every effort on our part to maintain traditionally friendly relations, the Government of Cuba is now following a course which raises serious question as to whether the United States can, in the long-run, continue to rely upon that country for such large quantities of sugar. I believe that we would fail in our obligation to our people if we did not take steps to reduce our reliance for a major food product upon a nation which has embarked upon a deliberate policy of hostility toward the United States.

The Government of Cuba has committed itself to purchase substantial quantities of goods from the Soviet Union under barter arrangements. It has chosen to undertake to pay for these goods with sugar—traded at prices well below those which it has obtained in the United States. The inescapable conclusion is that Cuba has embarked on a course of action to commit steadily increasing amounts of its sugar crop to trade with the Communist bloc, thus making its future ability to fill the sugar needs of the United States ever more uncertain.

It has been with the most genuine regret that this Government has been compelled to alter the heretofore mutually beneficial sugar trade between the United States and Cuba. Under the system which has existed up to this time, the people of Cuba, particularly those who labor in the cane fields and in the mills, have benefited from the maintenance of an assured market in the United States, where Cuban sugar commands a price well above that which could be obtained in the world market. These benefits also reached many others whose livelihood was related to the sugar industry on the island.

The American people will always maintain their friendly feelings for the people of Cuba. We look forward to the day when the Cuban Government will once again allow this friendship to be fully expressed in the relations between our two countries.

The summer of 1960 was a harsh one for the United States. The aftermath of the U-2 incident, the abortive Eisenhower trip to Japan, and the impending change in Administrations created a general climate of apprehension. Against this backdrop the Cuban crisis took on even more significance. Upon Castro's insistence that the sugar quota reduction was a prelude to invasion, Premier Nikita Khrushchev pledged Soviet protection of Cuba (July 9). Some Americans feared that Castro might trigger a Russo-American war, and Eisenhower reacted to the situation in Cold War terms on July 9.

Statement by President Eisenhower
Concerning Premier Khrushchev's Announcement of Support
for the Castro Government
July 9, 1960
[*Public Papers of the Presidents: 1960–61* (Washington, 1961), 567–68.]

The statement which has just been made by Mr. Khrushchev in which he promises full support to the Castro regime in Cuba is revealing in two respects. It underscores the close ties that have developed between the Soviet and Cuban governments. It also shows the clear intention to establish Cuba in a role serving Soviet purposes in this hemisphere.

The statement of the Soviet Premier reflects the effort of an outside nation and of international Communism to intervene in the affairs of the Western Hemisphere. There is irony in Mr. Khrushchev's portrayal of the Soviet Union as the protector of the independence of an American nation when viewed against the history of the enslavement of countless other peoples by Soviet imperialism.

The Inter-American system has declared itself, on more than one occasion, beginning with the Rio Treaty, as opposed to any such interference. We are committed to uphold those agreements. I affirm in the most emphatic terms that the United States will not be deterred from its responsibilities by the threats Mr. Khrushchev is making. Nor will the United States, in conformity with its treaty obligations, permit the establishment of a regime dominated by international Communism in the Western Hemisphere.

Cuba was inevitably a major issue in the 1960 presidential election. Although the candidates debated various policy proposals, neither suggested any American withdrawal from the naval base at Guantanamo Bay, an action that Castro had long desired. The President's statement on November 1 reiterated a view held by a vast majority of Americans.

Statement by President Eisenhower
Regarding the American Naval Base at Guantanamo
November 1, 1960
[*Public Papers of the Presidents: 1960–61* (Washington, 1961), 822.]

While the position of the Government of the United States with respect to the Naval Base at Guantanamo has, I believe, been made very clear, I would like to reiterate it briefly.

Our rights in Guantanamo are based on international agreements with Cuba, and include the exercise by the United States of complete jurisdiction and control over the area. These agreements with Cuba can be modified or abrogated only by agreement between the two parties, that is, the United States and Cuba. Our Government has no intention of agreeing to the modification or abrogation of these agreements and will take whatever steps may be appropriate to defend the Base.

The people of the United States, and all of the peoples of the world, can be assured that the United States' presence in Guantanamo and use of the Base pose no threat whatever to the sovereignty of Cuba, to the peace and security of its people or to the independence of any of the American countries. Because of its importance to the defense of the entire hemisphere, particularly in the light of the intimate relations which now exist between the present Government of Cuba and the Sino-Soviet bloc, it is essential that our position in Guantanamo be clearly understood.

Following the presidential election, relations with Cuba deteriorated even further. On January 2, 1961, the Cuban government demanded a drastic reduction in United States embassy personnel in Havana. Eisenhower, ignoring his "lame duck" status, terminated diplomatic relations with Cuba. Even as he acted, the training of exiles continued in Guatemala. Although Eisenhower failed to see his plans for liberating Cuba fulfilled, he did leave behind a well-defined program for his successor.

Statement by President Eisenhower
Terminating Diplomatic Relations with Cuba
January 3, 1961
[*Public Papers of the Presidents: 1960–61* (Washington, 1961), 891.]

Between one and two o'clock this morning, the Government of Cuba delivered to the United States Chargé d'Affaires ad interim of the United States Embassy in Havana a note stating that the Government of Cuba had decided to limit the personnel of our Embassy and Consulate in Havana to eleven persons. Forty-eight hours was granted for the departure of our entire staff with the exception of eleven. This unusual action on the part of the Castro Government can have no other purpose than to render impossible the conduct of normal diplomatic relations with that Government.

Accordingly, I have instructed the Secretary of State to deliver a note to the Chargé d'Affaires ad interim of Cuba in Washington which refers to the demand of his Government and states that the Government of the United States is hereby formally terminating diplomatic and consular relations with the Government of Cuba. Copies of both notes are being made available to the press.

This calculated action on the part of the Castro Government is only the latest of a long series of harassments, baseless accusations, and vilification. There is a limit to what the United States in self-respect can endure. That limit has now been reached. Our friendship for the Cuban people is not affected. It is my hope and my conviction that in the not too distant future it will be possible for the historic friendship between us once again to find its reflection in normal relations of every sort. Meanwhile, our sympathy goes out to the people of Cuba now suffering under the yoke of a dictator.

4. THE SPIRIT OF CAMP DAVID

Throughout the latter part of 1958 the recurrent problem of a German peace treaty continued to strain Soviet-American relations. Russia threatened to sign a separate peace treaty with East Germany unless the Western powers removed their forces from Berlin. This demand challenged the NATO alliance and brought firm assurances from the Western allies that the status quo would be maintained. Under these circumstances any reduction in tension between the United States and the Soviet Union seemed remote. Yet, even as Premier Nikita Khrushchev issued ultimatums over Berlin, rumors circulated that a summit conference appeared in the offing. Several times in the early months of 1959 Eisenhower had discounted the possibility of a meeting. However, while the President objected to a formal conference of heads of states, he did feel that an exchange of visits between himself and the Soviet Premier might have positive results. Ignoring the failure of a recent foreign ministers' conference convened to discuss the German crisis (May-June), he invited Khrushchev to visit the United States. Despite a press "leak" which suggested that the United States would carry on unilateral negotiations with the Soviet Union, Eisenhower made it clear that he had no intention of acting without consulting his allies. Indeed, the President quickly embarked on a trip to western Europe (August 26–September 7) to explain American policy. An urgently called news conference of August 3 outlined the board details of the Khrushchev visit, and a contemplated Soviet Union tour by the President.

Presidential News Conference
August 3, 1959
[*Public Papers of the Presidents: 1959* (Washington, 1960), 560.]

THE PRESIDENT: I asked this morning for this special press conference on the subject of the impending exchange of visits between Mr. Khrushchev and myself.

Now, while in Europe this has been for the past few days one of the worst kept secrets of a long time, still I think there may be enough special interest in the matter as to justify you people taking your time to come here this morning.

First of all, a little bit of the history:

Some time back, I suggested to the State Department that I believed in the effort to melt a little bit of the ice that seems to freeze our relationships with the Soviets, that possibly a visit such as I now have proposed would be useful. We studied this thing, and in early July I initiated the correspondence that finally brought about an agreement. Some of the details, exact details, are yet to be agreed between the diplomatic agencies of our separate, several governments.

Now, at this identical time, an identical statement is being issued in Moscow. The statement is as follows—and there will be copies at the door when you leave, so that you don't have to take the time to write it down:

[*Reading*] The President of the United States has invited Mr. Nikita Khrushchev, Chairman of the Council of Ministers of the U.S.S.R., to pay an official visit to the United States in September. Mr. Khrushchev has accepted with pleasure.

The President has also accepted with pleasure Mr. Khrushchev's invitation to pay an official visit to the U.S.S.R. later this fall.

Mr. Khrushchev will visit Washington for 2 or 3 days and will also spend 10 days or so travelling in the United States. He will have informal talks with the President, which will afford an opportunity for an exchange of views about problems of mutual interest.

On his tour of the United States, Mr. Khrushchev will be able, at first hand, to see the country, its people, and to acquaint himself with their life.

President Eisenhower will visit Moscow and will also spend some days travelling in the Soviet Union. This will provide further opportunity for informal talks and exchange of views about problems of mutual interest with the Chairman of the Council of Ministers of the U.S.S.R.

On his tour of the Soviet Union, President Eisenhower likewise will be able at first hand to see the country, its people, and to acquaint himself with their life.

Both Government express the hope that the forthcoming visits will help create better understanding between the U.S. and the U.S.S.R. and will promote the cause of peace. [*Ends reading*]

That is the end of the quoted statement.

Now, one or two other items.

We have, of course, been consulting for a couple of weeks through the foreign ministers about this possibility—our Western foreign ministers; they have, of course, agreed.

And then, the heads of state were notified just recently about this impending visit, and some of them have been able to answer. All of them have agreed—I think all of them have been able to answer; all have agreed that the matter is one that should produce plus rather than negative values. In other words, on balance, they think it's a very good thing to do.

In the meantime, I might tell you that this morning I have taken considerable trouble to inform some of the leaders of Congress, and those that I've heard from have been quite favorably disposed toward this plan.

I want to make this clear: by no means am I intending to be or can I be any spokesman for the Western powers in my talks with Mr. Khrushchev. I can be a spokesman only for America and for its Government. Nevertheless, I have already suggested that prior to these meetings, I go to meet our friends in Europe and to discuss with them problems of mutual interest.

The visit itself has no direct connection with any possible later summit meeting. I of course would hope that the mere announcement would inspire the foreign ministers to a greater activity, and probably some greater effort at conciliation, so that there might be results before Wednesday, when they temporarily adjourn at least, that would justify the scheduling of such a later meeting, at what time I don't know.

But in any event, even if they have to reassemble, I would hope that they could do that, if they found it reasonable and proper.

So, I merely want to make clear that this is a personal visit for the purposes that I have outlined and are given in the statement, but with the hope that it will do something to promote understanding and possibly progress toward peace in the world.

Now, as long as we talked on this one subject, because this is a special conference, I am perfectly ready to take 10 minutes or so for questions.

QUESTION. Edward T. Folliard, *The Washington Post:* Mr. President, Governor Meyner, who is one of the nine Governors who called on you the other day after their return from Russia, was talking about the possibility of a Khrushchev visit and he said there was the possibility of what he called "incidents," brought on by refugees in this country, and he thought that Premier Khrushchev should be told that there are such people, and that we didn't try to stifle people in this country.

Have you given some thought to the possibility of incidents, Mr. President?

THE PRESIDENT: Naturally, because this is always a possibility in our country, as is evidenced by the fact that we found it so necessary to provide protection for the members of the President's family.

Now, we do have these uncontrolled individuals, and of course we talked about that, and they know it. We have not failed to point out this fact to the U.S.S.R. representatives. I am certain, however, that we can control this matter.

QUESTION. Robert J. Donovan, *The New York Herald-Tribune:* Do you know, sir, whether Mr. Khrushchev will come directly to Washington first, or will he go to New York and then here, or how?

THE PRESIDENT: I can't tell you a thing about details. I can't give you the exact dates, the exact times, the exact schedules, or exactly how he will come here.

QUESTION. Chalmers M. Roberts, *The Washington Post:* On this schedule, sir, do you know when you will go to Europe——

THE PRESIDENT: No—oh, excuse me. Finish your question.

QUESTION. Mr. Roberts:—— to see the allied heads of state?

THE PRESIDENT: Sometime later in this month I would like to; that is my suggestion.

QUESTION. Mr. Roberts: And then you will come back here?

THE PRESIDENT: That is right.

QUESTION. Mr. Roberts: And Khrushchev will come here?

THE PRESIDENT: Yes. . . .

>─●━0━●━0━●━0━●━0━●━0━0━0━●━0━●━0━●━0━0━0━●━0━●━0━●━0━●━0━0━0━●━

Khrushchev's impending visit quickly became a major topic of concern for Americans. From the official negotiations about the Premier's itinerary to the smallest details of what he should eat or see, literally thousands of people made suggestions. The White House received a voluminous correspondence recommending what Khrushchev should do while on American soil. A number of people suggested that the President take the communist leader to church. On a different level, the domestic political aspects of the tour emerged. Eisenhower, of course, had his own ideas about topics to be discussed with the Premier.

W. B. Hamilton to President Eisenhower
August 4, 1959
[Official File 225-B-1, Eisenhower Papers.]

Dear Mr. President:

Your decision to invite Mr. Krushchev to these United States is only headlines at this time, but were it possible to project ourselves to August 2059 we would read of your tremendous impact on the history of this world.

May I suggest that you and Mrs. Eisenhower invite Mr. Krushchev to attend Sunday worship services with you. This may be an impossible suggestion, but it might impress our visitor with the spiritual strength of our nation which backs our material might.

It is with much satisfaction that I can report an upsurge in the opinions favoring your policies and ideas. The firmness of Mr. Herter and the "sure-footedness" of Mr. Nixon are proof to many that your desires for the good of all outweigh shortsighted "ward politics." . . .

Governor Mark Hatfield
to Presidential Assistant Robert Merriam
August 26, 1959
[Official File 225-B-1, Eisenhower Papers.]

Dear Bob:

Thank you for your note concerning the Khrushchev visit. While I would have liked very much to have Mr. Khrushchev see Oregon and some of our accomplishments here, I am dismayed not so much by the fact that this possibility has failed as I am by the point that he will be hosted almost exclusively by Democratic governors. I realize there are too few of us left and apparently those who remain are located in the wrong states.

President Eisenhower to Paul Hoffman
September 9, 1959
[Official File 116-WW, Eisenhower Papers.]

Dear Paul:

Many thanks for your note about the telecast I did with Prime Minister Macmillan. Needless to say I greatly appreciate your more than generous comments.

I plan to repeat to Mr. Khrushchev my belief that aid to the less developed nations should be a cooperative effort—although I have no idea, at the moment, what reaction such a statement may evoke.

Khrushchev arrived in the United States on September 15, 1959, and after a brief stay in Washington, began a hectic 10-day trip around the country, escorted by United States Ambassador to the United Nations Henry Cabot Lodge, Jr. The trip spanned the continent, touching, besides the major cities, such places as Coon Rapids, Iowa, and Beltsville, Maryland. Khrushchev saw many phases of American life, including his first love, farming. In fact, farm experts drafted special notes to assist Ambassador Lodge in this part of the tour.

Notes for Ambassador Lodge on American Agriculture
n.d.
[Parlberg Files, Eisenhower Papers.]

1. Mr. K. is keenly interested in agriculture.
   a) Was an agricultural student in the Ukraine
   b) Helped bring about several major recent changes in the pattern of Soviet agriculture.
   c) Realizes the problems of Soviet agriculture.
      i) Provides only a limited diet
      ii) Ties down nearly half the population in food production
      iii) Permits little export.
2. Mr. K. will have two agricultural stops while here.
   a) Beltsville, Md., the agricultural experiment station
   b) Coon Rapids, Iowa, the home of Roswell Garst, Iowa farmer, agricultural pioneer, extrovert, armchair philosopher. Old friend of Mr. K.
3. The Garst farm (huge, ultra-modern) is by no means typical of American agriculture. It does have, however, a number of features in which Mr. K. is especially interested:
   a) Large-scale mechanized equipment
   b) Feed-Grain-livestock type, a type which Mr. K. is trying to promote.
   c) Modern technology of feeding and fertilization of special interests to Mr. K.
4. The points about American agriculture which could well be stressed to Mr. K. are these:
   a) Farmers make their own decisions on what to plant and how much to produce (except for a few crops).
   b) Technological advance in American agriculture is accomplished by free enterprise, coupled with government help in research, education, rural electrification, credit services.
   c) The American farm worker outproduces the farm worker of the Soviet Union by about four-to-one.

d) The U. S. is making good use of technological advances in agriculture. Diets are improving, food cost is relatively low, people have been released from farms for industrial production, American agricultural technology has been successfully exported to underdeveloped nations, food has been made available to hungry people overseas through special export programs. *Problems have developed where government has sought to regulate production and fix prices, as for cotton and wheat.*

5. This is a good but not a record year for crop yields.

Crops are good in Iowa, where Mr. K. will visit.

There has been some drought in the Dakotas, in the Ohio valley and other scattered areas.

More Notes on American Agriculture
n.d.
[Parlberg Files, Eisenhower Papers.]

I. *The People*

1. Farm people constitute 12 percent of our population.
2. Each farm worker, on the average, feeds himself and 22 others.
3. 76 percent of our farm people own their farms. This percentage is increasing. 24 percent of our farmers are tenants.
4. Our farms are typically family farms. 96 percent of our commercial farms are of this kind. This percentage has not changed in the last 30 years.
5. Labor on our farms is typically family labor. 75 percent of our farm labor is supplied by the farmer and his family. The other 25 percent is hired.
6. The general breakdown of American "farms" by kind is as follows:

	Number	*Percent of all farms*	*Percent of total U.S. value of farm products sold*
Large commercial farms	134,000	2.8	31.3
Family-scale farms	1,968,000	63.5	59.5
Small-family farms	1,225,000	25.7	7.1
Part-time farms	575,000	12.0	1.4
Rural residences	878,000	18.4	0.3
Institutional farms	3,000	0.1	0.3
Total	4,783,000	100.0	100.0

II. *The Plant*

   7. The average value per farm of assets used in production is $33,500. The average total debt per farm is $5,016, 11 percent of total assets.

   8. The average farm is thus characterized:

Labor force	1.6 persons
Acres	242 acres
Number of tractors	1 tractor
Realized net income	$2,767

III. *The Programs*

   9. Major services of the Federal Government to agriculture:

Education	(15,000 full-time professional extension workers)
Research	(4,700 full-time professional research workers)

  10. 83 percent of farm income is from farm products which are without production controls.

  11. 57 percent of farm income is from farm products without price supports.

  12. Government stocks of major price-supported commodities are as follows:
Wheat: Stocks equal to 1 year's production
Cotton: Stocks equal to ½ year's production
Corn: Stocks equal to 2/5 year's production

On September 24 Khrushchev returned to Washington and met privately with the President at Camp David. Although Eisenhower assured America's allies that no deals would be made behind their backs, he did feel free to use personal diplomacy to try to alleviate tensions. His greatest accomplishment at the meeting—Russia's withdrawal of any time limt over a German peace treaty—almost went awry when Khrushchev asked that the final communiqué exclude the concession. Eisenhower rejected this request but compromised by delaying the statement's publication for 48 hours. This gave Khrushchev an opportunity to explain his decision at home. For this reason the final joint statement was issued from Eisenhower's farm in Gettysburg.

Joint Statement by President Eisenhower and Premier Nikita Khrushchev Following Discussions at Camp David September 27, 1959

[*Public Papers of the Presidents: 1959* (Washington, 1960), 692–93.]

The Chairman of the Council of Ministers of the USSR, N. S. Khrushchev, and President Eisenhower have had a frank exchange of opinions at Camp David. In some of these conversations United States Secretary of State Herter and Soviet Foreign Minister Gromyko, as well as other officials from both countries, participated.

Chairman Khrushchev and the President have agreed that these discussions have been useful in clarifying each other's position on a number of subjects. The talks were not undertaken to negotiate issues. It is hoped, however, that their exchanges of view will contribute to a better understanding of the motives and position of each and thus to the achievement of a just and lasting peace.

The Chairman of the Council of Ministers of the USSR and the President of the United States agreed that the question of general disarmament is the most important one facing the world today. Both governments will make every effort to achieve a constructive solution of this problem.

In the course of the conversations an exchange of views took place on the question of Germany including the question of a peace treaty with Germany, in which the positions of both sides were expounded.

With respect to the specific Berlin question, an understanding was reached, subject to the approval of the other parties directly concerned, that negotiations would be reopened with a view to achieving a solution which would be in accordance with the interests of all concerned and in the interest of the maintenance of peace.

In addition to these matters useful conversations were held on a number of questions affecting the relations between the Union of Soviet Socialist Republics and the United States. These subjects included the question of trade between the two countries. With respect to an increase in exchanges of persons and ideas, substantial progress was made in discussions between officials and it is expected that certain agreements will be reached in the near future.

The Chairman of the Council of Ministers of the USSR and the President of the United States agreed that all outstanding international questions should be settled not by the application of force but by peaceful means through negotiation.

Finally it was agreed that an exact date for the return visit of the President to the Soviet Union next spring would be arranged through diplomatic channels.

On the evening of September 27, 1959, just prior to his departure for the Soviet Union, Khrushchev addressed the American people via television. In a cordial and friendly tone he thanked President Eisenhower for inviting him and he called for friendly relations between his nation and the United States.

Address by Premier Nikita Khrushchev
on American-Soviet Relations
September 27, 1959
[*The New York Times*, September 28, 1959]

Good evening, American friends.

I am glad of this opportunity of talking to you before leaving for my country. We liked your beautiful cities and fine roads, but most of all your amiable, kind-hearted people. And let these words of mine not be taken as the guest's customary tribute of courtesy and respect to his host.

Those who have visited the Soviet Union will have told you about the very good feelings which the Soviet people have for you and about their wish to live in peace and friendship with you. And I will now take with me the certainty that you feel the same way about the Soviet people. I am going to tell them about it.

I have had very pleasant talks with President Dwight Eisenhower. In all matters touched upon in our conversations, we had much in common, both as regards our appraisal of the situation and the need for better relations between our countries.

You will realize that it is not so easy to overcome all that has piled up in the many years of cold war. Think of all the speeches that did not promote better relations but, on the contrary, aggravated them! That being so, we cannot expect an abrupt change in the situation. The process of improving relations between our countries will require great effort and patience, but above all else a mutual desire to create conditions that will facilitate a shift from the present state of tension to normal relations, and then to friendship in the interests of durable peace throughout the world.

The Soviet Union, whose government and people I represent, is guided by the desire to promote peace and friendship among nations. We have always done our utmost to end the cold war and improve relations between our countries, and we do so now.

I have not the slightest doubt that the President sincerely desires better relations between our countries. It seems to me that the position of the U. S. President is more difficult than mine. It would appear that the forces obstructing better relations between our countries and a relaxation of international tension are still influential in the United States of America. And that must be taken into account. I think, however, that common sense will in the end suggest the right course in the settlement of international problems. And that course, the only correct course, is the termination of the cold war and the promotion of universal peace.

But it takes more than two states to end international tension. This can only be done if all states desire it and work for it.

There can be no stability or peace in the world as long as the two mightiest powers are at odds.

Picture two neighbors. Each disapproves of the way the other lives and runs his household. So they fence themselves off from each other. And together with their families, they revile each other day and night. Is that a happy life to live? Anyone will say that it is not; sooner or later the two neighbors may come to blows.

Bad neighbors have a way out, at least—one of them could sell his house and move into another. But what about states? They cannot move elsewhere, can they? What is the solution then?

You have capitalism in your country, and we have socialism. Must we on this account push things to the point of a world-wide free-for-all? Or shall we establish normal relations and live in peace, each in his own way? Everybody in the Soviet Union wants all countries to live in peace, everybody wants peaceful coexistence.

Have you ever given any thought to the following? Why do you and we need all these armaments if we have no intention of going to war? I have been told that your country annually spends an average of more than 40 billion dollars on armaments. What about us? There's been no point in concealing the fact that we spend about 25 billion dollars a year for the same purpose. Couldn't a better use be found for the people's money?

To be sure, it is not easy for any country to accept disarmament unless it is certain that the others will do likewise. Every country has fears of being attacked.

You probably know that a week ago the Soviet Government submitted to the United Nations a proposal for general and complete disarmament and for the most rigid, comprehensive control. What have we in mind? We propose that all armed forces be completely abolished, that all weapons, including atomic, hydrogen and rocket weapons, be destroyed. The states should retain no more than strictly limited contingents of police armed with small arms. But if our partners should be unwilling to take measures as far-reaching as that, we are prepared, for a start, to reach agreement on partial steps toward disarmament.

We are gratified that many statesmen and political leaders are giving serious thought to these proposals of ours and on their part are taking steps to bring about the necessary agreement on disarmament. Unfortunately, some people still cling to the arguments of the cold-war period. We should like to hope that the governments of the USA and other countries will take a correct view of our peaceful proposals and will, for their part, take appropriate steps in the same direction.

We discussed this problem in detail during our conversations with your President. The President, like ourselves, is concerned about the fact that so far we have not succeeded in ending the armaments fever. I am going home in the hope that the U. S. Government will be able to overcome deep-rooted prejudices and that sooner or later, in common with all the other countries, we will find the correct approach to the solution of the disarmament problem.

We have also discussed other pressing matters, of which quite a number have piled up these days. I will, first of all, single out the problem of removing the aftermath of the Second World War. Many people ask why the Soviet Union is so concerned about the question of removing those vestiges. After all, it's a thing of the distant past, they argue. I will speak plainly: We are not afraid of German militarism. But we know its insidious ways and habits only too well. The absence of a peace treaty creates an atmosphere which stimulates revanchist sentiment. Don't misunderstand me. The survivals of war must not be allowed to stay if we are to have peace.

The Soviet Union has proposed that a line be drawn through the Second World War. This can and must be done by signing a treaty with Germany.

The argument is sometimes used against us that since the war was waged against Germany when she was a single state, a peace treaty can only be concluded after Germany is unified. But it is well known that, at present, two German states exist in reality, and each of them lives in its own way. Neither of the German states wants to give up its social system. And surely there can be no question of forcing one German state to surrender to the other. Let the Germans themselves reach agreement on how they should live, on how they should shape their mutual relations.

Would it not be best to conclude a peace treaty with both German states without further delay, and thereby put out the sparks buried in the ashes before they set off a new conflagration? Conclusion of a peace treaty would also put out the live spark in West Berlin, with the result that a normal situation would be created.

The question of a German peace treaty, like the disarmament question, is not an easy one. But precisely because these are difficult questions, they must be settled and not shelved.

During my stay in your country I have acquainted myself with the life of the American people as best I could in so short a time, and have seen and heard a good deal. I am most grateful for the warm reception and cordiality accorded to me, as head of the Soviet Government, and to my companions. We were strengthened in the conviction that the American people are striving for friendship with our people and that they love peace and their country. They have created great riches and achieved a high standard of living. Like you the Soviet people love their country and want peace. They want to live in friendship with your people, and with all the other peoples of the world.

The peoples of the Soviet Union have made great progress, thanks to the victory of socialism. And though we are not yet as rich as you, we are on the right path that leads to the achievement of the highest standard of living. Our people are striving for it, and it shall be achieved.

The question of social and political structure, that is, whether to live under socialism or capitalism, is the internal affair of each people, and noninterference by states in each other's domestic affairs should be strictly adhered to.

If all countries are guided by these principles, there will be no particular difficulties in assuring international peace. To live in peace, we must know each other better. Allow me to tell you, if only briefly, about our country, the life of our people and our plans for the future. I hope you will not misunderstand me when I say that the impressions which I have gained here, and indeed the things that I liked in your country, have not shaken my conviction that the political, economic and social mode of life in the Soviet Union is the most progressive and just.

The Soviet Union is a state of working people. We have no capitalists. Our factories and mills belong to the people and so does all the land with its riches. Peasants work on that land as members of collective farms. Each has an income that depends on the amount of work he puts in, not on capital invested.

Under socialism, the remuneration paid to a worker depends on the quantity and quality of the work he performs for the good of society. When we have expanded production still more and accumulated greater wealth, we will go over to distribution according to the communist principle, which means that each will work according to his ability and enjoy the good things of life according to his needs.

The Constitution of our state is, in fact, the most democratic. It guarantees universal, direct and equal suffrage by secret ballot. It guarantees the right to work, to education and to rest and leisure.

Before the Revolution in our country, he who had capital was considered wise. For the first time in history, our country has established the just principle: He who works well enjoys social distinction.

Take the composition of the Supreme Soviet of the USSR, which is the country's highest organ of state power. There are 1,378 deputies elected to the Supreme Soviet of the USSR, of whom 366 are women. Over 1,000 deputies are directly engaged in industrial or agricultural production—they are workers, engineers, collective farmers, agronomists. The other deputies are statesmen, public leaders, scientific or cultural workers, men of letters, art workers, teachers, doctors. As you see, there are no capitalists in our country and no capitalist representatives in the Supreme Soviet. Those who make up our government are the sons and daughters of working people.

I will tell you about myself. My grandfather was an illiterate peasant. He was the landlord's property and could be sold or even, as was often the case, traded for a dog. My father was a coal miner, and I, too, worked in a coal pit as a fitter. I fought in our Civil War. Then the Soviet state sent me to a workers' school and later to the Industrial Academy. Now the people have entrusted me with the high office of Chairman of the Council of Ministers.

Recently, both my First Deputies, Anastas Mikoyan and Frol Kozlov, visited your country. Who are they? Anastas Mikoyan is the son of a carpenter, and Frol Kozlov is the son of a blacksmith and was himself a worker and later an engineer. There is no such thing as inheriting capital or high posts in our country.

All members of Soviet society enjoy genuine freedom. The only thing we do not have is the freedom to exploit other people's labor, to privately own factories or banks.

We people of the older generation started life in a capitalist environment. But why do we consider the socialist way more just? For hundreds of years mankind had developed under conditions where a minority appropriated the riches created by the majority. And always people had sought a better social structure under which there would be no exploitation of man by man.

We are grateful to Marx, Engels and Lenin who blazed the trail to that society, and we have taken that trail. And the same path was taken after us by many peoples of Europe and Asia. Having taken power into their hands, the working people put an end to the urge for profiting at other people's expense. Human greed is a terrible thing. Has there ever been a millionaire who did not want to be a multimillionaire?

I want to be understood correctly. It is one thing when a person has a pair of shoes and wants to have two or three pairs more, when he has one suit and wants to have a few more, or when he has a house and wants to build himself a better one. That is a legitimate desire. Socialism does not limit people's tastes or requirements. But it is quite another thing when a person owns a factory and wants to have two, or when he owns one mill and wants to have ten. It should be perfectly clear that no one, even if he is helped by his entire family, and even if he were to live more than one life, can earn a million, and still less a billion dollars, by his own labor. He can do that only if he appropriates the labor of others. But surely that is contrary to man's conscience. You will remember that even the Bible says that when they who engaged in trade turned the temple into a house of usurers and money-changers, Christ took a whip and drove them out.

That is why religious people should not oppose the new socialist system if, in accordance with their moral code, they are guided by the principles of peace on earth and love of one's neighbor. For it is a system which establishes the most human and truly just relations in society.

To help you understand why we are so proud of our Soviet country, I must say a few words about our pre-Revolutionary past. The people had a very hard life in those days. Almost 80 per cent of the population was illiterate. Hunger and disease killed millions of people.

You will now find it easier to understand why Soviet people are so happy that their country has in a short time become the world's second greatest industrial power. We have increased industrial output 36-fold, eliminated illiteracy, and are now graduating almost three times as many engineers as the USA.

Our people would still be better off today if, out of 40 years, we had not spent almost two decades on wars imposed upon us, and on postwar economic rehabilitation.

Do you know that during the war the German fascist invaders burned down or otherwise destroyed 1,710 towns and townships and upward of 70,000 villages, leaving about 25 million people homeless? We lost many millions of people and suffered material damage amounting to nearly 500 billion dollars.

But for these fearful losses and destruction, we would probably have caught up with the United States by now both in volume of output and in living standards.

Today our people are busy fulfilling the seven-year plan. In the current seven-year period we will double industrial output. In this period, we will invest the equivalent of nearly 750 billion dollars in the national economy.

Today the United States is economically the most highly-developed power. Your country's economic indices are the peak of what has been attained in the capitalist world. But don't forget that, on the average, the Soviet Union's annual rate of industrial growth is three to five times as high as yours. That means that in the next ten to twelve years we will exceed the United States both in physical volume of industry and in per capita output. And in agriculture this task will be fulfilled much earlier.

Our country is carrying on large-scale housing construction. Here is an example: In the past eight years alone more housing was built in Moscow than throughout the 800 years of its pre-Revolutionary history. Next year the people of Moscow will have additional housing whose total floor space will exceed one quarter of all the housing available in our capital before the Revolution. In the current seven-year period we will build about 15 million apartments in towns and 7 million houses in the countryside. That is roughly equivalent to some 50 new towns as large as San Francisco. An important point is that our country has the world's lowest rent—a mere 4 or 5 per cent of the family budget.

We are seeing to it that there are more comfortable homes and that Soviet people get more and better consumer goods. And we are as good as our word. In the last six years Soviet agriculture has trebled meat sales to the urban population, and more than doubled those of milk.

It will not be long before we abolish—I repeat, abolish—all taxation of the population. I believe you fully appreciate the significance of this measure.

The Communist Party, the Soviet Government and the trade unions are working for the welfare of all Soviet people.

Soviet people need not fear anything like unemployment, for example. The term "unemployment" is long forgotten in our country. In the Soviet Union, it is not people who look for work, but work that looks for people.

All our children go to school. In the Soviet Union tuition is free not only in secondary schools, but also in higher schools. Students receive state allowances. We give a very great deal of attention to the education of children. Nursery school, kindergarten, boarding-school, and then a start in life—such is the clear road of our rising generation.

The merits of the Soviet educational system are widely known. It is the people educated in Soviet schools—scientists, engineers, technicians and workers—who amazed the world with the first man-made earth satellites. We are proud that the Russian words "sputnik" and "lunik" are now understood all over the world, without having to be translated.

Two million teachers and almost 400,000 doctors are serving the welfare of Soviet people.

We are taking care of the health of our people; the sick rate has sharply declined in our country and the death rate is the lowest in the world. Every factory or office worker is granted paid leave every year. The working people have the best sanatoriums, health resorts and vacation resorts at their disposal. Medical treatment is free for all in our country, and neither a minor operation nor the most complicated one entails any expense for the patient. Sometimes you don't understand certain aspects of our way of life. And Soviet people find it hard to understand how it can be that when you are in trouble because someone in your family is seriously ill and has to be operated on or sent to a hospital, you have to pay money for it. And what if you have no money? What happens then—must the sick man die?

When somebody is ill in our country and cannot work, he gets his pay just the same. And when old age comes along he does not feel abandoned, for he gets a state pension. Peasants are pensioned out of the funds of their collective farms.

You may ask: "Is everything really so good and smooth in your country?" I am afraid not, because we also have our difficulties, shortcomings and unsolved problems. I can assure you that we Soviet people are the most scathing and uncompromising critics of our own shortcomings.

Esteemed citizens of the United States of America, in a few hours our plane will leave American soil. I wish once again to thank the American people, President Eisenhower and the U. S. Government for the hospitality and good feelings shown us. I credit these good feelings and the attention shown to me, as head of the Soviet Government, to the people of my country.

During my stay in your country I have received thousands of letters and telegrams of greeting from American citizens. They express friendship for the Soviet people. Many of them invited my companions and myself to visit their homes and meet their families and their children. I should like to go to all the places I was invited to, but unfortunately that is out of the question. To do it, I should have to stay here a long time. And that, you will realize, is something I cannot do. Allow me to give my heartfelt thanks to all who extended their friendly invitation, to all who expressed friendly sentiments.

Allow me, in conclusion, to wish the American people prosperity and happiness, and also to express the hope that our visit to the United States, and President Dwight Eisenhower's forthcoming visit to the Soviet Union, will be regarded not only by the American and Soviet peoples, but also by all the other peoples, as the beginning of joint efforts in the search for ways of bringing our countries closer together and promoting universal peace.

Good-bye and good luck, friends!

The Administration was very pleased with the Khrushchev visit but did not want to give the impression that the trip had ended all Soviet-American disagreements. On October 1, 1959, Assistant Secretary of State Andrew H. Berding accented this in an address before the League of Republican Women of the District of Columbia. Berding stressed what was obviously the Administration's interpretation of "peaceful coexistence."

Speech by Assistant Secretary Andrew Berding on the Visit of Premier Khrushchev October 1, 1959

[Department of State, *Bulletin,* XLI (November 10, 1959), 544–47.]

This is a time of many important visits by chiefs of state and heads of government to Washington.

We are proud to have with us now the Prime Minister of Italy, Antonio Segni, and the Foreign Minister, Giuseppe Pella, both of whom I had the pleasure of knowing during the early Marshall plan days in Italy. His conference yesterday with President Eisenhower is in the tradition of the ever stronger influence of Italy in foreign affairs. Testimony to this is the fact that Italy is one of the members of the 10-nation committee which will engage in vital disarmament negotiations some time after the beginning of the year. Italy's strategic position in the Mediterranean, her sense of cooperation, the energy, industry, and ingeniousness of her people, justify Italian participation in the discussions of major world problems. Our own relations with Italy are close and constructive. Prime Minister Segni's visit will solidify them still more.

Later this month Washington will receive the welcome visit of President Lopez Mateos of Mexico, to strengthen still further the friendship between our two countries. Toward the end of the month we shall cordially greet the President of the newest country on earth—Sekou Touré of Guinea.

But without doubt the most important state visit of recent times ended 4 days ago, when Chairman Khrushchev winged out over the Atlantic to return to Moscow.

Value of Visit and Talks

Now it may be of interest to draw a few conclusions and make a few comments on this visit by one of the outstanding personalities of our time.

To begin with, the visit, without question, was a plus. It was a plus in both its aspects—first, the trip itself in the United States; second, the talks with President Eisenhower. During these talks I had the honor of being at Camp David and Gettysburg.

As to the visit, Chairman Khrushchev certainly got a better, clearer idea of America and Americans than he had had before. He saw the strength of our economy, the high living standards, the freedom of expression, the diversity of our people. He finally admitted that people could live very well indeed under what he calls capitalism. He also recognized that our Government and our people are virtually as one when it comes to foreign policy. He acknowledged that Americans generally want peace. He recognized that only 10 percent of our gross national product goes into armaments as compared with a much larger percentage in the Soviet Union and that therefore it is illogical to think that our people are afraid that disarmament would bring economic collapse. This should help to remove from the pages of *Pravda* the specter of American capitalists evilly conniving at war in order to increase their profits.

As to the talks, they led, among other things, to the lifting of the threat on Berlin. This was confirmed in the statement day before yesterday [September 29] by Chairman Khrushchev. They also led to certain agreements, such as those on the resumption of negotiations to settle the Soviet lend-lease debt and a considerable expansion of exchanges of persons and information. To use the expression in Yesterday's communique on the President's meeting with Prime Minister Segni, "interchange of views has proved useful in the cause of peace."

Perhaps the most important gain from the talks is the intangible one—the establishment of personal contact between the President of the United States and the Chairman of the Council of Ministers of the Soviet Union. The last time the President saw Chairman Khrushchev was at the summit conference, in 1955. But then the chief Soviet representative, in rank at least, was Mr. [Nikolai] Bulganin, and there were two other heads of government present. This time the President and the Chairman were together for many hours, either alone with the interpreters or with Secretary Herter, Foreign Minister [Andrei] Gromyko, and others.

They had a good opportunity this time to exchange views and to get an estimate of each other's thinking and way of thinking. They had a good chance to evaluate each other's personality.

Their conversations, whether private or in a larger group, were conducted quietly and objectively. Neither one hesitated to put forward his position directly and cogently. The overall tone was good.

Question of Berlin

There is one very revealing index of the relationship achieved. This relates to the unwritten agreement the President and the Chairman reached with regard to the fact that the reopened negotiations on Berlin, while not to be prolonged indefinitely, would not have a fixed time limit on them. Although this language was not in the communique, the President and Mr.

Khrushchev agreed that the President would make a statement using this language and then Mr. Khrushchev would make a statement confirming it.

This procedure was faithfully carried out without delay. The agreement itself was perhaps the most important development at Camp David.

A large portion of the conversations between the President and the Chairman was devoted to the Berlin question.

As the President indicated at his press conference on Monday [September 28], the situation of West Berlin is unnatural. How could it be otherwise when you have a city divided into two parts, with one part under one economic system, the other under another, and with the western part of the city, with all its thinking oriented toward the west, lying 110 miles inside the territory of East Germany? Some conclusions have been drawn that, because the President recognized the extraordinary nature of this situation, we would rush headlong to settle it and thereby sacrifice Western interests in West Berlin. Nothing could be farther from the truth.

We remain convinced that the problem of Berlin can best be resolved by the reunification of Germany. Until this reunification takes place, we have certain rights and obligations arising from our military victory in World War II. Among these are the right to maintain military forces in the sectors of Berlin allotted to the Western Allies after the war and the obligation to protect the right of the people of West Berlin to live in freedom under the social system they choose for themselves. We hope that Mr. Khrushchev's confirmation that no time limit is to be placed upon negotiations leading toward a more stable arrangement in Berlin will provide a better atmosphere for a reasonable approach to this problem.

While Mr. Khrushchev's visit here, and his talks with President Eisenhower, certainly improved the atmosphere in which Soviet relations with the United States and the free world are conducted, they also made it clear once more that there are great differences between us. Those differences remain. Most importantly, the Soviet Premier took every occasion to tell us in his inimitable fashion, and to demonstrate to us by his actions, that he and his comrades in the leadership of the Soviet Communist Party have no intention whatsoever of withdrawing, or retreating from, their basic challenge to us and to the system of freedom by which we govern ourselves. I feel that Mr. Khrushchev's trip produced an increased awareness on the part of the American people of the profound nature of this challenge.

U.S. Adherence to Principle of Peace with Justice

On several occasions Chairman Khrushchev stated in essence that, although the President and the great majority of Americans want peace with the Soviet Union, there are certain groups and individuals in the United States working against peace.

It is, of course, obvious and desirable that in a free society there should be diversity of views. And naturally there is a diversity of views in the United States as to Mr. Khrushchev himself, the results of his trip, and our policy toward the Soviet Union.

But I think I can categorically say this: No American in his right mind wants war with the Soviet Union. All Americans without exception, from the President on down, want peace with the Soviet Union. We are intelligent enough to know that, with modern weapons, in a new war there would be no victors, only victims.

At the same time we will not deviate from our principles. The peace we seek to maintain must be an honorable peace, based on justice. We will not barter away the freedom of other people, such as the more than 2 million men, women, and children of West Berlin.

We also want—sincerely want—an end to the cold war. I believe this is true of all Americans. We should infinitely prefer to discard all manifestations of cold war and live in real friendship with the Soviet people. We want such friendship. This is as true today as it was on June 26, 1951, when the American people said through their Congress in a joint resolution that "the Congress of the United States reaffirms the historic and abiding friendship of the American people for all other peoples and declares—that the American people deeply regret the artificial barriers which separate them from the peoples of the Union of Soviet Socialist Republics, . . . and that, although they are firmly determined to defend their freedom and security, the American people . . . invite the peoples of the Soviet Union to cooperate in a spirit of friendship. . . ." And we believe the Soviet people want such friendship.

Mr. Khrushchev sought during his trip to sell to the American people the idea of peaceful coexistence. This phrase "peaceful coexistence" has a beguiling appearance, and at first glance everyone ought to be in favor of it. Many people in many parts of the world have, in fact, indicated their acceptance of it.

As we understand the Soviet definition of "peaceful coexistence," it means a peaceful living together side by side of the Communist bloc and the free world.

If that is what they mean by it, we have to say at once, "That is not good enough." In the first place, we do not feel that the world should be divided into blocs, even though they coexist in peace. We believe that nations should be truly independent and that nations, rather than blocs should be at peace one with another.

Second, coexistence is a bare-bones, negative state of affairs. Just as human beings do not solely coexist but live and cooperate for their mutual development, so nations should not solely coexist but live and cooperate for their mutual development.

Acceptance of peaceful coexistence has the effect of solidifying the *status quo*, with the Soviet Union dominating the Communist bloc. We do not wish to contribute to the perpetuation of this *status quo*.

And so, as to "peaceful coexistence," our policy is, "We need something better than peaceful coexistence, something more in keeping with the aspirations of mankind."

Soviet Economic Competition Welcomed

Chairman Khrushchev repeatedly challenged us to competition in production, saying that the Soviet Union would overtake us by 1970. We are not afraid of this competition. We welcome it, if it means bettering the condition of the people of the Soviet Union.

Yet I cannot help but draw the conclusion that what Chairman Khrushchev saw of the economic way of life in this country—the manifestly high standard of living of our people and the vitality of our economy—has weakened if not destroyed his expressed conviction that the Soviet Union would overtake us by 1970.

He may proclaim this more, but he believes it less.

U.S. Spiritual Values Unchallenged

There was one challenge that Chairman Khrushchev did not deliver, and that was in the field of spiritual values, human dignity, and human freedom.

I think that, if you carefully read Mr. Khrushchev's speeches and off-the-cuff comments, you will be struck, as I have been, by an emphasis that is deeply materialistic, to the exclusion of almost everything else. Even his references to the Bible were in this vein. He cited quotations and passages from the Scriptures in the spirit of one who is determined to use any text which will support his purpose.

I could wish that he understood better the importance which we in this country ascribe to the text: "Man does not live by bread alone." For in this idea resides a great deal of the essence of America. We Americans recognize that all men, everywhere, are linked by bonds which transcend the fates and fortunes of any individual or any isolated group. We reject the idea that the mere satisfaction of material needs, a competition in which one group surpasses another or a struggle in which one group strives to impose its will on another, is the be-all and end-all of human existence.

If Mr. Khrushchev correctly understood our devotion to these ideas, he would understand that we are motivated not by a desire to oppose the legitimate aspirations of any other nation but by the belief that only a harmonious and peaceful adjustment of interests, only honest cooperation on every level of human endeavor, can assure the peace we all are seeking. He would know that that pursuit must not be confined to the attainment of purely material goals but must go beyond that to the striving for a meeting of minds which will enrich the lives and work of all men.

If Mr. Khrushchev wishes to continue his references to the Bible, we can recommend to him the passages on the great Christian virtues of faith, hope, and charity. Certainly he will find that the American people will meet him more than halfway with regard to hope and charity. However, it is now up to Mr. Khrushchev to provide a firm basis for the development of faith in the possibility of good relations with the Soviet Union. If the Soviet Government wishes to undertake the deeds that would provide a firm basis for such faith, it will find a receptive audience in the United States.

5. EISENHOWER'S OVERSEAS TRIPS

Dwight Eisenhower saw personal diplomacy as an effective means of better-ing world understanding. Following John Foster Dulles' death in May, 1959, the President, acting virtually as his own Secretary of State, embarked on a series of world trips. On November 8, 1959, Eisenhower met with congressional leaders of both parties to stress the nonpartisan nature of this approach to diplomacy. In December he embarked on a trip that saw him visit 11 nations—Italy, Turkey, Pakistan, Afghanistan, India, Iran, Greece, Algeria, France, Spain, and Morocco. The most important diplomatic event occurred in Paris, where an agreement was reached to hold a summit meeting the following May. In February of 1960 the President departed for an extensive tour of Latin America. May of that year saw the ill-fated journey to Paris, and June the long-planned trip to the Far East. The latter trip, already marred by Khrushchev's withdrawal of the invitation to visit the Soviet Union, received a further setback when left-wing demonstrators precipitated riots which forced cancellation of a visit to Japan. Those who had criticized presidential trips found their position verified in the debacle over the abortive Japanese visit. They further emphasized that the Pres-ident's absence from Washington permitted mischievous elements to make policy, that his health would be impaired, and that there was a constant danger that American prestige would be diminished by hostile overseas reactions. Eisenhower, however, believed that his trips helped convince the people of other nations that the United States opposed imperialism and desired true self-determination. He expressed this belief to a conference of congressional leaders in November of 1959, just prior to the beginning of his 11-nation trip.

President Eisenhower to Congressional Leaders
November 8, 1959
[Official File 116-XX, Eisenhower Papers.]

You know, I am sure, of the extensive trip abroad that I have scheduled for early December. I have planned it as a journey to reaffirm and strengthen the common purposes of the non-Communist world rather than one to negotiate substantive issues with the various nations concerned. Nevertheless, it has occurred to me that a pre-departure discussion of the trip might be of interest to you, and if this should be the case, I would be glad to have you and a few of your colleagues for breakfast at the White House at which time we would have an opportunity to talk about these matters.

I am sending this same telegram to each of your colleagues listed below. Should it be the consensus that such a meeting would be of sufficient value as to outweigh the serious inconvenience it would cause you, I should be glad to schedule the meeting for not later than December first. I would appreciate a telephone call from you to my Deputy Assistant, Mr. Harlow, in Washington so that if such a meeting is desired, we can promptly complete the arrangements.

I would hope that this matter could be kept confidential until the reactions of yourself and your colleagues have been received. The meeting, if held, would be announced in normal course.

> *With warm regard,*
> Dwight D. Eisenhower

List:
Speaker Sam Rayburn
Senator Lyndon Johnson
Congressman John W. McCormack
Senator Everett Dirksen
Congressman Charles A. Halleck
Senator J. William Fulbright
Congressman Thomas E. Morgan
Senator Alexander Wiley
Congressman Robert Chiperfield

Eisenhower's trips were unique in the peacetime history of the United States. Woodrow Wilson had gone to Europe to negotiate peace after the armistice ending World War I, Franklin Roosevelt had traveled to South America in the 1930's and in the next decade to Casablanca, Teheran, and Yalta to plan strategy during World War II, and Harry Truman had gone to Potsdam in 1945 to resolve postwar problems. But long presidential journeys were the exception rather than the rule. By the 1950's, however, rapid transportation had made such travels feasible. Preparations for these trips were highly complex and involved the CIA.

CIA Director Allen Dulles to President Eisenhower
December 2, 1959
[Official File 116XX, Eisenhower Papers.]

Dear Mr. President:

Your forthcoming trip will mark an important milestone in the development of our foreign policy. According to all our reports there will be an outpouring toward you of popular enthusiasm representing the people's view of you as the man, above all others, who has brought them aid and the hope for peace.

More than 40 years ago in Paris, I helped prepare for the reception for Woodrow Wilson. He then bore the hopes of the peoples of wartorn Europe. Today your trip will have deep influence in impressing the peoples of the countries you visit that their hopes lie with the West under American leadership.

In the various places you will be visiting, my representatives have already been working with your Security people on plans for your reception. They will also be kept daily and hourly informed of any intelligence developments which can be brought to your attention through General Andy Goodpaster or Major Eisenhower.

Speech by President Eisenhower
Upon Arriving in Pakistan
Karachi, December 8, 1959
[*Public Papers of the Presidents: 1959* (Washington, 1960), 815–18.]

Mr. President, the officials of the City of Karachi, Your Excellencies and Ladies and Gentlemen of Pakistan:

It is a high honor indeed and a personal privilege for me to be a part of this great gathering in your city. And this meeting gives to me an opportunity that I have sought every moment since I first arrived at the outskirts of Karachi. I have never received in the world a warmer, more hospitable greeting than was given to me by the throngs in Karachi. For this greeting, ladies and gentlemen, I am profoundly grateful and I assure you my party, those attending me, feel exactly the same way. And indeed I am sure the people of America will understand that you are trying, through me, to say to them that you are their friend.

I have long desired to visit your magnificent country, and at first hand to learn something of this nation. I bring to you the friendly greetings and heartfelt salutations of the people of the United States for the people of Pakistan.

In the deepest values of life, we feel with you a very close kinship. We have always admired the courage and independent spirit of the Pakistan people, and have respected them because of their religious and spiritual devotion.

Our two countries both believe in human dignity and the brotherhood of man under God. And both of us are determined to be strong—spiritually, materially, militarily—not merely to ensure present security but also that we may be in a better position confidently and effectively to search out the paths to world peace with justice.

Our two countries are staunch allies, each to the other. To strengthen this partnership we must lose no opportunity to increase our mutual understanding.

It is certain that the fuller our knowledge of each other, the more effective will be our alliance for peace.

The many educational and cultural exchanges which have taken place between Pakistan and the United States have already helped greatly. I hope they will be continuously expanded. They will bring about a broader understanding of our common ideals, goals, and purposes. From this both nations will benefit.

Another thing is certain: friends such as Pakistan and the United States must cooperate in many fields, not only for their common security but so that their peoples may be enabled to enjoy more fully the advantages and blessings that modern science can open for mankind.

We are now in the nuclear age. No scientific discovery is of itself evil. It becomes evil only when devoted by unworthy men to wicked purposes. The atom can be used either for the benefit or for the destruction of man. Six years ago this very day, in an address before the United Nations General Assembly, I proposed a study and development of a worldwide program for the peaceful use of atomic energy. Since then, much has been learned in nuclear science, about the production of power and its application to medicine, agriculture, metallurgy, and the like. Very much more remains to be learned as to ways this colossal force can best be utilized to serve mankind.

In order that Pakistan may more rapidly develop its peaceful uses of the atom, the United States has given, in our country, specialized training to a number of your scientists, and has provided various types of equipment for research and medical uses here in your country. American consultants have come here to work with your own scientists. Many other nations are likewise cooperating to find ways by which the miraculous inventiveness of man may be consecrated solely to his progress and welfare.

Another certainty is this: by helping each other in many other ways, the free nations can vastly increase their combined productivity and thus provide both a fuller life and better material advantages for all their peoples.

On its part, the United States, in order to help develop this cooperation, has adopted and prosecuted programs of economic and military assistance to those free countries needing them. Your own country is one of those involved. Military assistance is provided to help you build and participate in the collective security of the free world, while your economy is developing and expanding to promote progress in your nation.

I assure you that the United States will continue to review and give sympathetic consideration to this kind of need in Pakistan.

A final certainty is that discoveries of science in the production of military power increasingly demand that some system of progressive and enforceable disarmament be agreed to among the nations. There is no reason to hesitate in this great undertaking. There can be no winner in any future global war. The world, the entire world, must insist that the conference table, rather than force, be used for the settlement of international disputes. Every national leader worthy of the name must participate in this effort.

The American people especially hope that Pakistan and the other nations in South Asia will succeed in their efforts to improve relations among themselves. Thus they will enhance and practice economic cooperation for the more efficient use and benefit of the resources available to them. Cooperation means prosperity for all—in food, in health, in knowledge, in wealth, in every shape and form of national well being.

The United States urges that good will and patience continue to be exercised, and that the governments concerned here persistently strive to reach mutually satisfactory understandings between themselves. The cause of peace and justice will thereby prosper.

I should like to say at this moment that President Ayub has told me of his very great ambitions and purposes in this very line. And he has, I assure you, the plaudits of America in so doing.

Since my arrival here I have become fortified in a personal certainty: it is my fixed conviction that Pakistan-American friendship is a lasting one, built firmly. Through it we shall have a safer, brighter, happier future together.

My conversations with President Ayub and some of his associates are on the basis that we are two nations with many common interests, two nations which share common goals and which cooperate for mutual security.

Our fruitful talks give me a better appreciation of your problems, and of the courageous manner in which you are attacking them. And when I return home, I shall tell my fellow Americans that the Pakistani are a courageous people, an energetic people, a loyal people who love peace, but who put justice and freedom—as do we—before all else.

All of us know that there is more than one kind of courage. Any courageous man will of course fight for the protection of his home, his family, and his rights. But there is also a patient kind of courage, the kind that in spite of disappointment and discouragement enables a man to persist in working tirelessly to improve the lot of himself, his family, and his community. Pakistani leaders are pointing out the work that needs to be done—America believes that Pakistan has also the kind of courage needed to bring these programs of improvement to fulfillment.

And I shall tell my fellow Americans that in Pakistan are leaders, chief among whom is President Ayub, who are dedicated to the welfare of all their citizens, to the furtherance of universal education, and to the creation of a free republic. In building a truly representative government, they and he are demonstrating themselves to be men of vision, of courage, and of decisive action.

May God prosper their noble purpose.

Thank you very much, ladies and gentlemen.

Typical of the cordial tone of Eisenhower's overseas addresses is the following made to the Iran parliament.

Address by President Eisenhower
to the Parliament of Iran
Teheran, December 14, 1959
[*Public Papers of the Presidents: 1959* (Washington, 1960), 850–53.]

Mr. Prime Minister, Mr. President, Mr. Speaker, Members of the Senate, Members of the Majlis:

The honor you do me with this reception in your handsome new Senate building is a clear indication of the high mutual regard which the Iranian and American peoples have for each other.

Personally, I am deeply touched by your welcome.

We know that people, by meeting together, even if for a limited time, can strengthen their mutual understanding. To increase this mutual understanding has been one of the purposes of my trip to Iran; as it has been to the other countries in which I have stopped along the way.

My conversation this morning with His Imperial Majesty, this convocation, my knowledge of the state of relations between our two countries—and indeed, the cordial warmth of the reception that I received upon the streets of your beautiful city—have all been heartening assurances that our two countries stand side by side. This visit reinforces my conviction that we stand together. We see eye to eye when it comes to the fundamentals which govern the relations between men and between nations.

The message I bring from America is this: "We want to work with you for peace and friendship, in freedom." I emphasize freedom—because without it there can be neither true peace nor lasting friendship among peoples.

Consequently, Americans are dedicated to the improvement of the international climate in which we live. Though militarily we in America devote huge sums to make certain of the security of ourselves and to assist our allies, we do not forget that—in the long term—military strength alone will not bring about peace with justice. The spiritual and economic health of the free world must be likewise strengthened.

All of us realize that while we must, at whatever cost, make freedom secure from any aggression, we could still lose freedom should we fail to cooperate in progress toward achieving the basic aspirations of humanity. The world struggle in which we are engaged is many sided. In one aspect it is ideological, political, and military; in others it is both spiritual and economic.

As I well know, you, and the people of Iran, are not standing on the sidelines in this struggle.

Without flinching, you have borne the force of a powerful propaganda assault, at the same time that you have been working at improving the living standards in your nation.

The people of Iran continue to demonstrate that quality of fortitude which has characterized the long annals of your history as a nation. I know I speak for the American people when I say we are proud to count so valiant a nation as our partner.

Your ideals, expressed in the wise and mature literature of your people, are a source of enrichment to the culture of the world.

By true cooperation with your friends—and among these, America considers herself one—we can proceed together toward success in the struggle for peace and prosperity.

Through trust in one another, we can trust in the fruitful outcome of our efforts together to build a brighter future.

This future—the world we will hand on to our children and to our grandchildren—must occupy our thinking and our planning and our working. The broad outline of our goal is, I think, clear to everyone—to achieve a just peace in freedom.

But peace will be without real meaning—it may even be unattainable—until the peoples of the world have finally overcome the natural enemies of humanity—hunger, privation, and disease. The American people have engaged considerable resources in this work. I am proud of the many dedicated American men and women who have gone out into the world with the single hope that they can ease the pain and want of others.

Some of them are at work in Iran, and I have heard that the people of Iran have found these efforts beneficial.

Of course, their work is effective only because the government of Iran has sturdily shouldered its responsibilities for the development of their country. There are reports of significant accomplishments throughout the length and breadth of your land.

America rejoices with you that this is so.

On the long and difficult climb on the road to true peace, the whole world must some day agree that suspicion and hate should be laid aside in the common interest.

Here, I think, is our central problem. I know that you, too, and all men of good will, are devoting thought and energy to the practical and realistic steps to this great objective.

One such step is, of course, an enforceable agreement on disarmament, or, to be more exact, arms reduction. To achieve this, the governments of the world have chosen a primary instrument, the United Nations.

It could seem that, as the realities of the awful alternative to peace become clearer to all, significant progress in the safeguarded reduction of the arms burden can be made. To such a realistic beginning, there is no feasible alternative for the world.

In the meantime, we cannot abandon our mutual effort to build barriers, such as the peaceful barrier of our Central Treaty Organization, against the persistent dangers of aggression and subversion. This organization, CENTO, has no ulterior or concealed purpose; it exists only to provide security.

Such an effort erects a shield of freedom for our honor and for our lives. With such a shield, we preserve the cherished values of our societies.

To be sure, the people of Iran need no reminder of these simple facts. Only yesterday you celebrated the anniversary of the day on which justice triumphed over force in Azerbaijan. The full weight of world public opinion, as represented in the United Nations, supported you in those difficult times. It will always support the rights of any people threatened by external aggression.

Justice—the rule of law—among nations has not yet been effectively established. But in almost every nation in the world there is a great awakening to the need for such a development. Certainly this is true among the free nations. Because there is such an awakening, the act of any government contrary to the rights of mankind is quickly resented and keenly sensed by people everywhere.

This is the wellspring of our hope. This is why we are right to believe as we do—despite centuries of human turmoil and conflict—that true peace can and will one day be realized.

The impulse toward justice, toward the recognition of the worth and dignity of each and every human being, will not be denied. This is the mainspring of the movement toward freedom and peace.

Now, may I offer my heartfelt thanks for the opportunity you have given me to speak to you, and through you, the representatives of the people of Iran, to your entire nation.

You have conferred upon me an honor which I shall always remember.

Thank you very much.

During the December of 1959 trip, Eisenhower admitted that he often thought of his late Secretary of State John Foster Dulles. Upon returning to Washington, the President wrote an affectionate letter to Mrs. Dulles.

President Eisenhower to Mrs. John Foster Dulles
December 23, 1959
[President's Personal File 359, Eisenhower Papers.]

Dear Janet:

I came home to learn that you are in the hospital. But Phyllis Bernau reports that you are much better today, which of course delights me.

As you may have gathered, our trip was exhausting but exhilerating. Everywhere I heard praise of Foster's tremendous contribution to the cause of the just peace we all so much want; his name was often mentioned and his words recalled in the many discussions I had with the distinguished leaders of the countries I visited.

Mamie joins me in deep regret that you must spend the holidays in the hospital. But I do understand you are comfortable and well taken care of; I hope that this plant will provide some measure of cheer. We shall be thinking of you.

With affectionate regard,

Devotedly,

An example of the extensive coverage of governmental agencies during the 11-nation trip was a report to the White House by the United States Information Agency.

USIA Assistant James Halsema
to White House Assistant Albert Toner
January 13, 1960
[Official File 116-XX, Eisenhower Papers.]

SUBJECT: Item for Staff Report for the President

No. 341. *USIA Coverage of President's Eleven-Nation Trip—December 1959.*—The USIA media devoted all their resources to bring fullest possible attention to the President's eleven-nation trip. Coverage started well in advance with preparatory build-up and reached maximum level during the President's visits to the various nations.

The *Voice* gave top billing to the good-will trip in seventeen daily round-the-clock newscasts, each of which averaged 25 to 30 lines, or from one-fifth to one-fourth of the total newscast time. The newscasts were in English and in thirty-seven other languages. Features, news analyses, on-the-spot feeds, and special USIA coverage reports rounded out the news treatment of the voyage.

Press Service—IPS carried 141 publishable items, totaling over 81,000 words; these included texts of presidential speeches, communiqués, back-grounders, columns, overseas and domestic press comment. In addition, IPS provided the Presidential party with material covering the US press play of the trip, US and foreign press comment thereon, and supplements to domestic news roundups. IPS distributed 103 photographs to each of the 93 USIS posts.

Motion Picture Service—The Motion Picture Service has completed a 40-minute film of the trip. Four hundred forty-five prints of this have been distributed to 85 countries. A special 10-minute film of the President in Pakistan is being made for theatrical distribution in that country, using Pakistani languages; and a similar project is going forward for Morocco, in Arabic. Throughout the trip, daily black and white 35-mm newsreel coverage was supplied to 45 newsreel operations in 45 countries.

Television—ITV supplied materials to TV operations in 10 countries, 7 of them in Latin America. Overnight service of TV footage went to Rome and Ankara to feed the TV operations in those countries, and one of the NBC programs "Journey to Understanding" was obtained for the TV operations in Lima, Peru.

6. THE "MISSILE GAP"

During Eisenhower's eight years in office, questions of the nation's defense invariably became political issues. The unification of the armed forces, begun during the Truman Administration, had not eliminated public and private bickering among the service branches. The "bomber gap" and the later "missile gap" reflected the partisan nature of American military planning. In both instances, each branch of the armed services tried to improve its own position by accusing the others of laxity, mismanagement, and inefficiency. Ultimately, this "battle of the Pentagon" required President Eisenhower to request legislation reorganizing the Defense Department. Despite vehement opposition, the Administration's bill passed Congress in the summer of 1958, but only after Eisenhower had thrown his full weight behind the measure. The vituperative arguments, however, did not diminish following the Pentagon's reorganization. In fact, they increased, with Democrats charging that Eisenhower had placed "fiscal responsibility" above national defense. The debates accelerated with the Soviet Union's launching of Sputnik in October, 1957, and with Administration critics raising the spectre of a nation at the mercy of the Soviet Union. As the presidential election of 1960 approached, the debate over defense became even more heated. On July 13, 1959, Democratic Majority Leader Lyndon Johnson used the issue of the missile gap to attack the Administration's defense posture.

Senate Speech by Lyndon Johnson on America's Defense
July 13, 1959

[U. S., *Congressional Record*, 85th Cong., 1st Sess., 1959, CV, Part 10, 13177–79.]

MR. DENNIS CHAVEZ [Dem., N.M.]: Mr. President, let me say to my good friend, the Senator from Texas, that this bill, together with the bill for military construction funds, will involve a total of $41 billion—more than the cost of running the rest of the Government.

LYNDON JOHNSON [Dem., Tex.]: I thank the Senator from New Mexico.

In view of the comprehensive accounting made by the distinguished Senator from New Mexico, I do not propose to discuss this bill in detail. My remarks today will be concerned largely with the relationship between this appropriation bill and certain facts that have come to the fore as a result of the hearings of the Preparedness Investigating Subcommittee, of which I have the honor to be chairman.

In January, at the very outset of the subcommittee's hearings, the Secretary of Defense informed us that the Joint Chiefs of Staff had stated in writing that he considered "that the fiscal year 1960 proposed expenditure is adequate to provide for the essential programs necessary for the defense of the Nation for the period under consideration."

It was admitted, however, that each service chief had expressed some reservations regarding some of the program items of his own service. The Preparedness Subcommittee went into this matter in considerable detail with the individual members of the Joint Chiefs of Staff. I think that the record of our hearings demonstrated that their reservations to the 1960 budget were quite significant.

General Taylor, Chief of Staff of the Army, expressed serious concern with respect to four major Army programs. They were: First, Army modernization; second, the antimissile missile—Nike-Zeus—program; third, the personnel strength of the Active Army and the Reserve forces—which the very able senior Senator from Louisiana [Mr. Ellender] has waged such an untiring fight to keep adequate; and, fourth, the Army surface-to-air missile program.

Admiral Burke, Chief of Naval Operations, expressed his reservations concerning five major areas. These were: First, maintenance and modernization of ships and aircraft; second, procurement of new ships, new aircraft, guided missiles, and associated electronic equipment; third, acceleration of the antisubmarine warfare program; fourth, rate of procurement of the Polaris program; and fifth, increased research and development effort.

General Pate, Commandant of the Marine Corps, had reservations in four areas. These were: First, reduction of Marine Corps personnel; second, lag in new ship construction; third, decline in naval air strength; and, fourth, maintenance and construction of facilities.

General Pate further stated that he considered the military personnel reduction to be paramount.

General White, Chief of Staff of the Air Force, was less specific as to his reservations. He did mention, however, four specific examples: First, B-47's are not being replaced as rapidly as requested; second, the aircraft nuclear-powered program should be accelerated; third BOMARC procurement was less than initially requested by the Air Force; and fourth, operation and maintenance funding is minimal.

We all recognize that it is never possible to satisfy all the requirements that can be presented by each of the Armed Forces. And the problem becomes particularly acute when there is a lack of central guidance and direction in establishing priorities among programs.

A good case in point is the fact that the Army and Navy each considered that inadequate funds had been provided for their individual surface-to-air missile programs. In large measure, this simply reflected the fact that the Department of Defense had failed to come up with a unified and consistent plan for continental air defense. It took the direct intervention of the Congress to force the Department of Defense to make long overdue decisions in this area. As a result, it has been possible to reduce the funds required for air defense against manned aircraft. If the Congress had not forced a decision, we would probably still have the Army and Air Force pursuing separate plans which were combined only by a paperclip.

The bill recommended by the Appropriations Committee goes part way toward meeting the reservations expressed by the Joint Chiefs of Staff. For example, the committee has recommended an increase of $425,300,000 over the original budget estimate for the Army appropriation for procurement and equipment and missiles. The committee has also directed the reprograming of $117,800,000 of funds previously contemplated for the Nike-Hercules program. This will permit a major stepup in the Nike-Zeus antimissile-missile program, as well as provide for additional firepower and modernization of the Army.

The committee has recommended funds for nuclear-powered aircraft carrier and for an additional antisubmarine submarine. The committee has also provided for maintaining the Army National Guard at a minimum strength of 400,000, the Army Reserve at a minimum strength of 300,000, and the regular Marine Corps at an end strength of not less than 200,000. This will prevent the reductions planned in the 1960 budget which had proposed to cut the Army Reserve by 30,000 men, the Army National Guard by 40,000, and the Marine Corps by 25,000.

These actions will help materially in overcoming deficiencies in the 1960 budget in two important areas—namely, our capabilities for limited warfare and for defense against ballistic missiles.

At the time that the military construction authorization bill was debated on this floor, the distinguished Senator from Mississippi, and the other members of his subcommittee, expressed their doubts as to whether the so-called master plan—or more properly, the revised plan for continental air defense—had gone far enough. Nevertheless, they reluctantly concluded that this plan should be adopted since it was a halting step in the right direction and would save the taxpayer some $1.4 billion over the next few years.

The subcommittee report made it clear that the Secretary of Defense and the Joint Chiefs of Staff were expected to review the proposed program again before construction was begun on the new sites authorized in the bill. The committee also wisely stated its conclusion that, "The best defense is a strong effective offense." In all the debate on the construction authorization, I can recall no disagreement with this point of view.

Strangely enough, the written reservations expressed by the Joint Chiefs of Staff to the 1960 budget did not deal with the inadequacy of the projected ballistic missile programs. The only exception to this was Admiral Burke's reservation concerning the inadequate rate of procurement for the Polaris fleet ballistic missile system. Despite this omission, the hearings of the Preparedness Investigating Subcommittee are replete with references to the fact that the 1960 budget placed too much emphasis on defense against manned aircraft and too little emphasis on our offensive retaliatory capabilities. This point of view was expressed not only by the military witnesses appearing before the subcommittee, but was also concurred in by Mr. Stans, the Director of the Bureau of the Budget. The hearings developed the fact that the Administration's program conceded to the Russians at least a 3-to-1 preponderance in ICBM's for the next few years.

Mr. President, this sort of finding confronts the Congress with a dilemma. On the one hand, we receive clear-cut evidence of the inadequacy of defense plans and programs presented for congressional approval. On the other hand, the Congress is not a military body and should not be placed in the position of making decisions as to specific weapons systems. Such decisions must be made by those bearing the responsibility—the Joint Chiefs of Staff, the Secretary of Defense, and the President. It is indeed unfortunate that the Congress is placed in the position of making such decisions because of the inability of the constituted authorities to do so promptly and decisively.

For this reason I wish to congratulate the committee for one of the major recommendations that they have made in connection with the 1960 budget for the Department of Defense. I refer to section 633 which provides the Secretary of Defense with additional authority to transfer up to 10 percent of the amounts planned for missile systems or continental air defense programs in order to accelerate any ballistic missile program or nonballistic strategic or tactical missile program, whenever such acceleration will be advantageous to the national defense.

Mr. President, the testimony given to the Preparedness Investigation Subcommittee points up the fact that some of the inadequacy of the defense budget for 1960 stems from the way in which it was prepared. Despite all the glowing statements and promises we have been given concerning unification in the Department of Defense, despite the action the last Congress took providing for greater unification, the 1960 budget was not developed on a Department-wide basis. Instead, each service was given an individual expenditure target. The only decisions as to priorities were made within each department in relation to its individual expenditure target. We could find no evidence to show that the importance of any particular Army program was weighed against the importance of some other Navy or Air Force program. As a matter of fact, testimony revealed the shocking fact that the Joint Chiefs as a group were given only two days to consider the end result of the budget process and never considered such important things as the size of the Army, the need for a new aircraft carrier or—most fundamental of all—what deterrent forces are needed.

I do not think that the American people will ever get a full dollar's worth of defense for every tax dollar devoted to this purpose until the Department of Defense stops budgeting on this basis—on the basis of preestablished dollar ceilings—and instead starts considering the job to be done and the best way of getting the job done. I do believe that the additional transfer authority provided by section 633 of the appropriation bill will provide a valuable tool for shifting funds, so that we can accelerate ballistic missile programs to the maximum extent feasible.

Before concluding, I would like to mention briefly one other aspect of the 1960 budget that has been highlighted by the excellent committee report, which I hope each Member of the Senate will have a full and adequate opportunity to consider thoroughly.

There has been a good deal of talk in this Chamber about fiscal responsibility and backdoor financing. I, for one, call the shots as I see them. I do not believe that there is any room for a double standard—whether it be in human affairs or fiscal affairs. Yet, that is precisely what the administration appears to be practicing.

We all know that there has been a good deal of partisan debate about who is responsible for increasing the budget and who has been responsible for cutting the budget. The *Congressional Record* is replete with speeches and tables on this matter.

Certainly, so far as the budget estimates for 1960 are concerned, any score card on the increases and decreases Congress makes on the budget estimates must start with the budget estimates. Even if it were not required by law, simple public morality would dictate that where changes occur following submission of the budget to the Congress, the executive branch should submit a budget amendment or supplemental estimate on the desired changes. I believe most Members of this body assume that this is, in fact, being done. However, this principle has certainly not been applied to the Defense budget.

As pointed out on page 6 of the committee report—and I ask each Senator to bear the report in mind—the Army testified that a deficiency of $267 million was now anticipated in fiscal year 1960 because certain reimbursements were not expected to materialize. This estimate was disputed by the Assistant Secretary of Defense—Comptroller—who informed the chairman of the subcommittee that the estimated shortage was approximately $117 million. I do not intend to debate the relative merits of these two estimates.

As to differences between the Army and the Comptroller of the Department of Defense, they ought to get together over in the Pentagon. The important thing is the fact that there is admittedly a deficiency of at least $117 million. Despite this, the executive branch refrained from submitting a budget amendment to the Congress, but urged the Senate to approve the $200 million added to the Army procurement request by the House, so that a portion of the admitted shortage could be met in this fashion.

A natural question, in view of the above circumstances, is whether the failure to submit a budget amendment was simply because of lack of time to do so. This is clearly not the case. This was a deliberate and, I believe, a considered decision.

On the very day that the Secretary of Defense appeared before the Appropriations Committee, Mr. Stans, Director of the Bureau of the Budget, resumed his testimony before the Preparedness Investigating Subcommittee. In questioning Mr. Stans, the Senator from Mississippi [Mr. Stennis] referred to the House committee report on the question of shortage of funds for the Army procurement program. He asked Mr. Stans whether such a shortage actually existed. Let me quote some of the colloquy that followed.

I think each Member of the Senate ought to be able to read this colloquy in the *Record*. I think it ought to be made a permanent part of the records of this country and of the Senate:

MR. STANS: As we understand it, the matter of Army's needs for its fiscal year 1960 programs is being handled in connection with the appeal to the Senate from the House action on the entire defense budget. I have talked to the Secretary of Defense about that, and my understanding is that if any further action is required after Senate action, it will be brought to our attention. The matter is in abeyance at the present time until the fiscal year 1960 appropriations have been made.

SENATOR STENNIS: You mean you deferred it until a supplemental bill could come in at this session?

MR. STANS: No; we deferred it until action is taken on the fiscal year 1960 appropriations for the Department of Defense.

SENATOR STENNIS: That is what this alleged shortage pertains to. Why would you defer it until the committee acted?

MR. STANS: The House added $200 million to the Army's programs, and there were a number of other adjustments. As I have said, I discussed this with the Secretary of Defense, and we agreed to hold off consideration of this matter until their determination as to whether or not they were going to accept within their program the add-on made by the House, or whether they were going to ask for Army's appropriations to be handled in some other way.

SENATOR STENNIS: Mr. Stans, that would not touch this problem, would it, because the House, as I understand it, provided that the extra money could not be used for any purpose except those they specified. . . . The House committee said with reference to the $200 million they added, that "The committee does not intend that any of the funds provided above in the budget estimates for Nike Zeus firepower modernization or the Reserve forces be used to make up the shortages. . . ."

SENATOR STENNIS: If you defer this until all those matters are settled, with this shortage of $217 million, I don't see any way for the Appropriations Committee to handle it. It would require a supplemental, don't you think?

MR. STANS: I understand that the matters will be presented to the Senate Appropriations Committee by the Department of Defense in such a way as to make a supplemental unnecessary, but we do not have all of the details of their testimony.

SENATOR STENNIS: Do you give them just carte blanche authority to handle it that way? I want to feel that all of the departments have cleared it through you gentlemen. Not that we mistrust them, but it gives us assurance that someone has brought it out and put the pieces together.

MR. STANS: We did not take issue with the Department of Defense determinations as to the position they should take on the House add-ons and on the House cuts. We did make suggestions as to what we thought might be the best way to handle them, but the determination was to be made by the Secretary of Defense, and I am not sure that we have all of the details yet as to how the Secretary is going to make the presentation.

The only limitation that was imposed upon him was that in the aggregate the Secretary would not ask for a greater budget for the Department of Defense than appeared in the budget document last January.

I would like to read the last paragraph again because I believe this is the clue to the strategy behind the decision not to submit a supplemental estimate to cover this $117 million, or $267 million, deficiency:

> The only limitation that was imposed upon him was that in the aggregate the Secretary would not ask for a greater budget for the Department of Defense than appeared in the budget document last January.

Now, if this were the only such deficiency the matter might not be so significant. However, there were at least two other acknowledged deficiencies involving large sums of money. There was a deficiency of approximately $43 million in the Air Force military personnel account for fiscal year 1959. In addition, the Secretary of Defense told the Appropriations Committee that there was a deficiency of approximately $60 million in the Air Force military personnel account for fiscal year 1960. But no supplemental estimates or budget amendments were submitted to the Congress. Instead, the Department of Defense tried to cover up this matter by merely asking for blanket authority to transfer whatever amounts were required to meet these deficiencies. The bill before you now provides such transfer authority for fiscal year 1959 but rejects it for fiscal year 1960.

I certainly do not mean to criticize the committee for providing this transfer authority for fiscal year 1959 since, as a practical matter, the funds in question have been spent and the Congress has no recourse but to make up this deficiency. However, this informal, back-door method of covering up deficiencies must not be permitted to set a precedent for the future. In this connection I agree wholeheartedly with the statement on page 9 of the very fine committee report, which states:

> The committee is emphatic in its belief that this deficiency should not again occur without the committee being promptly informed in accordance with the statutes on deficiencies.

With reference to the deficiency in the Air Force military personnel account for fiscal year 1959, there appears to be a definite violation of the provisions of the Antideficiency Act (sec. 3679, Revised Statutes) in the failure of the Bureau of the Budget to submit the detailed reports required by the statute, accompanied by the required supplemental estimates. Furthermore, the failure of the Bureau of the Budget to submit formally revised estimates to cover the admitted deficiencies in the Air Force military personnel account for fiscal year 1960 is in conflict with the applicable provisions of the Budget and Accounting Act of 1921, as amended. One of the applicable provisions of this act states:

"No estimate or request for an appropriation and no request for an increase in an item of any such estimate or request, and no recommendation as to how the revenue needs of the Government should be met, shall be submitted to Congress or any committee thereof by any officer or employee of any department or establishment, unless at the request of either House of Congress" (June 10, 1921, ch. 18, title II, sec. 206, 42 Stat. 21).

The three deficiencies, I have just mentioned, for which formal budget estimates have not been submitted, amount to either $220 million or $370 million—depending on whether the Army or the Assistant Secretary of Defense is correct with respect to the shortage in the Army procurement account.

In this connection I would like to call the Senate's attention to one other transaction in which, in my opinion, a revised budget estimate should have been submitted to the Congress. In presenting the revised air defense plan to the Congress several weeks ago, the Department of Defense requested approval of an additional $137 million for the Nike-Zeus program. We were told that this increase was approved by the President. The Budget Director testified that he also participated in consideration of this increase. Despite this, no budget amendment was submitted to the Congress.

Now the President vetoed the housing bill just the other day on the ground that it was inflationary. That bill would have increased spending during the current year by a maximum of some $70 million, according to the staff estimate. Yet, the administration thinks nothing of requesting the Congress to cover admitted deficiencies and supplemental requirements amounting to approximately one-half billion dollars without any formal budget submission whatsoever.

We have heard of double-entry bookkeeping but apparently the administration has revealed a new method altogether—triple-entry bookkeeping.

Eisenhower took great pride in his military expertise and often used it to counter his critics. After Sputnik, *however, this became more difficult, and increasingly he stressed the well-balanced nature of American defense. On several occasions when questioned about the "missile gap," he not only denied its existence but became annoyed at the use of the phrase. Even so, by 1959 the term had become part of the political vernacular and was used in discussions of space exploration as well as military rockets. Eisenhower had many exchanges with the press on this topic. Major General John Medaris, referred to in this news conference, headed the Army Ordnance Missile Command at Huntsville, Alabama.*

Presidential News Conference
October 22, 1959
[*Public Papers of the Presidents: 1959* (Washington, 1960), 733–35.]

QUESTION. Charles Roberts, *Newsweek:* Sir, before General Medaris announced his intention to resign, he said that we are straddling the issue of whether we are competing with the Russians in space. I wonder if our position is that we are competing with the Russians, and if we are, if their recent successes in launching luniks and probes into space indicate that we must spend more money in this field in our next budget?

THE PRESIDENT: Well, you open a big subject with a lot of questions along with it. Here is a thing that has been studied ever since 1955 on a very urgent basis. I need not go again into the history of missile development within the Military Establishment, and the launching of at least our interest into the outer space field. But as early as 1953 or '54, we began to get the recommendations of certain scientific groups, and then I established my own, under Dr. Killian, which reported early in 1955. From there on, missiles and space vehicles began to take first priority in both defense and, you might say, in scientific research affairs.

Where we got into the outer space field was through the International Geophysical Year, if you will recall. Dr. Waterman was the one that proposed this to me, and we went into the Vanguard proposal.

Well now, as time went on, we began to do very well in the missile field. Now there was one reason that we could do pretty well in the missile field, and fairly early; it was this: we were ahead, it seemed clear, of anybody else in the development of efficient and still very powerful bombs. This meant that we did not have the same power in our engines or in our boosters that was required if those warheads had not been so efficiently designed and built.

So we have developed and we now have operational ICBM's. Therefore we have the certainty, the fact, that starting in 1955 until this moment we have done—our scientists have done—a remarkable job in bringing this about. But since we had no great interest at that moment in putting heavy bodies into outer space, we were going along with the engines or the boosters that were capable of handling our Thors, Jupiters, and Atlases—that kind of thing.

As the space exploration studies went further, it began to be obvious that we needed big boosters for this particular thing. We started, I believe, three projects—three routes, you might say—towards their designing. I think the scientists have come pretty well to the conclusion that one of these shows more promise than any other. The team that has had more experience in this field than any other is that headed by Dr. von Braun, a very brilliant group of scientists which was brought together by the foresight and the wisdom of the Army, in the original sense. They have done largely the work that they want to do for the Army. The Pershing, one of those other small items on which they have been working, has been largely completed. They are the ones now that we are looking for to get and develop this big booster.

But this great booster is of no present interest to the Defense Department. Its interest is in NASA, and that's the reason that we have decided to take this very competent team of scientists and this facility—the ABMA—and put it into the space department so that it can get the kind of booster that it needs.

Now, this statement that we are straddling as far as competition with the Russians is concerned: I don't know exactly what it means. I know this: we have established, and it has been published at least in outline, a program of space exploration; and Dr. Glennan has pointed out some of the major things we want to do. Our plan is a positive one, and I see no reason for thinking of it merely as competition with somebody else. It is something we intend to do.

And just one point about this transfer of ABMA I might point out is this: there are two separate facilities there. One of them is the Army Ordnance Center, I believe it is—Army Ordnance Research Center, some such thing. The Army projects stay right there, and their contacts and their coordination and the help that they get from the space agency will be no less than it has been before. Such little items, some finishing touches that remain on Redstone or one or two other programs, will be completed.

But at the same time, Dr. von Braun and his group are going over to the NASA because, I say, the big booster has its primary place in space exploration and not in our missile program.

QUESTION. Art Barriault, *National Broadcasting Company:* Is any effort being made, sir, to retain General Medaris perhaps in a civilian capacity?

THE PRESIDENT: Well, as a matter of fact, I really don't know. I haven't seen his reasons for wanting to retire, but I understood, just a few days back, from the Army, that he was quite content and happy. I don't know exactly what his disappointments or his disagreements are, and I would like to hear them. . . .

>■●□■□■□■□□■□■□■□■□□■□■□■□□■□■□■□□■□■□■□■<

By late 1959 the "missile gap" had become a powerful political issue. The White House staff, in an effort to defuse the issue, drafted the following fact sheet which they hoped would put the missile and space programs in proper perspective.

Ballistic Missile and Space Programs—Draft—Fact Sheet
November 19, 1959
[Hess Files, Eisenhower Papers.]

Purposes of Programs. The ballistic missile programs are strictly military in purpose. Under them a device to deliver nuclear weapons to a target area has been developed.

The space programs have scientific objectives. Satellites developed under these programs are expected to have military applications for such purposes as communications, reconnaisance, and gathering meteorological data. It is not possible, however, to foresee circumstances under which satellites will be used to deliver nuclear weapons.

Status of Programs. With respect to achievement of primary objectives, and based on the best knowledge available, the U. S. programs are not behind the U.S.S.R. programs.

We can be reasonably sure that our military capability to use ballistic missiles is superior to that of the U.S.S.R. at the present time, both in the number of missiles available and in their quality.

Our space programs have put into orbit a larger number of more sophisticated (though smaller) satellites, and we can be reasonably sure that the scientific information which we have gained is at least equal to that obtained by the U.S.S.R. from fewer but larger satellites and space probes. Examples of the important scientific discoveries of the American Space Program: the Van Allen radiation belts; the solar hot spots; the Argus effects.

With respect to the size and power of rocket engines, the U.S.S.R. has developed engines larger and more powerful than any presently available to us.

Status of Programs—Collateral Objectives. Progress in space programs is presently being understood as a measure of technological advance all over the world. The resulting prestige may be taken as a collateral objective of the program.

The Russians have achieved a considerable prestige as a result of the capability of their larger rocket engines.

Why the Russians Have Bigger Engines. There are two reasons why the Russians are ahead in the development of high-powered rocket engines:

1. They started immediately after the war to develop such engines. We began serious development only under this Administration. Thus, they had about a six-year jump on us.

2. They were behind us on warhead technology. They had been unable to develop as compact and light a warhead as we had; consequently, they had to have a more powerful engine to lift their heavier warhead.

Evaluation of Present Situation. The Russians have "cashed in" on their larger rocket motors by lifting spectacular loads into orbit and to the moon. They have gained prestige from this accomplishment, largely because many people have concluded that the larger motor meant a larger military capability.

Actually, however, the larger motor reflected their difficulties in building a compact warhead. It is not an indication of superior military capability, but rather an indication of important limitations.

Outlook. Our present military ballistic missile program is making very satisfactory progress. There is no reason to expect that we will not continue to be ahead of the U.S.S.R. in military missile capability.

We are continuing to develop research instruments and power packs for use in satellites which will accomplish more for their weight than those available to the Soviets. We may, therefore, reasonably expect that we will continue abreast of them in the acquisition of scientific knowledge about outer space.

We are developing more powerful rocket engines. Within a matter of months we will be able to lift weights as great as they can. Still more powerful engines are under development. We may, therefore, expect that more and more powerful engines will be available to us. However, because of the Russians' head start and because of their requirement of a big engine for military purposes (a requirement we did not have), they may continue to have more powerful engines than we do for some time.

It is important to keep in mind that this *does not mean* that they will have a superior military capability nor that they will surpass us in the acquisition of knowledge about space.

Finances. Here are the large and rapidly expanding sums being spent by the U. S. on space programs: fiscal year 1958, $189 million; fiscal year 1959, $691 million; fiscal year 1960, $1,031 million. These are in addition to billions being spent on military missiles.

This Administration has recommended space expenditures which can be prudently and effectively used. No useful purpose would be served by pushing these expenditures to a higher rate.

Conclusions. 1. On the vital heading of military capability of ballistic missiles, we are ahead of the Russians. We have superior, compact, light warheads and we have, in the Atlas, a very satisfactory vehicle to deliver them. A larger rocket engine would not advance this essential program.

2. On the important heading of space exploration, we are at least equal to the Russians in scientific accomplishments, although behind them in weight-lifting capability. This is possible because we accomplish more with less weight. We will soon increase our weight-lifting ability to their present level.

3. Our programs are making very good and highly satisfactory progress; increasing expenditures at a pace more rapid than we have been doing would not produce proportionate benefits.

On January 13, 1960, Eisenhower stated at a press conference that those who claimed there was a "missile gap" were "doing a disservice to the United States." Throughout the defense debate the question was not the number of rockets each side had, but the quality of the missiles and other military capabilities. The Chief of Staff of the United States Air Force, General Thomas White, made several public appearances in early 1960 in which he discussed Administration defense policy.

Television Interview with General Thomas White
College News Conference
January 31, 1960
[Official File 103, Eisenhower Papers.]

QUESTION: General White, two Air Force Generals have recently commented on the present missile situation. General Thomas Power has said "It is conceivable that within about two years the Russians will have built up a sufficient stockpile of ballistic missiles to commit a massive attack on the United States."

General Schriever says there is no missile gap where we stand today. Where do you stand, sir?

GENERAL WHITE: I stand this way: The people in the government who are charged with the planning and the implementation of our national defense are just about the most dedicated people I know, and I can only say that they have not and will not put this country in jeopardy.

*   *   *

QUESTION: General White, sir, do you think the United States is strong enough militarily to prevent Russia from starting a Third World War?

GENERAL WHITE: I certainly do.

QUESTION: General White, it seems to me that there has been an apparent need on the part of some Generals to resign in order to speak their mind on this whole question, that both General Taylor and General Gavin apparently didn't feel that they could do this until after they were relieved of their responsibilities. Do you feel that this is a problem for yourself in your capacity?

GENERAL WHITE: That is a very interesting question. I am not sure that that is what happened in the case of General Taylor, particularly. I am not sure by any means that if one felt that strongly that that is really the way to do it. I believe sometimes you can do more from your experience, where you are, continuing to carry out your duties to the limit of your ability and at the same time remain in the organization. Because after all, this is a good organization and it is—I am part of it and I am not unhappy about being part of it.

QUESTION: I don't think that is the point. Do you feel free to speak your mind and your honest opinions without fear of punishment or retaliation from superiors?

GENERAL WHITE: In the proper places I have absolutely no fears at all. I don't have any fears anyhow, but obviously propriety has a bearing and in a properly constituted forum of this nation I have no problem with superiors or with the Congress, of saying exactly what I think should be said.

QUESTION: Then you do feel the American people are getting the full and complete truth about our defense production?

GENERAL WHITE: They are and will continue to do so.

QUESTION: General White, sir, before we get into details, in comparison with the United States and Russia in military strength, I would like one general question answered, please: There are many conflicting opinions between high-ranking civilian and military personnel as to our relative strengths. I wonder if you could give us a general answer at this time as to how we do compare to the Soviet Union in military strength?

GENERAL WHITE: Well, I think my first answer covered it, but I would say this, that we are very strong, now, and I am sure if we do the things we have planned and programmed to do we will continue to be so.

QUESTION: Well, General, you say we are very strong. However, Secretary Gates recently has said that Russia will have moderately more missiles than the United States until we begin catching up in 1962.

Now just how far behind are we to maintain this "safe position" as you said, deterring them from a Third World War?

GENERAL WHITE: I don't think we are behind at all. When you talk about one specific weapons system you are only talking about one element of the big picture. And while it is conceivable that they may have numerically more missiles than we, that is not the whole or even at the moment the major part of the problem.

QUESTION: Their striking force at present would be based on their bombers?

GENERAL WHITE: Their striking force at the moment is very much greater in bombers than in anything else.

QUESTION: General White, sir, General Power, the SAC Commander, has testified to the effect that with 300 intercontinental ballistic missiles, Russia could wipe out the deterrent force of our country. Do we have any adequate warning system against missile warfare today?

GENERAL WHITE: We do not have in operation such a system today. We have one under construction and it is coming along according to schedule, and incidentally, I would sort of feel it would be necessary to enlarge a little on the question you put.

I would like to point out that General Power stated this in a speech, which was cleared in the proper manner, and that he was taking an entirely hypothetical case, in which he did some rather elementary mathematics, and if you go on further with the speech you will find that what he was saying is that this hypothetical situation, if it existed—and he didn't say that it did, or it would—if we do certain things, there is an answer to it. That was really what the burden of his speech, as I read it, contained.

QUESTION: General White, comments from some of the Senators emerging from the closed testimony given by Allen Dulles, Director of the Central Intelligence Agency, yesterday indicated that Russia now has and will continue to have both a quantitative and qualitative lead in the missile field. What are we doing about catching up since this gap seems to be constantly widening.

GENERAL WHITE: Well, not commenting on what Mr. Dulles said, because as I said earlier, I can not get into figures for several reasons, I can only say that the U. S. missile program and its defense program as laid on, is a properly balanced one in my opinion.

QUESTION: Are we working 24 hours a day to catch up, General?

GENERAL WHITE: No, I can't say that we are working 24 hours—not three shifts.

QUESTION: Should we be?

GENERAL WHITE: I can only say this, that if you did work three shifts and you carried it out into all of the ramifications in electronics, in construction and so on, we undoubtedly would have more missiles.

QUESTION: Are the Russians working 24 hours a day?

GENERAL WHITE: That I can't say. I don't know.

QUESTION: General White, sir, in the light of this comparison in missiles just some few days ago the Russians fired this new missile of theirs that went some 7800 miles and supposedly within a mile and a quarter of the desired target.

Now where does this put them, sir, in comparison with us? Is this a significant step ahead of our missile defense?

GENERAL WHITE: I don't think we should downgrade the Russian accomplishment. I think that they have had some very great accomplishments. But we also have right now an operational missile which serves our purposes fully. The fact that they made a long-distance shot doesn't mean that we couldn't do the same. I think it is a well-known fact that they have some very large boosters which have their particular applications in space, but as applied to missiles it means that they can fire a heavy warhead either a shorter distance with a greater bang, or you can fire a longer distance with a smaller weight warhead.

Now in our own case and in the proper military application of missiles, what you need is a missile with adequate range for the targets, with proper accuracy and with proper bang and that fills the military requirement and we have just such a missile.

QUESTION: With the development of ground-to-air missiles in recent years, do you feel the policy of massive retaliation with SAC bombers is now becoming outmoded?

GENERAL WHITE: No, I do not. There is a lot of argument about that. I think it is the only answer to the problem.

QUESTION: How long, sir, would it take to have an operational unit of the SAC bombers hit a target somewhere in an aggressor country, after they once attacked our country?

GENERAL WHITE: Of course it would depend on where the bombers were. If they were on air alert it would be one type. If they were on the ground not on any kind of alert, it would be another thing. If they were on the ground, with 15 minutes alert, which many of the B-47's are, then obviously the time to target is 15 minutes plus the flight time to the bomb release line.

QUESTION: General, Newsweek has recently called the bombers in the Strategic Air Command obsolete. Would you comment on that? The B-47's and B-52's?

GENERAL WHITE: I would say unqualifiedly that I don't agree with that. The B-47s are the oldest bomber we have in the Strategic Air Command. It still packs a terrific punch. We have a great many of them. But we are phasing them out as we get new weapons. The B-52 is anything but obsolete. It is being improved with each new model. One of the most significant improvements is the addition of the Hound Dog air-to-surface missile which, when fired from the airplane, can reach a target 400 or more miles from where it is released.

We are working on an air launched ballistic missile which I have termed the Sky Bolt which will also go on the B-52 when it is developed. We have a new engine going into the B-52, which is the turbo fan engine which will improve its performance in all respects. In range, speed and in weight lifting capacity.

QUESTION: Sir, you described the B-70 as a major Air Force goal. How do you stand now that the administration has cut back the appropriations for the production of this bomber?

GENERAL WHITE: Well, I stand exactly where I think any good team member of an organization stands. A decision was made which was contrary to my recommendation. I accept that decision and I am going to do the very best I can with what we have.

QUESTION: Do you plan a direct appeal to Congress to restore the funds?

GENERAL WHITE: I certainly do not. I can say this, that if I am interrogated and I have been, obviously it is my proper duty to reply according to my convictions.

QUESTION: And these convictions are that we need the B-70?

GENERAL WHITE: I have said so in the past and while I did not win the decision, I do what I am told to the best of my ability and I certainly am not fighting it.

QUESTION: The administration has already spent about a half billion dollars on the development of the B-70 bomber, isn't that correct?

GENERAL WHITE: I couldn't give you the exact figures. The B-70 unquestionably is an expensive weapons system, as are all new weapons systems, today.

QUESTION: Do you believe it has been a budgetary blunder to have only developed two B-70 prototypes this year?

GENERAL WHITE: I have to be very frank about it. In my opinion the decision was not based on budgetary considerations. It was a difference in the evaluation of the technical need in the time period when this bomber would be available.

QUESTION: Do you feel, General, that perhaps there is a tendency to down-grade the importance of all manned aircraft, because of the glamour of the new missiles, the various missiles which are becoming available?

GENERAL WHITE: Well, it depends. I think some quarters certainly do. We in the Air Force feel, and I feel particularly strongly and there are many people—I would say the majority of the Air Force probably would agree with me that there is a requirement for manned aircraft just as far in the future as I can see. There are many, many attributes of manned aircraft that the missile cannot fulfill.

QUESTION: What would this B-70 be able to do, for example, that a missile could not do?

GENERAL WHITE: Well, a B-70, for one thing, can carry a multiple load, which a missile under the present state of the art can't do. It can carry a much heavier load. It is under the control of intelligent human—it is under human intelligence. It can do many things that an automatic missile which moves on a predictable course—that is, the ballistic trajectory—can't do. One of the most specific things that any bomber can do is to go out and then be recalled. Whereas, a missile once launched can't be recalled.

*   *   *

QUESTION: Wouldn't a unified command with the Navy's Polaris and some of the other missiles under it, wouldn't that better facilitate our program?

GENERAL WHITE: I have made such a recommendation and it is not the first time I have stated it publicly that I feel, because of the exceeding importance of the strategic forces, the very vital mission they would have to perform in time of war, their very high cost, the complexity of their operation, the need for perfect coordination, that they should all be placed under one command.

Now I have been misquoted as advocating that the Polaris submarine force be placed under the Strategic Air Command. I have never made such a recommendation. My recommendation was that under the provisions of the Reorganization Act of 1958, which permits and in fact encourages the creation of unified commands, that there be created a new command to be known as the United States Strategic Command, and that overall command would have under it two components, one which is now the Strategic Air Command, and a new component command which would be composed of the Naval submarine—Polaris submarine. The commander of this organization could be either Air Force or a Naval officer, and in any case the staff of this higher command would have to be a joint command with officers from both the Navy and the Air Force.

QUESTION: Sir, you said before that you don't think we are behind at all. Comment on the testimony given yesterday also indicated it was confirmed that the Soviet Union will have a three to one advantage in missiles over the United States. Is this accurate, sir?

GENERAL WHITE: I don't think I did say that we weren't behind at all in the missile field. I said in the overall military posture in my opinion we are not behind at all.

QUESTION: Secretary Gates said in relation to that, that we are expanding our missile program, putting missiles on our bomber force and bringing into operation Polaris submarines which we believe will offset any so-called missile gap at least from the point of view of the validity of our deterrent. Is this the way in which we are offsetting the so-called missile gap?

GENERAL WHITE: It is my belief that the programs which we have now, which include those things Mr. Gates specifically stated, plus some others, will continue to give us the deterrent capability that we require. It is not a question of one particular weapon system.

*   *   *

QUESTION: General, you talked a little while ago about the 15-minute ground alert, which some of our Air Force was on. In light of the fact that we have a policy which would never start a preventive war—we are committed to this—and the Russians would have the first striking power, do you not feel that we ought to have an air-borne alert?

GENERAL WHITE: Well, I feel that—

QUESTION: To preserve our retaliatory power?

GENERAL WHITE: Right. I feel until we get a warning system against ballistic missiles—we do have incidentally a very good warning system against the air breathing threat, and by that I mean aircraft and air-breathing missiles—we don't have as yet in operation a warning system against incoming ballistic missiles and until that time, we should have in my opinion, the capability to go on an air-borne alert.

QUESTION: Well, is there any reason except saving a little money that we don't have them?

GENERAL WHITE: Well, as a matter of fact we expect to have what we call an on-the-shelf capability. That is the capability to do this when ever it is decided it is required. That is contained in this year's budget.

QUESTION: Well, what would happen if there was a surprise attack?

GENERAL WHITE: Well, that is the point. The aircraft would be in the air.

QUESTION: Then we can look forward to having an air-borne alert?

GENERAL WHITE: I think we can look forward to that when it is required.

QUESTION: When you say on-the-shelf, you mean it is in the air?

GENERAL WHITE: No, by "on-the-shelf" I mean having the parts. Having the parts. Because with an air-borne alert you have to fly many more hours, the engines and the black boxes and so on wear out more rapidly, so we must have a stock of spares over and above the normal spares that we would have that would enable us to fly this number of air-borne alert aircraft continuously. And the main problem here is to, one, of course, to work out the technique which we have done. Two is to have the units trained and practiced, and then to have the logistic capability to maintain it. And instead of starting to fly for no good reason, we should have this what I call the on-the-shelf capability. I mean having the parts, having the know-how, having the training so that if it is decided that these conditions require it, that we go on air-borne alert, that we can do so.

*   *   *

QUESTION: Sir, if you say we have no missile warning system at the present time, and if at most we are working toward an on-the-shelf capability for an air alert, how can one say we have a strong defensive picture against a surprise missile attack by an aggressor?

GENERAL WHITE: Well, you have to consider the enemy's capabilities. And nobody gives them credit for having that kind of capability now, or before the time that we would be able to carry on this air-borne alert.

In sharp contrast to the opinions of General White were the remarks of Senator John Kennedy of Massachusetts, already an announced candidate for the Democratic presidential nomination. On February 29 he made a major Senate speech scathingly attacking Administration defense policy. At one point he said: "Unless immediate steps are taken, failure to maintain our relative power of retaliation may in the near future expose the United States to a nuclear missile attack."

Senate Speech by John Kennedy on American Defense Policy
February 29, 1960
[U.S., *Congressional Record*, 86th Cong., 2nd Sess., 1960, CVI, Part 3, 3801-04.]

MR. JOHN KENNEDY (Dem., Mass.) : I thank the Senator from Florida for his courtesy and understanding.

Mr. President, Winston Churchill said: "We arm—to parley." We prepare for war—in order to deter war. We depend on the strength of armaments, to enable us to bargain for disarmament. It is my intention, later this week, to make a second address on what positive preparations for disarmament we can make now. We compare our military strength with the Soviets, not to determine whether we should use it, but to determine whether we can persuade them that to use theirs would be futile and disastrous, and to determine whether we can back up our own pledges in Berlin, Formosa, and around the world.

In short, peace, not politics, is at the heart of the current debate—peace, not war, is the objective of our military policy. But peace would have no meaning if the time ever came when the deterrent ratio shifted so heavily in favor of the Soviet Union that they could destroy most of our retaliatory capacity in a single blow. It would then be irrelevant as to whether the Soviets achieved our demise through massive attack, through the threat of such attack, or through nibbling away gradually at our security.

Will such a time come?

The current debate has too often centered on how our retaliatory capacity compares today with that of the Soviets. Our striking force, the President said one week ago Sunday night, is "ample for today—far superior to any other" and large enough to deter any aggressor. But the real issue is not how we stand today but tomorrow—not in 1960 but in 1961, 1962 and particularly 1963 and thereafter. Nineteen hundred and sixty is critical because this is the year that the money must be appropriated—by this session of this Congress—if we are to obtain initial results in subsequent years.

This year, our "mix" of forces undoubtedly is "far superior." But it is indisputable that we are today deficient in several areas—and that in one of those areas, ballistic missiles, our deficiency is likely to take on critical dimensions in the near future.

Those who uphold the administration defense budget are right on one count: We cannot be certain that the Soviets will have, during the term of the next administration, the tremendous lead in missile striking power which they give every evidence of building—and we cannot be certain that they will use that lead to threaten or launch an attack upon the United States. Consequently those of us who call for a higher defense budget are taking a chance on spending money unnecessarily. But those who oppose these expenditures are taking a chance on our very survival as a nation.

The ironic fact of the matter is that, despite all the debates, predictions, claims and counterclaims, the electorate will never be able to credit properly whichever side is right. For if we are successful in boosting our defenses, and no Soviet attack is ever launched or threatened, we shall never know with certainty whether our improved forces deterred that attack, or whether the Soviets would never have attacked us anyway. But, on the other hand, if the deterrent gap continues to go against us and invites a Soviet strike sometime after the maximum danger period begins, a large part of our population will have less than 24 hours of life in which to reflect that the critics of this administration were right all along.

The only real question is, Which chance, which gamble, do we take—our money or our survival? The money must be appropriated now—the survival will not, we hope, be at stake for a few more years.

It is easier therefore to gamble with our survival: it saves money now. It balances the budget now. It reassures the voters now. And now, 1960, is an election year. If a future administration or Congress is confronted with peril—if they lack the means in early 1963, for example, to back up our commitments around the world—that will be their problem. Let them worry about how to get by then; as we are getting by now. We can honestly say our striking force is second to none now—what happens then is their responsibility.

That is the easier alternative—to gamble with our survival. But I would prefer that we gamble with our money—that we increase our defense budget this year—even though we have no absolute knowledge that we shall ever need it—and even though we would prefer to spend the money on other critical needs in more constructive ways.

That is the harder alternative. It is less convenient in an election year. It makes us pay now, with our cash—instead of putting it off, in the hope that we will not have to pay later, with our lives. It exposes us to voter retaliation at the polls now, while the alternative course—if proven wrong—might well leave no voters able to retaliate.

But I am convinced that every American who can be fully informed as to the facts today would agree to an additional investment in our national security now rather than risk his survival, and his children's survival, in the years ahead—in particular, an investment effort designed, first, to make possible an emergency stopgap air alert program, to deter an attack before the missile gap is closed; second, to step up our ultimate missile program that will close the gap when completed: Polaris, Minuteman and long-range air-to-ground missiles—meanwhile stepping up our production of Atlas missiles to cover the current gap as best we can; and third, to rebuild and modernize our Army and Marine Corps conventional forces, to prevent the brush-fire wars that our capacity for nuclear retaliation is unable to deter.

These additional efforts do not involve a small sum, to be spent carelessly. There are other uses—schools, hospitals, parks and dams—to which we would rather devote it. But the total amount, I am convinced, would be less than 1 percent of our gross national product. It would be less than the estimated budget surplus.

It is, I am convinced, an investment in peace that we can afford—and cannot avoid.

I should think that anyone who heard tonight's news to the effect that Mr. Khrushchev said if he could not get an agreement on Berlin, he would sign a peace treaty with East Germany, in which event West Berlin would be a part of East Germany, will consider that to be a crisis which the Soviet Union might not postpone so long.

We cannot avoid taking these measures any more than the average American can avoid taking out fire insurance on his home. We cannot be absolutely certain of the danger. But neither can we risk our future on our estimates of a hostile power's strength and intentions, particularly when secrecy is that power's dominant characteristic—and particularly in the light of our consistent history of underestimating Soviet strength and scientific progress. The chance that our military improvidence will invite a national catastrophe is substantially greater—many, many times greater if you work out the odds on an actuarial basis—than the chance that your house or my house will burn down this year or next. But as individuals we are willing to pay for fire insurance—and, although we hope we never need it, we are surely equally prepared as a nation to pay every dollar necessary to take out this kind of additional insurance against a national catastrophe.

I am calling, in short, for an investment in peace. And my purpose today is to set forth the facts that every American should have to back up this investment.

To the extent possible, I want to avoid the conflicting claims and confusion over dates and numbers. These largely involve differences of degree. I say only that the evidence is strong enough to indicate that we cannot be certain of our security in the future, any more than we can be certain of disaster—and if we are to err in an age of uncertainty, I want us to err on the side of security.

Whether the missile gap—that everyone agrees now exists—will become critical in 1961, 1962, or 1963—whether during the critical years of the gap the Russian lead will be 2 to 1, 3 to 1, or 5 to 1—whether the gap can be brought to a close—by the availability in quantity of Polaris and Minuteman missiles—in 1964 or in 1965 or ever—on all these questions experts may sincerely differ. I do not challenge the accuracy of our intelligence reports—I do not charge anyone with intentionally misleading the public for purposes of deception. For whichever figures are accurate, the point is that we are facing a gap on which we are gambling with our survival—and this year's defense budget is our last real chance to do something about it.

I do not want to be told either that we cannot afford to do what is required, or that our people are unwilling to do it. In terms of this budget's proportion of our gross national product, we are not making nearly the defense effort today we were in 1953—or one-fifth the effort we made during World War II when we knew it had to be done. The Russians, with a far poorer standard of living, and desperate shortages in some consumer goods and housing, are commanding a much greater proportional effort.

It is clear that our defense budget is capable of supporting new efforts by cutting waste and duplication—that our overall budget is capable of including further defense expenditures without causing a serious deficit—that our economy is capable of sustaining a much greater defense effort—and that, if necessary, our citizens are willing to pay more, in taxes and sacrifices, for our national security, just as they have before.

Where, then, do we need the money—and why? To answer those questions requires a review of the record: 1953 was the critical turning point—it was a year of three critical turning points. In that year the military situation was transformed by the creation of an H-bomb small enough to put in the nose of a rocket, enabling it to destroy a wide enough area to compensate for what was then the inaccuracy of rockets. In that same year—if not earlier— the Soviet Union made a clear-cut decision to plunge their resources into ballistic missiles—reorganizing a new Ministry of Defense Production to unify research, development and production of missiles—and reorganizing Soviet science, technology and engineering. And finally, in that same year, the United States of America embarked on a policy of emphasizing budgetary considerations in the formulation of defense goals.

By 1954, we had good evidence of the rapid progress of Soviet technicians in these radical new weapons. By 1955, the Killian Committee—an official administration body—was ready to report that our rate of missile development must be stepped up if the Russian lead was not to endanger our existence in the sixties. By 1956, on his trip to England, Khrushchev was able to introduce into European diplomacy the threat of attack by intermediate range ballistic missiles. By 1957, the Russians were able to announce the successful testing of an intercontinental ballistic missile. Also by 1957, another administration committee—the Gaither Committee—produced another secret report with another urgent plea for more unity, more priority and more funds for our missile effort.

But throughout this period we continued our emphasis on budgetary limitations. An Operation Candor was considered, to lay bare to the public the facts of Soviet missile development—but it was rejected when "wiser counsels" prevailed, to use Robert Cutler's term—fearing that it might spur demands for military spending that would unbalance the budget. We assigned a "national priority" to the Atlas missile, finally, in 1955; but basically our second-strike capacity was concentrated on bombers carrying nuclear weapons. An air defense scheme was, finally, accepted; but by the time it was well underway, it had become evident that the U.S.S.R. had chosen to concentrate upon the missiles against which our system would prove unavailing.

Then, in the autumn of 1957, the Soviets launched the Sputniks, demonstrating for all the world to see their capabilities in the field of missiles. For the first time since the War of 1812, foreign enemy forces potentially had become a direct and unmistakable threat to the continental United States, to our homes and to our people.

The Soviet sputniks aroused the country. But the then Secretary of Defense shrugged aside the satellites, saying that this was merely "a neat scientific trick." One of the President's advisers referred to sputnik as a "silly bauble." The President himself said that his apprehensions were not raised "one iota."

There was, to be sure, a second new reorganization of the Pentagon. There were new scientific committees appointed. But only belatedly were sufficient time and attention given to our missile program. And even then sufficient funds were not forthcoming—not even all of the funds appropriated by the Congress.

I have briefly reviewed this period of time, because today time is what really matters. The coming missile gap is forecast not so much as the result of any technical lag as of a time lag. The President, I am sure, is right in saying our striking force is "constantly developing to meet the needs of tomorrow"—that "new generations of long-range missiles are under urgent development"—and that our "first Polaris missile submarine will soon be at sea." But he is talking about what we hope to have in the future—all of which takes time—and the timelag which threatens a critical missile gap is roughly equal to the timelag between the Killian report and the postsputnik era.

The history of our current defense posture is not complete, however, without chronicling developments in United States and Soviet conventional forces over this same period.

In 1953, both the Russians and the United States adopted a "new look" policy deemphasizing ground forces. Generals Zhukov and Ridgway both opposed these cuts in their respective countries; and in 1955, Zhukov, with Khrushchev's help, won the battle which Ridgway lost. Khrushchev expanded, reorganized and, more importantly, modernized and made more mobile Soviet ground forces and conventional weapons. New tactical nuclear weapons and tanks were added to the arsenal. A whole new naval fleet was developed, including the world's largest submarine fleet—much of it equipped with missiles.

In the United States, the new look prevailed. We consistently cut the numbers and strength of our ground forces—our Army and Marines. We consistently failed to provide those forces with modern conventional weapons, with effective, versatile firepower. And we particularly failed to provide the airlift and sealift capacity necessary to give those forces the swift mobility they need to protect our commitments around the world—and to give us the time we need to decide on the use of our nuclear retaliatory power.

But both before and after 1953 events have demonstrated that our nuclear retaliatory power is not enough. It cannot deter Communist aggression which is too limited to justify atomic war. It cannot protect uncommitted nations against a Communist takeover using local or guerrilla forces. It cannot be used in so-called brush-fire peripheral wars. In short, it cannot prevent the Communists from gradually nibbling at the fringe of the free world's territory and strength, until our security has been steadily eroded in piecemeal fashion—each Red advance being too small to justify massive retaliation, with all its risks.

Small atomic weapons are not the answer, for they suffer from much the same handicaps as large atomic weapons. If we use them, the Russians use them. Even the smallest atomic weapon would unleash 100 times the destructive power of World War II's largest conventional bombs. And even the smallest atomic weapon today produces fission—and thus fallout—and thus can reduce to a complete shambles the area in which it is used—a friendly area presumably, in these limited wars. But the people would not regard our use of atomic weapons as a very friendly act or the resulting holocaust a very limited war. And as the enemy's losses increase, so will its temptation to raise the ante to allout nuclear warfare first.

In short, we need forces of an entirely different kind to keep the peace against limited aggression, and to fight it, if deterrence fails, without raising the conflict to a disastrous pitch.

So much for the record. The facts are not pleasant to record. But they are facts nevertheless. The President spoke a week ago Sunday night of our strength commanding the "respect of knowledgeable and unbiased observers." But every objective committee of knowledgeable and unbiased observers which he has appointed, such as the Killian and Gaither Committees; or which have functioned independently, such as the Rockefeller committee; every private or public study; every objective inquiry by independent military analysis; every statement by Generals Gavin, Ridgway, Taylor, Power, Medaris and others; every book and article by scholars in the field—all, regardless of party, have stated candidly and bluntly that our defense budget is not adequate to give us the protection for our security or the support for our diplomatic objectives which we may well need in the near future. The conclusions of every such study agreed with this conclusion of the Rockefeller Bros. report on military policy, published early in 1958:

> It is the judgment of the panel that prepared this report that all is not well with present U. S. security policies and operations.
> We are convinced that corrective steps must be taken now. We believe that the security of the United States transcends normal budgetary considerations and that the national economy can afford the necessary measures.

Let me summarize our situation before we turn to the solutions.

Unless immediate steps are taken, failure to maintain our relative power of retaliation may in the near future expose the United States to a nuclear missile attack. Until our own mobile solid-fuel missiles are available in sufficient quantities to make it unwise for any enemy to consider an attack, we must scrape through with what we can most quickly make available. At the present time there are no Polaris submarines on station ready for an emergency. There are no hardened missile bases. There is no adequate air defense. There is no capacity for an airborne alert in anything like the numbers admittedly needed. Our missile early warning system—BMEWS—is not yet completed. Our IRBM bases—"soft," immobile, and undispersed—invite surprise attack. And our capability for conventional war is insufficient to avoid the hopeless dilemma of choosing between launching a nuclear attack and watching aggressors make piecemeal conquests.

Time is short. This situation should never have been permitted to arise. But if we move now, if we are willing to gamble with our money instead of our survival, we have, I am sure, the wit and resource to maintain the minimum conditions for our survival, for our alliances, and for the active pursuit of peace.

This is not a call of despair. It is a call for action—a call based upon the belief that at this moment in history our security transcends normal budgetary considerations.

But merely calling for more funds is not enough. Money spent on the wrong systems would not only be wasteful, it could slow us down. Merely to criticize is not enough, without stating clearly and candidly that to correct the situation will cost money. That money is not either mysteriously or easily made available. But I have indicated that I think the money must and can be made available, from elsewhere in the Pentagon, elsewhere in the budget, and elsewhere in the economy—including, if necessary, from additional tax revenues.

I am suggesting, therefore, three major changes in the pending defense budget:

First. We must provide funds to protect our investment in SAC, as long as it is our chief deterrent, primarily by making possible an airborne alert, keeping 25 percent of our nuclear striking force in the air at all times, to prevent them from being destroyed along with their bases in the event of a sudden attack. The Congress cannot and should not order such an alert now—only the President has the information and responsibility necessary to make that decision. But no President will feel free to do so, in view of the enormous cost and the wear and tear involved, unless funds are provided for more flight and maintenance crews, more planes and parts, more tankers, and more fuel. Any portion of the money appropriated for this purpose not actually used for this purpose should be used to speed up construction of our new ballistic early warning system—so that our planes will be off the ground before the missiles arrive—and further to disperse our bases, to reduce the chances of one paralyzing blow.

Second. We must provide funds to step up our Polaris, Minuteman and air-to-ground missile development program, in order to hasten the day when a full, mobile missile force becomes our chief deterrent and closes any gap between ourselves and the Russians. In the meantime, we must step up our production of Atlas missiles to cover the current gap as best we can. As a power which will never strike first, our hopes for anything close to an absolute deterrent must rest on missiles which come from hidden, moving, or invulnerable bases which will not be wiped out by a surprise attack: Polaris missiles on atomic submarines, Minuteman missiles on moving flatcars or in underground complexes, or long-range air-to-ground missiles on slow-flying planes or launching platforms. A retaliatory capacity based on adequate numbers of these weapons would deter any aggressor from launching or even threatening an attack—an attack he knew could not find or destroy enough of our force to prevent his own destruction.

But long-range air-to-ground missiles and launching platforms are still in an early stage of development. Polaris submarine goals have been consistently pushed back, with the proposed budget providing funds for starting only three. The Minuteman program likewise is suffering from delay, with no real start on either the moving railway car concept or the elaborate underground launching facilities required. If we hope to close whatever missile gap exists in 1963 or thereafter, these funds must be provided in 1960.

Third. We must provide funds to augment, modernize and provide increased mobility and versatility for the conventional forces and weapons of the Army and Marine Corps. The more difficult a decisive nuclear war becomes the more important will be the forces designed to oppose nonnuclear aggression.

There are other essential needs requiring additional funds in this budget as well: to complete and improve our continental defense and warning systems and to disperse our bases, as already mentioned; to equip us for anti-submarine warfare; to restore our merchant marine; to expand our space and military research; and to initiate a realistic fallout shelter program.

But the three stated above are the most critical. Our hopes for peace—for disarmament—for the time when the money required for this effort can be used for more constructive and enlightened uses all over the world—depend upon our obtaining the deterrent strength to which these three categories are vital. That is our real goal—an end to war, an end to the arms race, an end to these vast military departments and expenditures. We want to show our greatness in peace, not in war. We want to demonstrate the strength of our ideas, not our arms. That is why, at the same time we prepare our deterrent, we must also prepare for disarmament, with specific, concrete plans and policies that will strengthen our position at the bargaining table. I shall propose some positive steps for peace in my second address this week. But to secure that peace, to make certain that we never invite war, to make it possible for us to negotiate on a basis of equality with the Soviet Union, we must act now to build our security.

I repeat: We shall never be able to prove beyond all doubts that the efforts I have outlined are necessary for our security. We are taking a gamble with our money. But the alternative is to gamble with our lives.

Some say that it is deplorable that these facts are discussed on the Senate floor. I agree. It is not the discussion that is deplorable, however, but the facts. The Russians already know these facts. The American people may not. The debate itself is not deplorable—it is deplorable that the situation deteriorated to this point, where it became a matter for debate. In matters of this kind, the only wise and safe course is to leave a margin so large as to preclude any doubt or debate.

For when we are in doubt, our allies are in doubt, and our enemy is in doubt, and such doubts are tempting to him. While those doubts persist, he will want to push, to probe, and possibly to attack. He will not want to talk disarmament. He will not want to talk peace at the summit. He will threaten as he did today.

I urge that this Congress, before the President departs for the summit, demonstrate conclusively that we are removing those doubts, and that we are prepared to pay the full costs necessary to insure peace. Let us remember what Gibbon said of the Romans:

> They kept the peace—by a constant preparation for war; and by making clear to their neighbors that they were as little disposed to offer as to endure injury.

*   *   *

7. THE U-2 CRISIS

In the winter of 1959–60, the major powers made plans for a summit conference to be held in Paris during the spring. Final arrangements called for mid-May talks, followed soon thereafter by Eisenhower's Soviet Union tour. Then, on May 5, 1960, almost on the eve of Eisenhower's departure for Paris, Nikita Khrushchev announced that an American airplane had been shot down over the Soviet Union. At first, the United States issued a statement that a "weather plane" had strayed inside Soviet territory. Two days later Khrushchev demolished this explanation by declaring to the world that Soviet authorities had captured the pilot and had recovered the plane almost intact—over 1300 miles inside the Soviet Union. Khrushchev's revelation, supported by photographic evidence, exposed American efforts to cover up the incident. In Washington, Administration officials quickly drafted a public statement admitting responsibility, but placing it at a level below the President. In the Soviet Union, according to most State Department experts, Khrushchev was under pressure to scuttle the forthcoming Paris conference. The Chinese Communists were also hostile to any rapprochement with the United States. Senate Majority Leader Lyndon Johnson, who no doubt was privy to the Administration's policy, immediately issued a public statement supporting the Government. Johnson's statement, followed by repeated attempts to rally the Senate behind the President, pleased a very grateful Eisenhower.

Senator Lyndon Johnson to President Eisenhower
May 7, 1960
[Official File 225-G, Eisenhower Papers.]

THE PRESIDENT
I HAVE JUST ISSUED THE FOLLOWING STATEMENT TO THE PRESS IN CONNECTION WITH THE INCIDENT INVOLVING THE UNARMED AIRPLANE SHOT DOWN IN THE SOVIET UNION. THERE IS NO DOUBT THAT A SERIOUS INTERNATIONAL CRISIS MAY BE IN THE MAKING. IT IS TIME FOR ALL AMERICANS TO KEEP THEIR HEADS. IT IS ALSO TIME FOR AMERICANS

TO DEDICATE THEMSELVES TO THE UNITY OF THE COUNTRY. THE SIGNIFICANT THING AT THE MOMENT IS THAT PRE-MIER KHRUSHCHEV SEEMS DETERMINED TO EXPLOIT THE IN-CIDENT IN ORDER TO INFLAME THE COMMUNIST WORLD. COMMUNIST LEADERSHIP NEVER ACTS WITHOUT CLEAR CUT PURPOSE.

WE DO NOT KNOW JUST HOW FAR PREMIER KHRUSHCHEV INTENDS TO PUSH HIS SABER RATTLING BUT WE DO KNOW JUST HOW FAR AMERICANS INTEND TO GO TO PRESERVE THEIR FREEDOMS—RIGHT TO THE LIMIT.

BY THAT, I MEAN ALL AMERICANS—REPUBLICANS AND DEM-OCRATS ALIKE. WE MAY WEAR PARTISAN LABELS AT THE POLLING PLACES BUT OUR PARTISANSHIP DOES NOT MEAN THAT EITHER PARTY WILL PERMIT OUR COUNTRY TO BE TERRORIZED. THE PRESIDENT CAN BE CERTAIN THAT HE WILL BE BACKED SOLIDLY BY BOTH PARTIES WHEN HE SPEAKS FOR THIS COUNTRY AND LET NO ONE THINK THAT THIS COUNTRY CAN BE DIVIDED WITH THREATS. THE IMPORTANT FACT IS THAT PREMIER KHRUSHCHEV IS TRYING TO SEIZE UPON THIS INCIDENT FOR SOME ULTERIOR PURPOSE. IF HE WANTS TO DISCUSS IT CLEARLY AND RATIONALLY, I AM SURE THIS COUNTRY WILL REPLY IN KIND. BUT IF HE SEEKS TO USE IT TO SPLIT OUR UNITY, HE WILL BE SADLY MISTAKEN.

President Eisenhower to Senator Lyndon Johnson
May 10, 1960
[Official File 225-G, Eisenhower Papers.]

Dear Lyndon:

I am profoundly appreciative of your telegram, bringing to me your generous assurance of support in the latest international incident. Such a statement could have been made only by an individual of strong conviction, deep understanding, and dedication to his country.

The May 7 statement that denied the President's responsibility for the flight created more problems than it solved. Criticism about subordinates assuming presidential authority forced him two days later to admit responsibility for not only the abortive mission but for an entire espionage program extending back to 1956. On May 11, following a conference with congressional leaders, he issued a statement to the press and responded to several questions.

Presidential News Conference
May 11, 1960

[*Public Papers of the Presidents: 1960–61* (Washington, 1961), 403–09.]

THE PRESIDENT [*reading*]: I have made some notes from which I want to talk to you about this U-2 incident.

A full statement about this matter has been made by the State Department, and there have been several statesmanlike remarks by leaders of both parties.

For my part, I supplement what the Secretary of State has had to say, with the following four main points. After that I shall have nothing further to say—for the simple reason I can think of nothing to add that might be useful at this time.

The first point is this: the need for intelligence-gathering activities.

No one wants another Pearl Harbor. This means that we must have knowledge of military forces and preparations around the world, especially those capable of massive surprise attacks.

Secrecy in the Soviet Union makes this essential. In most of the world no large-scale attack could be prepared in secret, but in the Soviet Union there is a fetish of secrecy and concealment. This is a major cause of international tension and uneasiness today. Our deterrent must never be placed in jeopardy. The safety of the whole free world demands this.

As the Secretary of State pointed out in his recent statement, ever since the beginning of my administration I have issued directives to gather, in every feasible way, the information required to protect the United States and the free world against surprise attack and to enable them to make effective preparations for defense.

My second point: the nature of intelligence-gathering activities.

These have a special and secret character. They are, so to speak, "below the surface" activities.

They are secret because they must circumvent measures designed by other countries to protect secrecy of military preparations.

They are divorced from the regular visible agencies of government which stay clear of operational involvement in specific detailed activities.

These elements operate under broad directives to seek and gather intelligence short of the use of force—with operations supervised by responsible officials within this area of secret activities.

We do not use our Army, Navy, or Air Force for this purpose, first, to avoid any possibility of the use of force in connection with these activities, and second, because our military forces, for obvious reasons, cannot be given latitude under broad directives but must be kept under strict control in every detail.

These activities have their own rules and methods of concealment which seek to mislead and obscure—just as in the Soviet allegations there are many discrepancies. For example, there is some reason to believe that the plane in question was not shot down at high altitude. The normal agencies of our Government are unaware of these specific activities or of the special efforts to conceal them.

Third point: how should we view all of this activity?

It is a distasteful but vital necessity.

We prefer and work for a different kind of world—and a different way of obtaining the information essential to confidence and effective deterrents. Open societies, in the day of present weapons, are the only answer.

This was the reason for my "open skies" proposal in 1955, which I was ready instantly to put into effect—to permit aerial observation over the United States and the Soviet Union which would assure that no surprise attack was being prepared against anyone. I shall bring up the "open skies" proposal again at Paris—since it is a means of ending concealment and suspicion.

My final point is that we must not be distracted from the real issues of the day by what is an incident or a symptom of the world situation today.

This incident has been given great propaganda exploitation. The emphasis given to a flight of an unarmed nonmilitary plane can only reflect a fetish of secrecy.

The real issues are the ones we will be working on at the summit—disarmament, search for solutions affecting Germany and Berlin, and the whole range of East-West relations, including the reduction of secrecy and suspicion.

Frankly, I am hopeful that we may make progress on these great issues. This is what we mean when we speak of "working for peace."

And as I remind you, I will have nothing further to say about this matter. [*Ends reading*].

QUESTION. Robert J. Donovan, *The New York Herald Tribune:* Mr. President, since our last visit, or conference, Prime Minister Khrushchev has made some pretty vigorous statements about your plans for bringing Mr. Nixon to the summit in case you had to come home. Do his comments in any way change your intentions?

THE PRESIDENT: No, indeed. And, I should clarify something. There seems to be some misunderstanding, because a friend from Congress, a friend indeed of the other party, told me the other day that he had never heard of the latter part of my press conference on this point where I said that if my absence from the conference had to be more than 2 or 3 days, I would be right back there. And I believe I remarked, although I am not sure, that the jet plane made this kind of a trip possible.

Now, as far as Mr. Khrushchev's statement, I can just say this: he has never asked me my opinion of some of his people. [*Laughter*]

QUESTION. Charles H. Mohr, *Time* magazine: In case, Mr. President, that the Soviet Union should reject your proposal for a surprise attack conference, or an "open skies" arrangement, do you think that the development of satellites like Samos and Midas will possibly in the next few years erase our worries on the score of surveillance; and also are you doing anything now to speed up those scientific projects?

THE PRESIDENT: I keep in touch with my Scientific Advisory Committee and operators, and I know of nothing we could do to speed these up. They are research items and as such no one can predict exactly what would be their degree of efficiency. So I couldn't make a real prediction of how useful they are going to be.

QUESTION. Mr. Mohr: Sir, do you think that their development will ease our worries on the question of secrecy?

THE PRESIDENT: Well, I say, I just can't predict what the final results will be. Now, we do know this, right now. I believe it's Tiros that is sending back constantly pictures on the cloud cover all around the earth. That is admittedly a rather rough example of what might be done in photography, but that is being done constantly; and I don't know how many thousands of photographs have been taken. And they send them back on command.

QUESTION. Laurence H. Burd, *The Chicago Tribune:* Mr. President, last week you used the word "if" in connection with your trip to Russia. Have you changed any plans about that, or think you might?

THE PRESIDENT: No, not at all. I have no idea, but you can never tell from one day to the other what is happening in this world, it seems, so I just said "if." I put it in the positive sense, I think. I expect to go; put it that way.

QUESTION. Merriman Smith, *United Press International:* Quite aside from your comment about the U-2 plane episode, sir, I wonder if you could give us your reaction to a rather denunciatory speech made this morning, right ahead of the summit meeting, by the Russian Foreign Minister. Mr. Gromyko attributes to this country deeds and efforts which he said amount to dangerous ways of balancing on the brink of war. He says that the United States has deliberately engaged in provocative acts in conjunction with some of our allies. Now, with statements like this, do you still maintain a hopeful attitude toward the summit?

THE PRESIDENT: I'd say yes. I have some hope, because these things have been said for many years, ever since World War II, and there is no real change in this matter.

I wonder how many of you people have read the full text of the record of the trial of Mr. Abel. Well, I think he was sentenced to 30 years. Now, this business of saying that you're doing things that are provocative, why, they had better look at their own record.

And I'll tell you this: the United States—and none of its allies that I know of—has engaged in nothing that would be considered honestly as provocative. We are looking to our own security and our defense and we have no idea of promoting any kind of conflict or war. This is just—it's absolutely ridiculous and they know it is. . . .

The furor over the U-2 continued. Under the circumstances, many questioned the advisability of holding the Paris conference. Eisenhower made it clear, however, that he would not torpedo the proceedings. Indeed, the ill will engendered by the U-2 crisis convinced him that no false benevolence should interfere with serious discussions.

The President landed at Orly Airport in Paris on May 15 and soon learned that Premier Khrushchev had placed preconditions in the path of the meetings. Eisenhower then arranged with French President Charles de Gaulle, the chairman of the conference, to answer Khrushchev as the first order of business. On the morning of May 16, the participants—de Gaulle, Eisenhower, Khrushchev, and British Prime Minister Harold Macmillan— gathered for the opening session. Before de Gaulle could convene the meeting and recognize Eisenhower, the Soviet leader began a tirade denouncing United States policy and withdrew the invitation to Eisenhower to visit the Soviet Union. The President was finally able to make a brief reply defending American actions, but at this point the meeting broke up before it ever formally got underway. Later, the President issued a statement concerning the day's events.

Statement by President Eisenhower on the Opening of the Summit Conference Paris, May 16, 1960

[*Public Papers of the Presidents: 1960–61* (Washington, 1961), 427–29.]

Having been informed yesterday by General de Gaulle and Prime Minister Macmillan of the position which Mr. Khrushchev has taken in regard to this conference during his calls yesterday morning on them, I gave most careful thought as to how this matter should best be handled. Having in mind the great importance of this conference and the hopes that the peoples of all the world have reposed in this meeting, I concluded that in the circumstances it was best to see if at today's private meeting any possibility existed through the exercise of reason and restraint to dispose of this matter of the overflights, which would have permitted the conference to go forward.

I was under no illusion as to the probability of success of any such approach but I felt that in view of the great responsibility resting on me as President of the United States this effort should be made.

In this I received the strongest support of my colleagues President de Gaulle and Prime Minister Macmillan. Accordingly, at this morning's private session, despite the violence and inaccuracy of Mr. Khrushchev's statements, I replied to him on the following terms:

"I had previously been informed of the sense of the statement just read by Premier Khrushchev.

"In my statement of May 11th and in the statement of Secretary Herter of May 9th, the position of the United States was made clear with respect to the distasteful necessity of espionage activities in a world where nations distrust each other's intentions. We pointed out that these activities had no aggressive intent but rather were to assure the safety of the United States and the free world against surprise attack by a power which boasts of its ability to devastate the United States and other countries by missiles armed with atomic warheads. As is well known, not only the United States but most other countries are constantly the targets of elaborate and persistent espionage of the Soviet Union.

"There is in the Soviet statement an evident misapprehension on one key point. It alleges that the United States has, through official statements, threatened continued overflights. The importance of this alleged threat was emphasized and repeated by Mr. Khrushchev. The United States has made no such threat. Neither I nor my government has intended any. The actual statements go no further than to say that the United States will not shirk its responsibility to safeguard against surprise attack.

"In point of fact, these flights were suspended after the recent incident and are not to be resumed. Accordingly, this cannot be the issue.

"I have come to Paris to seek agreements with the Soviet Union which would eliminate the necessity for all forms of espionage, including overflights. I see no reason to use this incident to disrupt the conference.

"Should it prove impossible, because of the Soviet attitude, to come to grips here in Paris with this problem and the other vital issues threatening world peace, I am planning in the near future to submit to the United Nations a proposal for the creation of a United Nations aerial surveillance to detect preparations for attack. This plan I had intended to place before this conference. This surveillance system would operate in the territories of all nations prepared to accept such inspection. For its part, the United

States is prepared not only to accept United Nations aerial surveillance, but to do everything in its power to contribute to the rapid organization and successful operation of such international surveillance.

"We of the United States are here to consider in good faith the important problems before this conference. We are prepared either to carry this point no further, or to undertake bilateral conversations between the United States and the U.S.S.R. while the main conference proceeds."

My words were seconded and supported by my Western colleagues who also urged Mr. Khrushchev to pursue the path of reason and common sense, and to forget propaganda. Such an attitude would have permitted the conference to proceed. Mr. Khrushchev was left in no doubt by me that his ultimatum would never be acceptable to the United States.

Mr. Khrushchev brushed aside all arguments of reason, and not only insisted upon this ultimatum, but also insisted that he was going to publish his statement in full at the time of his own choosing.

It was thus made apparent that he was determined to wreck the Paris conference.

In fact, the only conclusion that can be drawn from his behavior this morning was that he came all the way from Moscow to Paris with the sole intention of sabotaging this meeting on which so much of the hopes of the world have rested.

In spite of this serious and adverse development, I have no intention whatsoever to diminish my continuing efforts to promote progress toward a peace with justice. This applies to the remainder of my stay in Paris as well as thereafter.

On the day Eisenhower returned from Paris (May 20), Senator Francis Case, a prominent Republican from South Dakota, wrote to him praising his performance at Paris. Case also made several foreign policy suggestions.

Senator Francis Case to President Eisenhower
May 20, 1960
[Official File 225-G, Eisenhower Papers.]

My dear Mr. President:
Kipling could have written "IF" on your performance at Paris. You "kept your head when those about were losing theirs and blaming it on you."

Now, what next? In an effort to be helpful, may I suggest considering—

1. That you bring Ambassador Wadsworth from Geneva to fill the post vacant since Mr. Stassen left:—thereby saying you redouble efforts for disarmament and getting (a) his U.N. acquaintanceship; (b) his Geneva-gained "feel" of international influences; (c) his knowledge of nuclear cans and can-nots; (d) his stature to counterbalance those who mistakenly see more arms race as a road to peace. He could still supervise the negotiations on suspension of nuclear tests.

2. That you quietly let Prime Minister Macmillan negotiate a three-point plan for Berlin:—(1) Extension of the existing city-wide Bi-Sector surface transport authority to cover rail and road to Helmstedt and the Mittelland Canal; (2) Referendum elections supervised by the United Nations on Unification or Free City; and (3) Reduction of allied troops in the city. This would stymie his Laborite hecklers.

3. That you set aside for President de Gaulle's negotiation some surplus commodities that he may initiate a Joint Aid program (France supplying medicines, chemicals and tools) with some of the Arab countries, including Algiers. This might help to end the fighting in Morocco and even extend tenure for a base or two.

4. That through Vice President Nixon you offer *Poland* surplus corn and poultry in a P.L. 480 program akin to the Wheat deal with India. This would be recognition of the warm welcome given him in Warsaw and might make some of Mr. K.'s blasts bounce like lead.

5. Here I hesitate. But—you were eminently wise and correct in the judgment you expressed about the U-2 incident when a group of us were your breakfast guests the morning of your May eleventh Press Conference. At that time, you indicated you planned to say nothing more about the U-2. However, between that hour and your mid-morning meeting with the Press, you reached a decision to read a prepared statement on the whole subject. I earnestly hope that decision was not based, even in part, upon urgings of Department and Agency officials already publicly involved in the matter. Through my years in Washington, I have seen much too much of the clamor by lesser officials to have a President go fully on record where he need not do so, but where in doing so he bears the "heat" which in the Nation's interest they should have borne themselves. I trust sincerely no such factors intruded themselves in this decision, for you are entitled to better. And I bring this up, in this personal note to you, only because I am so convinced of the wisdom of your earlier inclination not to elaborate, and because I sense there will be other crisis points before we hear the last of this U-2 episode. No President should be beset by "spokesmen" who have a greater sensitivity to some prior position of their own than they have to White House judgment. As I see it, "parochialism" can exist at State and CIA as well as in the Pentagon.

You will, I am sure, understand that I desire only to be helpful and know that any suggestions herein can be refined by your knowledge and experience. But the issues are so great, all of us have some responsibility to try. The prayers of every American are with you these days.

President Eisenhower to Senator Francis Case
June 28, 1960
[Official File 225-G, Eisenhower Papers.]

Dear Francis:

Thank you for your recent letter. I appreciate very much your suggestions and your observations, and while I understand your concern I nevertheless feel that the course of action with respect to the U-2 matter was the proper one. I assure you my decision was my own; I felt it only fair to all concerned to get the whole story accurately told.

Your recommendations will certainly be examined, and I am told that you have had occasion to talk with some of my Staff about Poland and the P. L. 480 Program. You will be kept advised of any developments.

><del>+=o=+o=+o=+=o=+o=+o=+=o=+o=+o=+=o=+o=+o=+=o=+o=+o=+=o=+o=+=</del>+

On May 25 Eisenhower went on national radio and television to discuss the U-2 incident, the Paris debacle, and other issues in American foreign policy.

Address to the Nation by President Eisenhower
on the Events in Paris
May 25, 1960
[*Public Papers of the Presidents: 1960–61* (Washington, 1961), 437–45.]

My fellow Americans:

Tonight I want to talk with you about the remarkable events last week in Paris, and their meaning to our future.

First, I am deeply grateful to the many thousands of you, and to representatives in Congress, who sent me messages of encouragement and support while I was in Paris, and later upon my return to Washington. Your messages clearly revealed your abiding loyalty to America's great purpose—

that of pursuing, from a position of spiritual, moral and material strength—a lasting peace with justice.

You recall, of course, why I went to Paris ten days ago.

Last summer and fall I had many conversations with world leaders; some of these were with Chairman Khrushchev, here in America. Over those months a small improvement in relations between the Soviet Union and the West seemed discernible. A possibility developed that the Soviet leaders might at last be ready for serious talks about our most persistent problems—those of disarmament, mutual inspection, atomic control, and Germany, including Berlin.

To explore that possibility, our own and the British and French leaders met together, and later we agreed, with the Soviet leaders, to gather in Paris on May 16.

Of course we had no indication or thought that basic Soviet policies had turned about. But when there is even the slightest chance of strengthening peace, there can be no higher obligation than to pursue it.

Nor had our own policies changed. We did hope to make some progress in a Summit meeting, unpromising though previous experiences had been. But as we made preparations for this meeting, we did not drop our guard nor relax our vigilance.

Our safety, and that of the free world, demand, of course, effective systems for gathering information about the military capabilities of other powerful nations, especially those that make a fetish of secrecy. This involves many techniques and methods. In these times of vast military machines and nuclear-tipped missiles, the ferreting out of this information is indispensable to free world security.

This has long been one of my most serious preoccupations. It is part of my grave responsibility, within the over-all problem of protecting the American people, to guard ourselves and our allies against surprise attack.

During the period leading up to World War II we learned from bitter experience the imperative necessity of a continuous gathering of intelligence information, the maintenance of military communications and contact, and alertness of command.

An additional word seems appropriate about this matter of communications and command. While the Secretary of Defense and I were in Paris, we were, of course, away from our normal command posts. He recommended that under the circumstances we test the continuing readiness of our military communications. I personally approved. Such tests are valuable and will be frequently repeated in the future.

Moreover, as President, charged by the Constitution with the conduct of America's foreign relations, and as Commander-in-Chief, charged with the direction of the operations and activities of our Armed Forces and their supporting services, I take full responsibility for approving all the various programs undertaken by our government to secure and evaluate military intelligence.

It was in the prosecution of one of these intelligence programs that the widely publicized U-2 incident occurred.

Aerial photography has been one of many methods we have used to keep ourselves and the free world abreast of major Soviet military developments. The usefulness of this work has been well established through four years of effort. The Soviets were well aware of it. Chairman Khrushchev has stated that he became aware of these flights several years ago. Only last week, in his Paris press conference, Chairman Khrushchev confirmed that he knew of these flights when he visited the United States last September.

Incidentally, this raises the natural question—why all the furor concerning one particular flight? He did not, when in America last September, charge that these flights were any threat to Soviet safety. He did not then see any reason to refuse to confer with American representatives.

This he did only about the flight that unfortunately failed, on May 1, far inside Russia.

Now, two questions have been raised about this particular flight; first, as to its timing, considering the imminence of the Summit meeting; second, our initial statements when we learned the flight had failed.

As to the timing, the question was really whether to halt the program and thus forego the gathering of important information that was essential and that was likely to be unavailable at a later date. The decision was that the program should not be halted.

The plain truth is this: when a nation needs intelligence activity, there is no time when vigilance can be relaxed. Incidentally, from Pearl Harbor we learned that even negotiation itself can be used to conceal preparations for a surprise attack.

Next, as to our government's initial statement about the flight, this was issued to protect the pilot, his mission, and our intelligence processes, at a time when the true facts were still undetermined.

Our first information about the failure of this mission did not disclose whether the pilot was still alive, was trying to escape, was avoiding interrogation, or whether both plane and pilot had been destroyed. Protection of our intelligence system and the pilot, and concealment of the plane's mission, seemed imperative. It must be remembered that over a long period, these flights had given us information of the greatest importance to the nation's security. In fact, their success has been nothing short of remarkable.

For these reasons, what is known in intelligence circles as a "covering statement" was issued. It was issued on assumptions that were later proved incorrect. Consequently, when later the status of the pilot was definitely established, and there was no further possibility of avoiding exposure of the project, the factual details were set forth.

I then made two facts clear to the public: first, our program of aerial reconnaissance had been undertaken with my approval; second, this government is compelled to keep abreast, by one means or another, of military activities of the Soviets, just as their government has for years engaged in espionage activities in our country and throughout the world. Our necessity to proceed with such activities was also asserted by our Secretary of State who, however, had been careful—as was I—not to say that these particular flights would be continued.

In fact, before leaving Washington, I had directed that these U-2 flights be stopped. Clearly their usefulness was impaired. Moreover, continuing this particular activity in these new circumstances could not but complicate the relations of certain of our allies with the Soviets. And of course, new techniques, other than aircraft, are constantly being developed.

Now I wanted no public announcement of this decision until I could personally disclose it at the Summit meeting in conjunction with certain proposals I had prepared for the conference.

At my first Paris meeting with Mr. Khrushchev, and before his tirade was made public, I informed him of this discontinuance and the character of the constructive proposals I planned to make. These contemplated the establishment of a system of aerial surveillance operated by the United Nations.

The day before the first scheduled meeting, Mr. Khrushchev had advised President de Gaulle and Prime Minister Macmillan that he would make certain demands upon the United States as a precondition for beginning a Summit conference.

Although the United States was the only power against which he expressed his displeasure, he did not communicate this information to me. I was, of course, informed by our allies.

At the four power meeting on Monday morning, he demanded of the United States four things: first, condemnation of U-2 flights as a method of espionage; second, assurance that they would not be continued; third, a public apology on behalf of the United States; and, fourth, punishment of all those who had any responsibility respecting this particular mission.

I replied by advising the Soviet leader that I had, during the previous week, stopped these flights and that they would not be resumed. I offered also to discuss the matter with him in personal meetings, while the regular business of the Summit might proceed. Obviously, I would not respond to his extreme demands. He knew, of course, by holding to those demands the Soviet Union was scuttling the Summit Conference.

In torpedoing the conference, Mr. Khrushchev claimed that he acted as the result of his own high moral indignation over alleged American acts of aggression. As I said earlier, he had known of these flights for a long time. It is apparent that the Soviets had decided even before the Soviet delegation left Moscow that my trip to the Soviet Union should be cancelled and that nothing constructive from their viewpoint would come out of the Summit Conference.

In evaluating the results, however, I think we must not write the record all in red ink. There are several things to be written in the black. Perhaps the Soviet action has turned the clock back in some measure, but it should be noted that Mr. Khrushchev did not go beyond invective—a time-worn Soviet device to achieve an immediate objective. In this case, the wrecking of the Conference.

On our side, at Paris, we demonstrated once again America's willingness, and that of her allies, always to go the extra mile in behalf of peace. Once again, Soviet intransigence reminded us all of the unpredictability of despotic rule, and the need for those who work for freedom to stand together in determination and in strength.

The conduct of our allies was magnificent. My colleagues and friends—President de Gaulle and Prime Minister Macmillan—stood sturdily with the American delegation in spite of persistent Soviet attempts to split the Western group. The NATO meeting after the Paris Conference showed unprecedented unity and support for the alliance and for the position taken at the Summit meeting. I salute our allies for us all.

And now, most importantly, what about the future?

All of us know that, whether started deliberately or accidentally, global war would leave civilization in a shambles. This is as true of the Soviet system as of all others. In a nuclear war there can be no victors—only losers. Even despots understand this. Mr. Khrushchev stated last week that he well realizes that general nuclear war would bring catastrophe for both sides. Recognition of this mutual destructive capability is the basic reality of our present relations. Most assuredly, however, this does not mean that we shall ever give up trying to build a more sane and hopeful reality—a better foundation for our common relations.

To do this, here are the policies we must follow, and to these I am confident the great majority of our people, regardless of party, give their support:

First. We must keep up our strength, and hold it steady for the long pull—a strength not neglected in complacency nor overbuilt in hysteria. So doing, we can make it clear to everyone that there can be no gain in the use of pressure tactics or aggression against us and our Allies.

Second. We must continue businesslike dealings with the Soviet leaders on outstanding issues, and improve the contacts between our own and the Soviet peoples, making clear that the path of reason and common sense is still open if the Soviets will but use it.

Third. To improve world conditions in which human freedom can flourish, we must continue to move ahead with positive programs at home and abroad, in collaboration with free nations everywhere. In doing so, we shall continue to give our strong support to the United Nations and the great principles for which it stands.

Now as to the first of these purposes—our defenses are sound. They are tailored to the situation confronting us.

Their adequacy has been my primary concern for these past seven years—indeed throughout my adult life.

In no respect have the composition and size of our forces been based on or affected by any Soviet blandishment. Nor will they be. We will continue to carry forward the great improvements already planned in these forces. They will be kept ready—and under constant review.

Any changes made necessary by technological advances or world events will be recommended at once.

This strength—by far the most potent on earth—is, I emphasize, for deterrent, defensive and retaliatory purposes only, without threat or aggressive intent toward anyone.

Concerning the second part of our policy—relations with the Soviets—we and all the world realize, despite our recent disappointment, that progress toward the goal of mutual understanding, easing the causes of tensions, and reduction of armaments is as necessary as ever.

We shall continue these peaceful efforts, including participation in the existing negotiations with the Soviet Union. In these negotiations we have made some progress. We are prepared to preserve and build on it. The Allied Paris communiqué and my own statement on returning to the United States should have made this abundantly clear to the Soviet government.

We conduct these negotiations not on the basis of surface harmony nor are we deterred by any bad deportment we meet. Rather we approach them as a careful search for common interests between the Western allies and the Soviet Union on specific problems.

I have in mind, particularly, the nuclear test and disarmament negotiations. We shall not back away, on account of recent events, from the efforts or commitments that we have undertaken.

Nor shall we relax our search for new means of reducing the risk of war by miscalculation, and of achieving verifiable arms control.

A major American goal is a world of open societies.

Here in our country anyone can buy maps and aerial photographs showing our cities, our dams, our plants, our highways—indeed, our whole industrial and economic complex. We know that Soviet attachés regularly collect this information. Last fall Chairman Khrushchev's train passed no more than a few hundred feet from an operational ICBM, in plain view from his window. Our thousands of books and scientific journals, our magazines, newspapers and official publications, our radio and television, all openly describe to all the world every aspect of our society.

This is as it should be. We are proud of our freedom.

Soviet distrust, however, does still remain. To allay these misgivings I offered five years ago to open our skies to Soviet reconnaissance aircraft on a reciprocal basis. The Soviets refused. That offer is still open. At an appropriate time America will submit such a program to the United Nations, together with the recommendation that the United Nations itself conduct this reconnaissance. Should the United Nations accept this proposal, I am prepared to propose that America supply part of the aircraft and equipment required.

This is a photograph of the North Island Naval Station in San Diego, California. It was taken from an altitude of more than 70 thousand feet. You may not perhaps be able to see them on your television screens, but the white lines in the parking strips around the field are clearly discernible from 13 miles up. Those lines are just six inches wide.

Obviously most of the details necessary for a military evaluation of the airfield and its aircraft are clearly distinguishable.

I show you this photograph as an example of what could be accomplished through United Nations aerial surveillance.

Indeed, if the United Nations should undertake this policy, this program, and the great nations of the world should accept it, I am convinced that not only can all humanity be assured that they are safe from any surprise attack from any quarter, but indeed the greatest tensions of all, the fear of war, would be removed from the world. I sincerely hope that the United Nations may adopt such a program.

As far as we in America are concerned, our programs for increased contacts between all peoples will continue. Despite the suddenly expressed hostility of the men in the Kremlin, I remain convinced that the basic longings of the Soviet people are much like our own. I believe that Soviet citizens have a sincere friendship for the people of America. I deeply believe that above all else they want a lasting peace and a chance for a more abundant life in place of more and more instruments of war.

Finally, turning to the third part of America's policy—the strengthening of freedom—we must do far more than concern ourselves with military defense against, and our relations with, the Communist Bloc. Beyond this, we must advance constructive programs throughout the world for the betterment of peoples in the newly developing nations. The zigs and zags of the Kremlin cannot be allowed to disturb our worldwide programs and purposes. In the period ahead, these programs could well be the decisive factor in our persistent search for peace in freedom.

To the peoples in the newly developing nations urgently needed help will surely come. If it does not come from us and our friends, these peoples will be driven to seek it from the enemies of freedom. Moreover, those joined with us in defense partnerships look to us for proof of our steadfastness. We must not relax our common security efforts.

As to this, there is something specific all of us can do, and right now. It is imperative that crippling cuts not be made in the appropriations recommended for Mutual Security, whether economic or military. We must support this program with all of our wisdom and all of our strength. We are proud to call this a nation of the people. With the people knowing the importance of this program, and making their voices heard in its behalf throughout the land, there can be no doubt of its continued success.

Fellow Americans, long ago I pledged to you that I would journey anywhere in the world to promote the cause of peace. I remain pledged to pursue a peace of dignity, of friendship, of honor, of justice.

Operating from the firm base of our spiritual and physical strength, and seeking wisdom from the Almighty, we and our allies together will continue to work for the survival of mankind in freedom—and for the goal of mutual respect, mutual understanding, and openness among all nations.

Thank you, and good night.

In the aftermath of the U-2 incident, a subcommittee of the Senate Armed Forces Committee began an investigation into who was responsible. Although Secretary of State Christian Herter testified on behalf of the Administration (June 10), some members of the President's staff feared that the Secretary had not made his position clear enough. As a result, they drafted a letter intended to clarify matters, but the Department of State did not think any further explanation was needed.

Administrative Assistant Edward McCabe to Deputy Assistant Jerry Morgan and Special Assistant Gordon Gray
June 16, 1960
[Official File 225-G, Eisenhower Papers.]

Attached is a draft we might offer to Chris Herter.

I find that the hearing record is open, and that Mr. Herter will not return to Washington until early next week.

I have not seen Tom Gates' Jackson Committee testimony, so I recommend the NSC Staff check out tightly the references this draft makes to him. Also, if the last few sentences in this draft are agreeable to you, the Gates' record should be checked closely because I suggested the same responses to him if he were questioned about the wisdom of deciding this outside the NSC. If it is in Gates' testimony, we might want to omit it here—or use some different words.

Dear Mr. Chairman:

In your subcommittee's June tenth hearing, several references were made to U-2 flights, and I believe that as it now stands your record on that point might be somewhat misleading. While I appreciate your intention not to publish testimony relating to the U-2, I nevertheless want to clarify my testimony so that, to the extent your hearing touched the U-2 matter, your own record may be fully accurate.

Conforming to statute, the Central Intelligence Agency pursues various broad intelligence undertaking at the behest of the National Security Council. However, it should be emphasized that except for the issuance of the general policy directive under which the overflight program was undertaken by CIA, the U-2 matter was not brought into the NSC machinery. While the individual members of the NSC were, of course, aware of the program, the flights themselves were never the subject of a Council meeting.

In your June tenth hearing, references were made to a National Security Council meeting of May fifth. Since I was out of the United States on that date I, of course, did not participate in any May fifth meetings in Washington, and it is with respect to May fifth activities that my testimony might cause your hearing record to be unclear. I have now determined that Secretary Gates also testified before your subcommittee concerning the May fifth decision—a decision not taken in the NSC process—and a decision in which he personally participated. Secretary Gates' testimony on the point in question is precisely accurate.

I appreciate this opportunity to clarify your record, particularly in view of your subcommittee's great interest in the machinery of the National Security Council. On this, perhaps I should add one further general thought. As to making any matter the subject of a Council meeting, that is, of course, the President's business since the NSC function is clearly an advisory one. In my judgment, any President must be free to decide in what manner, and to what extent, he makes use of any advisory body. But as far as the U-2 is concerned, there is no doubt in my mind that the people who needed to know about it did know about it, and that it was properly and effectively coordinated all along the line.

Administrative Assistant Edward McCabe
to Secretary Christian Herter
June 21, 1960
[Official File 225-G, Eisenhower Papers.]

At the recent Jackson Committee hearing in which the U-2 was discussed, the record is left somewhat unclear on the function of the National Security Council.

It seemed to us that a letter from you to the Committee could clarify the matter—so we offer the attached draft [above] for your consideration.

The Senate Committee on Foreign Relations also reviewed the U-2 incident and the failure of the Paris summit meeting. At the end of the hearings, Committee Chairman J. William Fulbright addressed the Senate. The Democratic senator from Arkansas, a frequent critic of the Administration, summarized his ideas on the matter and requested that the views of other committee members be included in the report. The "Supplemental Individual Views" of Senator Alexander Wiley of Wisconsin, the ranking Republican on the Committee, appeared to represent the general views of the Administration.

Senate Speech by J. William Fulbright on the U-2 Crisis and the Paris Summit Meeting
June 28, 1960
[U.S., *Congressional Record*, 86th Cong., 2nd Sess., CVI, Part II, 14733–37.]

MR. J. W. FULBRIGHT (Dem., Ark.) : Mr. President, on behalf of the Committee on Foreign Relations, I submit a report entitled "Events Relating to the Summit Conference," together with individual views.

The report is the result of the committee's hearings on the same subject from May 27 to June 2. It was approved by the committee last Thursday, June 23, by a vote of 14 to 1. I may say that in all of my service on the Foreign Relations Committee, never before have I known a report to receive such careful, minute, prolonged attention from the committee. Thirteen committee meetings were held, during which the report was gone over, sentence by sentence, with the most exacting care. A second draft received the same attention. Every member of the committee had ample opportunity to comment on everything from the most delicate shades of phrasing to the most profound questions of policy.

I might also say that throughout these proceedings the committee had the wholehearted cooperation and support of the Senate leadership, particularly of the majority leader, the distinguished Senator from Texas [Mr. Johnson]. I discussed the matter in advance with the Senator, and he agreed that the inquiry was a proper one and that the Committee on Foreign Relations was the proper committee to conduct it.

As is inevitable in a case of this kind where compromise is involved, the end product is probably not wholly satisfactory to any member of the committee. Yet it is generally satisfactory to most members of the committee, and I venture the hope that it will be read and pondered by the Senate, by the public at large, and especially by the officials of the executive branch. Considering the number of cooks involved, and the diversity of their feelings about the matter, this broth has turned out rather well.

Nevertheless, Mr. President, it is with a heavy heart and with some regret that I present the report to the Senate and thereby to the people of the Nation. It is never pleasant to admit error in our private lives. It is far more painful for a great nation to admit that its policies have been lacking in wisdom and foresight and one may be sure that whoever calls attention to the errors will not be thanked for his effort.

In spite of the fact that I may well expect to receive criticism, I feel a duty to express my views for whatever they are worth.

In some systems of government, notably the Communist system, error is rarely admitted by those who govern. Infallibility of the ruler is accepted by the people, who, indeed, have nothing to say about, or any power to change, the policy in any case.

In a democratic system, such as ours, the people do have much to say about policy, and they decide who shall govern them. How, may I ask, can our people be expected to discharge their duty as citizens of a self-governing republic, if they are not told the truth about their affairs? It would be easier, more pleasant, and I am sure more popular, to join those who pretend that all is well, that the summit meeting was a triumph for the West and that the Japanese fiasco only demonstrates once again the viciousness of the Communists.

Mr. President, in this connection I call attention to an article entitled "Eisenhower's Tactic: His Procedure on U-2, Summit, and Trip Is To Ignore the Critics," written by James Reston, the head of the Washington bureau of the New York *Times,* and published in the New York *Times* of today, June 28, 1960. I think the article is most appropriate, and I ask unanimous consent that it be printed at this point in the RECORD.

There being no objection, the article was ordered to be printed in the RECORD, as follows:

(By James Reston) June 27.—President Eisenhower has devised a simple procedure for dealing with his critics and his defeats: He simply ignores the critics and claims victories.

This is what he did in his explanation of the U-2 and the summit incidents last month, and this is what he did in his report on the Japanese situation tonight. The effect of this is serious in a democracy, for it confuses the public, infuriates the political opposition, and leaves mistakes unexplained and uncorrected.

What the President did tonight was merely to say that everything that had been done on our side was all right, and that all that was necessary was to carry on steadily as before.

The demonstrations in Okinawa were ignored: "Relations with Okinawa have been strengthened," he said. The cancellation of the trip to Japan was a nuisance, perhaps, but it was all the fault of the Communists, he said.

There was no analysis of the effect of the U-2 incident on U.S. bases in Japan, or of the immense crowds demonstrating against the treaty, though they numbered considerably more at times than the total membership of the Japanese Communist Party.

LOSS OF PRESTIGE IGNORED

Nor was there any reference to the criticism in the American press of the Japanese incident, or to the widespread discussion of loss of U. S. prestige in the press of the allied world.

Beyond this, there was only one reference to the U-2 spy plane flight over the Soviet Union and the Paris summit meeting, which were clearly connected with the demonstrations against the Japanese treaty. This was a remark that the President's trip to the Soviet Union was canceled after a series of false and elaborate excuses by Premier Khrushchev.

There is, of course, much that can be said for the other trips made by President Eisenhower in the last year. It was perfectly fair to argue that these had done much to create good will for the United States in India, Pakistan, the Near East and Europe.

Nobody has denied this. But the President's two speeches on Paris and Tokyo were a blanket denial of the very misjudgments his own officials concede in private and Secretary of State Herter has actually made in public.

EFFECT IN ELECTION YEAR

As a political device in an election year, of course, this carries great weight. The President is immensely popular. The public does not like to be told that its Government has made mistakes, and when the President in effect denies that mistakes were made, he no doubt helps restore the political balance.

He does nothing, however, to restore confidence within his own Government or within the alliance, or to institute any review of the policies that may have gone wrong.

If the President had taken up the criticism that has preoccupied the Western World in his absence, and answered the serious points raised, for example, in the report of the Senate Foreign Relations Committee this last weekend, then it would have been possible to reach fair judgments on the events of these last few months.

This however, is what he did not do. His conclusion on the basis of his last two reports is inescapable: He feels no responsibility for anything that went wrong, and therefore no need to do anything except carry on as before.

PROBLEM REMAINS

Accordingly, even if everything he said was absolutely true and in perspective, a serious problem remains. For if his account of where the Western alliance now stands is correct, then his allies and even the American press which has been so favorable to him in the past, are wrong and guilty of misleading the people about the principal leader of the West.

Democracies cannot operate effectively when their leaders and their public opinion do not come to grips with widely publicized criticism. The special gift of this system is that it has the power of self-criticism which corrects mistakes as they go along.

But the President is not answering the criticism; he is merely brushing it aside as the work of Communists and opposition Democrats.

Mr. President, I believe the prestige of our country among nations has reached a new low, and I believe that before we can begin to regain our position in the world we must admit our errors and examine the causes thereof; then carefully plan and execute a program for the restoration of that power and influence.

The matter which I present to the Senate today is, of course, but a small facet of the total national picture, but it is a facet which is illustrative, I believe, of the grave problems which confront us and to which solutions must be found.

Mr. President, the complete report of the committee is before the Senate, but there are a few points which seem to me to require emphasis.

The first of these is that it was a serious error of judgment to order the U-2 flight of May 1. It is true, of course, as administration spokesmen have repeatedly said, that there is no good time for a failure.

MR. RALPH YARBOROUGH (Dem., Tex.): Mr. President, will the Senator yield?

MR. FULBRIGHT: I yield.

MR. YARBOROUGH: Has it been ascertained yet who ordered the U-2 flight?

MR. FULBRIGHT: All that we know about it, I think, is contained in the record which was made at the time of the hearings, and as was presented in the report of the committee.

MR. YARBOROUGH: I thank the Senator from Arkansas for yielding.

MR. FULBRIGHT: Mr. President, to say that there is no good time for a failure is to overlook the fact that there are bad times and worse times. Certainly May 1 was one of the worst times. Little or no consideration was given to the international consequences of a failure on May 1. It has been argued that in view of the unbroken success of almost 4 years, there was no reason to anticipate this failure. But, Mr. President, in an enterprise as risky as this, it is imprudent not to take into account the consequences of failure. Such consequences are routinely taken into account in thousands of decisions in the day to day conduct of our affairs. All of us are accustomed, in considering any plan of action affecting either our private or public affairs, to ask ourselves the question, "What happens if this does not work?" Nobody asked that question in connection with the May 1 flight.

We are told that this particular flight was in a special category: that it was seeking information of extraordinary importance which might not be available later. However, we are not told, even under conditions of the utmost secrecy, what that information was. In view of the sensitivity of some of the other things we were told, this reticence on the part of the executive branch raises the question of whether the information sought on May 1 was in fact as important as it has been represented. There is ground here for the conclusion that the alleged extraordinary importance of this information is the administration's cover story for its own costly mistake.

It might be argued that if we come now to the judgment that the May 1 flight should not have taken place, it is incumbent upon us to come also to a judgment as to what date prior to May 1 should have been fixed as a cutoff. I am not sure that this follows, but I should say that sometime around the middle of April, or perhaps after the flight of April 9, the flights should have been suspended. If the April 9 flight had failed, there would have remained time perhaps to restore some sort of normalcy to international relations before the summit conference. There was plainly not sufficient time after the May 1 failure.

Moreover, the time available was improperly used. So, although sending the May 1 flight at all was the first mistake, what we did after it failed was the second mistake.

There are three aspects of the U.S. reaction to the failure which should have been handled differently. The cover statements made about the flight were far too specific, and made us look ridiculous when the full extent of Soviet knowledge was revealed. The gravest mistake was made when the President assumed responsibility for the flight. Finally, after the truth became known, the State Department and the White House assumed a self-righteous attitude which further complicated our situation in Paris.

The crux of the matter is found in these last two points—the assumption of Presidential responsibility and the self-righteous attempts to justify the flights in terms which implied their continuation. These are interrelated and each served to compound the mischievous effects of the other.

As is pointed out in the report, it is unprecedented among civilized nations for a chief of state to assume personal responsibility for covert intelligence operations. The traditional method would have been to allow the chief of the intelligence agency to take the responsibility. One reason intelligence agencies exist is to serve as a whipping boy in cases of this kind.

Mr. President, I am not so hidebound as to argue that any departure from precedent is a mistake ipso facto. We must examine the reasons for the precedents and ask ourselves why, up until the 9th of May, 1960, it had been the unvarying practice in international relations for chiefs of state to hold themselves above and apart from espionage These reasons are sound and persuasive and go to the heart of a system of diplomatic conventions which have developed over the centuries and which make it possible for nation states of differing characteristics to carry on amicable, impersonal relations with each other.

In this system of diplomatic forms, the chief of state embodies in his person the sovereignty and dignity of his country. It is totally unacceptable for one chief of state because of this personal embodiment to impinge upon the sovereignty of another, and much less so for him to assert the right to do so. It is begging the question to say that the sovereignty of nations is violated all the time by espionage, and that the Soviet Union is the worst offender. The violations of this type, as carried out by the covert intelligence activities of any nation state, are institutional in nature, and hitherto have not been considered as challenging the sovereignty of the nation. This is a subtle, but an important distinction.

So long as international relations are kept on an institutional, impersonal basis, states can disagree strongly and still maintain channels of communication with each other. This is why the rather stylized language of diplomacy has been developed. This is why a diplomatic note may contain strong, even harsh, statements, but still close with the phrase, "Accept, sir, renewed assurances of my highest esteem."

Within our own Federal system of 50 States, even though the members are somewhat less jealous of their own dignity, and are more friendly and tolerant of one another, than are the members of the international community, nevertheless, similar impersonal conventions govern our conduct, even here in the Senate. We do not refer to each other even by name, but as "the Senator from X State." And we usually preface a reference to one of our colleagues with adjectives such as "able," "distinguished," or "eminent." These adjectives are used even by a Senator who is describing a colleague whom he does not admire. If Senators said on the floor of the Senate what they really feel about some of their colleagues, the orderly conduct of legislative business would quickly become impossible. It is against the rules of the Senate for a Member to question the motives of another Senator. This derives from the fact, not that Senators are different from others in their motives, but from the tradition that they represent sovereign States, and from the fact that without the rule, the work of the Senate would be disrupted.

It seems clear to me that if chiefs of state begin the practice of personally admitting the violation of each other' sovereignty, the orderly conduct of international affairs will quickly become impossible—as, indeed, it did become in Paris, last month.

Historically, the deliberate and intentional assertion by a head of state of the right to violate the territorial sovereignty of another nation has been considered an unfriendly act of the utmost seriousness.

It is quite unacceptable to any state to be in the position in which this Government put the Soviet Union last month. Although another man would have most likely been more temperate in his choice of language, it is difficult to see how anyone could have been expected to act substantially different from the way Chairman Khrushchev acted under the circumstances which confronted him in Paris.

This is not said in defense of Khrushchev; it is said in an attempt to bring understanding of our own difficulties. Either we have got to resign ourselves to the inevitability of war; or we have got to get along, somehow, some way, with the Soviet Union. And if we are going to get along with that country, we have got to preserve the traditional conventions by means of which we can at least talk to its representatives.

Suppose, Mr. President, that the U-2 incident had occurred the other way around. Suppose a Russian counterpart of the U-2 had come down over Kansas City on May 1. This event in itself, I daresay, would have brought speeches in the Senate powerful enough to rock the Capitol Dome with denunciations of the perfidy of the Soviets on the eve of the summit conference and with demands that the President not go to Paris. But then, Mr. President, reflect how much more violent the reaction here would have been if Mr. Khrushchev had said he was personally responsible for the flight, and at the same time left the impression that he had every intention of trying it again. In this connection, it is well to remember Dwight Morrow's observation that one of our troubles is that we judge ourselves by our motives, and others by their actions.

Although it was bad enough for our Chief of State to assume personal responsibility for the U-2, it was worse for us then to leave the impression that the flights were to be continued, and, even more, to go to such lengths to justify the flights. I am not arguing here that the flights were not justified as an espionage operation; but the justification rested solely and simply on the need of the United States for the kind of intelligence which the flights provided. This is the kind of justification which the Soviet Union, and every other government, for that matter, can understand. But it becomes quite intolerable to go beyond this, and attempt to make it appear that the flights were really the Soviet's own fault; that if the Soviets had not been so secretive, we would not have had to spy on them. This attitude of smug self-righteousness must have been unbearably provocative to the Soviet Government and contributed substantially to the violence and intemperate bad manners of their representative, Mr. Khrushchev, at Paris.

I suppose, Mr. President, that this statement will be twisted to have me saying that we must be nice to the Russians and to Khrushchev and not offend him. The truth is that in the orderly conduct of international relations, one ought not to be either nice or offensive; one ought to be impersonal and objective. Heaven knows our basic differences of substance with the Soviet Union make the conduct of our relations difficult enough, without our creating novel obstructions to the traditional means of communication and negotiation.

But a larger, and rather more elusive, issue is also involved here. It is one thing to say, "We tried to get intelligence, because we needed it." It is quite another thing to say, "We needed intelligence, and this gave us the right to try to get it."

If a man is starving to death, and if he robs a grocery store, we can understand his action on the basis of need; but his need does not give him a right to become a burglar. Hitler used to argue that Germany's need for lebensraum gave him the moral right to commit aggression. The same kind of argument was heard from Mussolini and from the Japanese war lords of the thirties. It has even been heard from the Soviet Union. I hope it will not be heard even by implication, in the United States.

Discussion of the wisdom of having our Head of State assume responsibility for the U-2 has frequently been confused by irrelevant arguments over whether or not President Eisenhower should lie or should tell the truth. Stated in these terms, the answer obviously always is that the President should tell the truth, and that he should be commended for following the rigorous standards of honesty set by young George Washington. But, Mr. President, although Washington admitted chopping down the cherry tree, he did not go on to say, "Yes, I did it, and I'm glad. The cherry tree was offensive to me, because it had grown so tall. I needed some cherries, and I shall chop down other cherry trees whenever I want more cherries."

In any event, Mr. President, my argument is not that the President should not have told the truth; my argument is that he should not, as the Head of our Nation, have become personally involved in the incident, one way or the other.

We have not yet seen the last of the results of the bumbling and fumbling of the U.S. Government during the first 2 weeks of May 1960. One result was that there was no summit conference. It is perfectly clear that the U-2 incident and our handling of it were the immediate cause of the collapse of the conference. It is irrelevant in this connection to argue that Khrushchev came to Paris with a predetermined position to prevent the conference from taking place. The determining factor in reaching this position was the U-2 incident which had occurred 2 weeks before the conference. We also have the testimony of the Secretary of State that there were no indications, prior to May 1, that the Soviets did not intend to go through with the conference. And we have the testimony of former Ambassador Bohlen, now a high-ranking official in the Department of State, and our outstanding expert on Soviet affairs, and who was at Paris, that—and I quote from the report:

> Had there been no plane incident, I believe the conference would have run its full course. The plane incident, the whole development connected with that, moved things into a totally new dimension.

It contributes little to our understanding of these events to say Khrushchev wrecked the conference. Of course he did. The essential point is that the U-2 was the reason he did. Secretary Gates said it was the tool Khrushchev used. Secretary Herter said it was a convenient handle for Khrushchev. This is not essentially different from saying he used it as a crowbar and sledgehammer. One might even go further and say that we forced Khrushchev to wreck the conference by our own ineptness. Walter Lippmann, one of the most eminent and respected of our commentators, has put it best. Referring to the implication that the flights would be continued, he wrote on May 12, before the Paris conference:

> To avow that we intend to violate Soviet sovereignty is to put everybody on the spot. [The Soviet Government] is compelled to react because no nation can remain passive when it is the avowed policy of another nation to intrude upon its territory.

What is unprecedented about the avowal is not the spying as such but the claim that spying, when we do it, should be accepted by the world as righteous. This is an amateurish and naive view of the nature of spying.

The spy business cannot be conducted without illegal, immoral, and criminal activities. But all great powers are engaged in the spy business, and as long as the world is as warlike as it has been in all recorded history there is no way of doing without spying.

All the powers know this and all have accepted the situation as one of the hard facts of life. Around this situation there has developed over many generations a code of behavior.

The cardinal rule, which makes spying tolerable in international relations, is that it is never avowed.

Another result of this unfortunate series of blunders has been a loss of confidence, worldwide, in the United States. It is true that our allies stood by us stanchly and loyally in Paris. It is equally true that the technical skill demonstrated by almost 4 years of U-2 flights aroused widespread admiration. The loss of confidence to which I refer has to do with faith in the ability of the United States to coordinate its governmental machinery and its vast power, and engage this power positively and effectively in the defense of the free world.

Lack of confidence leads to neutralism, and I daresay this was a contributing factor to the riots in Japan protesting our new treaty. I also call the Senate's attention to the following report from Mexico City in the New York *Times* of May 22:

> Pressures were put on the Mexican Government this week to force the United States out of a planned missile-tracking site in the State of Sonora.
> Mounting sentiment against the proposed installation apparently resulted from a combined public determination to maintain Mexico's neutrality following the shooting down of an American U-2 reconnaissance plane in the Soviet Union, the collapse of the summit conference and the whipping up of anti-United States emotion by leftist sources here.
> Mexican reaction to the U-2 incident and the summit breakdown could probably reflect with fair accuracy that of a large part of Latin America.

And I fear that we may see other manifestations of this same loss of confidence in other countries where we have military bases. . . . Mr. President, it will be a long time before we can get back to where we were on April 30.

In the meantime, if we can disabuse ourselves of the habit of self-delusion, of viewing defeats as victories and of advertising blunders as strokes of genius, there are some things we can learn from these sad events. One is the need for better coordination and much firmer direction of all governmental activities affecting foreign relations. If this is not to come from the White House, it should come from the State Department.

Much has been said about the lack of coordination in handling the U-2 incident and about the defects in our governmental machinery which this reveals. What is lacking, Mr. President, is not so much coordination as direction.

I shall read one sentence from the report itself, which appears on page 24:

> Further, there are few, if any, references in the record to direction, and this seems to the committee to be what was most lacking in this period. There were many interagency meetings to coordinate activities, but there was apparently no one official or agency to direct activities.

Mr. President, it is not the machinery which is at fault so much as the people who operate it. The need for coordination varies inversely with the strength and vigor of leadership. Elaborate arrangements for coordination are really nothing more than a poor substitute for a firm hand directing affairs. It is the difference between making a hurried phone call to Gettysburg for approval of a coordinated position and receiving clear instructions based upon reflective consideration from the White House.

Another thing we can learn is that there should be no direct, public link between the President, as Chief of State, and the covert activities of our intelligence agencies. This, I think, has been amply discussed. At the same time, it is equally clear that closer policy control needs to be exercised over these agencies. This can most appropriately be done by the executive branch. But if that branch will not do it, then Congress may have to try to do it along the line of the suggestion of the distinguished Senator from Montana [Mr. Mansfield].

Finally, Mr. President, I feel impelled to take note of a point of view which is beginning to be heard to the effect that the U-2 flights must be resumed and that it was a great mistake ever to stop them. This point of view is most clearly expressed in an interview in the June 27 issue of *U. S. News & World Report* with an anonymous source said to represent "the viewpoint of important groups of officials in the military services of this country and in the U.S. Department of State." The basic theme is that in abandoning the U-2 flights the United States has lost an important source of intelligence and that the Soviets have gained a corresponding advantage. There can be no great quarrel with that as a statement of fact. What really disturbs me about the interview is the attitude reflected in the statement that the "United States has given up a highly important device for reconnaissance without getting a single thing in return."

This clearly implies, Mr. President, that the United States should and could have used the U-2 flights as a bargaining counter and that we should not have given them up unless the Soviets had given something to us. This must be based on the premise that the United States had a real choice in the matter, that we had some kind of right to continue to overfly the Soviet Union, and that in the meantime we could negotiate about it. This is getting dangerously close to the point of view I mentioned earlier—

namely, that our need for this intelligence gives us a right to go after it. This is untenable, and completely ignores the realities of our position.

Those who deplore the giving up of these flights might well reflect that the renunciation of the flights in the future was a direct consequence of the assumption of responsibility by the Head of State. In the words of Walter Lippmann:

> Having avowed too much, the President has had to renounce too much, much more than was necessary.

Mr. President, short of the madness of preventive war, I can think of nothing more dangerous than to resume overflights of the Soviet Union. These overflights were useful while they lasted, but they have now obviously become, as the professionals describe it, compromised.

Mr. President, with the completion of this report in hand, I hope that all of us may now direct our thoughts and best efforts to the problem of improving the policymaking procedures and the executive machinery of our Government. There are lessons to be learned from these experiences, if we can avoid beclouding and obfuscating them with wishful thinking or partisan bickering.

In the deliberations of the committee, which were long and arduous, the members displayed a minimum of partisanship. They acted as good Senators and good Americans should, although there were, of course, legitimate differences of opinion. In the beginning I was doubtful that a report could be agreed upon. It has been and I wish to express my deep appreciation to all those who gave so much of their time and wisdom to its accomplishment.

Mr. President, I ask unanimous consent to have the individual views printed as a part of the committee report.

Report of the Committee on Foreign Relations on Events Relating to the Summit Conference June 28, 1960
[U.S., Congress, 86th Cong., 2nd Sess., 1960, 22–36.]

Conclusions

Let it be said at the outset that the gathering of intelligence with respect to foreign activities potentially inimical to our security and that of the free world is fully justified by precedent as well as by vital necessity. Since time immemorial, nations have found it necessary to engage in such activities of both the overt and covert variety. The Soviet Union itself has probably engaged in covert intelligence activities on a wider scale than any other nation in the history of the world. What the committee is concerned with respecting the U-2 program is not the propriety, desirability, or necessity of such operations, but the lessons, if any, which can be drawn from the failure of the May 1 flight and related events.

On the basis of classified testimony which cannot be discussed, the committee has no reason to believe that technical preparations for the flight were faulty or that the pilot was unreliable in any respect. From the technical point of view—that is, the preparation and equipment of plane and pilot—what befell the U-2 on May 1 was just plain bad luck.

There remains the question of the wisdom of sending the flight at all. The committee was told that the flight was after information of well above average importance, but it was not told what this information was. The committee cannot, therefore, come to any conclusion as to whether the importance of the information sought justified the risks which were taken. Although the committee recognizes the necessity for secrecy in intelligence operations, it is strongly of the opinion that a government based upon a separation of powers cannot exist on faith alone. It is disappointed that the responsible officials of the executive branch did not see fit to confide in it this one piece of information which is crucial to reaching an informed judgment. The committee recognizes that the administration has the legal right to refuse the information under the doctrine of executive privilege.

The U-2 overflights had a record of almost 4 years of unbroken success. The Soviet Union had been aware of these overflights during this time and had been unable to do anything about them. Against this background, there would seem to be no reason to assume that the May 1 flight would be any different from any of its predecessors.

In approving the flight, little, if any, consideration was given to the proximity of May 1 to the date of the summit conference. An argument was made to the committee that if diplomatic considerations were taken into account, there would always be some reason for canceling or postponing a flight. This argument is not really persuasive, because it fails fully to recognize the importance of the summit conference. Further, the record is extremely obscure as to whether or not flights had in fact been canceled or postponed in the past for diplomatic reasons. The question here is whether the information sought by the May 1 flight was of sufficient importance to justify the hazards to which the summit conference would be subjected by failure of the flight. The question cannot be answered, of course, for want of knowledge of what information was sought by the flight.

The fact that neither the President, the Secretary of State, the Acting Secretary of State, nor the Secretary of Defense knew that this particular flight was even in the air is an indication of how routine these flight operations had become.

In view of the almost psychopathic addiction to secrecy which has characterized the Russian Government, a probing of this secrecy such as that involved in the U-2 operations, coupled with the frustrations and chagrin of the Soviets over a period of almost 4 years, could only have been expected to result in the most violent reaction when this penetration of their territory was made public.[1]

In view of the combination of circumstances surrounding the loss of the U-2 on May 1, the next question which arises concerns the reaction of the U.S. Government. The first conclusion on this point is that the cover story, which had been designed in advance to meet such a contingency, was inadequate for the circumstances which in fact existed. The cover story which was used in regard to the U-2 for the period May 1 to 7 might have served its purpose if the plane had come down under different circumstances. Until May 7, it was not known in Washington where the U-2 had come down. The plane's flight plan was known, however, and it would have been a reasonable assumption that the chances were quite good that the plane was nowhere near the Soviet border.

At any rate, the cover story was quite obviously outflanked on May 7, and the responsible officials felt that it was then necessary to discuss the matter in greater detail. It was admitted that the U-2 was on a reconnaissance mission, but it was denied that the mission had been authorized from Washington.

In Khrushchev's early statements about the plane, he had implied doubt that President Eisenhower knew about the operation. The May 7 statement of the State Department seemed to confirm this doubt. However, on May 9 Secretary Herter said the program of flights—though not specific flights as such—had been authorized by the President. The substance of this statement was repeated by the President himself May 11.

---

[1]On May 5, in announcing the shooting down of the May 1 flight, Chairman Khrushchev said that there had been another flight on April 9 when "A United States plane intruded into the airspace of our country from the Afghanistan side." He said the Soviet Government decided against making a protest but ordered military commanders to act if another plane intruded.

On May 9, Mr. Khrushchev said: "The reconnaissance plane should have been brought down on April 9, too. But our military, to put it mildly, let a chance slip by. And we, as one says, took them to task for it." In the same speech, he added: "I shall say further, when Twining, the then Chief of Staff of the United States Air Force, arrived here we welcomed him as guest and entertained him. He left our country by air and next day sent a plane flying at great altitude to our country. This plane flew as far as Kiev. The question arose: Should we protest? I proposed that no protest be lodged. From such behavior we drew the conclusion: To improve rockets, to improve fighters" . . . General Twining ended his visit to the Soviet Union July 1, 1956.

In the statement at the summit conference in Paris May 16, Mr. Khrushchev said the May 1 flight "was not the only case of aggressive and espionage actions by the United States Air Force against the Soviet Union."

In his press conference in Paris May 17, Mr. Khrushchev said he "almost" spoke to President Eisenhower about the overflights at their Camp David meeting, but then "became apprehensive . . . and I didn't broach the subject."

The course which the President took is unprecedented in intelligence operations, so far as the committee knows or the record discloses. It is known that Allen Dulles was prepared to accept the full responsibility himself, which is the traditional procedure under the circumstances.

The committee feels that perhaps too much emphasis may have been placed on justification of the flights. If justification was to be made, it would have been enough simply to say we were seeking intelligence vital to our own security.

It seems clear that the situation was complicated by the unnecessarily elaborate NASA statement of May 5 and the categorical statements of the State Department Press Officer on May 5 and 6.

In regard to this whole period of May 1 to 9, the record is full of references to coordination among the various agencies of the government—and yet at crucial points, the coordination broke down, as for example, in NASA issuing a statement on May 5 within 2 or 3 hours after it had been decided that only the State Department would issue a statement. Further, there are few, if any, references in the record to direction, and this seems to the committee to be what was most lacking in this period. There were many interagency meetings to coordinate activities, but there was apparently no one official or agency to direct activities. If this direction is not to come from the White House, then it ought to be made clear, by the White House, that it is to come from the State Department. Indeed, one of the lessons to be learned from this whole affair is the need for reasserting the primacy of the State Department in these matters.

Given the situation which existed by the time the President arrived in Paris, it is difficult to see what course of action he could have reasonably followed other than the one he took.

The crucial questions in regard to the events in Paris are whether the U-2 incident was the reason or the excuse for Khrushchev's behavior and whether his behavior would have been significantly different if the U-2 incident had been handled differently.

In the view of Secretary Herter, the U-2 incident was a contributing factor to Khrushchev's attitude toward the summit. The Secretary also said that prior to May 1 there had been no indications that Khrushchev intended to wreck the summit. Without doubt, the U-2 was a contributing factor to the breakup of the summit conference, so far as the Soviet Government was concerned. The other factors which the Secretary mentioned as contributing to the Soviet attitude in Paris all existed prior to May 1. It can be accepted that they did play a part in Soviet policy formation, and still be reasonably concluded that they would not, in and of themselves, have led to the precipitate and violent action taken by the Soviet Government in Paris. The U-2 incident therefore was the immediate excuse seized upon for not proceeding with the conference.

This is not to say that the summit conference would have been a success if the U-2 incident had not occurred. It is to say simply that there probably would have been a summit conference. No one can say what would have happened at the conference if it had been held. At best, it would have perhaps made some slight progress on disarmament and nuclear testing, temporized on Berlin, and set a pattern for future summits. At worst, it would have resulted in complete deadlock. If it was in fact Khrushchev's purpose to prevent the summit, then if the U-2 incident had not occurred, he would have had to find other means to do so. In this sense, the U-2 incident made his task easier. On the other hand, the circumstances under which the conference would have been aborted in the absence of the U-2—if it would have been—are unknown. They might have been more favorable to the West or less favorable. But the crucial point here is that it is by no means certain what the outcome of the conference would have been, as a matter of deliberate Soviet policy, if the U-2 incident had not occurred.

It is more difficult to answer with assurance the question of whether, given the U-2 incident, Khrushchev's behavior in Paris would have been significantly different if the incident had been handled differently. Here one can only speculate. It seems reasonable to suppose, however, that the Soviet reaction was greatly intensified by two aspects: (1) the interpretation that the flights were going to continue; and (2) the assumption of personal responsibility by the President.

It can be argued, as Secretary Herter did at some length, that it was unreasonable to interpret the statements of May 7 and 9 as implying a continuation of the flights. Nevertheless, the fact is that Khrushchev, as well as many of the free world's newspapers, did so interpret the statements. Thus, by the time the President announced the suspension in Paris May 16, the Soviet position had already been set and Khrushchev did not depart from it.

In the end, one is left with the same two questions with which one started: (1) Should the U-2 flight have been sent at all on May 1? and (2) Once the flight failed, should the United States have reacted differently?

In regard to the first question, the committee is handicapped, as stated above, by its lack of knowledge of the specific mission of the U-2. In looking back, if one accepts the conclusion that the failure of the mission furnished an excuse for Khrushchev's wrecking of the summit conference, then, in the absence of compelling reasons to the contrary, there is good reason to conclude that the flight should not have gone.

In regard to the second question, for the reasons stated above, it seems that the U.S. reaction to the failure of the U-2 complicated the problems which resulted from that failure.

There remains the question of future policies in the light of the U-2 incident and the failure of the summit conference. The committee is inclined to agree with Secretary Herter that the basic realities of the world situation have not greatly changed. However, the changes, if any, which have taken place within the Soviet Government and between the Soviet Government and the Chinese Communists may well be of more than passing importance. Although the evidence is neither solid nor consistent, there are indications, as cited above, that Khrushchev's attitude in Paris was due at least in part to pressure from his own military and from the Chinese Communists. There are also indications that, as Secretary Herter related, Khrushchev, at least before the U-2 incident, was identified with the Soviet advocates of a less aggressive, more cooperative course. If this was true, then it would have been in our interest to have done what we could, which would have been marginal at best, to strengthen Khrushchev's position vis-a-vis the Soviet military and the Chinese Communists.

It remains in our interest, as the Secretary said, to encourage Soviet proponents of a peaceful course and to discourage Soviet proponents of an aggressive course. In the years ahead, this will require an unusual degree of maturity and discrimination which will challenge the discretion and intelligence of the American people and their leaders in their approach to foreign policy.

Finally, the U-2 incident has pointed up the need for international agreement on the question of how high sovereignty extends skyward. This question is certain to become more acute in the future as aircraft fly at higher altitudes and as space satellites, many of them equipped with cameras or other devices, become more common. It is a question full of difficulties and one which demands the full attention and consideration of the United Nations as well as of the individual nations themselves. The committee hopes that efforts will be pushed to pursue U.N. studies with a view to bringing about agreement.

Statement by Senators Frank J. Lausche and Alexander Wiley

These are the judgments that we have reached on the basis of the testimony presented to the committee:

1. The Congress of the United States has appropriated for a number of years the moneys that were needed for the development and operation of planes capable of reaching high altitudes and gathering information required as a guide for the evolvement in our country of defenses for national security. The Members of the Congress who have been responsible for reviewing the details of our intelligence-gathering activities knew of these flights and approved of them.

2. The U-2's have been operating successfully for a period of 4 years, and during that time have obtained information indispensable to the preparation of an adequate national defense. Without the information acquired by the U-2 operations, the present military posture of the United States would be less capable of meeting the Soviet military power.

3. When Premier Khrushchev left Moscow on Saturday, May 14, instead of Sunday, May 15, his previously declared date of departure, he had already decided not to participate in the conference. This decision was based on his conviction that the Allied Powers could not be divided at the

summit, and that because of allied unity he would not be able to accomplish his objectives at the conference. Thus, while the U-2 incident gave him an excuse for wrecking the conference, it was not the cause why he chose to do so. At the time of his departure from Moscow on May 14, he carried with him as a precondition to the Soviet's participation in the meeting, an ultimatum to be made upon the President of the United States which he knew the President could not accept.

4. The Soviet Union has the largest espionage organization of any nation in the world and possibly the largest in history. The activities of this organization which are carried on in this country and elsewhere were not suspended on May 1 or at any period preceding the summit meeting.

5. Those who launched the May 1 flight knew that these flights had a previous record for almost 4 years of unbroken success and they had no reason to assume that this flight would be any different from its predecessors. They were aware that there was almost always a diplomatic reason for not sending flights at a particular time and that if these reasons were made overriding, it would be difficult to find any time when such flights could be sent. They knew of the enormous value to the national security of these flights. These were the facts which had to be taken into account in deciding whether or not the flight should be launched.

Of course, if the failure of the May 1 flight could have been expected and foreseen, then the flight should not have been dispatched. This would hold true too for all the previous flights. But the fact is that when the May 1 flight started on its journey, every past experience justified the conclusion that it would not fail.

With the benefit of hindsight, no criticisms have been made against the flights which did not fail, but only against the May 1 flight. Bad luck not bad judgment was the true cause of the May 1 incident.

6. The May 1 flight having failed, representatives of the State Department, Defense Department, and NASA neglected to sufficiently coordinate the information which they gave to the public respecting the mission.

7. Conditions following the May 1 flight having developed as they did, it was unavoidable for the President to make a statement with regard to it. If he had to make a statement, *he had to state the truth*. Moreover, if he had not told the truth by avoiding personal responsibility, the four demands Khrushchev made upon him in Paris would not have been altered.

8. The gathering of intelligence has been practiced by nations from time immemorial and though it is an unsavory and hateful occupation, its omission would come fairly close to constituting criminal negligence in the responsibility of a nation to provide for its common defense.

Frank J. Lausche
Alexander Wiley

Statement by Senators Bourke B. Hickenlooper, George D. Aiken, Frank Carlson, and John J. Williams

We joined in approving the committee report, which is a result of composite committee views. We have read the views of Senator Frank J. Lausche, and Senator Alexander Wiley, above, and believe that overall they state concisely and succinctly reasonable and proper conclusions on the U-2 incident, and we express our general approval of their statement in connection with the entire report.

Bourke B. Hickenlooper
George D. Aiken
Frank Carlson
John J. Williams

Statement by Senator Homer E. Capehart

I voted against the report because I do not think it promotes the best interests of the United States and international relations.

Homer E. Capehart

Supplemental Individual Views of Senator Wiley

Unfortunately, I find the report—to a large degree—unsatisfactory.

Insofar as the document reflects the testimony of witnesses from the executive branch, I believe that it does "shed light" on the situation.

However, I find that the "interpretative" aspects of the report leave much to be desired.

In some instances the report gives the impression of trying to find evidence—by microscopic scrutiny of departmental activities—to blame somebody in the administration for the U-2 incident on May 1, and, consequently, the failure of the summit conference.

From the evidence, Khrushchev alone was responsible for the blow-up.

In addition, the program of overflying the Soviet Union, conducted in accordance with a basic law of national life—self-preservation—was deemed essential for our national security.

In 1947, Congress enacted a law setting up the National Security Council and the Central Intelligence Agency. Prior to that time, we had been a nation without a centralized effort—in peacetime—to coordinate intelligence in the interests of our security. The experiences of World War II, however, demonstrated that such an agency was necessary. Consequently, the Congress established the CIA to participate in acquiring, as well as coordinating from other agencies and departments, information relating to our national security.

The U-2 flight, under the direction of CIA, was a significant part of that Agency's attempt to gather information from behind the Iron Curtain to protect us from sneak attack by secret buildup for a military offensive within the Soviet Union.

Overall, the policy of such flights has been almost unanimously approved as serving the United States and the free-world interest.

Now, turning further to the Senate Foreign Relations report—the conclusions, in my humble judgment, are to a large degree falsely premised, illogical, and "politically loaded."

To help put the highlights of these events in better perspective. I would like to briefly review the following factors:

REFUTATION OF MAJORITY CONCLUSIONS

I disagree with certain basic conclusions and implications in the majority report.

First, I do not share the disappointment of the majority in not learning from the Executive the exact specific intelligence objective of the May 1 flight. This is not our business. I am puzzled by the extraordinary reasoning of the majority which at one point in the report declares that it is not possible, because this objective had not been revealed, for the committee "to come to any conclusion as to whether the information sought justified the risks that were taken (in sending the May 1 flight)." Yet in the closing passages of the report the majority, despite this stated inability to reach a conclusion on this vital point, proceeds nevertheless to conclude that the May 1 flight should not have been sent. This, despite their earlier complaint that they were not in a position to reach a conclusion on this point one way or the other.

The majority declares that "little, if any, consideration was given to the proximity of May 1 to the date of the summit conference." The record shows that approval for a flight during a specific period within which this date fell was given by the President, the Secretary of State, and the Secretary of Defense. The conclusion of the majority can rest only on the extraordinary assumption that these officials were unaware of the approaching summit.

I believe this to be an assumption that reasonable persons will not accept.

On the contrary, these officials were very much aware of the approaching conference. They were aware also of the importance of the flights and of the necessity of getting vital information during that particular period which would not be available later. They were aware, as the majority has stated, that these flights "had a record of almost 4 years of unbroken success"; that "against this background there would seem to be no reason to assume that the May 1 flight would be any different from any of its predecessors." They were aware that there is almost always at hand some diplomatic reason for not sending flights at a particular time and that if these reasons were made overriding it was difficult to ascertain when such flights could be sent. Further, they were aware that the Soviet knew of these flights and had not made an issue of them.

Under all these circumstances, the decision was made to proceed. It would seem apparent to the minority that this was a sound decision clearly made in the national interest of the United States.

The basic fact is that our difficulties arose not as a result of bad planning or judgment, but as a result, to use the majority's phrase, of "just plain bad luck." Frankly, I do not believe that we can survive in this world if we abandon all enterprise where just plain bad luck could mean failure.

The majority report makes the point that neither the President nor the Secretaries of State and Defense actually knew that this particular flight was in the air. I fail to see the significance of this. The majority alleges that this shows how routine these flights had become. The record shows that all three of these officials knew that such a flight was likely in this period and had given their considered consent to it. This is the matter of importance. I do not believe they had to know the exact details of the flight's progress. When there was trouble, they were immediately informed.

The majority states that the Executive should have expected, because "of the almost psychopathic addiction to secrecy which characterizes the Russian Government," the most violent reaction to be forthcoming when the U-2 penetration of their territory was made public. This statement overlooks the almost 4 years of perfect performance of this operation and the fact is that the majority has stated there was no reason to believe that this flight would be any different than its predecessors.

The majority states that with regard to the cover story the coordination within the Executive "broke down." This statement reflects on our judgment and lack of understanding of the purpose of the Executive in its employment of the cover story. The simple fact is that the cover story, which the records show had been thought out in advance, was maintained as long as, in the opinion of responsible officials, there was any possibility of protecting the security of this particular operation.

It is obvious that the cover story was maintained during a period when our officials did not know the extent of the Soviet's knowledge. Our officials knew that there was a possibility that the Soviets had complete knowledge of the circumstances surrounding the flight but as long as there was any possibility that this was not the case, they maintained the cover story. They did this, realizing that the cover story in the end might be totally repudiated, but, in my judgment, they had no choice but to persist in the cover story as long as there was any possibility of protecting the security of the operation.

Once it was apparent that this possibility had vanished, the cover story was properly abandoned. I continue to believe, however, that it was the proper exercise of judgment to maintain the cover as long as they did.

The majority stresses the fact that the President in ultimately assuming responsibility for the flight took a step unprecedented in intelligence operations. This flight was, itself, an unprecedented type of intelligence operation. Once it was compromised, it seems the President made the wise choice in assuming personal responsibility. I fail to see how, if he had not done so, the demands that Khrushchev made upon him in Paris would have been altered in any way. In addition, the United States would have been vulnerable to the allegation that the President was not in charge of the activities of the Executive and that our system was such that irresponsible subordinates could act on vital matters without the knowledge or approval of the President.

The majority concludes that the U-2 incident was the immediate "excuse" for not proceeding with the conference. While I concur that the U-2 incident provided the Soviets with an excuse, I do not believe the incident itself was the real reason why the conference did not go forward. The record of the hearings provides ample evidence that the Soviets had concluded some time in advance of the summit conference that they were not going to be able to accomplish the objectives which they sought there. What has been overlooked is the fact that the Soviets did not have to break up the conference because of the U-2 incident. Once the incident had taken place, the Soviet Government had a clear choice. On the one hand, it could have, during the days preceding the summit, simply used the incident as grist for their propaganda operations throughout the world. It could have done this at considerable advantage without at the same time carrying it to the point of actually jeopardizing the summit itself. In addition, it could have used it as an excuse after the summit had taken place to explain the failure of that meeting from their point of view.

On the other hand, the Soviets could choose to use this as an excuse to break up the conference before it began. The important point to remember is that the Soviet Government had these two clear alternative courses open to it. It was not inevitable that they chose the latter course. The U-2 incident gave them an excuse, but it does not provide the answer as to why they chose to use the excuse. The real answer is that they had concluded that the firmness and unity of the Western Powers would prevent them from accomplishing their objectives at the conference.

Hence, I reject the notion that the U-2 episode was a major factor in preventing a fruitful summit conference. In fact, I am convinced that the Soviets realized that, because of the unity of the three Western Powers, they could not gain any of their objectives and had decided in advance to wreck the conference either in its course or before it took place. Whether the conference was wrecked rudely or politely, at the beginning or at the end, is, in the long run, a matter of academic concern in our dealings with the Soviet Union.

Finally, I am disturbed by the criticism implicit in the majority report on the U-2 incident. I do not believe the U-2 operations on May 1, or previously, are something for which our Government should be criticized. Rather, I believe Americans have been heartened by this great demonstration of our country's capacity and that they take pride in the courage and vision of our Government and its leaders for this ingenious and highly successful operation which has immeasurably enhanced the security of our country.

BACKGROUND

For several years, the United States has carried on data-gathering, nonaggressive U-2 flights over Soviet territory. The purpose: to provide us with information necessary to protect ourselves—and the free world—from sneak attack resulting from the clandestine military buildups within the Soviet Union. These flights have been considered essential by our military and intelligence experts for our security.

On May 1, a U-2 plane on an intelligence mission was downed in Soviet territory.

Upon reports of the downing of the plane, the National Aeronautics and Space Administration—under standard procedure in such activities—provided a cover story.

After it became confirmed that the pilot, and possibly part of the plane and equipment, were in Communist hands, then President Eisenhower assumed responsibility for the U-2 flight.

In acknowledging responsibility, President Eisenhower established a new candidness—on a previously hush-hush topic—in international affairs.

Only history will portray the real significance of the decision. In supporting the President, however, I believe that the nations of the world cannot afford to play nuclear missile "hide-and-seek." The stakes are too high. The fate of nearly 3 billion people around the globe hangs in the balance.

As a world seeking to avoid a devastating nuclear missile war, we cannot afford to "fake" about—or "sweep under the rug"—the necessity of protecting nonaggressive nations against surprise attack—as long as war-oriented, domination-bent countries, like the Communist-dominated ones, exist on earth.

The so-called "rules of the game" for carrying on such information-gathering activities may also be obsolete. Traditionally, these required that a nation, if detected in information-gathering activities, deny them at high levels, or shunt responsibility to lower echelons.

Throughout history, however, almost all nations—in the spirit of self-preservation—have found it necessary to collect data essential to their security.

At the United Nations, Ambassador Lodge reviewed only a few of the many ways in which the Communists are engaged in sabotage, espionage, subversion, and other activities.

On May 16, the heads of the United States, France, England, and the Soviet Union—President Eisenhower, President de Gaulle, Prime Minister

Macmillan, and Premier Khrushchev, were scheduled to meet in Paris, France, for a so-called summit meeting.

Under the impression that the meeting would take place as scheduled, the heads of the Western Powers proceeded to the conference site. Unfortunately, Premier Khrushchev—for reasons unknown to the West—decided to torpedo the meeting.

Utilizing the U-2 flight as an excuse, the Soviet Premier, in an insulting manner, unfitting the leader of a powerful nation, made demands upon the United States that could not be met. As a result, Premier Khrushchev refused to attend a conference of the four powers.

In the light of the Khrushchev blowup at Paris, the question then arose: Did he know about the flights prior to the Paris conference? The answer is, "Yes." At a followup meeting in Berlin, he admitted such knowledge.

Why, then, did the Soviet Premier torpedo the meeting?

Although it is not possible to assess motivation—known, perhaps only to him—the following conclusions seem logical from the analysis of events:

In the face of the Western Powers' shoulder-to-shoulder stand against making one-sided concessions favoring the Communists in Berlin or anywhere else, the outlook for attaining Soviet goals was dim.

Behind the Iron Curtain, Mr. Khrushchev has his own troubles which include economic problems and unrest among the intellectuals, creating pressure and a need for a diversionary tactic.

Mao Tse-tung prodded Khrushchev for a tougher line against the West.

The Soviet Premier, too, may have been afraid of the favorable impact which President Eisenhower would have on the people of the Soviet Union if he visited them, as he had been invited to do. Consequently, Mr. Khrushchev "drummed up" an excuse to withdraw the invitation.

And, finally, after all his bragging about the rocket missile power of the Soviet armed services, Mr. K. found it difficult to "explain away" the freedom with which the United States has been overflying the country.

Was the U-2 flight program, with its inherent dangers—worth the risk? In my opinion, unquestionably yes. During the program, the United States was able to obtain information essential to our defense planning, on Soviet airfields, aircraft, missile testing and training, special weapons storage, submarine production, atomic production, and aircraft deployments.

The sequence of events prior to, and following, the unfortunate failure of the U-2 flight of May 1, and the torpedoing of the Paris conference by Soviet Premier Khrushchev, illustrates—

Not that the program of overflying the Soviet Union was the cause of the breakdown of the meeting;

But, rather, that the Soviet Premier came to Paris with the decision already made of breaking up the conference.

In the aftermath, it is important that the United States—and particularly, the Senate Foreign Relations Committee—not provide ammunition for the Soviet Premier to use against our country.

CONCLUSIONS

After a review of the facts of the flights and events surrounding the Paris affair, the following conclusions seem to follow:

(1) The U-2 flight program—a dramatically successful program for behind-the-lines acquisition of information—was a necessary effort in our national and free world defense.

(2) The U-2 program of overflying the Soviet Union was not the underlying cause of the blowup of the Paris conference by Khrushchev.

(3) While there are differences of opinion on the handling of the U-2 flight cover story, this in no way detracts from the significance of the program; nor did it, to any substantial degree, affect the outcome of the Paris conference.

(4) According to testimony before the committee, a decision—it is generally concluded—had been made to blow up the conference before Khrushchev went to Paris.

(5) The Soviet Premier is experiencing rising pressures at home, as well as greater competition from the Red Chinese, for ideological leadership of the Communist world.

Following the breakup of the Paris meeting, the Western Powers "closed ranks," demonstrating a greater degree of dignity, unity, and dedication to opposing communism.

The challenge now is to strengthen free world efforts to cope effectively with the seemingly "tougher" line emerging from Moscow; as well as with the voices emerging more strongly from Peiping, the citadel of communism in the Far East.

Alexander Wiley

IX

THE END OF THE GREAT CRUSADE

THE END OF THE GREAT CRUSADE

Introduction

The provisions of the 22nd Amendment precluded the possibility of Eisenhower running for a third term. This proved fortunate for the Democrats, for Eisenhower, despite his frequent illnesses and some occasional setbacks in foreign policy, remained a highly popular Chief Executive. Without his presence on the ticket, the GOP's outlook for 1960 was gloomy indeed. Actually, the Republican party had been in the doldrums since the 1958 election. Not only had it lost heavily in Congress, but it had sustained severe reverses at the state, county, and local levels—a turn of events that hardly bolstered the enthusiasm of the rank-and-file. Contributing to the general pessimism prevalent in Republican circles was the party's lack of any strong presidential candidate. Among the hopefuls was Nelson Rockefeller, the rich and powerful moderate who had bucked the Democratic trend in 1958 to become governor of New York. Although obviously a *potential* candidate, Rockefeller disclaimed as late as December of 1959 any interest in the Presidency. In addition to the New York governor there were several dark horses—Secretary of Labor James Mitchell; Secretary of State Christian Herter; Senator Barry Goldwater of Arizona; and former presidential advisor Harold Stassen. All had serious liabilities: Mitchell was relatively unknown nationally and had no real power base; Herter, John Foster Dulles' successor, displayed no strong political aspirations; Goldwater, outspokenly conservative, had little appeal to moderates, even within his own party; Stassen, a celebrated governor of Minnesota in the 1940's, had established himself as a perennial candidate, but one not to be taken too seriously. In the final analysis, then, there was really only one choice—Vice President Richard Nixon.

As the 1960 Convention drew near Nixon solidified his position by winning a series of primary victories in which he ran virtually unopposed. His strategy involved a low key approach in which he emphasized his experience and closeness to the Eisenhower Administration. This tactic worked well, and he had the necessary votes long before the Republicans gathered in Chicago on July 25.

Although the road to the GOP nomination had presented no serious difficulties, Nixon still had to maintain party unity and select a running mate acceptable to a broad segment of the party. The former was accomplished after a dramatic meeting (July 22–23) with Governor Rockefeller, a meeting that led to several changes in the Republican platform. Shortly thereafter, an all-night conference of party leaders resulted in Henry Cabot Lodge's selection as the vice presidential candidate. A few party conservatives criticized the "Treaty of Fifth Avenue" with Rockefeller, but the vice presidential choice seemed to appease them. Nixon, in his acceptance address (July 28), stressed that the nation faced great dangers despite "the best eight-year record in the history of this country." He went on to state that "we happen to believe that a record is not something to stand on but something to build on, and building on the great record of this Administration we shall build a better America." Although Eisenhower had previously declined to endorse any Republican candidate, he gave a rousing political speech in Chicago (July 26) and there seemed no doubt that he supported the ticket.

The Republicans left Chicago a unified party, and the Democrats, who had expected an easy victory following the 1958 recession and their nomination of the dashing young Senator John F. Kennedy, now found themselves in a fight. Eisenhower, who did not campaign actively until late in the contest, finally came to Nixon's aid in the final days, but still Kennedy managed a narrow victory. In the final analysis, it appeared that the Great Crusade had depended more on the personal popularity of Dwight Eisenhower than on any deep-seated support for the Republican party.

Eisenhower wanted a smooth transition. While Kennedy's election tended to take much of the pleasure out of the operation, the President nevertheless did his best to oversee an orderly change. Almost immediately he arranged guidelines for the "interregnum," scheduled an early conference with Kennedy (December 6), and continued without hesitation to carry out the constitutional responsibilities of his office. In fact, it was during his last month in the White House that Eisenhower terminated diplomatic relations with Cuba (January 3, 1961). His conversations with Kennedy, while polite and friendly, distressed him because he felt the President Elect did not comprehend certain fiscal considerations. As the Administration ended, feelings of achievement were clouded with apprehensions as he pondered his eight years in the White House.

The approach of January 20, 1961, brought Eisenhower numerous departmental reports. Most compilations praised the accomplishments of the originating agency over the previous eight years. Few raised questions about the quality of past decisions or about issues that remained for the future.

The President did not dwell on the final assessments; rather, he gave a Farewell Address (January 17) in which he raised anew his fears that the nation's defense requirements would engender an unhealthy coalition between the military and American industry. With his final duties completed, Eisenhower, like Harry Truman eight years before, rode down Pennsylvania Avenue with a successor not of his own choosing.

1. LAUNCHING THE FINAL YEAR

The President's 1960 State of the Union Message indicated that he believed that the previous 12 months had been rather successful. Despite the fact that he had only one more year in the White House, Eisenhower refused to concentrate on reviewing the Administration.

State of the Union Message by President Eisenhower
January 7, 1960

[*Public Papers of the Presidents: 1960–61* (Washington, 1961), 3–17.]

Mr. President, Mr. Speaker, Members of the 86th Congress:

Seven years ago I entered my present office with one long-held resolve overriding all others. I was then, and remain now, determined that the United States shall become an ever more potent resource for the cause of peace—realizing that peace cannot be for ourselves alone, but for peoples everywhere. This determination is shared by the entire Congress—indeed, by all Americans.

My purpose today is to discuss some features of America's position, both at home and in her relations to others.

First, I point out that for us, annual self-examination is made a definite necessity by the fact that we now live in a divided world of uneasy equilibrium, with our side committed to its own protection and against aggression by the other.

With both sides of this divided world in possession of unbelievably destructive weapons, mankind approaches a state where mutual annihilation becomes a possibility. No other fact of today's world equals this in importance—it colors everything we say, plan, and do.

There is demanded of us, vigilance, determination, and the dedication of whatever portion of our resources that will provide adequate security, especially a real deterrent to aggression. These things we are doing.

All these facts emphasize the importance of striving incessantly for a just peace.

Only through the strengthening of the spiritual, intellectual, economic and defensive resources of the Free World can we, in confidence, make progress toward this goal.

Second, we note that recent Soviet deportment and pronouncements suggest the possible opening of a somewhat less strained period in the relationships between the Soviet Union and the Free World. If these pronouncements be genuine, there is brighter hope of diminishing the intensity of past rivalry and eventually of substituting persuasion for coercion. Whether this is to become an era of lasting promise remains to be tested by actions.

Third, we now stand in the vestibule of a vast new technological age—one that, despite its capacity for human destruction, has an equal capacity to make poverty and human misery obsolete. If our efforts are wisely directed—and if our unremitting efforts for dependable peace begin to attain some success—we can surely become participants in creating an age characterized by justice and rising levels of human well-being.

Over the past year the Soviet Union has expressed an interest in measures to reduce the common peril of war.

While neither we nor any other Free World nation can permit ourselves to be misled by pleasant promises until they are tested by performance, yet we approach this apparently new opportunity with the utmost seriousness. We must strive to break the calamitous cycle of frustrations and crises which, if unchecked, could spiral into nuclear disaster; the ultimate insanity.

Though the need for dependable agreements to assure against resort to force in settling disputes is apparent to both sides yet as in other issues dividing men and nations, we cannot expect sudden and revolutionary results. But we must find some place to begin.

One obvious road on which to make a useful start is in the widening of communication between our two peoples. In this field there are, both sides willing, countless opportunities—most of them well known to us all—for developing mutual understanding, the true foundation of peace.

Another avenue may be through the reopening, on January twelfth, of negotiations looking to a controlled ban on the testing of nuclear weapons. Unfortunately, the closing statement from the Soviet scientists who met with our scientists at Geneva in an unsuccessful effort to develop an agreed basis for a test ban, gives the clear impression that their conclusions have been politically guided. Those of the British and American scientific representatives are their own freely-formed, individual and collective opinion. I am hopeful that as new negotiations begin, truth—not political opportunism—will be the guiding light of the deliberations.

Still another avenue may be found in the field of disarmament, in which the Soviets have professed a readiness to negotiate seriously. They have not, however, made clear the plans they may have, if any, for mutual inspection and verification—the essential condition for any extensive measure of disarmament.

There is one instance where our initiative for peace has recently been successful. A multi-lateral treaty signed last month provides for the exclusively peaceful use of Antarctica, assured by a system of inspection. It provides for free and cooperative scientific research in that continent, and prohibits nuclear explosions there pending general international agreement on the subject. The Treaty is a significant contribution toward peace, international cooperation, and the advancement of science. I shall transmit its text to the Senate for consideration and approval in the near future.

The United States is always ready to participate with the Soviet Union in serious discussion of these or any other subjects that may lead to peace with justice.

Certainly it is not necessary to repeat that the United States has no intention of interfering in the internal affairs of any nation; likewise we reject any attempt to impose its system on us or on other peoples by force or subversion.

This concern for the freedom of other peoples is the intellectual and spiritual cement which has allied us with more than forty other nations in a common defense effort. Not for a moment do we forget that our own fate is firmly fastened to that of these countries; we will not act in any way which would jeopardize our solemn commitments to them.

We and our friends are, of course, concerned with self-defense. Growing out of this concern is the realization that all people of the Free World have a great stake in the progress, in freedom, of the uncommitted and newly emerging nations. These peoples, desperately hoping to lift themselves to decent levels of living must not, by our neglect, be forced to seek help from, and finally become virtual satellites of, those who proclaim their hostility to freedom.

Their natural desire for a better life must not be frustrated by withholding from them necessary technical and investment assistance. This is a problem to be solved not by America alone, but also by every nation cherishing the same ideals and in position to provide help.

In recent years America's partners and friends in Western Europe and Japan have made great economic progress. Their newly found economic strength is eloquent testimony to the striking success of the policies of economic cooperation which we and they have pursued.

The international economy of 1960 is markedly different from that of the early postwar years. No longer is the United States the only major industrial country capable of providing substantial amounts of the resources so urgently needed in the newly-developing countries.

To remain secure and prosperous themselves, wealthy nations must extend the kind of cooperation to the less fortunate members that will inspire hope, confidence and progress. A rich nation can for a time, without noticeable damage to itself, pursue a course of self-indulgence, making its single goal the material ease and comfort of its own citizens—thus repudiating its own spiritual and material stake in a peaceful and prosperous society of nations. But the enmities it will incur, the isolation into which it will descend, and the internal moral and physical softness that will be engendered, will, in the long term, bring it to disaster.

America did not become great through softness and self-indulgence. Her miraculous progress and achievements flow from other qualities far more worthy and substantial—

—adherence to principles and methods consonant with our religious philosophy

—a satisfaction in hard work

—the readiness to sacrifice for worthwhile causes

—the courage to meet every challenge to her progress

—the intellectual honesty and capacity to recognize the true path of her own best interests.

To us and to every nation of the Free World, rich or poor, these qualities are necessary today as never before if we are to march together to greater security, prosperity and peace.

I believe the industrial countries are ready to participate actively in supplementing the efforts of the developing countries to achieve progress.

The immediate need for this kind of cooperation is underscored by the strain in our international balance of payments. Our surplus from foreign business transactions has in recent years fallen substantially short of the expenditures we make abroad to maintain our military establishments overseas, to finance private investment, and to provide assistance to the less developed nations. In 1959 our deficit in balance of payments approached $4 billion.

Continuing deficits of anything like this magnitude would, over time, impair our own economic growth and check the forward progress of the Free World.

We must meet this situation by promoting a rising volume of exports and world trade. Further, we must induce all industrialized nations of the Free World to work together in a new cooperative endeavor to help lift the scourge of poverty from less fortunate nations. This will provide for better sharing of this burden and for still further profitable trade.

New nations, and others struggling with the problems of development, will progress only if they demonstrate faith in their own destiny and possess the will and use their own resources to fulfill it. Moreover, progress in a national transformation can be only gradually earned; there is no easy and quick way to follow from the oxcart to the jet plane. But, just as we drew on Europe for assistance in our earlier years, so now do those new and emerging nations that have this faith and determination deserve help.

Over the last fifteen years, twenty nations have gained political independence. Others are doing so each year. Most of them are woefully lacking in technical capacity and in investment capital; without Free World support in these matters they cannot effectively progress in freedom.

Respecting their need, one of the major focal points of our concern is the

South Asian region. Here, in two nations alone, are almost five hundred million people, all working, and working hard, to raise their standards, and in doing so, to make of themselves a strong bulwark against the spread of an ideology that would destroy liberty.

I cannot express to you the depth of my conviction that, in our own and Free World interests, we must cooperate with others to help these people achieve their legitimate ambitions, as expressed in their different multi-year plans. Through the World Bank and other instrumentalities, as well as through individual action by every nation in position to help, we must squarely face this titanic challenge.

All of us must realize, of course, that development in freedom by the newly emerging nations, is no mere matter of obtaining outside financial assistance. An indispensable element in this process is a strong and continuing determination on the part of these nations to exercise the national discipline necessary for any sustained development period. These qualities of determination are particularly essential because of the fact that the process of improvement will necessarily be gradual and laborious rather than revolutionary. Moreover, everyone should be aware that the development process is no short term phenomenon. Many years are required for even the most favorably situated countries.

I shall continue to urge the American people, in the interests of their own security, prosperity and peace, to make sure that their own part of this great project be amply and cheerfully supported. Free World decisions in this matter may spell the difference between world disaster and world progress in freedom.

Other countries, some of which I visited last month, have similar needs.

A common meeting ground is desirable for those nations which are prepared to assist in the development effort. During the past year I have discussed this matter with the leaders of several Western Nations.

Because of its wealth of experience, the Organization for European Economic Cooperation could help with initial studies. The goal is to enlist all available economic resources in the industrialized Free World—especially private investment capital. But I repeat that this help, no matter how great, can be lastingly effective only if it is used as a supplement to the strength of spirit and will of the people of the newly-developing nations.

By extending this help we hope to make possible the enthusiastic enrollment of these nations under freedom's banner. No more startling contrast to a system of sullen satellites could be imagined.

If we grasp this opportunity to build an age of productive partnership between the less fortunate nations and those that have already achieved a high state of economic advancement, we will make brighter the outlook for a world order based upon security, freedom and peace. Otherwise, the outlook could be dark indeed. We face what may be a turning point in history, and we must act decisively.

As a nation we can successfully pursue these objectives only from a position of broadly based strength.

No matter how earnest is our quest for guaranteed peace, we must maintain a high degree of military effectiveness at the same time we are engaged in negotiating the issue of arms reduction. Until tangible and mutually enforceable arms reduction measures are worked out, we will not weaken the means of defending our institutions.

America possesses an enormous defense power. It is my studied conviction that no nation will ever risk general war against us unless we should be so foolish as to neglect the defense forces we now so powerfully support. It is world-wide knowledge that any nation which might be tempted today to attack the United States, even though our country might sustain great losses, would itself promptly suffer a terrible destruction. But I once again assure all peoples and all nations that the United States, except in defense, will never turn loose this destructive power.

During the past year, our long-range striking power, unmatched today in manned bombers, has taken on new strength as the Atlas intercontinental ballistic missile has entered the operational inventory. In fourteen recent test launchings, at ranges of over 5,000 miles, Atlas has been striking on an average within two miles of the target. This is less than the length of a jet runway—well within the circle of total destruction. Such performance is a great tribute to American scientists and engineers, who in the past five years have had to telescope time and technology to develop these long-range ballistic missiles, where America had none before.

This year, moreover, growing numbers of nuclear-powered submarines will enter our active forces, some to be armed with Polaris missiles. These remarkable ships and weapons, ranging the oceans, will be capable of accurate fire on targets virtually anywhere on earth. Impossible to destroy by surprise attack, they will become one of our most effective sentinels for peace.

To meet situations of less than general nuclear war, we continue to maintain our carrier forces, our many service units abroad, our always ready Army strategic forces and Marine Corps divisions, and the civilian components. The continuing modernization of these forces is a costly but necessary process, and is scheduled to go forward at a rate which will steadily add to our strength.

The deployment of a portion of these forces beyond our shores, on land and sea, is persuasive demonstration of our determination to stand shoulder-to-shoulder with our allies for collective security. Moreover, I have directed that steps be taken to program our military assistance to these allies on a longer range basis. This is necessary for a sounder collective defense system.

Next I refer to our effort in space exploration, which is often mistakenly supposed to be an integral part of defense research and development.

First, America has made great contributions in the past two years to the world's fund of knowledge of astrophysics and space science. These discoveries are of present interest chiefly to the scientific community; but they are important foundation-stones for more extensive exploration of outer space for the ultimate benefit of all mankind.

Second, our military missile program, going forward so successfully, does *not* suffer from our present lack of very large rocket engines, which are so necessary in distant space exploration. I am assured by experts that the thrust of our present missiles is fully adequate for defense requirements.

Third, the United States is pressing forward in the development of large rocket engines to place much heavier vehicles into space for exploration purposes.

Fourth, in the meantime, it is necessary to remember that we have only begun to probe the environment immediately surrounding the earth. Using launch systems presently available, we are developing satellites to scout the world's weather; satellite relay stations to facilitate and extend communications over the globe; for navigation aids to give accurate bearings to ships and aircraft; and for perfecting instruments to collect and transmit the data we seek. This is the area holding the most promise for early and useful applications of space technology.

Fifth, we have just completed a year's experience with our new space law. I believe it deficient in certain particulars and suggested improvements will be submitted shortly.

The accomplishment of the many tasks I have alluded to requires the continuous strengthening of the spiritual, intellectual, and economic sinews of American life. The steady purpose of our society is to assure justice, before God, for every individual. We must be ever alert that freedom does not wither through the careless amassing of restrictive controls or lack of courage to deal boldly with the giant issues of the day.

A year ago, when I met with you, the nation was emerging from an economic downturn, even though the signs of resurgent prosperity were not then sufficiently convincing to the doubtful. Today our surging strength is apparent to everyone. 1960 promises to be the most prosperous year in our history.

Yet we continue to be afflicted by nagging disorders.

Among current problems that require solution are:

—the need to protect the public interest in situations of prolonged labor-management stalemate;

—the persistent refusal to come to grips with a critical problem in one sector of American agriculture;

—the continuing threat of inflation together with the persisting tendency toward fiscal irresponsibility;

—in certain instances the denial to some of our citizens of equal protection of the law.

Every American was disturbed by the prolonged dispute in the steel industry and the protracted delay in reaching a settlement.

We are all relieved that a settlement has at last been achieved in that industry. Percentagewise, by this settlement the increase to the steel companies in employment costs is lower than in any prior wage settlement since World War II. It is also gratifying to note that despite the increase in wages and benefits several of the major steel producers have announced that there will be no increase in steel prices at this time. The national interest demands that in the period of industrial peace which has been assured by the new contract both management and labor make every possible effort to increase efficiency and productivity in the manufacture of steel so that price increases can be avoided.

One of the lessons of this story is that the potential danger to the entire Nation of longer and greater strikes must be met. To insure against such possibilities we must of course depend primarily upon the good commonsense of the responsible individuals. It is my intention to encourage regular discussions between management and labor outside the bargaining table, to consider the interest of the public as well as their mutual interest in the maintenance of industrial peace, price stability and economic growth.

To me, it seems almost absurd for the United States to recognize the need, and so earnestly to seek, for cooperation among the nations unless we can achieve voluntary, dependable, abiding cooperation among the important segments of our own free society.

Failure to face up to basic issues in areas other than those of labor-management can cause serious strains on the firm freedom supports of our society.

I refer to agriculture as one of these areas.

Our basic farm laws were written 27 years ago, in an emergency effort to redress hardship caused by a world-wide depression. They were continued—and their economic distortions intensified—during World War II in order to provide incentives for production of food needed to sustain a war-torn free world.

Today our farm problem is totally different. It is that of effectively adjusting to the changes caused by a scientific revolution. When the original farm laws were written, an hour's farm labor produced only one-fourth as much wheat as at present. Farm legislation is woefully out-of-date, ineffective, and expensive.

For years we have gone on with an outmoded system which not only has failed to protect farm income, but also has produced soaring, threatening surpluses. Our farms have been left producing for war while America has long been at peace.

Once again I urge Congress to enact legislation that will gear production more closely to markets, make costly surpluses more manageable, provide greater freedom in farm operations, and steadily achieve increased net farm incomes.

Another issue that we must meet squarely is that of living within our means. This requires restraint in expenditure, constant reassessment of priorities, and the maintenance of stable prices.

We must prevent inflation. Here is an opponent of so many guises that it is sometimes difficult to recognize. But our clear need is to stop continuous and general price rises—a need that all of us can see and feel.

To prevent steadily rising costs and prices calls for stern self-discipline by every citizen. No person, city, state, or organized group can afford to evade the obligation to resist inflation, for every American pays its crippling tax.

Inflation's ravages do not end at the water's edge. Increases in prices of the goods we sell abroad threaten to drive us out of markets that once were securely ours. Whether domestic prices, so high as to be noncompetitive, result from demands for too-high profit margins or from increased labor costs that outrun growth in productivity, the final result is seriously damaging to the nation.

We must fight inflation as we would a fire that imperils our home. Only by so doing can we prevent it from destroying our salaries, savings, pensions and insurance, and from gnawing away the very roots of a free, healthy economy and the nation's security.

One major method by which the Federal government can counter inflation and rising prices is to insure that its expenditures are below its revenues. The debt with which we are now confronted is about 290 billion dollars. With interest charges alone now costing taxpayers about 9½ billions, it is clear that this debt growth must stop. You will be glad to know that despite the unsettling influences of the recent steel strike, we estimate that our accounts will show, on June 30 this year, a favorable balance of approximately $200 million.

I shall present to the Congress for 1961 a *balanced* budget. In the area of defense, expenditures continue at the record peace-time levels of the last several years. With a single exception, expenditures in every major category of Health, Education and Welfare will be equal or greater than last year. In Space expenditures the amounts are practically doubled. But the over-all guiding goal of this budget is national *need*—not response to specific group, local or political insistence.

Expenditure increases, other than those I have indicated, are largely accounted for by the increased cost of legislation previously enacted.

I repeat, this budget will be a balanced one. Expenditures will be 79 billion 8 hundred million. The amount of income over outgo, described in the budget as a Surplus, to be applied against our national debt, is 4 billion 2 hundred million. Personally, I do not feel that any amount can be properly called a "Surplus" as long as the nation is in debt. I prefer to think of such an item as "reduction on our children's inherited mortgage." Once we have established such payments as normal practice, we can profitably make improvements in our tax structure and thereby truly reduce the heavy burdens of taxation.

In any event, this one reduction will save taxpayers, each year, approximately 2 hundred million dollars in interest costs.

This budget will help ease pressures in our credit and capital markets. It will enhance the confidence of people all over the world in the strength of our economy and our currency and in our individual and collective ability to be fiscally responsible.

In the management of the huge public debt the Treasury is unfortunately not free of artificial barriers. Its ability to deal with the difficult problems in this field has been weakened greatly by the unwillingness of the Congress to remove archaic restrictions. The need for a freer hand in debt management is even more urgent today because the costs of the undesirable financing practices which the Treasury has been forced into are mounting. Removal of this roadblock has high priority in my legislative recommendations.

Still another issue relates to civil rights.

In all our hopes and plans for a better world we all recognize that provincial and racial prejudices must be combatted. In the long perspective of history, the right to vote has been one of the strongest pillars of a free society. Our first duty is to protect this right against all encroachment. In spite of constitutional guarantees and notwithstanding much progress of recent years, bias still deprives some persons in this country of equal protection of the laws.

Early in your last session I recommended legislation which would help eliminate several practices discriminating against the basic rights of Americans. The Civil Rights Commission has developed additional constructive recommendations. I hope that these will be among the matters to be seriously considered in the current session. I trust that Congress will thus signal to the world that our Government is striving for equality under law for all our people.

Each year and in many ways our nation continues to undergo profound change and growth.

In the past 18 months we have hailed the entry of two more States of the Union—Alaska and Hawaii. We salute these two western stars proudly.

Our vigorous expansion, which we all welcome as a sign of health and vitality, is many-sided. We are, for example, witnessing explosive growth in metropolitan areas.

By 1975 the metropolitan areas of the United States will occupy twice the territory they do today. The roster of urban problems with which they must cope is staggering. They involve water supply, cleaning the air, adjusting local tax systems, providing for essential educational, cultural, and social services, and destroying those conditions which breed delinquency and crime.

In meeting these, we must, if we value our historic freedoms, keep within the traditional framework of our Federal system with powers divided between the national and state governments. The uniqueness of this system may confound the casual observer, but it has worked effectively for nearly 200 years.

I do not doubt that our urban and other perplexing problems can be solved in the traditional American method. In doing so we must realize that nothing is really solved and ruinous tendencies are set in motion by yielding to the deceptive bait of the "easy" Federal tax dollar.

Our educational system provides a ready example. All recognize the vital necessity of having modern school plants, well-qualified and adequately compensated teachers and of using the best possible teaching techniques and curricula.

We cannot be complacent about educating our youth.

But the route to better trained minds is not through the swift administration of a Federal hypodermic or sustained financial transfusion. The educational process, essentially a local and personal responsibility, cannot be made to leap ahead by crash, centralized governmental action.

The Administration has proposed a carefully reasoned program for helping eliminate current deficiencies. It is designed to stimulate classroom construction, not by substitution of Federal dollars for state and local funds, but by incentives to extend and encourage state and local efforts. This approach rejects the notion of Federal domination or control. It is workable, and should appeal to every American interested in advancement of our educational system in the traditional American way. I urge the Congress to take action upon it.

There is one other subject concerning which I renew a recommendation I made in my State of the Union Message last January. I then advised the Congress of my purpose to intensify our efforts to replace force with a rule of law among nations. From many discussions abroad, I am convinced that purpose is widely and deeply shared by other peoples and nations of the world.

In the same Message I stated that our efforts would include a re-examination of our own relation to the International Court of Justice. The Court was established by the United Nations to decide international legal disputes between nations. In 1946 we accepted the Court's jurisdiction, but subject to a reservation of the right to determine unilaterally whether a matter lies essentially within domestic jurisdiction. There is pending before the Senate, a Resolution which would repeal our present self-judging reservation. I support that Resolution and urge its prompt passage. If this is done, I intend to urge similar acceptance of the Court's jurisdiction by every member of the United Nations.

Here perhaps it is not amiss for me to say to the Members of the Congress, in this my final year of office, a word about the institutions we respectively represent and the meaning which the relationships between our two branches has for the days ahead.

I am not unique as a President in having worked with a Congress controlled by the opposition party—except that no other President ever did it for quite so long! Yet in both personal and official relationships we have weathered the storms of the past five years. For this I am grateful.

My deep concern in the next twelve months, before my successor takes office, is with our joint Congressional-Executive duty to our own and to other nations. Acting upon the beliefs I have expressed here today, I shall devote my full energies to the tasks at hand, whether these involve travel for promoting greater world understanding, negotiations to reduce international discord, or constant discussions and communications with the Congress and the American people on issues both domestic and foreign.

In pursuit of these objectives, I look forward to, and shall dedicate myself to, a close and constructive association with the Congress.

Every minute spent in irrelevant interbranch wrangling is precious time taken from the intelligent initiation and adoption of coherent policies for our national survival and progress.

We seek a common goal—brighter opportunity for our own citizens and a world peace with justice for all.

Before us and our friends is the challenge of an ideology which, for more than four decades, has trumpeted abroad its purpose of gaining ultimate victory over all forms of government at variance with its own.

We realize that however much we repudiate the tenets of imperialistic Communism, it represents a gigantic enterprise grimly pursued by leaders who compel its subjects to subordinate their freedom of action and spirit and personal desires for some hoped-for advantage in the future.

The Communists can present an array of material accomplishments over the past fifteen years that lends a false persuasiveness to many of their glittering promises to the uncommitted peoples.

The competition they provide is formidable.

But in *our* scale of values we place freedom first—our whole national existence and development have been geared to that basic concept and are responsible for the position of free world leadership to which we have succeeded. It is the highest prize that any nation can possess; it is one that Communism can never offer. And America's record of material accomplishment in freedom is written not only in the unparalleled prosperity of our own nation, but in the many billions we have devoted to the reconstruction of Free World economies wrecked by World War II and in the effective help of many more billions we have given in saving the independence of many others threatened by outside domination. Assuredly we have the capacity for handling the problems in the new era of the world's history we are now entering.

But we must use that capacity intelligently and tirelessly, regardless of personal sacrifice.

The fissure that divides our political planet is deep and wide.

We live, moreover, in a sea of semantic disorder in which old labels no longer faithfully describe.

Police states are called "people's democracies."

Armed conquest of free people is called "liberation."

Such slippery slogans make more difficult the problem of communicating true faith, facts and beliefs.

We must make clear our peaceful intentions, our aspirations for a better world. So doing, we must use language to enlighten the mind, not as the instrument of the studied innuendo and distorter of truth.

And we must live by what we say.

On my recent visit to distant lands I found one statesman after another eager to tell me of the elements of their government that had been borrowed from our American Constitution, and from the indestructible ideals set forth in our Declaration of Independence.

As a nation we take pride that our constitutional system, and the ideals which sustain it, have been long viewed as a fountainhead of freedom.

By our every action we must strive to make ourselves worthy of this trust, ever mindful that an accumulation of seemingly minor encroachments upon freedom gradually could break down the entire fabric of a free society.

So persuaded, we shall get on with the task before us.

So dedicated, and with faith in the Almighty, humanity shall one day achieve the unity in freedom to which all men have aspired from the dawn of time.

The proposed budget for fiscal 1961 recommended that a sizable surplus accrue during the Administration's final months. The Budget Message, considerably shorter than many previous, failed to spell out specific proposals for either defense or domestic spending.

Annual Presidential Budget Message
January 18, 1960

[*Public Papers of the Presidents: 1960–61* (Washington, 1961), 37–45.]

To the Congress of the United States:

With this message, transmitting the Budget of the United States for the fiscal year 1961, I invite the Congress to join with me in a determined effort to achieve a substantial surplus. This will make possible a reduction in the national debt. The proposals in this budget demonstrate that this objective can be attained while at the same time maintaining required military strength and enhancing the national welfare.

This budget attests to the strength of America's economy. At the same time, the budget is a test of our resolve, as a nation, to allocate our resources prudently, to maintain the Nation's security, and to extend economic growth into the future without inflation.

In highlight, this budget proposes:

1. Revenues of $84 billion and expenditures of $79.8 billion, leaving a surplus of $4.2 billion. This surplus should be applied to debt reduction, which I believe to be a prime element in sound fiscal policy for the Nation at this time.

2. New appropriations for the military functions of the Department of Defense amounting to $40.6 billion, and expenditures of $41 billion. These expenditures, which will be slightly higher than the 1960 level, will provide the strong and versatile defense which we require under prevailing world conditions.

3. Increased appropriations (including substantial restoration of congressional reductions in the 1960 budget), and a virtual doubling of expenditures, for nonmilitary space projects under the National Aeronautics and Space Administration. This furthers our plans to keep moving ahead vigorously and systematically with our intensive program of scientific exploration and with the development of the large boosters essential to the conquest of outer space.

4. Nearly $4.2 billion in new appropriations for mutual security programs, an increase of about $950 million above appropriations for the current year, with an increase of $100 million in expenditures. This increase in program is needed to accelerate economic and technical assistance, chiefly through the Development Loan Fund, and to strengthen free world forces, in particular the forces of the North Atlantic Treaty Organization, with advanced weapons and equipment.

5. A record total of expenditures, $1.2 billion, for water resources projects under the Corps of Engineers and the Bureau of Reclamation. In addition to funds for going work, this amount provides for the initiation of 42 new high priority projects, which will require $38 million in new appropriations for 1961, and will cost a total of $496 million over a period of years.

6. Substantially higher expenditures in a number of categories which under present laws are relatively uncontrollable, particularly $9.6 billion for interest; $3.9 billion to help support farm prices and income; $3.8 billion for veterans compensation and pensions; and $2.4 billion in aid to State and local governments for public assistance and employment security activities. The aggregate increase in these relatively uncontrollable expenditures is more than $1 billion over 1960.

7. Research and development expenditures of $8.4 billion—well over one-half of the entire Nation's expenditures, public and private, for these purposes—in order to assure a continuing strong and modern defense and to stimulate basic research and technological progress.

8. Recommendations for prompt legislative action to increase taxes on highway and aviation fuels, and to raise postal rates. These measures are needed to place on the users a proper share of the rising costs of the Federal airways and postal service, and to support the highway program at an increased level.

9. Recommendations to extend for another year present corporation income and excise tax rates.

10. A constructive legislative program to achieve improvements in existing laws relating to governmental activities and to initiate needed actions to improve and safeguard the interests of our people.

In short, this budget and the proposals it makes for legislative action provide for significant advances in many aspects of national security and welfare. The budget presents a balanced program which recognizes the priorities appropriate within an aggregate of Federal expenditures that we can soundly support.

I believe that the American people have made their wishes clear: The Federal Government should conduct its financial affairs with a high sense of responsibility, vigorously meeting the Nation's needs and opportunities within its proper sphere while at the same time exercising a prudent discipline in matters of borrowing and spending, and in incurring liabilities for the future.

Budget Totals

During the present fiscal year we have made encouraging progress in achieving sound fiscal policy objectives. The deficit of $12.4 billion in fiscal 1959, which was largely caused by the recession, is expected to be followed by a surplus of $217 million in the current year. To safeguard this small surplus, I am directing all Government departments and agencies to exercise strict controls over the expenditure of Federal funds. Even so, the slender margin of surplus can be attained only if economic growth is not interrupted.

For the fiscal year 1961, I am proposing a budget surplus of $4.2 billion to be applied to debt retirement. In my judgment this is the only sound course. Unless some amounts are applied to the reduction of debt in prosperous periods, we can expect an ever larger public debt if future emergencies or recessions again produce deficits.

In times of prosperity, such as we anticipate in the coming year, sound fiscal and economic policy requires a budget surplus to help counteract inflationary pressures, to ease conditions in capital and credit markets, and to increase the supply of savings available for the productive investment so essential to continued economic growth.

The budget recommendations for 1961 lay the groundwork for a sound and flexible fiscal policy in the years ahead. A continuance of economic prosperity in 1962 and later years can be expected to bring with it further increases in Federal revenues. If expenditures are held to the levels I am proposing for 1961 and reasonable restraint is exercised in the future, higher revenues in later years will give the next administration and the next Congress the choice they should rightly have in deciding between reductions in the public debt and lightening of the tax burden, or both. Soundly conceived tax revision can then be approached on a comprehensive and orderly basis, rather than by haphazard piecemeal changes, and can be accomplished within a setting of economic and fiscal stability.

Budget expenditures in 1961 are estimated at $79.8 billion, which is $1.4 billion more than the 1960 level. The total increase is attributable to (1) an increase of more than $1 billion in relatively uncontrollable expenditures for farm price supports fixed by law, interest on the public debt, veterans compensation and pensions, and public assistance grants, and (2) an increase of about $500 million in expenditures because of commitments made in prior years for Federal housing programs, for civil public works projects and other construction, for loans under the mutual security program, and for other programs.

New activities and expansion of certain other programs have been included on a selective basis of need. These increases are offset by reductions in other existing programs, including the proposed elimination of the postal deficit.

New obligational authority recommended for the fiscal year 1961 totals $79.4 billion. This is $306 million less than the amounts already enacted and recommended for 1960, and $401 million less than estimated expenditures in 1961.

Budget receipts under existing and proposed legislation are expected to rise substantially to $84 billion in 1961. This compares with the revised estimate of $78.6 billion for 1960 and actual receipts of $68.3 billion in 1959.

Management of the Public Debt

Achievement of the proposed budget surplus will provide an opportunity to offset part of the deficits incurred in the fiscal years 1958 and 1959 largely because of the recession. The corresponding reduction of the public debt will reduce Government competition with private industry, individuals, and State and local governments for investment funds and will help ease the pressure on interest rates. Along with the recommended removal of the interest rate ceiling on long-term Federal debt, this will help hold down budget expenditures for interest, which now amount to almost one-eighth of the whole budget.

Statutory debt limit.— It is estimated that the public debt, which stood at $284.7 billion on June 30, 1959, will be $284.5 billion on June 30, 1960, and will decline to $280 billion at the end of fiscal 1961. Thus, the budget surplus estimated for fiscal 1961 will permit the Government to end the year with desirable operating leeway within the permanent debt limit of $285 billion. However, the fluctuating seasonal pattern in receipts will again require a temporary increase in the debt limit during the fiscal year 1961, since the present temporary limit of $295 billion expires on June 30, 1960. It is expected that the request for a new temporary limit will be for less than the present $295 billion if the Congress accepts my budgetary proposals.

Interest ceiling.—Effective management of a debt of this size requires a reasonable distribution among securities maturing at different times. Three-fourths of all marketable Treasury securities outstanding today come due in less than five years, of which $80 billion will mature in less than a year. As long as the rate that would have to be paid on newly issued bonds exceeds the present statutory ceiling of $4\frac{1}{4}\%$, it is impossible to issue and sell any marketable securities of over five years' maturity.

Exclusive reliance on borrowing in a limited sector of the market is an expensive and inefficient way to manage the debt. Inflationary pressures increase as the volume of short-term and hence highly liquid securities mounts, especially if these securities are acquired by commercial banks. Further, effective monetary policy becomes more difficult when the Treasury has to refinance often. To make possible prudent and flexible management of the public debt, to permit sale of a modest amount of intermediate and longer term bonds when market conditions warrant such action, and to keep the average maturity of the debt from constantly shortening, it is imperative that the Congress immediately act to remove the 42-year-old $4\frac{1}{4}\%$ limitation on interest rates on Government securities maturing after five years.

Budget Receipts

Estimated budget receipts of $84 billion in the fiscal year 1961 assume a high and rising level of economic activity in calendar year 1960. Specifically, this revenue estimate is consistent with an increase in the gross national product from about $480 billion for calendar 1959 to about $510 billion for calendar 1960. Personal incomes and corporate profits are expected to rise considerably beyond last year's levels, which were depressed somewhat by the long duration of the steel strike. The accompanying table shows the sources of Government receipts for the fiscal years 1959, 1960, and 1961.

BUDGET RECEIPTS

[Fiscal years. In billions]

Source	1959 actual	1960 estimate	1961 estimate
Individual income taxes	$36.7	$40.3	$43.7
Corporation income taxes	17.3	22.2	23.5
Excise taxes	8.5	9.1	9.5
All other receipts	5.8	7.0	7.3
Total	68.3	78.6	84.0

The estimates for 1961 assume (1) extension of present tax rates and (2) the adoption of modifications recommended last year for certain tax laws. These are summarized in the following paragraphs.

Extension of present tax rates.—In order to maintain Federal revenues, it is necessary that the present tax rates on corporation profits and certain excises be extended for another year beyond their scheduled expiration date of June 30, 1960. The scheduled reductions in the excise tax rates on transportation of persons and the scheduled repeal of the tax on local telephone service, which were enacted in the last session of the Congress, should be similarly postponed.

Improvement of the tax system.—The recent tax revision hearings of the Ways and Means Committee have provided valuable information bearing on changes in the tax laws. The Treasury will continue to work in cooperation with the committees of the Congress in developing sound and attainable proposals for long-range improvement of the tax laws.

As the development of a comprehensive tax revision program will take time, the Congress should consider this year certain changes in the tax laws to correct inequities. These include amendments of the laws on taxation of cooperatives, now before the Congress, and a number of technical changes on which the Treasury Department has been working with committees of Congress. There is also before the Congress an amendment to prevent unintended and excessive depletion deductions resulting from the computation of percentage depletion allowances on the selling price of finished clay, cement products, and mineral products generally; unless the problem is satisfactorily resolved in a case now pending before the Supreme Court, the need for corrective legislation in this area will continue.

Under existing law, administration of the depreciation provisions is being hampered by the attempts of some taxpayers to claim excessive depreciation before disposing of their property. If gain from the sale of depreciable personal property were treated as ordinary income, the advantage gained in claiming excessive depreciation deductions would be materially reduced and the taxpayer's judgment as to the useful life of his property could more readily be accepted. Accordingly, I recommend that consideration be given to a change in the law which would treat such gain as ordinary income to the extent of the depreciation deduction previously taken on the property.

Aviation fuel taxes.—To help defray the cost of the Federal airways system, the effective excise tax rate on aviation gasoline should be promptly increased from 2 to 4½ cents per gallon and an equivalent excise tax should be imposed on jet fuels, which now are untaxed. The conversion from piston engines to jets is resulting in serious revenue losses to the Government. These losses will increase unless the tax on jet fuels is promptly enacted. The revenues from all taxes on aviation fuels should be credited to general budget receipts, as a partial offset to the budgetary costs of the airways system, and clearly should not be deposited in the highway trust fund.

Changes in fees and charges.—The cost of other Federal programs which provide measurable special benefits to identifiable groups or individuals should be recovered through charges paid by beneficiaries rather than by taxes on the general public. Whenever feasible, fees or charges should be established so that the beneficiaries will pay the full cost of the special services they receive. To help accomplish this purpose, I have directed that further work be done by the departments and agencies on a carefully defined inventory of Federal services which convey such special benefits. In the meantime, the Congress is requested to act favorably on the postal rate proposals described in this message and on a number of other specific proposals now pending before it or planned to be submitted this year for increased fees or charges for special services.

ESTIMATED SAVINGS TO THE GENERAL TAXPAYERS FROM MORE ADEQUATE FEES AND CHARGES

[In millions]

Proposal	Fiscal year 1961	Full annual effect
Increase postal rates	$554.0	$554.0
Support highway expenditures by highway-user taxes:		
Replace future diversion of general excise taxes to trust fund with increased motor fuel tax or other charges		850.0
Transfer financing of forest and public land highways to trust fund	39.0	36.0
Charge users for share of cost of Federal airways:		
Increase taxes on aviation fuels	72.0	88.0
Transfer aviation fuel taxes from highway trust fund to general fund	17.0	20.0
Revise fees for noncompetitive oil and gas leases		14.0
Recover administrative costs of Federal crop insurance		6.4
Increase patent fees	3.7	3.7
Increase miscellaneous fees now below costs	8.0	8.9
Total savings	693.7	1,581.0

Receipts From and Payments to the Public

The program of responsible fiscal policy represented by a balanced budget with a substantial surplus is reinforced by an even greater surplus of total cash receipts from the public over cash payments to the public. In this more comprehensive measure of Federal financial activity, obtained by consolidating budget, trust fund, and certain other Federal transactions, receipts from the public are estimated at $102.2 billion in 1961 and payments to the public at $96.3 billion, resulting in an excess of $5.9 billion of receipts.

This excess of receipts will be used to repay cash the Government has previously borrowed from the public. Repayment of such debt owed to the public will be greater than the amount of public debt retired, because the Government trust funds are expected to add to their holdings of public debt securities to the extent that trust fund receipts exceed trust fund expenditures. This will reduce the debt held by the public in like amount by shifting ownership to the trust funds.

For the fiscal year 1960, on the other hand, an excess of payments to the public of $542 million is estimated, despite the anticipated budget surplus of $217 million. This situation reflects the fact that total disbursements of trust funds will exceed their receipts in 1960, notably in the old-age and survivors insurance, unemployment, and highway trust funds.

FEDERAL GOVERNMENT RECEIPTS FROM AND PAYMENTS TO THE PUBLIC

[Fiscal years. In billions]

	1959 actual	1960 estimate	1961 estimate
Receipts from the public	$81.7	$94.8	$102.2
Payments to the public	94.8	95.3	96.3
Excess of payments over receipts	−13.1	−.5	....
Excess of receipts over payments	....	....	+5.9

2. THE 1960 ELECTION

During the months prior to the Republican National Convention, Eisenhower refused to endorse any candidate for the party's nomination. In fact, on numerous occasions he referred to the availability of many good possible candidates. Nevertheless, it seemed that he favored Vice President Richard Nixon. In April, 1960, before a large gathering of Republican women in Washington, he came close to an outright endorsement.

Speech by President Eisenhower on Republican Achievements
April 4, 1960
[*Public Papers of the Presidents: 1960–61* (Washington, 1961), 332–37.]

Madam Chairman, Mr. Vice President, delegates to the 8th Republican Women's National Conference, and friends:

For me it is invariably a joyous occasion when I meet with my friends of the Republican Women's National Conference. Your enthusiasm is infectious and it's good to feel it again.

As a matter of fact, I got so enthused this evening that sitting here I am thinking of running for the national—. Well, nevertheless, I am thinking of running for the legislature of my adopted State. At least, again I have the opportunity of thanking all of you—which I do most earnestly—for the support you have given me, both in political campaigns and in the day-to-day business of administering the Government of the United States.

Many of you here probably know of a fact concerning women in politics that I discovered only recently. The first woman to address any presidential nominating convention was a Republican, who, back in 1892, said, "We are here to help, and we have come to stay." I cannot tell you how deeply appreciative I am of the continuing validity of that 60-year-old pledge. For in politics, I early learned that the ladies not only produce "helping power" but also seem to have the most "staying power."

For example, I see plenty of evidence that you are standing firmly by a decision that many of you here helped to make in 1952. That year our Republican Convention turned to a highly talented man for the vice presidential nomination. None of us has ever regretted that choice.

Now in this little talk I wrote some things about Dick Nixon, and I was astonished when he talked a little bit about me, because I am not running. But Dick Nixon has been a credit to the administration, to our party, and to our country. Since 1952 he has gained nearly 8 years of added governmental experience at the highest level—a tour of seasoning unmatched in the Nation's history. All of us know him as a man of integrity and deep faith—one who is intelligent, mature, and uniquely knowledgeable in the problems and personalities in the world scene. And along with this, he has that priceless gift, a sense of humor—indispensable in politics.

And finally and most important, he has Pat.

Now, this year we want to and expect to elect a Republican President and are striving to regain control of the House of Representatives and make real gains in the Senate. The need for this effort is one on which I can speak with some feeling. Not since 1954 have I served with a Congress controlled by our party. More than 5 consecutive years with an opposition Congress is, I'm told, a record for any President—although it is hardly one I wanted to make. In any event, we are setting our sights on ·obtaining a Republican House to work with my Republican successor.

It's not my purpose tonight to take off into oratorical orbit—already we have a number of senatorial hopefuls doing that, each hoping in the scramble to get into the chair I shall soon vacate. Instead, might I make just a few comments about the coming campaign, about our party, our record, and how we shall serve our country in the coming years.

As we approach this presidential election, each party should be prepared to examine the corridors of its conscience, the record of its performance and its program for future action.

For this our party stands well prepared.

First of all, it believes that political programs should be based on moral law. Moreover, the Republican Party has never rested its case upon promises and platforms alone; it has been a party of accomplishment.

From 1860 to 1960 it has achieved a record of responsible and brilliant performance that is boldly written across the pages of history.

Let's take a look at just the past 7 years.

What have we done to redeem the platform pledges made to the American people in 1952 and 1956?

The record is filled with such advances as improvements in the health and welfare of our people, the greater soundness, freedom, and growth of our economy, increased modernization and strengthening of our defenses, greater prestige abroad, and the initiation of a roadbuilding program that dwarfs anything of its kind in all history of all nations.

To cite in more detail just two examples of the way in which we have kept faith with the American voter:

Foremost, we stopped, on honorable terms, the fighting in Korea and, since, have kept the peace.

That peace cannot, because of the threat hanging like a cloud over the world, achieve the perfection we desire. But we do remember that during the past 7 years no American boy has lost his life in battle, nor has our Nation been depressed by daily casualty lists.

Since 1953 we have lived in an atmosphere where, with our allies, we are able constantly to strengthen the bonds of peace, regardless of the undeniable uneasiness and tension in the world.

We are well aware of and well understand the powerful threats, both implicitly and explicitly expressed by Communist imperialism, and the sacrifices we must make to uphold peace in freedom. And wherever freedom is threatened we have never temporized nor compromised—nor ever shall.

In this spirit we have made certain of our Nation's defenses—well knowing that from a position of strength we provide not only for military security but establish the only platform from which we can effectively pursue the objective of mutual disarmament and world peace.

In programming America's defense, we have insisted not only on sufficiency, but on balance—a balance that makes maximum use of our material resources, human energies, and national spirit, and is designed to counter every foreseeable risk.

To do otherwise would be to court disaster.

Now some, I know, have felt and expressed themselves individually as highly qualified to criticize adversely the comprehensive and painstaking calculations that responsible military, scientific, and governmental personnel have made in satisfying our defense requirements. For myself, I assure you that I have the highest personal confidence in those calculations, made by a great cooperating group of able and dedicated people.

I am convinced that our whole defensive structure has been accurately tailored in the light both of national needs and operational efficiency.

Our Nation is the most powerful in the world, and only the ignorant or the blind insist it to be otherwise.

But we—we Republicans—owe it to our people to make this clear to every citizen in the land.

And I earnestly hope you will drive home something else.

Here I refer to a second major area of Republican promise and performance.

Some opponents apparently feel there is no problem that cannot be solved by a subsidy—that all social and economic difficulties can be speedily resolved by tapping the treasury.

What a myth that is!

Extravagance and statesmanship can never be happily wedded.

We stand squarely with Lincoln in the conviction that government should undertake only that which the citizen cannot do properly for himself—that government should always be ready to give a helping hand but never a heavy handout.

Now when we express our belief in such things as "fiscal responsibility," "balanced budgets," "refusal to debase our currency," and the importance of local authority, we no doubt sound unspectacular to those people who want to dive deeply into the Federal Treasury.

But these subjects are not unspectacular to the family that has, in the past, encountered the rising costs and prices resulting from governmental irresponsibility; or to the housewife who must make the family budget stretch to cover the necessaries of life, with its emergencies; or to the worker whose savings and pensions are endangered whenever government permits the debasing of our money.

All these matters are basic to sound government. Moreover, good government does not seek to be spectacular; it seeks rather the progress and the happiness of the people it serves.

So we shall not deviate from principle; but our job is to make sure that the public better understands the Republican accomplishments of the past and the sound and enduring good to be found in its programs for the future.

If we do this, I have no doubt about which party the American people will turn to next November.

If we do our work well, all our people will appreciate the great advances in American influence in the world, and the growing effectiveness of foreign programs. They will realize that we have had marked success in preserving stability and promoting a great expansion in our economy.

Moreover, in two small cyclic recessions we have remained true to principle, refusing to heed the councelors of fear. We have pursued sane and helpful programs tailored to the true needs of our people. The result has been in each case a rebounding economy and a record rise in prosperity.

Under the policies our party has supported, our people are assured of becoming ever more prosperous according to the best judgment of the finest economic experts we can muster. Indeed, this year's Gross National Product —the broadest measure of the Nation's output of goods and services—will be more than $500 billion.

And if we spread the good news properly, the public will pay no attention to those who have developed an amazing, and what is to them seemingly an enjoyable, habit of making forecasts that drip with gloom, lack of faith, and self-doubt.

Although the political pessimist may voice despair about our future, I know that this audience will never believe that our Nation has lost the hardy traits of mind and spirit, the self-confidence and self-dependence, that have characterized the American people for over 300 years. Rather all of us here tonight assert that the history of our Nation—including that of its past 7 years—justifies fully our confidence in America for the journey ahead.

Our party is about to enter the second century since it first came to power. Over the years the core of Republican purpose has been to exalt individual opportunity and human dignity and to enthrone freedom. This purpose we all share, but we must remember that the driving force in a successful political party is the strength of spirit of its members. Only as we renew this spiritual power and enthusiasm will we bring our party up the slow climb to the summit where the election of a Republican President and a Republican Congress will again become the normal pattern.

And so, as I thank you again for your courtesy and express my admiration for the effort you are making, may I say this: in the confident spirit of the final resolution introduced at the convention that nominated Lincoln, we read, "we adjourn to meet at the White House on March 4th next"—I bid you good night and I hope to see you at the Capitol when my Republican successor takes over on January 20th.

Congress recessed on July 3, 1960, for the national conventions. When Congress reconvened on August 8, the President took the opportunity to reiterate his legislative proposals in a manner reminiscent of Harry Truman's famous "Turnip Day Session" message of 1948. Eisenhower's extensive list of requests undermined the plans of Democratic candidate John Kennedy, who had planned to use the session as a launching pad for his own campaign.

Special Message to the Congress from President Eisenhower upon its Reconvening August 8, 1960

[*Public Papers of the Presidents: 1960–61* (Washington, 1961), 612–19.]

To the Congress of the United States:

I welcome the return of the Congress. There is much important legislative work still pending that cannot await the selection and assembly of a new Congress and a new Administration. The Executive and Legislative branches must act together on these pressing needs these next few weeks. I shall do my part. I am sure that the Congress will be similarly disposed.

First, the world situation, with its great significance to us.

Fundamentally, it is as it was. The free world still faces a Communist imperialism fixed upon conquest of all the world.

Vigilance, therefore, must still be our watchword. Continuing strength, military, economic, spiritual, must remain our reliance. Our basic objective—

to secure a permanent peace—is yet to be won. Our programs have long been keyed to this situation. They must continue.

During the Congressional recess events have dramatized tensions that still plague the world.

We have seen an intensification of Communist truculence.

Indeed, the Soviet dictator has talked loosely and irresponsibly about a possible missile attack on the United States.

An American aircraft has been attacked over international waters. Our resolution requesting an investigation of this matter has been vetoed by the Soviets in the United Nations Security Council. Surviving crew members are still being held prisoner.

The Soviet Delegation has walked out of the Geneva disarmament negotiations.

The Communists continue to exploit situations of unrest, flagrantly striving to turn to their ends the struggles and hopes of peoples for a better world. These Communist efforts have recently reached new extremes in Central Africa.

All of us know about Cuba.

As a result of continuous appraisal of changing Communist tactics and attitudes, I have ordered the military services to take certain practical measures affecting the readiness and posture of our military commands. These include the deployment of additional aircraft carriers to the Sixth and Seventh Fleets. A number of B-47 medium bombers and their accompanying tankers, which had been scheduled to be phased out of our forces, will be retained in service for the time being; and the tempo of operation of the Strategic Air Command will be increased and its deployment further dispersed. The readiness of our ground forces will be further improved by expanding the number and scope of strategic field and airborne exercises.

I have also directed expansion of certain long-range programs. The Strategic Air Command capability to conduct a continuous airborne alert will be further strengthened. More funds will be applied to the modernization of the Army combat equipment and to military airlift. Additional effort will be devoted to the development of the B-70 and the reconnaissance satellite SAMOS.

During the Congressional recess we have made extraordinary progress in testing one of America's most important weapons systems—the Polaris Ballistic Missile Submarine. It is with great satisfaction that I report to the Congress that the first test firings of the Polaris missile from the submerged nuclear submarine GEORGE WASHINGTON had rifle shot accuracy at great ranges. Never in my long military career has a weapon system of such complexity been brought from its original conception to the operational stage with such sureness and speed—an achievement that in its entirety has taken less than five years.

The time is now right to increase the scope of the Polaris program and five instead of three more submarines have been started this fiscal year. Furthermore, I have directed the development of a much longer range version of the Polaris missile, which will give America a weapon of even greater versatility, power and invulnerability.

The Defense Department will carry out these defense measures with its available resources insofar as possible. Measures pertaining to weapons systems programs will be carried out by utilizing appropriations already made in this session. Total resources are adequate, although a modest increase in military personnel and in operation and maintenance funds may prove to be necessary to carry out the readiness measures. If such an increase should be required, I shall promptly request the necessary funds.

Incidentally, provision will have to be made after the first of the year to fund the civilian pay increases imposed by Congress a few weeks ago. These will add permanently to our defense costs some $200 million a year.

Once again I assure the Congress that this Nation's military power is second to none and will be kept that way. Our long range strategic bombers and air to ground missiles, our intermediate and long range ballistic missiles, our Polaris submarines, our attack carriers, the tactical air units overseas, the air defense forces, and the atomic and conventional firepower of our ground forces world-wide are indeed a retaliatory and defensive force unmatched anywhere.

So much for administrative actions which I have recently taken. Congressional actions, too, are required.

Our national security needs encompass more than excellence and strength in our own military establishment. They include measures to build free world strength everywhere. These require, and I therefore request, appropriations of the full amount authorized by the Congress for the Mutual Security Program. At this point in the legislative process, these appropriations have been cut by well over a half billion dollars. The Nation's security and our inescapable interest in a stable world require that these amounts be restored.

In addition, I request a $100 million increase in the authorization and appropriation for the Mutual Security Contingency Fund. This increase is needed to keep America poised for sudden developments such as those in the Congo where a United States airlift and other efforts were needed suddenly and critically. Happily, in this instance, we were able to respond in a matter of hours. We must maintain ourselves in a position to give rapid backing to the efforts of the United Nations in this troubled region.

At my direction, two other matters will be presented to Congress, their purpose being to promote free world stability by stimulating the hopes, morale and efforts of our friends everywhere. These programs are:

First, an authorization in the magnitude of $600 million to help our Latin American neighbors accelerate their efforts to strengthen the social and economic structure of their nations and improve the status of their individual citizens. This program, which should include further assistance for the rehabilitation of devastated Chile, will promote the dynamism and effectiveness of all our efforts in this Hemisphere. I urgently request enactment of this authorization prior to the Economic Conference of the American Republics, which convenes at Bogota on September 5, so that discussions leading to the development of detailed plans may be initiated there.

Second, a proposal to be presented in September before the General Assembly of the United Nations, whereby we and other fortunate nations can, together, make greater use of our combined agricultural abundance to help feed the hungry of the world. The United Nations provides a multilateral forum admirably suited to initiate consideration of this effort.

I consider it important that Congress approve a Resolution endorsing such a program before the United Nations Assembly convenes.

Turning to domestic problems, clearly we face a legislative log jam, the possibility of which I suggested, by special message, on the third of May.

Only one major measure—civil rights—had then been passed, and this had two major deletions which I hope will not be restored in keeping with the bipartisan support evidenced for these items last month.

Legislating time is now short, and so far in this session only six of the twenty-seven measures I cited last May as required by the Nation's interests have been enacted into law. Because those that fail of enactment before adjournment will go begging for months to come, I urge the Congress to attend to them now. In addition to those already mentioned, I cite these:

—Federal assistance in the construction of facilities for colleges, universities and elementary and secondary schools;

—assistance to older people to meet serious illnesses;

—expansion of coverage of the Fair Labor Standards Act;

—a moderate upward adjustment of the minimum wage;

—constructive measures to meet existing farm problems;

—a sound area assistance program directed specifically to the areas in need;

—the authorizing of 40 new judgeships to expedite the rendering of justice;

—proper financing to avoid delays in our Interstate Highway Program;

—an increase in the aviation fuel tax to facilitate proper financing of our Airways Modernization Program;

—removal of the interest rate limitation on long-term Treasury bonds;

—a postal rate increase to avoid saddling the next administration and taxpayers generally, wholly unjustifiably, with a postal deficit nearing a billion dollars a year;

—liberalization of our immigration laws;

—continuation of the long-established authority for the President to reorganize the Executive branch;

—and a grouping of measures generally in the conservation field.

Also still needed and long ago recommended are Senate ratification of the important Antarctica Treaty, amendments to speed our space exploration efforts, and a restoration of the traditional relationship between the active duty and the retired pay of our military personnel.

All of these items are at least as urgently needed for America as when first recommended. So I urge that we stay on the job until it is done.

Certainly we cannot adjourn the public interest.

I have a special comment on two of these matters.

First, agriculture. I reiterate the theme of my February ninth and May third messages on this subject. The well-being of our farm people still demands that we act with good sense on their pressing problems, notably wheat. The public will have every right to register its serious protest should the Congress adjourn without responsible action in this area.

The recent history of this problem has been deadlock. The Congress has refused to accept my recommendations and insisted upon unrealistic programs which, of course, I have rejected.

Last January I made one further attempt to resolve this issue. I urged Congress simply to work its will, provided only that the end result fitted within broad guidelines assuring a truly beneficial result for the farmer and the Nation. My own preferred program, leading to greater freedom for the farmer, is widely known. I repeat, however, what I have said many times—if a different approach is desired, and kept within the guidelines, I will unhesitatingly approve it.

Our farmers need constructive action and for years have been entitled to it. They know, as does all America, that this Administration has been unable substantially to alter the existing type of wheat program because of lack of Congressional cooperation. It has been a program attuned to calamity—war, depression or drought—but which in these years of peace and great productivity has resulted in staggering surpluses which overhang the market, depress prices, and threaten the farmer's future.

The Congress should promptly provide the constructive remedies for agriculture so long and so urgently needed.

For five years in a row I have recommended area assistance legislation. Regrettably I had no choice but to veto the legislation the Congress did pass this session. It would have frittered the taxpayers' money away in areas where it was not needed and on programs that would not have benefited those truly in need of help.

A new area assistance bill, with Administration backing, was introduced immediately after my veto. It would channel more help directly into stricken areas than any previous measure proposed. Failure to act will deny this help for months to come. Human distress demands action now. If later we find there should be changes either in the dollar amounts or the methods used, experience will dictate the kind of adjustments to be made.

Last January I estimated that, if the Congress would adhere to my appropriation and revenue recommendations, we could look forward to a budgetary surplus of $4 billion. Since then, however, the spending programs enacted and pending—coupled with the failure of Congress to enact proposed new revenue measures—threaten to consume the entire expected surplus.

This situation relates very importantly to your forthcoming deliberations because of the need of avoiding further deficit spending and of making, in years of prosperity, savings to be applied either to debt reduction or to tax reform.

In meeting this need I shall not abdicate my responsibility to use the Executive power to help keep the Nation's economy strong and sound while we carry forward our urgent work at home and in the world.

This means that I shall not be a party to reckless spending schemes which would increase the burden of debt of our grandchildren, by resuming, in prosperous times, the practice of deficit financing. I shall not fail to resist inflationary pressures by whatever means are available to me.

This truth we must take to heart: in good times, we must at the very least pay our way. This is the fundamental condition for a dependable future for our working men and women, for management, for consumers, and for the Government. If we will but handle responsibly the taxpayers' money, as I am firmly determined that we shall, private and public action can continue to move confidently ahead.

This simply means that we must adhere to necessary programs and sensible priorities. I have herein suggested those in which I believe.

If the Congress prefers other priorities at greater national cost, responsibility dictates that it accompany them with the additional taxes to pay the bill.

I recognize the magnitude of the task still before the Congress, and, of course, I am not unaware of the other matters attracting public attention in this year 1960.

But I repeat—if during the critical months ahead we hold to the standard of national interest, the future will be bright for America—indeed, for all the free world.

Throughout the 1960 campaign Nixon stressed his experience. Part of this strategy involved emphasizing his decision-making role within the Eisenhower Administration. This tactic was not intended to alienate the President; indeed, to the contrary, it represented an attempt to identify Nixon as the President's right-hand man. However, the approach backfired, because Eisenhower and his staff insisted in the strongest terms that the President made his own decisions. Partially a natural reaction, it also reflected a response to widespread press criticism. As early as August 24, 1960, the Nixon organization had been distressed by the President's answer at a press conference to a question concerning what decisions the Vice President had made during his Administration. Eisenhower said: "If you give me a week, I might think of one. I don't remember."

Early in the campaign the President made what the White House described as a series of "nonpolitical" speeches. To the dismay of Nixon and his staff these speeches were indeed non-political. As the campaign heated up, Nixon aides began pressing Eisenhower's staff to acknowledge the Vice President's importance in making policy. This issue came to a head in late October. As the President prepared a major speech for delivery in Philadelphia on October 28, Nixon supporters proposed to the White House staff textual changes in the address. By this time the Kennedy bandwagon seemed to be rolling and Nixon appeared in desperate need of help. Yet, the Philadelphia speech, as presented over national television and radio, reflected none of the advice offered by the Nixon staff. However, the President did say, "And clearly the best is the team of Nixon and Lodge."

Administrative Assistant Edward McCabe
to Presidential Assistants Wilton Persons
and Bryce Harlow
October 27, 1960
[Harlow Files, Eisenhower Papers.]

By phone this afternoon, Hugh Scott lodged an urgent plea for the President's Philadelphia talk tomorrow night.

He most earnestly asks the President to say not only that he is for Dick Nixon—but to forcefully say he is opposed to Senator Kennedy, spelling out some of the reasons why.

Scott reports he has been repeatedly confronted, in Pennsylvania and elsewhere, with this type observation: "Obviously the President must be for Nixon. After all they are in the same Party. But he hasn't said that he is against Kennedy—so it seems that he probably really doesn't feel too strongly either way."

Administrative Assistant Edward McCabe
to Presidential Assistant Bryce Harlow
or Special Assistant Kevin McCann
n.d.
[Harlow Files, Eisenhower Papers.]

Bryce or Kevin

Bill Robinson called about the section about the President making decision. He said (and I quarrelled with him) that the President has said all along that Nixon has participated in many of these decisions. I tried to tell him that what the President has said is that the decisions are his, but that advice has been sought and offered by many of the top people in government, including the Vice President.

Bill is afraid that the press will make a big point of this.

Speech by President Eisenhower on the Issues
in the Presidential Campaign
Philadelphia, October 28, 1960
[White House Press Release Section, Eisenhower Papers.]

General Baker and my Fellow Citizens—

We have ten critical days left in which to evaluate the issues and personalities of this campaign. We are thankful that we vote secretly in America—that regardless of party affiliation or party registration we can freely and conscientiously choose the best leader for our country.

Almost eight years have gone by since millions of us—Republicans, Democrats and Independents—enthusiastically joined together to build a better America. We have had, I feel, a happy and fruitful partnership.

Measured in the dollars that have remained relatively stable these past 8 years, you—the American people—have come a long way since 1952—

You have increased personal income by 132 billion dollars—by 48 percent.

You have increased average weekly earnings from 68 dollars a week to 91 dollars a week—by over a third.

You have increased your individual annual savings by 7 billion dollars—up 37 percent.

You are building 70 thousand elementary classrooms this year alone. That is 22 thousand more than were built in 1952—or 46 percent.

You have increased college enrollments from 2 million to almost 3½ million—up 75 percent.

You have built 9 million new homes—more than ever were built before in the same length of time.

You have added $280 billion in capital expenditures on plants and equipment—more in this job-making field than in the preceding 30 years.

You have increased the gross national product by 158 billion dollars—almost 45 percent.

Our Interstate Highway System was talked about for many years, but not started. Now we are building 41 thousand miles of these great new avenues of commerce—and paying for them as we go. When completed, they will save four thousand American lives a year.

The St. Lawrence Seaway was for decades a dream; finally, it came true. At last we have brought the oceans of the world to the very heart of America.

In the meantime, you expanded social security, improved our national parks, forced passage of a good labor reform bill, and took the only significant steps in civil rights in 80 years. You the American people kept inflation down, balanced the budget four times, with another one on the way. You did these and a multitude of other things—and all this with a reduction of a quarter of a million in governmental positions.

Now, in all these years, a primary contribution of government and national leadership was to create a climate fostering confidence, enterprise, and a willingness to venture and risk. At the same time, we stopped a wasteful war and prevented others, always with honor. By removing stifling economic controls, we allowed the men and women of America once again to concentrate on getting ahead. Under enlightened governmental policies you the American people have been responsible for all this surging progress.

And what about our military strength?

It is the most powerful on earth.

Into our armed forces we integrated weapons of tremendous deterrence, many of them unknown eight years ago, through a program more than three times larger, in dollar amount, than only ten years ago. And we have proof of the respect the Soviets have for our power and our resolution: the Communists have been turned from a strategy of military penetration to a strategy of infiltration by political and economic means.

So, I am proud of you—proud of what you have done, and proud of what has been done by America. Let no one diminish your pride and confidence in yourselves or belittle these accomplishments. My friends, never have Americans achieved so much in so short a time.

Now in glib political oratory we have heard this progress called "standing still".

Now if the great things you have done are "standing still," then I say America needs more of it.

Now, shortly you must select a new leader for our country. Because I know what he must face—because I feel so earnestly that your choice will have far-reaching effects—possibly for decades—I trust you will think it fitting that I share with you my deep personal convictions on this matter.

There are four key qualities by which I believe America would like to measure the candidates in this election. They are:

Character; Ability; Responsibility; Experience.

From eight years of intimate association, I know Richard Nixon has these qualities and will use them wisely and decisively. And so will Cabot Lodge. This is why I trust and I believe that the American people will elect this splendid team on November 8.

My friends, this is a subject on which I will have more to say next Wednesday from New York.

Your President, of course, will have to be many things. As Chief of State and of Government, he will be your spokesman, presenting to the world your ideals; your firmness in the right; your strength—in fact, the true image of your country.

To perform this task he must thoroughly think through the problems of our time. In this he cannot succeed unless he is free of rashness; of arrogance; of headlong action; of the inclination to easy compromise. I hear that one candidate says he will act first and act fast. My friends, America needs a man who will think first, and then act wisely.

We need a leader who will not, one day, say that the United States Government should intervene in Cuba and then retract it the next day.

We need a leader who will not, one day, say he would give up territory to the Communists, then change his mind on it a day or so later.

Because, my friends, upon such decisions can hinge peace or war. Upon your President will fall problems like disarmament—like nuclear testing—like Berlin and Quemoy—like Cuba—and, beyond these, the task of continuing to win the hearts and minds of millions of struggling peoples. By the morality, justice and steadiness of his decisions, he must be able to rally world support.

Your President will also be the Commander-in-Chief of your Armed Forces. National security will be one of his basic responsibilities and will depend greatly upon his understanding, born of experience. Just wanting to keep out of war will not be enough—as our three major wars in this century have proved. Your President must see to it that your Armed Forces are kept alert and modern, always ready to meet whatever threat may exist in this world. They are that now.

Now a strong defense necessarily rests upon a strong economy. Defense is vastly expensive. Even now you the people are spending ten million dollars a day on long-range ballistic missiles alone—more each day, every day, than the total spent for this purpose in all the years before I took office. Now as long as high level spending is necessary for your security, the Commander-in-Chief will need to be mindful that unless he holds firmly to policies that promote the growth of free, competitive economic enterprise in the United States, the entire defense effort will be weakened.

Now I have given these few examples of Presidential duties to make clear the momentous significance to you and your children of your vote on November 8.

I have lived a fairly long and full life, so I tend to think of this nation in terms of my children's and grandchildren's problems. In thinking of their future I am profoundly concerned by some statements in this campaign that have had world-wide circulation and have cruelly distorted the image of America. These statements demonstrate an amazing irresponsibility. They demand, from me, emphatic correction.

This week *Pravda,* one of Moscow's propaganda newspapers, reproduced speeches by some American politicians—you know who they are—bewailing alleged weaknesses in our country. The Soviet leaders are gleefully quoting from these same speeches in their effort to prove that our influence with other governments of the world is shrinking.

My friends, too many people are talking carelessly and ignorantly about America's standing, as if our Republic were in a popularity contest.

The word prestige has become so badly used and misused as to have lost any real meaning. But of this we can be sure: the Nation's prestige is not measured by the stridency of a politician's voice; it is measured by proved accomplishment. Aside from the great economic development for which you have been responsible, we have, among other things, stopped a futile and costly war, moved to halt Communist advances in Viet-Nam, prevented attacks on Formosa, helped our Philippine friends eliminate Communist guerrilla warfare, achieved, through the United Nations, a decent solution for the Suez affair, saved Iran, removed the sore spot of Trieste, by our sacrifices and cooperative effort strengthened free nations all along the periphery of the Communist bloc, and forged new and strong ties with our neighbors to the South. Now these successes were not won by any lack of strength or decisiveness. It is on such a record that Americans measure prestige rather than upon self-serving political assertions.

The important thing in our foreign affairs is that our Nation's purposes and programs be right. I should like to ask you all to give your closest study to this thing of foreign relations and foreign activities. Foreign problems color every other problem we have in the world—indeed, they cause almost every other problem we have. This is the basic problem that all of us must think about, and select leaders that will know how to handle them. That these programs are right is proved in one area by the eagerness with which the heads of other governments seek our counsel and support, and by our record in the United Nations.

More than 120 heads of state and government have visited our Nation's Capital in the past eight years, an unprecedented occurrence. The heads of government who went to the United Nations in its last session, excepting those from behind the Iron Curtain, requested to see me, as your chief spokesman, to assure me of their purpose of keeping their relations with us sound and firm. And all the new nations formed—gaining their independence since World War II, have chosen a democratic form of government— not communist. They, at least, have no doubts about America's prestige.

And too many of our people talk loosely about relative military strength. Such talk is an exercise in calculated confusion. I remind these self-appointed experts that the past eight years comprise the only period in the entire history of the United States in which peacetime military preparation has been adequate and tailored to meet any possible emergency. I remind you that I have served in these Forces for more than forty years. I think I know whereof I speak. Moreover, our defense has been tuned to the continuity of the threat and to long-range goals, avoiding the wild fluctuations that too often follow upon the incidence of either panic or complacency. This is one of the important reasons why the United States is today militarily the strongest nation in the world.

In any case: Whatever was America's image abroad at the beginning of this political campaign, it tends to become blurred today. This is because of unwarranted disparagement of our own moral, military and economic power. And what American is entitled to criticize the accomplishments of 180 million other Americans?

My friends, anyone who seeks to grasp the reins of world leadership should not spend all his time wringing his hands.

As another example of unwise politicking, I call attention to the recent speculations in gold on the London market.

Today your dollar is still the strongest currency in the world. We can keep it that way if we continue to hold firmly to the right policies on our budget, our money, and our national debt.

This we have worked tirelessly to achieve for eight years. We have successfully fought against the big-spending schemes and irresponsible monetary policies that lead to currency debasement and a weak dollar.

But recently, the price of gold in the free market has risen above our official price of $35 per ounce. The foreign press—the European press, reports that this development is based in part on a growing fear of the cheap money policies and radical spending promised in the Los Angeles platform.

If these promises should be carried out, the impact on our economic position—and on the free world—could be catastrophic. Very quickly, confidence in our dollar could be impaired.

This places an immediate obligation upon the political leaders who support that platform.

That obligation is to spell out, specifically, in dollars and cents, how they would pay for the many billions of additional Federal spending pledged by that platform. We know that they could not pay for them with high hopes alone.

If they would pay for these lavish programs by raising taxes, let them say so.

And if they would cut going programs of the government, let them specify what they are.

But if they would pay for these programs by deficit spending, raising the debt of our children and grandchildren, and thereby debase our currency, let them so confess.

In such a case let them understand that they and their party assume not only full responsibility for the present dangerous speculation in gold, but also for the developing fear about the future worth of the American dollar.

In all these things, my friends, we will need judgment and experience as our surest guide.

Of course "America must move." But forward—not backward. Not back to inflation—not back to bureaucratic controls—not back to deficit spending—not back to higher taxes, and bigger government. We found all these in 1952.

America must continue to go forward—with maturity, with judgment, with balance. I see no sense in America galloping in reverse to what has been called a New Frontier.

This is why, my fellow Americans, we must not settle for leadership other than the very best. We cannot afford anything less.

And clearly the best is the team of Nixon and Lodge.

Dick Nixon is superbly experienced, maturely conditioned in the critical affairs of the world. For eight years he has been a full participant in the deliberations that have produced the great decisions affecting our Nation's security and have kept us at peace. He has shared more intimately in the great affairs of government than any Vice President in all our history.

He has traveled the world, studying at first hand the hopes and needs of more than 50 nations. He knows in person the leaders of those nations—knowledge of immeasurable value to a future President. He has represented us with distinction in situations demanding diplomacy, wisdom, tact and courage.

By all odds, Richard Nixon is the best qualified man to be the next President of the United States.

Likewise unique in experience is Ambassador Henry Cabot Lodge. Where could we find a man, better qualified by stature and service in the world arena, to assume the responsibility whose burden must always be the knowledge that at any instant he may have to assume the Presidency of the United States? Cabot Lodge will be prepared.

Here is a superlative team, prepared in every respect to lead our country responsibly and well.

Fellow Americans—in the days ahead, I ask you to reflect soberly on these thoughts. However you are registered, consider it only a passkey to a secret ballot governed solely by your own convictions and your own conscience. Cast your ballot not for party, nor for any other lesser consideration. Vote for the team that can more fully lead us toward peace with justice. Vote what is best for America.

In that spirit, and joined, I hope by a vast majority of Americans regardless of party, I shall vote for Vice President Nixon and Ambassador Lodge on November eighth.

Once having given an unqualified endorsement, the President took the campaign trail in a style reminiscent of his 1954 efforts to return a Republican Congress. The high point of the President's activities came in Ohio. At Cleveland on November 4, he reviewed his Administration and without mentioning any names cast doubts on the ability of the Democratic candidate. The President's tour seemed to move Ohio from the Kennedy to the Nixon column. Yet in the end, the pundits would claim that Eisenhower had entered the campaign too late.

Speech by President Eisenhower on Republican Achievements
Cleveland, November 4, 1960
[Public Papers of the Presidents: 1960–61 (Washington, 1961), 841–43.]

My friends:

Of course we don't have to be reminded we are in the midst of a political campaign, and I have been a little amused by some of the descriptions of my part in this campaign. This morning my headlines in the Washington papers said that I was a member of a rescue squad.

I said this is right, in 1952 I joined with a good many million Americans to rescue us from a lot. We were able to rescue the Nation from a war that no longer had any real meaning except calling for casualties every day, where we had already the objective we said we wanted, which was to gain the safety of South Korea. So that was solved—and with honor. Then we rescued it from inflation, and George Humphrey and I were called a good many names in trying to rescue it from a lot of controls that were then over our economy, prices on both labor and the costs of things and services. And we were rescued from military weakness which was the principal cause of ever getting into the Korean struggle in the first place.

And finally we were rescued from the philosophy that could see China go down the drain with five hundred million people, by far the vast majority of whom wanted to stay on this side of freedom and indeed looked to America as their great friend and champion.

So I am very proud to be in this rescue squad, because I think that the millions with whom I joined at that time have done a very splendid job.

And then of course we hear about the country standing still. I would just like to see this one test: when we say America and the American economy, in a way sort of an amorphous idea, the entity that we are thinking about is just so vast we don't grasp it very well. But I would like to see on billboards around this town—I would like to see Cleveland put up somewhere, what they have done, how many more homes you have built, how many hospitals, how many more roads, how many businesses have come in, what is the increase in population, the increase in its real wages, and the very great flattened-out curve of the cost of living since 1952. I would like to see those things just on a billboard to remind ourselves that we haven't exactly stood still. Either that, or I don't understand the word—the term.

Now I am on my way today to go to Pittsburgh for a little politicking, but I just want to make one observation: too many candidates—and here I am talking about the one on the opposing side, seems to me to think of this election as a little bit like we do a hundred-yard sprint. You put everything you have got into it, you call on every resource of mind and heart and muscles just to get over that line. That's the election day. Now the proper way to look at election day, in my opinion, is: what are you going to do after you get over that line? It is not in the race. In the race, all you have to do is break that tape and that's that. You are number one. In this race it is not good enough to be just number one. What are you going to do now?

I think of going back to the sports field again, and let's take a baseball game. Well, you have cracked out a grounder and you put in your last ounce of energy and you just happen to make first base. But you don't stop there. First base is the beginning. Now you call on all your alertness, your skill, your energy—and you count on your teammates, you count on the people that are working with you. And the purpose of that getting on first base was to get you around to count a run.

Now we want to think of the things that are coming behind this election. It is necessary to be number one over the line, but after you get there, we are going to do something about it, not merely to stand up and "huzza" after the results and say, "Well, we were number one," and go on about our business.

The Nation is too important to think of this race in those terms, and I think it is too often thought of in exactly that way.

And then finally I have this one observation: we talk so much or we hear so much about a second-rate country, second-rate in this and that and the other thing, whether it's space or whether it's schoolrooms or whatever. By the way, all these things are so ridiculous that they don't have to be refuted, but it leads me to this observation: suppose you had one of the players on Ohio State and he was forever saying, "You are a second-rate bunch of 'muckers.'" "You don't look good to me." "Now if you just make me your coach, this will be a much better team and we would go places, we would be world champions without even walking on the field."

Now I submit that any of the players that is running down his own squad all through the season, all through the year, is not himself going to make a very good coach.

Thank you very much and goodbye.

><⊂●━◗●━◗●━◗●━◗●━◗●━◗●━◗●━◗●━◗●━◗●━◗●━◗●━◗●━◗●━◗●<

Eisenhower's feelings about the outcome of the election found expression in a letter to New York Governor Nelson Rockefeller.

Presidential Secretary Ann Whitman
to Governor Nelson Rockefeller
November 19, 1960
[President's Personal File 149, Eisenhower Papers.]

PERSONAL
Dear Nelson:

The President asked me to send this letter off to you under my signature, in order to assure its getting in the mails today. (He is out playing a certain game!)

He is anxious to see you when you are in Washington week after next. He said particularly he wanted to be sure "we are all talking the same language. I feel there has been too much promising to the American people and not enough stress laid on the tremendous problems that have to be solved before we begin to eat the pie that so far is just in the sky!"

There you have it. I know Tom will set up an appointment for you at any time that is convenient to you both.

Fondly,
Ann C. Whitman

P.S.: I am assuming you want this appointment when you come down to Washington for the Cabinet dinner, but of course any time after next Wednesday the President will be (I think) back.

3. THE TRANSITION

Because Eisenhower was the first President to have his tenure limited to two terms, there was no question, even before the party conventions, about his retirement. Thus, in a July press conference he set forth broad ideas, which were shortly expanded by his aides, on the transfer of government. As early as July 26, a staff member wrote a memorandum on the problem.

Presidential Assistant Bradley Patterson, Jr., to Special Counsel David Kendall
July 26, 1960
[Kendall Files, Eisenhower Papers.]

The President has forthrightly set the objective: in November this government is going to witness the smoothest, most comprehensive and best organized transition in its history. As he stated at the July 6 press conference:

> When the election is carried out and the results known, my successor, no matter who he may be, will be given every facility to familiarize himself with every going policy, every activity, every connection we have, and he and his associates that he will appoint to take the place of my associates will be given like opportunity."

Equally firm is his parallel decision that *between* now and November transition planning should be low-key and be under White House control. The Departments have been instructed in the Cabinet Record of Action

> . . . action on transition matters should in the main be conducted in the post-election period. Such actions as may be appropriate now are to be taken only after White House coordination through the Assistant to the President.

How is the White House to make sure this control is effective?

There will be tendencies—perhaps even "pressure"—to make a "big thing" out of the transition planning prior to the President's own timing. These tendencies will come from four directions:

1324

a) from the Congress, as witness Representative Murray's letter to Roger Jones of June 23, 1960.

b) from Brookings, which on its own is holding consultations and which will be issuing a series of publications.

c) from the career people of government who with good intent and pride in their capability, may want to "start now".

d) from the press, to whom this subject is dramatic and who will take every opportunity supplied by the above three to make a story about the subject.

A possible fifth source might even be the associates of the candidates who may be prematurely eager to "get into the act".

To repeat, the three questions which you and Jerry now face are:

1. How to keep White House control over what the Executive Branch, egged on by these pressures, may be starting?

2. How to authorize and police the limited "getting ready" which will be legitimate if the President's objective is going to be met promptly in November?

3. How, after November 8, to continue to ensure Presidential control over and consistency within what will be a widespread activity?

Recommendations:

A. Very informally designate a White House staff officer to keep on top of the situation. (This has been done and you are he.)

B. Enlist the aid of the Executive Office, particularly of the Bureau of the Budget which is uniquely equipped to begin low-key preparations. (This has been started; it should have continuing, informal liaison and follow-up from here.)

C. Collect information. Quietly and informally, by personal contact rather than written instruction, get in touch with the Departments and major agencies and inform ourselves on what kinds of activities are underway in this area.

D. Clarify as may be necessary with General Persons our own ideas as to what would be the minimum legitimate preparations the Departments should now undertake.

E. Transmit guidance. By the same personal, informal channel as in "C", let the Departments know what you consider are the proper boundaries in the pre-election phase of these preparations and then arrange to see that each does what is necessary now but no more.

F. Later on, draw up a private, internal outline of the shape and magnitude of White House transition-coordinating responsibilities in the November 9–January 19 period.

On the day after the election, the Cabinet received information on how they should conduct themselves. Although the tone seemed less enthusiastic than the July memo, cooperation was still the keynote.

Cabinet Paper-Privileged
November 9, 1960
[Kendall Files, Eisenhower Papers.]

THE CABINET
Preparatory Arrangements for Turn-Over
of Executive Responsibility

For consideration by the Cabinet, attached is a memorandum which is proposed for transmittal by the President to the Heads of Departments and Agencies.

Robert Gray
Secretary to the Cabinet

The President-elect will undoubtedly wish to appoint representatives to prepare for the exercise of Executive responsibilities following January 20th. It will be the policy of this Administration to cooperate in this matter, with the double objective of facilitating an orderly transfer of responsibility on that date, while maintaining until then, without compromise, Executive authority and responsibility in this Administration. Under the Constitution, there can be no "sharing" of responsibility with the new Administration prior to that time.

The following telegram, sent to the President-elect, sets out the broad pattern of arrangements:

> I refer to my initial telegram to you, sent a few hours ago. I would like you to know that I stand ready to meet with you at any mutually convenient time to consider problems of continuity of government and orderly transfer of Executive responsibility on January 20th from my administration to yours. In the meantime—or even in lieu thereof—in order to facilitate and prepare for this transfer, I would be happy to have one of your assistants meet with my principal staff assistant, Wilton B. Persons, to whom I am assigning coordinating responsibility. He will be prepared to make arrangements by which representatives designated by you could meet with the present heads of the Executive Departments.
>
> Meetings of this kind over the coming weeks with the Director of the Bureau of the Budget might, for example, be important in providing information to you concerning the budget now in preparation. In addition, the Secretary of State will be prepared for meetings to provide information on foreign policy activities on which there will be special need for continuity until you shall have had opportunity, after inauguration, to arrange these matters to your satisfaction.

Contact by representatives of the President-elect within the Executive Branch is to be limited and controlled. Normally, no more than one designated representative, who may of course be the individual intended for appointment to the Cabinet post in the new Administration, should be in contact in any Department, and arrangements should first be cleared with General Persons; within the Department, contacts with the representative should be as directed and controlled by the head of the Department, and should normally be limited to senior or policy-level personnel. The representatives of the President-elect will be there to observe and to receive appropriate information. Obviously, there is to be no general movement into the Executive Branch by personnel from the Administration to come.

Documentary material is to be furnished to these representatives only as approved by the Department head concerned, and in accordance with security regulations where classified material is involved.

The foregoing is to guide this Administration, with Department heads bearing responsibility for their Departments. In case of questions, General Persons should be consulted before action is taken.

Eisenhower and the incoming President met on December 6, 1960. Even before this formal encounter the internal arrangements for the transfer of power had begun. The White House staff had checked in detail on what each major agency would do to facilitate the transition. By November 19 the process seemed well in hand.

Presidential Assistant Bradley Patterson, Jr. to Staff Secretary Andrew Goodpaster, Jr. and Special Assistant Wilton Persons
November 19, 1960
[Kendall Files, Eisenhower Papers.]

As requested, I have gone around to see each of the senior Departmental and Agency officers to find out their respective preparations for briefing their new Chiefs when designated by the President-elect. Facts were obtained; no recommendations were made.

The results are reported in the attachment, with specific illustrative material under the Tabs.

To summarize: The spectrum of response varies from "Why should we help this new guy do a better job?" (Labor), to the most comprehensive collections of advance, written briefing materials (State). Most of the agencies are toward the State end of the spectrum.

All emphasize their willingness to meet with the new men; all have been familiarized with Cabinet Paper 110/1 and Record of Action 159 setting forth the President's wishes as to procedures and as to the role of General Persons.

All stressed the personal role which the outgoing Chief will play and the personal control he will exercise over the subsequent contacts. Many of the agencies expressed concern that security clearances must be afforded before the briefing process can get very far. It seems quite clear, however, that once the security clearance is obtained, the briefings will by no means be limited to administrative and organizational matters alone.

If the President-elect starts making designations right after Thanksgiving, some of the due-dates on the briefing materials will have to be accelerated. (The slow start may be partly a result of not wanting to "jump the gun" before the election.)

The kinds of advance briefing materials contemplated vary; all include basic organizational and administrative facts, some include program summaries and a few envisage the identification of "tough problems" with recommendations thereon probably being made personally by the outgoing Chief. Defense plans a series of important trips. A few agencies apparently interpret "program briefings" to mean "accomplishments"; they and others often asked if there were any uniform guidance which the White House could offer.

Questions:

1. Should the White House offer some general guidance as to what kinds of advance briefing materials should in fact be prepared, i.e., covering
   a) Organization
   b) Program facts
   c) Tough problems and issues, dealt with in terms of alternatives, with recommendations reserved to outgoing Chief?
   (An outline could be prepared expanding on these three basic points but avoiding over-specificness.)

2. Should we ask that due-dates be accelerated and should we set any given deadline?

3. What wishes should we express concerning White House review of the materials being prepared?

4. Should the affected Departments and Agencies be informed of what arrangements are being made for security clearances?

State

State, through Assistant Secretary Macomber, is currently referring the numerous unclassified incoming messages from foreign nations are congratu-

lations, invitations to visit, etc. to the President-Elect via Mr. Halborn of
Mr. Kennedy's Senate Office staff.

The Executive Secretariat has the responsibility of pulling together the
briefing material for the Secretary-designate. This material will be of three
kinds:

1) A factual briefing book on organization and administration, being
prepared by Mr. Dwinnell's office (outline under Tab 1)

2) A series of policy briefing papers (no recommendations) on an
extensive list of specific subjects (list attached under Tab 2). Material will
be up through Top Secret (will not include "Q" or "Crypto"). The papers
are being prepared in State's respective Bureaus, each of which has a
designated liaison officer for this purpose. They are due November 28 and
the Secretary is expected to review them personally when he returns on
December 4.

3) A separate briefing book on the operation of the Secretary's immediate office is being prepared by the Executive Secretariat.

Treasury

Assistant Secretary Weatherbee is pulling together for completion by
Thanksgiving two kinds of briefing materials:

1) Organization and management
    a) A basic briefing book for the Secretary-designate
    b) A notebook on the functions of the Treasury Department (for
       other key officials)
    c) A briefing book on the work and programs of the individual
       bureaus (for the use of new Assistant Secretaries)
    d) A book on detailed administrative matters (for a possible new
       Administrative Assistant Secretary)

2) Two "Issues and Problems" briefing books (to be reviewed by Mr.
Scribner), one classified, one unclassified. They will state facts on both sides
of various issues, but present neither alternatives nor recommendations.

Defense

Some time ago, General Wheeler gave Mr. Kennedy the Top Secret
"Relative Strength of Forces" briefing (the kind given by Defense on the
Hill), and he has seen the SAC briefing along with Messrs. Symington and
Jackson.

The military assistants to the Secretary and Mr. Livesay contemplate the
following for a new Secretary-designate (assuming security clearance):

1) Giving him the unclassified Orientation Briefing Book given to every
new Presidential appointee, which deals with the organization and administration of the Department.

2) Suggesting a series of trips to most Unified and Specified Commands
(e.g., accompanying Mr. Gates to Paris on December 10 and thus meeting

General Norstad, to CINCPAC in Hawaii, etc.) and, en route, visiting the appropriate important field installations. The purpose: to have the Secretary-designate become personally acquainted with each major military Command and Officer. He would be accompanied on such visits by the appropriate Service Chief and by one of Secretary Gates' military assistants.

3) Having available for short notice selected oral briefings (e.g., the 1½ hour "pros and cons" briefing on Defense Organization Alternatives which was recently presented to the B.A.C., War Room Briefings, budget-alternatives briefing, etc.).

Except for #1, most of this would be oral. Point emphasized: the above program involves *time* and Defense is hoping therefore for an early designation.

Justice

The Attorney General has been absent for some time but his Executive Assistant, Mr. Cushman, contemplates the following:

1) Books are available on (a) the statutory citations specifying the duties of the Attorney General, and (b) the delegations of responsibilities within the Justice Department.

2) Each of the ten Division-heads in the Department will summarize in a document the status of the case-work in his Division (since most of the Department's activities are in terms of litigation).

Other supplementary materials and briefings may be put together.

Post Office

Mr. McKibbin and Mr. Sponsler are pulling together a briefing book which ought to be ready before December 15. The accomplishments of the Post Office Department will be stressed. Mr. Summerfield can be expected to take up various problems and issues (facsimile mail, obscenity, automation) directly with the Postmaster General Designate.

Interior

Mr. Kennedy and Mr. Beasley report that nothing specific has been started as yet.

Personnel information is available readily; there has recently been a codification of the delegations of authority within the Department. An existing Orientation Book for new top-level executives can be brought up to date within ten days.

The Secretary has a *personal* compilation of briefing books, one of each State and each Territory, and each containing a summary of every significant Interior Department activity and problem in that State. This is considered a personal possession and Messrs. Kennedy and Beasley doubt if the Secretary would release it for his successor's use. The same information could be re-compiled from its respective Bureau sources.

Agriculture

Administrative Assistant Secretary Ralph Roberts will have ready by November 21 a two-volume briefing notebook the table of contents of which appears under Tab 3.

This material is primarily organizational and administrative, but will include, without recommendations, a discussion of "budget issues" and of "legislative issues", the latter including a spotlight on the need for decision on the Sugar Act, which expires this coming March 31. Other Agriculture programs to be covered include the Rural Development, Mobilization Planning, and Centennial Planning.

Mr. Roberts and other Agriculture officials feel that advance written briefing materials on other programs, and especially on current problems (e.g. price supports) should be left for each Bureau Head to bring out on an individual basis.

Commerce

Assistant Secretary Moore is preparing a briefing handbook, the outline for which appears under Tab 4. The first draft will be ready December 10, the final material by December 15.

As is seen, it starts and ends with organizational and administrative matters, including an identification of important interdepartmental and public advisory committees with which the Secretary would be concerned. Its Section 5 is titled "Major Programs and Objectives"; the present intention of Commerce is to list some eight principal programs, emphasize their present status and accomplishments and point to the policy direction now current in each as in effect a recommendation for the future. Only one of these sections is expected to contain classified material.

Labor

The Secretary has not yet expressed his views, but those of Mr. Wallace, his Executive Assistant, are:

No advance materials will be prepared. The new Secretary-designate will be received courteously and his questions answered. The functions of the Department are on the statute books; the organization of the Department is in the public record; the budget of the Department can be found in the Appropriations Hearings for 1960–61.

Health, Education and Welfare

At the Secretary's direction, Messrs. Jarold Kieffer, Rufus Miles and Charles Saunders are pulling together materials following an outline circulated within the Department as early as last June (see Tab 5). What this will add up to is:

1) A new 1961 edition of the published "Handbook on Programs of HEW" (some 200 pages).

2) A memorandum on "Program decisions needed" from each of the six Bureaus of the Department. These memos, due November 21, will include recommendations as to immediate, pressing issues—some of which the Secretary may be able to settle between now and January 20.

3) A compendium of organizational materials due December 7, including an identification of some sixteen management policy issues which a new Secretary-designate will need to look into.

4) Some of the first drafts of the "10-Year Goals" Studies now being done by the Bureaus in a dozen or more program areas. Six or seven of these are moving along and may be ready with recommendations; others will have completed at least the factual staff-study stage.

5) The Secretary may have a personal series of "sign-off" papers to give to his successor which he will have prepared based on the above materials.

Bureau of the Budget

The Bureau's comprehensive preparations are well along and are summarized under Tab 6. Director Stans has not yet reviewed the material being prepared.

Office of Civil and Defense Mobilization

Governor Hoegh has just designated Mr. Emil Reutzel as in charge of pulling together appropriate advance materials. Each Assistant Director has now been asked to propose an outline of the program facts and questions which should be prepared for a new Director; the outlines will be reviewed beginning November 21 and assignments then made.

Briefings on the National Plan for Civil and Defense Mobilization would be featured and would be unclassified; Plans C and D and other OCDM activities involve high classification.

National Aeronautics and Space Administration

Dr. Glennan and Mr. Frank Phillips contemplate a full, no-holds-barred treatment of the new Administrator once he is designated and cleared for security. Dr. Glennan will personally supervise and control the briefing procedures, which he plans to include:

1) Written organizational and administrative materials on "what makes NASA tick", including biographies of top people. Due November 23.

2) Oral program briefings to be given by the top program directors. These will be general, factual, classified, will make no recommendations and are ready now.

3) A briefing on "critical problems" which Dr. Glennan will do personally, aided by some advance written materials which he personally is preparing. Problems will be identified and in some cases recommendations made.

Atomic Energy Commission

Assistant General Manager Hollingsworth and Mr. Dwight Ink point out that the Commission now has one vacancy in its membership; the designation of its Chairman is Presidential.

Assuming security clearance and assuming that the Chairman-designate is not a present Commission member, the staff will begin now (they were waiting for word) to pull together:

1) Organizational and administrative materials.

2) Program outlines, such as Raw Materials (where simplified summaries are available), Reactor Development and Weapons (complex and highly sensitive).

3) Policy questions, especially the three major ones of testing, custody and reactor development. Long papers are either ready or can be updated on each of these.

Council of Economic Advisers

Mr. Stocking points out that the Council will routinely prepare two documents which can be used for the Chairman-designate:

1) The CEA Budget justification for FY 1962 which will cover the Council's establishment, function and duties.

2) The Council's annual Report to the President on its activities which is always an appendix to the Economic Report of the President.

The Council has no "programs" of its own and the President's 1962 Economic Report will, of course, be a legacy statement of policy over-all, as well as a collection of statistical material.

Civil Service Commission

Roger Jones summarizes the Commission's plans as follows:

1) He is urging the Departments and agencies to identify for the incoming Administration the facts about the three major controls over program and policy: personnel, money and the governing statutes.

2) The Commission is assisting individual agencies on questions of personnel information.

3) Two publications are planned for the very near future:

    a) "Civil Service at Your Service"—a booklet designed for new political executives.

    b) A pamphlet explaining the benefits available to outgoing people.

4) The Career Roster of GS 16-17-18's is being accelerated to be ready in time for reference by the new Administration.

5) Specific briefing papers are being developed on particular personnel management problems. These papers will state the chief alternative approaches and their pros and cons.

The Senate Post Office and Civil Service Committee is keeping a very close track of the Commission's activities in this whole change-over field.

Federal Aviation Agency

Mr. Alan Dean, who has been designated in charge of transfer preparations, reports the following plans:

1) Two important program-management devices are always current and would be used for an Administrator-designate:

    a) The "green book" on "Program Status and Evaluation" consisting of charts and written materials on the critical program areas of interest to the Administration.

    b) The supplement to the above which is much broader and in more detail.

2) Written materials will be assembled covering organizational and administrative questions, including budget, legislative program and personnel.

3) Special memoranda will be prepared for Mr. Quesada's use with an Administrator-designate covering certain major substantive problems, e.g.: Air Cargo, the supersonic commercial aircraft, Project Friendship, and user charges.

Veterans Administration

Deputy Administrator Lamphere explains that VA plans to use its Chart Room as the focal point for briefing an Administrator-designate. Using the 100-odd currently-maintained charts around the walls, Mr. Whittier could give a full picture of budget, organization, short-range problems, and long-range problems. Each group of charts is backed up with a system of notebooks going into more details.

For management and organizational depth, the newly-completed Booz-Allen-Hamilton Management Survey of VA would be referred to.

Housing and Home Finance Agency

Mr. Lewis Williams is pulling together the material outlined under Tab 7, with a due date of December 1.

In addition, some 25-35 "problems of a new Administrator" will be identified as subjects for oral briefings under Mr. Mason's control. These will include problems of relationships with Commerce, with FNMA, with special-interest lobbies, the question of a Department of Urban Affairs, etc.

General Services Administration

Mr. Floete would personally handle the briefing of an Administrator-designate, using the following materials now on hand:

1) A row of black notebooks which he keeps currently maintained behind his desk—covering all the programs of GSA and the problems of each. (Bureau heads update these pages every two weeks; Regional Directors every month.)

2) The Eleventh Annual Report of GSA to the Congress, dated June 30, 1960, and published as a pamphlet just recently.

Mr. Floete would personally go over with a new man some of the major open questions which he would face: organization for the new Unified Federal Civil Agency Communications System, Federal office space management, relations with the military on Federal supply, stockpiling, etc. He would expect to make his own recommendations as a legacy to the incoming Administrator.

National Science Foundation

Acting Director Carothers points out that Director Waterman's term doesn't expire until 1962 and that there are no Schedule C appointments in the Foundation.

If there is to be a new Presidential Assistant for Science and Technology, however, he would expect the Foundation to provide briefing materials and this could be done from such basic resources as the current NSC "legacy" papers, several of which deal with science, as well as those of the Federal Council on Science and Technology. The current deliberations of these two groups are providing much "food" for a new Special Assistant concerned with the future of science on both the American and the world scene.

4. THE EISENHOWER YEARS—A SUMMARY

In one of his last official acts the President called for various executive departments to submit summaries of their activities during the course of his Administration. Most of these accentuated achievements while ignoring or down-playing unresolved problems. Quite typical was the State Department's summary. Most obvious by their exclusion were the pressing situations in Cuba and Laos, which consumed most of Eisenhower's time during his final days.

Assistant Secretary Gerard Smith
to Deputy Assistant Robert Merriam
December 27, 1960
[Hess Files, Eisenhower Papers.]

Dear Bob:

Herewith is an uncleared version of the paper requested in your letter of December 20. I understand that Secretary Herter has informed you he wants to go over it when he returns on January 3.

Sincerely,
Gerard C. Smith

UNITED STATES FOREIGN POLICY
UNDER THE EISENHOWER ADMINISTRATION
1953–1961

Introduction

During the past eight years while the United States has experienced stability and growth at home, abroad there have been widespread and profound changes.

Great historical forces have been at work which our country has only marginal ability to control.

Man's developing control over disease is unbalancing nature's past ratios of deaths and births. Since President Eisenhower's first inaugural, the human race has been growing at a rate of about 40 million additional persons per year. Our world has about 300 million more people as President Eisenhower leaves office than in 1953. Since 1953 the nations of the world have increased by 20%.

There are two important elements in the deep unrest and change we are witnessing around the world. Peoples are realizing that scientific and technological gains give promise for them and their children of a better life—if only the needed skills and treasure can be accumulated. There is a new and indignant awareness that although the misery of man is so, it need not continue to be so.

Just as strong is the yearning of peoples to govern themselves. Under bursting pressures for political independence, dependent territories are being transformed almost overnight into nations—some without much benefit of the nation-building process which is indispensable if they are to become responsible members of a world community.

The masses of people of the Soviet and Chinese empires, harnessed to do the work and the will of their master Communist parties, have sharply increased the power of the USSR and Red China. Although Communist imperialism has not captured any more governments since 1954, Communist hostility toward free nations has intensified.

While gradually becoming aware of the catastrophic nature of nuclear war—the recognition of which lead the US in 1946 to propose internationalization of atomic energy—the Communists have yet to show serious interest in a responsible approach to disarmament. And so the world is in a highly disturbed and dangerous situation.

In these past perilous years what have we in the State Department (USIA and ICA) been doing to preserve the security and freedom of the United States and constructively to channel, as best we can, these surging forces which are rolling over our world?

The United States has sought to strengthen collective security, deter the use of force, create international status in new frontiers of activity, progress toward safeguarded arms control, promote negotiation of outstanding international disputes, increase the role of the United Nations and make of the interdependence of a shrunken world a force for peace rather than a breeding ground for war. Each of these efforts is discussed in turn below.

A. Collective Security

Since 1953, some fifty countries have associated with the United States in regional or bilateral security pacts. These mutual security arrangements no longer are mere military alliances. They are the framework of consultative processes that day by day are steadily improving the collaboration of free nations.

During these years NATO has evolved into an effective military and political instrument enabling the Atlantic Community to thwart Soviet efforts to dominate Western Europe.[1]

In 1954, the Southeast Asia Treaty Organization was created to strengthen the determination and capability of the nations of that area to resist the expansionist thrusts of Communist China. In recent years, certain nations of the area which are not members of the Southeast Asia Treaty Organization have come to understand and appreciate its importance for the preservation of freedom.

The Anzus treaty which has strengthened the close ties between Australia, New Zealand and the U. S. is another illustration of how our security alliances contribute to the development of common purposes in other fields than military.

In 1954 at the Tenth Inter-American Conference at Caracas, there was promulgated the "Declaration of Solidarity" of the American States. It declared that the domination or control by the International Communist Movement of the political institutions of any American state would threaten us all and endanger the peace of the Americas. During recent years, the Organization of American States has further developed as an instrument of hemispheric cooperation. The August 1959 Conference of the Foreign Ministers of the American Republics in Santiago clearly demonstrated the determination of these Republics to maintain peace in the hemisphere through common action on problems creating international tensions. An outstanding example of this common action came in early 1959 when Panama was threatened by revolution fomented outside her borders. Prompt action by the Inter-American Peace Commission was an important factor in ending this threat. We are working continuously with the other American Republics in the Organization of American States and in the Inter-American Peace Commission to reduce international tensions in this Hemisphere, particularly in the Caribbean area where they are now most acute.

In the Middle East, the United States, although not a member, has strongly supported the Baghdad Pact organization which was established in 1955. Although the Government of Iraq recently indicated its withdrawal, this organization—now known as the Central Treaty Organization—remains a solid instrument of collective security for the Northern Tier of States in the Middle East.

The situation in the Middle East today is clearly improved as compared with 1958 as a result of actions by the United States, United Nations and the States in the area.

President Eisenhower's phenomenal reception during his "good will" trips has shown how significant these travels have been in the battle for the

---

[1] Witnessing the importance attached to NATO by the United States for several years the U. S. representative to the North Atlantic Council has participated in meeting of the Cabinet and NSC when in Washington.

minds of men. His world-wide reputation as a man of peace has served strikingly to strengthen the cause of peace wherever he has gone.

Most of the countries he visited had never before welcomed an American President.

The purpose of such trips by the leader of the strongest free-world country was to demonstrate tangibly and at first hand to the people of other lands that we value their friendship, and that we share their hopes and aspirations. The purpose was not to "negotiate" or to arrange treaties or take other concrete steps which are properly handled in regular diplomatic channels.

By the Declaration of Common Purpose of 1957 the US and the UK demonstrated the extremely close relation which bind our two nations.

With American support, Germany has made a rapid economic recovery and is now among our strongest allies. In France, we are witnessing an inspiring example of national renewal. Free China's extraordinary economic development is a symbol to the entire Far East of how much more freedom can do to improve the lot of people than can slavery.

B. Deterrence of Force

The United States has sought to establish the principle of renunciation of aggressive force and has shown its ability and will to deter use of force.

At the time of the Suez episode in 1956 and the Israeli-Egyptian hostilities, the United Kingdom and France, and then Israel, responding to the overwhelming opinion of the United Nations, withdrew their armed forces and accepted a United Nations solution.

When Lebanon considered itself threatened from without and appealed to the United States for emergency aid, we responded with promptness and efficiency. When the emergency was relieved by United Nations action, we promptly withdrew our forces.

In the Far East, the Chinese Communists, with Soviet backing, initiated military action in 1958 designed, as they put it, to "expel the United States" from the Western Pacific. We stood beside the Republic of China in its successful resistance to that attack.

In October 1958, the Dulles-Chiang Declaration memorialized the undertaking by the Republic of China that it would rely primarily upon peaceful principles and not upon force to secure the freeing of the mainland.

The United States and Japan signed in 1960 a new Security Treaty providing more equitable and workable relationships with this important Far Eastern ally.

C. International Status

We have sought acceptance for a new principle of international law— where national control has not been established, the nations should seek a maximum scope for international status.

Three United States proposals exemplify this approach.

1. *Polar Areas*

In April 1958, the United States proposed in the United Nations Security Council a system of international inspection of the Arctic area to reduce the danger of surprise attack over the north polar region and to reduce the danger of miscalculation. This proposal was vetoed by the Soviet Union.

In May 1958, the United States proposed that the countries which heretofore have shown particular interest in Antarctica, including the Soviet Union, join in negotiating a treaty to guarantee the peaceful use of Antarctica and continue international scientific cooperation there. The treaty is now in process of ratification.

2. *Atoms for Peace*

In his famous address at the United Nations on December 8, 1953, President Eisenhower proposed a method to "find the way by which the miraculous inventiveness of man shall not be dedicated to his death, but consecrated to his life."

Under the "Atoms for Peace" program, we have negotiated bilateral agreements with some forty nations. Research reactor grants have been approved for seventeen nations. Negotiations are under way with others. We have developed close and constructive relations with EURATOM, the Atomic Energy Community of France, Germany, Italy, Netherlands, Belgium, and Luxembourg.

The International Atomic Energy Agency, proposed by President Eisenhower, designed to promote peaceful uses of atomic energy around the world, was finally established in 1957. It gives promise of the beginnings of an international approach to the problems of atomic energy.

3. *Outer Space*

In January 1958, President Eisenhower proposed to the Soviet Union "that we agree that outer space should be used only for peaceful purposes." This bilateral proposal was subsequently advanced in the broader forum of the United Nations, since it is of concern to all nations, and an *ad hoc* committee on peaceful uses of outer space was created. The Soviet Union at first refused to participate, but was eventually brought to join, in December 1959, a United Nations 24-member committee on the peaceful uses of outer space. This committee is responsible for studying means for giving effect to programs in peaceful uses of outer space and to make preparations for an international conference in 1961.

During the past eight years the United States has proposed several comprehensive disarmament programs which the Soviet Union has rejected out of hand.

The U.S. has also proposed a number of specific arms control measures which met a similar fate.

The test suspension negotiations which at one time gave promise of success after many months have yet to reach any conclusion.

D. International Negotiation

India-Pakistan Dispute

The United States has encouraged and assisted the World Bank in the successful settlement of the serious dispute between India and Pakistan over the Indus Waters.

Negotiations with the Communists

1. We made the Korean armistice which ended the hostilities in Korea.

2. We participated in the Geneva Conference of 1954 which ended the hostilities in Indochina.

3. We continue to seek in the Warsaw talks with the Chinese Communists to assure that in the Taiwan area force should not be relied upon by either side to bring about the reunification of China.

4. We joined with the Soviet Union in concluding the Austrian Peace Treaty which liberated Austria.

5. In 1955, President Eisenhower met with the Soviet leaders at the Summit in Geneva. At that time, he presented his famous "Open Skies" proposal.

6. In 1958, we made a comprehensive agreement with the Soviet Union for exchanges in the fields of culture, technology and education. This agreement operated successfully for two years and recently has been extended for two more.

We have endeavored to bring home to the people of the USSR a true picture of the United States. Vice President Nixon's trip to the Soviet Union in 1959 served to emphasize directly to the Soviet people the desire of the United States for peace and friendship.

7. In November 1958, the Soviet Union threatened to take unilateral action against Western rights in Berlin by May 1959 unless the three Western powers accepted the Soviet proposal for a so-called free city. The United States, United Kingdom and France refused, with full NATO support, to compromise their rights or to negotiate under duress. When the Soviet Union then indicated that its deadline was of no particular significance, the three Western powers agreed to negotiate concerning the question of Germany, including Berlin and a peace treaty, at a Foreign Ministers' Conference. I spent ten weeks in Geneva in 1959 seeking a settlement of the German problem and, failing that, of a *modus vivendi* on Berlin. This conference clarified and narrowed our differences with the Soviet Union but did not produce agreement. West Berlin remains free.

At the invitation of President Eisenhower the Chairman of the Council of Ministers of the USSR visited the United States in 1959 and saw at first hand the power and the peacefulness of the American people.

In the spring of 1960 the United States stood ready to meet the Soviet leader at the planned Summit meeting in Paris. Soviet policy torpedoed the meeting.

E. United Nations

In the last eight years, the United States has repeatedly taken the lead in trying to strengthen the United Nations and the processes of international cooperation which the United Nations represents. A few examples follow.

1. In December, 1953, President Eisenhower proposed the "Atoms for Peace" program to the United Nations.

2. In the economic field, we played a leading role in bringing about two new entities linked with the United Nations: the International Finance Corporation, and the Special Fund. The International Finance Corporation, which came into being in July 1956 as an affiliate of the World Bank, invests in private enterprise abroad, thus stimulating the vital private sector of developing economies. The Special Fund, which was set up by the United Nations General Assembly, provides funds for broad regional and basic technical assistance and survey projects more extensive than those financed by the United Nations Technical Assistance Program.

3. The United States also took the lead at the General Assembly in creating a committee on outer space.

4. We have continued to try to strengthen the United Nations Procedures. Thus in January 1958 the United States renewed its proposal to restrict use of the veto in the Security Council. This offer was refused by the Soviet Union.

5. When a Middle Eastern crisis arose in 1958, we promptly notified the United Nations of the action that we were taking in Lebanon to meet that crisis and called for an emergency session of the General Assembly to deal with the crisis. President Eisenhower proposed to counter the immediate threat in Lebanon and Jordan, and also long-range measures to improve basic conditions in the Middle East: An Arab Development Institution, a stand-by United Nations force, and possibly a United Nations study of Middle Eastern arms control.

6. We cooperated vigorously with other United Nations in the General Assembly to resist Soviet attempts to weaken or destroy the Organization during the Congo crisis. We have supported the UN's complex task of keeping the peace in chaotic Congo.

7. We have strongly supported the General Assembly in the adoption of resolutions condemning offenses against mankind, such as the wholesale murder of the people of Tibet by the Chinese Communists and the brutal Soviet repression in Hungary.

8. We have welcomed to the community of nations the new countries of Africa.

From the outset of this Administration the United States Ambassador to the United Nations has sat in the President's Cabinet, an arrangement which was inaugurated to strengthen the Ambassador's hand in carrying out his responsibilities.

In recent years, there has been a growing clarification of understanding around the world of the real purpose of the Communist leaders—to subject all the world to the dominant influence and control of international Communism. In the Middle East, the deadly designs of Communism are now far more clearly realized than a few years ago. Brutal Chinese Communist repression in Tibet and border incursions and demands against India have brought home aggressive Communist designs more clearly to the peoples of South Asia. In Southeast Asia, liberty-loving peoples are struggling successfully to remain masters in their newly built national homes. In Europe, there are a number of inspiring examples of national renewal and recession of Communist influence.

F. Interdependence

President Eisenhower's policies have been based on a belief that economic growth and interdependence are necessary conditions for stable and free nations. Here are a number of things that the Eisenhower Administration has done in the last eight years to promote that growth and interdependence:

1. It has strongly supported the Reciprocal Trade Agreements Program. At President Eisenhower's request the Congress in 1958 strengthened and extended this program for a period of four years, the longest single extension during the 25-year history of the program. The value of American foreign trade (excluding military exports) in 1953 was 23.2 billion and in 1959 was 31.5 billion.

2. In 1957 the Congress, at the request of President Eisenhower, established the United States Development Loan Fund with a capitalization of $300 million. This was a major step to meet the needs of less developed countries for loans on terms less rigorous than those offered from existing sources. In 1958 and 1959 the Congress appropriated $1.1 billion more for the Development Loan Fund. It was the first United States financial institution set up specifically to help less developed countries. In its short life the Fund has made a significant contribution to economic growth. Qualifying projects awaiting its review are far more numerous than the Fund can handle.

3. The United States has also moved vigorously to encourage the flow of private investment to less developed and other free nations. Under the Eisenhower Investment Guarantee Program which provides insurance against noncommercial risks nearly 40 nations have signed agreements and considerably over $200 million in insurance contracts have been issued. The United States has negotiated and sought to negotiate treaties designed to create more favorable conditions for private investment abroad. We have encouraged and assisted the creation in foreign countries of development banks to make loans to private enterprise and of local productivity centers

to render that enterprise more productive. We encouraged the creation in 1955 of the International Finance Corporation, as an affiliate of the World Bank, to make investments in private enterprise abroad.

4. In February 1959, at presidential request, the Congress authorized $3.175 and $1.375 billion increases in the United States subscriptions to the World Bank and International Fund.

5. The President also authorized the Secretary of the Treasury to discuss with other governments the possible establishment of an International Development Association, as an affiliate of the World Bank. These discussions were fruitful, and we may expect to see this agency in operation in the near future, helping to mobilize free world resources to meet the less developed countries' need for financing on flexible terms.

6. At US initiative, eighteen European nations have joined Canada and the United States in reconstituting the Organization for European Economic Cooperation. This organization will permit more effective cooperation in promoting sound economic growth in the free world and in mobilizing the resources of its industrialized members to help the newly-developing lands.

7. The United States took the lead in establishment of an institution to promote economic development in Latin America. On April 9, 1959, the charter of a $1 billion Inter-American Bank was initialed in Washington. The ratification of this agreement by the United States and by all the other American states—except Cuba—has brought into being a sizeable new source of funds for economic development loans to our good neighbors. The Bank's charter also provides for assisting in the development of managerial and technical skills, and the Bank will assist in social development projects where necessary.

In the Act of Bogota (1960) we joined with Latin American states to assist in a large-scale attack on the problem of improving living standards.

8. In August 1958, President Eisenhower offered the cooperation of the United States in the establishment of an Arab regional development financing program if the Middle Eastern states concerned were prepared to support such a venture. Exchanges of views among these states have taken place and the initiative now lies with them.

9. A Common Market for Europe has long been officially supported by President Eisenhower and in January 1959 the six-nation Common Market of Western Europe became a reality. Measures have also been taken to create an area of freer trade among seven other nations of Western Europe. In addition, Western European currencies have become more freely exchangeable and there is a strong movement for broader economic cooperation in Western Europe. The support of the United States played no small part in these accomplishments.

10. The United States has also moved to encourage and participate in the study of key raw material problems of particular concern to less developed countries. Through our good offices and on our initiative, the International

Coffee Study Group was established in June 1958 to consider possible means of dealing with problems arising in international trade of coffee. Through this study group the Mexico City Emergency Coffee Agreement was continued and expanded to consider the present imbalance in world coffee supply and demand. The United States at the ECOSOC meeting in July 1958 agreed also to become a member of the Commission on International Commodity Trade, which considers general problems relating to international trade in basic commodities.

11. On the initiative of President Eisenhower an International Food for Peace Conference was held in May 1959 to discuss ways and means of utilizing wheat to relieve hunger and to promote economic development among the less developed countries of the free world. It was participated in by the five major wheat exporting countries. It established a Food for Peace Wheat Utilization Committee to consider specific problems, such as, how to make more effective use of wheat in improving living standards, in raising nutritional levels, and in strengthening the economies of free countries. This committee met in June. At the conclusion of the meeting the other wheat exporting countries expressed their willingness to cooperate to the fullest possible extent in carrying out the objectives of the President's Food for Peace program.

The President's address at the United Nations General Assembly, September 22, 1960, contained a five-point program designed to promote the security and well-being of the new African nations.

12. Parallel with these new initiatives, the Eisenhower Administration has continued vigorously to support and strengthen the Mutual Security Program, which provides economic and military aid to free countries around the world.

13. The Administration has moved energetically and successfully toward eliminating our unfavorable balance of trade with other nations. At our urging, more than a dozen nations have removed trade restrictions on American goods, and several others have indicated an intention to take similar action.

In conclusion, President Eisenhower's foreign policy rests on two simple propositions: We want peace, liberty and well-being for ourselves; and we cannot be sure of peace, liberty and well-being unless other nations also have them.

Eisenhower used his last State of the Union Message to review his eight years in office. In methodical fashion he cataloged the major domestic achievements and foreign policy decisions of his Administration.

State of the Union Message by President Eisenhower
January 12, 1961

[*Public Papers of the Presidents: 1960–61* (Washington, 1961), 913–30.]

To the Congress of the United States:

Once again it is my Constitutional duty to assess the state of the Union.

On each such previous occasion during these past eight years I have outlined a forward course designed to achieve our mutual objective—a better America in a world of peace. This time my function is different.

The American people, in free election, have selected new leadership which soon will be entrusted with the management of our government. A new President shortly will lay before you his proposals to shape the future of our great land. To him, every citizen, whatever his political beliefs, prayerfully extends best wishes for good health and for wisdom and success in coping with the problems that confront our Nation.

For my part, I should like, first, to express to you of the Congress, my appreciation of your devotion to the common good and your friendship over these difficult years. I will carry with me pleasant memories of this association in endeavors profoundly significant to all our people.

We have been through a lengthy period in which the control over the executive and legislative branches of government has been divided between our two great political parties. Differences, of course we have had, particularly in domestic affairs. But in a united determination to keep this Nation strong and free and to utilize our vast resources for the advancement of all mankind, we have carried America to unprecedented heights.

For this cooperative achievement I thank the American people and those in the Congress of both parties who have supported programs in the interest of our country.

I should also like to give special thanks for the devoted service of my associates in the Executive Branch and the hundreds of thousands of career employees who have implemented our diverse government programs.

My second purpose is to review briefly the record of these past eight years in the hope that, out of the sum of these experiences, lessons will emerge that are useful to our Nation. Supporting this review are detailed reports from the several agencies and departments, all of which are now or will shortly be available to the Congress.

Throughout the world the years since 1953 have been a period of profound change. The human problems in the world grow more acute hour by hour; yet new gains in science and technology continually extend the promise of a better life. People yearn to be free, to govern themselves; yet a third of the people of the world have no freedom, do not govern themselves. The world recognizes the catastrophic nature of nuclear war; yet it sees the wondrous potential of nuclear peace.

During the period, the United States has forged ahead under a constructive foreign policy. The continuing goal is peace, liberty, and well-being—for others as well as ourselves. The aspirations of all peoples are one—peace with justice in freedom. Peace can only be attained collectively as peoples everywhere unite in their determination that liberty and well-being come to all mankind.

Yet while we have worked to advance national aspirations for freedom, a divisive force has been at work to divert that aspiration into dangerous channels. The Communist movement throughout the world exploits the natural striving of all to be free and attempts to subjugate men rather than free them. These activities have caused and are continuing to cause grave troubles in the world.

Here at home these have been times for careful adjustment of our economy from the artificial impetus of a hot war to constructive growth in a precarious peace. While building a new economic vitality without inflation, we have also increased public expenditures to keep abreast of the needs of a growing population and its attendant new problems, as well as our added international responsibilities. We have worked toward these ends in a context of shared responsibility—conscious of the need for maximum scope to private effort and for State and local, as well as Federal, governmental action.

Success in designing and executing national purposes, domestically and abroad, can only come from a steadfast resolution that integrity in the operation of government and in our relations with each other be fully maintained. Only in this way could our spiritual goals be fully advanced.

Foreign Policy

On January 20, 1953, when I took office, the United States was at war. Since the signing of the Korean Armistice in 1953, Americans have lived in peace in highly troubled times.

During the 1956 Suez crisis, the United States government strongly supported United Nations' action—resulting in the ending of the hostilities in Egypt.

Again in 1958, peace was preserved in the Middle East despite new discord. Our government responded to the request of the friendly Lebanese Government for military help, and promptly withdrew American forces as soon as the situation was stabilized.

In 1958 our support of the Republic of China during the all-out bombardment of Quemoy restrained the Communist Chinese from attempting to invade the off-shore islands.

Although, unhappily, Communist penetration of Cuba is real and poses a serious threat, Communist dominated regimes have been deposed in Guatemala and Iran. The occupation of Austria has ended and the Trieste question has been settled.

Despite constant threats to its integrity, West Berlin has remained free.

Important advances have been made in building mutual security arrangements—which lie at the heart of our hopes for future peace and security in the world. The Southeast Asia Treaty Organization has been established; the NATO alliance has been militarily strengthened; the Organization of American States has been further developed as an instrument of inter-American cooperation: the Anzus treaty has strengthened ties with Australia and New Zealand, and a mutual security treaty with Japan has been signed. In addition, the CENTO pact has been concluded, and while we are not officially a member of this alliance we have participated closely in its deliberations.

The "Atoms for Peace" proposal to the United Nations led to the creation of the International Atomic Energy Agency. Our policy has been to push for enforceable programs of inspection against surprise attack, suspension of nuclear testing, arms reduction, and peaceful use of outer space.

The United Nations has been vigorously supported in all of its actions, including the condemnations of the wholesale murder of the people of Tibet by the Chinese Communists and the brutal Soviet repression of the people of Hungary, as well as the more recent UN actions in the Congo.

The United States took the initiative in negotiating the significant treaty to guarantee the peaceful use of vast Antarctica.

The United States Information Agency has been transformed into a greatly improved medium for explaining our policies and actions to audiences overseas, answering the lies of communist propaganda, and projecting a clearer image of American life and culture.

Cultural, technological and educational exchanges with the Soviet Union have been encouraged, and a comprehensive agreement was made which authorized, among other things, the distribution of our Russian language magazine Amerika and the highly successful American Exhibition in Moscow.

This country has continued to withhold recognition of Communist China and to oppose vigorously the admission of this belligerent and unrepentant nation into the United Nations. Red China has yet to demonstrate that it deserves to be considered a "peace-loving" nation.

With communist imperialism held in check, constructive actions were undertaken to strengthen the economies of free world nations. The United States government has given sturdy support to the economic and technical assistance activities of the UN. This country stimulated a doubling of the capital of the World Bank and a 50 percent capital increase in the International Monetary Fund. The Development Loan Fund and the International Development Association were established. The United States also took the lead in creating the Inter-American Development Bank.

Vice President Nixon, Secretaries of State Dulles and Herter and I travelled extensively through the world for the purpose of strengthening the cause of peace, freedom, and international understanding. So rewarding were these visits that their very success became a significant factor in causing the Soviet Union to wreck the planned Summit Conference of 1960.

These vital programs must go on. New tactics will have to be developed, of course, to meet new situations, but the underlying principles should be constant. Our great moral and material commitments to collective security, deterrence of force, international law, negotiations that lead to self-enforcing agreements, and the economic interdependence of free nations should remain the cornerstone of a foreign policy that will ultimately bring permanent peace with justice in freedom to all mankind. The continuing need of all free nations today is for each to recognize clearly the essentiality of an unbreakable bond among themselves based upon a complete dedication to the principles of collective security, effective cooperation and peace with justice.

National Defense

For the first time in our nation's history we have consistently maintained in peacetime, military forces of a magnitude sufficient to deter and if need be to destroy predatory forces in the world.

Tremendous advances in strategic weapons systems have been made in the past eight years. Not until 1953 were expenditures on long-range ballistic missile programs even as much as a million dollars a year; today we spend ten times as much each day on these programs as was spent in all of 1952.

No guided ballistic missiles were operational at the beginning of 1953. Today many types give our armed forces unprecedented effectiveness. The explosive power of our weapons systems for all purposes is almost inconceivable.

Today the United States has operational ATLAS missiles which can strike a target 5000 miles away in a half-hour. The POLARIS weapons system became operational last fall and the TITAN is scheduled to become so this year. Next year, more than a year ahead of schedule, a vastly improved ICBM, the solid propellant MINUTEMAN, is expected to be ready.

Squadrons of accurate Intermediate Range Ballistic Missiles are now operational. The THOR and JUPITER IRBM, based in forward areas, can hit targets 1500 miles away in 18 minutes.

Aircraft which fly at speeds faster than sound were still in a developmental stage eight years ago. Today American fighting planes go twice the speed of sound. And either our B–58 Medium Range Jet Bomber or our B–52 Long Range Jet Bomber can carry more explosive power than was used by all combatants in World War II—Allies and Axis combined.

Eight years ago we had no nuclear-powered ships. Today 49 nuclear warships have been authorized. Of these, 14 have been commissioned, including three of the revolutionary POLARIS submarines. Our nuclear submarines have cruised under the North Pole and circumnavigated the earth while submerged. Sea warfare has been revolutionized, and the United States is far and away the leader.

Our tactical air units overseas and our aircraft carriers are alert; Army units, guarding the frontiers of freedom in Europe and the Far East, are in the highest state of readiness in peacetime history; our Marines, a third of whom are deployed in the Far East, are constantly prepared for action; our Reserve establishment has maintained high standards of proficiency, and the Ready Reserve now numbers over 2½ million citizen-soldiers.

The Department of Defense, a young and still evolving organization, has twice been improved and the line of command has been shortened in order to meet the demands of modern warfare. These major reorganizations have provided a more effective structure for unified planning and direction of the vast defense establishment. Gradual improvements in its structure and procedures are to be expected.

United States civil defense and nonmilitary defense capacity has been greatly strengthened and these activities have been consolidated in one Federal agency.

The defense forces of our Allies now number five million men, several thousand combatant ships, and over 25,000 aircraft. Programs to strengthen these allies have been consistently supported by the Administration. U.S. military assistance goes almost exclusively to friendly nations on the rim of the communist world. This American contribution to nations who have the will to defend their freedom, but insufficient means, should be vigorously continued. Combined with our Allies, the free world now has a far stronger shield than we could provide alone.

Since 1953, our defense policy has been based on the assumption that the international situation would require heavy defense expenditures for an indefinite period to come, probably for years. In this protracted struggle, good management dictates that we resist overspending as resolutely as we oppose underspending. Every dollar uselessly spent on military mechanisms decreases our total strength and, therefore, our security. We must not return to the "crash-program" psychology of the past when each new feint by the Communists was responded to in panic. The "bomber gap" of several years ago was always a fiction, and the "missile gap" shows every sign of being the same.

The nation can ill afford to abandon a national policy which provides for a fully adequate and steady level of effort, designed for the long pull; a fast adjustment to new scientific and technological advances; a balanced force of such strength as to deter general war, to effectively meet local situations and to retaliate to attack and destroy the attacker; and a strengthened system of free world collective security.

The Economy

The expanding American economy passed the half-trillion dollar mark in gross national product early in 1960. The Nation's output of goods and services is now nearly 25 percent higher than in 1952.

In 1959, the average American family had an income of $6,520, 15 percent higher in dollars of constant buying power than in 1952, and the real wages of American factory workers have risen 20 percent during the past eight years. These facts reflect the rising standard of individual and family well-being enjoyed by Americans.

Our Nation benefits also from a remarkable improvement in general industrial peace through strengthened processes of free collective bargaining. Time lost since 1952 because of strikes has been half that lost in the eight years prior to that date. Legislation now requires that union members have the opportunity for full participation in the affairs of their unions. The Administration supported the Landrum-Griffin Act, which I believe is greatly helpful to the vast bulk of American Labor and its leaders, and also is a major step in getting racketeers and gangsters out of labor-management affairs.

The economic security of working men and women has been strengthened by an extension of unemployment insurance coverage to 2.5 million ex-servicemen, 2.4 million Federal employees, and 1.2 million employees of small businesses, and by a strengthening of the Railroad Unemployment Insurance Act. States have been encouraged to improve their unemployment compensation benefits, so that today average weekly benefits are 40 percent higher than in 1953.

Determined efforts have improved workers' safety standards. Enforceable safety standards have been established for longshoremen and ship repair workers; Federal Safety Councils have been increased from 14 to over 100; safety awards have been initiated, and a national construction safety program has been developed.

A major factor in strengthening our competitive enterprise system, and promoting economic growth, has been the vigorous enforcement of antitrust laws over the last eight years and a continuing effort to reduce artificial restraints on competition and trade and enhance our economic liberties. This purpose was also significantly advanced in 1953 when, as one of the first acts of this Administration, restrictive wage and price controls were ended.

An additional measure to strengthen the American system of competitive enterprise was the creation of the Small Business Administration in 1953 to assist existing small businesses and encourage new ones. This agency has approved over $1 billion in loans, initiated a new program to provide long-term capital for small businesses, aided in setting aside $3½ billion in government contracts for award to small business concerns, and brought to the attention of individual businessmen, through programs of information and education, new developments in management and production techniques. Since 1952, important tax revisions have been made to encourage small businesses.

Many major improvements in the Nation's transportation system have been made:

—After long years of debate, the dream of a great St. Lawrence Seaway, opening the heartland of America to ocean commerce, has been fulfilled.

—The new Federal Aviation Agency is fostering greater safety in air travel.

—The largest public construction program in history—the 41,000 mile national system of Interstate and Defense highways—has been pushed rapidly forward. Twenty-five percent of this system is now open to traffic.

Efforts to help every American build a better life have included also a vigorous program for expanding our trade with other nations. A 4-year renewal of the Reciprocal Trade Agreements Act was passed in 1958, and a continuing and rewarding effort has been made to persuade other countries to remove restrictions against our exports. A new export expansion program was launched in 1960, inaugurating improvement of export credit insurance and broadening research and information programs to awaken Americans to business opportunities overseas. These actions and generally prosperous conditions abroad have helped push America's export trade to a level of $20 billion in 1960.

Although intermittent declines in economic activity persist as a problem in our enterprise system, recent downturns have been moderate and of short duration. There is, however, little room for complacency. Currently our economy is operating at high levels, but unemployment rates are higher than any of us would like, and chronic pockets of high unemployment persist. Clearly, continued sound and broadly shared economic growth remains a major national objective toward which we must strive through joint private and public efforts.

If government continues to work to assure every American the fullest opportunity to develop and utilize his ability and talent, it will be performing one of its most vital functions, that of advancing the welfare and protecting the dignity, rights, and freedom of all Americans.

Government Finance and Administration

In January 1953, the consumer's dollar was worth only 52 cents in terms of the food, clothing, shelter and other items it would buy compared to 1939. Today, the inflationary spiral which had raised the cost of living by 36 percent between 1946 and 1952 has all but ceased and the value of the dollar virtually stabilized.

In 1954 we had the largest tax cut in history, amounting to $7.4 billion annually, of which over 62 percent went to individuals mostly in the small income brackets.

This Administration has directed constant efforts toward fiscal responsibility. Balanced budgets have been sought when the economy was advancing, and a rigorous evaluation of spending programs has been maintained at all times. Resort to deficit financing in prosperous times could easily erode international confidence in the dollar and contribute to inflation at home. In this belief, I shall submit a balanced budget for fiscal 1962 to the Congress next week.

There has been a firm policy of reducing government competition with private enterprise. This has resulted in the discontinuance of some 2,000 commercial industrial installations and in addition the curtailment of approximately 550 industrial installations operated directly by government agencies.

Also an aggressive surplus disposal program has been carried on to identify and dispose of unneeded government-owned real property. This has resulted in the addition of a substantial number of valuable properties to local tax rolls, and a significant monetary return to the government.

Earnest and persistent attempts have been made to strengthen the position of State and local governments and thereby to stop the dangerous drift toward centralization of governmental power in Washington.

Significant strides have been made in increasing the effectiveness of government. Important new agencies have been established, such as the Department of Health, Education, and Welfare, the Federal Aviation Agency, and the National Aeronautics and Space Administration. The Council of Economic Advisers was reconstituted.

The operation of our postal system has been modernized to get better and more efficient service. Modernized handling of local mail now brings next-day delivery to 168 million people in our population centers, expanded carrier service now accommodates 9.3 million families in the growing suburbs, and 1.4 million families have been added to the rural delivery service. Common sense dictates that the Postal Service should be on a self-financing basis.

The concept of a trained and dedicated government career service has been strengthened by the provision of life and health insurance benefits, a vastly improved retirement system, a new merit promotion program, and the first effective incentive awards program. With no sacrifice in efficiency, Federal civilian employment since 1953 has been reduced by over a quarter of a million persons.

I am deeply gratified that it was under the urging of this Administration that Alaska and Hawaii became our 49th and 50th States.

Agriculture

Despite the difficulties of administering Congressional programs which apply outmoded prescriptions and which aggravate rather than solve problems, the past eight years brought notable advances in agriculture.

Total agricultural assets are approximately $200 billion—up $36 billion in eight years.

Farm owner equities are at the near record high of $174 billion.

Farm ownership is at a record high with fewer farmers in a tenant and sharecropper status than at any time in our nation's history.

The "Food-for-Peace" program has demonstrated how surplus of American food and fiber can be effectively used to feed and clothe the needy abroad. Aided by this humanitarian program, total agricultural exports have grown from $2.8 billion in 1953 to an average of about $4 billion annually for the past three years. For 1960, exports are estimated at $4.5 billion, the highest volume on record. Under the Food-for-Peace program, the largest wheat transaction in history was consummated with India in 1960.

The problems of low-income farm families received systematic attention for the first time in the Rural Development Program. This program has gone forward in 39 States, yielding higher incomes and a better living for rural people most in need.

The Rural Electrification Administration has helped meet the growing demands for power and telephones in agricultural areas. Ninety-seven percent of all farms now have central station electric power. Dependence upon Federal financing should no longer be necessary.

The Farm Credit Administration has been made an independent agency more responsive to the farmer's needs.

The search for new uses for our farm abundance and to develop new crops for current needs has made major progress. Agricultural research appropriations have increased by 171 percent since 1953.

Farmers are being saved approximately $80 million a year by the repeal in 1956 of Federal taxes on gasoline used in tractors and other machinery.

Since 1953, appropriations have been doubled for county agents, home agents and the Extension Service.

Eligibility for Social Security benefits has been extended to farmers and their families.

Yet in certain aspects our agricultural surplus situation is increasingly grave. For example, our wheat stocks now total 1.3 billion bushels. If we did not harvest one bushel of wheat in this coming year, we would still have all we could eat, all we could sell abroad, all we could give away, and still have a substantial carryover. Extraordinary costs are involved just in management and disposal of this burdensome surplus. Obviously important adjustments must still come. Congress must enact additional legislation to permit wheat and other farm commodities to move into regular marketing channels in an orderly manner and at the same time afford the needed price protection to the farmer. Only then will agriculture again be free, sound, and profitable.

Natural Resources

New emphasis has been placed on the care of our national parks. A ten year development program of our National Park System—Mission 66—was initiated and 633,000 acres of park land have been added since 1953.

Appropriations for fish and wildlife operations have more than doubled. Thirty-five new refuges, containing 11,342,000 acres, have been added to the national wildlife management system.

Our Nation's forests have been improved at the most rapid rate in history.

The largest sustained effort in water resources development in our history has taken place. In the field of reclamation alone, over 50 new projects, or project units, have been authorized since 1953—including the billion dollar Colorado River Storage Project. When all these projects have been completed they will have a storage capacity of nearly 43 million acre-feet—an increase of 50 percent over the Bureau of Reclamation's storage capacity in mid-1953. In addition, since 1953 over 450 new navigation flood control and multiple purpose projects of the Corps of Engineers have been started, costing nearly 6 billion dollars.

Soil and water conservation has been advanced as never before. One hundred forty-one projects are now being constructed under the Watershed Protection Program.

Hydroelectric power has been impressively developed through a policy which recognizes that the job to be done requires comprehensive development by Federal, State, and local governments and private enterprise. Teamwork is essential to achieve this objective.

The Federal Columbia River power system has grown from two multipurpose dams with a 2.6 million kilowatt capacity to 17 multipurpose projects completed or under construction with an ultimate installed capacity of 8.1 million kilowatts. After years of negotiation, a Columbia River Storage Development agreement with Canada now opens the way for early realization of unparalleled power, flood control and resource conservation benefits for the Pacific Northwest. A treaty implementing this agreement will shortly be submitted to the Senate.

A farsighted and highly successful program for meeting urgent water needs is being carried out by converting salt water to fresh water. A 75 percent reduction in the cost of this process has already been realized.

Continuous resource development is essential for our expanding economy. We must continue vigorous, combined Federal, State and private programs, at the same time preserving to the maximum extent possible our natural and scenic heritage for future generations.

Education, Science, and Technology

The National Defense Education Act of 1958 is already a milestone in the history of American education. It provides broad opportunities for the intellectual development of all children by strengthening courses of study in science, mathematics, and foreign languages, by developing new graduate programs to train additional teachers, and by providing loans for young people who need financial help to go to college.

The Administration proposed on numerous occasions a broad new five-year program of Federal aid to help overcome the classroom shortage in public elementary and secondary schools. Recommendations were also made to give assistance to colleges and universities for the construction of academic and residential buildings to meet future enrollment increases.

This Administration greatly expanded Federal loans for building dormitories for students, teachers, and nurses training, a program assisting in the construction of approximately 200,000 living accommodations during the past 8 years.

There has been a vigorous acceleration of health, resource and education programs designed to advance the role of the American Indian in our society. Last fall, for example, 91 percent of the Indian children between the ages of 6 and 18 on reservations were enrolled in school. This is a rise of 12 percent since 1953.

In the field of science and technology, startling strides have been made by the new National Aeronautics and Space Administration. In little more than two years, NASA has successfully launched meteorological satellites, such as Tiros I and Tiros II, that promise to revolutionize methods of weather forecasting; demonstrated the feasibility of satellites for global communications by the successful launching of Echo I; produced an enormous amount of valuable scientific data, such as the discovery of the Van Allen Radiation Belt, successfully launched deep space probes that maintained communication over the greatest range man has ever tracked; and made real progress toward the goal of manned space flights.

These achievements unquestionably make us preeminent today in space exploration for the betterment of mankind. I believe the present organizational arrangements in this area, with the revisions proposed last year, are completely adequate for the tasks ahead.

Americans can look forward to new achievements in space exploration. The near future will hold such wonders as the orbital flight of an astronaut, the landing of instruments on the moon, the launching of the powerful giant Saturn rocket vehicles, and the reconnaissance of Mars and Venus by unmanned vehicles.

The application of atomic energy to industry, agriculture, and medicine has progressed from hope and experiment to reality. American industry and agriculture are making increasing use of radioisotopes to improve manufacturing, testing, and crop-raising. Atomic energy has improved the ability of the healing professions to combat disease, and holds promise for an eventual increase in man's life span.

Education, science, technology and balanced programs of every kind— these are the roadways to progress. With appropriate Federal support, the States and localities can assure opportunities for achieving excellence at all levels of the educational system; and with the Federal government continuing to give wholehearted support to basic scientific research and technology, we can expect to maintain our position of leadership in the world.

Civil Rights

The first consequential Federal Civil Rights legislation in 85 years was enacted by Congress on recommendation of the Administration in 1957 and 1960.

A new Civil Rights Division in the Department of Justice has already moved to enforce constitutional rights in such areas as voting and the elimination of Jim Crow laws.

Greater equality of job opportunity in Federal employment and employment with Federal contractors has been effectively provided through the President's Committees on Government Contracts and Government Employment Practices.

The Civil Rights Commission has undertaken important surveys in the fields of housing, voting, and education.

Segregation has been abolished in the Armed Forces, in Veterans' Hospitals, in all Federal employment, and throughout the District of Columbia— administratively accomplished progress in this field that is unmatched in America's recent history.

This pioneering work in civil rights must go on. Not only because discrimination is morally wrong, but also because its impact is more than national—it is world-wide.

Health and Welfare

Federal medical research expenditures have increased more than fourfold since 1954.

A vast variety of the approaches known to medical science has been explored to find better methods of treatment and prevention of major diseases, particularly heart diseases, cancer, and mental illness.

The control of air and water pollution has been greatly strengthened.

Americans now have greater protection against harmful, unclean, or misrepresented foods, drugs, or cosmetics through a strengthened Food and Drug Administration and by new legislation which requires that food additives be proved safe for human consumption before use.

A newly established Federal Radiation Council, along with the Department of Health, Education, and Welfare, analyzes and coordinates information regarding radiological activities which affect the public health.

Medical manpower has been increased by Federal grants for teaching and research.

Construction of new medical facilities has been stepped up and extended to include nursing homes, diagnostic and treatment centers, and rehabilitation facilities.

The vocational rehabilitation program has been significantly expanded. About 90,000 handicapped people are now being rehabilitated annually so they are again able to earn their own living with self-respect and dignity.

New legislation provides for better medical care for the needy aged, including those older persons, who, while otherwise self-sufficient, need help in meeting their health care costs. The Administration recommended a major expansion of this effort.

The coverage of the Social Security Act has been broadened since 1953 to make 11 million additional people eligible for retirement, disability or survivor benefits for themselves or their dependents, and the Social Security benefits have been substantially improved.

Grants to the States for maternal and child welfare services have been increased.

The States, aided by Federal grants, now assist some 6 million needy people through the programs of Old Age Assistance, Aid to Dependent Children, Aid to the Blind, and Aid to the Totally and Permanently Disabled.

Housing and Urban Development

More houses have been built during the past eight years—over nine million—than during any previous eight years in history.

An historic new approach—Urban Renewal—now replaces piecemeal thrusts at slum pockets and urban blight. Communities engaged in urban renewal have doubled and renewal projects have more than tripled since 1953. An estimated 68 projects in 50 cities will be completed by the end of the current fiscal year; another 577 projects will be underway, and planning for 310 more will be in process. A total of $2 billion in Federal grants will ultimately be required to finance these 955 projects.

New programs have been initiated to provide more and better housing for elderly people. Approximately 25,000 units especially designed for the elderly have been built, started, or approved in the past three years.

For the first time, because of Federal help and encouragement, 90 metropolitan areas and urban regions and 1140 smaller towns throughout the country are making comprehensive development plans for their future growth and development.

American communities have been helped to plan water and sanitation systems and schools through planning advances for 1600 public works projects with a construction cost of nearly $2 billion.

Mortgage insurance on individual homes has been greatly expanded. During the past eight years, the Federal Housing Administration alone insured over 2½ million home mortgages valued at $27 billion, and in addition, insured more than ten million property improvement loans.

The Federal government must continue to provide leadership in order to make our cities and communities better places in which to live, work, and raise families, but without usurping rightful local authority, replacing individual responsibility, or stifling private initiative.

Immigration

Over 32,000 victims of Communist tyranny in Hungary were brought to our shores, and at this time our country is working to assist refugees from tyranny in Cuba.

Since 1953, the waiting period for naturalization applicants has been reduced from 18 months to 45 days.

The Administration also has made legislative recommendations to liberalize existing restrictions upon immigration while still safeguarding the national interest. It is imperative that our immigration policy be in the finest American tradition of providing a haven for oppressed peoples and fully in accord with our obligation as a leader of the free world.

Veterans

In discharging the nation's obligation to our veterans, during the past eight years there have been:

The readjustment of World War II veterans was completed, and the five million Korean conflict veterans were assisted in achieving successful readjustment to civilian life;

Increases in compensation benefits for all eligible veterans with service connected disabilities;

Higher non-service connected pension benefits for needy veterans;

Greatly improved benefits to survivors of veterans dying in or as a result of service;

Authorization, by Presidential directive, of an increase in the number of beds available for sick and disabled veterans;

Development of a 12-year, $900 million construction program to modernize and improve our veterans hospitals;

New modern techniques brought into the administration of Veterans Affairs to provide the highest quality service possible to those who have defended us.

Conclusion

In concluding my final message to the Congress, it is fitting to look back to my first—to the aims and ideals I set forth on February 2, 1953: To use America's influence in world affairs to advance the cause of peace and justice, to conduct the affairs of the Executive Branch with integrity and efficiency, to encourage creative initiative in our economy, and to work toward the attainment of the well-being and equality of opportunity of all citizens.

Equally, we have honored our commitment to pursue and attain specific objectives. Among them, as stated eight years ago: strengthening of the mutual security program; development of world trade and commerce; ending of hostilities in Korea; creation of a powerful deterrent force; practicing fiscal responsibility; checking the menace of inflation; reducing the tax burden; providing an effective internal security program; developing and conserving our natural resources; reducing governmental interference in the affairs of the farmer; strengthening and improving services by the Department of Labor, and the vigilant guarding of civil and social rights.

I do not close this message implying that all is well—that all problems are solved. For progress implies both new and continuing problems and, unlike Presidential administrations, problems rarely have terminal dates.

Abroad, there is the continuing Communist threat to the freedom of Berlin, an explosive situation in Laos, the problems caused by Communist penetration of Cuba, as well as the many problems connected with the development of the new nations in Africa. These areas, in particular, call for delicate handling and constant review.

At home, several conspicuous problems remain: promoting higher levels of employment, with special emphasis on areas in which heavy unemployment has persisted; continuing to provide for steady economic growth and preserving a sound currency; bringing our balance of payments into more reasonable equilibrium and continuing a high level of confidence in our national and international systems; eliminating heavily excessive surpluses of a few farm commodities; and overcoming deficiencies in our health and educational programs.

Our goal always has been to add to the spiritual, moral, and material strength of our nation. I believe we have done this. But it is a process that must never end. Let us pray that leaders of both the near and distant future will be able to keep the nation strong and at peace, that they will advance the well-being of all our people, that they will lead us on to still higher moral standards, and that, in achieving these goals, they will maintain a reasonable balance between private and governmental responsibility.

The budget presented by an outgoing President does not go into effect until approximately six months after he has left office. Therefore, a new Administration can dramatically change fiscal policies. Just as Eisenhower looked for ways to cut Truman's final proposal, the Kennedy Administration would modify the outgoing President's economic goals.

Annual Presidential Budget Message
January 16, 1961
[*Public Papers of the Presidents: 1960–61* (Washington, 1961), 934–47.]

To the Congress of the United States:

For the fiscal year 1962 I send you budget and legislative proposals which will meet the essential domestic needs of the Nation, provide for the national defense, and at the same time preserve the integrity and strength of our Federal Government's finances.

With this budget, I leave to the new administration and the Congress a progressive and workable financial plan which recognizes national priorities and which reflects my confidence in the strength of our economy now and in the years to come.

A budget surplus was achieved in the fiscal year which ended on June 30, 1960. A narrowly balanced budget is anticipated for fiscal year 1961. The recommendations in this budget provide for still another balanced budget, with a surplus, in fiscal year 1962. The achievement of balanced budgets this year and in the coming fiscal year will help foster noninflationary prosperity at home and strengthen confidence in the dollar abroad.

Despite the persistence of hardship in some local areas, economic activity continues at a high level. It is imperative for the extension of economic growth at a high and sustainable rate that the budget be kept balanced and that we act responsibly in financial matters.

For 1962 the budget estimates reflect expected gains in the national economy and provide for carrying programs forward in an efficient and orderly manner. The estimates also reflect, as in previous years, the budgetary effects of proposed changes in legislation, including the cost of certain new programs. Most of the legislative proposals have been previously recommended. I again urge their enactment.

In total and in its parts, this budget embodies a sensible and forward-looking plan of action for the Government. In brief, it provides for:

1. Increasing our own military capabilities and promoting increased strength in other free world forces;

2. Advancing activities important to economic growth and domestic welfare;

3. Continuing assistance to the less-developed nations of the world whose peoples are striving to improve their standards of living;

4. Increasing support for scientific activities in outer space;

5. Achieving savings by making desirable modifications in existing programs and by charging users the costs of special benefits received by them; and

6. Continuing present tax rates to maintain the revenues needed for a sound fiscal plan.

The policies and proposals in this budget will enable us to meet fully our national and international responsibilities and to promote real and sustainable national progress.

General Budget Policy

This budget, like each of the seven which I have previously sent to the Congress, reflects the conviction that military strength and domestic advancement must be based on a sound economy, and that fiscal integrity is essential to the responsible conduct of governmental affairs. A surplus in good times, as provided in this budget, helps make up the deficits which inevitably occur during periods of recession. To ignore these principles is to undermine our strength as a Nation through deficits, unmanageable debt, and the resulting inflation and cheapening of our currency.

An 8-year effort has been made by this administration to stabilize the purchasing power of the dollar. This effort, which was a necessary undertaking in view of the heavy depreciation of the dollar's purchasing power following World War II, has had a large measure of success, but the problem of maintaining reasonable price stability will require close and continuing attention in the future.

Our national economy is strong and our national welfare continues to advance. Despite a leveling out in economic activity during the latter part of the calendar year just ended, the total market value of all goods and services produced in our country in the calendar year 1960 increased by approximately $20 billion over the preceding year and crossed the half-trillion-dollar mark for the first time in our history. Personal incomes increased more than 5% over 1959, the previous record high. The Economic Report will describe the trends which indicate that further substantial increases can be expected during the calendar year 1961, carrying the gross national product and personal incomes to new highs.

The budgetary outlook for the future reinforces the need for self-discipline in meeting current national demands. Over the next 10 years and beyond, we will be faced with the consequences of many commitments under present laws for nondefense expenditures, in addition to the heavy military burden we must continue to bear.

We can confidently expect that a growing economy will help pay for these commitments. As the labor force grows and employment expands, as business discovers new techniques of production and invests in a larger and more efficient productive base, the national output and income will grow, and with them our ability to finance needed public services. But our resources will not be unlimited. New and expanded Federal programs being urged by special groups are frequently appealing, but, added to existing commitments, they threaten to swell expenditures beyond the available resources.

The Federal Government cannot reasonably satisfy all demands at the same time. We must proceed first to meet those which are most pressing, and find economies to help pay their costs by reappraising old programs in the light of emerging priorities. We must encourage States and localities to increase further their participation in programs for meeting the needs of their citizens. And we must preserve and strengthen the environment in which individual initiative and responsibility can make their maximum contribution.

Our unsatisfactory balance of international payments provides another compelling reason for pursuing sound financial policies. The relationship between our budgetary actions and the balance of payments needs to be carefully examined to assure a minimum adverse effect. Whether the dollar will continue to enjoy high prestige and confidence in the international financial community will depend on the containment of inflation at home and on the exercise of wise restraint and selectivity in our expenditures abroad.

The need for concern about our spending abroad is not strange or surprising. It results from the recovery, profoundly desired and deliberately encouraged by our country, of the major centers of production in Western Europe and Japan following the devastation and disruption caused by war. To reflect this developing state of affairs, changes are now required in some policies established in earlier years. Therefore, I have prescribed certain actions in international transactions under direct governmental control and others are under study. Such measures, combined with proper financial prudence in the handling of domestic affairs and strong export promotion, should significantly improve our balance of payments.

In summary, if we plan wisely and allocate our resources carefully, we can have both public and private advancement. Sound fiscal policies and balanced budgets will sustain sound economic growth and, eventually, will make possible a reduced tax burden. At the same time, we can have necessary improvements in Federal programs to meet the demands of an ever-changing world. If, however, we deliberately run the Government by credit cards, improvidently spending today at the expense of tomorrow, we will break faith with the American people and their children, and with those joined with us in freedom throughout the world.

Budget Totals—1961

Current estimates indicate a close balance in the 1961 budget. On the newly adopted basis of excluding interfund transactions, expenditures are estimated at $78.9 billion and receipts of $79.0 billion, resulting in a budget surplus of $0.1 billion. The revenue estimate reflects a justifiably optimistic view as to the course of our economy, based on circumstances described in my Economic Report.

Last January, I proposed a budget for 1961 that showed a surplus of $4.2 billion. The enactment by the Congress of unrecommended expenditures and the unwillingness of the Congress to increase postal rates reduced this prospect by approximately $2 billion. In the meantime, lower corporate profits have materially reduced our expectation of tax collections from this source.

The small surplus of $79 million currently estimated for 1961 takes into account an assumption that postal rates will be increased not later than April 1, 1961.

Despite the congressional increases in the budget last year, the present estimate of $78.9 billion for 1961 expenditures is about $900 million less than the figure of $79.8 billion which appeared in the budget a year ago. The apparent reduction results from (1) the elimination, as announced in last year's budget, of certain interfund transactions totaling $0.7 billion from the current estimate of expenditures and (2) the shift of employment security grants of $0.3 billion to trust fund financing as provided by law. As explained elsewhere in this budget, these changes affect receipts as well as expenditures and do not affect the surplus.

Apart from these accounting adjustments, the increases and decreases from last year's estimate of 1961 expenditures are approximately offsetting.

Major increases from the original budget include $766 million for Federal employee pay raises; $554 million in losses of the postal service because rates were not increased as proposed; $269 million for defense programs;

$188 million for health, education, and welfare activities; and $164 million for civil space activities.

Major decreases from the original estimates include $600 million for interest on the public debt; $496 million for the activities of the Commodity Credit Corporation; $311 million for veterans compensation, pensions, and readjustment benefits; $93 million for the Export-Import Bank; and $50 million for military assistance. In addition, a reduction of $160 million is estimated under the proposal to reduce the postal deficit in 1961 by increasing postal rates effective April 1. Other reductions, including a normal downward revision in the allowance for contingencies, total $210 million.

Budget Totals—1962

For the fiscal year 1962, my recommendations provide for $82.3 billion in budget receipts and $80.9 billion in budget expenditures. The resulting budgetary surplus of $1.5 billion will permit another modest payment on the public debt.

The estimate of receipts in 1962 is $3.3 billion higher than the current estimate for 1961, and $4.6 billion more than the receipts actually collected in 1960. Expenditures are also increasing, from a total of $76.5 billion in 1960 to $78.9 billion currently estimated for 1961 and $80.9 billion proposed for 1962.

BUDGET EXPENDITURES.—The increase of $1.9 billion in estimated expenditures between 1961 and 1962 reflects several factors which are worthy of special note.

First, outlays for our Nation's defenses are estimated to rise by $1.4 billion in 1962 to a total of $42.9 billion. Much of this increase reflects continued emphasis on certain expanding defense programs, such as Polaris submarines, the Minuteman missile, the B–70 long-range bomber, a strengthened airborne alert capability, airlift modernization, and modernization of Army equipment. These improvements are for the purpose of keeping our military might the strongest in the world.

Second, the budget provides for substantial continuing efforts to support the cause of freedom through the mutual security program. Expenditures for this program in 1962 are estimated at $3.6 billion, an increase of $250 million over 1961.

Third, civil space vehicles and space exploration will require $965 million in 1962, up $195 million from 1961, and $564 million more than in 1960. In total, the recommendations in this budget provide for $9.4 billion in expenditures in 1962 for carrying forward research and development efforts, of which $7.4 billion is for major national security purposes. The total represents an increase of $770 million over 1961. As part of the overall research and development effort, increasing Federal support for basic research is being provided. This budget includes $1 billion for the conduct and support of basic research in universities, industrial establishments, Government laboratories, and other centers of research.

Fourth, increases in expenditures are proposed for certain activities important to domestic well-being and to the future development of our Nation. These include, among others, broadening medical care for the aged; making major improvements in transportation programs; continuing development of our natural resources at a new record level of expenditures; improving our health and welfare programs; providing assistance for construction of elementary and secondary schools and college facilities; assisting areas of substantial and persistent unemployment; and fostering rural development. Expenditures in 1962 for labor, education, health, welfare, community development, transportation aids and services, and conservation of natural resources are estimated to total $8.6 billion, an increase of $627 million over 1961.

To some extent these recommended budget increases are offset by proposed reductions which can be effected in existing programs through improved operations and through changes in present laws. These reductions result from a continuous search for ways to restrain unnecessary expenditures in going activities, to recognize real priorities of need, and to assure that Federal programs are carried out in an efficient manner.

Savings are proposed and can be achieved through modification of activities which, in their existing form, require a disproportionate or wasteful expenditure of Federal funds. For example, States, localities, and other non-Federal interests should assume a greater share of the costs of urban renewal, local flood protection, and the building and operating of schools in federally affected areas. The Congress should act on proposals to encourage nongovernmental financing, and reduce reliance on direct Federal financing, in such activities as home loans for veterans and for military personnel, and the expansion of rural electrification and telephone systems. Certain grants and benefits should also be reviewed and revised, including those for agricultural conservation, civil airport construction, airline subsidies, housing aids no longer needed for readjustment of World War II veterans, and agricultural price supports, particularly for wheat.

Benefits to the general taxpayer are also proposed in the coming fiscal year and later years through the enactment of measures to charge users for special services which they derive from particular Government activities. Among these are proposals to eliminate the postal deficit and to provide more adequate taxes on aviation and highway fuels.

BUDGET RECEIPTS.—Estimated budget receipts of $82.3 billion in 1962 are based on an outlook for higher production, employment, and income as the calendar year 1961 progresses. The accompanying table shows the sources of budget receipts for the fiscal years 1960, 1961, and 1962.

BUDGET RECEIPTS

[Fiscal years. In billions]

Source	1960 actual	1961 estimate	1962 estimate
Individual income taxes	$40.7	$43.3	$45.5
Corporation income taxes	21.5	20.4	20.9
Excise taxes	9.1	9.3	9.7
All other receipts	7.1	6.7	6.9
Total	78.5	79.7	83.0
Deduct interfund transactions (included in both receipts and expenditures)	.7	.7	.7
Budget receipts	77.8	79.0	82.3

Extension of present tax rates.—It is necessary to extend for another year the present tax rates on corporation income and the excise taxes which are scheduled for reduction or termination on July 1, 1961. The excise tax rates scheduled for reduction include those on distilled spirits, beer, wines, cigarettes, passenger automobiles, automobile parts and accessories, and transportation of persons; the 10% tax on general telephone service is scheduled to expire. Unless these tax rates are extended, the Federal Government will lose an estimated $2.6 billion in revenues in 1962, and $3.7 billion on a full annual basis.

Changes in fees and charges.—In the conduct of certain of its activities, the Government provides special services, sells products, and leases federally owned resources, which convey to the recipients benefits above and beyond those which accrue to the public at large. In fairness to the general taxpayer, the cost of these services or the fair market value of the products and resources which are transferred to private use should be recovered, wherever feasible, through adequate fees and charges. To this end, the Congress was requested last year to provide increased fees and charges for a number of special benefits. With the one exception of fees for non-competitive oil and gas leases no final action was taken. The Congress is again requested to raise postal rates to eliminate the postal deficit and to act favorably on the proposals for increased highway and aviation fuel taxes and for a number of other fees or charges.

The present highway fuel tax rate should be increased by one-half cent per gallon and the resulting rate of 4½ cents should be continued through 1972. This step is necessary to permit timely completion of the Interstate System. It will also make possible the repeal of the unwise diversion from the general fund to the trust fund of excise tax receipts amounting to 5% of the manufacturers' price of passenger automobiles and automobile parts and accessories; this diversion is presently scheduled by law to begin July 1,

1961, and to continue for the fiscal years 1962 through 1964. The Congress should also raise the excise tax rate on aviation gasoline from 3 to 4½ cents per gallon; impose the same excise tax rate on jet fuels, now untaxed; and retain the receipts from these taxes in the general fund to help pay the cost of the Federal airways system. Other aspects of these recommendations are set forth in the discussion of transportation programs in this message.

ESTIMATED SAVINGS TO THE GENERAL TAXPAYERS FROM MORE ADEQUATE FEES AND CHARGES

[In millions]

Proposal	Fiscal year 1962
Increase postal rates	$843
Support highway expenditures by highway use taxes:	
Repeal pending diversion of general fund excise taxes to trust fund (and increase motor fuel tax)	810
Transfer financing of forest and public lands highways to trust fund	38
Charge users for share of cost of Federal airways:	
Increase taxes on aviation gasoline and retain in general fund	38
Tax jet fuels	62
Increase patent fees	7
Increase miscellaneous fees now below costs	9
Total savings	1,807

PUBLIC DEBT.—Achievement of the proposed budget surplus for 1962 will enable the Federal Government to make another modest reduction in the public debt. It is estimated that the public debt, which stood at $286.3 billion on June 30, 1960, will decline to $284.9 billion by the end of fiscal year 1961 and to $283.4 billion on June 30, 1962.

If the Congress accepts the proposals in this budget, and the proposed budget surplus for fiscal year 1962 is achieved, at the end of that year the Government will have some operating leeway within the permanent debt limit of $285 billion. Due to the seasonal pattern of tax collections, however, it will again be necessary for the Congress to provide a temporary increase in the debt limit during 1962. The present temporary debt limit of $293 billion expires June 30, 1961.

The Congress is again urged to remove the 4¼% statutory limitation on new issues of Treasury bonds, which remains a serious obstacle to efficient long-run management of the public debt. The marketable debt is still too heavily concentrated in securities of relatively short maturity, with almost 80% of the total coming due within 5 years. Although interest rates have declined in recent months, the continued existence of the interest rate ceiling limits the flexibility of debt operations by the Treasury. It effectively prevents the Treasury under certain circumstances from lengthening the debt by offering longer term securities or exchanges at maturity and, more importantly, it reduces considerably the possible use of the advance refunding technique, which offers the greatest promise for lengthening the average maturity of the debt.

Receipts From and Payments to the Public

The budget totals exclude the transactions of funds held in trust by the Federal Government as well as certain other transactions affecting the flow of money between the public and the Federal Government as a whole. Trust fund operations are an important factor in this flow and are consolidated with budget transactions to measure the Federal Government's cash receipts from and payments to the public. In this consolidation, certain transactions involving no flow of cash between the Government and the public are eliminated.

Expenditures from trust funds are financed through taxes and other receipts which are specifically designated to serve the special purposes for which the funds were established. About one-half of total trust fund transactions are accounted for by the old-age and survivors insurance system. Other important programs carried on through trust funds include the railroad retirement system, the Federal employees' retirement systems, disability insurance, unemployment compensation, grants for highway construction, purchase of insured and guaranteed mortgages, and veterans life insurance. In certain areas of Government activity, notably labor and welfare, trust fund expenditures far exceed the amounts spent through budget funds and, with the taxes levied to finance them, exert a considerable influence on the economy of the Nation.

Total receipts and expenditures of trust funds more than tripled during the decade of the fifties, and passed the $20 billion mark in 1960. In 1962, they are both estimated to total $25.2 billion. Total receipts from the public in 1962 are estimated at 103.1 billion and payments to the public at $101.8 billion, with a resulting excess of receipts of $1.3 billion.

FEDERAL GOVERNMENT RECEIPTS FROM AND PAYMENTS TO THE PUBLIC

[Fiscal years. In billions]

	1960 actual	1961 estimate	1962 estimate
Receipts from the public	$95.1	$99.0	$103.1
Payments to the public	94.3	97.9	101.8
Excess of receipts over payments	+.8.	+1.1	+1.3

Improvements in the Tax System

There is a continuing need for a reappraisal of the tax system to assure that it operates equitably and with a minimum of repressive effects on incentives to work, save, and invest. Continued close cooperation between the Treasury and the committees of the Congress is necessary to formulate sound and attainable proposals for the long-range improvement of the tax laws.

However, as the development of a comprehensive tax revision program will take time, the Congress should consider promptly this year certain changes in the tax laws to correct inequities. For example, it is again recommended that the Congress promptly consider amending the laws on taxation of cooperatives to provide for more equitable taxation by insuring that taxes are paid on the income of these businesses either by the cooperative or by its members.

It has been many years since certain of the tax laws which now apply to the Nation's various private lending institutions and to fire and casualty insurance companies became effective. The Congress should review these statutes and the tax burdens now carried by lending institutions and insurance companies to determine whether or not inequities exist and to remedy any inequitable situations which may be found. The Treasury Department has under way studies relating to the operation of the existing statutes in this area. These studies should be of assistance to the Congress in any such review.

There is a need for review of present depreciation allowances and procedures. More liberal and flexible depreciation can make a major contribution toward neutralizing the deterrent effects of high tax rates on investment. A better system of capital recovery allowances would provide benefits to those who invest in productive plant and equipment and would encourage business expenditures for modernization and greater efficiency, thus helping to foster long-range economic growth. By bringing the allowances for American business more nearly into line with those available to many foreign producers, improved depreciation procedures would not only strengthen the competitive position of American producers, but their benefits would also accrue to American workers through increased productivity and greater job opportunity.

The depreciation rules should not be substantially liberalized, however, without accompanying remedial legislation with respect to the taxation of gains from sale of depreciable property. The legislation recommended last year to treat income on disposition of depreciable property as ordinary income to the extent of the depreciation deductions previously taken on the property is an essential first step.

Improvements in Government Organization

During the past 8 years major improvements have been made in the organization of the executive branch of the Government. An executive

Department of Health, Education, and Welfare was established to give Cabinet status to its important programs. The organization of the Department of Defense was strengthened to bring it more closely into line with the requirements of modern warfare. A National Aeronautics and Space Administration was created to provide effective civilian leadership over appropriate parts of our national space program. The Council of Economic Advisers was reconstituted and reorganized to strengthen its internal administration and clarify its relationships with the President. Functions of coordinating governmental planning for defense mobilization and civil defense were consolidated. The establishment of the Federal Aviation Agency brought about substantial improvements in aviation programs.

Many of the numerous organizational improvements were effected by Presidential reorganization plans authorized by the Reorganization Act of 1949, which has now expired. The Congress should renew that authority and make it permanently available for all future Presidents in the effective form as originally enacted. The task of conforming Government organization to current needs is a continuing one in our everchanging times.

Executive Office of the President.—The duties placed on the President by the Constitution and the statutes demand the most careful attention to the staffing and organization of the President's Office. While the present organization of the Executive Office of the President reflects many constructive steps taken over a period of years, much remains to be done to improve the facilities available to the President. The first requirement for improvement is for the Congress to give the President greater flexibility in organizing his own Office to meet his great responsibilities.

Specifically, the Congress should enact legislation authorizing the President to reorganize the Executive Office of the President, including the authority to redistribute statutory functions among the units of the Office; to change the names of units and titles of officers within the Office; to make changes in the membership of statutory bodies in the Office; and, within the limits of existing laws and available appropriations, to establish new units in the Executive Office and fix the compensation of officers. Such action would insure that future Presidents will possess the latitude to design the working structure of the Presidential office as they deem necessary for the effective conduct of their duties under the Constitution and the laws. Enactment of such legislation would be a major step forward in strengthening the Office of the President for the critical tests that will surely continue to face our Nation in the years to come. These matters are obviously devoid of partisan considerations.

My experience leads me to suggest the establishment of an Office of Executive Management in the Executive Office of the President in which would be grouped the staff functions necessary to assist the President in the discharge of his managerial responsibilities. In an enterprise as large and diversified as the executive branch of the Government, there is an imperative need for effective and imaginative central management to strengthen program planning and evaluation, promote efficiency, identify and eliminate waste and duplication, and coordinate numerous interagency operations within approved policy and statutory objectives. The establishment of an Office of Executive Management is highly desirable to help the President achieve the high standards of effective management that the Congress and the people rightfully expect.

I have given much personal study to the assistance the President needs in meeting the multitude of demands placed upon him in conducting and correlating all aspects of foreign political, economic, social, and military affairs. I have reached the conclusion that serious attention should be given to providing in the President's Office an official ranking higher than Cabinet members, possibly with the title of First Secretary of the Government, to assist the President in consulting with the departments on the formulation of national security objectives, in coordinating international programs, and in representing the President at meetings with foreign officials above the rank of Foreign Minister and below the rank of Head of State.

Recognizing the personal nature of the relationship of each President to his Cabinet and staff, I am not submitting formal legislative proposals to implement these latter two suggestions, but I do commend them for earnest study.

Other improvements.—Several other organizational reforms should be considered by the Congress:

First, a Department of Transportation should be established so as to bring together at Cabinet level the presently fragmented Federal functions regarding transportation activities.

Second, legislation should be enacted to strengthen the position of the chairmen of the Interstate Commerce Commission, the Federal Communications Commission, and the National Labor Relations Board by vesting in them the executive and administrative duties of their agencies. The legislation should provide that the Chairman of the Interstate Commerce Commission be designated by the President. These steps would place these chairmen generally on a comparable basis with the chairmen of other regulatory bodies. In the case of the National Labor Relations Board, the legislation should vest all regulatory responsibilities under the National Labor Relations Act in the Board. Additionally, the responsibility of the President to control and supervise the exercise of executive functions by all Federal regulatory bodies should be clarified.

Third, action should be taken to consolidate the civil water resources functions of the Corps of Engineers of the Department of the Army, the Department of the Interior, and the responsibilities of the Federal Power Commission for river basin surveys, in order to bring about long needed improvements in the coordination of the increasingly important Federal civil water resources activities.

Harking back to a little used tradition, Eisenhower decided to give a farewell address to the American people. Over national radio and television he covered many items, but his reference to the dangers inherent in the "military industrial complex" received the most attention. Most people missed his main intent—to warn against excessive and wasteful spending. And almost no one noticed that the greatest conqueror of modern times ended his last major public address as President with the word "love."

Farewell Radio and Television Address to the American People by President Eisenhower January 17, 1961

[*Public Papers of the Presidents: 1960–61* (Washington, 1961), 1035–40.]

My fellow Americans:

Three days from now, after half a century in the service of our country, I shall lay down the responsibilities of office as, in traditional and solemn ceremony, the authority of the Presidency is vested in my successor.

This evening I come to you with a message of leave-taking and farewell, and to share a few final thoughts with you, my countrymen.

Like every other citizen, I wish the new President, and all who will labor with him, Godspeed. I pray that the coming years will be blessed with peace and prosperity for all.

Our people expect their President and the Congress to find essential agreement on issues of great moment, the wise resolution of which will better shape the future of the Nation.

My own relations with the Congress, which began on a remote and tenuous basis when, long ago, a member of the Senate appointed me to West Point, have since ranged to the intimate during the war and immediate post-war period, and, finally, to the mutually interdependent during these past eight years.

In this final relationship, the Congress and the Administration have, on most vital issues, cooperated well, to serve the national good rather than mere partisanship, and so have assured that the business of the Nation should go forward. So, my official relationship with the Congress ends in a feeling, on my part, of gratitude that we have been able to do so much together.

II

We now stand ten years past the midpoint of a century that has witnessed four major wars among great nations. Three of these involved our own country. Despite these holocausts America is today the strongest, the most influential and most productive nation in the world. Understandably proud of this pre-eminence, we yet realize that America's leadership and prestige depend, not merely upon our unmatched material progress, riches and military strength, but on how we use our power in the interests of world peace and human betterment.

III

Throughout America's adventure in free government, our basic purposes have been to keep the peace; to foster progress in human achievement, and to enhance liberty, dignity and integrity among people and among nations. To strive for less would be unworthy of a free and religious people. Any failure traceable to arrogance, or our lack of comprehension or readiness to sacrifice would inflict upon us grievous hurt both at home and abroad.

Progress toward these noble goals is persistently threatened by the conflict now engulfing the world. It commands our whole attention, absorbs our very beings. We face a hostile ideology—global in scope, atheistic in character, ruthless in purpose, and insidious in method. Unhappily the danger it poses promises to be of indefinite duration. To meet it successfully, there is called for, not so much the emotional and transitory sacrifices of crisis, but rather those which enable us to carry forward steadily, surely, and without complaint the burdens of a prolonged and complex struggle—with liberty the stake. Only thus shall we remain, despite every provocation, on our charted course toward permanent peace and human betterment.

Crises there will continue to be. In meeting them, whether foreign or domestic, great or small, there is a recurring temptation to feel that some spectacular and costly action could become the miraculous solution to all current difficulties. A huge increase in newer elements of our defense; development of unrealistic programs to cure every ill in agriculture; a dramatic expansion in basic and applied research—these and many other possibilities, each possibly promising in itself, may be suggested as the only way to the road we wish to travel.

But each proposal must be weighed in the light of a broader consideration: the need to maintain balance in and among national programs—balance between the private and the public economy, balance between cost and hoped for advantage—balance between the clearly necessary and the comfortably desirable; balance between our essential requirements as a nation and the duties imposed by the nation upon the individual; balance between actions of the moment and the national welfare of the future. Good judgment seeks balance and progress; lack of it eventually finds imbalance and frustration.

The record of many decades stands as proof that our people and their government have, in the main, understood these truths and have responded to them well, in the face of stress and threat. But threats, new in kind or degree, constantly arise. I mention two only.

IV

A vital element in keeping the peace is our military establishment. Our arms must be mighty, ready for instant action, so that no potential aggressor may be tempted to risk his own destruction.

Our military organization today bears little relation to that known by any of my predecessors in peacetime, or indeed by the fighting men of World War II or Korea.

Until the latest of our world conflicts, the United States had no armaments industry. American makers of plowshares could, with time and as required, make swords as well. But now we can no longer risk emergency improvisation of national defense; we have been compelled to create a permanent armaments industry of vast proportions. Added to this, three and a half million men and women are directly engaged in the defense establishment. We annually spend on military security more than the net income of all United States corporations.

This conjunction of an immense military establishment and a large arms industry is new in the American experience. The total influence—economic, political, even spiritual—is felt in every city, every State house, every office of the Federal government. We recognize the imperative need for this development. Yet we must not fail to comprehend its grave implications. Our toil, resources and livelihood are all involved; so is the very structure of our society.

In the councils of government, we must guard against the acquisition of unwarranted influence, whether sought or unsought, by the military-industrial complex. The potential for the disastrous rise of misplaced power exists and will persist.

We must never let the weight of this combination endanger our liberties or democratic processes. We should take nothing for granted. Only an alert and knowledgeable citizenry can compel the proper meshing of the huge industrial and military machinery of defense with our peaceful methods and goals, so that security and liberty may prosper together.

Akin to, and largely responsible for the sweeping changes in our industrial-military posture, has been the technological revolution during recent decades.

In this revolution, research has become central; it also becomes more formalized, complex, and costly. A steadily increasing share is conducted for, by, or at the direction of, the Federal government.

Today, the solitary inventor, tinkering in his shop, has been overshadowed by task forces of scientists in laboratories and testing fields. In the same fashion, the free university, historically the fountainhead of free ideas and scientific discovery, has experienced a revolution in the conduct of research. Partly because of the huge costs involved, a government contract becomes virtually a substitute for intellectual curiosity. For every old blackboard there are now hundreds of new electronic computers.

The prospect of domination of the nation's scholars by Federal employment, project allocations, and the power of money is ever present—and is gravely to be regarded.

Yet, in holding scientific research and discovery in respect, as we should, we must also be alert to the equal and opposite danger that public policy could itself become the captive of a scientific-technological elite.

It is the task of statesmanship to mold, to balance, and to integrate these and other forces, new and old, within the principles of our democratic system—ever aiming toward the supreme goals of our free society.

V

Another factor in maintaining balance involves the element of time. As we peer into society's future, we—you and I, and our government—must avoid the impulse to live only for today, plundering, for our own ease and convenience, the precious resources of tomorrow. We cannot mortgage the material assets of our grandchildren without risking the loss also of their political and spiritual heritage. We want democracy to survive for all generations to come, not to become the insolvent phantom of tomorrow.

VI

Down the long lane of the history yet to be written America knows that this world of ours, ever growing smaller, must avoid becoming a community of dreadful fear and hate, and be, instead, a proud confederation of mutual trust and respect.

Such a confederation must be one of equals. The weakest must come to the conference table with the same confidence as do we, protected as we are by our moral, economic, and military strength. That table, though scarred by many past frustrations, cannot be abandoned for the certain agony of the battlefield.

Disarmament, with mutual honor and confidence, is a continuing imperative. Together we must learn how to compose differences, not with arms, but with intellect and decent purpose. Because this need is so sharp and apparent I confess that I lay down my official responsibilities in this field with a definite sense of disappointment. As one who has witnessed the horror and the lingering sadness of war—as one who knows that another war could utterly destroy this civilization which has been so slowly and painfully built over thousands of years—I wish I could say tonight that a lasting peace is in sight.

Happily, I can say that war has been avoided. Steady progress toward our ultimate goal has been made. But, so much remains to be done. As a private citizen, I shall never cease to do what little I can to help the world advance along that road.

VII

So—in this my last good night to you as your President—I thank you for the many opportunities you have given me for public service in war and peace. I trust that in that service you find some things worthy; as for the rest of it, I know you will find ways to improve performance in the future.

You and I—my fellow citizens—need to be strong in our faith that all nations, under God, will reach the goal of peace with justice. May we be ever unswerving in devotion to principle, confident but humble with power, diligent in pursuit of the Nation's great goals.

To all the peoples of the world, I once more give expression to America's prayerful and continuing aspiration:

We pray that peoples of all faiths, all races, all nations, may have their great human needs satisfied; that those now denied opportunity shall come to enjoy it to the full; that all who yearn for freedom may experience its spiritual blessings; that those who have freedom will understand, also, its heavy responsibilities; that all who are insensitive to the needs of others will learn charity; that the scourges of poverty, disease and ignorance will be made to disappear from the earth, and that, in the goodness of time, all peoples will come to live together in a peace guaranteed by the binding force of mutual respect and love.

SECRETARIES AND UNDERSECRETARIES OF DEPARTMENTS OF THE GOVERNMENT 1953–1961

Secretaries of State
John Foster Dulles—January 21, 1953, to April 21, 1959
Christian A. Herter—April 22, 1959, to January 20, 1961

Under Secretaries of State
Walter Bedell Smith—February 9, 1953, to October 1, 1954
Herbert Hoover, Jr.—October 4, 1954, to February 21, 1957
Christian A. Herter—February 21, 1957, to April 22, 1959
C. Douglas Dillon—June 12, 1959, to January 4, 1961

Under Secretaries of State for Administration
Donald B. Lourie—February 16, 1953, to March 5, 1954
Charles E. Saltzman—June 28, 1954, to December 31, 1954

Under Secretary of State for Economic Affairs
C. Douglas Dillon—July 1, 1958, to June 12, 1959

Under Secretary of State for Political Affairs
Livingston T. Merchant—December 4, 1959, to February 20, 1961

Secretaries of the Treasury
George M. Humphrey—January 21, 1953, to July 28, 1957
Robert B. Anderson—July 29, 1957, to January 20, 1961

Under Secretaries of the Treasury
Marion B. Folsom—January 27, 1953, to August 1, 1955
H. Chapman Rose—August 3, 1955, to January 31, 1956
Fred C. Scribner, Jr.—August 9, 1957, to January 20, 1961

Under Secretaries of the Treasury for Monetary Affairs
W. Randolph Burgess—August 3, 1954, to September 26, 1957
Julian B. Baird—September 26, 1957, to January 20, 1961

Secretaries of Defense
  Charles E. Wilson—January 28, 1953, to October 8, 1957
  Neil H. McElroy—October 9, 1957, to December 1, 1959
  Thomas S. Gates, Jr.—December 2, 1959, to January 20, 1961

Deputy Secretaries of Defense
  Roger M. Kyes—February 2, 1953, to May 1, 1954
  Robert B. Anderson—May 3, 1954, to August 4, 1955
  Reuben B. Robertson, Jr.—August 5, 1955, to April 25, 1957
  Donald A. Quarles—May 1, 1957, to May 8, 1959
  Thomas S. Gates, Jr.—June 8, 1959, to December 1, 1959
  James H. Douglas, Jr.—December 11, 1959, to January 20, 1961

Secretaries of the Army
  Robert T. Stevens—February 4, 1953, to July 20, 1955
  Wilber M. Brucker—July 21, 1955, to January 20, 1961

Secretaries of the Navy
  Robert B. Anderson—February 4, 1953, to May 2, 1954
  Charles S. Thomas—May 3, 1954, to April 1, 1957
  Thomas S. Gates, Jr.—April 1, 1957, to June 8, 1959
  William B. Franke—June 8, 1959, to January 20, 1961

Secretaries of the Air Force
  Harold E. Talbott—February 4, 1953, to August 13, 1955
  Donald A. Quarles—August 15, 1955, to April 30, 1957
  James H. Douglas, Jr.—May 1, 1957, to December 11, 1959
  Dudley C. Sharpe—December 11, 1959, to January 20, 1961

Chairmen of the Joint Chiefs of Staff
  General Omar N. Bradley—August 16, 1949, to August 14, 1953
  Admiral Arthur W. Radford—August 15, 1953, to August 14, 1957
  General Nathan F. Twining—August 15, 1957, to September 30, 1960
  General Lyman L. Lemnitzer—October 1, 1960, to September 30, 1962

Chiefs of Staff of the U. S. Army
  General J. Lawton Collins—August 16, 1949, to August 14, 1953
  General Matthew B. Ridgway—August 15, 1953, to June 30, 1955
  General Maxwell D. Taylor—June 30, 1955, to June 30, 1959
  General Lyman L. Lemnitzer—July 1, 1959, to September 30, 1960
  General George H. Decker—September 30, 1960, to September 30, 1962

Chiefs of Naval Operations
  Admiral William M. Fechteler—August 16, 1951, to August 17, 1953
  Admiral Robert B. Carney—August 17, 1953, to August 17, 1955
  Admiral Arleigh A. Burke—August 17, 1955, to August 1, 1961

Chiefs of Staff of the U. S. Air Force
General Hoyt S. Vandenberg—April 30, 1948, to June 29, 1953
General Nathan F. Twining—June 30, 1953, to June 30, 1957
General Thomas D. White—July 1, 1957, to June 30, 1961

Commandants of the Marine Corps
General Lemuel C. Shepherd, Jr.—January 1, 1952, to December 31, 1955
General Randolph McC. Pate—January 1, 1956, to December 31, 1959
General David M. Shoup—January 1, 1960, to December 31, 1963

Attorneys General
Herbert Brownell, Jr.—January 21, 1953, to November 8, 1957
William P. Rogers—November 8, 1957, to January 20, 1961

Deputy Attorneys General
William P. Rogers—January 28, 1953, to November 8, 1957
Lawrence E. Walsh—December 27, 1957, to December 31, 1960

Postmaster General
Arthur E. Summerfield—January 21, 1953, to January 20, 1961

Deputy Postmasters General
Charles R. Hook, Jr.—January 29, 1953, to October 1, 1955
Maurice H. Stans—October 1, 1955, to September 15, 1957
Edson O. Sessions—September 20, 1957, to October 20, 1959
John M. McKibbin—November 2, 1959, to January 20, 1961

Secretaries of the Interior
Douglas McKay—January 21, 1953, to April 15, 1956
Fred A. Seaton—June 18, 1956, to January 20, 1961

Under Secretaries of the Interior
Ralph A. Tudor—March 31, 1953, to September 1, 1954
Clarence A. Davis—September 1, 1954, to January 4, 1957
O. Hatfield Chilson—March 18, 1957, to September 20, 1958
Elmer F. Bennett—October 3, 1958, to January 20, 1961

Secretary of Agriculture
Ezra Taft Benson—January 21, 1953, to January 20, 1961

Under Secretary of Agriculture
True D. Morse—January 29, 1953, to January 20, 1961

Secretaries of Commerce
Sinclair Weeks—January 21, 1953, to November 10, 1958
Lewis L. Strauss—November 13, 1958, to June 30, 1959
Frederick H. Mueller—August 10, 1959, to January 20, 1961

Under Secretaries of Commerce
   Walter Williams—January 28, 1953, to November 1, 1958
   Frederick H. Mueller—November 3, 1958, to August 10, 1959
   Philip A. Ray—August 31, 1959, to January 20, 1961

Under Secretaries of Commerce for Transportation
   Robert B. Murray, Jr.—January 28, 1953, to January 20, 1955
   Louis S. Rothschild—March 2, 1955, to October 24, 1958
   John J. Allen, Jr.—December 20, 1958, to January 20, 1961

Secretaries of Labor
   Martin P. Durkin—January 21, 1953, to September 10, 1953
   James P. Mitchell—October 8, 1953, to January 20, 1961

Under Secretaries of Labor
   Lloyd A. Mashburn—February 24, 1953, to October 9, 1953
   Arthur Larson—April 12, 1954, to November 14, 1956
   James T. O'Connell—February 3, 1957, to January 20, 1961

Secretaries of Health, Education and Welfare
   Oveta Culp Hobby—April 11, 1953, to August 1, 1955
   Marion B. Folsom—August 1, 1955, to July 31, 1958
   Arthur S. Flemming—August 1, 1958, to January 20, 1961

Under Secretaries of Health, Education and Welfare
   Nelson A. Rockefeller—June 11, 1953, to December 16, 1954
   Herold C. Hunt—September 12, 1955, to February 4, 1957
   John A. Perkins—March 26, 1957, to March 1, 1958
   Bertha S. Adkins—August 18, 1958, to January 20, 1961

Chairmen of the Atomic Energy Commission
   Gordon Dean—July 11, 1950, to June 30, 1953
   Lewis L. Strauss—July 2, 1953, to June 30, 1958
   John A. McCone—July 14, 1958, to January 20, 1961

Directors of the Bureau of the Budget
   Joseph M. Dodge—January 21, 1953, to April 15, 1954
   Rowland R. Hughes—April 15, 1954, to April 1, 1956
   Percival F. Brundage—April 2, 1956, to March 17, 1958
   Maurice H. Stans—March 18, 1958, to January 20, 1961

Chairmen of the Council of Economic Advisers
   Arthur F. Burns—August 8, 1953, to December 1, 1956
   Raymond J. Saulnier—December 1, 1956, to January 20, 1961

BIBLIOGRAPHICAL ESSAY

The materials cited from the Eisenhower Papers are part of the holdings of the Dwight D. Eisenhower Library in Abilene, Kansas. The Eisenhower Center is composed of four major structures: the Eisenhower home where Dwight lived as a child; the Museum, constructed by the Eisenhower Foundation; the Library, completed with private contributions after Eisenhower left the Presidency; and the Place of Meditation, which contains a small chapel and the family tomb. The Center has become a major tourist attraction—approximately 850,000 people visit it each year. In contrast to this huge number of tourists is the relatively small group of scholars who use the Library.

The Library's holdings fall into numerous designations. The major segment of the Presidential Papers is entitled the White House Central Files, consisting of a massive collection of correspondence, memoranda, reports, and other records. The Official File of the White House Central Files contains 958 archive boxes and includes what the President's staff considered "high level" material—for example, a memorandum from a White House aide advocating a certain course of action on the St. Lawrence Seaway, or a letter from the President to a congressman on national security. This is by far the most meaningful portion of the White House Central Files. The General File of the White House Central Files, 1,318 archive boxes, includes bulk mail on a variety of subjects received from the public. This "low level" material went for the most part unanswered. Occasionally, when the President did answer letters from the public, his reply found its way into other files. The Personal Papers File of the White House Central Files (986 boxes) does not contain the private correspondence of President Eisenhower. Rather, it includes the "public personal correspondence"; that is, birthday greetings, condolences, Christmas cards, anniversary announcements, and personal messages that deal with an individual's public career. The private personal correspondence of the President is not included in this file, and indeed, is closed to researchers. However, the Personal Files of General of the Army Dwight D. Eisenhower, 1916–52, which cover the pre-presidential period are mostly open and contain personal material that is considered no longer sensitive to national security. This material contains letters written to close friends, plus personal, family, and financial records. The largest segment of the White House Central Files is the Alpha File (1,154 archive boxes), which is the cross reference and name file. Containing no original documents, the Alpha File assisted the White House staff in identifying topics and individuals contained in other files. Generally speaking, the work of the archivists at the Eisenhower Library has superceded this file and researchers seldom use it. These four divisions of the White House Central Files form the backbone of this study.

There are several other major collections at the Library dealing with the Administration. By far the most important are the Staff Files. These are the papers of the White House aides who worked closely and directly with the President. This material is part of the Eisenhower Papers simply because it was included in the original shipment of manuscripts from the White House. These papers deal with the day-to-day activities of individual staff members. In contrast, the files of staff members who chose to take their papers with them when leaving office and who subsequently donated them to the Library, are designated as Personal Papers. Another useful collection is the Bill Files, which include the reaction of interested departments and agencies to legislation that had passed Congress but was awaiting the President's signature. The Bureau of the Budget carried out the surveys on bills which comprise this series. This collection is immensely helpful in seeking attitudes within the Administration to completed legislation. In addition, the Library contains the drafts, papers, and reports of numerous presidential commissions and committees. These deal with topics as diverse as civil rights and tariff legislation.

A file that far exceeds the time span of the Eisenhower Presidency is that of the Republican National Committee, 1932–1965. It is officially described as containing "news clippings and publications." Of interest are the reports dealing with political trends and conditions. Researchers interested in broad topics dealing with the Republican party will find this file helpful.

Out of the Library's total holdings of approximately 15,000,000 manuscript pages, slightly under 5 per cent are closed. While the percentage is low, the total quantity of closed material is quite high, filling some 1,200 archive boxes and running to about 800,000 pages. The decision to close material is based on legislative authority or on terms of a "letter of gift." The former involves mostly matters affecting national security. The latter restriction, authorized by the Presidential Library Act of 1955, allows a somewhat wider scope for the individual donating papers. President Eisenhower's "letter of gift" of April 13, 1960, stated: "It is my purpose to make the papers and other documentary materials . . . available . . . for serious research as soon as possible and to the fullest extent possible. However, since the President of the United States is the recipient of many confidences from others, and since the inviolability of such confidences is essential to the functioning of the office of the Presidency, it will be necessary to withhold from public scrutiny certain papers and classes of papers for varying periods of time." While it is true that rescreening of materials at the Library goes on constantly, there is no doubt that vast quantities of highly sensitive materials will be closed for many years to come.

The Library also has an outstanding collection of still photographs, motion pictures, phonograph records, and audio tapes. Of the 50,000 still photographs, many are from the President's personal scrapbooks, compiled over the course of his Administration. This collection continues to grow and affords many research opportunities.

The quantity of printed material about Dwight D. Eisenhower is overwhelming. However, publications specifically dealing with his Administration are relatively limited and uneven in quality. In the memoir catagory, Eisenhower's own two volumes, *Mandate for Change* (1963) and *Waging Peace* (1965), give the President's point of view about his tenure in office. His Vice President, Richard Nixon, describes a number of important problems that confronted the Administration in *Six Crises* (1962). The only cabinet member who has thus far written a memoir is Ezra Taft Benson, whose *Cross Fire: The Eight Years with Eisenhower* (1962) describes his trials and tribulations as Secretary of Agriculture. Staff members have written several accounts of their work with Eisenhower. These include Emmet John Hughes, *The Ordeal of Power* (1962), E. Frederic Morrow, *Black Man in the White House* (1963), Robert K. Gray, *Eighteen Acres Under Glass* (1962), Arthur Larson, *Eisenhower: The President Nobody Knew* (1968), and Sherman Adams, *Firsthand Report* (1961). Three contemporary journalistic accounts of the Administration are: Robert J. Donovan, *Eisenhower: The Inside Story* (1956), Richard Rovere, *Affairs of State: The Eisenhower Years* (1956), and Marquis Childs, *Eisenhower: Captive Hero* (1958). Several other important books include: Merlo J. Pusey, *Eisenhower the President* (1956), Samuel Lubell, *Revolt of the Moderates* (1956), and David A. Frier, *Conflict of Interest in the Eisenhower Administration* (1969). Most of the books listed above were completed before the Eisenhower Library opened for research and all would have been appreciably better had the Library's resources been available during their writing.

ACKNOWLEDGMENTS

In the preparation of this work, we incurred many agreeable debts of gratitude. Early financial assistance came in the form of a faculty research grant from the School of Graduate Studies of the University of Missouri-Kansas City. We wish to thank Dean Wesley Dale for his continued interest in our project. John Wickman, the Director of the Eisenhower Library, welcomed our interest in the Eisenhower Administration and provided a skilled staff to assist us. We want to thank archivists Roland Doty and Donald Wilson, and photographer Willie Scott. Not only were we courteously received in Abilene, but as the project progressed into the final stages, the library staff gave us invaluable help in solving numerous technical problems. Kenneth LaBudde, Director of the General Library of the University of Missouri-Kansas City, despite supervising the moving of the library to a new building in the midst of our project, offered every assistance. The Government Documents Librarian, Bernice Miller, and her assistant Frieda Rowbottom, unraveled for us the mysteries of government document cataloging. Mrs. Frances Miller frequently juggled her schedule in order to provide rapid copying service, while Eugene Moulton understood our need to borrow reference materials. Michael Renner provided off-campus research space at the reasonable rental of $1.50 per pitcher. Gary Abernathy gave us continued encouragement.

A special note of thanks goes to William Petrowski, Alton Lee, Donald Beaver, Herman Hattaway, Donald Carlson, John Graham, Theodore Freidell, Stanley Parsons, Jesse Clardy, Harold Smith, and Richard McKinzie. Departmental secretaries that assisted us are Marjory Smith, Sharon Steiner, Claire Hildebrand, and Debra Sturgeon. While all these people receive our thanks, Sharon Steiner typed and retyped an overwhelming amount of material. Our heartfelt thanks go out to her for always making time for "Ike." Our wives frequently delayed dinners, tolerated constant discussions of obscure details, and suffered through the many traumas.

Acknowledgment also is extended to the following: President Richard Nixon for permission to quote from *Six Crises,* New York, Doubleday & Company, Inc., 1962; Arthur Larson for permission to quote from *A Republican Looks At His Party,* New York, Harper & Row, Publishers, 1956; E. Frederic Morrow for permission to quote from his personal papers; Thomas F. Daly for permission to quote from Ross Roy, "What Businessmen Can Do to Relieve the Tax Burden," *Vital Speeches of the Day,* XXIII, No. 11 (March 15, 1957); Harper & Row, Publishers, Inc. for permission to quote from Sherman Adams, *Firsthand Report,* Copyright © 1961 by Sherman Adams.

INDEX

INDEX